Watering

A good quality **hose** is a sound investment. The extra expense is worthwhile if the hose kinks less and lasts longer. Look for a hose that has no visible veining and features a long brass nozzle and brass screw-ends. Even if you have a sprinkler system, you'll need a garden hose for supplying water to freshly planted trees and shrubs.

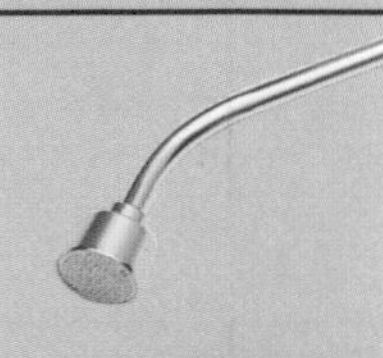

A **watering wand** attaches to the end of your hose. Its long handle makes it easy to water hard-to-reach corners of beds as well as containers and hanging baskets. The wand head showers plants like raindrops instead of blasting them with a hard stream of water.

A **watering can** always comes in handy. Choose one with a large head to disperse water gently. A rounded handle makes the can easier to grip when it's full.

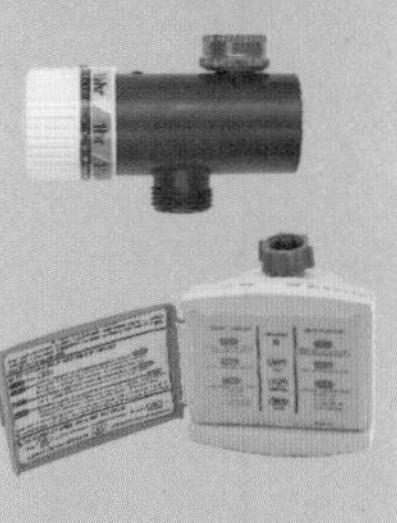

Timers are great for regulated watering. Use timers to turn on garden hoses, soaker hoses, or drip systems. Automatic irrigation systems with underground piping can also be controlled by specialized timers. Because watering early in the day is better than later, rely on timers to get the watering done while you're still asleep. They're also useful for keeping your landscape healthy while you're out of town.

Soaker hoses have tiny holes that allow water to seep into the soil and deliver moisture directly to roots. Snake these special hoses around the roots of plants beneath a layer of mulch.

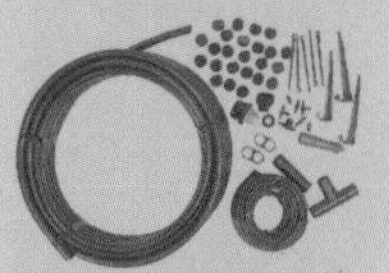

Drip irrigation kits are another way to supplement Mother Nature. Like soaker hoses, small plastic tubing lies on top of the ground beneath a bed of mulch. Tiny emitters release water where needed.

Automatic irrigation systems, also called **underground sprinklers,** rely on a series of pipes buried in trenches to carry water throughout the landscape. Pop-up heads, like this one, or heads attached to risers spray water when turned on manually or by a timer.

Weeding

A **weed hound** helps dig out weeds from a standing position.

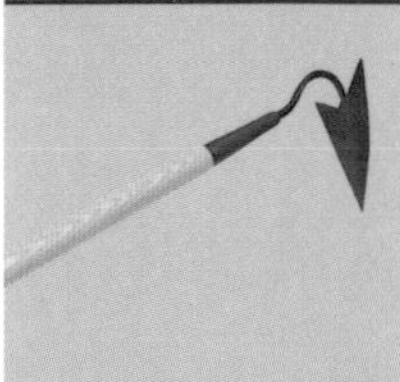

Use a **warren hoe** to chop out weeds by their roots. The pointed blade of the warren hoe makes it easy to cut away and remove established root systems.

Pruning

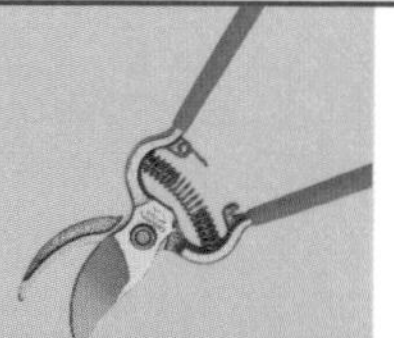

Bypass hand pruners are essential. Buy a good pair with blades you can sharpen. Bypass pruners work like scissors, with both blades moving. They make cleaner cuts than anvil pruners, which feature one fixed edge and one moving cutting blade.

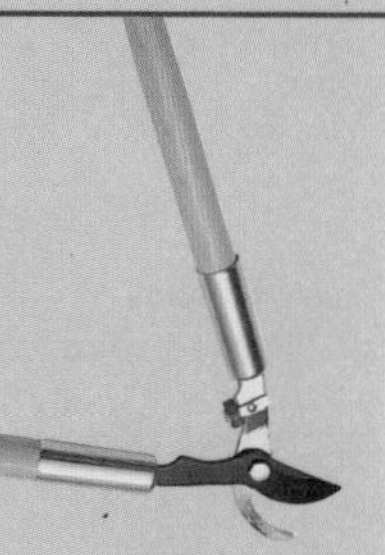

Bypass loppers should find a home in your toolshed. With longer handles for leverage and bigger blades than hand pruners, loppers are necessary for cutting branches that are thicker than a pencil. Using hand pruners on a large stem can hurt both your hand and the plant. Clean cuts are essential to good plant health. Torn, jagged edges invite insects and diseases. Loppers guarantee a good cut.

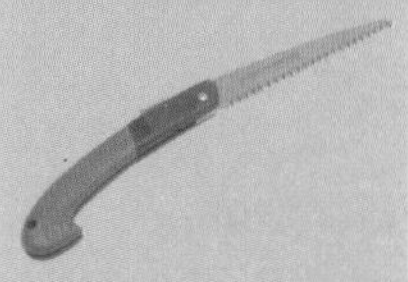

A **pruning saw** is needed for removing large branches that are too big for loppers to grasp. The small, serrated blade is strong enough to cut into green wood but light enough for easy handling.

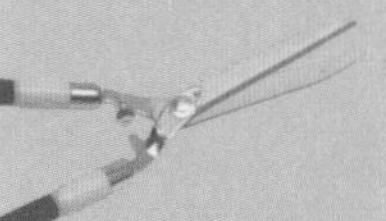

Hedge trimmers have long blades and handles. They are designed for cutting along the surfaces of shrubs to trim, maintain, and shape them.

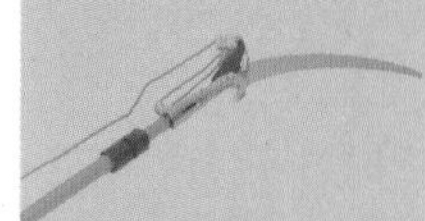

A **pole pruner** easily removes overhead branches and fronds. Wear eye protection when you're working above your head.

Safety

Work boots are essential. You need work boots with sturdy soles to press down on shovels. The tough exteriors offer foot protection and provide ankle support.

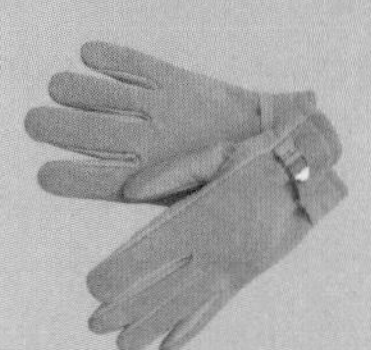

Leather gloves are necessary for landscaping projects; cotton garden gloves won't do. Good leather gloves protect your hands against thorns, sharp branches, and tools. Look for gloves with laces that tighten at the wrist to keep out dirt. (Rubber gloves might be required for handling chemicals.)

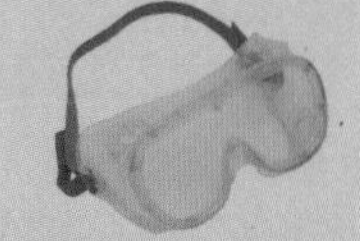

Eye protection is a must. You need to wear safety goggles whenever debris or chemicals might become airborne, such as when you're digging, tilling, or spraying.

Face masks prevent you from breathing airborne particles into your mouth and nose. If you need eye protection, you also need a face mask. When spraying chemicals, you might need a special **respirator** that provides more protection.

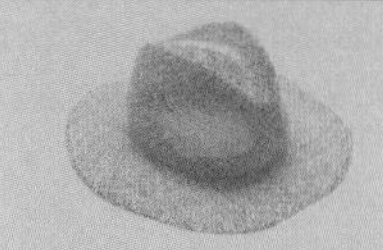

A **straw hat** protects your face from the sun. Open-weave material breathes to keep you from overheating. Use a sun hat and sunscreen when you're working outdoors.

Landscaping 1-2-3™ *(For Zones 2, 3, and 4)*

Meredith Book Development Team
Project Editor: John P. Holms
Art Director: John Eric Seid
Writer and Illustrator: Jo Kellum, ASLA
Contributing Writers: Elizabeth Conner, Julie Martens, Jennie McIlwain, Lisa Wolfe Williams
Photographer: Doug Hetherington
Designer: Ann DuChaine—Ann DuChaine Creative
Contributing Designer: Tim Abramowitz
Copy Chief: Catherine Hamrick
Copy and Production Editor: Terri Fredrickson
Contributing Copy Editors: Lorraine Ferrell, Sherry Rindels
Contributing Proofreaders: Janet Anderson, Maria Duryee, Dan Degen, Margaret Smith
Indexer: Donald Glassman
Managers, Book Production: Pam Kvitne, Marjorie J. Schenkelberg
Electronic Production Coordinator: Paula Forest
Editorial Assistants: Renee McAtee, Karen Schirm

Meredith® Books
Editor in Chief: James D. Blume
Design Director: Matt Strelecki
Managing Editor: Gregory H. Kayko
Executive Editor, Home Depot Books: Benjamin W. Allen

Director, Retail Sales and Marketing: Terry Unsworth
Director, Sales, Special Markets: Rita McMullen
Director, Sales, Premiums: Michael A. Peterson
Director, Sales, Retail: Tom Wierzbicki
Director, Book Marketing: Brad Elmitt
Director, Operations: George A. Susral
Director, Production: Douglas M. Johnston

Vice President, General Manager: Jamie L. Martin

Meredith Publishing Group
President, Publishing Group: Stephen M. Lacy
Vice President, Finance and Administration: Max Runciman

Meredith Corporation
Chairman and Chief Executive Officer: William T. Kerr

Chairman of the Executive Committee: E. T. Meredith III

The Home Depot®
Senior Vice President, Marketing and Communications: Dick Hammill
Marketing Manager: Nathan Ehrlich
Wisdom of the Aisles: Countless Home Depot store associates

First Edition. Printing Number and Year: 4 3 2 1 0 04 03 02 01 00
Library of Congress Catalog Card Number: 00-135013
ISBN: 0-696-21160-2 Distributed by Meredith Corporation

Note to the Reader: Due to differing conditions, tools, and individual skills, Meredith Corporation and The Home Depot assume no responsibility for any damages, injuries suffered, or losses incurred as a result of following the information published in this book. Before beginning any project, review the instructions carefully, and if any doubts or questions remain, consult local experts or authorities. Because codes and regulations vary greatly, you should always check with authorities to ensure that your project complies with all applicable local codes and regulations. Always read and observe all of the safety precautions provided by any tool or equipment manufacturer, and follow all accepted safety procedures.

Contact us by any of these methods:
1 Leave a voice message at (800) 678-2093
2 Write to **Meredith Books, Home Depot Books, 1716 Locust Street, Des Moines, IA 50309-3023**
3 Send e-mail to **hi123@mdp.com.** Visit The Home Depot website at **homedepot.com**

Landscaping 1-2-3™

Selection & Design

Trees

Shrubs

Groundcovers & Vines

STEP-BY-STEP

Landscaping 1-2-3 for Zones 2, 3, and 4

How to Use this Book . . . 4

Chapter 1 design 10

Elements of Design 10
Professional Principles 12
Growing in Style 14
Assessing Your Yard 16
Prioritizing Your Plans 18

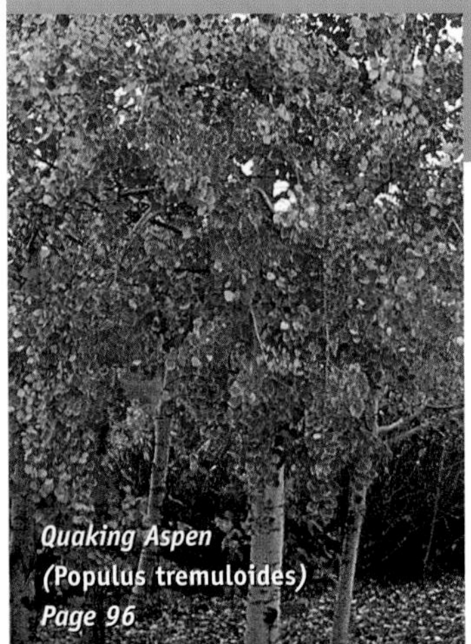

Quaking Aspen (Populus tremuloides) Page 96

Chapter 2 selection 20

The Right Plant in the Right Place 20
Choosing Plants for Zone 2 22
Choosing Plants for Zone 3 24
Choosing Plants for Zones 4 26
Screening and Privacy 28
Sun and Shade 32
Choosing Plants for Full Sun 34
Choosing Plants for Shade 36
Soil Conditions 38
Project: Perc Test 38
Soil pH 40
Choosing Plants for Special Site Conditions 42
Plants for Windbreaks 44

Chapter 3 how-to 46

Getting the Job Done 46
Project: Marking a Bedline 47
Project: Making a Bed 48
Project: Grass Removal 49
Bed Preparation 50
Keeping Plants Happy 52
Project: Drainage Solutions 53
Fertilizing 54
Project: Planting Bare-Root Roses 56
Project: Planting Containerized Roses 57
Caring for Roses 58
Project: Winterizing Roses 60

Vermont Sun Forsythia (Forsythia mandschurica 'Vermont Sun') Page 133

Japanese Flowering Crabapple
(Malus floribunda)
Page 91

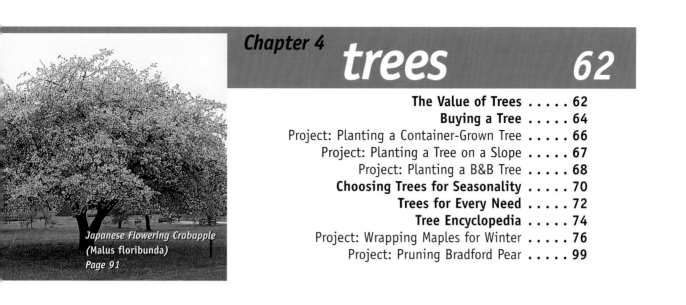

Chapter 4 trees 62

The Value of Trees 62
Buying a Tree 64
Project: Planting a Container-Grown Tree 66
Project: Planting a Tree on a Slope 67
Project: Planting a B&B Tree 68
Choosing Trees for Seasonality 70
Trees for Every Need 72
Tree Encyclopedia 74
Project: Wrapping Maples for Winter 76
Project: Pruning Bradford Pear 99

Chapter 5 shrubs 106

Depend on Shrubs 106
Foundation Planting 108
Project: Planting a Container Shrub 110
Project: Planting Shrubs on Slopes 111
Project: Pruning Evergreen Shrubs 112
Project: Pruning Hedges 113
Project: Pruning Flowering Shrubs 114
Project: Bundling Shrubs for Winter 116
Choosing Shrubs by Characteristics 118
Choosing Shrubs by Needs 120
Choosing Shrubs for Seasonal Interest 122
Shrub Encyclopedia 124
Project: Pruning Rhododendrons 146
Project: Rejuvenating Overgrown Lilacs 160

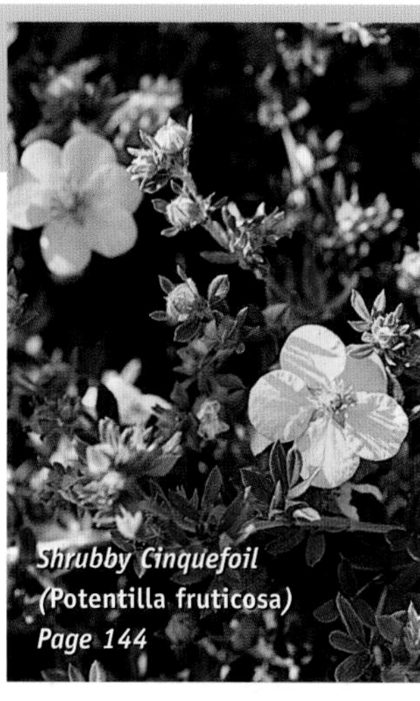

Shrubby Cinquefoil
(Potentilla fruticosa)
Page 144

Chapter 6 groundcovers/vines 168

Boston Ivy
(Parthenocissus tricuspidata)
Page 213

Adding the Final Layers 168
Project: Planting Groundcovers 169
Choosing Groundcovers by Characteristics 170
Choosing Groundcovers for Special Areas 172
Project: Winterizing Groundcovers 174
Project: Dividing Groundcover Clumps 176
Groundcover Encyclopedia 177
Vines 206
Choosing Vines for Seasonal Interest 208
Project: Pruning Vines 209
Vine Encyclopedia 210

Index....214

Landscaping 1-2-3

How to Use this Book

Landscaping 1-2-3 Overview 4
Find Your Climate Zone 5
Planning and Executing Your Landscape . . 6
How to Pick the Right Plants 8
Special Features 9

Learn Landscaping from the Experts

Landscaping 1-2-3 **from the landscaping experts at The Home Depot® is specifically tailored for Climate Zones 2, 3, and 4. Inside you'll find everything you need to help you plan, design, select, install, and care for a landscape that will make your yard a showcase.** First, you will become familiar with some basic landscaping terminology. Then you'll learn how to find your climate zone. Pages 6 and 7 explain how the book is arranged and lay out the steps to creating a great landscape. Pages 8 and 9 introduce you to features in this book that will make putting your plans to work quick and easy.

The Language of Landscaping

Knowing a few basic landscaping terms will help you understand what the pros are talking about when they're making a plan.

- **Evergreen** An evergreen keeps fresh-looking leaves all year, even in winter. Evergreens shed leaves and grow new ones but never lose their leaves completely.
- **Deciduous** A deciduous plant sheds its leaves and goes through a yearly period of dormancy. Deciduous plants are often noted for fall colors.
- **Perennial** Most perennials, with the exception of some evergreens, go into dormancy during the winter months and reappear in spring.
- **Tree** A tree is a woody plant that has one or more main trunks. It grows at least to the height of an adult person. Trees can be evergreen or deciduous. Some palms are listed as trees, according to their use in the landscape.
- **Shrub** Shrubs are evergreen or deciduous. They vary in height and width but are generally lower and have a wider spread than trees. Some palms are listed as shrubs, according to their use in the landscape.

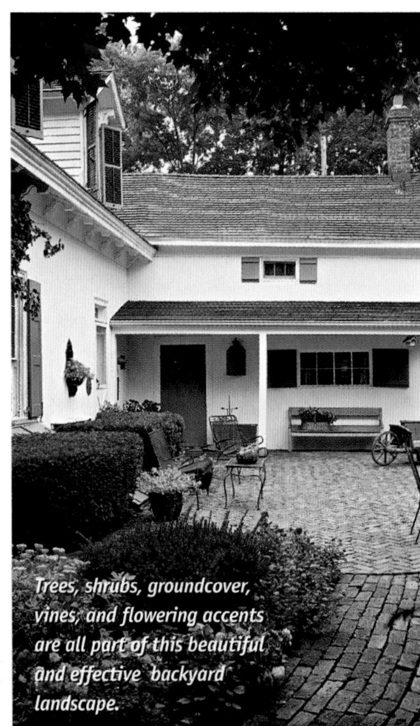

Trees, shrubs, groundcover, vines, and flowering accents are all part of this beautiful and effective backyard landscape.

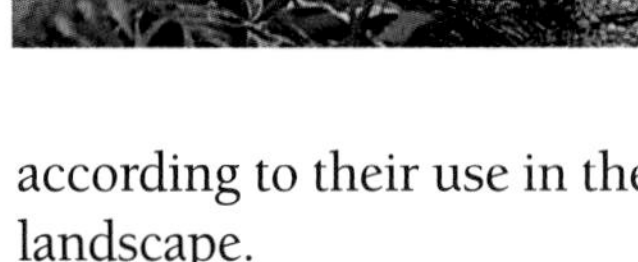

- **Groundcover** This is not a true horticultural term. There are differing opinions on what is or is not a groundcover. Groundcovers here are evergreen or deciduous plants that spread to cover large areas of ground or to act as the low, front layer of a planting bed. Vines growing prostrate, spreading shrubs, low compact shrubs, ornamental grasses, clumping plants, flat spreading plants, or even perennials might be considered groundcovers.
- **Vine** Vines are climbers. Some have tendrils to grasp any nearby support. Others twist and twine over anything in their path. Still others attach themselves with tiny aerial rootlets to cover hard surfaces. Though some trailing plants are included as groundcovers, plants listed as vines are those used primarily to grow vertically on fences, posts, arbors, trellises, and walls.

Find Your Climate Zone

The first step to landscaping success is understanding climate zones and their effect on plant selection and care. Plants that are right for your climate zone, soil type, and watering needs will make themselves at home in your yard and are less likely to be troubled by insects and disease. *All the plant selection guides, projects, and landscaping information in the book are specific to Zones 2, 3, and 4.*

United States, Canada, and Mexico

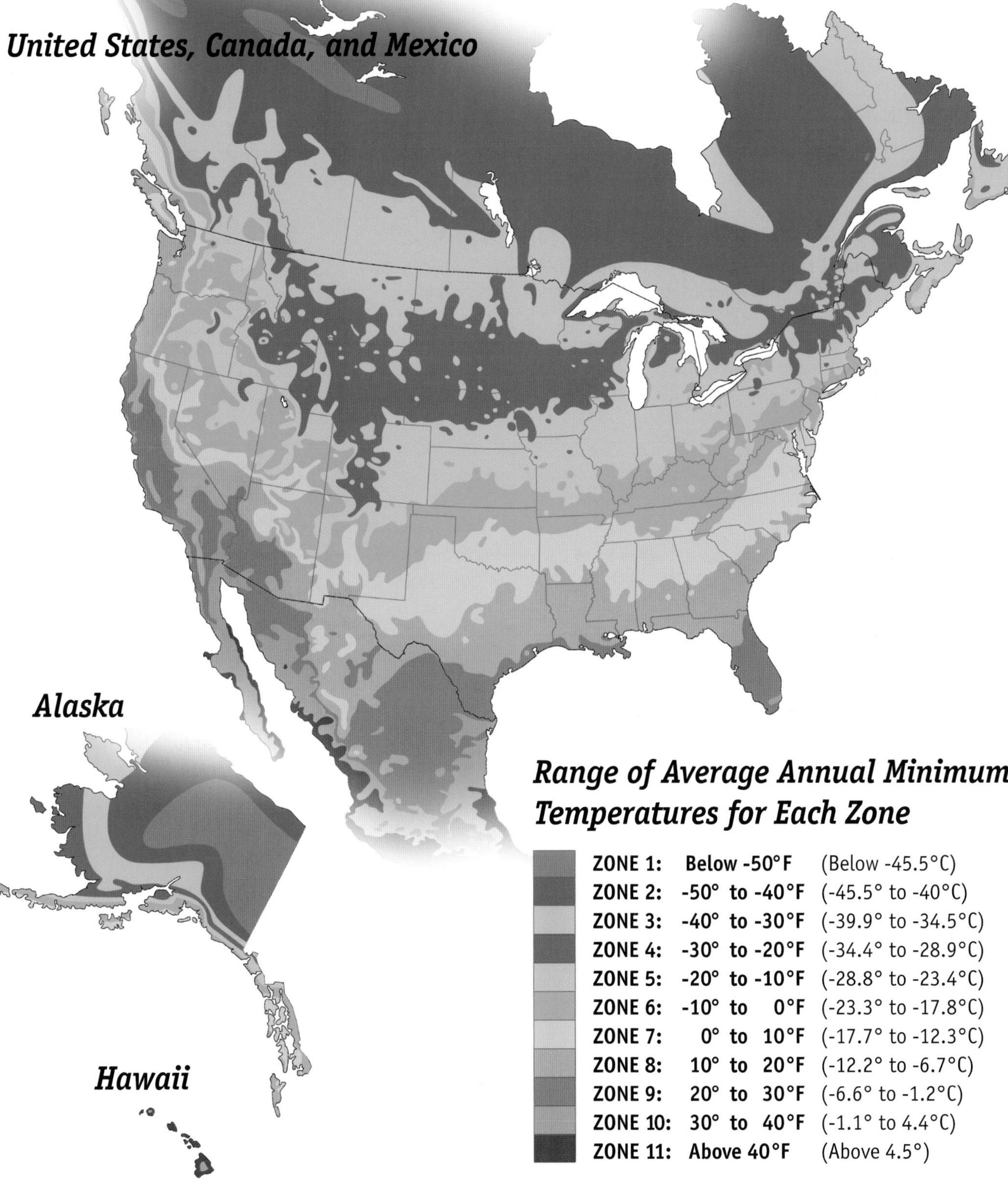

Range of Average Annual Minimum Temperatures for Each Zone

ZONE 1:	Below -50°F	(Below -45.5°C)
ZONE 2:	-50° to -40°F	(-45.5° to -40°C)
ZONE 3:	-40° to -30°F	(-39.9° to -34.5°C)
ZONE 4:	-30° to -20°F	(-34.4° to -28.9°C)
ZONE 5:	-20° to -10°F	(-28.8° to -23.4°C)
ZONE 6:	-10° to 0°F	(-23.3° to -17.8°C)
ZONE 7:	0° to 10°F	(-17.7° to -12.3°C)
ZONE 8:	10° to 20°F	(-12.2° to -6.7°C)
ZONE 9:	20° to 30°F	(-6.6° to -1.2°C)
ZONE 10:	30° to 40°F	(-1.1° to 4.4°C)
ZONE 11:	Above 40°F	(Above 4.5°)

Planning and Executing Your Landscape

This book is organized the way you should organize your landscaping plans.

Chapter One–*Design* gives you basic design concepts.

Chapter Two–*Selection* helps you choose the right plant for your yard. All the selection guides are specific to Zones 2, 3, and 4.

Chapter Three–*How-To* shows you how to install and care for plants.

Chapters Four, Five, and Six–*Trees, Shrubs, Groundcovers, and Vines* guide you through the specifics of selection, care, and feeding.

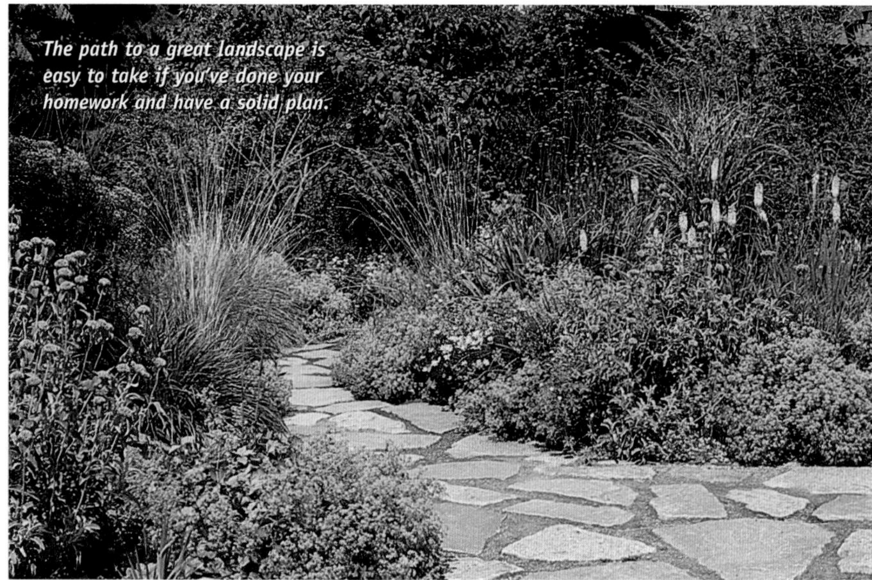

The path to a great landscape is easy to take if you've done your homework and have a solid plan.

Four Steps to a Great Landscape

1) Plan Before You Plant

Make landscaping decisions in an orderly manner to create an orderly landscape. Like building a house, planning comes first, then the foundation, walls, and roof.

2) Layout Bedlines

Lay out shapes for lawn areas and planting beds first. Work around existing plants you'd like to keep within new planting beds. Fill new beds by starting with trees. Then add shrubs. Complete the design with groundcovers and vines.The goal is an attractive, balanced composition that makes the most of outdoor areas while defining and complementing your home.

Because plants mature at different rates, be patient as your landscape takes shape. Balance rapid and slow growers in the design mix so you can have plants to enjoy as you move through the growing phases.

3) Place Trees and Shrubs

Trees and shrubs are the foundation, forming the structure of the landscape. Make decisions about these big plants first. They are also the walls of outdoor rooms, shaping the space within your yard and providing protection and privacy.

4) Add Groundcover and Vines

Groundcovers define the landscape by filling in planting beds that frame lawns. They give planting areas a lush, rich look, adding layers of greenery and flowers. Vines emphasize overhead structures, such as trellises and arbors, drawing the eye down and into the landscape.

Ideally, grass should be added when the rest of the work is done. However, you might want to incorporate some of your present lawn into a new landscape design. The key is to not let the current shape of grassy areas dictate where planting areas should go. Changing the size and shape of an old lawn can give you a refreshing new look.

Finishing Touches

Seasonal flowers are accessories, giving the finished landscape interest and accent. However, they can be in the way while you're working. Grow them in pots instead of beds while the yard is a work-in-progress. You should be focused on the basics—layout and structure—not tiptoeing around plants that have been placed out of order in the landscape.

The Bottom Line

Unless you've done your homework and your plan is well thought out, all the flowers in the world won't make your landscape a success. That's why you should go step-by-step through the entire landscaping process, starting with design in Chapter One. Before you begin, check pages 8 and 9 for special features that will help you along the way.

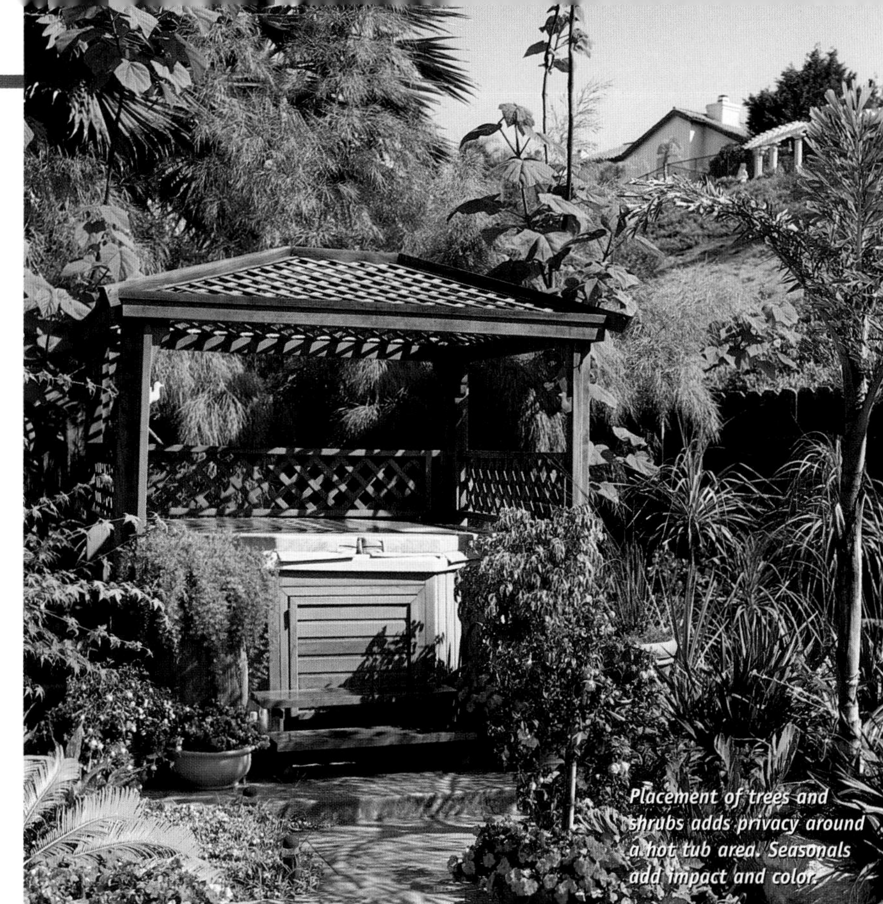

Placement of trees and shrubs adds privacy around a hot tub area. Seasonals add impact and color.

Call Before You Dig

Cutting through a cable or gas line is potentially dangerous and can be hazardous to your pocketbook as well. Utility and cable companies are happy to mark the locations of underground lines for you at no charge. Pick up the phone before you pick up a shovel to avoid cutting lines and cutting off your service.

If You Want to Hire a Pro

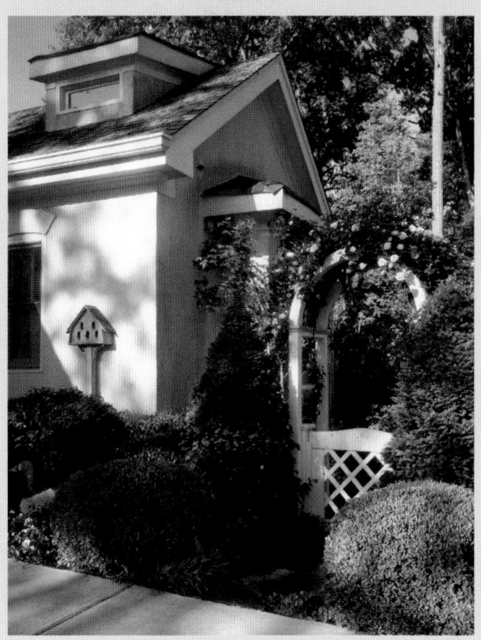

If design and planning have you stumped, consult an expert. Associates at home and garden centers often offer informal design advice as part of their service. If you want to consult a professional gardener, you have several options. **Landscape architects** are professionals licensed to prepare plans and guide planting, grading, and landscape construction. **Garden designers** might not be licensed, but they are often very qualified and can offer advice on planning and preparing your landscape. **Design/build contractors** will often provide free design services as long as they're hired to do the work as well.

Always ask for references, visit sites in progress, and see completed jobs before you negotiate a contract. Show the designer yardscapes you like. Don't be satisfied until you get what you want. Set a budget and stick to it. Never pay the entire fee up-front. Expect a licensed architect to charge a higher fee.

How to Pick the Right Plants

Rapid-growing deciduous trees for filtered views

Rapid-growing deciduous vines for screening

Combining Plants and Materials

Deciduous shrubs for screening

selection 2

Plant Selection 31

1) Selection Guides

Plant selection guides that range from the general to the specific make shopping decisions easier. First you'll find comprehensive lists of plants that grow within Zones 2, 3, and 4. (See Chapter Two: "Selection," page 20.) Then throughout the book there are lists designed to help you narrow your choices into groups of plants that will work in your landscape and stay healthy. These lists will also spark your imagination and offer plant choices you might not otherwise have considered.

Use these dedicated selection guides to determine the right plant for the right job. Establishing privacy or blocking poor views might be a top priority. Selection guides, such as the one shown above, list plants suitable for screening and filtering. There are lists for sun or shade, for different soil conditions, and for particular site conditions (slopes, small spaces, or salt spray). You'll find selection guides that group plants by similar characteristics or solve similar landscaping problems. Each plant listed in a selection guide refers you to the page where the plant is described in detail.

2) Plant Descriptions

These entries, as shown below, tell you about outstanding features, growth rate, mature size, light requirements, and form. You'll see from the photos what each plant looks like.There's also a description of how to grow each plant and its purpose in the landscape. Each description contains both botanical and common names. The "More Choices" entry will refer you to specific selection guides for proper use of the featured plant.

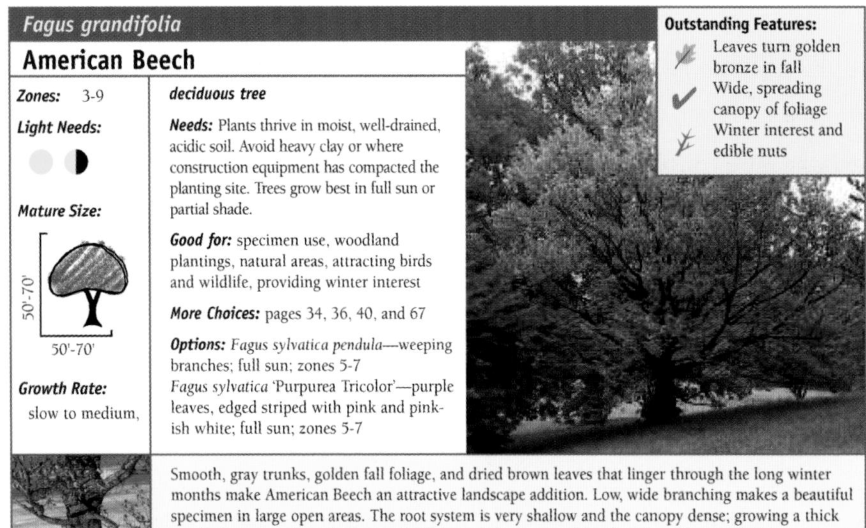
Fagus grandifolia

American Beech

Zones: 3-9

Light Needs:

Mature Size:

Growth Rate: slow to medium

deciduous tree

Needs: Plants thrive in moist, well-drained, acidic soil. Avoid heavy clay or where construction equipment has compacted the planting site. Trees grow best in full sun or partial shade.

Good for: specimen use, woodland plantings, natural areas, attracting birds and wildlife, providing winter interest

More Choices: pages 34, 36, 40, and 67

Options: *Fagus sylvatica pendula*—weeping branches; full sun; zones 5-7
Fagus sylvatica 'Purpurea Tricolor'—purple leaves, edged striped with pink and pinkish white; full sun; zones 5-7

Outstanding Features:
- Leaves turn golden bronze in fall
- Wide, spreading canopy of foliage
- Winter interest and edible nuts

Smooth, gray trunks, golden fall foliage, and dried brown leaves that linger through the long winter months make American Beech an attractive landscape addition. Low, wide branching makes a beautiful specimen in large open areas. The root system is very shallow and the canopy dense; growing a thick stand of grass can be a challenge. Mulch instead for improved tree health and less work for you. Nuts are edible and enjoyed by several species of birds and squirrels.

Understanding Rates of Growth

How fast a plant will grow depends on site conditions, how quickly it settles into its new home, and length of the growing season. With so many variables, it isn't possible to predict the number of inches or feet you can expect a plant to grow per year, but they can be generally classified as rapid, medium, and slow growers.

The Name Game

Common vs. Botanical

Cross-Referencing by Common and Botanical Names Makes Plants Easy to Identify.

Common names for plants vary greatly from region to region. The same plant can even have several different common names. This creates the potential for confusion. Plant experts have agreed to use botanical (Latin) names to maintain consistency and make sure everyone is talking about the same thing.

***Selection Guides* are alphabetized by common names.** Because most people recognize plants by their common names, the Selection Guides reflect the most common usage.

***Plant Descriptions* are alphabetized by botanical names.** Latin is the language for accurate plant identification. It's a good idea to know the botanical name even if you're not sure how to say it. Don't worry about how the words are pronounced. Knowing a little Latin will help you get the right plant.

Multiple Indexes *Selection Guides* and *Plant Descriptions* are cross-referenced throughout the book. Beginning on page 214 you'll find a **general index** for easy access to projects and landscaping information. There's also an **index** of **botanical** and **common names** to make plants easy to find no matter what they're called.

Note: Availability of specific plants varies by area and local conditions (see page 21). Check with your garden center for plants that will thrive in your particular area.

Special Features for Quick Reference

✔ *Information about hardiness and climate will help you eliminate plants that won't live where you do and help you pick the right ones for your planting zone.*

In the Zone

New plants need daily watering for the first few weeks, especially during hot weather. In cooler seasons, you can water every other day for the first week. fter that, cut back to once a week r 2 to 3 months, then reduce to ıce a month, until shrubs have eathered a full growing season. 'ater faithfully unless nature ıpplies at least one-half inch of ater during the week. Once tablished, properly sited plants ill need supplemental water only ıring hot, dry spells.

✔ *Every project includes a list of tools and materials you'll need to get the job done right.*

STUFF YOU'LL NEED

- ✔ Garden hose that you don't mind getting paint on
- ✔ Sharp-shooter or trenching shovel
- ✔ Marking paint (not regular spray paint)
- ✔ Inexpensive gloves
- ✔ Old shoes

What to Expect

You'll probably try several patterns with the hose before you're satisfied with the bedline. Don't rush the process. You'll live with your choice for a long time.

Step-by-Step Projects

3 how-to

Planting Bare-Root Roses

Whether you're planting bare-root roses or plants grown in containers, learn how to get new roses off to the best start.

Bare-root roses are shipped without soil, making them less expensive. They look like stubby sticks. You'll find these plants for sale in late winter or early spring. Plant them soon after purchasing.

STUFF YOU'LL NEED

- ✔ Bucket
- ✔ Root stimulator
- ✔ Hand pruners
- ✔ Organic matter such as bagged compost
- ✔ Round-point shovel

What to Expect

Your newly planted bare-root rose will look like a stick poking up out of the ground until new shoots and leaves appear in a few weeks.

1 **Carefully open the packaging.** Avoid cutting roots. Gently remove packing material from roots and discard. Place the roots in a bucket of water mixed with root stimulator and allow them to soak in a dark, cool, dry location such as a garage. Soak roots no longer than eight hours.

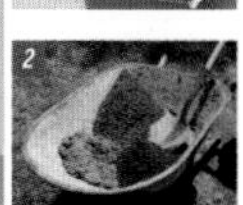

2 **Dig a hole in a spot that receives at least six hours of sun daily.** The hole should be 12 to 18 inches deep. Mix bagged compost with some of the native soil in a wheelbarrow or on a tarp to create a mixture that's about two-thirds organic matter and one-third native soil. The soil mixture should appear dark and rich.

BUYER'S GUIDE

Pick up several bare-root roses before you buy one. If one feels heavier than the others or has water dripping from its packaging, it's not the one you want to take home to plant in your yard. Roots that are bare should stay moist but not wet during shipping.

3 **Shovel the good soil mixture into the hole until it's nearly full.** Use your hands to form a cone of soil in the center of the hole. Make the top of the cone slightly below the level of adjacent, undisturbed soil. Position the rose on top of the cone, spreading roots evenly around it.

4 **Backfill around the rose with soil.** Make sure the scion (the ridge where the rose was grafted to the rootstock) is still visible above the soil. Add a thick layer of compost for mulch. Use excess native soil to form a moat around the freshly planted rose. Fill moat with a slowly trickling hose.

Good idea! **Before plant... hand...**

54 How-to

TOOL TIP

Round-point shovels are great for digging holes and scooping out soil. Shovels with fiberglass handles usually last longer than those with wooden handles.

✔ *Having the right tool and knowing how to use it can make a world of difference.*

Homer's Hindsight

When I landscaped our first home, I picked out plants by purchasing whatever caught my eye at the garden center. The yard looked all right at first, but after a while, it was a mess! And it was a lot of work trying to keep that many different kinds of plants healthy and neat. Landscaping is easier with a strategy.

✔ *Homer helps you avoid mistakes before you make them.*

Design Tip

The front yard is more heavily influenced by architecture than the backyard. Your house and front yard landscape are seen together from the street. On the other hand, the backyard is usually seen when looking from the house, not at it. If the architecture makes a formal style appropriate, use a traditional approach to design in front; if you also like informally styled outdoor spaces, grow a m free-form landscape in the back.

✔ *Hints from a landscape architect will make your yard look its best.*

BUYER'S GUIDE

If you want a larger tree than those in stock, ask a garden associate about ordering a B&B tree for you. Some stores stock balled-and-burlapped trees only upon request. Inquire about the approximate measurements of the root ball and dig the proper-sized hole before the tree arrives. Ask if delivery is available for a fee when you order your tree. If so, find out where the tree will be left—don't be surprised if the delivery driver will take it no farther than the curb. You'll probably need to have a sturdy wheelbarrow waiting to get the tree to the hole. You might want to hire a professional or get a friend to help with a big tree; B&B trees are heavy.

✔ *Solid shopping tips from the pros.*

✔ *Great advice you can't get anywhere else—tried-and-true wisdom of the aisles from the experts at Home Depot.*

Wisdom of the Aisles

Most trees and shrubs require no fertilizer at all during their first year in your landscape. That's because they've been heavily fertilized during nursery production to make them look their best on the shelves. If you add fertilizer at planting and then apply more fertilizer later in the growing season, you've probably given your new plants a double-dose of chemicals they don't need. Wait until the second year of growth.

✔ *Good ideas go along with step-by-step instructions to make projects even easier.*

Put the Best Face on Things. Before backfilling, turn your shrub so that its best side is facing the direction from which it will be viewed. Once the dirt's in the hole, it's harder to adjust the shrub's direction.

Chapter 1
design

A successful landscape design defines the function of outdoor spaces. Lush foliage around the pond on the left creates a sense of privacy and tranquility for this backyard getaway, while carefully placed combinations of color and form beckon along garden paths.

Four Elements of Design

This is where you unlock the secrets of landscape design. Start with the four building blocks that form the basis of outdoor composition.

1) Color is the first element—easy to identify, but challenging to use correctly. So many colors are appealing that it can be hard to limit your choices.

Flowerbeds are obvious sources of color, but trees, shrubs, groundcovers, and vines are bloomers as well. Leaf color, seasonal variations, and the hues of bark and branches also have impact. Both flowers and foliage need to work with other features—paving, outdoor furniture and fabrics, and the colors of your home.

Color evokes an emotional response. Bright colors give a garden a cheerful, pleasing look. Just one noticeable color contrasting with green leaves gives a landscape a sophisticated appearance. Too many colors in too many places compete for attention and overwhelm the design. Carefully placed color directs your guests right to your front door.

2) Texture is a subtle but important element of good design. The more you know about texture and how it works, the more professional your landscape will be.

You might think of texture as something you touch—the roughness of sandpaper or the smoothness of silk—but it's also something you see. Coarsely textured plants have big leaves, large flowers, or rough, peeling bark. They are characterized as bold or architectural. Finely textured plants have tiny leaves and twigs, or flowers with many small petals. Many species of plants fall somewhere between. Leaf texture matters in landscape design because flowering time is usually brief.

Textures blend or contrast. If you're using a lot of different colors in your landscape, minimize the difference in textures. Conversely, if you have a shady yard with few hues, a variety of textures adds interest. Place a large-leaf, coarsely textured plant, such as Catawba Rhododendron, behind a tiny-leaf, finely textured plant, such as Maidenhair Fern. The contrast in textures will be eye-catching.

3) Line impacts landscape design. The horizontal outlines of walkways, patios, driveways, and bedlines carve fluid shapes and create spaces. They separate planting areas from the lawn, creating areas for trees, shrubs, groundcovers, and vines. Bedlines should complement existing landscaping—the shape of your house on the land, paved areas, trees, and fences.

Vertical lines are also important. If everything is the same height, your landscape will appear flat and dull. Trees are the most obvious example. Upright, spiky foliage, such as iris leaves, also add a vertical accent to the landscape. Fencing and posts will contribute vertical lines to your yard. Too many vertical lines, however, will make a yard small and crowded. The goal is to frame and balance open spaces with vertical lines.

A picture is still worth a thousand words. Colors that seem so attractive in the store might not work when planted near your home. Picking complementary colors from memory is tough. Even if you're sure of the color scheme, take some snapshots of the outside of your house with you when you go plant shopping. It'll help the salespeople and possibly eliminate a return trip.

4) Form defines the physical presence of a plant and the space it takes up in your yard. Knowing the mature shape of a plant is critical when plant shopping. If you want a plant that will stay low and neat, don't buy one that is naturally large and arching. You won't be able to prune it into a compact shape, and the plant won't be attractive when confined to an unnatural form.

The shape of a young plant is not necessarily the same as it will be when it matures. Study the form symbols with the plant descriptions in this book or on plant tags. Ask before you buy. You will hear the terms regular or irregular. Regular forms are symmetrical—neatly rounded, compact, pyramidal, or oval. Irregular forms are uneven, resist pruning, and are described as airy, natural, loose, arching, spreading, or sculptural. What you buy depends on your design. Choose regular shrubs for a neatly clipped hedge or formal garden. If you're seeking an airy backdrop for a cottage garden or a woodland scene, irregular forms are best. A single plant with uneven form can serve as a living sculpture.

A garden bench becomes a focal point because it contrasts with its setting. The texture of ornamental grasses, the curving lawn, and arching and mounded plant forms provide visual contrast.

Choosing Colors That Work with Your Home

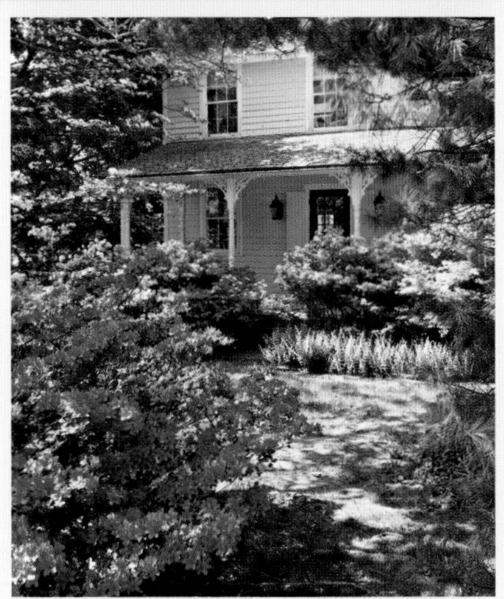

Welcome the seasons by choosing plants to color your landscape with spring or summer flowers, fall foliage, or bright winter stems.

If your home is a neutral color, such as tan, buff, gray, beige, brown, or white, just about any flower or foliage color will look good beside it. Houses featuring unusual colors, such as lavender-painted siding or pink-tinted stucco, should depend heavily on dark greens and whites. But keep things fun by repeating the house color in nearby plants. Matching the color or using flower hues a little darker will emphasize the scheme.

Bold color schemes present other challenges. Hot pink flowers and yellow, golden, or bluish foliage won't work well with a red brick house. Plant lots of dark green instead, and stick to white, dark purple, or pale pink flowers. Yellow can work if separated from the brick by a layer of dark green leaves. Oranges and reds will clash; use them elsewhere in your yard, away from the house.

Professional Principles of Design

Now that you've gone through the elements of design, the next step is learning how to apply them in your landscape. The methods professionals use to manipulate design elements are known as the principles of design. Here's what they are and how they can help you create a beautiful and functional landscape. If you need help planning your landscape, work with a professional designer to give your yard style.

A walkway leading to the front door winds through a landscape unified by color. Roses repeat the pink blossoms of Anthony Waterer Spirea, (Spiraea japonica 'Anthony Waterer'), page 157.

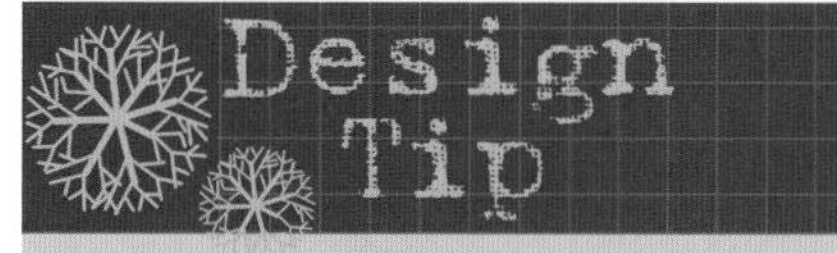

Planting the same kind of plant in more than one place is a surefire way to add unity to your landscape through repetition. But you can also repeat a characteristic common to different kinds of plants. For example, wispy ornamental grasses have fine texture. So do delicate ferns, some grasslike clumping groundcovers, and shrubs with tiny leaves. Plant them together to create a mass of fine texture, which makes an excellent background for showing off a coarse-textured, large-leafed plant as an accent. Set plants with similar textures in different places throughout your yard. This makes it easier to deal with different conditions. In the example above, you can plant ferns in the shade and ornamental grasses in the sun, repeating the fine textures of both plants and unifying your landscape. Texture isn't the only element you can repeat. Using similar colors, lines, or forms will also add unity.

1) ***Unity*** is the glue that holds a landscape together, and repetition is the means to achieve it. Without unity a yard is a hodgepodge of plants. Trees, shrubs, groundcovers, and vines are lovely individually, but they must work together to make your design cohesive.

At first, examples of unity can be hard to spot. But look closely at yards you admire in your neighborhood or study attractive landscapes in books and magazines. You will notice that, no matter how much styles vary, well-designed landscapes all share a certain elusive quality: The plants in well-designed landscapes seem to belong where they are placed. The secret is unity, and here's how to get it.

Repetition gives your landscape a unified look. Even cottage gardens, which contain a multitude of flowers, are held together by repetition of one or more elements: color, texture, line, or form. For example, in a cottage garden the flowers might be united by a color theme of mostly pinks or shades of yellow. Perhaps there are many bright colors tied together with generous helpings of white. Landscapes that feature multitudes of flowers need a good solid background for structure. Evergreen trees and shrubs, walls, or picket fences are common choices of unifying materials.

You don't have to have a cottage garden to need unity in your landscape. Start by selecting the trees and shrubs that form the backbone of your composition. Limit yourself to a core group of plants that grow well in your area. Using 8-2-2 (8 kinds of shrubs, 2 kinds of trees, and 2 kinds of groundcovers) is a proven combination. You can vary this, but

When color schemes are simplified, other design elements become more noticeable. The textures and forms of a bed of conifers and heathers capture attention.

don't be tempted to introduce too many different plants at this early stage. Think of these core plants as wardrobe basics; you can mix and match them for different looks. Using the same kind of plant in more than one place in your yard is an example of repetition and a good way to achieve unity.

When you're ready to add more plants to your basic landscape, keep the value of repetition in mind. Set showier plants together in groups, known as masses, so they'll have an attractive impact on the composition. (Scattering plants tends to dilute their effect.) Adding masses of the same species of plant in more than one place will create a cohesive and unified look.

2) Accent is the second principle of landscape design. This is the fun stuff: eye-catching plants with brightly colored flowers, unusual forms, or noticeable leaves. Just because a plant is showy doesn't make it an accent. Like real estate, it's all about location.

A plant must stand out from its surroundings to serve as an accent. Too many varieties of showy plants too close together will compete for attention. Contrast is the key. A plant becomes distinctive when its color, texture, line, or form contrasts with its setting.

Create contrast by placing an eye-catching plant in a mass of similar plants. Your accent plant will be showcased, making its special qualities noticeable. You can choose a single accent plant, known as a specimen, to stand alone, or set a few of the same kind of accent plants together for a bigger impact. Groups of three work well in many settings.

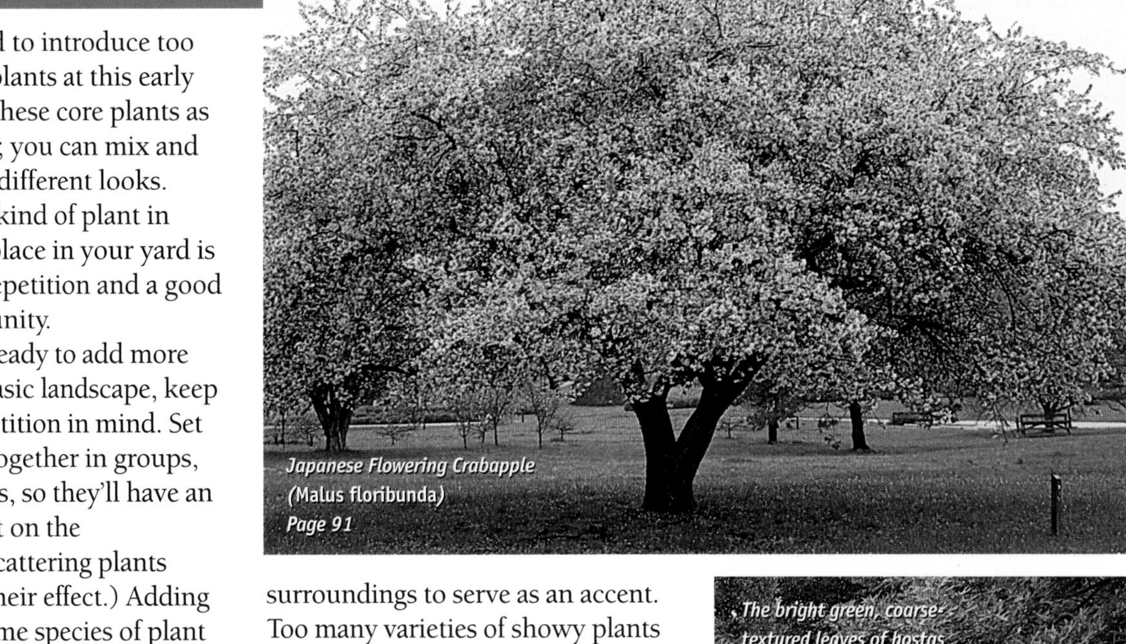

Japanese Flowering Crabapple (Malus floribunda)
Page 91

The bright green, coarse-textured leaves of hostas contrast with darker, lacy leaves to create an accent in the garden.

Homer's Hindsight

When I landscaped our first home, I picked out plants by purchasing whatever caught my eye at the garden center. The yard looked all right at first, but after a while, it was a mess! And it was a lot of work trying to keep that many different kinds of plants healthy and neat. I'm doing things differently at our second house. I have a pretty good idea of what characteristics a plant should have and where it will go in my yard before I buy it. I still purchase some plants from time to time just because they're pretty, but it's a lot easier to work them into the landscape now that I have a strategy.

Creating Focal Points

Evergreen trees and shrubs offer ample opportunity for dressing up an entry walk with beds and containers of seasonal flowers. The bright colors lead the way to the front door.

Position colorful plants where they'll draw attention to what you want your visitors to see. Your landscape should focus first on the house and then on your front door. If it's hard to tell which house is yours, add an address plate near a bright, eye-catching planting so the mailbox isn't the only indication of your house number. This way, you'll focus attention on your home, not your mailbox. Use attractive plantings at property entrances and in parking areas. This makes guests feel welcome. Lead them to the door with landscaping—putting the brightest colors there denotes a destination.

Growing in Style

The exterior of your home should fit your personal style, just as the interior does. The appearance of your home—its architectural style—has a big role in setting the scene. Bungalows, colonial mansions, rustic log homes, and adobe houses each have their own distinctive look. Though you could choose the same plants for any of these houses, the way you arrange the plants to create a setting is the essence of style. Setting a style for your landscape is the result of a combination of influences. Understanding them will make it easier for you to create a landscape in the style that's right for you.

1) Formal style will complement many traditional types of architecture, characterized by an even number of windows symmetrically placed, balanced wings, or formal columns. This style also works well in small city gardens. Formality is achieved by arranging plants, walkways, benches, and other outdoor features along an invisible line, known as an axis. Plants on one side of the axis match, or mirror, those on the opposite, creating symmetry. Arrange plants in groups that are evenly divisible by two. Pairs of plants establish instant symmetry as do two matching shrubs on each side of a walkway. Plants set in rows or in recognizable geometric patterns, such as squares, diamonds, rectangles, and circles, also lend a formal style to a landscape. (Repeat shapes found on your house, such as windows or trim.) The more symmetry, the more formal your design. Formal landscaping shows the designer's hand in nature. Your choice of plant material also affects formality. Plants that can be clipped into smooth hedges, round balls, or neat cones add a formal touch.

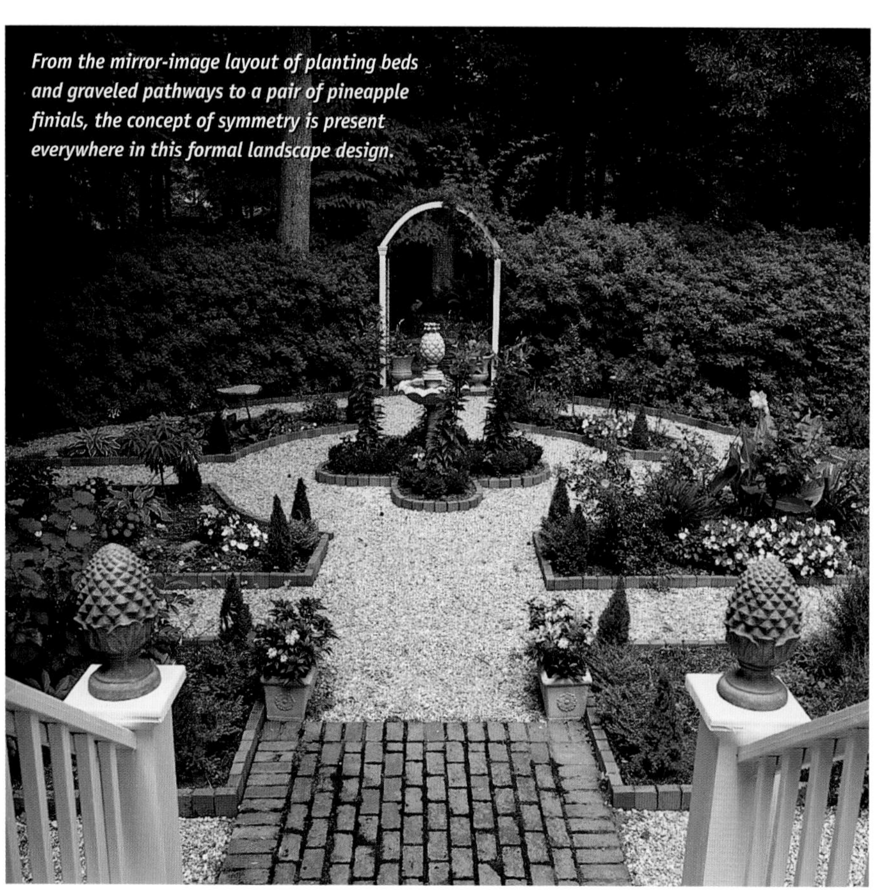

From the mirror-image layout of planting beds and graveled pathways to a pair of pineapple finials, the concept of symmetry is present everywhere in this formal landscape design.

Regional Styles

Let where you live influence the style of your landscape. Including native plants will make your landscape look appropriate for its location, and the plants will be more likely to survive. Using other indigenous materials will also give your landscape a local flavor. Local plants and materials look best when paired with architectural styles that are typical of the region. Paving materials, such as brick, stone, tile, or pebbles, might be produced in your region, as well as the kind of wood and finish you choose for fences, gates, benches, rails, and arbors. A Cape Cod will look wonderful with a weathered picket fence covered with climbing roses framing the entry. Such a design reflects the English heritage of the Northeast.

If your house features a look borrowed from elsewhere, design the landscape's style to match the architecture first and the region second. Include native plants whenever their natural forms are appropriate to the landscape style that suits your house.

2) *Informal style* is the natural arrangement of elements. It complements a wide range of architectural styles. Informal landscapes are asymmetrical—their components don't match up like a mirror. Instead of dividing the landscape with an axis, arrange planting beds in broad, sweeping curves. This will soften the hard lines of any house and make it seem nestled into the landscape.

Though they don't feature mirror images, asymmetrical landscapes must be balanced. If you have a large shade tree at one end of a planting bed, balance it with three large shrubs at the far end. This approach sets a scene that looks balanced instead of lopsided.

Plants with natural and irregular forms are informal. Those that arch, spread, twist, or seem fluffy or airy give landscapes a casual style.

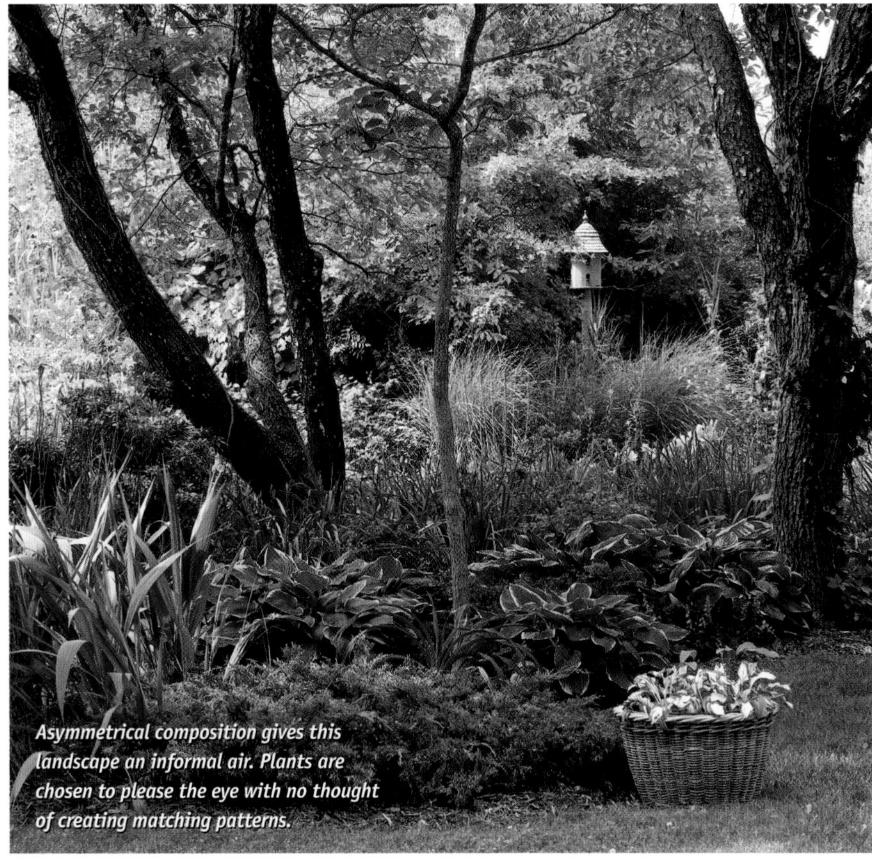

Asymmetrical composition gives this landscape an informal air. Plants are chosen to please the eye with no thought of creating matching patterns.

3) *Combining styles* should be done carefully. As long as you don't have formal features competing with informal ones, you can combine styles successfully. Use one style to set the dominant tone of your landscape, then create little accent areas of the opposite style. A landscape full of curving bedlines without a central axis is informal, but you can add a few formal touches. For example, a pair of ornamental trees framing a view add a touch of formality, but won't be out of place in an informal setting.

Combining styles can also add contrast. A formally clipped hedge surrounding a bed of plants with delicate flowers and foliage on lanky stems will create an appealing scene showing off both kinds of plants to their best advantage.

How much work do you want to do? Maintenance considerations affect choice of style. If you enjoy pruning, try a formal landscape with lots of plants clipped into neat shapes. If you want to spend more time admiring your landscape than working in it, an informal style might suit your needs. To reduce maintenance chores, avoid mixing many different kinds of plants closely together. You'll find it difficult to meet their individual needs unless you enjoy puttering with plants. Consider growing conditions when choosing plants. The right plant in the right place is still the first rule of landscaping.

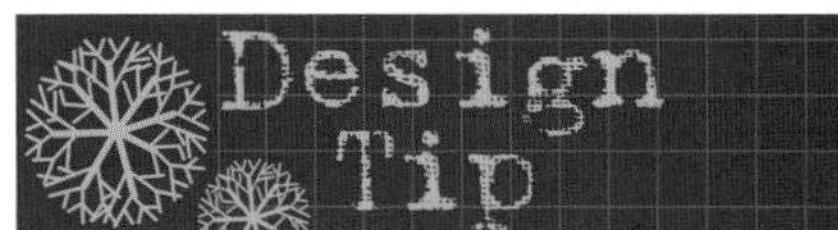

The front yard is more heavily influenced by architecture than the backyard. Your house and front yard landscape are seen together from the street. On the other hand, the backyard is usually seen when looking from the house, not at it. If the architecture makes a formal style appropriate, use a traditional approach to design in front; if you also like informally styled outdoor spaces, grow a more free-form landscape in the back.

A pair of pots adds a formal touch to an informally designed landscape, drawing attention to the bench. A pair of matching shrubs or small trees could do the same.

Assessing Your Yard

Great landscapes start at home, not at the store. The first things you need to decide are what you have that's worth keeping, what you need to get rid of, and what problems need to be solved before you can start making improvements.

1) Create a Base Map and Site Analysis

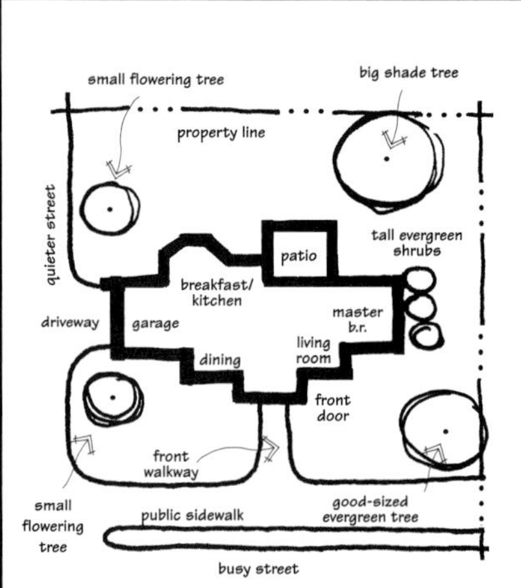

A base map doesn't have to be neat or accurate. It's just the first step in assessing your property.

To assess your yard, you'll need to take an objective look at your property. It helps to have a sketch on which you can take notes. Make a photocopy of your original survey if you have one. If you can't find your survey, make a rough sketch showing the shape of your lot with the house and any paving on it. Don't worry about making the drawing neat and pretty or getting accurate dimensions. The purpose of this sketch is to make it easier to take notes about different areas. Mark approximate locations of trees, water features, and existing bedlines to indicate the locations and shapes of planting beds and lawn areas. The result is a rough base map.

With your base map in hand, walk your property. Look at the exterior spaces from different angles, including from across the street. Note the parking areas and walkways. Go inside the house and look out windows; views from the inside are part of landscaping, too.

You're looking for assets and liabilities for the site analysis. Assets are things that you want to keep. Attractive planting areas, healthy shrubs, big shade trees, small accent trees, good stands of lawn, and pretty vines are assets. Mark good views looking into your property and looking outward. Nicely paved areas, welcoming walkways, and interesting architectural features on your home are also worth noting. Anything you like is an asset.

Now it's time to be blunt. List all the liabilities you see. Scribble notes and arrows all over your sketch. Use a different color ink to contrast with the notes you made about assets.

Liabilities include unattractive or unhealthy plants, trees or shrubs that block good views or make interior rooms dark and gloomy, plants that are messy or require constant maintenance, scraggly lawn areas, or deteriorating paving, walls, or fences. Include poor views seen while looking at your home, out the windows, or from within your yard looking out toward adjacent properties. Note areas that don't have enough privacy, shade, or seating to be comfortable.

Other common liabilities include traffic noises, glare, inadequate parking, and noticeable utility areas.

TOOL TIP

A camera is a valuable landscaping tool. Snapshots can give you an objective perspective. You might be surprised at what you've become used to seeing. Take pictures from across the street and from different angles to get different views. Shoot one or two that will show what's behind you. Take pictures that can be taped together to form a panoramic view by holding the camera steady and pivoting slightly as you shoot. (Panoramic cameras make this job easier.) Take your photos shopping with you. They're a helpful tool for communicating with salespeople.

Scribble notes on a sketched base map to get a clear picture of exterior assets and liabilities. When you're done, you'll have a site analysis.

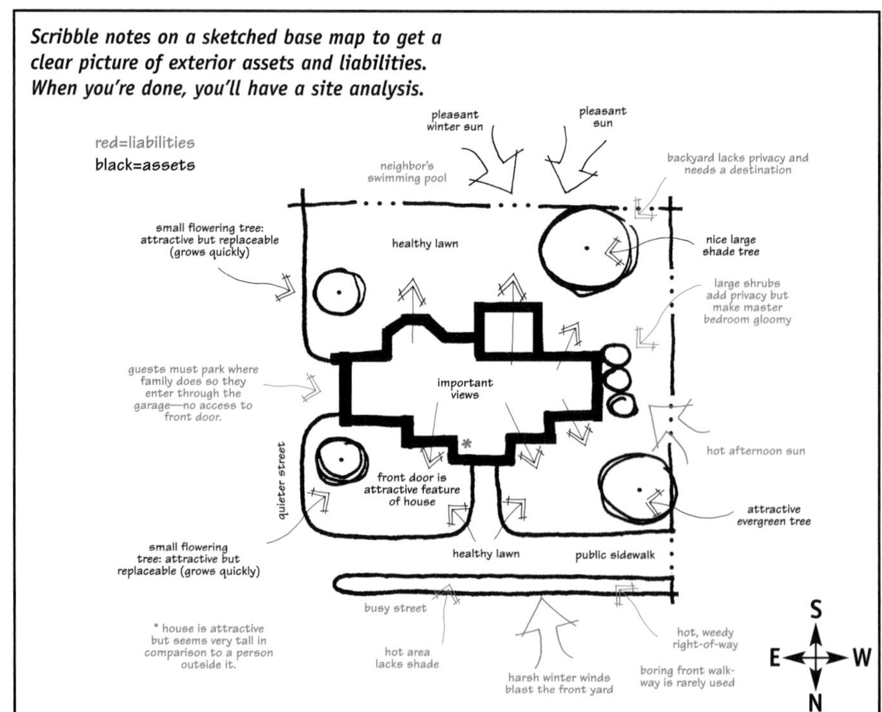

Look for unattractive aspects of your house. Blank, windowless walls; old closed-in garages with driveways leading nowhere; and tall foundations will make your list. Drainage problems should be noted, too: Spots that stay wet or are difficult to keep moist are important factors in plant selection.

Good landscaping overcomes liabilities and makes the most of the assets of your home. It could be painful to be objective now, but it's easier to fix problems if you know what they are.

2) Inventory Your Needs

Landscape architects and garden designers visit with their clients before beginning work. They learn about a family's likes and dislikes, their budget, and their priorities before they begin. You'll need to do the same thing. Though it seems as though all the answers would be obvious (after all, you're your own client), a little research goes a long way toward setting obtainable landscaping goals.

List your needs and your goals. Some things might be obvious, such as providing additional parking or adding more shade. Others will take more thought—making your walkway more inviting or adding privacy to make your patio more usable or more intimate.

Follow these observations with notations about the cause of the current condition. For example, if your walkway is uncomfortable, it might be too narrow. Adding borders of bricks, pavers, or stones can widen the paving to make it more inviting. Or, crumbling, uneven paving might need to be replaced.

3) Set a Budget Decide how much you'd like to spend and then research the costs of plants, materials, delivery, and labor if you're hiring help. Most people find that landscaping costs more than they think, so budgets have to be flexible. Compared with the cost of your house, landscaping is a reasonable investment. If you're building a new home, set aside 10 percent of the cost for landscaping. If that's impossible, find a percentage you can live with and stick to it. You'll be glad you didn't spend all your money on the interior when it comes time to dress up the exterior—after all, that's the area most people will see.

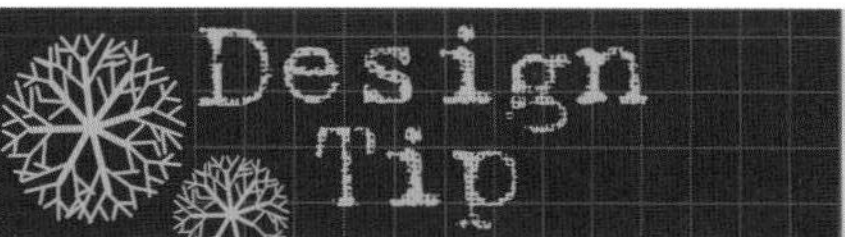

Smart Design—Inside and Out

You're missing a design bet if you don't plan your landscape to work from both the inside and outside of your home. Windows are picture frames that invite you into a living world. Creating great views from favorite interior spaces such as bedrooms, family rooms, kitchens, and living rooms will give you hours of enjoyment when you can't be outside.

Landscape Assessment Quiz

How well do you know your property?

Answer these questions before you head for the garden center. Prepare a packet with all the notes you've gathered, including the snapshots of your home and yard, and bring it along. Accurate information will help you get you what you want.

1) What's your exposure?
Knowing the direction your house faces (the exposure) will help you design your landscape and select the right plant. Some plants will thrive on southern exposure but freeze on the northern side of your house. Others grow in eastern sun but wilt in hot, western sun. Use a compass to find north or track where the sun rises (east) and sets (west). If you're facing west, north is to your right.

2) How's your sun and shade?
Knowing how the amount of sun or shade affects plants is essential to their survival. (See pages 32-33.) Observe at various times of the day (10 a.m., noon, 3 p.m., and 5 p.m.) to see how the sun affects your property. Buildings, walls, evergreen trees, and shrubs also might provide shade most of the year. Trees, shrubs, and vines will allow winter sunlight to filter through during dormancy but will cast shade during the summer. Does the project area receive morning sun or afternoon sun? Refer to your notes and combine that with information about exposure: East-facing areas receive morning light unless shaded, and west-facing spots generally receive afternoon sun.

3) What's your soil like? Dig a few sample holes in your project area and examine the soil. (See page 38 for information on soil and percolation tests.) Some basic questions are: What color is the soil a few inches beneath the surface? Is the soil moist or dry? The ideal soil will roll into a ball yet crumble easily, will be dark in color, and will hold water and nutrients. For a detailed analysis, visit your county extension service and arrange for a soil test.

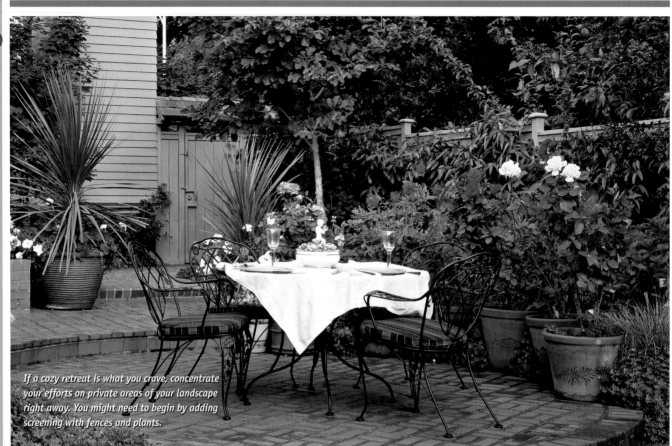

If a cozy retreat is what you crave, concentrate your efforts on private areas of your landscape right away. You might need to begin by adding screening with fences and plants.

Prioritizing Your Plans

Plan your design and then break it down into manageable projects. Completing work on specific areas is more satisfying than scattering your efforts. Improving your landscape in phases stretches your budget, too. Before you choose which project area to work on first, prioritize your needs. First, look at your public and private spaces.

1) *Public Spaces* The exterior area around your house can be broadly classified in two categories—public and private. Public spaces are the parts of your yard that you present to guests and the public, including passersby and workers who access your property. For many people, these public areas are a top priority. Completing this portion of a landscape makes a home look its best from the street and beautifies the neighborhood. Making public areas the first priority is a practical decision, too. A well-designed landscape welcomes people, gives them a place to park, and provides clear access to the house. Good landscaping adds value to your home by enhancing curb appeal. If you're making improvements to enhance sales value, public spaces will be your priority.

On most lots, the front yard is the public space, and many people begin their landscape efforts there. That's fine if public space is your top priority. In fact, most builders will spend the entire landscape allowance on the front yard because that's what helps sell the house. But don't automatically concentrate on the front yard if you'd really rather begin by working on more private family areas. Prioritize your efforts to meet your family's needs, or you might never get around to sprucing up the area you'd use the most.

Pay attention to the public spaces of your yard. Landscaping around the front door will make your home welcoming and attractive.

2) *Private Spaces* Family entries, entertainment areas, and spots to sit, read, talk, or snooze in the fresh air are quiet private spaces. Active private areas include children's play areas and places for growing vegetables or favorite flowers. Utility areas are also

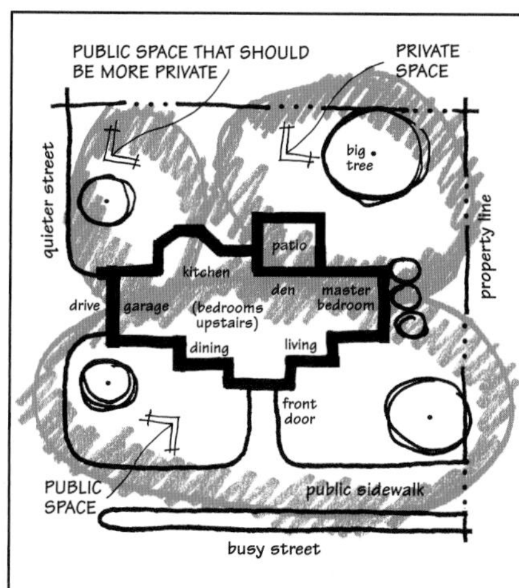

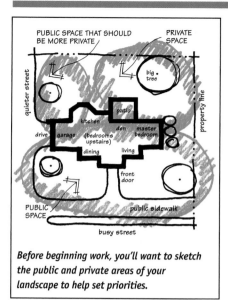

Before beginning work, you'll want to sketch the public and private areas of your landscape to help set priorities.

Brick steps, pots of flowers, and a pretty garden gate mark the entry to somewhere special. Lush plantings and walls make this backyard patio private and comfortable.

private—there's no need for neighbors to share a view of garbage cans, dog runs, and storage spots.

Most backyards and some side yards are private spaces. If you don't enjoy being in your backyard, or feel you're on display when you sit there, make some changes. A lack of destination, poor views, no privacy, drainage problems, too little or too much shade, and unattractive plants are common backyard problems. If some of these descriptions sound like your backyard, working on it might be more important than working on the public spaces. Let family members have a say. The landscape is part of your home and should meet everyone's needs—including pets.

Focus Your Work Dividing your landscaping goals into phases makes achieving them more likely. It's much more satisfying to complete a project area within your yard than it is to get bogged down trying to do all the work at once. Doing the job in phases is also a good way to stretch a budget. Set priorities to concentrate your efforts.

Design Tip

Multiple Priorities Planning phases for landscaping public and private spaces isn't an either/or proposition. You can devise a plan that includes major work on a private space, such as the backyard, as well as minor improvements for the front. Those changes can make it immediately more presentable and create the groundwork for a bigger overhaul later on.

Combined Spaces

Lots don't always divide neatly in half, with the front as public space and the back as private space. You can also carve out private spaces within the front yard, increasing the area's usefulness. Low hedges, walls, or fences distinguish a private space from a public one. Waist-high barriers seem friendly and unchallenging, giving you the best of both worlds—you can have a public conversation and still offer privacy with outdoor seating behind the hedge.

You might need to separate a private area to make the public space more appealing. If everyone is entering your house through a messy garage strewn with toys and tools, rethink your landscape. Block views of doors that you don't want people to use. A vine-covered trellis or artfully arranged trees and shrubs keep family entries from becoming visible targets for guests. Make the public area welcoming by including a wide, inviting, well-lit walkway close to where people get out of their cars or approach from public sidewalks. (Consider creating separate guest parking.) Keep the landscape fresh and tidy around the door you'd like guests to use. If it looks like no one ever goes there, no one ever will.

Chapter 2

selection

White Fir
(Abies concolor)
Page 74

A thriving landscape full of healthy plants isn't an accident. It's the result of thorough research and careful planning. Good plant selection is the key.

Sweetshrub
(Calycanthus floridus)
Page 129

The Right Plant in the Right Place

If there's a common equation for good results in the landscaping trade, it would be something like this: right + right + right = success. But you don't need chalk and a blackboard to figure out that the *right* plant in the *right* place with the *right* care will guarantee landscaping success.

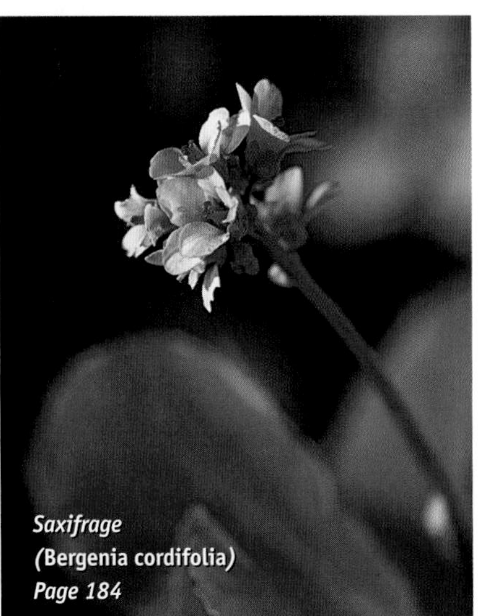

Saxifrage
(Bergenia cordifolia)
Page 184

Proper plant selection is critical. A lovely plant in the wrong place won't thrive or serve its intended purpose, and will require constant attention. A poorly chosen plant might grow too large for the space and require excessive pruning. Choosing the wrong location for a plant means that conditions are unfavorable for growth, resulting in more work on your part. Finally, there's an artistic issue. The wrong plant in the wrong place just won't work well within your landscape design.

Follow these steps to choose the right plant for the right place:

1) Determine Your Needs

Chapter One is a road map for figuring out what you want; if you skipped it, go back and work through the exercises so you'll understand the roles each plant plays within your landscape design. You might need some plants to supply privacy, others to dress up the front of your house, and still others to add interest to a backyard patio. Before plant shopping, pick a specific project area within your yard and list the purposes new plants should serve to make that area work.

Wisdom of the Aisles

Reduce yard work. Proper plant selection in the beginning will help keep maintenance requirements at a manageable level later on. That's because plants that thrive in their setting are less susceptible to insects and disease problems than those that struggle to survive. Plants that are right for their location require less coaxing to grow. Plants that are correctly sited have room to mature. Their natural forms fit their chosen sites well and require little pruning.

Make existing elements on your site work for you. Selecting plants that thrive in rocky soil and full sun turns this barren stone outcropping into a garden.

2) Define Existing Conditions

You need to know what conditions exist within your project area and which plants will thrive there. Refer to notes you made during your site analysis (see page 16), but repeat the exercise focusing on your project area. Note whether the area is hilly or flat; wet, moist, or dry; and sunny or shady in mornings and afternoons. Learn which direction your area faces and whether it's protected from harsh winds or exposed to them. Check to see whether the soil is hard and compacted or rich and soft. Look for any special conditions, such as salt spray from ocean breezes, confined root space, or city conditions such as car exhaust.

BUYER'S GUIDE

Don't overlook a good plant just because it isn't in full bloom at the store. You're better off buying a vigorous plant that's shaped properly according to its species than you would be if you made flowers the top shopping criteria. Your purchases are for the long run.

3) Study Your Options

Use the selection guides that follow to help you get started in the decisionmaking process. These lists of plants are a good first step toward choosing the right plants for the right places in your yard. They'll help you match your needs, your desires, and the conditions of your yard with a variety of suitable plants. To get a complete picture of your options, you'll need to look up descriptions of plants on the pages listed. It's also important to supplement your research with observations about what grows in your area. Seek the advice of local experts, too. Talented gardeners and associates at garden centers are valuable sources of information when it comes to choosing plants for your region.

Examine the selection guides and eliminate any plant that doesn't include your climate zone within its growing range (see page 5 to determine your climate zone). But keep in mind that not every plant with a zone number that matches yours will grow where you live. That's because climate zones are based on the minimal temperatures at which plants will thrive. This information is valuable, but it's not the final word in plant selection. Other climate factors such as annual rainfall and humidity also play a role in choosing plants. Local soil conditions and soil pH affect which plants you'll find for sale in your area, too. Availability is also dependent in part upon local growers who supply plants to stores.

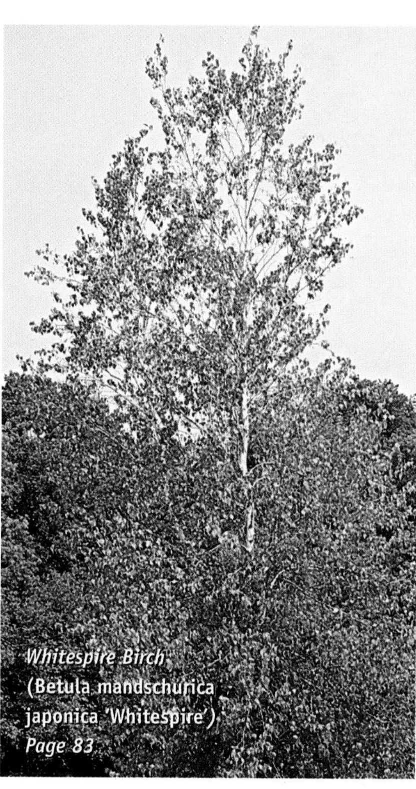

Whitespire Birch (Betula mandschurica japonica 'Whitespire') *Page 83*

Plants for Zone 2

Locate your area on the map on page 5 to determine the number of your climate zone. The plants in the following lists will thrive in Zone 2. These lists categorize plants by height. Follow the pages listed to the encyclopedia entries that will give you complete information on the plants you're considering. Availability varies by area and conditions (see page 21). Check with your garden center.

Trees for Zone 2

Common Name	Zones	Page
◆ Small Trees (30 feet or under)		
Amur Maple *Acer tataricum ginnala*	2-6	77
◆ Medium Trees (30 to 60 feet)		
Amur Chokecherry *Prunus maackii*	2-6	97
Colorado Blue Spruce *Picea pungens glauca*	2-7	93
Jack Pine *Pinus banksiana*	2-6	94
Norway Spruce *Picea abies*	2-7	92
Quaking Aspen *Populus tremuloides*	2-6	96
White Spruce *Picea glauca*	2-6	92
◆ Large Trees (60 feet or more)		
American Linden *Tilia americana*	2-8	105
Canoe Birch *Betula papyrifera*	2-7	82
European White Birch *Betula pendula*	2-7	82
Red Spruce *Picea rubens*	2-5	93

Amur Maple (Acer tataricum ginnala) Page 77

Moss Phlox (Phlox subulata) Page 200

Shrubs for Zone 2

Common Name	Zones	Page
◆ Small Shrubs (3 feet or under)		
Adelaide Hoodless Rose *Rosa 'Adelaide Hoodless'*	2-9	148
Bird's Nest Spruce *Picea abies 'Nidiformis'*	2-7	142
Dwarf Alberta Spruce *Picea glauca 'Conica'*	2-8	143
Green Mound Alpine Currant *Ribes alpinum 'Green Mound'*	2-7	147
Morden Centennial Rose *Rosa 'Morden Centennial'*	2-9	152
Nearly Wild Rose *Rosa 'Nearly Wild'*	2-9	152
Shrubby Cinquefoil *Potentilla fruticosa*	2-7	144
◆ Medium Shrubs (3 to 6 feet)		
Compact Amer. Cranberrybush *Viburnum trilobum 'Alfredo'*	2-7	167
Fru Dagmar Hastrup Rose *Rosa 'Fru Dagmar Hastrup'*	2-9	149
Hetz's Midget Arborvitae *Thuja occidentalis 'Hetz's Midget'*	2-8	164
Mugo Pine *Pinus mugo*	2-7	143
Purple-Leaf Sand Cherry *Prunus x cistena*	2-8	145
Sir Thomas Lipton Rose *Rosa 'Sir Thomas Lipton'*	2-7	153
◆ Large Shrubs (6 feet or more)		
Coral Embers Willow *Salix alba 'Britzensis'*	2-8	156
Emerald Arborvitae *Thuja occidentalis 'Emerald'*	2-7	163
Northern Bayberry *Myrica pensylvanica*	2-6	141
Redtwig Dogwood *Cornus alba*	2-8	130
William Baffin Rose *Rosa 'William Baffin'*	2-9	154

Groundcovers for Zone 2

Common Name	Zones	Page
◆ Low Groundcovers (12" or less)		
Bunchberry *Cornus canadensis*	2-7	186
Creeping Phlox *Phlox stolonifera*	2-8	199
Kinnikinick *Arctostaphylos uva-ursi*	2-7	181
Lily-of-the-Valley *Convallaria majalis*	2-9	185
Moss Phlox *Phlox subulata*	2-9	200
◆ Tall Groundcovers (12" or more)		
Blanket Flower *Gaillardia x grandiflora*	2-9	190
Bog Rosemary *Andromeda polifolia*	2-6	180

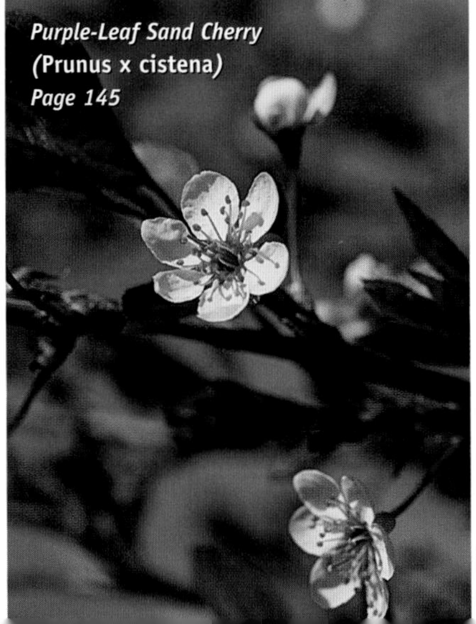

Purple-Leaf Sand Cherry (Prunus x cistena) Page 145

Preventing Deicer Damage

The salts in chemical deicers can harm plants. Protect your landscape by following some simple guidelines to minimize damage to plants.

The deicer story Salt makes it difficult for plants to absorb water. All chemical deicers contain some type of salt. Rock salt and common salt have been proven to damage plants, contaminate soil, and pollute water sources by mixing with spring runoff. Fertilizers containing urea might not do much damage to the soil itself, but they do harm plants and pollute water. Fertilizers and chemical deicers are not effective below 15 degrees F.

Safer deicers **Calcium magnesium acetate** is less harmful to plants and soil and is not considered a water pollutant, making it a better choice if used sparingly. **Calcium chloride** is effective at -20 degrees F and doesn't contaminate water through snowmelt, but it can cause some damage. Extension services might recommend calcium chloride, but it must be applied and cleaned up with care.

Use a shovel first Don't rely on any chemical product to melt all the snow and ice. Blow, shovel, scrape, or sweep away as much as you can. Apply deicer sparingly to melt the final layers and remove them by hand. Don't dump snow and ice around or onto plants.

Add drainage Salt builds up in soils with poor drainage, particularly in clay. Good drainage makes it easier to flush salts from the soil after the ground thaws. See page 53 for tips on installing drainage.

Improve soil Add organic matter to planting beds. This is good for drainage and helps plants become slightly more tolerant of salt. Weak, struggling plants in poor soil are more likely to be damaged by chemical deicers than flourishing, healthy plants growing in good soil. See page 38 for information on soil conditions.

Mix chemical deicers with sterile sand or kitty litter. You'll reduce the amount of chemicals you're applying and the abrasives will help improve traction. Use sand or litter without chemical deicers to reduce salt damage to plants.

Excess Salt Harms Plants

When snowmelt containing deicers gets on plants and in the soil around them the damage can be fatal. Foliage can be burned by direct contact. Though the symptoms won't show up right away, the needles of evergreen trees and shrubs can turn brown or yellow and twigs may die. Some plants may produce clusters of new twigs—known as "witches brooms"—in an attempt to recover from twig dieback. Even if you don't use deicers on your property, salts from roadways can end up in your yard. This is particularly troublesome for plants growing in or near the right-of-way. Avoid planting salt-sensitive plants in such areas. Though all plants will suffer under excess amounts of salt, choosing plants known for their salt tolerance will increase their chances of survival and minimize damage.

Salt-tolerant plants

Common Name	Zones	Page
◆ **Trees**		
Cockspur Hawthorn *Crataegus crus-galli 'Inermis'*	4-7	86
Eastern Red Cedar *Juniperus virginiana*	3-9	90
European Mountain Ash *Sorbus aucuparia*	4-7	103
Honeylocust *Gleditsia triacanthos inermis*	3-9	89
Pyramidal Japanese Yew *Taxus cuspidata 'Capitata'*	4-7	104
Russian Olive *Elaeagnus angustifolia*	2-7	87
Weeping Willow *Salix babylonica*	4-8	102
◆ **Shrubs**		
Amur Privet *Ligustrum amurense*	3-7	139
Arrowwood Viburnum *Viburnum dentatum*	3-8	165
Coral Embers Willow *Salix alba 'Britzensis'*	2-8	156
Fru Dagmar Hastrup Rose *Rosa 'Fru Dagmar Hastrup'*	2-9	149
Green Mound Alpine Currant *Ribes alpinum 'Green Mound'*	2-7	147
Inkberry *Ilex glabra 'Compacta'*	3-10	136
Northern Bayberry *Myrica pensylvanica*	2-6	141
Parson's Juniper *Juniperus chinensis 'Parsonii'*	3-9	137
Sea Green Juniper *Juniperus chinensis 'Sea Green'*	4-8	138
Snowberry *Symphoricarpos albus*	3-7	159
Summersweet *Clethra alnifolia*	3-9	130
Therese Bugnet Rose *Rosa 'Therese Bugnet'*	3-9	154
White Rugosa Rose *Rosa rugosa 'Alba'*	3-10	155
◆ **Groundcovers**		
Andorra Compact Juniper *Juniperus horizontalis 'Plumosa Compacta'*	3-9	194
Bar Harbor Juniper *Juniperus horizontalis 'Bar Harbor'*	3-9	193
Blanket Flower *Gaillardia x grandiflora*	2-9	190
Blue Chip Juniper *Juniperus horizontalis 'Blue Chip'*	3-9	193
Blue Rug Juniper *Juniperus horizontalis 'Wiltonii'*	3-9	194
Kinnikinick *Arctostaphylos uva-ursi*	2-7	181
Sea Thrift *Armeria maritima*	3-8	182
Silver Brocade Artemisia *Artemisia stelleriana 'Silver Brocade'*	3-9	182
◆ **Vines**		
Virginia Creeper *Parthenocissus quinquefolia*	4-9	213

Plants for Zone 3

Locate your home on the map on page 5 to determine your climate zone. The plants in the following lists are good for Zone 3. Availability varies by area and conditions (see page 21). Check with your garden center. Plants on these lists are categorized by height. Turn to the pages listed for more information about growth rate and for ranges of height and spread.

Trees for Zone 3

Common Name	Zones	Page
◆ Small Trees (30 feet or under)		
Amur Maple *Acer tataricum ginnala*	2-6	77
Japanese Flowering Crabapple *Malus floribunda*	3-8	91
Japanese Tree Lilac *Syringa reticulata*	3-7	104
Redbud *Cercis canadensis*	3-9	85
Russian Olive *Elaeagnus angustifolia*	2-7	87
Shadblow Serviceberry *Amelanchier canadensis*	3-8	80
Washington Hawthorn *Crataegus phaenopyrum*	3-9	86
◆ Medium Trees (30 to 60 feet)		
American Arborvitae *Thuja occidentalis*	2-7	105
American Hornbeam *Carpinus caroliniana*	3-9	84
Amur Chokecherry *Prunus maackii*	2-6	97
Balsam Fir *Abies balsamea*	3-6	74
Colorado Blue Spruce *Picea pungens glauca*	2-7	93
Eastern Red Cedar *Juniperus virginiana*	3-9	90
Green Ash *Fraxinus pennsylvanica*	3-9	88
Jack Pine *Pinus banksiana*	2-6	94
Mayday Tree *Prunus padus commutata*	3-6	97
Norway Maple *Acer platanoides*	3-7	77
Norway Spruce *Picea abies*	2-7	92
Ohio Buckeye *Aesculus glabra*	3-7	79
Quaking Aspen *Populus tremuloides*	2-6	96
Red Maple *Acer rubrum*	3-9	78
White Fir *Abies concolor*	3-7	74
White Spruce *Picea glauca*	2-6	92
◆ Large Trees (60 feet or more)		
American Beech *Fagus grandifolia*	3-9	87
American Linden *Tilia americana*	2-8	105
Canoe Birch *Betula papyrifera*	2-7	82
Common Horsechesnut *Aesculus hippocastanum*	3-7	80
European White Birch *Betula pendula*	2-7	82
Ginkgo *Ginkgo biloba*	3-9	88
Golden Weeping Willow *Salix alba 'Tristis'*	3-8	102
Honeylocust *Gleditsia triacanthos inermis*	3-9	89
Red Spruce *Picea rubens*	2-5	93
Scots Pine *Pinus sylvestris*	3-7	95
Silver Maple *Acer saccharinum*	3-9	78
Veitch Fir *Abies veitchii*	3-6	75
White Oak *Quercus alba*	3-6	75
White Pine *Pinus strobus*	3-8	95

Shrubs for Zone 3

Common Name	Zones	Page
◆ Small Shrubs (3 feet or under)		
Adelaide Hoodless Rose *Rosa 'Adelaide Hoodless'*	2-9	148
Bird's Nest Spruce *Picea abies 'Nidiformis'*	2-7	142
Dwarf Alberta Spruce *Picea glauca 'Conica'*	2-8	143
Green Mound Alpine Currant *Ribes alpinum 'Green Mound'*	2-7	147
Morden Centennial Rose *Rosa 'Morden Centennial'*	2-9	152
Nearly Wild Rose *Rosa 'Nearly Wild'*	2-9	152
Parson's Juniper *Juniperus chinensis 'Parsonii'*	3-9	137
Russian Cypress *Microbiota decussata*	3-7	140
Shrubby Cinquefoil *Potentilla fruticosa*	2-7	144
◆ Medium Shrubs (3 to 6 feet)		
Annabelle Hydrangea *Hydrangea arborescens 'Annabelle'*	3-9	134
Anthony Waterer Spirea *Spiraea japonica 'Anthony Waterer'*	3-9	157
Compact Amer. Cranberrybush *Viburnum trilobum 'Alfredo'*	2-7	167
Dwarf Burning Bush *Euonymus alatus 'Compacta'*	3-8	133
Dwarf Norway Spruce *Picea abies 'Pumila'*	3-8	142
Fru Dagmar Hastrup Rose *Rosa 'Fru Dagmar Hastrup'*	2-9	149
Hetz's Midget Arborvitae *Thuja occidentalis 'Hetz's Midget'*	2-8	164
Inkberry *Ilex glabra 'Compacta'*	3-10	136
Little Giant Arborvitae *Thuja occidentalis 'Little Giant'*	3-7	164
Mugo Pine *Pinus mugo*	2-7	143
Purple-Leaf Sand Cherry *Prunus x cistena*	2-8	145
Sir Thomas Lipton Rose *Rosa 'Sir Thomas Lipton'*	2-7	153
Snowberry *Symphoricarpos albus*	3-7	159
Tam Juniper *Juniperus sabina 'Tamariscifolia'*	3-7	138
Therese Bugnet Rose *Rosa 'Therese Bugnet'*	3-9	154

PeeGee Hydrangea (Hydrangea paniculata 'Grandiflora') Page 135

PeeGee Hydrangea (Hydrangea paniculata 'Grandiflora') Page 135

Common Name	Zones	Page
◆ Large Shrubs (6 feet or more)		
Amur Privet *Ligustrum amurense*	3-7	139
Arnold's Red Tatarian Honeysuckle *Lonicera tatarica 'Arnold's Red'*	3-9	140
Arrowwood Viburnum *Viburnum dentatum*	3-8	165
Blackhaw Viburnum *Viburnum prunifolium*	3-9	167
Common Lilac *Syringa vulgaris*	3-7	162
Common Witch Hazel *Hamamelis virginiana*	3-8	134
Coral Embers Willow *Salix alba 'Britzensis'*	2-8	156
Cut-Leaf Staghorn Sumac *Rhus typhina 'Laciniata'*	3-8	147
Dwarf Balsam Fir *Abies balsamea 'Nana'*	3-6	124
Emerald Arborvitae *Thuja occidentalis 'Emerald'*	2-7	163
European Cranberrybush *Viburnum opulus 'Roseum'*	3-8	166
Henry Kelsey Rose *Rosa 'Henry Kelsey'*	3-9	150
Miss Kim Lilac *Syringa patula 'Miss Kim'*	3-7	161
Northern Bayberry *Myrica pensylvanica*	2-6	141
PeeGee Hydrangea *Hydrangea paniculata 'Grandiflora'*	3-8	135
Persian Lilac *Syringa x persica*	3-7	161
Redtwig Dogwood *Cornus alba*	2-8	130
Summersweet *Clethra alnifolia*	3-9	130
White Rugosa Rose *Rosa rugosa 'Alba'*	3-10	155
William Baffin Rose *Rosa 'William Baffin'*	2-9	154
Winterberry *Ilex verticillata*	3-9	136
Yellow-Twig Dogwood *Cornus stolonifera 'Flaviramea"*	3-8	132

Winterberry
(Ilex verticillata)
Page 136

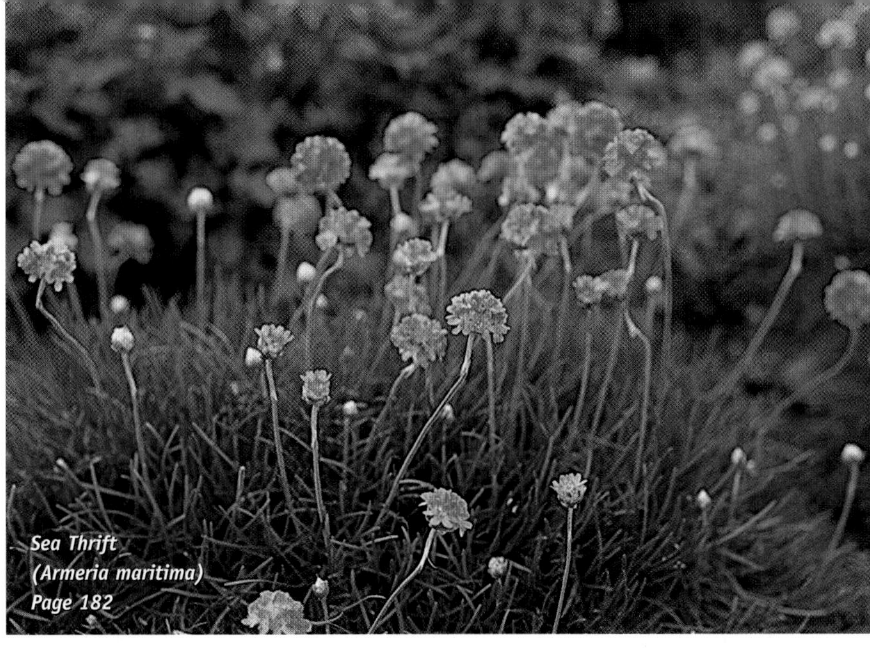

Sea Thrift
(Armeria maritima)
Page 182

Groundcover for Zone 3

Common Name	Zones	Page
◆ Low Groundcovers (12" or less)		
Alpine Strawberry *Fragaria vesca*	3-9	189
Bar Harbor Juniper *Juniperus horizontalis 'Bar Harbor'*	3-9	193
Blue Chip Juniper *Juniperus horizontalis 'Blue Chip'*	3-9	193
Blue Rug Juniper *Juniperus horizontalis 'Wiltonii'*	3-9	194
Bunchberry *Cornus canadensis*	2-7	186
Creeping Phlox *Phlox stolonifera*	2-8	199
Forget-Me-Not *Myosotis scorpioides*	3-8	197
Kinnikinick *Arctostaphylos uva-ursi*	2-7	181
Lily-of-the-Valley *Convallaria majalis*	2-9	185
Moss Phlox *Phlox subulata*	2-9	200
Mountain Sandwort *Arenaria montana*	3-6	181
Pink Panda Strawberry *Fragaria 'Pink Panda'*	3-9	189
Rockcress *Arabis caucasica*	3-7	180
Sea Thrift *Armeria maritima*	3-8	182
Snow-in-Summer *Cerastium tomentosum*	3-7	185
Spotted Dead Nettle *Lamium maculatum*	3-9	196
Waldesteinia *Waldsteinia ternata*	3-8	205
Wintergreen *Gaultheria procumbens*	3-8	190
◆ Tall Groundcovers (12" or more)		
Andorra Compact Juniper *Juniperus horizontalis 'Plumosa Compacta'*	3-9	194
Blanket Flower *Gaillardia x grandiflora*	2-9	190
Bloody Cranesbill *Geranium sanguineum*	3-8	191
Blue Star *Amsonia tabernaemontana*	3-9	179
Bog Rosemary *Andromeda polifolia*	2-6	180
Cliff Green *Paxistima canbyi*	3-7	199
Coral Bells *Heuchera sanguinea*	3-8	191
Hay-Scented Fern *Dennstaedtia punctilobula*	3-8	186
Hosta *Hosta species*	3-8	192
Maidenhair Fern *Adiantum pedatum*	3-8	177
Saxifrage *Bergenia cordifolia*	3-8	184
Siberian Forget-Me-Not *Anchusa myosotidiflora*	3-7	179
Silver Brocade Artemisia *Artemisia stelleriana 'Silver Brocade'*	3-9	182
Snow-on-the-Mountain *Aegopodium podagraria 'Variegatum'*	3-9	177
Stonecrop *Sedum spectabile*	3-10	202
Yellow Archangel *Lamiastrum galeobdolon 'Variegatum'*	3-9	195

Vines for Zone 3

Common Name	Zones	Page
American Bittersweet *Celastrus scandens*	3-8	211
Dropmore Scarlet Honeysuckle *Lonicera x brownii 'Dropmore Scarlet'*	3-7	212

American Bittersweet
(Celastrus scandens)
Page 211

Plants for Zone 4

If you live in Zone 4, check out the plants on these lists. Availability varies by area and conditions (see page 21). Check with your garden center. These lists are organized by plant height. Turn to the pages listed for more information about growth rate and for ranges of height and spread.

Trees for Zone 4

Common Name	Zones	Page
◆ Small Trees (30 feet or under)		
Allegheny Serviceberry *Amelanchier laevis*	4-8	81
American Smoke Tree *Cotinus obovatus*	4-8	85
Amur Maple *Acer tataricum ginnala*	2-6	77
Cockspur Hawthorn *Crataegus crus-galli 'Inermis'*	4-7	86
Corkscrew Willow *Salix 'Golden Curls'*	4-8	103
European Mountain Ash *Sorbus aucuparia*	4-7	103
Japanese Flowering Crabapple *Malus floribunda*	3-8	91
Japanese Tree Lilac *Syringa reticulata*	3-7	104
Newport Plum *Prunus cerasifera 'Newport'*	4-8	96
Plumleaf Crabapple *Malus prunifolia*	4-9	91
Redbud *Cercis canadensis*	3-9	85
Russian Olive *Elaeagnus angustifolia*	2-7	87
Shadblow Serviceberry *Amelanchier canadensis*	3-8	80
Skyrocket Juniper *Juniperus scopulorum 'Skyrocket'*	4-8	89
Star Magnolia *Magnolia stellata*	4-9	90
Washington Hawthorn *Crataegus phaenopyrum*	3-9	86
◆ Medium Trees (30 to 60 feet)		
American Arborvitae *Thuja occidentalis*	2-7	105
American Hornbeam *Carpinus caroliniana*	3-9	84
Amur Chokecherry *Prunus maackii*	2-6	97
Balsam Fir *Abies balsamea*	3-6	74
Bradford Pear *Pyrus calleryana 'Bradford'*	4-8	98
Colorado Blue Spruce *Picea pungens glauca*	2-7	93
Eastern Red Cedar *Juniperus virginiana*	3-9	90
European Hornbeam *Carpinus betulus*	4-7	83
Frasier Fir *Abies fraseri*	4-7	75
Green Ash *Fraxinus pennsylvanica*	3-9	88
Jack Pine *Pinus banksiana*	2-6	94
Katsura Tree *Cercidiphyllum japonicum*	4-8	84
Mayday Tree *Prunus padus commutata*	3-6	97
Norway Maple *Acer platanoides*	3-7	77
Norway Spruce *Picea abies*	2-7	92
Ohio Buckeye *Aesculus glabra*	3-7	79
Pyramidal Japanese Yew *Taxus cuspidata 'Capitata'*	4-7	104
Quaking Aspen *Populus tremuloides*	2-6	96
Red Maple *Acer rubrum*	3-9	78
Weeping Willow *Salix babylonica*	4-8	102
White Fir *Abies concolor*	3-7	74
White Spruce *Picea glauca*	2-6	92
Whitespire Birch *Betula mandschurica japonica 'Whitespire'*	4-7	83
◆ Large Trees (60 feet or more)		
American Beech *Fagus grandifolia*	3-9	87
American Linden *Tilia americana*	2-8	105
Canoe Birch *Betula papyrifera*	2-7	82
Common Horsechesnut *Aesculus hippocastanum*	3-7	80
Douglas Fir *Pseudotsuga menziesii*	4-6	98
European White Birch *Betula pendula*	2-7	82
Ginkgo *Ginkgo biloba*	3-9	88
Golden Weeping Willow *Salix alba 'Tristis'*	3-8	102
Honeylocust *Gleditsia triacanthos inermis*	3-9	89
Lacebark Pine *Pinus bungeana*	4-7	94
Northern Red Oak *Quercus rubra*	4-7	101
Pin Oak *Quercus palustris*	4-8	101
Red Spruce *Picea rubens*	2-5	93
River Birch *Betula nigra*	4-9	81
Scarlet Oak *Quercus coccinea*	4-9	100
Scots Pine *Pinus sylvestris*	3-7	95
Silver Maple *Acer saccharinum*	3-9	78
Sugar Maple *Acer saccharum*	4-8	79
Veitch Fir *Abies veitchii*	3-6	75
White Oak *Quercus alba*	3-9	100
White Pine *Pinus strobus*	3-8	95

Shrubs for Zone 4

Common Name	Zones	Page
◆ Small Shrubs (3 feet or under)		
Adelaide Hoodless Rose *Rosa 'Adelaide Hoodless'*	2-9	148
Anglojap Yew *Taxus x media 'Densiformis'*	4-7	162
Bird's Nest Spruce *Picea abies 'Nidiformis'*	2-7	142
Blue Star Juniper *Juniperus squamata 'Blue Star'*	4-8	139
Carol Mackie Daphne *Daphne x burkwoodii 'Carol Mackie'*	4-8	132
Dwarf Alberta Spruce *Picea glauca 'Conica'*	2-8	143
Dwarf Hinoki False Cypress *Chamaecyparis obtusa 'Nana Gracilis'*	4-8	129
Green Mound Alpine Currant *Ribes alpinum 'Green Mound'*	2-7	147
Hunter Rose *Rosa 'Hunter'*	4-8	151
Limemound Spirea *Spiraea japonica Limemound*	4-9	157
Morden Centennial Rose *Rosa 'Morden Centennial'*	2-9	152
Nearly Wild Rose *Rosa 'Nearly Wild'*	2-9	152
Old Gold Juniper *Juniperus chinensis 'Old Gold'*	4-10	137
Parson's Juniper *Juniperus chinensis 'Parsonii'*	3-9	137
Russian Cypress *Microbiota decussata*	3-7	140
Shrubby Cinquefoil *Potentilla fruticosa*	2-7	144
The Fairy Rose *Rosa The Fairy'*	4-9	153
Wintergreen Boxwood *Buxus microphylla 'Wintergreen'*	4-6	128
◆ Medium Shrubs (3 to 6 feet)		
Annabelle Hydrangea *Hydrangea arborescens 'Annabelle'*	3-9	134
Anthony Waterer Spirea *Spiraea japonica 'Anthony Waterer'*	3-9	157
Betty Prior Rose *Rosa 'Betty Prior'*	4-9	148
Carefree Beauty Rose *Rosa Carefree Beauty*	4-8	149
Carolina Azalea *Azalea carolinianum*	4-9	126
Compact Amer. Cranberrybush *Viburnum trilobum 'Alfredo'*	2-7	167
Coralberry *Symphoricarpos orbiculatus*	4-7	159
Dwarf Burning Bush *Euonymus alatus 'Compacta'*	3-8	133
Dwarf Flowering Almond *Prunus glandulosa 'Rosea'*	4-8	144
Dwarf Norway Spruce *Picea abies 'Pumila'*	3-8	142
Exbury Azalea *Azalea 'Exbury Hybrids'*	4-7	126
French Pussy Willow *Salix caprea 'Kilmarnock'*	4-8	156
Fru Dagmar Hastrup Rose *Rosa 'Fru Dagmar Hastrup'*	2-9	149
Hetz's Midget Arborvitae *Thuja occidentalis 'Hetz's Midget'*	2-8	164
Inkberry *Ilex glabra 'Compacta'*	3-10	136
Japanese Barberry *Berberis thunbergii*	4-8	128
Little Giant Arborvitae *Thuja occidentalis 'Little Giant'*	3-7	164
Mugo Pine *Pinus mugo*	2-7	143
Northern Lights Azalea *Azalea 'Northern Lights'*	4-7	127
Purple-Leaf Sand Cherry *Prunus x cistena*	2-8	145
Rosa Rubrifolia *Rosa rubrifolia*	4-9	155
Sea Green Juniper *Juniperus chinensis 'Sea Green'*	4-8	138
Shibori Spirea *Spiraea japonica 'Shibori'*	4-8	158
Sir Thomas Lipton Rose *Rosa 'Sir Thomas Lipton'*	2-7	153

Common Name	Zones	Page
Snowberry *Symphoricarpos albus*	3-7	159
Tam Juniper *Juniperus sabina 'Tamariscifolia'*	3-7	138
Therese Bugnet Rose *Rosa 'Therese Bugnet'*	3-9	154
White Forsythia *Abeliophyllum distichum*	4-8	124
Yukon Belle Firethorn *Pyracantha angustifolia Yukon Belle*	4-9	145

◆ Large Shrubs (6 feet or more)

Common Name	Zones	Page
Amur Privet *Ligustrum amurense*	3-7	139
Arnold's Red Tatarian Honeysuckle *Lonicera tatarica 'Arnold's Red'*	3-9	140
Arrowwood Viburnum *Viburnum dentatum*	3-8	165
Black Chokeberry *Aronia melanocarpa*	4-9	125
Blackhaw Viburnum *Viburnum prunifolium*	3-9	167
Catawba Rhododendron *Rhododendron catawbiense*	4-8	146
Common Lilac *Syringa vulgaris*	3-7	162
Common Witch Hazel *Hamamelis virginiana*	3-8	134
Coral Embers Willow *Salix alba 'Britzensis'*	2-8	156
Cornelian Cherry *Cornus mas*	4-8	131
Cornell Pink Azalea *Azalea mucronulatum 'Cornell Pink'*	4-7	127
Cut-Leaf Staghorn Sumac *Rhus typhina 'Laciniata'*	3-8	147
Cutleaf Lilac *Syringa x laciniata*	4-8	160
Doublefile Viburnum *Viburnum plicatum tomentosum*	4-8	166
Dwarf Balsam Fir *Abies balsamea 'Nana'*	3-6	124
Emerald Arborvitae *Thuja occidentalis 'Emerald'*	2-7	163
European Cranberrybush *Viburnum opulus 'Roseum'*	3-8	166
Gray Dogwood *Cornus racemosa*	4-7	131
Green Lustre Japanese Holly *Ilex crenata 'Green Lustre'*	4-6	135
Henry Kelsey Rose *Rosa 'Henry Kelsey'*	3-9	150
Hick's Upright Yew *Taxus x media 'Hicksii'*	4-7	163
Miss Kim Lilac *Syringa patula 'Miss Kim'*	3-7	161
Mohican Viburnum *Viburnum lantana 'Mohican'*	3-8	165
Northern Bayberry *Myrica pensylvanica*	2-6	141
Oriental Photinia *Photinia villosa*	4-7	141
PeeGee Hydrangea *Hydrangea paniculata 'Grandiflora'*	3-8	135
Persian Lilac *Syringa x persica*	3-7	161
Redtwig Dogwood *Cornus alba*	2-8	130
Serviceberry *Amelanchier alnifolia*	4-5	125
Summersweet *Clethra alnifolia*	3-9	130
Sweetshrub *Calycanthus floridus*	4-9	129
Vermont Sun Forsythia *Forsythia mandshurica 'Vermont Sun'*	4-8	133
White Rugosa Rose *Rosa rugosa 'Alba'*	3-10	155
William Baffin Rose *Rosa 'William Baffin'*	2-9	154
Winterberry *Ilex verticillata*	3-9	136
Yellow-Twig Dogwood *Cornus stolonifera 'Flaviramea"*	3-8	132

Groundcover for Zone 4

◆ Low Groundcovers (12" or less)

Common Name	Zones	Page
Ajuga *Ajuga reptans*	3-9	178
Allegheny Foam Flower *Tiarella cordifolia*	4-9	204
Alpine Strawberry *Fragaria vesca*	3-9	189
Bar Harbor Juniper *Juniperus horizontalis 'Bar Harbor'*	3-9	193
Basket-of-Gold *Aurinia saxatilis*	4-8	183
Bath's Pink *Dianthus gratianopolitanus 'Bath's Pink'*	4-9	187
Blue Chip Juniper *Juniperus horizontalis 'Blue Chip'*	3-9	193
Blue Rug Juniper *Juniperus horizontalis 'Wiltonii'*	3-9	194
Blue Star Bellflower *Campanula poscharskyana*	4-9	184
Bunchberry *Cornus canadensis*	2-7	186
Creeping Phlox *Phlox stolonifera*	2-8	199
Cypress Spurge *Euphorbia cyparissias*	4-8	188
Dwarf Blue Fescue *Festuca glauca*	4-9	188
Forget-Me-Not *Myosotis scorpioides*	3-8	197
Kinnikinick *Arctostaphylos uva-ursi*	2-7	181
Lady's Mantle *Alchemilla mollis*	4-7	178
Lily-of-the-Valley *Convallaria majalis*	2-9	185
Littleleaf Periwinkle *Vinca minor*	4-8	205
Moss Phlox *Phlox subulata*	2-9	200
Mountain Sandwort *Arenaria montana*	3-6	181
Pachysandra *Pachysandra terminalis*	4-9	198
Pink Panda Strawberry *Fragaria 'Pink Panda'*	3-9	189
Rockcress *Arabis caucasica*	3-7	180
Sea Thrift *Armeria maritima*	3-8	182
Snow-in-Summer *Cerastium tomentosum*	3-7	185
Spotted Dead Nettle *Lamium maculatum*	3-9	196
Spring Cinquefoil *Potentilla tabernaemontani*	4-8	200
Sundrop Primrose *Oenothera missouriensis*	4-8	198
Sweet Woodruff *Asperula odorata*	4-8	183
Waldesteinia *Waldsteinia ternata*	3-8	205
Wintergreen *Gaultheria procumbens*	3-8	190

◆ Tall Groundcovers (12" or more)

Common Name	Zones	Page
Alba Meidiland Rose *Rosa Alba Meidiland*	4-8	201
Andorra Compact Juniper *Juniperus horizontalis 'Plumosa Compacta'*	3-9	194
Blanket Flower *Gaillardia x grandiflora*	2-9	190
Bloody Cranesbill *Geranium sanguineum*	3-8	191
Blue Star *Amsonia tabernaemontana*	3-9	179
Bog Rosemary *Andromeda polifolia*	2-6	180

Trumpet Vine
(Campsis radicans)
Page 210

Common Name	Zones	Page
Catmint *Nepeta x faassenii*	4-8	197
Cliff Green *Paxistima canbyi*	3-7	199
Coral Bells *Heuchera sanguinea*	3-8	191
Dwarf Japanese Garden Juniper *Juniperus procumbens 'Nana'*	4-9	195
Flower Carpet Rose *Rosa 'Flower Carpet'*	4-10	201
Germander *Teucrium prostratum*	4-9	204
Goldmoss *Sedum acre*	4-9	202
Hay-Scented Fern *Dennstaedtia punctilobula*	3-8	186
Hosta *Hosta species*	3-8	192
Lamb's Ear *Stachys byzantina*	4-8	203
Maidenhair Fern *Adiantum pedatum*	3-8	177
Partridge Berry *Mitchella repens*	4-9	196
Prostrate Chenault Coralberry *Symphoricarpos x chenaultii 'Hancock'*	4-7	203
Purple-Leaf Wintercreeper *Eunoymus fortunei 'Coloratus'*	3-9	187
Saxifrage *Bergenia cordifolia*	3-8	184
Siberian Forget-Me-Not *Anchusa myosotidiflora*	3-7	179
Silver Brocade Artemisia *Artemisia stelleriana 'Silver Brocade'*	3-9	182
Snow-on-the-Mountain *Aegopodium podagraria 'Variegatum'*	3-9	177
Stonecrop *Sedum spectabile*	3-10	202
Yellow Archangel *Lamiastrum galeobdolon 'Variegatum'*	3-9	195

Vines for Zone 4

Common Name	Zones	Page
American Bittersweet *Celastrus scandens*	3-8	211
Boston Ivy *Parthenocissus tricuspidata*	4-8	213
Climbing Hydrangea *Hydrangea petiolaris*	4-7	211
Dropmore Scarlet Honeysuckle *Lonicera x brownii 'Dropmore Scarlet'*	3-7	212
Hardy Kiwi *Actinidia arguta*	4-8	210
Trumpet Honeysuckle *Lonicera sempervirens*	4-9	212
Trumpet Vine *Campsis radicans*	4-9	210
Virginia Creeper *Parthenocissus quinquefolia*	4-9	213

Screening and Privacy

The results of your assessment revealed some views that should be blocked, such as unappealing garbage cans or air-conditioners within your own yard. Other scenes might be off your property—a neighbor's messy garage, ugly signs, or unkempt alleyways will spoil your time outdoors. The beauty of landscaping is that you don't have to look at anything you don't want to. You can make unwanted views disappear behind plants, fences, arbors, or walls.

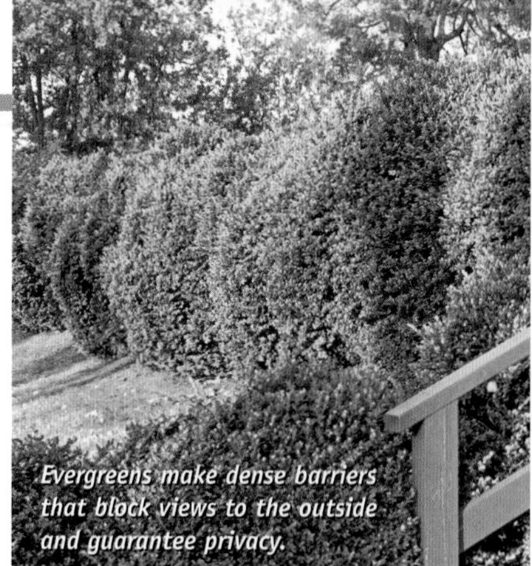

Evergreens make dense barriers that block views to the outside and guarantee privacy.

1) Define Privacy Needs

In addition to pinpointing unpleasant views, your site analysis reveals areas that might be unusable because they lack privacy. Blocking views to add or enhance privacy is important. However, it's rarely necessary to block every view from every angle. Doing so turns your home into a fortress. Instead, look at your yard notes on public and private spaces. Are the private spaces truly private? Do you need to make changes to increase privacy and make these spaces more usable? Would some public areas be better as private spaces?

2) Concentrate Efforts

When you've answered these questions, you'll know where to add privacy. Walk those areas. Identify the directions from which people can see into private areas. (Don't forget to look up; a neighboring multistory home or building might pose a problem.) These directions are angles of view. Identifying them will help you place plants to block views and enhance privacy without walling in your entire yard.

3) Filter Views

Now that you know which views to block, it's time to add screening. This term describes plants or objects positioned to block views. There are several screening options: fences, arbors, walls, and plants.

Evergreen plants are often used as screens because they retain their foliage year-round. Some are so dense they form screens like living walls.

Adding privacy can be as simple as planting a hedge or as elaborate as creating a beautiful hillside garden.

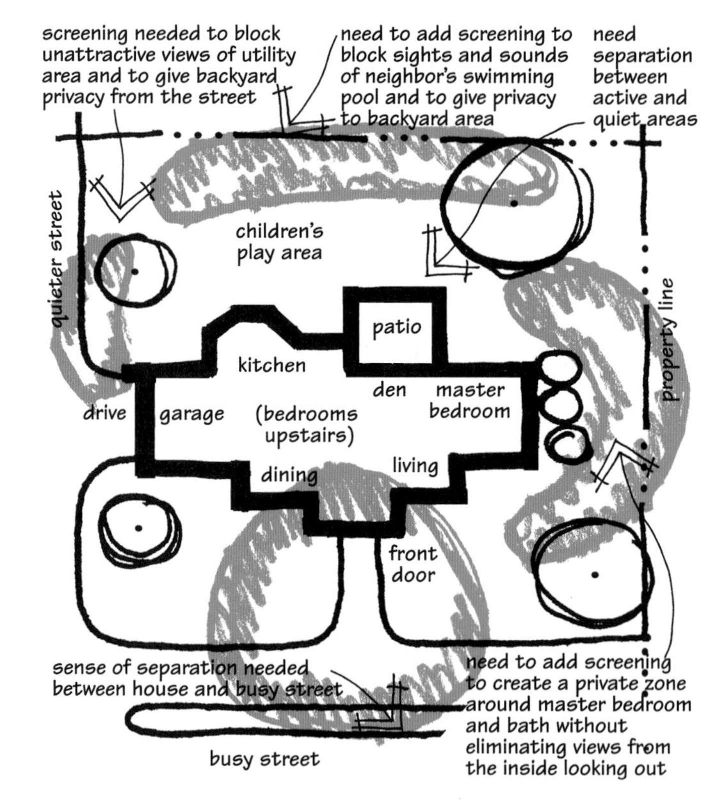

screening needed to block unattractive views of utility area and to give backyard privacy from the street
need to add screening to block sights and sounds of neighbor's swimming pool and to give privacy to backyard area
need separation between active and quiet areas
quieter street
children's play area
patio
kitchen
den
master bedroom
drive
garage
(bedrooms upstairs)
dining
living
property line
front door
sense of separation needed between house and busy street
need to add screening to create a private zone around master bedroom and bath without eliminating views from the inside looking out
busy street

You might want to make a second sketch that focuses only on where you need to add screening to provide privacy, to block views looking outward, to conceal unattractive areas on your property, or to provide a sense of separation between areas of your yard. Use your earlier sketches and notes as references.

Strong climbers such as Climbing Hydrangea (H. petiolaris, Page 211) add texture to fences.

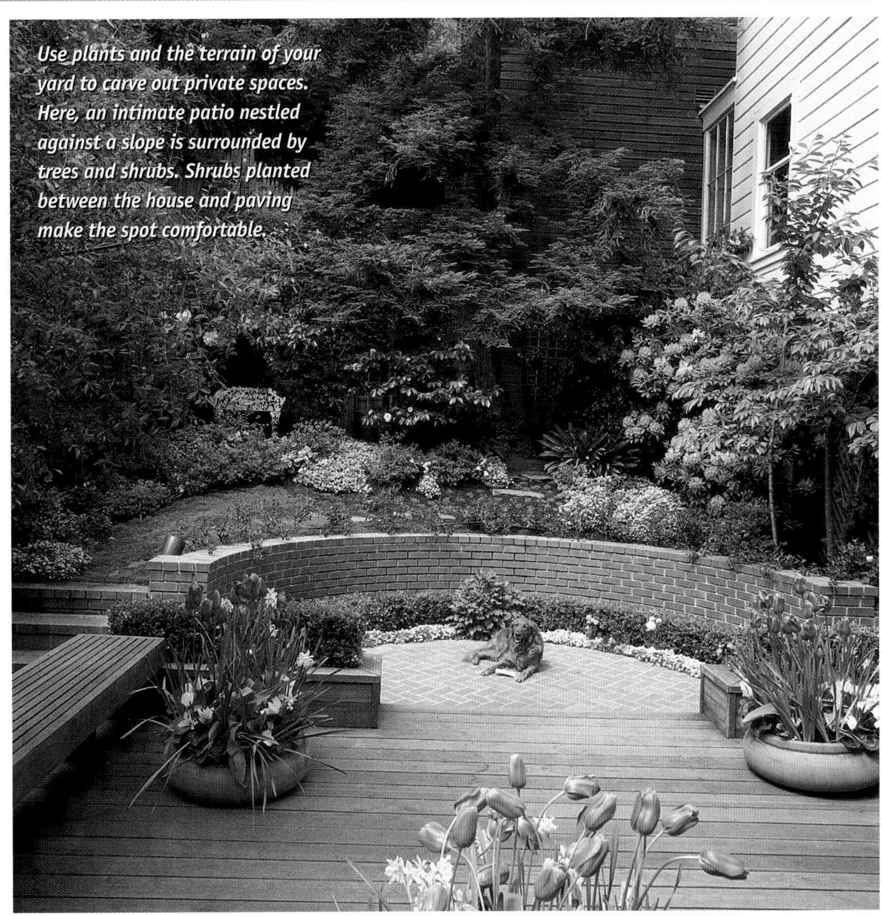

Use plants and the terrain of your yard to carve out private spaces. Here, an intimate patio nestled against a slope is surrounded by trees and shrubs. Shrubs planted between the house and paving make the spot comfortable.

Deciduous plants can also be used for screening, though you'll rarely find such notations in their descriptions. Look for plants with a rapid growth rate or ones described as good choices for informal hedges.

Rapid-growing deciduous plants are good choices when you need to establish a sense of separation. This means that you add screening to distinguish between your public and private space. Instead of blocking views completely, you enhance some spots in your yard by filtering the views that look inward or out toward another area. A filtered view is not blocked completely. There is enough screening to establish some distinction between areas. Adding a filtered screen to your yard creates an illusion of privacy without sacrificing breezes or views you enjoy. Though you can see out through the filtered screen and others can see in through it, the presence of something between areas creates a sense of separation necessary for a feeling of privacy.

Design Tip

During warm months when you're out in your yard, deciduous trees, shrubs, and vines block unwanted views with their foliage. These views will become visible again in fall, winter, and early spring when plants are bare. The structure of the plant (its trunk and branches) still filters views after leaves have fallen, which may provide a sense of adequate separation. If not, combine fast-growing deciduous plants with slower-growing evergreens. Deciduous plants are good choices for screening along the southern exposure. When leaves fall, they'll let in winter sunlight.

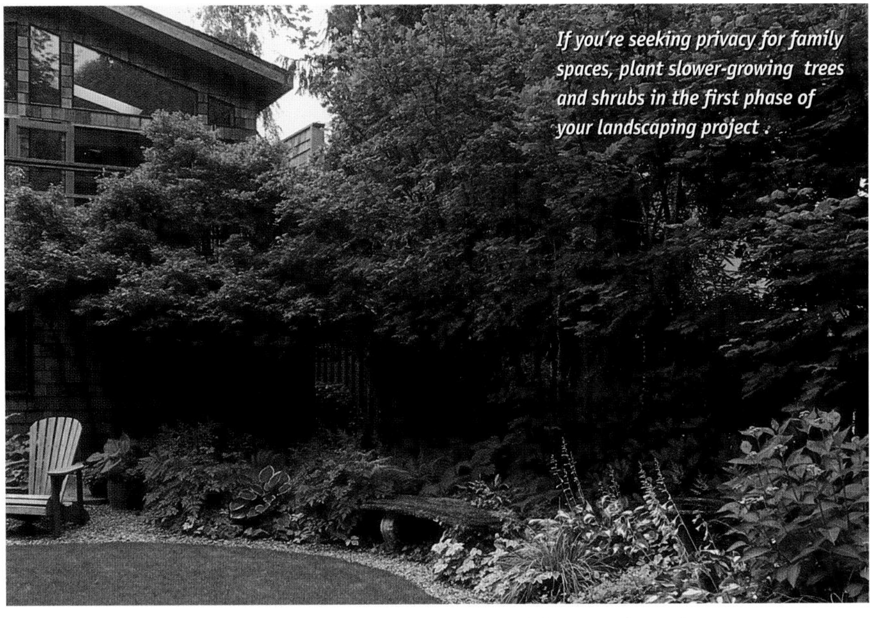

If you're seeking privacy for family spaces, plant slower-growing trees and shrubs in the first phase of your landscaping project.

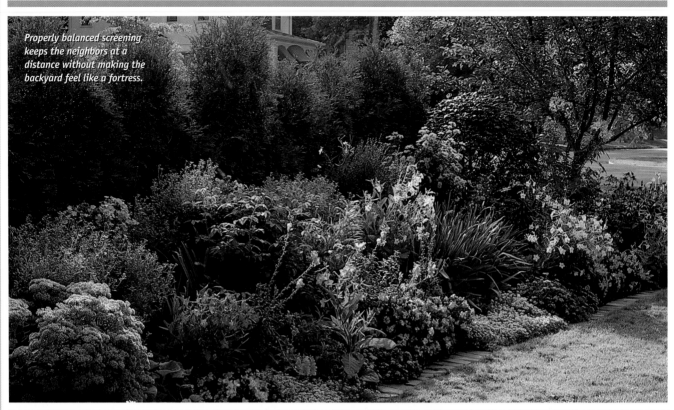

Properly balanced screening keeps the neighbors at a distance without making the backyard feel like a fortress.

Plants for Privacy

Evergreen trees for screening

Common Name	Zones	Page	Growth
American Arborvitae *Thuja occidentalis*	2-7	105	S
Balsam Fir *Abies balsamea*	3-6	74	S
Colorado Blue Spruce *Picea pungens glauca*	2-7	93	S
Douglas Fir *Pseudotsuga menziesii*	4-6	98	M
Eastern Red Cedar *Juniperus virginiana*	3-9	90	M
Frasier Fir *Abies fraseri*	4-7	75	S
Jack Pine *Pinus banksiana*	2-6	94	M
Lacebark Pine *Pinus bungeana*	4-7	94	S
Norway Spruce *Picea abies*	2-7	92	M
Pyramidal Japanese Yew *Taxus cuspidata 'Capitata'*	4-7	104	S
Red Spruce *Picea rubens*	2-5	93	M
Scots Pine *Pinus sylvestris*	3-7	95	M
Skyrocket Juniper *Juniperus scopulorum 'Skyrocket'*	4-8	89	S
Veitch Fir *Abies veitchii*	3-6	75	R
White Fir *Abies concolor*	3-7	74	M
White Pine *Pinus strobus*	3-8	95	R
White Spruce *Picea glauca*	2-6	92	M

Evergreen shrubs for screening

Common Name	Zones	Page	Growth
Catawba Rhododendron *Rhododendron catawbiense*	4-8	146	S
Dwarf Balsam Fir *Abies balsamea 'Nana'*	3-6	124	S
Emerald Arborvitae *Thuja occidentalis 'Emerald'*	2-7	163	S
Green Lustre Japanese Holly *Ilex crenata 'Green Lustre'*	4-6	135	S
Hick's Upright Yew *Taxus x media 'Hicksii'*	4-7	163	R
Inkberry *Ilex glabra 'Compacta'*	3-10	136	M
Little Giant Arborvitae *Thuja occidentalis 'Little Giant'*	2-7	164	S
Northern Bayberry *Myrica pensylvanica*	2-6	141	R

Evergreen vines for screening

Common Name	Zones	Page	Growth
Dropmore Scarlet Honeysuckle *Lonicera x brownii 'Dropmore Scarlet'*	3-7	212	M

Wisdom of the Aisles

Though you might be eager to plant flowers, adding privacy and blocking poor views should be one of your top priorities. The sooner you get trees, shrubs, and vines in the ground, the sooner they can start growing. Even if you've picked a particular area of your yard to concentrate on, plant living screens in other areas you've identified so plants can get a head start on growth.

Rate of Growth:

R: Rapid M: Medium S: Slow

Botanical name in italics

Availability varies by area and conditions (see page 21). Check with your garden center.

Deciduous shrubs for screening

Common Name	Zones	Page	Growth
Amur Privet *Ligustrum amurense*	3-7	139	R
Arnold's Red Tatarian Honeysuckle *Lonicera tatarica 'Arnold's Red'*	3-9	140	R
Arrowwood Viburnum *Viburnum dentatum*	3-8	165	R
Bridalwreath Spirea *Spiraea prunifolia*	5-8	158	R
Coralberry *Symphoricarpos orbiculatus*	4-7	159	R
Cutleaf Lilac *Syringa x laciniata*	4-8	160	M
Dwarf Burning Bush *Euonymus alatus 'Compacta'*	3-8	133	S
Miss Kim Lilac *Syringa patula 'Miss Kim'*	3-7	161	S
Northern Bayberry *Myrica pensylvanica*	2-6	141	R
Oriental Photinia *Photinia villosa*	4-7	141	M
PeeGee Hydrangea *Hydrangea paniculata 'Grandiflora'*	3-8	135	R
Purple-Leaf Sand Cherry *Prunus x cistena*	2-8	145	S
Sir Thomas Lipton Rose *Rosa 'Sir Thomas Lipton'*	2-7	153	R
Vermont Sun Forsythia *Forsythia mandshurica 'Vermont Sun'*	4-8	133	S
White Forsythia *Abeliophyllum distichum*	4-8	124	R
Winterberry *Ilex verticillata*	3-9	136	S

Rapid-growing deciduous trees for filtered views

Common Name	Zones	Page
Bradford Pear *Pyrus calleryana 'Bradford'*	4-8	98
Green Ash *Fraxinus pennsylvanica*	3-9	88
Pin Oak *Quercus palustris*	4-8	101
Red Maple *Acer rubrum*	3-9	78
Redbud *Cercis canadensis*	3-9	85
River Birch *Betula nigra*	4-9	81
Scarlet Oak *Quercus coccinea*	4-9	100
Silver Maple *Acer saccharinum*	3-9	78
Weeping Willow *Salix babylonica*	4-8	102

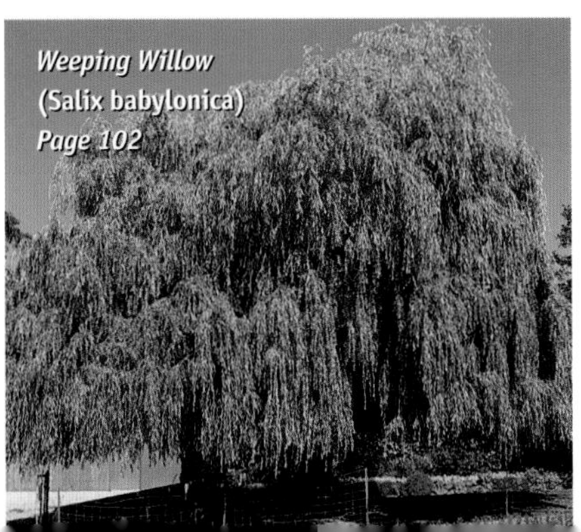
Weeping Willow (Salix babylonica) Page 102

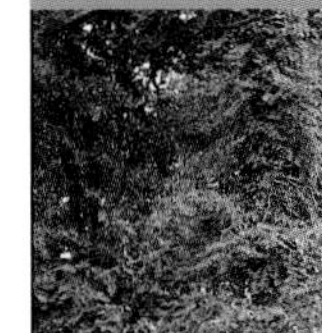

Rapid-growing deciduous vines for screening

Common Name	Zones	Page
American Bittersweet *Celastrus scandens*	3-8	211
Boston Ivy *Parthenocissus tricuspidata*	4-8	213
Hardy Kiwi *Actinidia arguta*	4-8	210
Trumpet Honeysuckle *Lonicera sempervirens*	4-9	212
Trumpet Vine *Campsis radicans*	4-9	210
Virginia Creeper *Parthenocissus quinquefolia*	4-9	213

American Bittersweet (Celastrus scandens) Page 211

Combining Plants and Materials

Choose a variety of evergreen or deciduous plants to screen for privacy or to block unpleasant views.

Plant a combination of the two to enjoy the advantages of both. This works particularly well when rapid-growing deciduous trees are planted among slower-growing evergreen shrubs. The trees quickly establish a sense of separation, while the shrubs slowly fill in to block views completely from a lower angle. Such combinations add privacy to low decks, patios, and other outdoor seating areas. The shrubs eventually block views from eye-level while you're seated, making the area seem comfortably private. The trees filter higher views that need not be obscured completely. Open space between the top of the shrubs and the bottom of the tree canopies will be filtered by tree trunks but won't be closed in. This permits sunlight and breezes to enter without walling off the seating area.

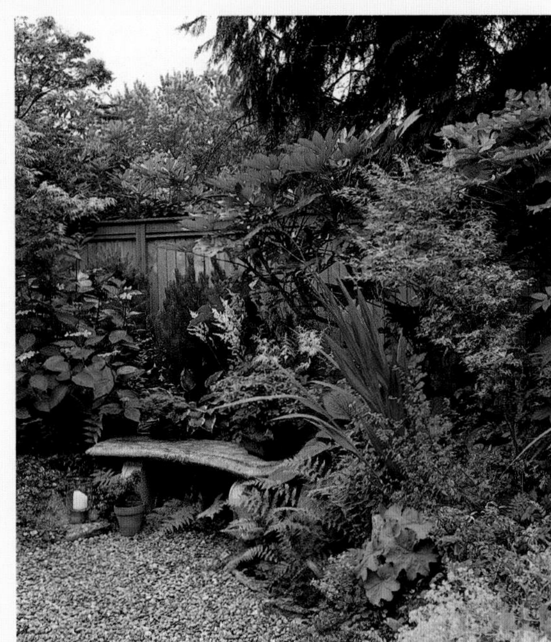

You can also combine evergreen and deciduous plants with fences, walls, trellises, or arbors to enhance privacy and block unattractive sights. These structures have the advantage of immediate impact. Use them where you can't wait for plants to grow. (First compare the cost of construction to the expense of adding big plants.) Use vines, shrubs, and trees to give the hard surfaces of these structures a softer look. Leaves, stems, branches, and trunks will also make the screen denser and block unwanted views more completely.

Choose sun-loving plants for open areas to enjoy profuse blossoms and lush foliage. Such plants usually need midday and afternoon sun to grow well.

Sun and Shade

Understanding sun and shade requirements for your plants is important. The symbols for sun and shade on plant tags tell you how much sunlight a plant needs to thrive. To find the right plants for your yard, learn to interpret the tags. If you find a tag with all three symbols, the plant can grow successfully in any light condition.

Full sun A tag with a circle or sun shape that isn't blackened indicates a plant that will tolerate a full day of hot, direct sun. The hottest climates are a possible exception; protection from the sun might be necessary during the hottest part of the day. The intensity and heat of the sun diminishes as you move into northern zones. Plants that have only the full-sun symbol on their tags will not grow as well in partially shaded spots; flowers and foliage might be reduced.

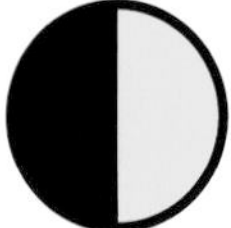

Part shade A circle half shaded and half open indicates that partial shade is the optimum condition. Morning sunlight followed by afternoon shade is best for these plants. The term partial shade also describes areas where the sun is filtered by overhead canopies, allowing some rays to penetrate during the day. Plant tags describe this condition as dappled or filtered shade. Both terms mean the same thing and are different types of partial shade.

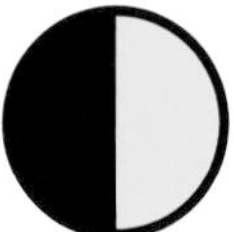

Full sun/part shade
Though plant tags don't differentiate between morning and afternoon sun, you can still decide what a plant needs by looking for combinations of symbols. Tags with both full-sun and partial-shade symbols indicate a plant can grow in conditions ranging from sunny all day long to sunny for just part of the day. Choose plants with both of these symbols to grow in areas of your yard that are sunny all day or

Homer's Hindsight

I had always heard that roses need a lot of sun, but I wasn't sure how much was enough. After several seasons of skimpy blooms and puny foliage, I finally cut my rose plants back, dug them up, and moved them to a brighter location. Now I know that, unless a particular kind of rose is known for its shade tolerance, I need to find a spot in my yard that gets at least six hours of direct sun each day to grow bountiful roses.

sunny in the afternoons. In hotter climates, intense midday and afternoon sun can be deadly to plants requiring some shade. If the plant tag has a full-sun symbol, the plant should tolerate a half day of hot afternoon sun. Remember, the partial-shade symbol tells you the plant can thrive with less than a full day of sun.

If you have dappled shade areas that receive some direct sunlight during a portion of the day, look for plants that include both the full-sun circle and the partial-shade symbol on their tags.

Design Tip

Light levels in your landscape vary during the day and during the year. Areas that are full sun early in the spring can turn to deep shade when your oak and maple trees leaf out. Make sure you consider the light levels over the entire growing season, not just for a single day.

Choosing plants that thrive in shade turns dim corners into lovely and useful areas of your landscape.

Stop, Look, and Listen

Plants can't talk, but they will tell you when something is wrong. Look for signs that plants aren't seeing the right kind of light. After allowing a few months for them to establish, the only solution is to move your plants where the light better suits them.

Too much sun: Leaves wilt (even shortly after watering) and quickly become brown and crispy as though they've been fried.

Too much shade: Growth is tall, weak, and spindly; stems lean toward the light; foliage and flowers are sparse.

Part shade/deep shade

Plants that need some sunlight filtered through other plant canopies but should stay deeply shaded most of the day have both the deep-shade symbol and the partial-shade symbol. These plants thrive in conditions that range from almost no light to a half-day's sun. Morning sun is usually best for plants with these symbols, though the weaker rays of an afternoon winter sun are likely to be OK.

Deep shade

If you need plants where there is little or no direct sunlight, look for plants with a solid dark circle on their tags. These plants thrive with low light levels, though nothing grows in the dark. In hotter climates, it's important that plants tagged for deep shade do not receive any midday or afternoon sun, especially during the hottest months of the year. Too much sun is fatal for deep shade-loving plants.

Plants for Full Sun

You can take the guesswork out of buying plants. This section groups plants into selection guides by light requirements. Check out the lists on the following pages for plants that thrive in full sun, partial shade, and deep shade. You'll see plants on more than one list; they grow in varying amounts of sunlight. Look for plants that include your zone within their growing range. (If you don't know what planting zone you live in, see page 5.) Then, turn to the pages listed for photos and a complete description of plants you'd like to know more about. Availability varies by area and conditions (see page 21). Check with your garden center.

Trees for full sun

Common Name	Zones	Page
Allegheny Serviceberry *Amelanchier laevis*	4-8	81
American Arborvitae *Thuja occidentalis*	2-7	105
American Beech *Fagus grandifolia*	3-9	87
American Hornbeam *Carpinus caroliniana*	3-9	84
American Linden *Tilia americana*	2-8	105
American Smoketree *Cotinus obovatus*	4-8	85
Amur Chokecherry *Prunus maackii*	2-6	97
Amur Maple *Acer tataricum ginnala*	2-6	77
Bradford Pear *Pyrus calleryana 'Bradford'*	4-8	98
Canoe Birch *Betula papyrifera*	2-7	82
Cockspur Hawthorn *Crataegus crus-galli 'Inermis'*	4-7	86
Colorado Blue Spruce *Picea pungens glauca*	2-7	93
Common Horsechesnut *Aesculus hippocastanum*	3-7	80
Corkscrew Willow *Salix 'Golden Curls'*	4-8	103
Douglas Fir *Pseudotsuga menziesii*	4-6	98
Eastern Red Cedar *Juniperus virginiana*	3-9	90
European Hornbeam *Carpinus betulus*	4-7	83
European Mountain Ash *Sorbus aucuparia*	4-7	103
European White Birch *Betula pendula*	2-7	82
Frasier Fir *Abies fraseri*	4-7	75
Ginkgo *Ginkgo biloba*	3-9	88
Golden Weeping Willow *Salix alba 'Tristis'*	3-8	102
Green Ash *Fraxinus pennsylvanica*	3-9	88
Honeylocust *Gleditisia triacanthos inermis*	3-9	89
Jack Pine *Pinus banksiana*	2-6	94
Japanese Flowering Crabapple *Malus floribunda*	3-8	91
Japanese Tree Lilac *Syringa reticulata*	3-7	104
Katsura Tree *Cercidiphyllum japonicum*	4-8	84
Lacebark Pine *Pinus bungeana*	4-7	94
Mayday Tree *Prunus padus commutata*	3-6	97
Newport Plum *Prunus cerasifera 'Newport'*	4-8	96
Northern Red Oak *Quercus rubra*	4-7	101
Norway Maple *Acer platanoides*	3-7	77
Norway Spruce *Picea abies*	2-7	92
Ohio Buckeye *Aesculus glabra*	3-7	79
Pin Oak *Quercus palustris*	4-8	101
Plumleaf Crabapple *Malus prunifolia*	4-9	91
Pyramidal Japanese Yew *Taxus cuspidata 'Capitata'*	4-7	104
Quaking Aspen *Populus tremuloides*	2-6	96
Red Spruce *Picea rubens*	2-5	93
Redbud *Cercis canadensis*	3-9	85
River Birch *Betula nigra*	4-9	81
Russian Olive *Eleagnus angustifolia*	2-7	87
Scarlet Oak *Quercus coccinea*	4-9	100
Scots Pine *Pinus sylvestris*	3-7	95
Shadblow Serviceberry *Amelanchier canadensis*	3-8	80
Silver Maple *Acer saccharinum*	3-9	78
Skyrocket Juniper *Juniperus scopulorum 'Skyrocket'*	4-8	89
Sugar Maple *Acer saccharum*	4-8	79
Washington Hawthorn *Crataegus phaenopyrum*	3-9	86
Weeping Willow *Salix babylonica*	4-8	102
White Fir *Abies concolor*	3-7	74
White Oak *Quercus alba*	3-9	100
White Pine *Pinus strobus*	3-8	95
White Spruce *Picea glauca*	2-6	92
Whitespire Birch *Betula mandschurica japonica 'Whitespire'*	4-7	83

Doublefile Viburnum (Viburnum plicatum tomentosum) Page 166

Shrubs for full sun

Common Name	Zones	Page
Adelaide Hoodless Rose *Rosa 'Adelaide Hoodless'*	2-9	148
Amur Privet *Ligustrum amurense*	3-7	139
Anglojap Yew *Taxus x media 'Densiformis'*	4-7	162
Annabelle Hydrangea *Hydrangea arborescens 'Annabelle'*	3-9	134
Anthony Waterer Spirea *Spiraea japonica 'Anthony Waterer'*	3-9	157
Arnold's Red Tatarian Honeysuckle *Lonicera tatarica 'Arnold's Red'*	3-9	140
Arrowwood Viburnum *Viburnum dentatum*	3-8	165
Betty Prior Rose *Rosa 'Betty Prior'*	4-9	148
Bird's Nest Spruce *Picea abies 'Nidiformis'*	2-7	142
Black Chokeberry *Aronia melanocarpa*	4-9	125
Blackhaw Viburnum *Viburnum prunifolium*	3-9	167
Blue Star Juniper *Juniperus squamata 'Blue Star'*	4-8	139
Bridalwreath Spirea *Spiraea prunifolia*	5-8	158
Carefree Beauty Rose *Rosa Carefree Beauty*	4-8	149
Carol Mackie Daphne *Daphne x burkwoodii 'Carol Mackie'*	4-8	132
Carolina Azalea *Azalea carolinianum*	4-9	126
Catawba Rhododendron *Rhododendron catawbiense*	4-8	146
Common Lilac *Syringa vulgaris*	3-7	162
Common Witch Hazel *Hamamelis virginiana*	3-8	134
Compact Amer. Cranberrybush *Viburnum trilobum 'Alfredo'*	2-7	167
Coralberry *Symphoricarpos orbiculatus*	4-7	159
Coral Embers Willow *Salix alba 'Britzensis'*	2-8	156
Cornelian Cherry *Cornus mas*	4-8	131
Cornell Pink Azalea *Azalea mucronulatum 'Cornell Pink'*	4-7	127
Cut-Leaf Staghorn Sumac *Rhus typhina 'Laciniata'*	3-8	147
Cutleaf Lilac *Syringa x laciniata*	4-8	160
Doublefile Viburnum *Viburnum plicatum tomentosum*	4-8	166
Dwarf Alberta Spruce *Picea glauca 'Conica'*	2-8	143
Dwarf Burning Bush *Euonymus alatus 'Compacta'*	3-8	133
Dwarf Flowering Almond *Prunus glandulosa 'Rosea'*	4-8	144

Common Name	Zones	Page
Dwarf Hinoki False Cypress *Chamaecyparis obtusa 'Nana Gracilis'*	4-8	129
Dwarf Norway Spruce *Picea abies 'Pumila'*	3-8	142
Emerald Arborvitae *Thuja occidentalis 'Emerald'*	2-7	163
European Cranberrybush *Viburnum opulus 'Roseum'*	3-8	166
Exbury Azalea *Azalea 'Exbury Hybrids'*	4-7	126
French Pussy Willow *Salix caprea 'Kilmarnock'*	4-8	156
Fru Dagmar Hastrup Rose *Rosa 'Fru Dagmar Hastrup'*	2-9	149
Graham Thomas Rose *Rosa Graham Thomas*	5-9	150
Gray Dogwood *Cornus racemosa*	4-7	131
Green Lustre Japanese Holly *Ilex crenata 'Green Lustre'*	4-6	135
Green Mound Alpine Currant *Ribes alpinum 'Green Mound'*	2-7	147
Henry Kelsey Rose *Rosa 'Henry Kelsey'*	3-9	150
Hetz's Midget Arborvitae *Thuja occidentalis 'Hetz's Midget'*	2-8	164
Hick's Upright Yew *Taxus x media 'Hicksii'*	4-7	163
Hunter Rose *Rosa 'Hunter'*	4-8	151
Inkberry *Ilex glabra 'Compacta'*	3-10	136
Japanese Barberry *Berberis thunbergii*	4-8	128
Limemound Spirea *Spiraea japonica Limemound*	4-9	158
Little Giant Arborvitae *Thuja occidentalis 'Little Giant'*	2-7	164
Margo Koster Polyantha Rose *Rosa 'Margo Koster'*	5-8	151
Miss Kim Lilac *Syringa patula 'Miss Kim'*	3-7	161
Mohican Viburnum *Viburnum lantana 'Mohican'*	3-8	165
Morden Centennial Rose *Rosa 'Morden Centennial'*	2-9	152
Mugo Pine *Pinus mugo*	2-7	143
Nearly Wild Rose *Rosa 'Nearly Wild'*	2-9	152
Northern Bayberry *Myrica pensylvanica*	2-6	141
Northern Lights Azalea *Azalea 'Northern Lights'*	4-7	127
Old Gold Juniper *Juniperus chinensis 'Old Gold'*	4-10	137
Oriental Photinia *Photinia villosa*	4-7	141
Parson's Juniper *Juniperus chinensis 'Parsonii'*	3-9	137
PeeGee Hydrangea *Hydrangea paniculata 'Grandiflora'*	3-8	135
Persian Lilac *Syringa x persica*	3-7	161
Purple-Leaf Sand Cherry *Prunus x cistena*	2-8	145
Redtwig Dogwood *Cornus alba*	2-8	130
Rosa Rubrifolia *Rosa rubrifolia*	4-9	155
Russian Cypress *Microbiota decussata*	3-7	140
Sea Green Juniper *Juniperus chinensis 'Sea Green'*	4-8	138
Serviceberry *Amelanchier alnifolia*	4-5	125
Shibori Spirea *Spiraea japonica 'Shibori'*	4-8	157
Shrubby Cinquefoil *Potentilla fruticosa*	2-7	144
Sir Thomas Lipton Rose *Rosa 'Sir Thomas Lipton'*	2-7	153
Snowberry *Symphoricarpos albus*	3-7	159
Sweetshrub *Calycanthus floridus*	4-9	129
Tam Juniper *Juniperus sabina 'Tamariscifolia'*	3-7	138
The Fairy Rose *Rosa 'The Fairy'*	4-9	153
Therese Bugnet Rose *Rosa 'Therese Bugnet'*	3-9	154
Vermont Sun Forsythia *Forsythia mandshurica 'Vermont Sun'*	4-8	133
White Forsythia *Abeliophyllum distichum*	4-8	124
White Rugosa Rose *Rosa rugosa 'Alba'*	3-10	155
William Baffin Rose *Rosa 'William Baffin'*	2-9	154
Winterberry *Ilex verticillata*	3-9	136
Wintergreen Boxwood *Buxus microphylla 'Wintergreen'*	4-6	128
Yellow-Twig Dogwood *Cornus stolonifera 'Flaviramea'*	3-8	132
Yukon Belle Firethorn *Pyracantha angustifolia Yukon Belle*	4-9	145

Boston Ivy (Parthenocissus tricuspidata) Page 213

Groundcovers for full sun

Common Name	Zones	Page
Ajuga *Ajuga reptans*	3-9	178
Alba Meidiland Rose *Rosa Alba Meidiland*	4-8	201
Alpine Strawberry *Fragaria vesca*	3-9	189
Andorra Compact Juniper *Juniperus horizontalis 'Plumosa Compacta'*	3-9	194
Bar Harbor Juniper *Juniperus horizontalis 'Bar Harbor'*	3-9	193
Basket-of-Gold *Aurinia saxatilis*	4-8	183
Bath's Pink *Dianthus gratianopolitanus 'Bath's Pink'*	4-9	187
Blanket Flower *Gaillardia x grandiflora*	2-9	190
Bloody Cranesbill *Geranium sanguineum*	3-8	191
Blue Chip Juniper *Juniperus horizontalis 'Blue Chip'*	3-9	193
Blue Rug Juniper *Juniperus horizontalis 'Wiltonii '*	3-9	194
Blue Star Bellflower *Campanula poscharskyana*	4-9	184
Bog Rosemary *Andromeda polifolia*	2-6	180
Catmint *Nepeta x faassenii*	4-8	197
Cliff Green *Paxistima canbyi*	3-7	199
Coral Bells *Heuchera sanguinea*	3-8	191
Cypress Spurge *Euphorbia cyparissias*	4-8	188
Dwarf Blue Fescue *Festuca glauca*	4-9	188
Dwarf Japanese Garden Juniper *Juniperus procumbens 'Nana'*	4-9	195
Flower Carpet Rose *Rosa 'Flower Carpet'*	4-10	201
Forget-Me-Not *Myosotis scorpioides*	3-8	197
Germander *Teucrium prostratum*	4-9	204
Goldmoss *Sedum acre*	4-9	202
Kinnikinick *Arctostaphylos uva-ursi*	2-7	181
Lamb's Ear *Stachys byzantina*	4-8	203
Littleleaf Periwinkle *Vinca minor*	4-8	205
Moss Phlox *Phlox subulata*	2-9	200
Mountain Sandwort *Arenaria montana*	3-6	181
Pink Panda Strawberry *Fragaria 'Pink Panda'*	3-9	189
Prostrate Chenault Coralberry *Symphoricarpos x chenaultii 'Hancock'*	4-7	203
Purple-Leaf Wintercreeper *Eunoymus fortunei 'Coloratus'*	3-9	187
Rockcress *Arabis caucasica*	3-7	180
Saxifrage *Bergenia cordifolia*	3-8	184
Silver Brocade Artemisia *Artemisia stelleriana 'Silver Brocade'*	3-9	182
Snow-in-Summer *Cerastium tomentosum*	3-7	185
Spring Cinquefoil *Potentilla tabernaemontani*	4-8	200
Stonecrop *Sedum spectabile*	3-10	202
Sundrop Primrose *Oenothera missouriensis*	4-8	198
Sweet Woodruff *Asperula odorata*	4-8	183
Waldesteinia *Waldsteinia ternata*	3-8	205

Vines for full sun

Common Name	Zones	Page
American Bittersweet *Celastrus scandens*	3-8	211
Boston Ivy *Parthenocissus tricuspidata*	4-8	213
Climbing Hydrangea *Hydrangea petiolaris*	4-7	211
Dropmore Scarlet Honeysuckle *Lonicera x brownii 'Dropmore Scarlet'*	3-7	212
Hardy Kiwi *Actinidia arguta*	4-8	210
Trumpet Honeysuckle *Lonicera sempervirens*	4-9	212
Trumpet Vine *Campsis radicans*	4-9	210
Virginia Creeper *Parthenocissus quinquefolia*	4-9	213

Plants for Shade

Need help finding plants to grow in shaded areas? These lists are guides to help you find trees, shrubs, groundcovers, and vines for partial or deep shade. If you see plants on more than one list, they grow in varying degrees of shade. Look for plants that include your zone within their growing range and skip plants that don't. (If you don't know what planting zone you live in, see page 5.) Then turn to the pages listed for photos and a complete description of plants you'd like to know more about. Availability varies by area and conditions (see page 21). Check with your garden center.

Trees for shade

Common Name	Zones	Page	Shade
Allegheny Serviceberry *Amelanchier laevis*	4-8	81	P
American Beech *Fagus grandifolia*	3-9	87	P
American Hornbeam *Carpinus caroliniana*	3-9	84	P
American Linden *Tilia americana*	2-8	105	P
Amur Chokecherry *Prunus maackii*	2-6	97	P
Amur Maple *Acer tataricum ginnala*	2-6	77	P
Balsam Fir *Abies balsamea*	3-6	74	P
Cockspur Hawthorn *Crataegus crus-galli 'Inermis'*	4-7	86	P
Common Horsechesnut *Aesculus hippocastanum*	3-7	80	P
Corkscrew Willow *Salix 'Golden Curls'*	4-8	103	P
European Hornbeam *Carpinus betulus*	4-7	83	P
European Mountain Ash *Sorbus aucuparia*	4-7	103	P
European White Birch *Betula pendula*	2-7	82	P
Frasier Fir *Abies fraseri*	4-7	75	P
Norway Maple *Acer platanoides*	3-7	77	P
Ohio Buckeye *Aesculus glabra*	3-7	79	P
Pin Oak *Quercus palustris*	4-8	101	P
Pyramidal Japanese Yew *Taxus cuspidata 'Capitata'*	4-7	104	D
Red Maple *Acer rubrum*	3-9	78	P
Red Spruce *Picea rubens*	2-5	93	P
Redbud *Cercis canadensis*	3-9	85	P
River Birch *Betula nigra*	4-9	81	P
Shadblow Serviceberry *Amelanchier canadensis*	3-8	80	P
Silver Maple *Acer saccharinum*	3-9	78	P
Star Magnolia *Magnolia stellata*	4-9	90	P
Sugar Maple *Acer saccharum*	4-8	79	P
Veitch Fir *Abies veitchii*	3-6	75	P
Washington Hawthorn *Crataegus phaenopyrum*	3-9	86	P
White Spruce *Picea glauca*	2-6	92	P

Level of Shade:
P: Partial D: Deep
Botanical name in italics

Shrubs for shade

Common Name	Zones	Page	Shade
Amur Privet *Ligustrum amurense*	3-7	139	P
Anglojap Yew *Taxus x media 'Densiformis'*	4-7	162	D
Annabelle Hydrangea *Hydrangea arborescens 'Annabelle'*	3-9	134	P
Anthony Waterer Spirea *Spiraea japonica 'Anthony Waterer'*	3-9	157	P
Arrowwood Viburnum *Viburnum dentatum*	3-8	165	P
Black Chokeberry *Aronia melanocarpa*	4-9	125	P
Blackhaw Viburnum *Viburnum prunifolium*	3-9	167	P
Bridalwreath Spirea *Spiraea prunifolia*	5-8	158	P
Carol Mackie Daphne *Daphne x burkwoodii 'Carol Mackie'*	4-8	132	P
Catawba Rhododendron *Rhododendron catawbiense*	4-8	146	D
Common Lilac *Syringa vulgaris*	3-7	162	P
Common Witch Hazel *Hamamelis virginiana*	3-8	134	P
Compact American Cranberrybush *Viburnum trilobum 'Alfredo'*	2-7	167	P
Coralberry *Symphoricarpos orbiculatus*	4-7	159	D
Cutleaf Lilac *Syringa x laciniata*	4-8	160	P
Doublefile Viburnum *Viburnum plicatum tomentosum*	4-8	166	P
Dwarf Alberta Spruce *Picea glauca 'Conica'*	2-8	143	P
Dwarf Balsam Fir *Abies balsamea 'Nana'*	3-6	124	P
Dwarf Burning Bush *Euonymus alatus 'Compacta'*	3-8	133	P
Dwarf Flowering Almond *Prunus glandulosa 'Rosea'*	4-8	144	P
Green Lustre Japanese Holly *Ilex crenata 'Green Lustre'*	4-6	135	P
Green Mound Alpine Currant *Ribes alpinum 'Green Mound'*	2-7	147	D
Hick's Upright Yew *Taxus x media 'Hicksii'*	4-7	163	D
Inkberry *Ilex glabra 'Compacta'*	3-10	136	P
Japanese Barberry *Berberis thunbergii*	4-8	128	D
Miss Kim Lilac *Syringa patula 'Miss Kim'*	3-7	161	P
Mohican Viburnum *Viburnum lantana 'Mohican'*	3-8	165	P
Mugo Pine *Pinus mugo*	2-7	143	P
Northern Bayberry *Myrica pensylvanica*	2-6	141	P
Oriental Photinia *Photinia villosa*	4-7	141	P
PeeGee Hydrangea *Hydrangea paniculata 'Grandiflora'*	3-8	135	P
Persian Lilac *Syringa x persica*	3-7	161	P
Russian Cypress *Microbiota decussata*	3-7	140	P
Serviceberry *Amelanchier alnifolia*	4-5	125	P
Shibori Spirea *Spiraea japonica 'Shibori'*	4-8	157	P
Shrubby Cinquefoil *Potentilla fruticosa*	2-7	144	P
Sir Thomas Lipton Rose *Rosa 'Sir Thomas Lipton'*	2-7	153	P
Snowberry *Symphoricarpos albus*	3-7	159	D
Summersweet *Clethra alnifolia*	3-9	130	P
Sweetshrub *Calycanthus floridus*	4-9	129	D
The Fairy Rose *Rosa 'The Fairy'*	4-9	153	P
Vermont Sun Forsythia *Forsythia mandshurica 'Vermont Sun'*	4-8	133	P
Winterberry *Ilex verticillata*	3-9	136	P
Wintergreen Boxwood *Buxus microphylla 'Wintergreen'*	4-6	128	P
Yellow-Twig Dogwood *Cornus stolonifera 'Flaviramea'*	3-8	132	P
Yukon Belle Firethorn *Pyracantha angustifolia Yukon Belle*	4-9	145	P

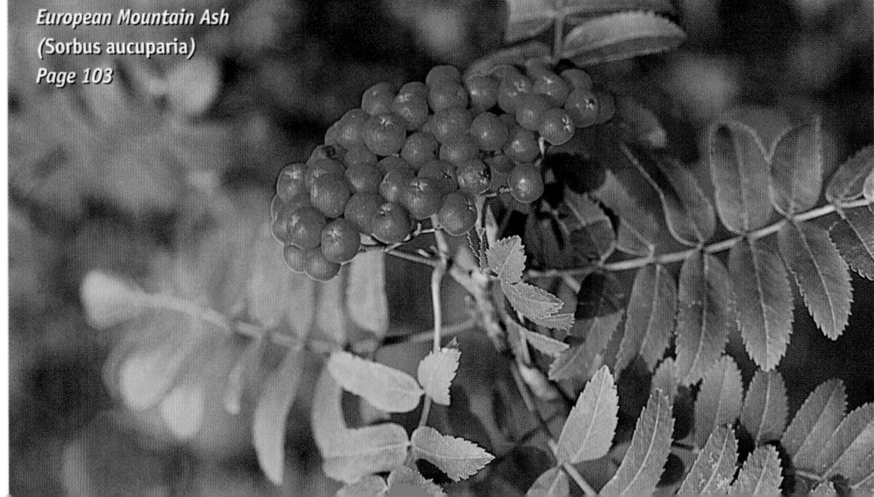
European Mountain Ash (Sorbus aucuparia) Page 103

Groundcovers for shade

Common Name	Zones	Page	Shade
Ajuga *Ajuga reptans*	3-9	178	P
Alba Meidiland Rose *Rosa Alba Meidiland*	4-8	201	P
Allegheny Foam Flower *Tiarella cordifolia*	4-9	204	D
Alpine Strawberry *Fragaria vesca*	3-9	189	P
Bath's Pink *Dianthus gratianopolitanus 'Bath's Pink'*	4-9	187	P
Bloody Cranesbill *Geranium sanguineum*	3-8	191	P
Blue Star *Amsonia tabernaemontana*	3-9	179	P
Blue Star Bellflower *Campanula poscharskyana*	4-9	184	P
Bog Rosemary *Andromeda polifolia*	2-6	180	P
Bunchberry *Cornus canadensis*	2-7	186	D
Catmint *Nepeta x faassenii*	4-8	197	P
Cliff Green *Paxistima canbyi*	3-7	199	P
Coral Bells *Heuchera sanguinea*	3-8	191	P
Creeping Phlox *Phlox stolonifera*	2-8	199	D
Cypress Spurge *Euphorbia cyparissias*	4-8	188	P
Forget-Me-Not *Myosotis scorpioides*	3-8	197	P
Hay-Scented Fern *Dennstaedtia punctilobula*	3-8	186	D
Hosta *Hosta species*	3-8	192	D
Kinnikinick *Arctostaphylos uva-ursi*	2-7	181	P
Lady's Mantle *Alchemilla mollis*	4-7	178	P
Lily-of-the-Valley *Convallaria majalis*	2-9	185	D
Littleleaf Periwinkle *Vinca minor*	4-8	205	P
Maidenhair Fern *Adiantum pedatum*	3-8	177	D
Pachysandra *Pachysandra terminalis*	4-9	198	D
Partridge Berry *Mitchella repens*	4-9	196	D
Pink Panda Strawberry *Fragaria 'Pink Panda'*	3-9	189	P
Prostrate Chenault Coralberry *Symphoricarpos x chenaultii 'Hancock'*	4-7	203	D
Rockcress *Arabis caucasica*	3-7	180	P
Saxifrage *Bergenia cordifolia*	3-8	184	P
Sea Thrift *Armeria maritima*	3-8	182	P
Siberian Forget-Me-Not *Anchusa myosotidiflora*	3-7	179	D
Snow-on-the-Mountain *Aegopodium podagraria 'Variegatum'*	3-9	177	D
Spotted Dead Nettle *Lamium maculatum*	3-9	196	D
Sweet Woodruff *Asperula odorata*	4-8	183	P
Waldesteinia *Waldsteinia ternata*	3-8	205	P
Wintergreen *Gaultheria procumbens*	3-8	190	P
Yellow Archangel *Lamiastrum galeobdolon 'Variegatum'*	3-9	195	D

Sweet Woodruff (Asperula odorata) Page 183

Bath's Pink (Dianthus gratianopolitanus 'Bath's Pink') Page 187

Vines for shade

Common Name	Zones	Page	Shade
American Bittersweet *Celastrus scandens*	3-8	211	D
Boston Ivy *Parthenocissus tricuspidata*	4-8	213	P
Climbing Hydrangea *Hydrangea petiolaris*	4-7	211	D
Hardy Kiwi *Actinidia arguta*	4-8	210	P
Trumpet Vine *Campsis radicans*	4-9	210	D
Virginia Creeper *Parthenocissus quinquefolia*	4-9	213	P

Soil Conditions

Knowing what kind of soil you have is the first step in choosing plants that will thrive. Here are the basics; visit your county extension service if you want a specific soil analysis. No matter what condition you have, working the soil is beneficial to new plants, which need all the help you can offer them. Improving soil with amendments is a bonus for good growth (see pages 54-55), but don't think you can fool Mother Nature. Choose plants that thrive naturally in existing soil conditions.

Get Your Hands Dirty

Begin evaluating the soil in your yard by pushing up your sleeves and digging a few inches below the surface. You're looking for three indicators—water retention, nutrient content, and drainage or percolation rate. (See "Wisdom of the Aisles," below.) Scoop up a handful of soil and squeeze it to check for water content. If water dribbles out, it's wet. If it can't form a lump, it's dry. If the soil forms a lump that firmly holds its shape, you might have clay. If it forms a lump that easily crumbles again, the soil is moist. Next, roll it between your palms with light pressure.

Heavy Soil If it forms a snakelike form on rolling, the soil has a high clay content and is described as heavy. The pores between soil particles are very small. Nutrients do not leach out as quickly as in other soil types. However, water can be trapped in pores, resulting in sticky, wet soil. This situation creates standing water surrounding roots causing nonadapted plants to suffocate and die. When clay is dry, it is dense and hard, much like concrete. Roots can have difficulty penetrating these soils. Choose plants that can tolerate clay soil.

Porous Soil If the soil in your hand is too sandy or rocky to hold together well, it is porous. Water percolates quickly through such soil. There's no problem with water collecting around roots, but nutrients wash rapidly away. These soils are known as poor and dry. You'll need to regularly water and fertilize plants in porous soil. Select plants that tolerate poor, dry soils.

Moderate Soil Many soil types fall somewhere between these two extremes. You might be able to roll your soil into a ribbon, indicating some clay content, but it will break apart when just a few inches long. If you're able to crumble the soil easily between your fingers to its original state, your soil is moderate. Many different plants thrive in moderate soil, but they'll grow even better if you work the soil prior to planting.

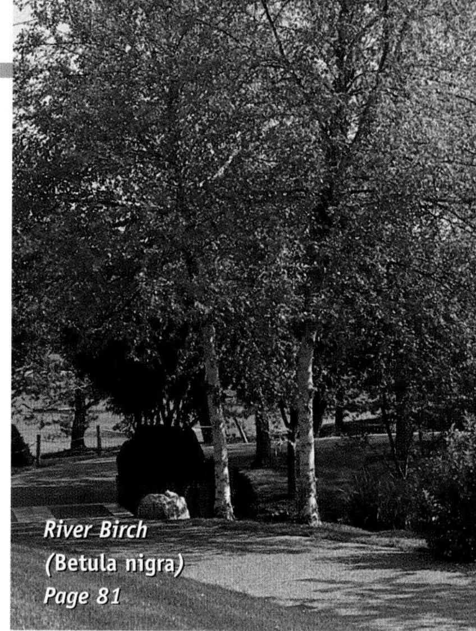

River Birch (Betula nigra) Page 81

Do a perc test. Percolation is the way water drains through soil and is one of the guides for plant selection. Determine your soil's rate of percolation by digging test holes 12 to 18 inches deep in several spots around your yard. Fill them with water and measure the water depth with a stick. After 30 minutes measure the water depth again. If the hole empties or water levels drop an inch or more within half an hour, your soil drains very quickly. Choose plants that thrive in poor, dry soil. If water remains, check levels hourly. If the hole drains about an inch an hour, it's well-drained and should support many different plant types. Less than an inch an hour indicates poor drainage. Choose plants that grow well in wet, boggy areas or will tolerate compacted soil.

Plants for poor, dry soil

Common Name	Zones	Page
◆ Trees		
American Smoketree *Cotinus obovatus*	4-8	85
Amur Maple *Acer tataricum ginnala*	2-6	77
Eastern Red Cedar *Juniperus virginiana*	3-9	90
Ginkgo *Ginkgo biloba*	3-9	88
Green Ash *Fraxinus pennsylvanica*	3-9	88
Pin Oak *Quercus palustris*	4-8	101
Pyramidal Japanese Yew *Taxus cuspidata 'Capitata'*	4-7	104
Red Maple *Acer rubrum*	3-9	78
River Birch *Betula nigra*	4-9	81
Scots Pine *Pinus sylvestris*	3-7	95
Silver Maple *Acer saccharinum*	3-9	78
Skyrocket Juniper *Juniperus scopulorum 'Skyrocket'*	4-8	89
Washington Hawthorn *Crataegus phaenopyrum*	3-9	86
Weeping Willow *Salix babylonica*	4-8	102
White Oak *Quercus alba*	3-9	100
White Pine *Pinus strobus*	3-8	95
Whitespire Birch *Betula mandschurica japonica 'Whitespire'*	4-7	83
◆ Shrubs		
Amur Privet *Ligustrum amurense*	3-7	139
Black Chokeberry *Aronia melanocarpa*	4-9	125

Common Name	Zones	Page
Blue Star Juniper *Juniperus squamata ‘Blue Star’*	4-8	139
Carol Mackie Daphne *Daphne x burkwoodii ‘Carol Mackie’*	4-8	132
Coralberry *Symphoricarpos orbiculatus*	4-7	159
Cut-Leaf Staghorn Sumac *Rhus typhina ‘Laciniata’*	3-8	147
Dwarf Alberta Spruce *Picea glauca ‘Conica’*	2-8	143
Emerald Arborvitae *Thuja occidentalis ‘Emerald’*	2-7	163
Fru Dagmar Hastrup Rose *Rosa ‘Fru Dagmar Hastrup’*	2-9	149
Green Mound Alpine Currant *Ribes alpinum ‘Green Mound’*	2-7	147
Northern Bayberry *Myrica pensylvanica*	2-6	141
Old Gold Juniper *Juniperus chinensis ‘Old Gold’*	4-10	137
Parson’s Juniper *Juniperus chinensis ‘Parsonii’*	3-9	137
Sea Green Juniper *Juniperus chinensis ‘Sea Green’*	4-8	138
Tam Juniper *Juniperus sabina ‘Tamariscifolia’*	3-7	138
Therese Bugnet Rose *Rosa ‘Therese Bugnet’*	3-9	154
◆ **Groundcovers**		
Basket-of-Gold *Aurinia saxatilis*	4-8	183
Bath’s Pink *Dianthus gratianopolitanus ‘Bath’s Pink’*	4-9	187
Blanket Flower *Gaillardia x grandiflora*	2-9	190
Blue Chip Juniper *Juniperus horizontalis ‘Blue Chip’*	3-9	193
Cliff Green *Paxistima canbyi*	3-7	199
Dwarf Blue Fescue *Festuca glauca*	4-9	188
Goldmoss *Sedum acre*	4-9	202
Hay-Scented Fern *Dennstaedtia punctilobula*	3-8	186
Kinnikinick *Arctostaphylos uva-ursi*	2-7	181
Lily-of-the-Valley *Convallaria majalis*	2-9	185
Moss Phlox *Phlox subulata*	2-9	200
Mountain Sandwort *Arenaria montana*	3-6	181
Prostrate Chenault Coralberry *Symphoricarpos x chenaultii ‘Hancock’*	4-7	203
Sea Thrift *Armeria maritima*	3-8	182
Snow-in-Summer *Cerastium tomentosum*	3-7	185
Snow-on-the-Mountain *Aegopodium podagraria ‘Variegatum’*	3-9	177
Spotted Dead Nettle *Lamium maculatum*	3-9	196
Spring Cinquefoil *Potentilla tabernaemontani*	4-8	200
Stonecrop *Sedum spectabile*	3-10	202
Sundrop Primrose *Oenothera missouriensis*	4-8	198
◆ **Vines**		
American Bittersweet *Celastrus scandens*	3-8	211
Boston Ivy *Parthenocissus tricuspidata*	4-8	213
Trumpet Vine *Campsis radicans*	4-9	210
Virginia Creeper *Parthenocissus quinquefolia*	4-9	213

Availability varies by area and conditions (see page 21). Check with your garden center.

Plants for heavy, clay soil

Common Name	Zones	Page
◆ **Trees**		
American Arborvitae *Thuja occidentalis*	2-7	105
American Linden *Tilia americana*	2-8	105
Cockspur Hawthorn *Crataegus crus-galli ‘Inermis’*	4-7	86
Common Horsechesnut *Aesculus hippocastanum*	3-7	80
Eastern Red Cedar *Juniperus virginiana*	3-9	90
European Mountain Ash *Sorbus aucuparia*	4-7	103
Ginkgo *Ginkgo biloba*	3-9	88
Green Ash *Fraxinus pennsylvanica*	3-9	88
Norway Maple *Acer platanoides*	3-7	77
Norway Spruce *Picea abies*	2-7	92
Pin Oak *Quercus palustris*	4-8	101
River Birch *Betula nigra*	4-9	81
Shadblow Serviceberry *Amelanchier canadensis*	3-8	80
Silver Maple *Acer saccharinum*	3-9	78
Weeping Willow *Salix babylonica*	4-8	102
White Pine *Pinus strobus*	3-8	95
◆ **Shrubs**		
Annabelle Hydrangea *Hydrangea arborescens ‘Annabelle’*	3-9	134
Anthony Waterer Spirea *Spiraea japonica ‘Anthony Waterer’*	3-9	157
Arrowwood Viburnum *Viburnum dentatum*	3-8	165
Bird’s Nest Spruce *Picea abies ‘Nidiformis’*	2-7	142
Black Chokeberry *Aronia melanocarpa*	4-9	125
Common Lilac *Syringa vulgaris*	3-7	162
Compact Amer. Cranberrybush *Viburnum trilobum ‘Alfredo’*	2-7	167
Dwarf Alberta Spruce *Picea glauca ‘Conica’*	2-8	143
Dwarf Norway Spruce *Picea abies ‘Pumila’*	3-8	142
Emerald Arborvitae *Thuja occidentalis ‘Emerald’*	2-7	163
Hetz’s Midget Arborvitae *Thuja occidentalis ‘Hetz’s Midget’*	2-8	164
Japanese Barberry *Berberis thunbergii*	4-8	128
Little Giant Arborvitae *Thuja occidentalis ‘Little Giant’*	2-7	164
Mohican Viburnum *Viburnum lantana ‘Mohican’*	3-8	165
Mugo Pine *Pinus mugo*	2-7	143
Snowberry *Symphoricarpos albus*	3-7	159
◆ **Groundcovers**		
Bath’s Pink *Dianthus gratianopolitanus ‘Bath’s Pink’*	4-9	187
Snow-on-the-Mountain *Aegopodium podagraria ‘Variegatum’*	3-9	177

Plants for wet, boggy soil

Common Name	Zones	Page
◆ **Trees**		
Allegheny Serviceberry *Amelanchier laevis*	4-8	81
American Hornbeam *Carpinus caroliniana*	3-9	84
Eastern Red Cedar *Juniperus virginiana*	3-9	90
Golden Weeping Willow *Salix alba ‘Tristis’*	3-8	102
Green Ash *Fraxinus pennsylvanica*	3-9	88
River Birch *Betula nigra*	4-9	81
Shadblow Serviceberry *Amelanchier canadensis*	3-8	80
Weeping Willow *Salix babylonica*	4-8	102
◆ **Shrubs**		
Black Chokeberry *Aronia melanocarpa*	4-9	125
Coral Embers Willow *Salix alba ‘Britzensis’*	2-8	156
European Cranberrybush *Viburnum opulus ‘Roseum’*	3-8	166
French Pussy Willow *Salix caprea ‘Kilmarnock’*	4-8	156
Inkberry *Ilex glabra ‘Compacta’*	3-10	136
Red Maple *Acer rubrum*	3-9	78
Redtwig Dogwood *Cornus alba*	2-8	130
Summersweet *Clethra alnifolia*	3-9	130
Sweetshrub *Calycanthus floridus*	4-9	129
Winterberry *Ilex verticillata*	3-9	136
Yellow-Twig Dogwood *Cornus stolonifera ‘Flaviramea’*	3-8	132
◆ **Groundcovers**		
Forget-Me-Not *Myosotis scorpioides*	3-8	197
Snow-on-the-Mountain *Aegopodium podagraria ‘Variegatum’*	3-9	177

White Pine (Pinus strobus) Page 95

Soil pH

Soil can be categorized three ways based on its pH: neutral, acidic, or alkaline. Knowing which category your yard fits into will help you choose the right plants to grow there. Most soil in a given geographic area will be similar in pH, so your local garden center associates will know what's typical of where you live. For a pH reading, purchase a soil testing kit or visit your county extension agent. Your results will show a number between 0 and 14. Neutral soils test around 7. Acidic soils are usually between 4 and 6. Alkaline soils yield readings higher than 7. Observing characteristics native to your area will also give you clues about soil pH. For example, areas where limestone is plentiful are naturally alkaline. Regions with high annual rainfall tend to have acidic soil because of nutrient washing. Areas with high amounts of decaying pine straw or oak leaves usually have acidic soil, too.

Catawba Rhododendron (Rhododendron catawbiense) Page 146

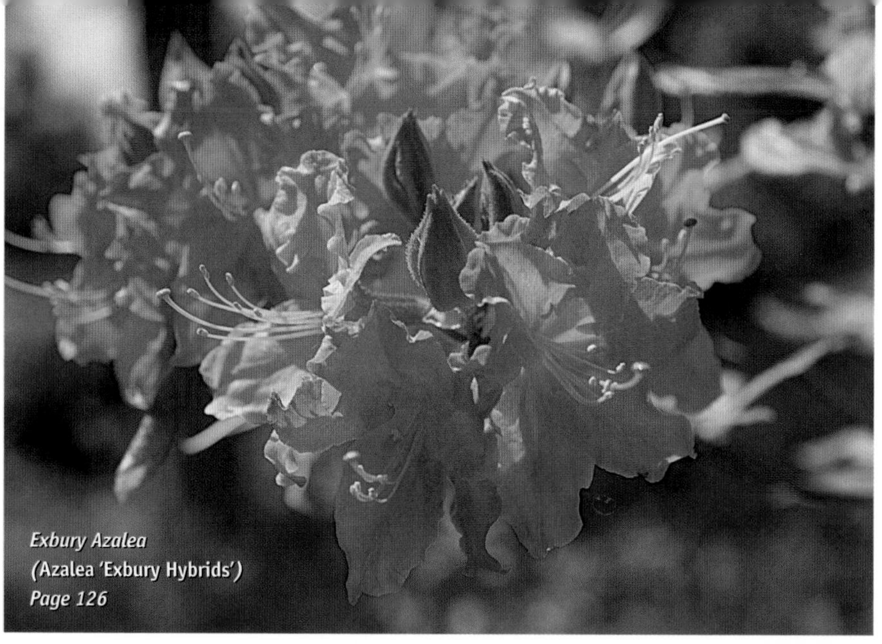

Exbury Azalea (Azalea 'Exbury Hybrids') Page 126

Plants for Special Soil Conditions

Plants for acidic soil

Common Name	Zones	Page
◆ **Trees**		
Allegheny Serviceberry *Amelanchier laevis*	4-8	81
American Beech *Fagus grandifolia*	3-9	87
American Hornbeam *Carpinus caroliniana*	3-9	84
Balsam Fir *Abies balsamea*	3-6	74
Canoe Birch *Betula papyrifera*	2-7	82
Cockspur Hawthorn *Crataegus crus-galli 'Inermis'*	4-7	86
Douglas Fir *Pseudotsuga menziesii*	4-6	98
Eastern Red Cedar *Juniperus virginiana*	3-9	90
European Hornbeam *Carpinus betulus*	4-7	83
European Mountain Ash *Sorbus aucuparia*	4-7	103
European White Birch *Betula pendula*	2-7	82
Ginkgo *Ginkgo biloba*	3-9	88
Green Ash *Fraxinus pennsylvanica*	3-9	88
Jack Pine *Pinus banksiana*	2-6	94
Japanese Tree Lilac *Syringa reticulata*	3-7	104
Katsura Tree *Cercidiphyllum japonicum*	4-8	84
Lacebark Pine *Pinus bungeana*	4-7	94
Newport Plum *Prunus cerasifera 'Newport'*	4-8	96
Northern Red Oak *Quercus rubra*	4-7	101
Norway Spruce *Picea abies*	2-7	92
Pin Oak *Quercus palustris*	4-8	101
Plumleaf Crabapple *Malus prunifolia*	4-9	91
Red Maple *Acer rubrum*	3-9	78
Red Spruce *Picea rubens*	2-5	93
Redbud *Cercis canadensis*	3-9	85
River Birch *Betula nigra*	4-9	81
Russian Olive *Eleagnus angustifolia*	2-7	87
Shadblow Serviceberry *Amelanchier canadensis*	3-8	80
Silver Maple *Acer saccharinum*	3-9	78
Star Magnolia *Magnolia stellata*	4-9	90
Sugar Maple *Acer saccharum*	4-8	79
Veitch Fir *Abies veitchii*	3-6	75
Washington Hawthorn *Crataegus phaenopyrum*	3-9	86
White Oak *Quercus alba*	3-9	100
White Spruce *Picea glauca*	2-6	92
Whitespire Birch *Betula mandschurica japonica 'Whitespire'*	4-7	83
◆ **Shrubs**		
Adelaide Hoodless Rose *Rosa 'Adelaide Hoodless'*	2-9	148
Anglojap Yew *Taxus x media 'Densiformis'*	4-7	162
Annabelle Hydrangea *Hydrangea arborescens 'Annabelle'*	3-9	134
Arrowwood Viburnum *Viburnum dentatum*	3-8	165
Black Chokeberry *Aronia melanocarpa*	4-9	125
Blackhaw Viburnum *Viburnum prunifolium*	3-9	167
Carolina Azalea *Azalea carolinianum*	4-9	126
Catawba Rhododendron *Rhododendron catawbiense*	4-8	146
Compact Amer. Cranberrybush *Viburnum trilobum 'Alfredo'*	2-7	167
Cornell Pink Azalea *Azalea mucronulatum 'Cornell Pink'*	4-7	127
Cut-Leaf Staghorn Sumac *Rhus typhina 'Laciniata'*	3-8	147
Dwarf Alberta Spruce *Picea glauca 'Conica'*	2-8	143

Availability varies by area and conditions (see page 21). Check with your garden center.

Common Name	Zones	Page
Dwarf Balsam Fir *Abies balsamea 'Nana'*	3-6	124
Dwarf Burning Bush *Euonymus alatus 'Compacta'*	3-8	133
Dwarf Hinoki False Cypress *Chamaecyparis obtusa 'Nana Gracilis'*	4-8	129
Dwarf Norway Spruce *Picea abies 'Pumila'*	3-8	142
Exbury Azalea *Azalea 'Exbury Hybrids'*	4-7	126
Green Mound Alpine Currant *Ribes alpinum 'Green Mound'*	2-7	147
Henry Kelsey Rose *Rosa 'Henry Kelsey'*	3-9	150
Hick's Upright Yew *Taxus x media 'Hicksii'*	4-7	163
Hunter Rose *Rosa 'Hunter'*	4-8	151
Inkberry *Ilex glabra 'Compacta'*	3-10	136
Mohican Viburnum *Viburnum lantana 'Mohican'*	3-8	165
Morden Centennial Rose *Rosa 'Morden Centennial'*	2-9	152
Nearly Wild Rose *Rosa 'Nearly Wild'*	2-9	152
Northern Lights Azalea *Azalea 'Northern Lights'*	4-7	127
Old Gold Juniper *Juniperus chinensis 'Old Gold'*	4-10	137
Oriental Photinia *Photinia villosa*	4-7	141
PeeGee Hydrangea *Hydrangea paniculata 'Grandiflora'*	3-8	135
Serviceberry *Amelanchier alnifolia*	4-5	125
Sir Thomas Lipton Rose *Rosa 'Sir Thomas Lipton'*	2-7	153
Summersweet *Clethra alnifolia*	3-9	130
White Forsythia *Abeliophyllum distichum*	4-8	124
White Rugosa Rose *Rosa rugosa 'Alba'*	3-10	155
William Baffin Rose *Rosa 'William Baffin'*	2-9	154
Winterberry *Ilex verticillata*	3-9	136
◆ **Groundcovers**		
Allegheny Foam Flower *Tiarella cordifolia*	4-9	204
Bath's Pink *Dianthus gratianopolitanus 'Bath's Pink'*	4-9	187
Bog Rosemary *Andromeda polifolia*	2-6	180
Bunchberry *Cornus canadensis*	2-7	186
Cliff Green *Paxistima canbyi*	3-7	199
Creeping Phlox *Phlox stolonifera*	2-8	199
Dwarf Japanese Garden Juniper *Juniperus procumbens 'Nana'*	4-9	195
Hay-Scented Fern *Dennstaedtia punctilobula*	3-8	186
Maidenhair Fern *Adiantum pedatum*	3-8	177
Partridge Berry *Mitchella repens*	4-9	196
Purple-Leaf Wintercreeper *Eunoymus fortunei 'Coloratus'*	3-9	187
Snow-on-the-Mountain *Aegopodium podagraria 'Variegatum'*	3-9	177
Sweet Woodruff *Asperula odorata*	4-8	183
Wintergreen *Gaultheria procumbens*	3-8	190
◆ **Vines**		
Boston Ivy *Parthenocissus tricuspidata*	4-8	213
Virginia Creeper *Parthenocissus quinquefolia*	4-9	213

Green Mound Alpine Currant (Ribes alpinum 'Green Mound') Page 147

Common Horsechesnut (Aesculus hippocastanum) Page 80

Plants for alkaline soil

Common Name	Zones	Page
◆ **Trees**		
American Arborvitae *Thuja occidentalis*	2-7	105
American Linden *Tilia americana*	2-8	105
American Smoketree *Cotinus obovatus*	4-8	85
Cockspur Hawthorn *Crataegus crus-galli 'Inermis'*	4-7	86
Common Horsechesnut *Aesculus hippocastanum*	3-7	80
Eastern Red Cedar *Juniperus virginiana*	3-9	90
European Hornbeam *Carpinus betulus*	4-7	83
European White Birch *Betula pendula*	2-7	82
Ginkgo *Ginkgo biloba*	3-9	88
Green Ash *Fraxinus pennsylvanica*	3-9	88
Honeylocust *Gleditsia triacanthos inermis*	3-9	89
Japanese Flowering Crabapple *Malus floribunda*	3-8	91
Katsura Tree *Cercidiphyllum japonicum*	4-8	84
Lacebark Pine *Pinus bungeana*	4-7	94
Newport Plum *Prunus cerasifera 'Newport'*	4-8	96
Norway Maple *Acer platanoides*	3-7	77
Redbud *Cercis canadensis*	3-9	85
Silver Maple *Acer saccharinum*	3-9	78
Washington Hawthorn *Crataegus phaenopyrum*	3-9	86
◆ **Shrubs**		
Carol Mackie Daphne *Daphne x burkwoodii 'Carol Mackie'*	4-8	132
Cut-Leaf Staghorn Sumac *Rhus typhina 'Laciniata'*	3-8	147
Dwarf Burning Bush *Euonymus alatus 'Compacta'*	3-8	133
Dwarf Hinoki False Cypress *Chamaecyparis obtusa 'Nana Gracilis'*	4-8	129
Emerald Arborvitae *Thuja occidentalis 'Emerald'*	2-7	163
Green Mound Alpine Currant *Ribes alpinum 'Green Mound'*	2-7	147
Little Giant Arborvitae *Thuja occidentalis 'Little Giant'*	2-7	164
Old Gold Juniper *Juniperus chinensis 'Old Gold'*	4-10	137
PeeGee Hydrangea *Hydrangea paniculata 'Grandiflora'*	3-8	135
Persian Lilac *Syringa x persica*	3-7	161
Serviceberry *Amelanchier alnifolia*	4-5	125
White Forsythia *Abeliophyllum distichum*	4-8	124
◆ **Groundcovers**		
Alpine Strawberry *Fragaria vesca*	3-9	189
Andorra Compact Juniper *Juniperus horizontalis 'Plumosa Compacta'*	3-9	194
Bar Harbor Juniper *Juniperus horizontalis 'Bar Harbor'*	3-9	193
Bath's Pink *Dianthus gratianopolitanus 'Bath's Pink'*	4-9	187
Blue Chip Juniper *Juniperus horizontalis 'Blue Chip'*	3-9	193
Blue Rug Juniper *Juniperus horizontalis 'Wiltonii'*	3-9	194
Blue Star Bellflower *Campanula poscharskyana*	4-9	184
Cliff Green *Paxistima canbyi*	3-7	199
Coral Bells *Heuchera sanguinea*	3-8	191
Dwarf Japanese Garden Juniper *Juniperus procumbens 'Nana'*	4-9	195
Germander *Teucrium prostratum*	4-9	204
Goldmoss *Sedum acre*	4-9	202
Purple-Leaf Wintercreeper *Eunoymus fortunei 'Coloratus'*	3-9	187
Snow-on-the-Mountain *Aegopodium podagraria 'Variegatum'*	3-9	177
◆ **Vines**		
Boston Ivy *Parthenocissus tricuspidata*	4-8	213
Virginia Creeper *Parthenocissus quinquefolia*	4-9	213

Plants for Special Site Conditions

Special site conditions require special plants. These selection guides will help you choose plants suitable for growing on slopes, on low-water sites, and in areas that receive ocean salts or salt from winter road crews. If parts of your yard suffer from car exhaust, reflected heat from paving, or confined root spaces, check out the list of plants for urban areas on page 43.

Plants for slopes

Common Name	Zones	Page
◆ Trees		
Eastern Red Cedar *Juniperus virginiana*	3-9	90
Golden Weeping Willow *Salix alba 'Tristis'*	3-8	102
Quaking Aspen *Populus tremuloides*	2-6	96
Weeping Willow *Salix babylonica*	4-8	102
◆ Shrubs		
Black Chokeberry *Aronia melanocarpa*	4-9	125
Coralberry *Symphoricarpos orbiculatus*	4-7	159
Cut-Leaf Staghorn Sumac *Rhus typhina 'Laciniata'*	3-8	147
Nearly Wild Rose *Rosa 'Nearly Wild'*	2-9	152
Old Gold Juniper *Juniperus chinensis 'Old Gold'*	4-10	137
Russian Cypress *Microbiota decussata*	3-7	140
Sea Green Juniper *Juniperus chinensis 'Sea Green'*	4-8	138
Sir Thomas Lipton Rose *Rosa 'Sir Thomas Lipton'*	2-7	153
Snowberry *Symphoricarpos albus*	3-7	159
Vermont Sun Forsythia *Forsythia mandshurica 'Vermont Sun'*	4-8	133
White Forsythia *Abeliophyllum distichum*	4-8	124
White Rugosa Rose *Rosa rugosa 'Alba'*	3-10	155
◆ Groundcovers		
Alba Meidiland Rose *Rosa Alba Meidiland*	4-8	201
Alpine Strawberry *Fragaria vesca*	3-9	189

Common Name	Zones	Page
Andorra Compact Juniper *Juniperus horizontalis 'Plumosa Compacta'*	3-9	194
Bar Harbor Juniper *Juniperus horizontalis 'Bar Harbor'*	3-9	193
Basket-of-Gold *Aurinia saxatilis*	4-8	183
Bath's Pink *Dianthus gratianopolitanus 'Bath's Pink'*	4-9	187
Blanket Flower *Gaillardia x grandiflora*	2-9	190
Blue Chip Juniper *Juniperus horizontalis 'Blue Chip'*	3-9	193
Blue Rug Juniper *Juniperus horizontalis 'Wiltonii'*	3-9	194
Blue Star Bellflower *Campanula poscharskyana*	4-9	184
Cliff Green *Paxistima canbyi*	3-7	199
Cypress Spurge *Euphorbia cyparissias*	4-8	188
Goldmoss *Sedum acre*	4-9	202
Littleleaf Periwinkle *Vinca minor*	4-8	205
Moss Phlox *Phlox subulata*	2-9	200
Partridge Berry *Mitchella repens*	4-9	196
Prostrate Chenault Coralberry *Symphoricarpos x chenaultii 'Hancock'*	4-7	203
Purple-Leaf Wintercreeper *Eunoymus fortunei 'Coloratus'*	3-9	187
Snow-in-Summer *Cerastium tomentosum*	3-7	185
Snow-on-the-Mountain *Aegopodium podagraria 'Variegatum'*	3-9	177
Spring Cinquefoil *Potentilla tabernaemontani*	4-8	200
Stonecrop *Sedum spectabile*	3-10	202

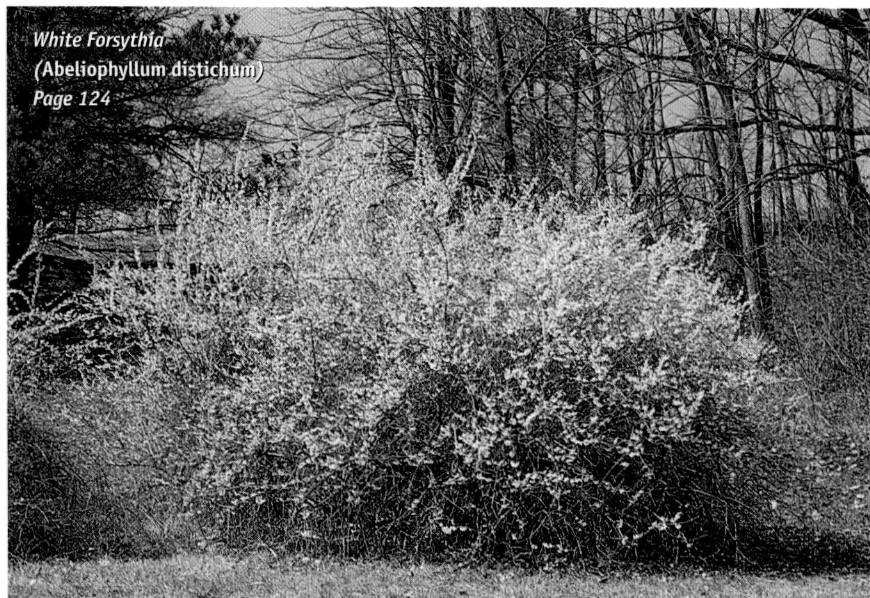
White Forsythia (Abeliophyllum distichum) Page 124

Dwarf Flowering Almond (Prunus glandulosa 'Rosea') Page 144

Plants for low-water sites

Common Name	Zones	Page
◆ Trees		
Russian Olive *Eleagnus angustifolia*	2-7	87
Skyrocket Juniper *Juniperus scopulorum 'Skyrocket'*	4-8	89
◆ Shrubs		
Fru Dagmar Hastrup Rose *Rosa 'Fru Dagmar Hastrup'*	2-9	149
Old Gold Juniper *Juniperus chinensis 'Old Gold'*	4-10	137
Parson's Juniper *Juniperus chinensis 'Parsonii'*	3-9	137
Sea Green Juniper *Juniperus chinensis 'Sea Green'*	4-8	138
Therese Bugnet Rose *Rosa 'Therese Bugnet'*	3-9	154
◆ Groundcovers		
Basket-of-Gold *Aurinia saxatilis*	4-8	183
Bath's Pink *Dianthus gratianopolitanus 'Bath's Pink'*	4-9	187
Catmint *Nepeta x faassenii*	4-8	197
Moss Phlox *Phlox subulata*	2-9	200
Snow-in-Summer *Cerastium tomentosum*	3-7	185
Spring Cinquefoil *Potentilla tabernaemontani*	4-8	200
Stonecrop *Sedum spectabile*	3-10	202
◆ Vines		
American Bittersweet *Celastrus scandens*	3-8	211
Boston Ivy *Parthenocissus tricuspidata*	4-8	213
Trumpet Vine *Campsis radicans*	4-9	210
Virginia Creeper *Parthenocissus quinquefolia*	4-9	213

Plants for urban areas

Common Name	Zones	Page
◆ **Trees**		
Allegheny Serviceberry *Amelanchier laevis*	4-8	81
American Smoketree *Cotinus obovatus*	4-8	85
Bradford Pear *Pyrus calleryana 'Bradford'*	4-8	98
Cockspur Hawthorn *Crataegus crus-galli 'Inermis'*	4-7	86
European Hornbeam *Carpinus betulus*	4-7	83
Ginkgo *Ginkgo biloba*	3-9	88
Green Ash *Fraxinus pennsylvanica*	3-9	88
Honeylocust *Gleditsia triacanthos inermis*	3-9	89
Japanese Flowering Crabapple *Malus floribunda*	3-8	91
Northern Red Oak *Quercus rubra*	4-7	101
Norway Maple *Acer platanoides*	3-7	77
Pin Oak *Quercus palustris*	4-8	101
Plumleaf Crabapple *Malus prunifolia*	4-9	91
Pyramidal Japanese Yew *Taxus cuspidata 'Capitata'*	4-7	104
Red Maple *Acer rubrum*	3-9	78
Skyrocket Juniper *Juniperus scopulorum 'Skyrocket'*	4-8	89
Washington Hawthorn *Crataegus phaenopyrum*	3-9	86
◆ **Shrubs**		
Anthony Waterer Spirea *Spiraea japonica 'Anthony Waterer'*	3-9	157
Bridalwreath Spirea *Spiraea prunifolia*	5-8	158
Common Lilac *Syringa vulgaris*	3-7	162
Cut-Leaf Staghorn Sumac *Rhus typhina 'Laciniata'*	3-8	147
Dwarf Burning Bush *Euonymus alatus 'Compacta'*	3-8	133
Old Gold Juniper *Juniperus chinensis 'Old Gold'*	4-10	137
Parson's Juniper *Juniperus chinensis 'Parsonii'*	3-9	137
Snowberry *Symphoricarpos albus*	3-7	159
◆ **Groundcovers**		
Andorra Compact Juniper *Juniperus horizontalis 'Plumosa Compacta'*	3-9	194
Bar Harbor Juniper *Juniperus horizontalis 'Bar Harbor'*	3-9	193
Blanket Flower *Gaillardia x grandiflora*	2-9	190
Blue Chip Juniper *Juniperus horizontalis 'Blue Chip'*	3-9	193
Blue Rug Juniper *Juniperus horizontalis 'Wiltonii'*	3-9	194
Catmint *Nepeta x faassenii*	4-8	197
Dwarf Japanese Garden Juniper *Juniperus procumbens 'Nana'*	4-9	195
Flower Carpet Rose *Rosa 'Flower Carpet'*	4-10	201
Goldmoss *Sedum acre*	4-9	202
Littleleaf Periwinkle *Vinca minor*	4-8	205
Moss Phlox *Phlox subulata*	2-9	200
Prostrate Chenault Coralberry *Symphoricarpos x chenaultii 'Hancock'*	4-7	203
Purple-Leaf Wintercreeper *Eunoymus fortunei 'Coloratus'*	3-9	187
Spotted Dead Nettle *Lamium maculatum*	3-9	196
Stonecrop *Sedum spectabile*	3-10	202

Availability varies by area and conditions (see page 21). Check with your garden center.

Flower Carpet Rose (Rosa 'Flower Carpet') Page 201

Plants for small spaces

Common Name	Zones	Page
◆ **Trees**		
American Hornbeam *Carpinus caroliniana*	3-9	84
Bradford Pear *Pyrus calleryana 'Bradford'*	4-8	98
Ginkgo *Ginkgo biloba*	3-9	88
Japanese Flowering Crabapple *Malus floribunda*	3-8	91
Redbud *Cercis canadensis*	3-9	85
Star Magnolia *Magnolia stellata*	4-9	90
Washington Hawthorn *Crataegus phaenopyrum*	3-9	86
◆ **Shrubs**		
Annabelle Hydrangea *Hydrangea arborescens 'Annabelle'*	3-9	134
Compact Amer. Cranberrybush *Viburnum trilobum 'Alfredo'*	2-7	167
Dwarf Alberta Spruce *Picea glauca 'Conica'*	2-8	143
Dwarf Burning Bush *Euonymus alatus 'Compacta'*	3-8	133
Green Lustre Japanese Holly *Ilex crenata 'Green Lustre'*	4-6	135
Inkberry *Ilex glabra 'Compacta'*	3-10	136
Limemound Spirea *Spiraea japonica Limemound*	4-9	158
The Fairy Rose *Rosa 'The Fairy'*	4-9	153
◆ **Groundcovers**		
Alpine Strawberry *Fragaria vesca*	3-9	189
Andorra Compact Juniper *Juniperus horizontalis 'Plumosa Compacta'*	3-9	194
Bar Harbor Juniper *Juniperus horizontalis 'Bar Harbor'*	3-9	193
Bath's Pink *Dianthus gratianopolitanus 'Bath's Pink'*	4-9	187
Blanket Flower *Gaillardia x grandiflora*	2-9	190
Bloody Cranesbill *Geranium sanguineum*	3-8	191
Blue Chip Juniper *Juniperus horizontalis 'Blue Chip'*	3-9	193
Blue Rug Juniper *Juniperus horizontalis 'Wiltonii'*	3-9	194
Catmint *Nepeta x faassenii*	4-8	197
Coral Bells *Heuchera sanguinea*	3-8	191
Dwarf Japanese Garden Juniper *Juniperus procumbens 'Nana'*	4-9	195
Germander *Teucrium prostratum*	4-9	204
Goldmoss *Sedum acre*	4-9	202
Hosta *Hosta species*	3-8	192
Lamb's Ear *Stachys byzantina*	4-8	203
Maidenhair Fern *Adiantum pedatum*	3-8	177
Moss Phlox *Phlox subulata*	2-9	200
◆ **Vines**		
Climbing Hydrangea *Hydrangea petiolaris*	4-7	211

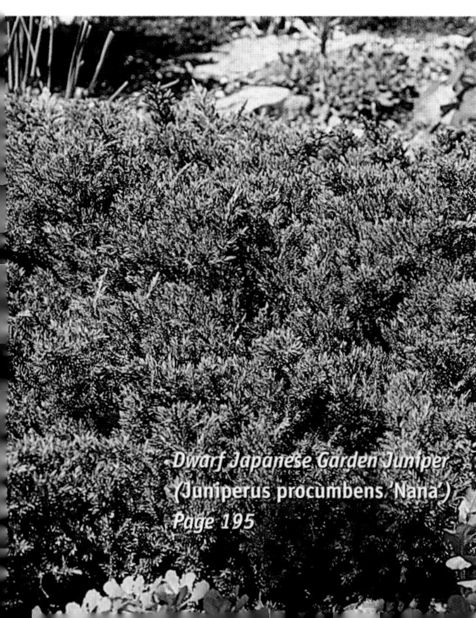

Dwarf Japanese Garden Juniper (Juniperus procumbens 'Nana') Page 195

Creating an effective windbreak means more than planting a single row of trees. Combine layers of trees and shrubs for functional and beautiful windbreaks.

Plants for Windbreaks

Strategically positioning plants to deflect harsh winds can make your home and yard more pleasant. The first step in planting a windbreak is to figure out where you need one. Winds come from different directions in different seasons. Cold winter winds frequently blow from the northwest, but the direction is often affected by local terrain. It's best to make your plans based upon personal observation. You can also filter summer winds that are too gusty. Make sure you're not taking notes about prevailing wind direction during warm weather if winter or autumn winds are your main concern.

Get a Sense of Direction Once you know the direction undesirable wind is coming from, you can figure out what area you want to shelter. The side of the windbreak opposite the direction wind is coming from is called the leeward side. A 20-foot-wide area on the leeward side next to the windbreak is the most sheltered spot. This means you should plant trees and shrubs within 20 feet of sitting areas, such as decks and patios, if winds presently make these spots less than comfortable. Adding a windbreak can extend the season of use for a favorite outdoor spot and make it cozy a little longer. Strategically positioned trees and shrubs can also shield walkways from wind. Think about the routes you walk to retrieve your newspaper, bring in firewood, or get into your car. If icy winds make even short trips miserable in winter, planting a windbreak can make a big difference.

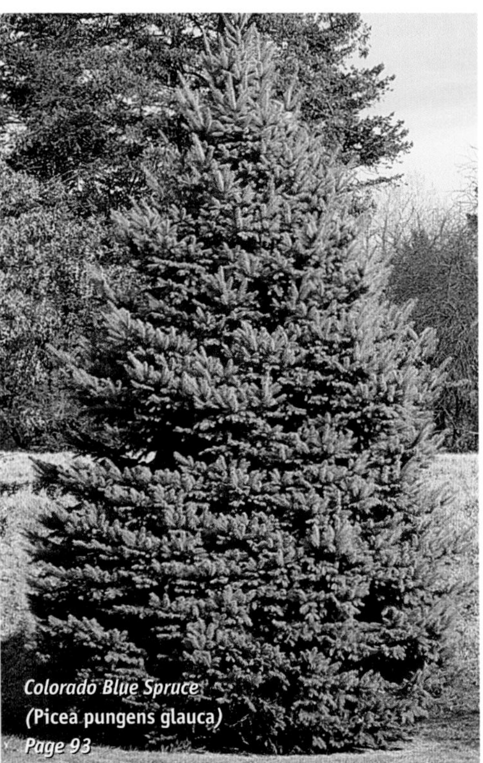
Colorado Blue Spruce (Picea pungens glauca)
Page 93

Plants that deflect wind can keep your house snug, too. Blasting winter winds make interior rooms colder and drive heating costs up. Position windbreaks to shelter windows that face into the paths of harsh winds. You don't have to plant a dense screen close to your house; you can position the windbreak in the background. Though the first 20 feet of the leeward side will be the most sheltered, areas farther away will be affected, too. Wind speeds can be reduced for areas within 200 feet of a windbreak that's 20 feet tall.

Find an Informal Look

You'll have the most success with a planted windbreak if you give it an informal look. That's because letting plants grow to different heights—instead of flat-topping them to create a formal hedge—will have an impact on wind speed. A group of plants with staggered tops is less aerodynamic than an even-topped hedge or fence. The uneven heights create drag, slowing wind. If the rest of your yard is clipped formally, you can still have a windbreak by using it

Windbreaks affect the way snow accumulates.

Though the area that's closest to the leeward side of a windbreak is the most sheltered from wind, this area also receives the most snow buildup because of altered wind patterns. If drifts are a problem in your area, make sure your house and driveway are not within the first 25 percent of the sheltered area that's downwind of the windbreak; drifts will pile up there. To calculate the sheltered area, see Design Tip, below.

Trees for windbreaks

Common Name	Zones	Page
American Arborvitae *Thuja occidentalis*	2-7	105
Colorado Blue Spruce *Picea pungens glauca*	2-7	93
Eastern Red Cedar *Juniperus virginiana*	3-9	90
Jack Pine *Pinus banksiana*	2-6	94
Lacebark Pine *Pinus bungeana*	4-7	94
Norway Maple *Acer platanoides*	3-7	77
Norway Spruce *Picea abies*	2-7	92
Scots Pine *Pinus sylvestris*	3-7	95
Skyrocket Juniper *Juniperus scopulorum 'Skyrocket'*	4-8	89
White Fir *Abies concolor*	3-7	74
White Pine *Pinus strobus*	3-8	95
White Spruce *Picea glauca*	2-6	92

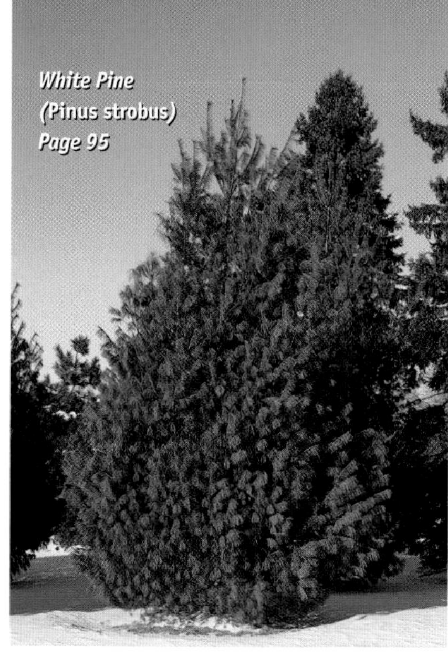
White Pine (*Pinus strobus*) Page 95

as a background to set off your formal garden areas. Setting plants in a zigzag pattern creates a more effective windbreak than planting trees and shrubs in straight rows. Layers of plants do a better job than groupings that are only one plant wide.

Form a Solid Mass

Windbreaks work by deflecting winds up and over, not by stopping them. So it's important to arrange plantings so that they form a solid mass from top to bottom. Any openings below the top of the highest plant are invitations for winds to squeeze through. Such winds will blow faster as the airstream is funneled through to the leeward side of your windbreak. To prevent this, plant two or three kinds of shrubs so the forms and sizes of plants will vary and fill in gaps. Select trees that grow branches all the way to the ground and don't trim lower branches. Trees that have exposed trunks and high branches can leave gaps in your windbreak that allow air to rush through. Evergreen plants that don't lose their leaves all at once usually make the best windbreaks because they have foliage during all the seasons, even winter.

Sea Green Juniper (*Juniperus chinensis* 'Sea Green') Page 138

Shrubs for windbreaks

Common Name	Zones	Page
Arnold's Red Tatarian Honeysuckle *Lonicera tatarica 'Arnold's Red'*	3-9	140
Common Lilac *Syringa vulgaris*	3-7	162
Emerald Arborvitae *Thuja occidentalis 'Emerald'*	2-7	163
Green Mound Alpine Currant *Ribes alpinum 'Green Mound'*	2-7	147
Hick's Upright Yew *Taxus x media 'Hicksii'*	4-7	163
Inkberry *Ilex glabra 'Compacta'*	3-10	136
Little Giant Arborvitae *Thuja occidentalis 'Little Giant'*	2-7	164
Mugo Pine *Pinus mugo*	2-7	143
Northern Bayberry *Myrica pensylvanica*	2-6	141
Sea Green Juniper *Juniperus chinensis 'Sea Green'*	4-8	138
Tam Juniper *Juniperus sabina 'Tamariscifolia'*	3-7	138

Availability varies by area and conditions (see page 21). Check with your garden center.

Design Tip

How to calculate the area that will be protected by a windbreak.

Multiply the mature height of the trees you are planting by 10. The resulting number indicates how many feet on the leeward side of the windbreak will be sheltered when the trees reach their mature heights. The taller the trees, the more area you will shelter. Remember to combine trees with shrubs to keep wind from forcing through the windbreak below treetops. The denser your windbreak is, the more effective it will be.

Chapter 3
how-to

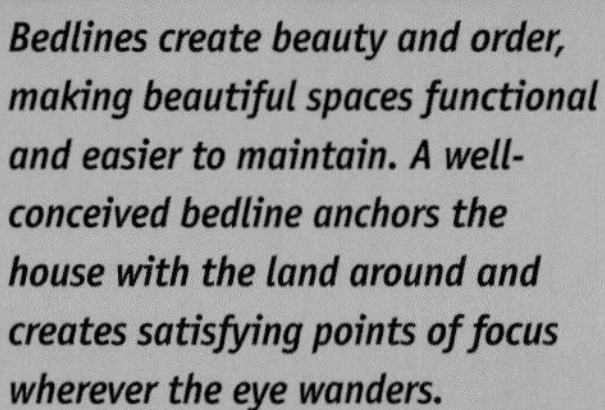

Bedlines create beauty and order, making beautiful spaces functional and easier to maintain. A well-conceived bedline anchors the house with the land around and creates satisfying points of focus wherever the eye wanders.

Getting the Job Done

Here's where you'll learn to plant and care for your new landscape. We'll show you step-by-step how to get your carefully selected plants into the ground and keep them happy for years to come.

1) Begin with a Bedline

You can usually tell if a landscape was designed before planting or if trees and shrubs were put in without a great deal of thought. The first clue is the bedline. The bedline separates planting areas from lawns. How you draw the line determines the shape of the planting bed on one side and the shape of the lawn area on the other side of it.

Smooth, curving bedlines complement most homes. Such bedlines wrap around corners of houses, decks, patios, walkways, parking areas, and swimming pools. Curving bedlines nestle man-made structures within the landscape.

2) Keep It Simple

It's important to keep bedlines simple. Complicated lines with little curves will make the bedline appear unnatural and the lawn more difficult to mow. Part of your goal is functionality. You should be able to easily mow a perimeter strip around the edge of the bedline before cutting the entire lawn. Plants in a bed that grow to fill in a single, smooth curve will make your landscape attractive, neat, and easy to maintain.

3) Get It on Paper

Lay a piece of tracing paper over your site analysis and sketch bedline schemes. The sketch will show how planting areas in your yard connect. Leave some areas open for access to doorways and utility areas. Leave access to walk around your house. Build easy routes or pathways into your design to set out trash cans, move the mower from one lawn area to another, and receive deliveries.

Once you've designed a bedline that's both artistic and functional, you're ready to get to work.

Marking a Bedline

Stuff You'll Need

- ✔ Garden hose that you don't mind getting paint on
- ✔ Sharpshooter or trenching shovel
- ✔ Marking paint (not regular spray paint)
- ✔ Inexpensive gloves
- ✔ Old shoes

What to Expect

You'll probably try several patterns with the hose before you're satisfied with the bedline. Don't rush the process. You'll live with your choice for a long time.

Design Tip

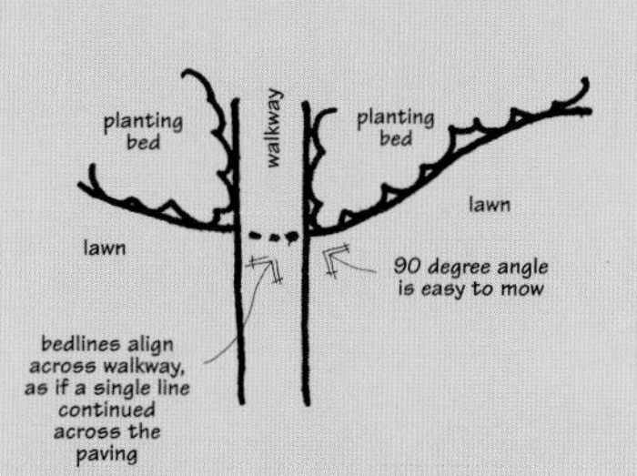

▲ ***Right*** Aligning bedlines on either side of a walkway makes the entrance lead into the landscape instead of interrupting it. Always make sure bedlines meet paving or structures at 90 degrees so that lawn areas are wide enough to mow easily.

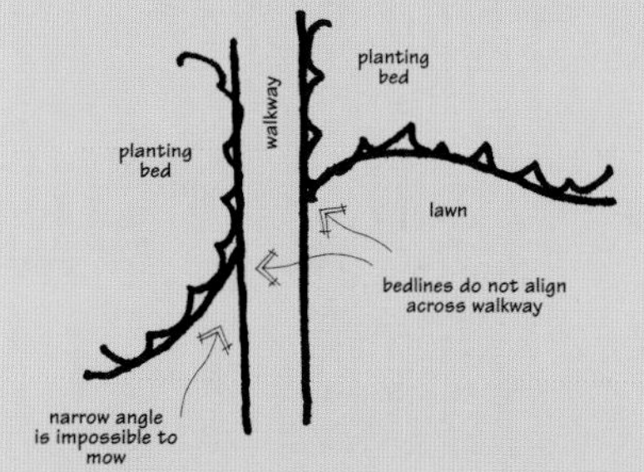

▲ ***Wrong*** Bedlines that don't align across a walkway make the paving look like an afterthought. Bedlines that meet paving or structures at narrow angles create slivers of lawn that are difficult to mow, inviting weed growth.

1 Use a garden hose to create an outline. Spread a garden hose in the sun on a driveway or patio for about 15 minutes to make it flexible. Lay the garden hose on the ground in the shape of your proposed bedline. The area inside the hose will become the planting bed; the area outside the hose will remain unchanged.

2 Adjust the hose as needed. Reposition the hose until you like the outline. Smooth the hose to eliminate any dips that give the bedline an unnatural shape. The object is to create a gently flowing curve. If that curve connects to another bedline, flow them smoothly together.

Push your mower alongside the hose to see if you can cut the grass easily. This will help you make the final decision about the shape of your bedline.

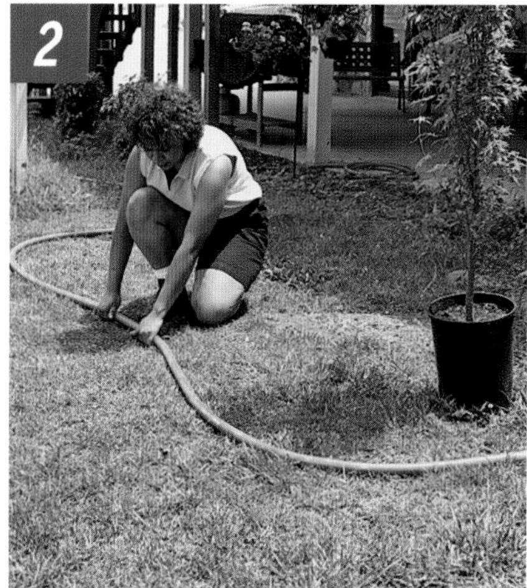

3 Spray the grass or ground with marking paint. Don't use regular spray paint and don't spray paving, stones, or plants you want to keep. Remove the hose and examine the shape of the bedline. Make sure you're happy with it before you begin digging. You can substitute flour for marking paint. If you do, make sure you finish the job in a day. Flour will wash away if it rains.

Don't spray a thick line until you're sure. You might change your mind. Try spraying small dashes and then standing back to look. Scuff out and correct areas you don't like, then connect the dashes into a digging line.

Making a Bed

Once you lay out your bedline, it's time to prepare the area inside it for planting. Chances are, the spot you want to convert to a lovely landscape is now full of grass. Here's how to remove it to create a fresh planting area.

Stuff You'll Need

- ✔ Tiller
- ✔ Sharpshooter
- ✔ Work boots

What to Expect

Running a tiller is a lot like running a floor sander—it can get away from you. Practice some cuts before you carve out the tighter portions of the bedline.

1 Turn live grass under by tilling it into the soil. You can turn live grass under by tilling it into the soil. The grass will decay and add extra nutrients to your planting bed. Make several passes with a tiller so grass is torn to bits and turned under the surface of the soil. To improve the soil you should now add amendments such as organic matter or gypsum for clay soils.

Plan ahead so you can till planting beds in the fall before planting in spring. Winter precipitation fills the exposed gaps in tilled soil. Water will freeze, expand, and thaw, creating a heaving action that helps break up soil.

BUYER'$ GUIDE

If you don't have a tiller and don't think you'll use it often enough to buy one, look into renting one instead. Many stores offer lawn equipment available for rental. If the rental company doesn't deliver, you'll need a truck to get the tiller home.

2 Delineate your bedline with a neat shovel cut. Use a narrow-bladed shovel to cut a nearly vertical edge along the grass side of your planting bed. This line separates the new planting bed from the existing lawn that will remain. Scrape soil away so that the opposite side of the trench rolls upward into the bed area. Make your V-cut about 6 inches deep so it will hold a thick layer of mulch. If you're planning to install edging, do so now. (See "Edging Choices" on page 49.)

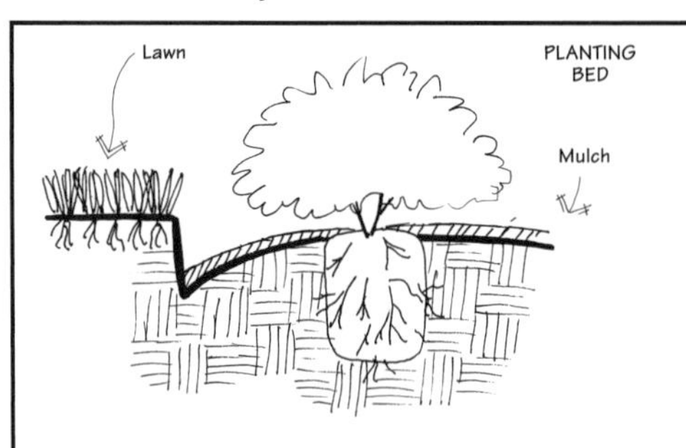

TOOL TIP

A sharpshooter is another name for trenching shovel. It features a long, narrow blade that's straight and sharp. This light shovel is easy to use and good for digging straight down.

A sod lifter has a blade attached at an angle from the handle. It's easy to slide the flat, sharp end beneath grass roots. Use a sod lifter if you need to remove grass completely from a bed instead of tilling it under.

Edging Choices

You can keep bedlines neat by cutting the edges with a sharp shovel every few months. Or, install edging to form a barrier.

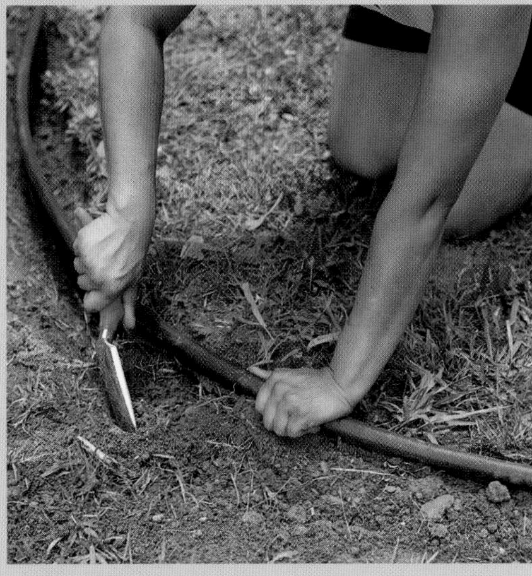

The purposes of edging are to delineate the bedline, to make it more difficult for grass to grow into the bed or for groundcovers to spread into the lawn, and to provide a solid edge for mowing or trimming against. Brick, stone, or steel can do the job. Plastic edging is another choice. Install it carefully so the edging is inserted into the ground all the way to the rounded plastic lip. Pack soil firmly on both sides of the edging to keep it from popping out.

Edging creates neatly shaped bedlines to resist encroaching grass and weeds.

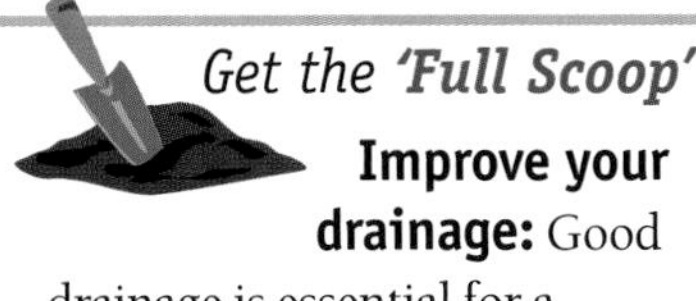

Get the 'Full Scoop'

Improve your drainage: Good drainage is essential for a thriving bed. **—See page 53**

'Organic Grass Removal'

If you want to replant a large amount of grass you're removing from a new planting bed elsewhere in your yard, rent a sod cutter. This machine uses sharp, scissors-action blades to cut sod so you can lift sections of grass. Have the associate at the rental house teach you how to use the cutter before you go to work. For smaller jobs, a manual sod cutter can do the job. Keep cut sod moist. Replant as soon as possible and water thoroughly. When laying sod, stagger cut pieces so the seams don't line up but instead resemble brick paving. This will make seams disappear more quickly as the grass grows in.

A well-prepared planting bed adds more than beauty and order to your landscape. The proper balance of nutrients and good drainage helps new plants succeed.

Bed Preparation

Think of the soil in your yard as an aquarium and the plants you're adding as fish. They both have requirements for survival. Fish need the right kind of water, and plants need the right kind of soil. Prepare your bed correctly and you'll give your landscape the right start.

The more you prep the soil prior to planting, the more hospitable it becomes for plants. Tilling, digging, and turning the ground loosens soil and makes it easier for water to percolate. Loose soil allows air to reach roots and makes it easier for them to spread.

Ideally, you should till your entire planting bed area before setting out the first plant. Prepping the entire bed is especially important when planting groundcover. Usually, these plants are set out at a smaller size than shrubs and are planted closer together. Tilling the whole bed is more efficient than digging lots of little holes and makes arranging the plants more efficient. Save the shovel for planting individual trees, shrubs, and vines. Though working the entire bed is preferable, you can improve the soil you use to fill planting holes—known as backfill—to give new trees and shrubs a good start. Whether you till or dig, mix in amendments prior to planting. Organic matter—such as well-composted manure, composted plant debris, or leaf mold—is an excellent amendment for any soil type. When mixed into sandy or rocky soil, organic matter slows the flow of water, giving roots a chance to absorb moisture. Organic matter mixed into heavy clay soil does the opposite. It creates air spaces between the densely packed soil particles, improving drainage. Organic matter also supplies nutrients to roots.

Tilling the entire planting bed guarantees a consistent mixture of amendments in the soil. Tillers are available at most rental outlets. Get a lesson and safety tips from a qualified salesperson.

Mix soil amendments with native soil at a ratio of 1:1. This helps plants adapt to native soil as roots spread. When you dig holes, pile the

TOOL TIP

Prevention helps keep weeds down, but you'll still need to do some digging. The classic garden hoe is a great weeder, but here are some tools to make the job easier:

- **Warren hoe—**This hoe has a pointed blade for hooking into roots and pulling them out.
- **Hula hoe—**Use this hooped hoe to grub away weeds.
- **Hoe-Matic—**This hand tool has a rake on one end and an ax head on the other.
- **Hoe mattock—**This hand tool has a claw on one end and an ax head on the other.

soil on a tarp or in a wheelbarrow. Mix in amendments, chopping and sifting lumps with your shovel before backfilling the hole around the roots of new plants. If the soil in the hole contains no native soil, roots are discouraged from spreading beyond the backfill. In areas with high rainfall and heavy clay soil, mix native soil with organic matter at a ratio of 4:1.

Keeping Weeds Down

Weeds will like your freshly prepared bed as much as your new plants do. Here's how to keep weeds down while your landscape gets started.

- **Apply pre-emergent herbicide.** Use on bare soil before you set out container-grown or balled-and-burlapped plants. (Follow product label instructions, and don't use this kind of herbicide if you plan to sow your new bed with seeds.) Pre-emergents prevent seeds from germinating and will stop weed growth during the first growing season. Reapply each spring as needed by scratching into the soil around plants. Pre-emergents won't hurt plants that are already growing.
- **Mulch, mulch, mulch.** The thicker the layer, the harder it is for weeds to penetrate and grow. Organic mulches, such as shredded wood, bark, or compost, are ideal because they also break down to supply nutrients to plants. Replenish mulch annually to keep layers about 3 inches thick. Tuck mulch carefully around stems of plants you want to keep; never pile mulch at the base of plants. Rock mulches also cover the ground, retarding weed growth. No matter what you do, tough weeds will eventually push their way upward. Plastic weed mats discourage weeds but trap heat beneath them, raising soil temperatures higher than many plant roots prefer.
- **The best defense against plants you don't want is plenty of plants that you do want.** Bare soil is an invitation to weed growth. Crowd weeds out with groundcovers and shrubs. Though it's necessary to leave some soil surface bare to allow new plants room to grow, fill in bare spots with groundcover as quickly as possible.

Wisdom of the Aisles

Dealing with heavy clay:

- Gypsum is a valuable soil amendment for improving the structure of clay soils. (It also adds calcium; don't introduce it to soil with high calcium content.) Instead of adding gypsum to backfill, mix it into native soil first, tilling or digging it in deeply to separate sticky soil particles. This works little pockets of air into the soil, allowing water to flow through more freely instead of trapping it around roots and causing plants to drown. A couple of pounds of gypsum will amend about 100 square feet of bed area.
- When planting trees and shrubs in hard clay soil, use your shovel to scrape and roughen the sides of the hole. Slick-sided holes function much like clay pots, keeping the roots confined to the hole and trapping water.
- Some plants—such as azaleas—are particularly sensitive to standing water collecting around their roots. When landscaping in clay soil, plant such shrubs high so root balls protrude an inch or two above the surface of the ground, ensuring that water will drain away from the roots.
- Gypsum does not affect soil pH.

Raised Beds

Building the soil up is an alternative to digging down. Raised beds offer the advantage of filling the entire planting area with good soil. Raised beds are good choices for spots with compacted or clay soils that don't drain well and for areas where the soil is full of tree roots. Make sure raised beds are open to the soil beneath. Sealing them with paving traps water.

Sweet and Sour Soils

Alkaline soil (sweet) and acidic soil (sour) occupy different ends of the pH scale and present different growing issues.

The easiest way to deal with sweet or sour soils is to grow plants that love them. You can also balance the pH to suit your needs. A pH reading of 7 (the pH of water) is considered neutral. Alkaline soils have pH numbers greater than 7. Acidic soils have pH numbers lower than 7. Average garden soil has a pH between 5 and 7. The ideal level for the largest range of plants is a pH reading between 6 and 7.

Peat moss is extremely acidic. Add it to reduce the pH of alkaline soil.

Add **ground dolomitic limestone** to raise the pH of acidic soils. See pages 40-41 for plants that prefer alkaline or acidic soil.

A watering wand attached on a hose produces a spray similar to rainfall and gets in hard-to-reach places.

Keeping Plants Happy

**aking sure plants get the proper amount of water is critical.** Rainfall is the best source of water for plants, but it isn't always plentiful. Here's the scoop on watering.

Deep Watering

Deep Watering makes plants tougher. You can't actually drought-proof your plants, but you can prepare them for dry spells to give your landscape a fighting chance. To deep water, apply water slowly for long periods of time at infrequent intervals. Roots learn to follow water that seeps down into soil, making them less prone to suffering during dry spells. If you water often and quickly, you'll only dampen the top layer of soil. As a result, roots tend to stay within this area instead of digging deeper to seek moisture. Roots near the surface are more likely to wither during dry periods than roots that grow downward.

An automatic sprinkler system makes watering easy. Valves control water flow through pipes buried underground to sprinkler heads placed at ground level. Sprinklers are turned on and off by timers. Install automatic watering systems before you plant; trenching to lay pipes can damage existing plants.

Drip irrigation systems deliver water directly to the roots instead of through the air. Watering roots conserves water and prevents many fungal problems caused by wet foliage. Most drip systems are installed by burying flexible tubing beneath mulch. They can also be controlled by timers.

Hand watering works if you're diligent and patient. Many people enjoy the time spent watering their yards—it's therapeutic. The key to hand watering is consistency. If you get off schedule, your plants suffer, especially if you go away for an extended period of time. Trees and large shrubs need water, too. A good soaking beneath the entire dripline is best, not just a quick spray while you're watering the flowers.

Winter watering will help your plants survive. Winter weather is stressful on trees and shrubs planted in late fall and for spring flowering plants. Both should be deep watered during dry winter months.

Troubleshooting

Troubleshooting is always a part of landscaping. Here are some common conditions and solutions to watering problems:

- **Too Much or Too Little** Those plants that prefer poor, dry soil will struggle with too much water. Plants requiring rich, moist soil will not thrive in dry locations.

Solution: Research plant needs thoroughly before you install.

- **Underwatering** Broad-leaved plants wilt in order to expose less leaf surface. Foliage becomes crispy around the edges as though burned. Evergreens maintain their form, but foliage becomes dry and discolored.

Solution: Check in-ground plants weekly and container plants daily for water needs. Poke a finger or dig a small hole a few inches below the soil surface near the plant. If the soil feels dry, the plant needs water. Apply a slow, gentle stream of water to the base, allowing the water to soak down to the roots.

- **Overwatering** Too much water produces the same symptoms as underwatering. Check the soil as above. If the soil is moist but still crumbly, lack of water is probably not the problem.

Solution: If the soil has any of the four "s" symptoms—soupy, sticky, soggy, or smelly—cut back on your watering schedule. Let the soil dry out between waterings.

When you water is as important as how you water. The earlier in the day the better. (That's when timers come in handy.) If you wait until plants are struggling, watering becomes a form of first-aid instead of a regular part of their care. Watering in the late afternoon or evening means your plants will have suffered during the longest hours of the day. Foliage might not have a chance to dry before nightfall, making conditions ripe for fungal problems. Soil and mulch that stay damp overnight invite soft-bodied pests, such as slugs and snails.

Timers can attach directly to the hose and be programmed to provide regular watering cycles.

Drainage Solutions

Too much water can harm plants by filling air pockets in the soil and drowning roots or by washing plants away. Here are some methods for making soggy soil drier, keeping storm water from blasting plants from their beds, and preventing puddles from forming. Keep in mind that it usually isn't legal to increase the amount of water that drains across property lines, so don't dump your excess water on your neighbor's property.

French Drains

French drains disperse water that becomes trapped in soil. They're used where pounding rain spills from roof edges, confined planting beds meet paving, or retaining walls cause ground water to accumulate. To install:

- **Dig a trench that's 8 to 12 inches wide and deep.** Slope the trench downhill about one-eighth inch per foot. Extend as far from the problem area as possible.
- **Fill the trench with a layer of coarse gravel an inch or two thick.** Rinse the gravel first to keep debris from clogging pipes later. Maintain the downward slope of the trench when adding gravel.
- **Place a 3- to 4-inch-wide perforated plastic pipe on top of the gravel bed.**
- **Wrap the pipe in a filter sleeve.** This will prevent holes from clogging. You can also buy perforated plastic pipe that's already wrapped in a filter sleeve. If the pipe has holes on just one side, lay this side face down.
- **Fill the rest of the trench with washed gravel, surrounding the pipe completely.** The top of the gravel in the trench should be level with the adjacent soil.

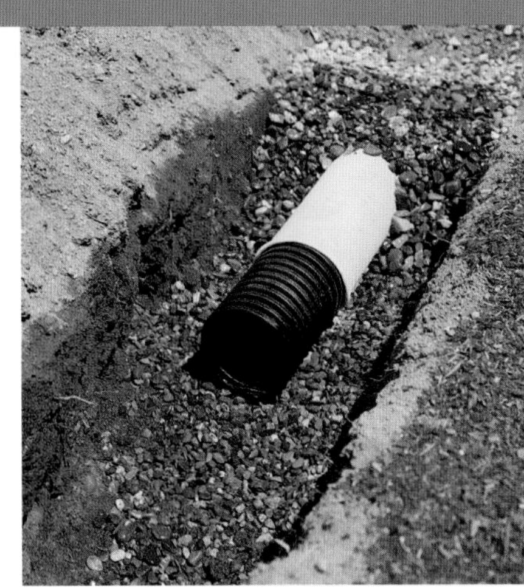

Downspouts

Downspouts are often the culprits when plants, topsoil, and mulch are washed away by a blast of water.

Solve the problem by connecting a flexible pipe to the end of the downspout. Bury the pipe in a trench. If you can, run the pipe to a lower spot in the yard where water can flow from the far end. Wedge a flat stone beneath the end of a drain pipe where it empties onto the ground. This helps prevent erosion. If it isn't possible to "daylight" the pipe—letting the low end open onto the soil's surface—build a long French drain to disperse the water, instead (see above).

Catch Basins

Catch basins collect excess surface water so it can be moved elsewhere through underground pipes.

Set a catch basin at a low point where water puddles. Dig a hole just big enough to house the catch basin. This drainage device is topped with a grate to admit water. (Hint: Domed grates help prevent mulch from washing into catch basins.) You'll need to dig a trench leading from your catch basin to an area where you want to release the water, such as a natural area or storm drainage system. Lay plastic drain pipe in the trench and connect it to the catch basin.

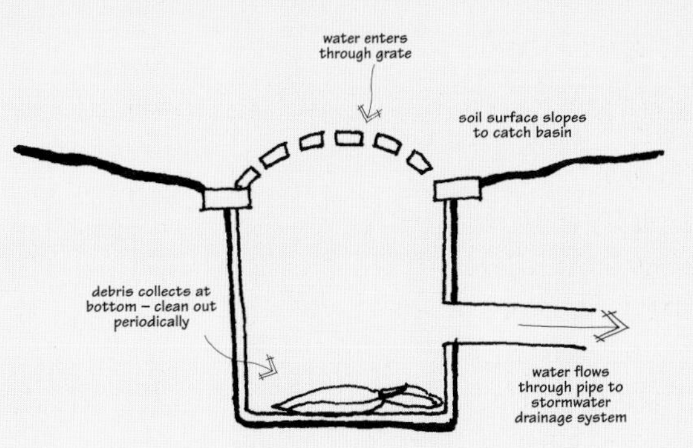
water enters through grate
soil surface slopes to catch basin
debris collects at bottom – clean out periodically
water flows through pipe to stormwater drainage system

Plants have varying nutritional needs. Choosing the right fertilizer and applying the right amount at the right time will keep your landscape a showplace.

Wisdom of the Aisles

Most trees and shrubs require no fertilizer at all during their first year in your landscape. That's because they've been heavily fertilized during nursery production to make them look their best on the shelves. If you add fertilizer at planting and then apply more fertilizer later in the growing season, you've probably given your new plants a double-dose of chemicals they don't need. Wait until the second year of growth before giving supplemental nutrients to most plants.

Fertilizing

Fertilizing provides plants a good, balanced diet. Adding plenty of organic amendments at planting gives plants a healthy start. Properly applied fertilizers keeps them flourishing.

The Key is N-P-K Fertilizers are combinations of major elements nitrogen (N), phosphorus (P), and potassium (K) along with other minor elements such as calcium (Ca), magnesium (Mn), and iron (Fe). N, P, and K are listed on the label in order. Bags labeled as complete fertilizers contain various percentages of N, P, and K and might contain minor elements as well. Balanced fertilizers contain equal amounts of N, P, and K. A label that reads 6-6-6 means there is 6 percent of each element; the remainder is inert matter. The larger the numbers, the higher the proportion of fertilizer. Use fertilizers with lower matching numbers in hot, dry weather to avoid chemical burns on plants. Higher matching numbers are good for cool, wet conditions when plants absorb elements easily. Different numbers indicate that the product contains N, P, and K in unequal amounts. Select fertilizers with higher percentages of specific elements to solve problems and match growing requirements. (See "It's Elemental—Know Your N-P-K," right.) A fertilizer labeled 8-12-4 contains 8 percent nitrogen, 12 percent phosphorus, and 4 percent potassium. Always read labels on fertilizers before applying. If you're confused, look for plant lists on the label or a general description that fits the plant you want to feed.

Liquid or slow-release fertilizers are the best choice for tightly clustered plants to avoid burning foliage.

Synthetic Fertilizers are man-made. They are dry—in granular, powder, or pellet form—or liquid. All come with instructions for proper use. Keep dry fertilizer away from foliage and avoid mounding it at the base of plants. Instead, scratch it into the soil around plants and water well. Slow-release fertilizers have coated pellets that disintegrate, releasing fertilizer over a longer period of time and are unlikely to

Root Stimulator

You can give new plants a boost with a dose of root stimulator at planting. Root stimulators prompt growth of feeder roots, helping new plants become at home in their new environments. Follow package directions; apply to holes just prior to setting plants in them. Soak bare-root roses in liquid root stimulator before planting.

burn plants. Mix them into the soil at planting or around established plants. Apply liquid fertilizers directly to plant leaves or spray onto moistened soil. Liquid fertilizers allow quick plant uptake.

Natural Fertilizers also come in dry or liquid forms. Many provide only one nutrient and are not complete fertilizers. For example, bloodmeal supplies nitrogen that will quickly green up failing plants. Bonemeal provides phosphorus for root growth and flower formation. You might need to use more than one product to provide complete fertilization. Fish emulsion is a liquid fertilizer that can be applied to damp soil or directly to leaves. Benefits of natural fertilizers are listed on each product label. Natural fertilizers are more difficult to balance than synthetics. Natural products can also be used to amend the soil pH. Cottonseed meal makes soil more acidic, while limestone makes it more alkaline. Natural fertilizers work best on warm days.

Troubleshooting

- **Overfertilizing** Plants that are overfertilized compensate by shutting down and slowing growth. Foliage turns yellow or brown but remains on branches. Plants take on a burned appearance. Flowering plants produce more leaves than blossoms.

  Solution: Check the soil; you could have a watering problem. If the soil moisture is normal and you've been fertilizing frequently, stop immediately. Supply the plant with plenty of water to leach excess chemicals from the soil.

- **Underfertilizing** Foliage becomes discolored, turning a more yellowish hue. Growth becomes distorted or stunted.

  Solution: Give the soil a finger-test first to find if it is too wet or too dry before fertilizing. Find a fertilizer that describes or lists your plant on the label. Follow directions carefully.

When a few of my shrubs began to wilt and discolor, I headed out into the yard to give them a good dose of fertilizer. Fortunately, my neighbor saw what I was up to and pointed out that the soil in the area was soggy. He went on to say that fertilizing overwatered shrubs is like shoving a cheeseburger in the mouth of a drowning man! I put the fertilizer back in my shed, temporarily raked the mulch away to speed up drying, and cut back on watering. These days my shrubs are in great shape.

how-to 3

It's Elemental–Know Your N-P-K

Understanding package labels is necessary for using fertilizers correctly.

You'll see the letters N-P-K on lots of fertilizer labels. Here's what they mean:

N is for nitrogen. This element promotes green growth and lush foliage. But if you use too much of it, you could end up with more leaves than flowers. That's why a balanced fertilizer is a good idea.

P is for phosphorus. Your plants need phosphorus for good root growth and strong production of flowers and fruit.

K is for potassium. This element is vital for the general well-being of plants. Potassium helps neutralize ground salts that can make soil less than hospitable for growth.

You can feed at different speeds. The kind of granular fertilizer you choose affects the rate at which plants will absorb nutrients.

Slow-release. Fertilizers that are coated break down slowly so plants don't get all the good stuff at one time. This is valuable because plants have access to a longer-lasting supply of nutrients. Because slow-release fertilizers are coated, there's no need to worry about burning plants when fertilizer is freshly applied.

Fast-release. These fertilizers are good for a quick fix. But they don't last long and must be "watered in" when applied to avoid burning plants. Keep away from foliage.

Planting Bare-Root Roses

Whether you're planting bare-root roses or plants grown in containers, learn how to get new roses off to the best start.

Bare-root roses are shipped without soil, making them less expensive. They look like stubby sticks. You'll find these plants for sale in late winter or early spring. Plant them soon after purchasing.

STUFF YOU'LL NEED

- ✔ Bucket
- ✔ Root stimulator
- ✔ Hand pruners
- ✔ Organic matter such as bagged compost
- ✔ Round-point shovel

What to Expect

Your newly planted bare-root rose will look like a stick poking up out of the ground until new shoots and leaves appear in a few weeks.

1 **Carefully open the packaging.** Avoid cutting roots. Gently remove packing material from roots and discard. Place the roots in a bucket of water mixed with root stimulator. Allow them to soak in a dark, cool, dry location such as a garage. Soak roots no longer than eight hours.

2 **Dig a hole in a spot that receives at least six hours of sun daily.** The hole should be 12 to 18 inches deep. Mix bagged compost with some of the native soil in a wheelbarrow or on a tarp to create a mixture that's about two-thirds organic matter and one-third native soil. The soil mixture should appear dark and rich.

3 **Shovel the good soil mixture into the hole until it's nearly full.** Use your hands to form a cone of soil in the center of the hole. Make the top of the cone slightly below the level of adjacent undisturbed soil. Position the rose on top of the cone, spreading roots evenly around it.

BUYER'$ GUIDE

Pick up several bare-root roses before you buy one. If one feels heavier than the others or has water dripping from its packaging, it's not the one you want to take home to plant in your yard. Roots that are bare should stay moist but not wet during shipping.

4 **Backfill around the rose with soil.** Make sure the scion (the ridge where the rose was grafted to the rootstock) is still visible above the soil. Add a thick layer of compost for mulch. Use excess native soil to form a moat around the freshly planted rose. Fill moat with a slowly trickling hose.

Good idea!

Before planting, use a pair of good-quality hand pruners to trim away any roots that have jagged ends. This replaces rough edges with a good clean cut. Without overdoing it, remove any excessively long, dead, or broken roots.

Grafted and Nongrafted Roses

Keep the scion of grafted roses above ground. The scion is the ridge where the preferred variety is grafted onto sturdier rootstock. If buried, shoots might grow from the rootstock instead of the rose you want. When planting, keep the scion above the soil line. If a freeze is predicted, temporarily cover the scion with mulch.

Bury the crowns of nongrafted roses. The crown of the plant is the point where branches emerge from the main stem just above the roots. Make sure it's low enough to be covered with an inch or two of soil at planting.

Planting Containerized Roses

Roses grown in containers cost more than bare-root plants, but you get leaves and often buds right away.

1 **Dig a hole to the proper depth.** Check the depth by setting the rose, still in its container, into the hole. The soil in the container should be level with undisturbed soil around the hole. If the hole is too deep, remove the rose and add some soil to the bottom of the hole. If it's too shallow, you'll need to dig a little more.

2 **Gently slide the rose from its container and place it in the hole.** Remember, it's better to destroy the pot than the plant; cut the container with a utility knife if necessary. Don't pull on the plant and don't disturb the root ball.

3 **Fill the hole to the proper depth.** Mix bagged compost with native soil to create a mixture that's about two-thirds organic matter and one-third native soil and fill around the plant. Do not add any soil to the top of root ball. Use excess soil to form a moat around the plant as wide as the depth of the hole. Mulch this area with compost before filling it slowly with a small, gentle stream from a hose. Mist newly planted roses frequently during the first week or so if the weather is hot and wilting occurs. Keep the soil around roots moist but not soggy while the plant adjusts to its new home.

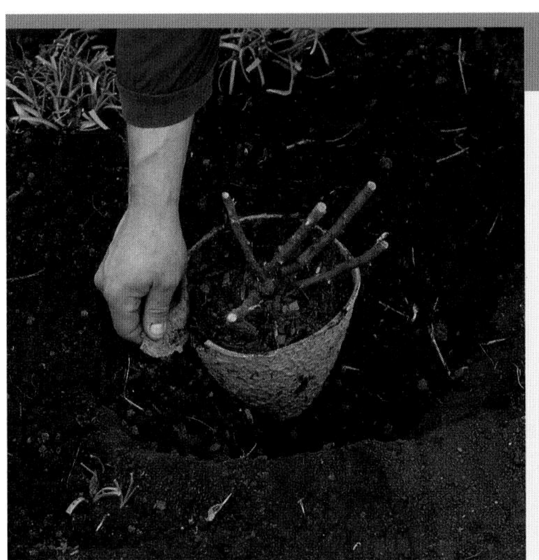

Planting Peat-Pot Roses

Roses sold in biodegradable containers such as peat pots can be planted in their containers. This method keeps the root ball firmly intact and prevents damage to it. When set in the planting hole, the base of the plant should be level with adjacent undisturbed soil. It is critical that you bury the entire peat pot with soil. If you leave some protruding from the ground, the peat pot will dry out and wick moisture away from the rose plant's roots. But don't pile soil around your rose plant. Instead, carefully tear off the top inch or two of the peat pot, working your way all the way around the pot. This makes it easy to cover the pot entirely without planting your rose too deep. Continue planting per instructions in step 3, above.

Caring for Roses

Pruning roses is important to keep plants vigorous.

Prune roses at any time except before a freeze; trimming while plants are dormant makes it easier to see the structure of the plant and what you are doing.

Cut angles away from bud and about 1/4 inch above.

1 Make the right cut. The first order of business is making a proper cut. Cuts should be made on live canes about one-fourth inch above an outward facing bud. Angle your pruners so the tip is cut at a 45-degree slant away from the bud. Apply pruning sealer to fresh cuts to prevent damage from insects and diseases.

Cut angles toward bud; rain washes to the bud.

Cut is too far above the bud and it's flat, not angled.

Cut is too close to the bud.

2 Cut away darkened, dead wood. Live canes will be green and buds will be visible.

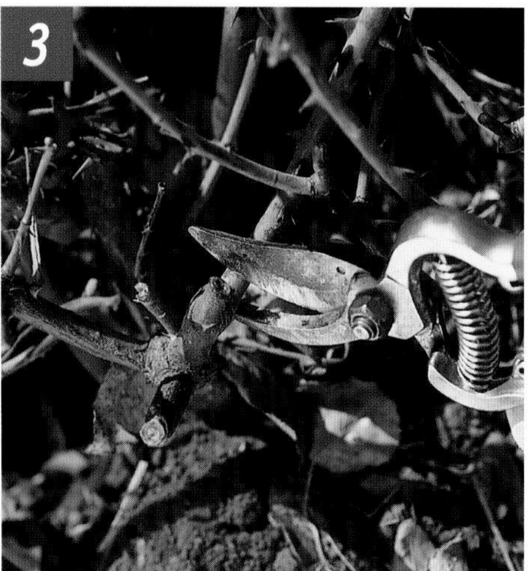

3 Locate any canes that rub together. Remove the one that is angling into the center of the plant near the base. Do not cut into the main stem; instead, prune the offending cane where it emerges from the main stem, leaving a little knob of growth known as a collar. If the cane is thicker than a pencil, use bypass loppers instead of hand pruners.

STUFF YOU'LL NEED

- ✔ Bypass hand pruners
- ✔ Bypass loppers
- ✔ Pruning sealer

What to Expect

Many roses have thorns; arm yourself with long sleeves and gloves while pruning.

Why Prune?

Proper pruning keeps plants healthy. You'll need to trim roses each year to remove dead wood, improve air circulation, eliminate rubbing canes, reduce height, and encourage new, vigorous growth with plenty of blossoms.

Wisdom of the Aisles

Preventive medicine. A few simple steps now will prevent problems later on. Dip cutting tools in rubbing alcohol or bleach after each cut. This helps prevent the spread of disease. Always collect rose clippings instead of letting them fall into garden beds. Clippings might harbor pests or diseases, so you'll need to destroy them. Do not compost rose clippings.

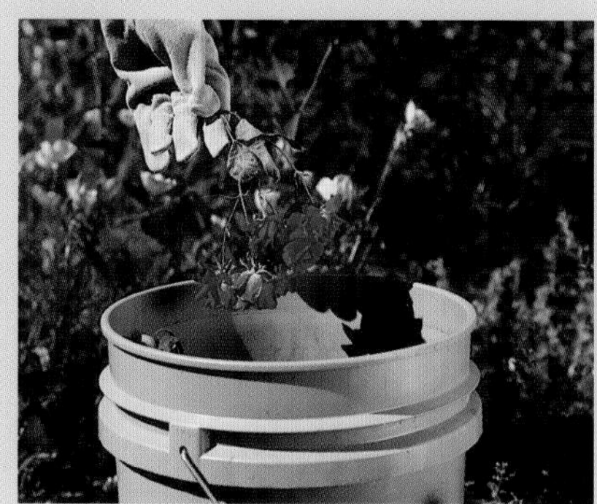

4 Thin the center of thick shrub roses to improve air circulation. Leave strong main stems uncut, and prune away selected thin, twiggy canes. Remove canes from the center of the plant only, not the outside. Choose canes randomly from the plant's center, leaving nubs of growth so cuts don't go completely back to main stems. Reduce the overall size of a shrub rose if needed. Select your desired height and cut individual canes to that level.

5 Remove individual fading blooms. This encourages new buds for more flowers. A good rule of thumb is to remove spent flowers by cutting the stem below the first set of five healthy leaves.

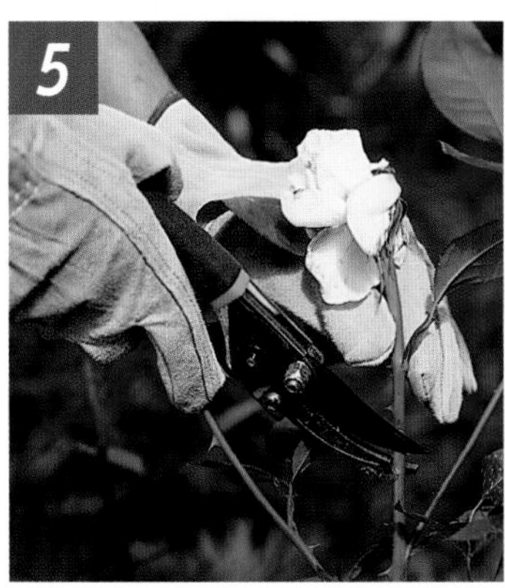

6 Before protecting roses for winter, apply a dormant spray. This preventive step makes sure that insect and diseases don't overwinter in your rose plants. Follow product directions.

Rose Care – Symptoms & Solutions

Roses might require spraying to control problems.

If you know what to look for and what product to use, you've already won half the battle. Here are some common culprits. When seeking advice from a garden staffer, take a sample with you. Begin your spray program as soon as first leaves appear for preventive care.

Symptom: Holes in rose blossoms; small green or tan beetles noticeable.
Solution: Hand-pick if possible. Spray large infestations with an insecticide containing carbaryl or rotenone that's labeled for roses. Erect a cheesecloth cage around plants to keep new beetles from flying in. Barrier should be taller than the plant but can be open at the top. Remove when beetles cease feeding.

Symptom: A grayish-white coating covers foliage, distorting young shoots.
Solution: Spray powdery mildew with a fungicide containing triforine, folpet, or thiophanate-methyl. Prevent by watering early in the day so leaves can dry.

Symptom: Black spots appear on foliage; leaves fall off.
Solution: Spray with a fungicide containing thiophante-methyl, chlorothalonil, mancozeb, or triforine. Allow foliage to dry by watering early in the day to prevent this problem. Rake up and destroy fallen leaves.

Symptom: Brown buds develop and flowers are few and oddly shaped. Probably caused by tiny bugs such as thrips or mites.
Solution: Spray with a systemic insecticide containing acephate. Remove buds and blooms by hand and destroy.

Symptom: New leaves are curled and stunted; foliage is shiny and sticky. Little green bugs called aphids are visible.
Solution: Knock them off with a stiff spray of water. Control with insecticidal soap or a contact-killer spray. For long-term control, apply a systemic insecticide containing acephate.

Feeding Roses

Most roses are heavy feeders—they require more fertilizer than many other landscape plants. A fertilizer that contains higher amounts of phosphorus and potassium than nitrogen will encourage the growth of flowers instead of just leaves. Look for a fertilizer that lists a smaller first number (N) on its label than the next two numbers (P and K). Fertilizers identified as rose foods make it easy. They contain elements balanced to give roses just what they need. Slow-release fertilizers are coated to prevent all the nutrients from entering the soil at once. They supply benefits over a longer period of time than noncoated fertilizers. Some granular fertilizers also supply systemic insecticides for preventive care.

Feed roses each year when new growth is about 3 inches long. Rake away mulch and scratch dry fertilizers into the soil around plants, watering well before covering with mulch again. Feed roses again in autumn, at least a month before the first frost.

Foliar feeding. Liquid fertilizer (foliar feed) can be applied directly to leaves. Temperatures should be below 90 degrees when applying. You can use liquid fertilizer as often as every week to correct nutrient deficiencies. Always apply liquid fertilizers in the early morning to allow leaves to dry thoroughly as quickly as possible. Damp leaves lead to fungal problems, especially if foliage is left wet overnight.

Nearly Wild Rose (Rosa 'Nearly Wild') Page 152

Winterizing Roses

Take steps in fall to protect your roses from winter cold damage. Here's how to employ the "Minnesota Tip" method, which uses earth as an insulator.

1 You're actually going to tip your rose plant over and bury it in the ground until spring. The first thing you'll need to do is to water thoroughly for a few days to keep the plant pliable and soil soft. The day before you plan to bury your rose, apply a dormant spray to prevent pests from overwintering. Do not prune your rose plant at this time. Wounds won't heal properly late in the season.

2 Gently tie the stems of your rose plant together to make a neat, upright package. Wrap plastic twine around the plant, starting at the bottom and working up. Cut the string, leaving an extra foot at the top.

3 Dig a trench in the soil beside your rose plant. The trench should start at the base of the plant. Make it long and wide enough to hold the entire plant when you tip it over into the trench. Dig the trench deep enough for you to place the plant into it and add 2 or 3 inches of soil to cover it without forming a mound. When your rose is buried, the soil covering it should be level or nearly level with the rest of the soil in the bed.

4 Carefully remove soil from the base of the plant, exposing the very tops of the roots. Loosen soil around roots by hand. It isn't necessary to expose all the roots; your goal is to loosen them just enough to be able to tip the plant over without forcing it. It's OK to cut a few minor roots.

STUFF YOU'LL NEED

- ✔ Spading fork
- ✔ Any shovel you prefer
- ✔ Dormant spray for roses
- ✔ Hose connected to a water source within reach of project site
- ✔ Mulch
- ✔ Extra topsoil (optional)
- ✔ Rose fungicide and insecticide (the following spring)
- ✔ Plastic twine

What to Expect

It isn't easy to tip an established rose all the way over. If your plant resists, don't force it; doing so could break canes or tear roots. Insert a spading fork into the moistened root area and rock the plant gently to loosen it.

BUYER'S GUIDE

Hardy roses are the best bet for cold-climate gardens. Though all roses require winter protection, choose tough ones for a better survival rate. Here are some terms you need to know when shopping for hardy roses.

- **Species roses** are sometimes called wild roses. These tough roses are original plants, not the results of breeding. Species roses have only two words in their botanical names.
- **Old Garden roses** have been around for a long time. At the end the 18th century the repeat-blooming China rose was introduced and modern roses (such as hybrid teas and floribundas) were developed from it. Old Garden roses predate China rose breeding. These old-fashioned favorites produce large plants that bloom only once but produce many fragrant flowers.
- **Shrub roses** are the results of crossing Species roses with Old Garden roses or with hybrids. Plants are usually large. Flowers are often semi-double and grow in masses.

Other Methods

The Minnesota Tip method of protecting roses from freeze damage requires the most effort, but it's also proven by horticulturists to be reliable.

Other methods take less work, but they don't insulate plants as well and can attract rodents seeking winter nests.

Chicken wire can be fashioned to make cages around rose plants. Fill cages completely with hay or leaves, making sure the tops of plants are well covered.

Rose cones cover plants with a plastic foam igloo to block bitter winter winds. Always anchor rose cones with bricks or rocks to keep them from blowing away. Mulch the base of plants before covering with cones.

5 **Gently tip the plant into the trench** by using a spading fork to push it over. Some of the roots might protrude from the soil after the plant is laid in the trench.

6 **Cover the entire rose plant with a 2- to 3-inch-thick layer** of rich garden soil, leaving the extra plastic twine protruding from the surface. You'll use this plastic twine next spring to locate your plant to uncover it. Don't skimp on soil; if you don't have enough left over from digging the trench, add bagged topsoil or dig some more soil from another planting bed. Make sure that all roots are well covered with soil. Finally, add a layer of mulch to form a pile that's about a foot and a half deep. Hay or leaves can do this job.

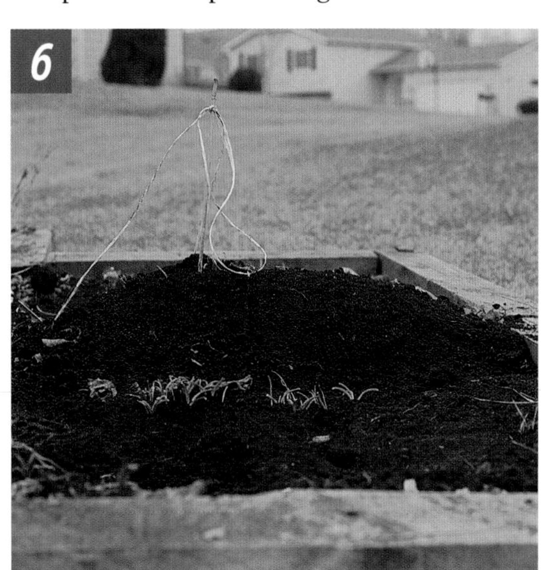

7 **After the last frost the following spring,** begin uncovering your buried rose plant in stages. First, remove the pile of mulch. Gradually remove soil as it thaws to expose the plant over about a 15-day period, completing the process by mid-April. Gently raise the uncovered plant to an upright position and press soil around roots as needed to anchor it, but avoid piling soil around the stem. Spray the entire plant with water several times to keep canes hydrated. Apply a combination fungicide and insecticide that lists roses on the label; follow product directions for application rates and methods, safety, and clean-up. Water your rose plant regularly to help it adjust to exposure to light and air after months spent underground.

Chapter 4
trees

Trees are the backbone of good design, providing color, texture, line, and form. They also offer shade, protection from wind and rain, and shelter for other plants in your yard. Because most trees take longer than other plants to mature, the sooner you get new trees started in your landscape, the better.

The Value of Trees

Start your landscape with trees. A single, well-placed tree impacts your yard more than any other landscaping item. Most trees are long-lasting and embody the elements of good design—color, texture, line, and form. Planting trees first shapes planting beds and gives them a head start on growth while you work on other parts of your landscape.

Trees Solve Problems

Look over the notes from your site analysis. Trees might solve the problem areas you identified. Carefully chosen trees put privacy where you need it, add shade, dress up patios and entries, deflect wind, and establish a background for your landscape. Good selection is more important than quantity. Picking the right trees to fill the right needs is more effective than planting whatever you happen to find on sale. Look at the selection guides on the following pages, then go to the tree encyclopedia later in this book to help make your final decisions.

Consider These Factors

Defining the jobs you want new trees to do helps identify desirable characteristics. Think about whether you need a tree that keeps its foliage year-round (evergreen) or sheds its leaves once a year (deciduous). Evergreen trees offer more privacy but usually grow more slowly than deciduous trees. Deciduous trees make good choices for producing summer shade.

Keep in mind that the right plant in the right place is critical to success. Before adding a tree to your yard, you need to know its ultimate size and how long it will take to reach maturity. After all, it's a shame to prune a tall, stately tree severely because you didn't take telephone or power lines into account at planting. Knowing how big a tree will get also helps you avoid the common problem of planting a tree that will grow large too close to your house. You'll also want to know if the tree has any characteristics that make it undesirable for the purpose you have in mind. For example, trees

Rapid Growers

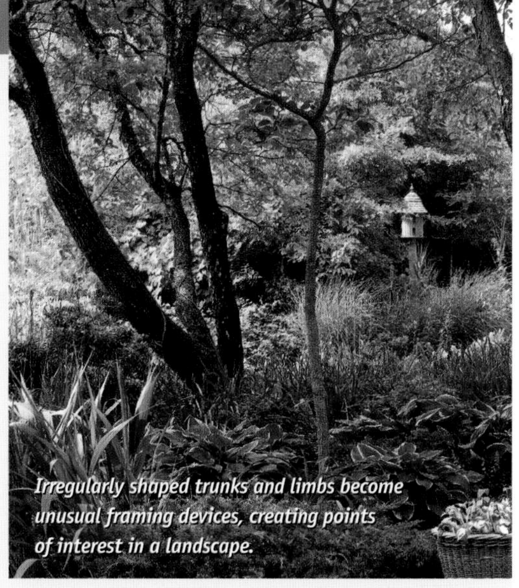
Irregularly shaped trunks and limbs become unusual framing devices, creating points of interest in a landscape.

Rapidly growing trees can improve your landscape in a hurry. Position new trees properly in the landscape, dig large-sized planting holes, provide good soil, water adequately (see page 52), and watch your trees take off. Find out all you can about the trees you are considering for your landscape. Growth rate is just one bit of information provided in the tree encyclopedia pages. Look on plant tags and ask garden associates for additional information if needed. Knowing the growth rate will help you decide the size of tree to purchase. If you've decided on a slow grower, consider planting one that's larger in size so you won't have to wait several years before enjoying it. A Star Magnolia used as a focal point in an entry area or courtyard is a tree worth buying big. Other trees, such as River Birches, grow so quickly that you needn't go to the expense of purchasing large ones. Remember that faster-growing trees usually have weaker wood and shorter lifespans than their slower-growing counterparts. ***Availability varies by area and conditions (see page 21). Check with your garden center.***

Common Name	Zones	Page
Amur Chokecherry *Prunus maackii*	2-6	97
Bradford Pear *Pyrus calleryana 'Bradford'*	4-8	98
Canoe Birch *Betula papyrifera*	2-7	82
Corkscrew Willow *Salix 'Golden Curls'*	4-8	103
European White Birch *Betula pendula*	2-7	82
Golden Weeping Willow *Salix alba 'Tristis'*	3-8	102
Green Ash *Fraxinus pennsylvanica*	3-9	88
Honeylocust *Gleditsia triacanthos inermis*	3-9	89
Katsura Tree *Cercidiphyllum japonicum*	4-8	84
Newport Plum *Prunus cerasifera 'Newport'*	4-8	96
Northern Red Oak *Quercus rubra*	4-7	101
Norway Spruce *Picea abies*	2-7	92
Pin Oak *Quercus palustris*	4-8	101
Quaking Aspen *Populus tremuloides*	2-6	96
Red Maple *Acer rubrum*	3-9	78
Redbud *Cercis canadensis*	3-9	85
River Birch *Betula nigra*	4-9	81
Russian Olive *Elaeagnus angustifolia*	2-7	87
Scarlet Oak *Quercus coccinea*	4-9	100
Silver Maple *Acer saccharinum*	3-9	78
Veitch Fir *Abies veitchii*	3-6	75
Weeping Willow *Salix babylonica*	4-9	102
White Pine *Pinus strobus*	3-8	95
Whitespire Birch *Betula mandschurica japonica 'Whitespire'*	4-7	83

with large root systems that buckle paving are poor choices for planting next to patios, sidewalks, parking areas, or streets. These areas need trees that have well-behaved roots. They should also thrive next to the reflected heat of paving. (Always check easements and right-of-way restrictions before planting.) Find out if trees have invasive roots so you can avoid planting them around septic and drainage systems. Finally, know what it takes to care for your new trees before you plant them. Don't make high-maintenance choices if you desire a low-maintenance landscape. Throughout the following pages, you'll find the details to help you choose the right trees for your landscape.

Design Tip

Legacy Trees

Celebrating a major family event by planting a tree is a time-honored tradition. Trees that are known for slow growth and large size are good choices for longevity. Ginkgos, White Oaks, and Sugar Maples are trees that will commemorate great moments for many generations to come.

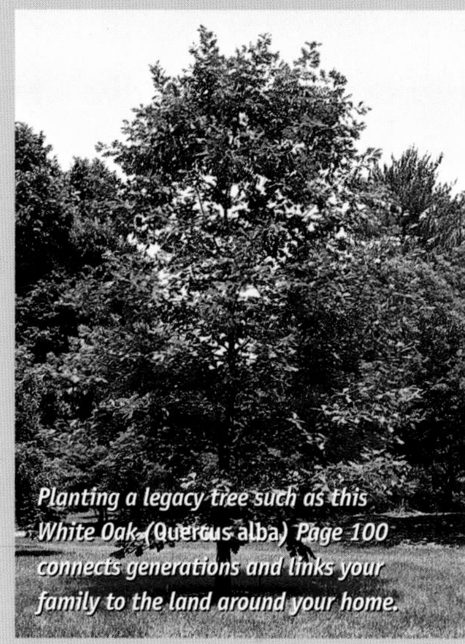
Planting a legacy tree such as this White Oak (*Quercus alba*) Page 100 connects generations and links your family to the land around your home.

Wisdom of the Aisles

Trees can actually affect the climate around your home. Trees suitable for use as windbreaks make a big difference when positioned to deflect harsh northwestern winter winds. Deciduous trees planted along the southern and southeastern sides of your home offer cooling shade during the warm seasons. Then they shed their leaves allowing winter rays to light and warm your home. Choosing trees known for providing leafy shade can make a big difference when positioned to block hot, afternoon summer sun coming from the west.

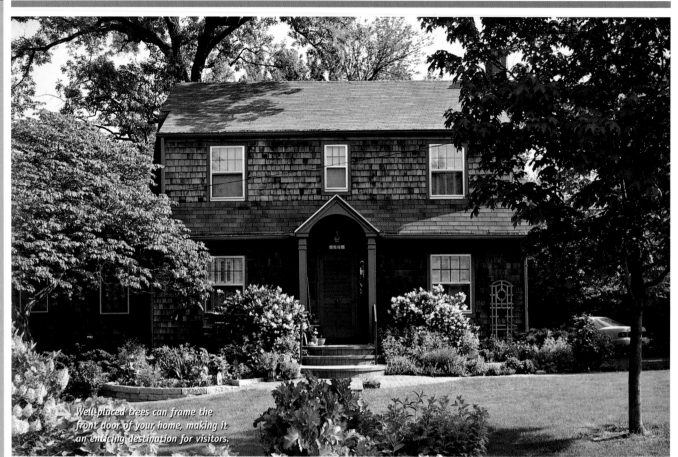

Well-placed trees can frame the front door of your home, making it an enticing destination for visitors.

Buying a Tree

Choosing a good tree and getting it home from the store safely are the first steps in creating a landscape. Trees are sold as container-grown, balled-and-burlapped, and bare-root. Containerized trees have lived their lives in nursery pots. Balled-and-burlapped trees—also known as B&B—start their lives in tree farm fields. After they're dug up with tree spades, their root balls are wrapped with fabric for shipping. Bare-root types (such as fruit trees) come with roots carefully surrounded with packing inside a plastic bag or set in sawdust.

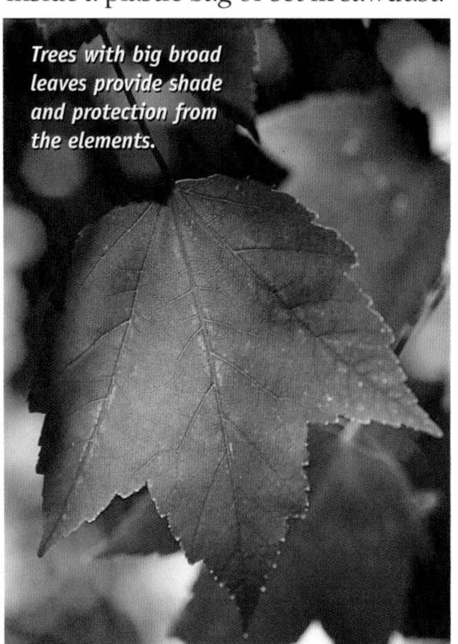
Trees with big broad leaves provide shade and protection from the elements.

Container vs. B&B

Trees grown in containers are often smaller than ones wrapped in burlap. Root growth is limited by the size of the container. Because they don't have to be removed from the ground, container-grown trees are less likely to go into shock and lose their leaves when planted. Garden shops, home centers, and nurseries carry wide selections of container-grown trees. They are often easier for most consumers to handle and are available for a longer period of time during the growing season. The best times to buy B&B trees are early spring or late fall.

Shopping Tips

- **Choose a tree with bigger caliper.** A thick trunk is sturdier than a tall, skinny-trunked tree.
- **Check the firmness of the root ball.** If the tree and root ball move as one, it has developed a good, firm root ball. If the tree is loose within the soil in the container, it has only recently been "stepped up" from a smaller pot into the larger container. Roots are the most important thing you buy when you purchase any plant. Bypass a tree that hasn't been in its container long enough to develop roots to fill the container. If the root ball of a B&B tree is cracked or crumbling, find another tree.
- **Look at the tree roots.** A tree that has long, white roots protruding from the bottom drainage hole has been in its container too long and is root-bound. A root-bound tree can be grown successfully but takes longer to put out fresh feeder roots in its new home.

• **Avoid trees that have nicks or wounds to their trunks.** These trees are damaged and might attract insects or develop disease problems.

• **Know the form of the mature tree.** If a tree is supposed to have multiple trunks, that's one thing. But if a particular kind of tree normally has a single, straight trunk, don't purchase one that divides into a double trunk. Water collecting in the crotch can cause splitting because of rot or the formation of ice. High winds can damage an improperly formed tree, too. It pays to know what form is correct before you buy.

• **Check the tree container.** Trees with burlap-wrapped root balls are sometimes set in containers for easier handling. A layer of bark is then added to cover the burlap and keep the root ball moist. These are good trees, just not container grown. Check beneath the mulch to see what you're getting. If you see burlap, the tree was dug from a nursery field and is balled-and-burlapped, not container grown.

Evergreens have their place, but don't forget to choose some trees to help you celebrate the changing of the seasons.

Fall is for Planting Autumn is an excellent time to plant woody trees and shrubs. Cold weather slows growth above ground, so a plant's energy is put into expanding roots beneath the ground. Cool weather puts less stress on new trees than hot weather does. Regular watering is not as critical. Insect and disease problems are fewer in fall and winter than in spring and summer. Planting in the fall gives you a jump start on next spring.

Tree Mortality

Plants that have been transported from one location to another and then replanted are under a great deal of stress. Some will die through no fault of yours. If the plant is mishandled at any point during the shipping process, the damage has been done before you buy it.

Newly planted trees and shrubs that turn completely brown and hold their leaves instead of dropping them are not going into transplant shock (see page 68). This symptom usually indicates that the plant has died. To test whether your tree is dead or alive, use your fingernail to scratch the thin bark of a branch. If you see green, your tree is alive. If you see brown or gray beneath the bark, try again on other branches or even on the trunk. If none are green, your tree is dead.

Trunk damage is one of the leading reasons that healthy trees die. Trunk wounds destroy the tissues that transport water and nutrients from the roots to the upper portions of the tree. Wounds also invite insects and disease. In the landscape, string trimmers and mowers often cause this damage. Avoid planting grass near tree trunks to eliminate potential problems.

Don't ignore mature trees. They can suffer during the stress of drought. Shallow-rooted trees such as dogwoods are particularly vulnerable during prolonged periods of extremely hot, dry weather. Curling leaves that turn crispy brown along the edges are a sign that a tree needs water. Foliage may also drop prematurely. Water trees by turning a hose on to a slow trickle and placing it around the base of the tree and at various places under the dripline for several hours at a time to give the tree a good soaking. If water flows across the surface of the ground, your hose is turned on too hard.

Homer's Hindsight

I bought a new tree and was eager to get it home. My first mistake was putting it in the trunk with the top sticking out. The tree was destroyed by the time I got home. Even though I'd driven slowly, the wind shredded the leaves and dried them out. Next time, I'll get a tarp and bungie cords to bundle up the tree or at least lay it down in the bed of a pickup truck to give it some wind protection during the ride home.

Planting a Container-Grown Tree

It's easy to add trees to your landscape. Follow these guidelines for planting those that are container-grown.

1 Dig a hole that's one-and-a-half to two times as wide as the tree's container. The hole should be as deep as the container is tall. Use a shovel handle to take a rough measurement; if your hole is too deep, add soil to the bottom and tamp it in place to keep the tree from settling. If you're planting in an area with heavy clay soil, scrape the sides of the hole with a shovel to roughen them. A slick-sided hole acts like a big clay pot and restricts root growth. Add gypsum to clay soil, too (see page 51).

Have a tarp or wheelbarrow handy. As you shovel, place soil onto a tarp or in a wheelbarrow instead of on your lawn. This will make it easier to mix amendments into the soil before putting it back into the hole around the root ball. This trick also makes cleaning up easier.

2 Mix amendments into the removed soil. Amendments vary according to existing soil conditions and plant requirements. Compost or bagged, composted manure are good organic amendments to use. The amended mixture should contain half native soil and half organic matter. The use of native soil helps the tree adapt to its new home and spread roots out into the soil beyond the planting hole.

3 Gently slide the tree from its container. Cut the container with a utility knife if you can't get it off without tugging. (Pulling on the trunk can damage roots.) When the container is off, lay the tree on its side. Gently score the root ball with a sharp shovel or utility knife to encourage the growth of new roots outside the pot-shaped mass of roots. It's important to keep the root ball intact; limit the scores on the root ball.

STUFF YOU'LL NEED

- ✔ Round-point shovel
- ✔ Hose connected to water supply within reach of work site
- ✔ Organic matter (such as bagged compost)
- ✔ Wheelbarrow
- ✔ Mulch
- ✔ Gypsum (for clay soil)

What to Expect

Your newly planted tree will look shorter than it did at the garden center because the container itself seems to add height. When the tree is planted, the roots are buried beneath the soil surface.

Moving a tree correctly

▲ ***Right*** Support the heavy root ball from below to prevent damaging tree roots.

▲ ***Wrong*** Transport trees to the planting site by the container, not the tree trunk.

4 Position the tree in its hole. The top of the root ball should be level with adjacent, undisturbed soil. In areas with heavy clay soil, trees should be planted higher so the root ball protrudes an inch or two above the soil surface. This prevents water from puddling around roots. Before filling the hole, gently swivel the tree so it looks best at the angle from which you'll see it the most. Check to make sure the tree is straight from all directions.

5 Fill the hole with amended soil mixture. Add soil around the root ball, pressing it firmly with your hands as you go. If planting during hot weather, water the soil as you fill in the hole. Avoid stomping on the soil to tamp it down. This destroys soil porosity, making it difficult for water and air to reach plant roots. Because you have dug the hole only as deep as the container is tall, the tree is sitting on a firm base that won't settle.

Unless your yard has heavy clay soil that will retain water easily, use the excess soil to form a moat around the tree. Make the moat as wide as the hole. Pat the soil firmly in place with your hands. The moat walls should be 3 inches wide and tall. Mulch the area inside the moat and fill with water from a slowly trickling hose. Place the hose at the base of the tree's trunk to soak the root ball; otherwise, the water will run past the root ball into the looser soil in the hole. The moat allows the water to seep down to the roots instead of running off the soil's surface. Weather will eventually melt your moat; but by then, your tree will no longer need it.

TOOL TIP

Round-point shovels are great for digging holes and scooping out soil. Shovels with fiberglass handles usually last longer than those with wooden handles.

Planting a Tree on a Slope

Hilly terrain can make growing trees difficult. If a new tree is not properly secured, gravity will cause the root ball to pivot in its hole before roots grow into the adjacent soil. When this happens, the tree leans downhill and grows at an angle instead of straight up and down. Use a tree-staking kit to secure the tree on the uphill side. (To secure a newly planted tree on level soil in areas prone to high winds, use three cables to anchor the tree from all sides.) Watering is also a major concern. Here's how to solve both potential problems:

1) Form a moat on the downhill side of the tree. Now the soil is level and prevents water runoff (see A). Deep watering (see page 52) is particularly important for trees planted on slopes. Roots growing downward seeking water give the tree stability.

2) Pass the roping through plastic tubes. Loop tubes around the trunk above a limb, and position the hose to prevent wire from cutting into the tree (see B).

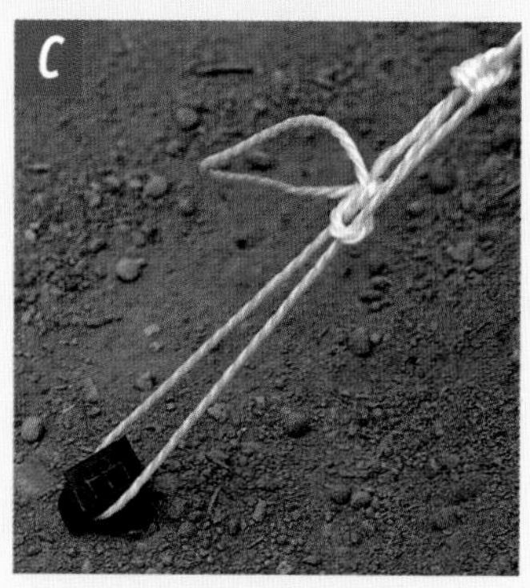

3) Secure each rope to a stake driven into the soil on the uphill side. (The two stakes should form the points of a triangle, with the tree at the apex.) Wrap the ropes around the hook in each stake, pulling until taut. Make sure the tree is straight from all angles. Tie a brightly colored flag to each rope (see C).

Remove the ropes after the tree has been in place for one complete growing season. If your area is prone to high winds, leave trees—even those not planted on slopes—roped for a year. Check the lines periodically and tighten as needed. As the root system develops, the tree becomes securely anchored in the ground.

Planting a B&B Tree

Trees that come from the store with balled-and-burlapped root balls are known as B&B trees. Planting them is slightly different than planting container-grown trees.

1 Dig a hole that's twice as wide as the tree's root ball. The hole should be as deep as the root ball is tall. Use a shovel handle to take a rough measurement. If your hole is too deep, add soil to the bottom and tamp it in place to keep the tree from settling. If you're planting in an area with heavy clay soil, scrape the sides of the hole with a shovel to roughen them. A slick-sided hole acts like a big clay pot and restricts root growth.

2 Mix amendments into the removed soil. The resulting mixture is usually half native soil and half organic matter. Amendments vary according to existing soil conditions and plant requirements. In areas with high rainfall and heavy clay soil, mix native soil with organic matter at a reduced ratio of 4:1. Organic materials such as bagged compost make excellent soil additions.

3 Cut back all metal or plastic fasteners from the root ball and peel back the top third of the burlap after the tree is set in the hole. It's important to remove metal or plastic fasteners wrapped around the burlap at the base of the trunk. Leaving these will eventually girdle the tree, killing it. However, if the B&B root ball is sitting in a wire basket, do not remove it. This helps keep the root ball intact. The roots will grow through the wire and the wire will eventually rust away.

Wisdom of the Aisles

Topping trees. **Don't flat-top your trees.** Cutting branches so they're all the same level encourages the development of many fast-growing sprouts from the tips of remaining stubs. Though the tree's canopy will appear dense and bushy for a while, the sprouts will shoot upward, requiring more pruning. Thick, gnarled scars can appear after cuts are made in the same place year after year. Cutting branches off to make the tree resemble a lollipop prohibits the development of the tree's natural form. Instead, shoots angle upward, close to the trunk. Narrow crotches result, which may accumulate water and rot wood or form ice that will split the branches from the tree. Topping trees also severely limits the size of a tree's canopy; eventually, the trunk grows thicker, making it appear out of proportion to the limited canopy. Topping is also known as pollarding or dehorning.

Stuff You'll Need

- ✔ Round-point shovel
- ✔ Water supply and hose within reach of work site
- ✔ Organic matter such as bagged compost
- ✔ Tarp (optional)
- ✔ Gypsum for clay soil

What to Expect

It can be difficult to pry fasteners from root balls with your fingers; try using a flat-head screwdriver, instead.

TOOL TIP

A digging bar is essential when you're digging holes in rocky, compacted, or hard clay soil. Use a sledgehammer to drive it into the soil to pry chunks loose and get your hole started.

Transplant Shock

If your new tree drops all its leaves shortly after planting, don't give it up for dead. A balled-and-burlapped tree has many roots severed when it is dug from the ground. It is more likely to experience transplant shock than a container-grown tree. Trees in shock shed their foliage and go into a survival mode. Given enough time and water, such trees will most likely recover. Keep the soil lightly moist. Though it appears a little silly to be watering something that looks dead, keep doing it!

BUYER'S GUIDE

If you want a larger tree than those in stock, ask a garden associate about ordering a B&B tree for you. Some stores stock balled-and-burlapped trees only upon request. Inquire about the approximate measurements of the root ball and dig the proper-sized hole before the tree arrives. Ask if delivery is available for a fee when you order your tree. If so, find out where the tree will be left—don't be surprised if the delivery driver will take it no farther than the curb. You'll probably need to have a sturdy wheelbarrow waiting to get the tree to the hole. You might want to hire a professional or get a friend to help with a big tree; B&B trees are heavy.

Plan your bedlines around existing or future trees

Though you shouldn't plant right up to the trunks of trees, you can surround them with a bed of shrubs and groundcovers. Keep lawns away from the base of trees to avoid trunk damage from mowers and string trimmers and to avoid problems caused by different watering needs for trees and grass.

4 Position the tree in its hole. Peel back the fabric to reveal the top third of the root ball. Leave the fabric in place unless it is nonbiodegradable plastic, which will need to be removed before the ball goes in the hole. The top of the root ball should be level with adjacent, undisturbed soil. This is easily checked with the handle of a shovel. In clay soil, trees need to be planted so the root ball is an inch or two above the soil surface so water won't puddle around roots. Make sure the tree is straight from all sides.

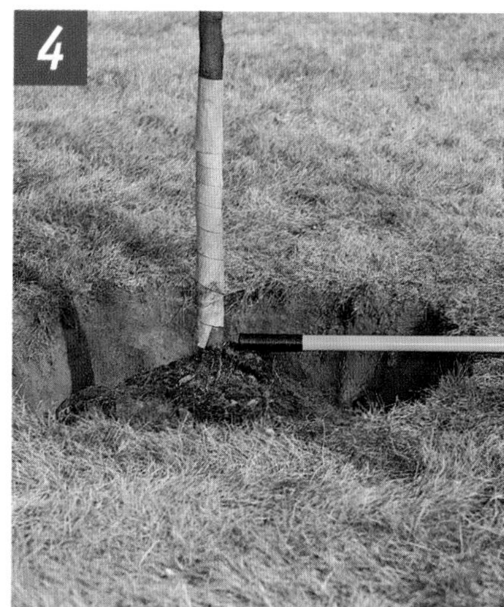

5 Fill the hole with the amended soil mixture. Add soil around the root ball, pressing it firmly with your hands as you go. If planting during hot weather, water the soil as you fill in the hole. Avoid stomping on the soil to tamp it down. This destroys soil porosity, and makes it difficult for water and air to reach plant roots. Because you have dug the hole only as deep as the root ball is tall, the tree is sitting on a firm base and shouldn't settle.

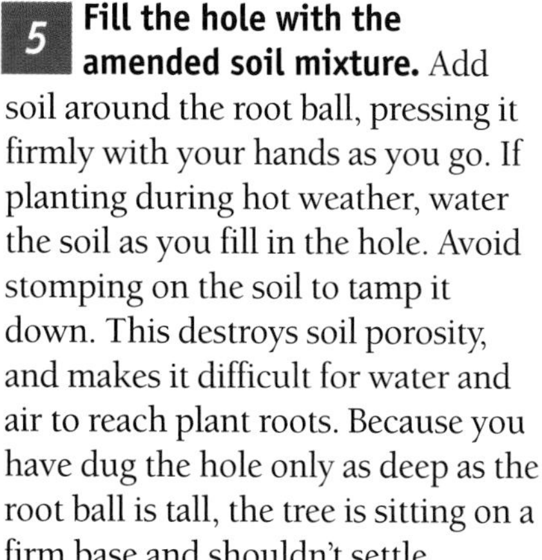

Good idea! **Capture a wonderful family occasion by taking pictures as you plant your new tree**. Everyone will treasure the memories, and the moment will become part of your family history.

6 Use the excess soil to form a moat around the tree. The moat should be as wide as the hole and 3 inches wide and tall. Pat it in place with your hands to make it sturdy. Mulch the inside and fill the area with water from a trickling hose placed at the base of the trunk. The moat allows the water to seep down to the roots instead of running off the surface of the soil. Fill the moat slowly several times, letting the water soak in each time. Weather will eventually wear away your moat, but after establishment, your tree will no longer need it.

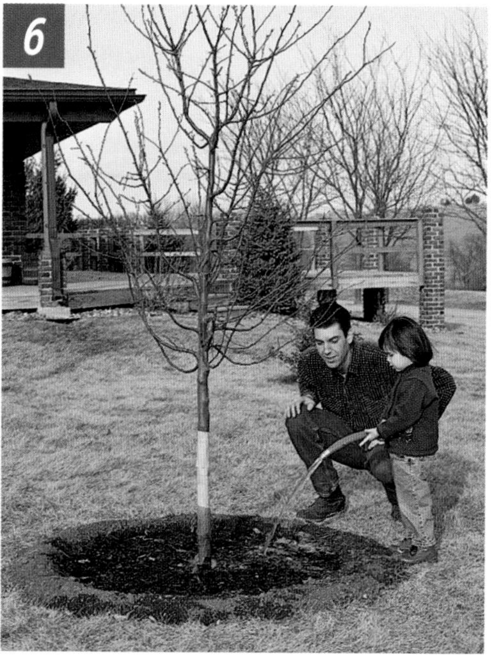

Lush summer foliage provides a rich backdrop for the spray from a fountain in a backyard pond.

Choosing Trees for Seasonality

Decorate the seasons. Choose trees for beauty throughout the year. You'll find plenty of different kinds with attractive flowers, foliage, berries, or bark. The selection guides on these pages offer a range of choices. Eliminate any trees that don't include your planting zone within their range. Turn to the pages listed for photographs and more information.

Plumleaf Crabapple (Malus prunifolia) *Page 91*

Autumn has arrived when the fan-shaped leaves of a Ginkgo turn golden.

Japanese Flowering Crabapple
(Malus floribunda)
Page 91

Japanese Tree Lilac
(Syringa reticulata)
Page 104

Trees with colorful fall foliage

Common Name	Zones	Page
Allegheny Serviceberry *Amelanchier laevis*	4-8	81
American Beech *Fagus grandifolia*	3-9	87
American Hornbeam *Carpinus caroliniana*	3-9	84
American Smoke Tree *Cotinus obovatus*	4-8	85
Amur Chokecherry *Prunus maackii*	2-6	97
Amur Maple *Acer tataricum ginnala*	2-6	77
Bradford Pear *Pyrus calleryana 'Bradford'*	4-8	98
Canoe Birch *Betula papyrifera*	2-7	82
Cockspur Hawthorn *Crataegus crus-galli 'Inermis'*	4-7	86
European Hornbeam *Carpinus betulus*	4-7	83
European Mountain Ash *Sorbus aucuparia*	4-7	103
European White Birch *Betula pendula*	2-7	82
Ginkgo *Ginkgo biloba*	3-9	88
Green Ash *Fraxinus pennsylvanica*	3-9	88
Honeylocust *Gleditsia triacanthos inermis*	3-9	89
Katsura Tree *Cercidiphyllum japonicum*	4-8	84
Mayday Tree *Prunus padus commutata*	3-6	97
Northern Red Oak *Quercus rubra*	4-7	101
Norway Maple *Acer platanoides*	3-7	77
Pin Oak *Quercus palustris*	4-8	101
Quaking Aspen *Populus tremuloides*	2-6	96
Red Maple *Acer rubrum*	3-9	78
Redbud *Cercis canadensis*	3-9	85
Scarlet Oak *Quercus coccinea*	4-9	100
Shadblow Serviceberry *Amelanchier canadensis*	3-8	80
Silver Maple *Acer saccharinum*	3-9	78
Star Magnolia *Magnolia stellata*	4-9	90
Sugar Maple *Acer saccharum*	4-8	79
Washington Hawthorn *Crataegus phaenopyrum*	3-9	86
White Oak *Quercus alba*	3-9	100
Whitespire Birch *Betula mandschurica japonica 'Whitespire'*	4-7	83

Availability varies by area and conditions (see page 21). Check with your garden center.

Spring-flowering trees

Common Name	Zones	Page
Allegheny Serviceberry *Amelanchier laevis*	4-8	81
Amur Chokecherry *Prunus maackii*	2-6	97
Bradford Pear *Pyrus calleryana 'Bradford'*	4-8	98
Cockspur Hawthorn *Crataegus crus-galli 'Inermis'*	4-7	86
European Mountain Ash *Sorbus aucuparia*	4-7	103
Japanese Flowering Crabapple *Malus floribunda*	3-8	91
Mayday Tree *Prunus padus commutata*	3-6	97
Newport Plum *Prunus cerasifera 'Newport'*	4-8	96
Plumleaf Crabapple *Malus prunifolia*	4-9	91
Red Maple *Acer rubrum*	3-9	78
Redbud *Cercis canadensis*	3-9	85
Russian Olive *Elaeagnus angustifolia*	2-7	87
Shadblow Serviceberry *Amelanchier canadensis*	3-8	80
Star Magnolia *Magnolia stellata*	4-9	90
Washington Hawthorn *Crataegus phaenopyrum*	3-9	86

Summer-flowering trees

Common Name	Zones	Page
American Linden *Tilia americana*	2-8	105
Common Horsechesnut *Aesculus hippocastanum*	3-7	80
Japanese Tree Lilac *Syringa reticulata*	3-7	104
Ohio Buckeye *Aesculus glabra*	3-7	79
Russian Olive *Elaeagnus angustifolia*	2-7	87

Trees with winter interest

Common Name	Zones	Page
American Beech (bark) *Fagus grandifolia*	3-9	87
American Hornbeam (bark) *Carpinus caroliniana*	3-9	84
American Smoke Tree(bark) *Cotinus obovatus*	4-8	85
Amur Chokecherry (bark) *Prunus maackii*	2-6	97
Amur Maple (shape) *Acer tataricum ginnala*	2-6	77
Canoe Birch (bark) *Betula papyrifera*	2-7	82
Cockspur Hawthorn (berries) *Crataegus crus-galli 'Inermis'*	4-7	86
Eastern Red Cedar (bark) *Juniperus virginiana*	3-9	90
European White Birch (bark) *Betula pendula*	2-7	82
Lacebark Pine (bark) *Pinus bungeana*	4-7	94
Plumleaf Crabapple (berries) *Malus prunifolia*	4-9	91
Red Spruce (bark) *Picea rubens*	2-5	93
River Birch (bark) *Betula nigra*	4-9	81
Scots Pine (bark) *Pinus sylvestris*	3-7	95
Silver Maple (bark) *Acer saccharinum*	3-9	78
Washington Hawthorn (berries) *Crataegus phaenopyrum*	3-9	86
Whitespire Birch (bark) *Betula mandschurica japonica 'Whitespire'*	4-7	83

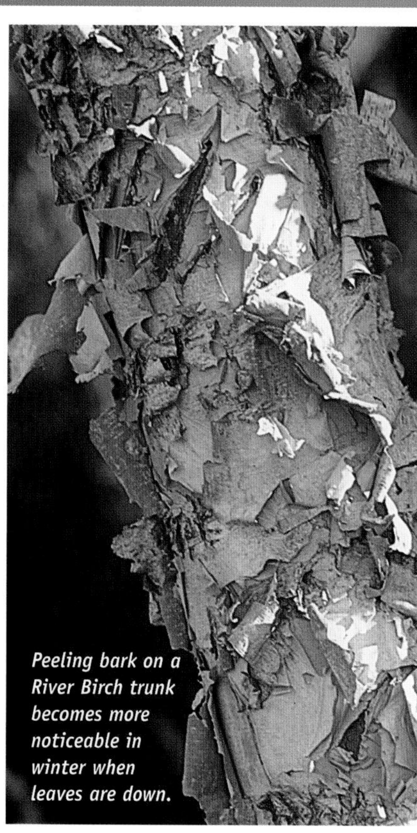

Peeling bark on a River Birch trunk becomes more noticeable in winter when leaves are down.

Honeylocust (Gleditsia triacanthos inermis) is known for its bright-green foliage. The leaf color is especially noticeable in spring.

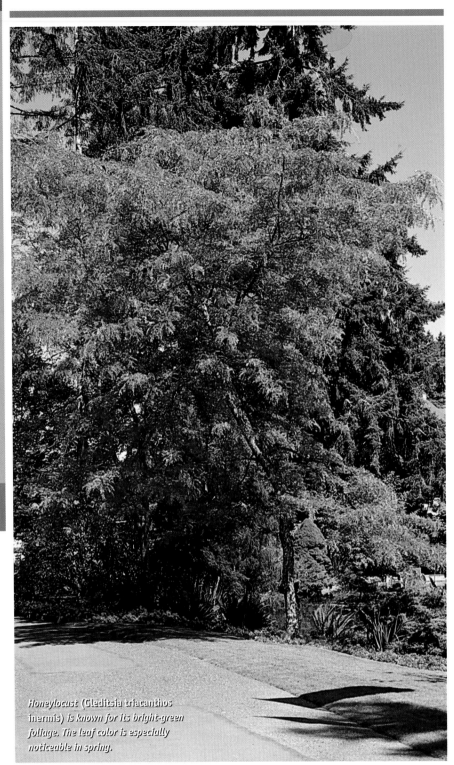

Weeping Willow (Salix babylonica) Page 102

Streetside trees

Common Name	Zones	Page
American Hornbeam *Carpinus caroliniana*	3-9	84
American Linden *Tilia americana*	2-8	105
American Smoke Tree *Cotinus obovatus*	4-8	85
European Hornbeam *Carpinus betulus*	4-7	83
Ginkgo *Ginkgo biloba*	3-9	88
Green Ash *Fraxinus pennsylvanica*	3-9	88
Honeylocust *Gleditsia triacanthos inermis*	3-9	89
Katsura Tree *Cercidiphyllum japonicum*	4-8	84
Northern Red Oak *Quercus rubra*	4-7	101
Norway Maple *Acer platanoides*	3-7	77
Pin Oak *Quercus palustris*	4-8	101
Pyramidal Japanese Yew *Taxus cuspidata 'Capitata'*	4-7	104
Red Maple *Acer rubrum*	3-9	78
River Birch *Betula nigra*	4-9	81
Russian Olive *Elaeagnus angustifolia*	2-7	87

Patio trees

Common Name	Zones	Page
American Hornbeam *Carpinus caroliniana*	3-9	84
American Smoke Tree *Cotinus obovatus*	4-8	85
Amur Maple *Acer tataricum ginnala*	2-6	77
Bradford Pear *Pyrus calleryana 'Bradford'*	4-8	98
Cockspur Hawthorn *Crataegus crus-galli 'Inermis'*	4-7	86
European Hornbeam *Carpinus betulus*	4-7	83
European Mountain Ash *Sorbus aucuparia*	4-7	103
Green Ash *Fraxinus pennsylvanica*	3-9	88
Japanese Flowering Crabapple *Malus floribunda*	3-8	91
Japanese Tree Lilac *Syringa reticulata*	3-7	104
Katsura Tree *Cercidiphyllum japonicum*	4-8	84
Newport Plum *Prunus cerasifera 'Newport'*	4-8	96
Pin Oak *Quercus palustris*	4-8	101
Red Maple *Acer rubrum*	3-9	78
Redbud *Cercis canadensis*	3-9	85
River Birch *Betula nigra*	4-9	81
Russian Olive *Elaeagnus angustifolia*	2-7	87
Washington Hawthorn *Crataegus phaenopyrum*	3-9	86
Whitespire Birch *Betula mandschurica japonica 'Whitespire'*	4-7	83

Trees for Every Need

Some trees are better suited for special jobs than others. Use these selection guides as a starting point for choosing the right tree for the right place. You will find other choices for sale, too. Availability varies by area and conditions (see page 21). Check with your garden center.

Quaking Aspen (Populus tremuloides) - Page 96

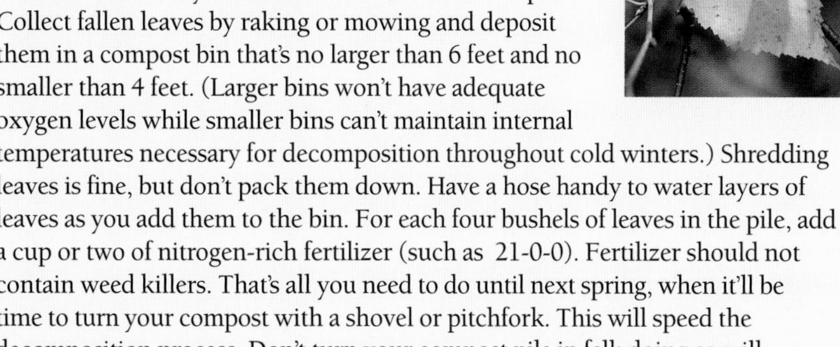

Composting Fallen Leaves

Natural Recycling is Nature's Bonus

Turn the leaves on your lawn into carbon-rich compost. Collect fallen leaves by raking or mowing and deposit them in a compost bin that's no larger than 6 feet and no smaller than 4 feet. (Larger bins won't have adequate oxygen levels while smaller bins can't maintain internal temperatures necessary for decomposition throughout cold winters.) Shredding leaves is fine, but don't pack them down. Have a hose handy to water layers of leaves as you add them to the bin. For each four bushels of leaves in the pile, add a cup or two of nitrogen-rich fertilizer (such as 21-0-0). Fertilizer should not contain weed killers. That's all you need to do until next spring, when it'll be time to turn your compost with a shovel or pitchfork. This will speed the decomposition process. Don't turn your compost pile in fall; doing so will allow heat to escape and keep internal temperatures too low for leaves to begin decomposing.

Accent trees

Common Name	Zones	Page
American Smoke Tree *Cotinus obovatus*	4-8	85
Amur Chokecherry *Prunus maackii*	2-6	97
Balsam Fir *Abies balsamea*	3-6	74
Bradford Pear *Pyrus calleryana 'Bradford'*	4-8	98
Cockspur Hawthorn *Crataegus crus-galli 'Inermis'*	4-7	86
Corkscrew Willow *Salix 'Golden Curls'*	4-8	103
European Mountain Ash *Sorbus aucuparia*	4-7	103
Ginkgo *Ginkgo biloba*	3-9	88
Japanese Flowering Crabapple *Malus floribunda*	3-8	91
Japanese Tree Lilac *Syringa reticulata*	3-7	104
Mayday Tree *Prunus padus commutata*	3-6	97
Newport Plum *Prunus cerasifera 'Newport'*	4-8	96
Plumleaf Crabapple *Malus prunifolia*	4-9	91
Quaking Aspen *Populus tremuloides*	2-6	96
Red Spruce *Picea rubens*	2-5	93
Redbud *Cercis canadensis*	3-9	85
Shadblow Serviceberry *Amelanchier canadensis*	3-8	80
Skyrocket Juniper *Juniperus scopulorum 'Skyrocket'*	4-8	89
Star Magnolia *Magnolia stellata*	4-9	90
Sugar Maple *Acer saccharum*	4-8	79
Washington Hawthorn *Crataegus phaenopyrum*	3-9	86

Trees for open areas

Common Name	Zones	Page
Common Horsechesnut *Aesculus hippocastanum*	3-7	80
Eastern Red Cedar *Juniperus virginiana*	3-9	90
Ginkgo *Ginkgo biloba*	3-9	88
Golden Weeping Willow *Salix alba 'Tristis'*	3-8	102
Northern Red Oak *Quercus rubra*	4-7	101
Ohio Buckeye *Aesculus glabra*	3-7	79
River Birch *Betula nigra*	4-9	81
Silver Maple *Acer saccharinum*	3-9	78
Sugar Maple *Acer saccharum*	4-8	79
Weeping Willow *Salix babylonica*	4-9	102

Availability varies by area and conditions (see page 21). Check with your garden center.

Shade trees

Common Name	Zones	Page
Common Horsechesnut *Aesculus hippocastanum*	3-7	80
Green Ash *Fraxinus pennsylvanica*	3-9	88
Honeylocust *Gleditsia triacanthos inermis*	3-9	89
Northern Red Oak *Quercus rubra*	4-7	101
Norway Maple *Acer platanoides*	3-7	77
Ohio Buckeye *Aesculus glabra*	3-7	79
Pin Oak *Quercus palustris*	4-8	101
Red Maple *Acer rubrum*	3-9	78
Redbud *Cercis canadensis*	3-9	85
Scarlet Oak *Quercus coccinea*	4-9	100
Silver Maple *Acer saccharinum*	3-9	78
Sugar Maple *Acer saccharum*	4-8	79
White Oak *Quercus alba*	3-9	100

Amur Chokecherry (Prunus maackii) Page 97

Abies balsamea

Balsam Fir

Outstanding Features:

- Tolerates cold weather, wind, and shade
- Dark green foliage all year-round
- Narrow, upright form for specimen use

Zones: 3-6

Light Needs:

Mature Size:

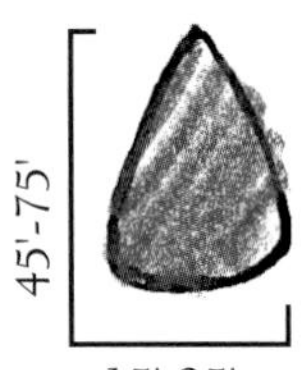

Growth Rate: slow to medium

evergreen tree

Needs: Plant in moist, acidic soils; trees will also grow in boggy areas and windswept summits. Plants look their best when grown in well-drained soil. Grow in partial shade. Prune only diseased or broken branches. Won't tolerate pollution.

Good for: screening for privacy or blocking poor views, vertical accent, providing background for trees and shrubs

More Choices: pages 30, 36, 40, and 73

Though it grows more than 50 feet high, a Balsam Fir may fit in a small yard. This pretty tree only gets about 15 to 20 feet wide. This tree is a good choice for higher elevations and temperature extremes. Trees are widely used for Christmas trees and wreaths.

Abies concolor

White Fir

Outstanding Features:

- Conical shape like a Christmas tree
- Bluish foliage stays fresh year-round
- Low maintenance and wide adaptability

Zones: 3-7

Light Needs:

Mature Size:

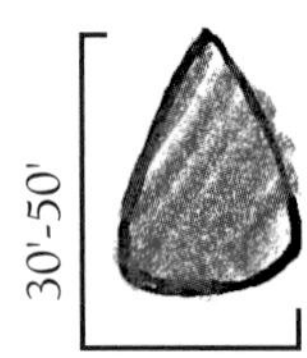

Growth Rate: slow to medium

evergreen tree

Needs: Plant in rich, moist, well-drained, sandy loam soil. Trees will tolerate rocky or dry soil, but growth is slower. Tolerates heat and cold equally well. Grow in full sun. Plant in a location where you won't need to prune.

Good for: specimen tree use, windbreaks, screening, background, adding fine texture, winter interest, and blue color to landscape compositions

More Choices: pages 30, 34, and 45

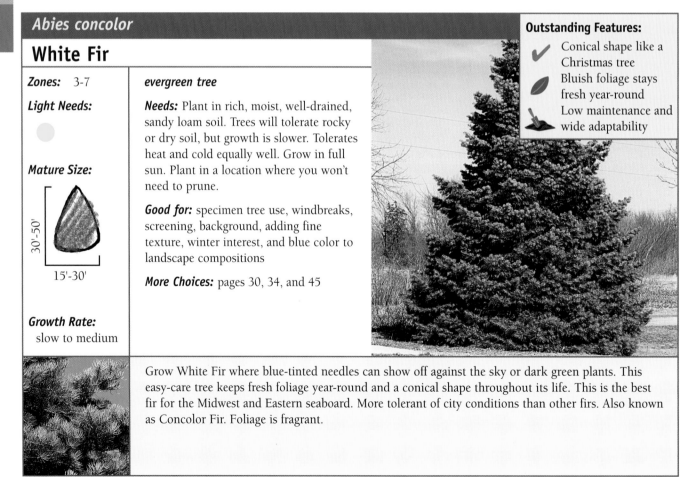

Grow White Fir where blue-tinted needles can show off against the sky or dark green plants. This easy-care tree keeps fresh foliage year-round and a conical shape throughout its life. This is the best fir for the Midwest and Eastern seaboard. More tolerant of city conditions than other firs. Also known as Concolor Fir. Foliage is fragrant.

Abies fraseri

Frasier Fir

Zones: 4-7

Light Needs:

Mature Size:

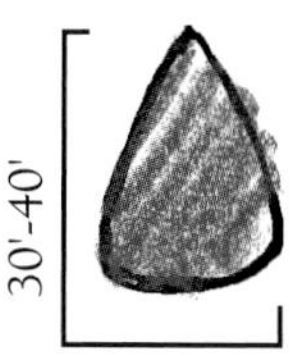

Growth Rate:
slow

evergreen tree

Needs: Grow in full sun or partial shade. Plant in moist, well-drained soil. Trees tolerate drier soil, but young trees will require watering during the first few years until well established. Not tolerant of heat or excessive drought.

Good for: specimen use, winter interest, screening to add privacy or to block poor views, providing background for shrubs and other trees

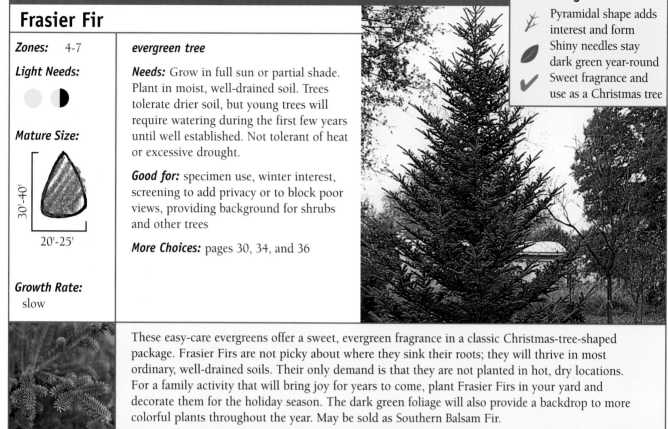

More Choices: pages 30, 34, and 36

Outstanding Features:

- Pyramidal shape adds interest and form
- Shiny needles stay dark green year-round
- Sweet fragrance and use as a Christmas tree

These easy-care evergreens offer a sweet, evergreen fragrance in a classic Christmas-tree-shaped package. Frasier Firs are not picky about where they sink their roots; they will thrive in most ordinary, well-drained soils. Their only demand is that they are not planted in hot, dry locations. For a family activity that will bring joy for years to come, plant Frasier Firs in your yard and decorate them for the holiday season. The dark green foliage will also provide a backdrop to more colorful plants throughout the year. May be sold as Southern Balsam Fir.

Abies veitchii

Veitch Fir

Zones: 3-6

Light Needs:

Mature Size:

Growth Rate:
medium to rapid

evergreen tree

Needs: Plant in acidic soils that are moist but well-drained. Grow in sun or partial shade. Prune only diseased or broken branches. Somewhat tolerant of urban growing conditions.

Good for: screening for privacy or blocking poor views, winter interest, providing background for deciduous trees and shrubs, cold regions of the country

More Choices: pages 30, 36, 40, and 63

Outstanding Features:

- Dark green needles; silvery undersides
- Immature cones have bright blue-gray color
- Pyramidal form with horizontal branches

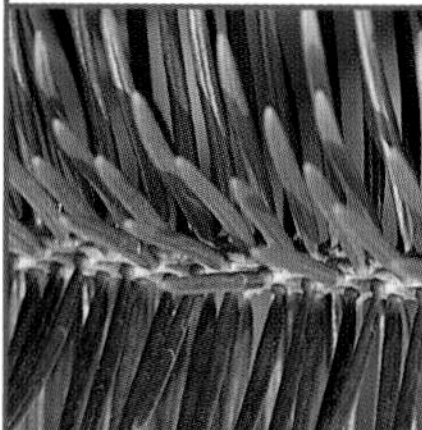

Evergreens are traditionally slow growing. Choose this species of fir when you need an evergreen tree that grows relatively quickly. Veitch Fir will provide pyramidal form even in urban areas.

Wrapping Maples for Winter

Maples make great shade trees and their leaves turn lovely colors in autumn. But come winter, these thin-barked trees need trunk protection.

On sunny winter days, the sun's rays warms the trunks, causing sap to rise. But when temperatures drop at night, the sap freezes and the thin bark splits. Not only are the resulting gashes unsightly, but they also damage trees and leave them vulnerable to harmful insects and diseases. Here's how to prevent this problem.

STUFF YOU'LL NEED

- ✔ Paper tree wrap
- ✔ Duct tape
- ✔ Scissors

What to Expect

Even big, healthy maple trees can suffer bark damage in winter. Don't forget to wrap them, too.

1

1 Wrap your maples in fall before the first freeze. Start at the base of the tree. You're going to work from the ground up. Loop the end of the tree wrap around the bark and tape it firmly to itself. Do not adhere tape to bark.

Wisdom of the Aisles

Paper or Plastic?

Paper tree wrap is superior to plastic because it's permeable, allowing the trunk to "breath". But plastic wrapping is worth the price if you have a problem each winter with hungry rodents gnawing your maples' bark away. Plastic wrapping is more of a deterrent than paper wrapping. Both types of wrapping must be removed promptly in spring after the last frost.

2

2 Work your way up the trunk, wrapping tightly. Each new layer should overlap the previous layer by half.

If you've never wrapped a tree trunk before, have a buddy help you. He can hold the wrap tightly in place as you continue working your way upward, much like a person holding a ribbon in place while you tie a bow. With a little practice, you'll soon be able to do the job without assistance.

3

3 Wrap the trunk all the way up to just beneath the first set of limbs. Cut the paper wrap and use duct tape to secure the cut end tightly in place. Do not adhere tape to bark.

4

4 Leave maple trunks wrapped all winter. Unwrap trees in spring after the danger of a final freeze has passed. It's important to remove wrapping from trees promptly when spring arrives. At first, leftover wrap can prevent the sun's rays from warming the trunk, delaying sap flow and leaf production. But as temperatures continue to climb, old wrapping left on trunks can trap heat and moisture between the wrapping and the bark. This is an ideal place for harboring pests and diseases.

Acer tataricum ginnala

Amur Maple

Outstanding Features:

- Leaves turn bright red or yellow in fall
- Small size and wide, spreading form
- Multitrunk form adds interest to winter scenes

Zones: 2-6

Light Needs:

Mature Size:

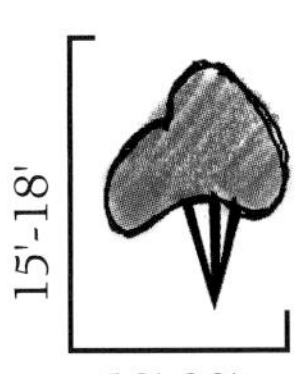

Growth Rate: slow

deciduous tree

Needs: Amur Maple grows best in moist, well-drained soil, but will thrive in drier soils as well. Plant in full sun or partial shade. Prune in summer or fall to minimize bleeding sap. Can withstand heavy pruning. Easy to transplant.

Good for: planting beside patios or decks, entries, or in front of blank walls, multi-stemmed specimen tree, containers

More Choices: pages 34, 36, 38, 71, and 72

Options: 'Red Fruit' boasts large quantities of bright red-winged seeds
'Flame' has outstanding fall color

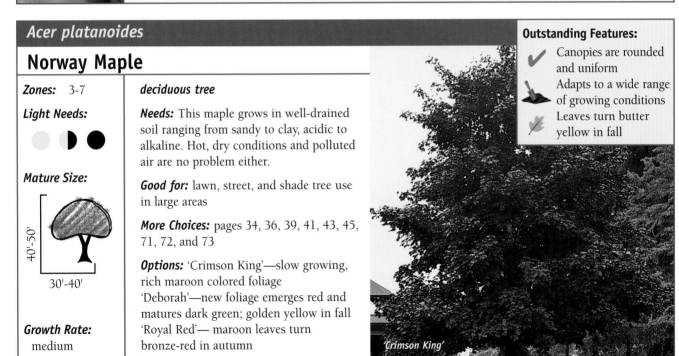

You can grow this hardy little maple as a traditional single-stemmed tree or in a multitrunk form. Trees grown in full sun develop the best fall color. Ornamental seed turns from green to red to brown in late summer and fall. Trees are pest-free and adaptable. They adapt well to life in above-ground containers. Known as a hard maple.

Acer platanoides

Norway Maple

Outstanding Features:

- Canopies are rounded and uniform
- Adapts to a wide range of growing conditions
- Leaves turn butter yellow in fall

Zones: 3-7

Light Needs:

Mature Size:

Growth Rate: medium

deciduous tree

Needs: This maple grows in well-drained soil ranging from sandy to clay, acidic to alkaline. Hot, dry conditions and polluted air are no problem either.

Good for: lawn, street, and shade tree use in large areas

More Choices: pages 34, 36, 39, 41, 43, 45, 71, 72, and 73

Options: 'Crimson King'—slow growing, rich maroon colored foliage
'Deborah'—new foliage emerges red and matures dark green; golden yellow in fall
'Royal Red'— maroon leaves turn bronze-red in autumn

'Crimson King'

Plant this tough tree for its large leaves that cast cooling shade in summer. Varieties are available with varying foliage colors and mature tree size. Roots can buckle nearby concrete. Grass doesn't grow well under its dense shade or shallow roots. Known as a hard maple. Try this cultivar as well: 'Schwedleri'—new leaves are purple, turning dark green in summer and changing to gold in fall.

Acer rubrum

Red Maple

Zones: 3-9

Light Needs:

Mature Size:

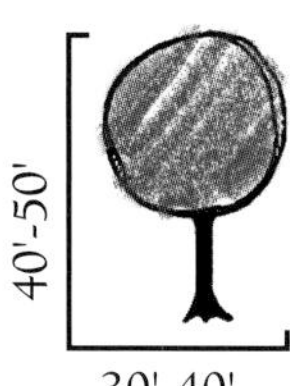

Growth Rate: rapid

deciduous tree

Needs: Grow in any kind of soil, from alkaline to acidic, rich to poor, or wet to dry. Grow in full sun or partial shade. Water new trees regularly for the first growing season; after that, trees rarely need water. Tolerates heat and car exhaust.

Good for: shade trees, parking areas, street trees, lining long driveways, woodlands, patios, decks, fast-growing deciduous screens, beside ponds or creeks, in boggy areas or in hot, dry spots, natural areas

More Choices: pages 31, 36, 38, 39, 40, 43, 63, 71, 72, and 73

Outstanding Features:

- Leafy shade gives way to bright fall color
- Tolerant of a range of soil conditions
- Flowers and seeds appear before leaves

Grow this tough, native tree for a delicate blush of red in spring, leafy shade in summer, and brightly colored foliage in fall. Red Maples adapt to a variety of growing conditions. These trees grow naturally in swamps but are equally at home in a hot, dry parking area. Known as a hard maple. Try these cultivars: 'Autumn Flame'—leaves turn vivid red in early fall; 'October Glory'—brilliant orange or red fall foliage; 'Red Sunset'—foliage turns red in early fall; 'Bowhall'—symmetrical, narrow canopy; yellow to red fall leaves; 'Columnare'—narrow canopy about 10' wide, red fall foliage.

Acer saccharinum

Silver Maple

Zones: 3-9

Light Needs:

Mature Size:

Growth Rate: rapid

deciduous tree

Needs: Plant in full sun or partial shade. Tolerates a variety of soils, from acidic to alkaline and sandy loam to clay. Plant away from buildings, paving, and pipes.

Good for: shading, screening, adding quick shade and height to new yards, large open spaces.

More Choices: pages 31, 34, 36, 38, 39, 40, 41, 63, 71, and 73

Options: 'Silver Queen'—oval form, bears fewer seeds
'Skinneri'—stronger wood, deeply cut green leaves

Outstanding Features:

- Grows quickly; transplants easily
- Large leaves cast abundant shade
- Grows in a variety of soil conditions

Plant a Silver Maple to provide quick shade in broad, open areas. Silvery-back leaves turn lemon yellow in autumn. Because of its rapid growth, wood is weak and trees can break apart during storms; keep trees away from power lines or houses for this reason. Plant where roots can't invade septic or drainage systems. Keep roots away from paving. Short-lived compared to other maples. Known as a soft maple.

Acer saccharum

Sugar Maple

Zones: 4-8

Light Needs:

Mature Size:

Growth Rate: slow

deciduous tree

Needs: Plant in acidic soil that's moist but well-drained; avoid compacted clay, wet soil, or city conditions. Grow in full sun or partial shade. Fall color is best in sun.

Good for: shade trees, lawn trees, lining driveways and streets, large open spaces, seasonal accent, natural areas, large estates, formal landscapes, mountainsides

More Choices: pages 34, 36, 40, 71, and 73

Options: 'Green Mountain'—thick, deep green foliage
'Bonfire'—grows slightly faster
'Green Column'—leaves turn yellow-orange

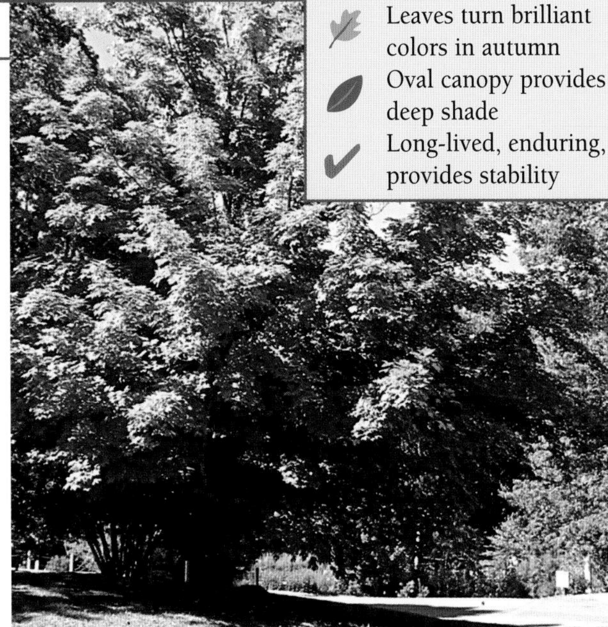

Outstanding Features:

- Leaves turn brilliant colors in autumn
- Oval canopy provides deep shade
- Long-lived, enduring, provides stability

Leafy summer shade followed by traffic-stopping fall color makes Sugar Maple an excellent choice for growing in large lawns or in rows along streets or driveways. Roots require large open spaces rather than restricted growing areas. Plants will grow well in the cooler areas of Zone 8. Known as a hard maple. Try these cultivars: 'Legacy'—drought-resistant; 'Flax Mill Majesty'—faster growing, red-orange leaves.

Aesculus glabra

Ohio Buckeye

Zones: 3-7

Light Needs:

Mature Size:

Growth Rate: medium

deciduous tree

Needs: Plant in deep, fertile soil that's moist but well-drained. Grow in full sun or partial shade. Mulch to keep roots moist and cool; avoid dry conditions.

Good for: shade tree or specimen use, natural areas, riverbanks, woodlands, large, open areas, parks

More Choices: pages 34, 36, 71, and 73

Outstanding Features:

- Large, yellow-green flowers in summer
- Low branched, broad rounded form
- Dense canopy of coarse-textured foliage

Give this tree room to grow and you'll enjoy cool, leafy shade for many years. Scented flowers in summer are an added bonus. Flowers are followed by inedible fruit. The seed is actually poisonous. Trees prefer moist locations and will not tolerate drought.

Aesculus hippocastanum

Common Horsechestnut

Zones: 3-7

Light Needs:

Mature Size:

Growth Rate: medium

deciduous tree

Needs: Plant in deep, fertile soil that's moist but well-drained. Tolerates acidic or alkaline soils. Grow in full sun or partial shade. Mulch to keep roots moist and cool; avoid dry conditions.

Good for: large open areas, shade tree use, contributing seasonal color and coarse texture, large estates

More Choices: pages 34, 36, 39, 41, 71, and 73

Outstanding Features:

- Large, dark green, coarse-textured leaves
- White flowers with yellow and pink
- Produces spiny fruit known as buckeyes

This attractive tree gets big and is best planted in large open spaces. Spikes of white flowers rise above coarse-textured leaves in late spring. Individual flowers have hints of yellow and pink on each petal. The buckeyes ripen in September. Dry soils bring on the condition called leaf scorch; don't let trees dry out. These large trees should not be planted in small yards.

Amelanchier canadensis

Shadblow Serviceberry

Zones: 3-8

Light Needs:

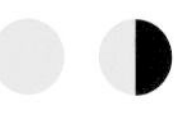

Mature Size:

Growth Rate: medium

deciduous tree

Needs: Plant in acidic, fertile soil. Trees thrive in moist soils that is well-drained or boggy; they're native to swamps. Grow in full sun to partial shade. For an upright, multi-stemmed form, remove suckers from the base of plants to encourage several main trunks.

Good for: specimen use, edges of woodlands, waterside areas, wet, boggy soils, seasonal accent, naturalized areas

More Choices: pages 34, 36, 39, 40, 71, and 73

Outstanding Features:

- White flowers in spring before leaves
- Tolerates wet, boggy soil conditions
- Leaves turn yellow to orange and red in fall

The wet, boggy soils found beside ponds and streams is ideal for growing this pretty little tree. Spring brings a cloud of white flowers; blue-black fruit attracts birds in summer; autumn brings beautifully colored foliage. Can be grown as a large shrub or multi-stemmed tree. Try: *A.* x *grandiflora* (Apple Serviceberry)—young leaves purplish, red fall color, 25' tall by 30' wide.

Amelanchier laevis

Allegheny Serviceberry

Zones: 4-8

Light Needs:

Mature Size:

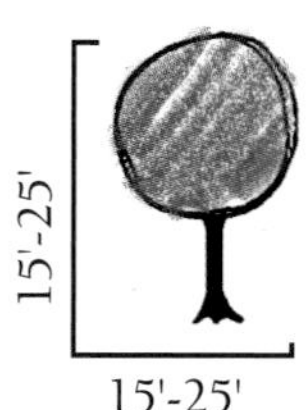

Growth Rate: medium

deciduous tree

Needs: Grow this tree in moist soil that's fertile and acidic. Wet, boggy soils are ideal. Provide a location with full sun or partial shade.

Good for: small specimen tree use, woodland gardens, naturalized areas, fall color, waterside locations, areas with wet soils

More Choices: pages 34, 36, 39, 40, 43, and 71

Outstanding Features:

- Tolerates moist, acidic soil conditions
- Sweet, black berries attract birds
- Attractive, orange-red fall color

This small, shrubby tree boasts white flowers followed by bronze leaves in spring. Foliage is green in summer and changes to a brilliant orange-red in fall. You can grow Allegheny Serviceberry in damp soil. Sweet, blue-black fruit attracts birds in July.

Betula nigra

River Birch

Zones: 4-9

Light Needs:

Mature Size:

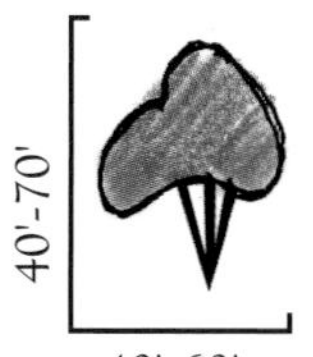

Growth Rate: rapid

deciduous tree

Needs: Plant in almost any soil from dry to soggy, poor or fertile. Acidic pH suits it best. Grow in full sun or partial shade. Prune only to remove obstructing low-hanging branches.

Good for: boggy areas, watersides, natural areas, beside patios and decks, along walkways, groves, open areas, deciduous screens, winter interest

More Choices: pages 31, 34, 36, 38, 39, 40, 63, 71, 72, and 73

Options: 'Heritage'—outstanding peely bark

Outstanding Features:

- Coarse-textured, peeling bark
- Fast-growing and adaptable
- Multiple trunks have instant presence

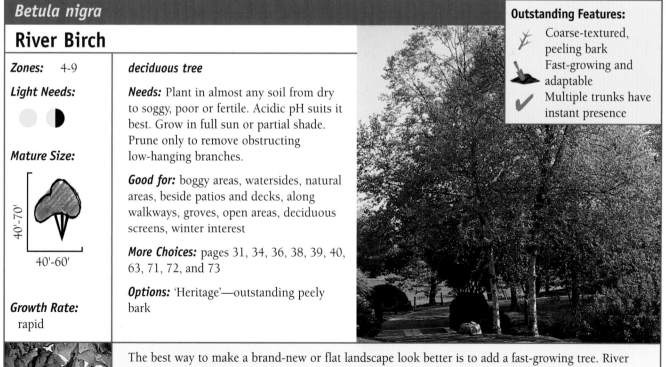

The best way to make a brand-new or flat landscape look better is to add a fast-growing tree. River Birch adds height, shade, and texture quickly. Peeling bark adds to its ornamental value throughout the year. River Birch is tolerant of a variety of growing conditions; it will even tolerate standing in water. Heat-tolerant too, this is the best birch tree for the South. Other birches become stressed when temperatures rise, making them more susceptible to damaging and potentially deadly pests. River Birch is NOT susceptible to borers; definitely an added landscaping bonus.

Betula papyrifera

Canoe Birch

Zones: 2-7

Light Needs:

Mature Size:

Growth Rate: medium to rapid

deciduous tree

Needs: Plant in full sun in acidic soil that's moist but well-drained. This birch thrives in cool, northern climates and transplants easily. Plant where low branches are not a problem. Or, remove obstructing branches in summer or fall when sap flow is less and bleeding from cuts is reduced.

Good for: specimen tree use, planting in groves, natural areas, adding interest to winter landscapes, large yards

More Choices: pages 34, 40, 63, and 71

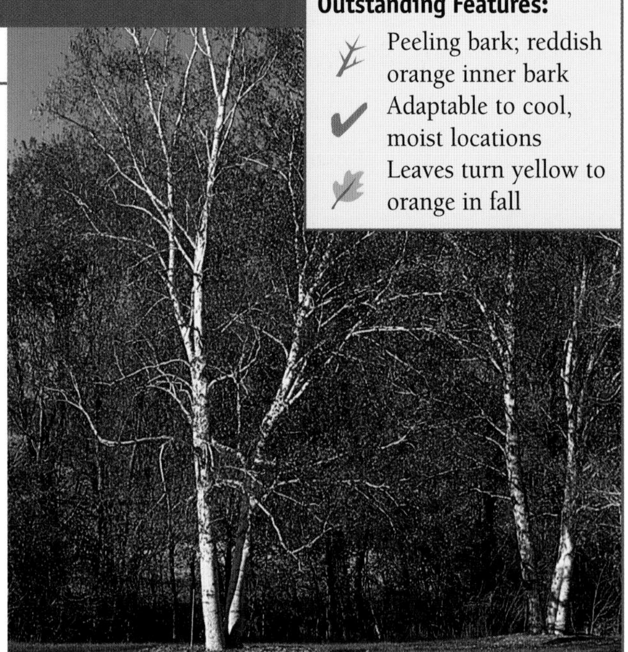

Outstanding Features:
- Peeling bark; reddish orange inner bark
- Adaptable to cool, moist locations
- Leaves turn yellow to orange in fall

When you plant a Canoe Birch, you're planting a piece of history. Native American Indians used the bark for making utensils, wigwam covers, and—hence the name—canoes. You'll want nothing more than to enjoy the beauty of its chalky white bark that peels away in papery layers. Canoe Birch is especially striking when planted against a backdrop of evergreens. The trees tower over 70 feet tall and add to fall's color show with leaves that turn shades of yellow and orange. Will not thrive in polluted areas. Also sold as Paper Birch.

Betula pendula

European White Birch

Zones: 2-7

Light Needs:

Mature Size:

Growth Rate: medium to rapid

deciduous tree

Needs: Plant in moist, well-drained soil. Keep roots cool with mulch or groundcover. Adaptable to alkaline soil pH. Grow in full sun to partial shade. Prune in summer or fall to prevent excessive bleeding of sap.

Good for: specimen tree, winter interest, groves, deciduous screen, corners of yards, cold growing regions,

More Choices: pages 34, 36, 40, 41, 63, and 71

Outstanding Features:
- White bark with distinct black marks
- Yellow fall foliage for seasonal appeal
- Multi-stemmed forms grow quickly

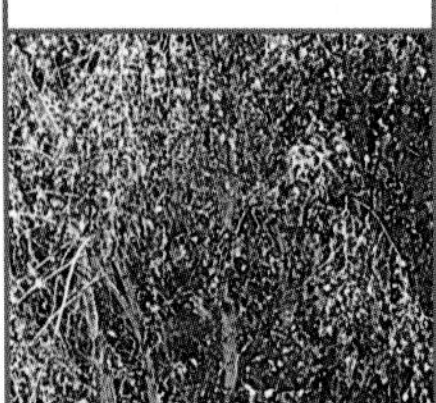

Striking black-and-white bark is the hallmark of this birch species. Trees grow best where summers are cool and moist. Glossy green, summer leaves turn yellow in the fall. Very attractive planted against evergreens. This is not a tree for heat and drought. Stressful growing conditions like these invite birch borer insects resulting in short-lived trees.

Betula mandschurica japonica 'Whitespire'

Whitespire Birch

Zones: 4-7

Light Needs:

Mature Size:

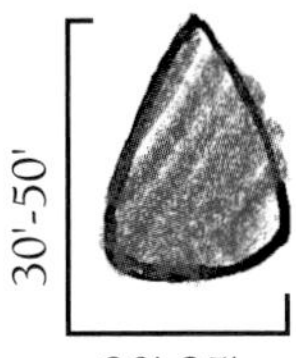

Growth Rate: medium to rapid

deciduous tree

Needs: Plant in acidic soil that's either moist or dry. Grow in full sun. Prune in summer or fall to prevent bleeding of sap. Plants are resistant to potentially deadly bronze birch borer infestations.

Good for: specimen tree, planting in groves, natural areas, adding winter interest, planting beside patios

More Choices: pages 34, 38, 40, 63, 71, and 72

Outstanding Features:

- Showy, chalk-white bark on trunks
- Yellow fall foliage adds seasonal interest
- Very resistant to bronze birch borer problems

The glossy, green leaves of this tree shimmer in summer breezes, turn yellow in autumn, and fall to reveal showy white branches in winter. Bark doesn't turn white until branches are about three to four years old. Bark does not peel like other species of birch.

Carpinus betulus

European Hornbeam

Zones: 4-7

Light Needs:

Mature Size:

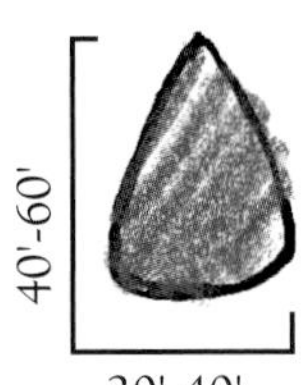

Growth Rate: slow to medium

deciduous tree

Needs: Grow in full sun or partial shade and provide well-drained soil. Roots won't tolerate standing water. Plants are tolerant of acidic or alkaline soil pH.

Good for: parking areas, entries, street trees, including in small yards, lawns, using near patios, in paving cut-outs, lining driveways, or as a high hedge

More Choices: pages 34, 36, 40, 41, 43, 71, and 72

Options: *C. caroliniana* (American Hornbeam)—multi-stemmed or single-stemmed tree, 20' to 30' tall by 40' to 50' wide; Zones 2-9

Outstanding Features:

- Shade tree suitable for small landscapes
- Roots won't disturb concrete paving
- Insect-free leaves are lush green in summer

This adaptable tree is easy to grow. Branches are arranged around trunks like a spiral staircase to form dense, tidy canopies. Trees are pest- and disease-free. Foliage turns yellow in fall. Also look at: 'Columnaris'—slow-growing columnar form, 30' tall by 20' wide; 'Fastigiata' (also sold as 'Pyramidalis')—vase-shaped tree, 30' to 50' tall by 20' to 40' wide; 'Pendula'—mound-forming with pendulous branches, 8' tall by 12' wide, often grafted.

Carpinus caroliniana

American Hornbeam

Outstanding Features:

- Thrives in soggy, acidic soils
- Leaves turn yellow, orange, and red in fall
- Long-lived tree when sited properly

Zones: 3-9

Light Needs:

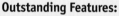

Mature Size:

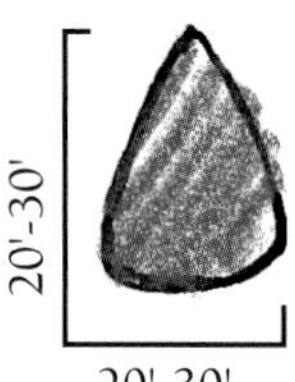

Growth Rate: slow

deciduous tree

Needs: Plant in deep, rich, soil that's slightly acidic. Trees thrive in moist soil but will tolerate drier ground. Wet, boggy soil is fine. Will grow in partial to full shade. Plant in spring.

Good for: small street trees, lawn trees, wet, boggy areas, waterside locations, natural areas, woodlands, beside patios

More Choices: pages 34, 36, 39, 40, 43, 71, and 72

Plant an American Hornbeam now and you'll enjoy it for many years to come. Brightly colored fall foliage is one good reason; tolerance of boggy soils is another. Smooth, gray bark earns this tree its nickname of Musclewood. Trees are best used in naturalized areas as an understory tree.

Cercidiphyllum japonicum

Katsura Tree

Outstanding Features:

- Leaves provide multiseason interest
- Roots will not disturb paving or sidewalks
- No special care; maintenance-free

Zones: 4-8

Light Needs:

Mature Size:

Growth Rate: medium to rapid

deciduous tree

Needs: Plant in full sun in soil that's well-drained and fertile. Grow in alkaline or acidic soils. Water young trees during periods of heat and drought. If several main stems emerge, prune the tree to a single trunk in late winter or early spring.

Good for: specimen use, patio areas, small yards, street trees, entries, courtyards, and parking areas

More Choices: pages 34, 40, 41, 63, 71, and 72

Here's a tree anyone can grow. Its size fits well with small home landscapes. Foliage emerges a reddish color in the spring, matures to a blue-green hue, and turns red and gold in the fall providing three-season interest. Fall color is best when grown in acidic soil. Fallen leaves smell of cinnamon or burnt sugar. Avoid planting in areas with northwestern exposure in the winter or where winds are extremely harsh.

Cercis canadensis

Redbud

Zones: 3-9

Light Needs:

Mature Size:

Growth Rate: medium

deciduous flowering tree

Needs: Will tolerate many soil types from sandy to clay and soil pH from acidic to alkaline. Prefers dry over soggy soil. Grow in full sun to partial shade. Prune to remove dead wood and open the canopy for light penetration.

Good for: specimen, patio, understory, and lawn tree use, seasonal accent, shrub and groundcover beds, woodland areas

More Choices: pages 31, 34, 36, 40, 41, 43, 63, 71, 72, and 73

Options: 'Alba'—white flowers
'Forest Pansy'—purple foliage in spring and fall

'Alba'

Outstanding Features:

- Purplish pink flowers appear before leaves
- Heart-shaped leaves turn yellow in fall
- Native tree proves tough and adaptable

Spring arrives early if you have a Redbud in your yard. April blooms appear on trees just a few years old. Older trees may form flower buds on tree trunks and provide conversation for the entire neighborhood. Attractive, heart-shaped leaves turn yellow in fall; color quality varies with genetics and light levels. Trunks divide close to the ground and develop graceful, ascending branches.

Cotinus obovatus

American Smoke Tree

Zones: 4-8

Light Needs:

Mature Size:

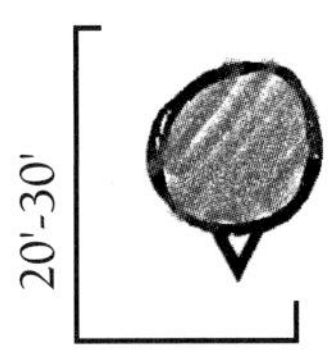

Growth Rate: slow

deciduous tree

Needs: Grow in full sun. Plant in soil that is moist or dry, poor or fertile, as long as it is well-drained. Trees thrive in alkaline soil pH. Tolerates urban conditions.

Good for: seasonal accent, small street tree, growing beside patios, parking areas, shrub border, mass plantings

More Choices: pages 34, 38, 41, 43, 71, 72, and 73

Options: *C. coggygria* –10' to 15' high and wide, Zones 5-8

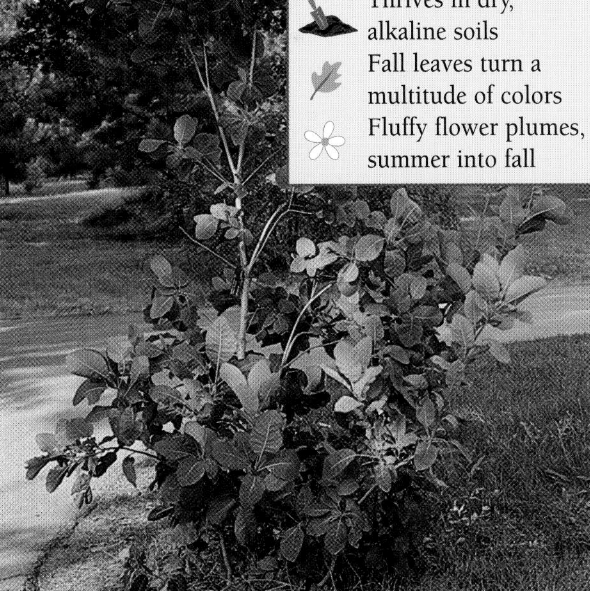

Outstanding Features:

- Thrives in dry, alkaline soils
- Fall leaves turn a multitude of colors
- Fluffy flower plumes, summer into fall

Plant this tree in your yard and everyone will want to know what it is. Flowering plumes are smokey pink in color and appear from June to September. Flowering is followed by head-turning fall foliage in colors ranging from yellow to orange and red to purple. Bark becomes scaly with age. Plants may be sold as *C. americanus*.

Crataegus crus-galli 'Inermis'

Cockspur Hawthorn

Zones: 4-7

Light Needs:

Mature Size:

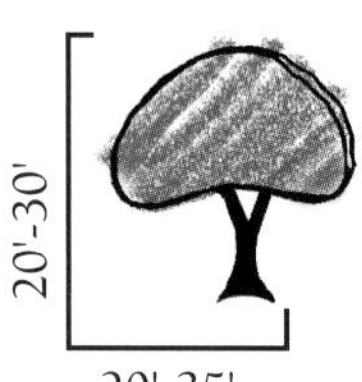

Growth Rate: medium

deciduous flowering tree

Needs: Plant in any soil that's well-drained, including acidic, alkaline, sandy, or clay. Grow in full sun to partial shade. Tolerates wind, coastal conditions, cold weather, and urban pollution. Little pruning is required.

Good for: specimen trees, seasonal accents, entries and courtyards, patio areas, coastal or urban landscapes, tall hedges, planting at corners of houses

More Choices: pages 23, 34, 36, 39, 40, 41, 43, 71, 72, and 73

Outstanding Features:

- White flowers appear in early spring
- Orange fall color; red berries last into winter
- Thornless stems and drought-resistant

This tough little tree provides flowers in spring, bright leaves in fall, and showy red fruit in winter. Look for the variety *inermis,* other kinds have thorns that can be dangerous to children and adults walking by. Plants grow vigorously in the landscape.

Crataegus phaenopyrum

Washington Hawthorn

Zones: 3-9

Light Needs:

Mature Size:

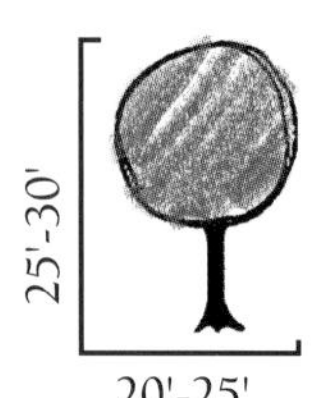

Growth Rate: medium

deciduous flowering tree

Needs: Plant in any soil, from acidic to alkaline, dry to moist, or poor to fertile. Grow in full sun or partial shade. Tolerates urban pollution and paving. Remove low-hanging branches for clearance if desired. Avoid planting in high-traffic areas because of the thorns.

Good for: specimen trees, seasonal accents, natural areas, growing in clusters, attracting birds, winter interest, narrow spaces, and hedges

More Choices: pages 34, 36, 38, 40, 41, 43, 71, 72, and 73

Outstanding Features:

- Clusters of white flowers in spring

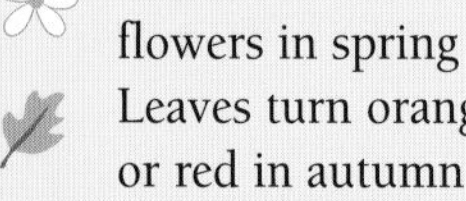

- Leaves turn orange or red in autumn

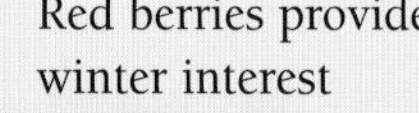

- Red berries provide winter interest

Here's a small tree that isn't picky about its growing conditions. Plant a few anywhere you want to add year-round color in the yard. White flowers tinged with pink start off the spring season followed by glossy green summer foliage. Colorful fall foliage raises the curtain for red fruit that persist throughout the winter. Thorny twigs add texture during the winter as well.

Elaeagnus angustifolia

Russian Olive

Outstanding Features:
- Tolerates salt, drought, and wind
- Fragrant flowers in late spring, summer
- Silvery, gray-green foliage adds contrast

Zones: 2-7

Light Needs:

Mature Size:

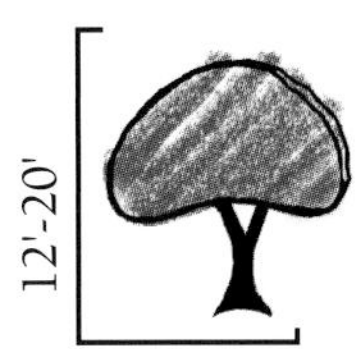

Growth Rate: medium to rapid

deciduous tree

Needs: This tough tree tolerates coastal winds; salty, poor soil; and drought. It can actually be planted in any kind of soil except soggy. Grow in full sun. Prune after flowering for a rounded shape. Or, let trees grow naturally into irregular forms. Roots will not disturb paving.

Good for: coastal areas, Xeriscaping, patio trees, street trees (withstands road salt), specimen use, natural areas, entries

More Choices: pages 23, 34, 40, 42, 63, 71, and 72

This tough tree takes cold, salt, wind, and dry soil. Foliage has silvery undersides and can't be beat for providing foliage contrast in the landscape. Trees add interest to areas enjoyed in the evening and tolerate troublesome areas. Tiny, yellowish flowers are fragrant. Keep plants growing vigorously for best performance.

Fagus grandifolia

American Beech

Outstanding Features:
- Leaves turn golden bronze in fall
- Wide, spreading canopy of foliage
- Winter interest and edible nuts

Zones: 3-9

Light Needs:

Mature Size:

Growth Rate: slow to medium

deciduous tree

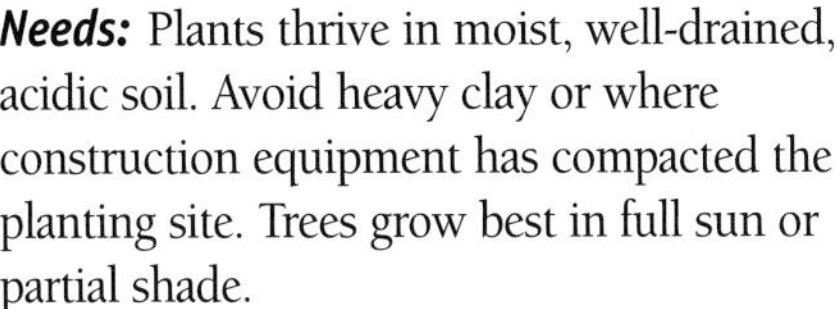

Needs: Plants thrive in moist, well-drained, acidic soil. Avoid heavy clay or where construction equipment has compacted the planting site. Trees grow best in full sun or partial shade.

Good for: specimen use, woodland and naturalized areas, attracting birds and wildlife, providing winter interest

More Choices: pages 34, 36, 40, and 71

Options: *Fagus sylvatica pendula*—weeping branches, full sun, Zones 5-7
Fagus sylvatica 'Purpurea Tricolor'—purple leaves, edged with pink and pinkish white, full sun, Zones 5-7

Smooth, gray trunks, golden fall foliage, and dried brown leaves that linger through the long winter months make American Beech an attractive landscape addition. Low, wide branches make a beautiful specimen in large open areas. The root system is very shallow and the canopy dense; growing a thick stand of grass can be a challenge. Mulch instead for improved tree health and less work for you. Nuts are edible and enjoyed by several species of birds and squirrels.

Fraxinus pennsylvanica

Green Ash

Outstanding Features:

- Transplants easily for fast-growing shade
- Leafy, spreading canopy turns yellow in fall
- Tolerates a range of growing conditions

Zones: 3-9

Light Needs:

Mature Size:

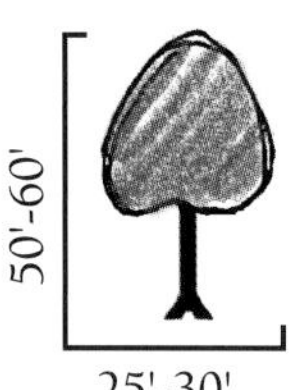

Growth Rate: rapid

deciduous tree

Needs: Plant in soils ranging from acidic to alkaline, wet to dry, compacted or loose. Tolerates drought, reflected heat from paving, and car exhaust. Roots won't buckle paving.

Good for: providing shade; lining walkways, driveways, or roadsides, planting in open lawns and parking areas

More Choices: pages 31, 34, 38, 39, 40, 41, 43, 63, 71, 72, and 73

Options: 'Marshall's Seedless'—rapid growth, seedless, insect-resistant
F. americana Autumn Purple—purple to chocolate brown fall color

Need shade? Grow Green Ash. This tree grows fast, lives a long life, and tolerates whatever growing conditions are thrown its way. Roots are well-behaved and will not buckle paving, though they will clog drains if given the opportunity. Trees are widely planted because of their ease of growth. Choose seedless varieties for less mess in the landscape. For a tree with a narrow, egg-shaped crown, choose 'Summit'.

Ginkgo biloba

Ginkgo

Outstanding Features:

- Striking golden fall foliage color
- Adaptable, easy to grow, and pest-free
- Angular limbs, pyramidal form

Zones: 3-9

Light Needs:

Mature Size:

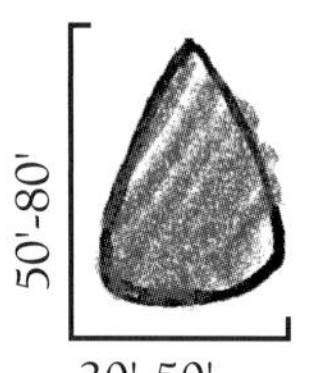

Growth Rate: slow

deciduous tree

Needs: Plant in a range of soils including acidic, alkaline, sandy, or clay. Ginkgo grows best in full sun. Trees are drought-resistant but grow faster with regular watering and a spring feeding of balanced fertilizer. No pruning is necessary except to remove lower limbs for clearance. Tolerates urban conditions, confined root spaces, heat, and cold.

Good for: specimen use, seasonal accents, street trees, lining walkways or drives, parking areas, open lawns, large estates

More Choices: pages 34, 38, 39, 40, 41, 43, 71, 72, and 73

Hold that rake; let the fallen leaves stay on the ground awhile. When Ginkgo's fan-shaped leaves turn golden in autumn, they hold their color even after dropping to the ground. This tree is considered to be one of the most attractive deciduous trees grown. Female trees produce messy fruit with an objectionable odor. There are several male clones available that do not produce fruit, including 'Autumn Gold', and the narrow-formed 'Fastigiata'.

Gleditsia triacanthos inermis

Honeylocust

Zones: 3-9

Light Needs:

Mature Size:

Growth Rate: rapid

deciduous tree

Needs: Plant in fertile, well-drained soil in full sun. Trees tolerate salt, drought, polluted air, and alkaline soils. Prune as needed to shape or remove dead wood.

Good for: shade, lawn, street, or specimen use; coastal areas, city conditions, areas prone to salting by winter road crews

More Choices: pages 23, 34, 41, 43, 63, 71, 72, and 73

Options: 'Shademaster'—seedless, 30' to 45' tall and wide
'Skyline'—pyramidal shape, to 50' tall
'Sunburst'—conical shape, new leaves yellow, 40' tall by 30' wide

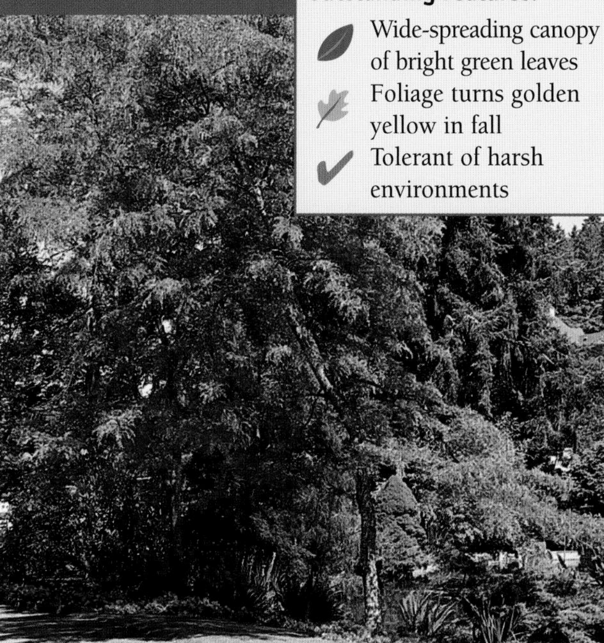

Outstanding Features:

- Wide-spreading canopy of bright green leaves
- Foliage turns golden yellow in fall
- Tolerant of harsh environments

You can grow grass beneath this broad shade tree. Fine-textured leaves are yellow-green in spring, bright green in summer, and golden yellow in fall. The true Honeylocust tree has dangerous thorns present on the trunk. Named selections are all thornless and most are seedless as well. Selections are widely available in the nursery trade today. Select one with the growth habit you desire for your yard.

Juniperus scopulorum 'Skyrocket'

Skyrocket Juniper

Zones: 4-8

Light Needs:

Mature Size:

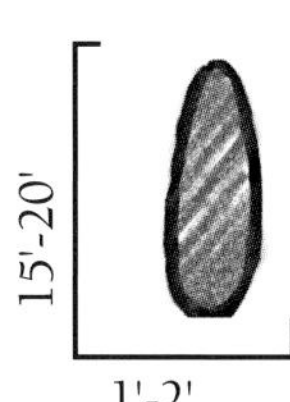

Growth Rate: slow

evergreen tree

Needs: Plant in full sun. This tree thrives in moist, well-drained soil but will grow in poor, dry soil, too. Tolerant of city conditions. Do not plant in soggy soil.

Good for: vertical accent, arid landscapes, hedges, screens, growing in groups as windbreaks, urban landscapes, Xeriscaping

More Choices: pages 30, 34, 38, 42, 43, 45, and 73

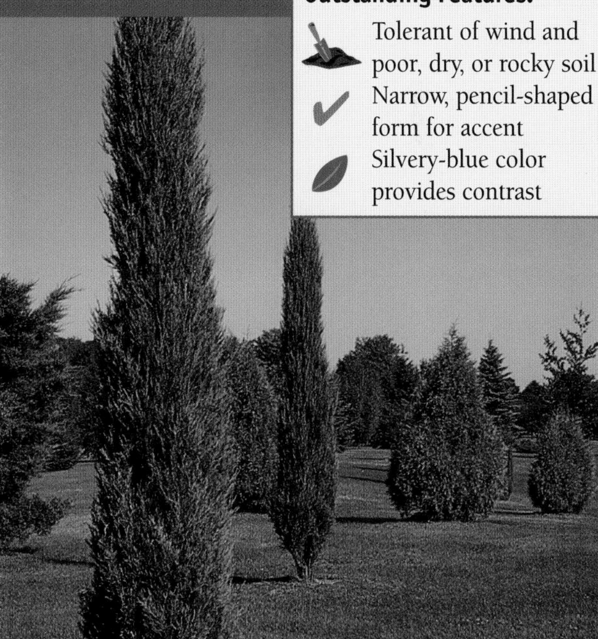

Outstanding Features:

- Tolerant of wind and poor, dry, or rocky soil
- Narrow, pencil-shaped form for accent
- Silvery-blue color provides contrast

Don't despair if your soil is dry and rocky and your region is windy. None of these conditions will faze 'Skyrocket' Juniper. Sometimes sold as Rocky Mountain Juniper, 'Skyrocket' is a preferred selection chosen especially for its narrow upright form and silvery-blue coloration. Plants tolerate the harsh growing conditions of the Midwest. Growth may be limited in clay soils.

Juniperus virginiana

Eastern Red Cedar

Outstanding Features:

- Dense foliage stays green year-round
- Withstands wind, salt, and dry conditions
- Conical form becomes pendulous with age

Zones: 3-9

Light Needs:

Mature Size:

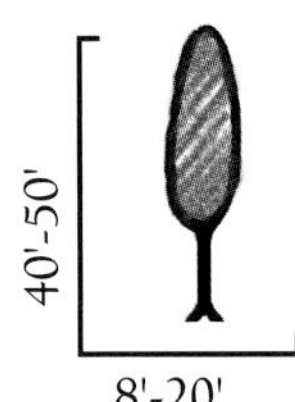

Growth Rate: medium

evergreen tree

Needs: Grow in any soil from acidic to alkaline, sandy to clay, wet to dry. Plant in full sun for densest growth. Trees grown in partial shade will be more open. Tolerates wind, salt, and drought. Water new trees regularly the first year to help them establish.

Good for: screening, privacy, windbreaks, shelter belts, seaside landscapes, hillsides, natural areas, providing background for deciduous trees and shrubs, attracting birds, hedges, topiaries

More Choices: pages 23, 30, 34, 38, 39, 40, 41, 42, 45, 71, and 73

Grow this durable native to block winds and screen poor views, provide a background for your garden, or to add needed privacy in the landscape. Trees are tough enough to plant at the beach and anywhere else you need its wide adaptability. Numerous cultivars are available with varying sizes, forms, and foliage color.

Magnolia stellata

Star Magnolia

Outstanding Features:

- Fragrant, white, starry blooms in early spring
- Green summer foliage turns yellow in fall
- Neat, small size for foundation planting

Zones: 4-9

Light Needs:

Mature Size:

Growth Rate: slow

deciduous flowering tree

Needs: Plant in moist, well-drained soil that's rich in organic matter and acidic in pH. Mulch trees well and water regularly to keep soil moist during summer months. Grows best in partial shade. Plant in warmer parts of Zone 4.

Good for: small specimen use, seasonal accent, foundation planting, narrow spaces, planting beside walkways or steps, natural areas, understory tree, woodlands, shaded courtyards

More Choices: pages 36, 40, 43, 71, and 73

Starry white blooms brighten shady spots during the gray days between winter and spring. This tree stays small and tidy. This is the earliest-blooming magnolia. Planting on a northern exposure may delay flowering and reduce flower loss due to freezing temperatures. Trees look great planted against red brick walls and buildings.

Malus floribunda

Japanese Flowering Crabapple

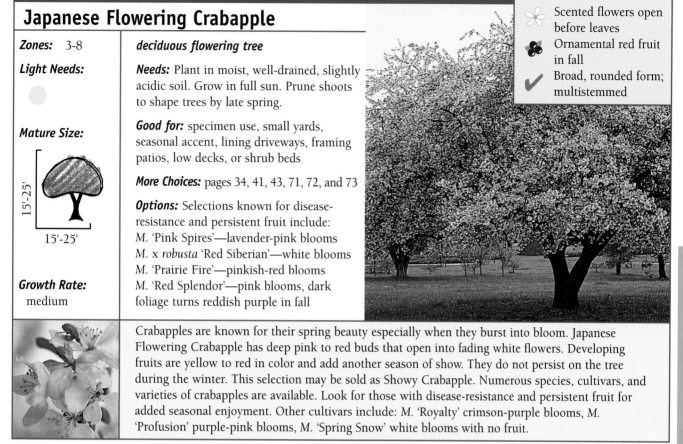

Outstanding Features:

- Scented flowers open before leaves
- Ornamental red fruit in fall
- Broad, rounded form; multistemmed

Zones: 3-8

Light Needs:

Mature Size:

Growth Rate: medium

deciduous flowering tree

Needs: Plant in moist, well-drained, slightly acidic soil. Grow in full sun. Prune shoots to shape trees by late spring.

Good for: specimen use, small yards, seasonal accent, lining driveways, framing patios, low decks, or shrub beds

More Choices: pages 34, 41, 43, 71, 72, and 73

Options: Selections known for disease-resistance and persistent fruit include:
M. 'Pink Spires'—lavender-pink blooms
M. x *robusta* 'Red Siberian'—white blooms
M. 'Prairie Fire'—pinkish-red blooms
M. 'Red Splendor'—pink blooms, dark foliage turns reddish purple in fall

Crabapples are known for their spring beauty especially when they burst into bloom. Japanese Flowering Crabapple has deep pink to red buds that open into fading white flowers. Developing fruits are yellow to red in color and add another season of show. They do not persist on the tree during the winter. This selection may be sold as Showy Crabapple. Numerous species, cultivars, and varieties of crabapples are available. Look for those with disease-resistance and persistent fruit for added seasonal enjoyment. Other cultivars include: *M.* 'Royalty' crimson-purple blooms, *M.* 'Profusion' purple-pink blooms, *M.* 'Spring Snow' white blooms with no fruit.

Malus prunifolia

Plumleaf Crabapple

Outstanding Features:

- Pinkish buds open into white flowers
- Edible red fruit adds winter interest
- Small size and overall rounded shape

Zones: 4-9

Light Needs:

Mature Size:

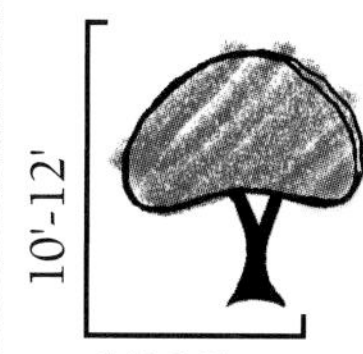

Growth Rate: medium

deciduous flowering tree

Needs: Grow in full sun. A heavy loam soil that's well-drained, moist, and acidic is ideal, but trees will grow in sites less than ideal. Remove water sprouts—non-blooming, thin twigs growing straight up from main branches.

Good for: specimen use, lawn tree, seasonal accent, lining driveways, planting along fences, adding winter interest, attracting birds

More Choices: pages 34, 40, 43, 71, and 73

Spring brings clouds of fragrant, white flowers before leaves emerge on this tree. Red fruit dangles like holiday ornaments through winter snows. One-inch fruit can be messy. Avoid planting near patios and walkways. Rake away fallen leaves and fruit to help control apple scab disease.

Picea abies

Norway Spruce

Zones: 2-7

Light Needs:

Mature Size:

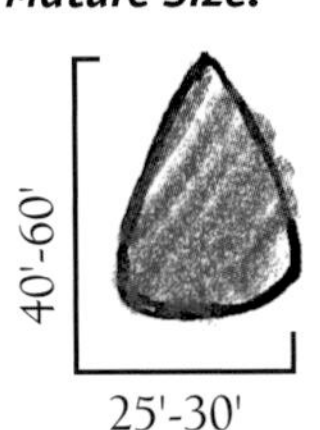

Growth Rate: medium to rapid

evergreen tree

Needs: Plant in acidic soil that's moist but well-drained. Water diligently during the early years of growth. After establishment, spruces can tolerate drier conditions. Clean air is necessary. Plants require little pruning. Grow best in cool climates.

Good for: windbreaks, background planting, large specimen use, defining property lines, screening, large estates, sheltering wild birds

More Choices: pages 30, 34, 39, 40, 45, and 63

Options: 'Aurea'—yellow-green needles

Outstanding Features:

- Pyramidal shape adds formality to landscapes
- Tolerates harsh winds and cold temperatures
- Evergreen foliage on pendulous branches

Spruce have the toughness and durability necessary to survive in colder climates. Wind and below zero temperatures are no problem for Norway Spruce. Trees grow to be quite large, so give them plenty of room from the start. Big cones, 4 to 6 inches long, persist on branches through winter. Also try: 'Pendula'—weeping shrub.

Picea glauca

White Spruce

Zones: 2-6

Light Needs:

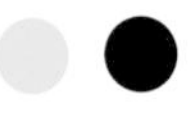

Mature Size:

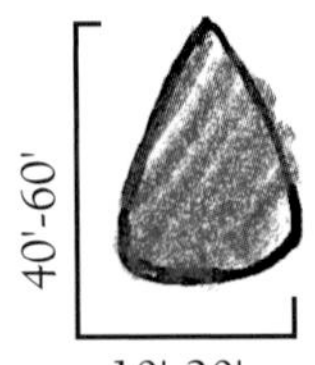

Growth Rate: medium

evergreen tree

Needs: Plant in acidic soil that's moist but well-drained. Water diligently during the early years of growth. After establishment, spruces can tolerate drier conditions. Clean air is necessary. Little pruning is needed. Grow in full sun or shade.

Good for: windbreaks, large specimen trees, screening to add privacy or block poor views, tall hedges

More Choices: pages 30, 34, 36, 40, and 45

Outstanding Features:

- Tolerates a wide range of harsh conditions

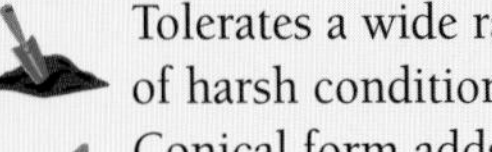

- Conical form adds formality in the yard

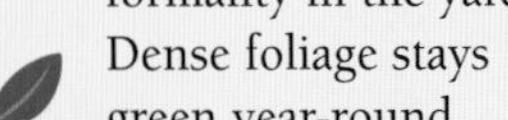

- Dense foliage stays green year-round

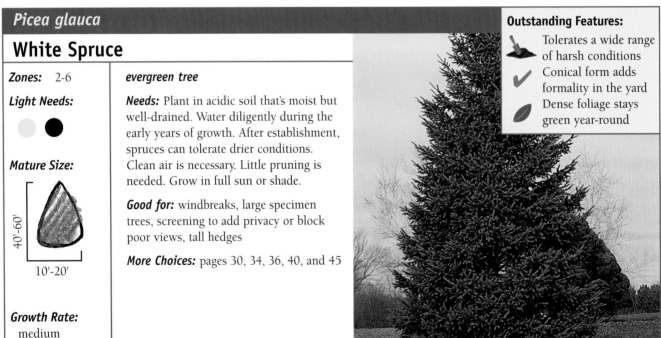

This tree withstands wind, heat, cold, shade, and drought—all the growing conditions found in the Plains States. No wonder it thrives there. Trees can tolerate overcrowding and transplant easily. Dense foliage stays green year-round. Cones are less than 2 inches long, green at first, then turning brown upon maturity.

Picea pungens glauca

Colorado Blue Spruce

Outstanding Features:

- Blue to blue-green needles year-round
- Dense branches extend to the ground
- Adaptability to a range of soil conditions

Zones: 2-7

Light Needs:

Mature Size:

Growth Rate: slow

evergreen tree

Needs: Grow in full sun. Trees grow best in rich, moist soil. They will tolerate dry soil conditions.

Good for: large specimen use, winter interest, windbreaks, grouping beside long driveways or in the corners of large yards, screening, sheltering wild birds

More Choices: pages 30, 34, and 45

Options: 'Koster'—silvery foliage
'Hoopsii'—blue-white needles; dense, pyramidal form

The blue foliage color of a Colorado Blue Spruce is attractive year-round. The degree of blueness can vary from tree to tree. Compare the colors and select the trees that fit your needs. Blue tree color can conflict with house colors. Select the color appropriately or plant trees away from the house. Cones grow 2 to 4 inches long.

Picea rubens

Red Spruce

Outstanding Features:

- Reddish-brown bark and cones
- Needlelike foliage on upturned branches
- Adapted to high mountain areas

Zones: 2-5

Light Needs:

Mature Size:

Growth Rate: medium

evergreen tree

Needs: Plant in deep, well-drained, neutral to acidic soil. Grow in full sun to partial shade. Prune only as needed to shape. Allow lower branches to remain on the tree and maintain conical form. Does not tolerate air pollution well.

Good for: vertical accent, specimen, winter interest, sheltering wild birds, screening, providing evergreen background for deciduous shrubs and trees

More Choices: pages 30, 34, 36, 40, 71, and 73

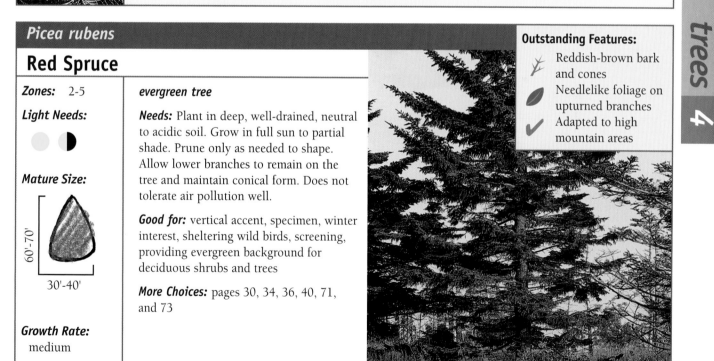

Choose Red Spruce when you want a tall, evergreen tree that is well adapted to the cold. The conical form and evergreen branches are attractive year-round, especially in snow. Attractive bark and cones add ornamental interest as well.

Pinus banksiana

Jack Pine

Zones: 2-6

Light Needs:

Mature Size:

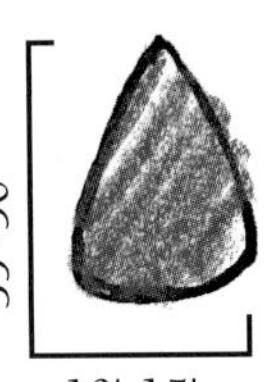

Growth Rate: slow to medium

evergreen tree

Needs: Plant in acidic soil; trees won't thrive in areas with alkaline soils. However, very poor, sandy soil or clay soil is fine. Grow in full sun. Tolerates extreme cold and wind.

Good for: arctic areas, windbreaks, mass plantings, screening, providing background in the landscape

More Choices: pages 30, 34, 40, and 45

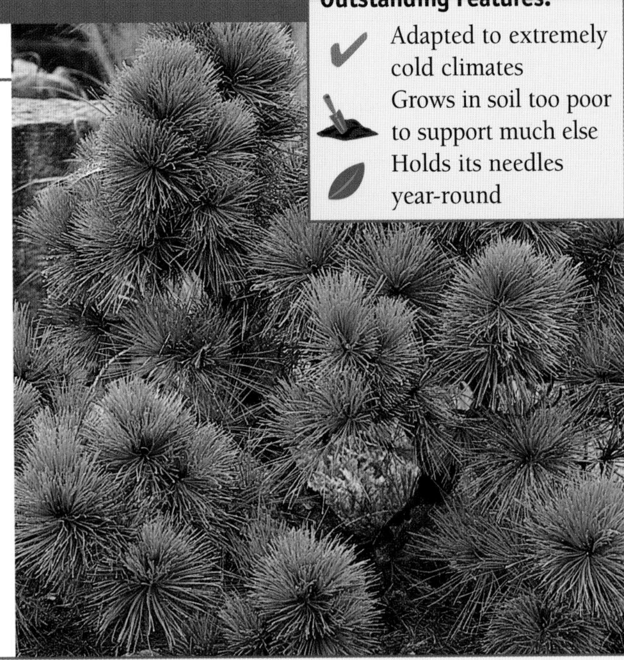

Outstanding Features:

- Adapted to extremely cold climates
- Grows in soil too poor to support much else
- Holds its needles year-round

Blasting wind, frigid temperatures, and impoverished soil are too harsh for most trees. If this describes your area, Jack Pine is the right plant for the place. A tough, evergreen tree, its form is irregular. Young trees are pyramidal while older trees may appear flat-topped.

Pinus bungeana

Lacebark Pine

Zones: 4-7

Light Needs:

Mature Size:

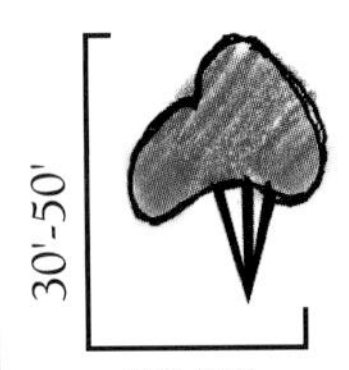

Growth Rate: slow

evergreen tree

Needs: Plant in any well-drained soil; acidic or alkaline pH is fine. Grow in full sun. Prune as desired to form multi- or single-stemmed trees. Trees grow best in cool climates.

Good for: specimen use, windbreaks, fine-textured background, dense, year-round screening for privacy or to block poor views, winter interest

More Choices: pages 30, 34, 40, 41, 45, and 71

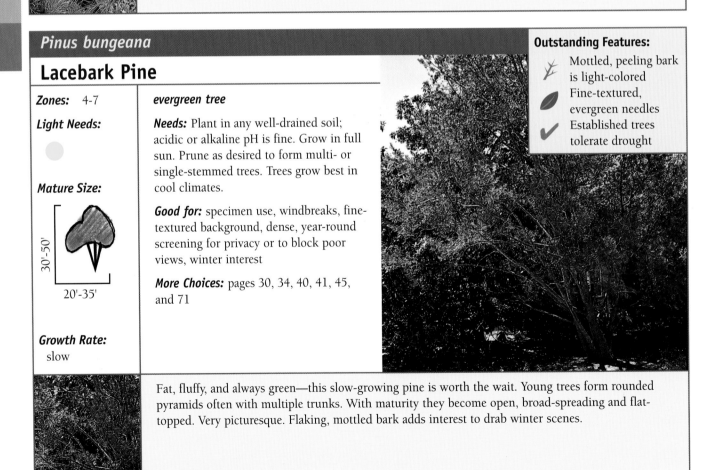

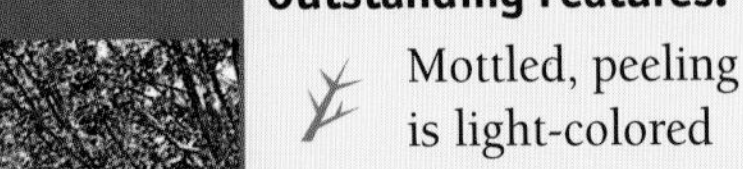

Outstanding Features:

- Mottled, peeling bark is light-colored
- Fine-textured, evergreen needles
- Established trees tolerate drought

Fat, fluffy, and always green—this slow-growing pine is worth the wait. Young trees form rounded pyramids often with multiple trunks. With maturity they become open, broad-spreading and flat-topped. Very picturesque. Flaking, mottled bark adds interest to drab winter scenes.

Pinus strobus

White Pine

Zones: 3-8

Light Needs:

Mature Size:

50'-80'

20'-40'

Growth Rate: rapid

evergreen tree

Needs: Plant in any well-drained soil; trees thrive in many extremes except heavy, clay soil. Grow in full sun. Trees transplant easily into the landscape. They are not tolerant of high pollution levels.

Good for: screening for privacy and blocking poor views, filling large empty areas, background plantings, clustering together or planting in rows or groves

More Choices: pages 30, 34, 38, 39, 45, and 63

Outstanding Features:

- Fluffy, soft needles have a bluish hue
- Grows quickly for screen and hedge use
- Full-skirted, graceful, pyramidal form

It's hard to find a screening tree that grows as quickly or is as pretty as White Pine. Bluish green needles are three to five inches long, soft, and touchable. Given them room to grow, trees may reach 150 feet in height. They can also be sheared for hedging use. Allow fallen needles to accumulate as water-conserving, weed-controlling mulch. Water during dry spells. In colder areas, protect from sweeping winds and road salt. Also try: 'Nana'—dwarf globe white pine, a rounded shrub.

Pinus sylvestris

Scots Pine

Zones: 3-7

Light Needs:

Mature Size:

30'-60'

30'-40'

Growth Rate: medium

evergreen tree

Needs: Plant in full sun. Adapts to a wide range of soil types, but prefers acidic pH. Requires well-drained sites. Tolerates poor, dry soils. Trees are easy to transplant.

Good for: screening for privacy or to block poor views, specimen use, winter interest, natural areas, planting in masses

More Choices: pages 30, 34, 38, 45, and 71

Options: 'Aurea'—bright, golden yellow foliage in winter
'Edwin Hiller'—silvery blue needles
'Fastigiata'—narrow, upright with ascending branches, 25' tall, 3' to 10' wide

Outstanding Features:

- Peeling, textured bark; reddish-brown color
- Open, wide-spreading, flat-topped form
- Blue-green or yellow-green needles

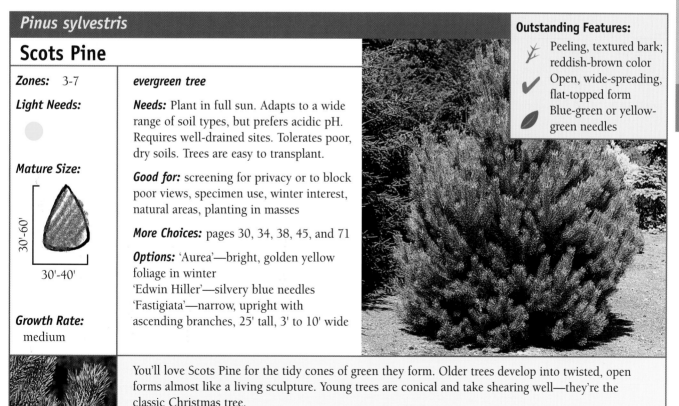

You'll love Scots Pine for the tidy cones of green they form. Older trees develop into twisted, open forms almost like a living sculpture. Young trees are conical and take shearing well—they're the classic Christmas tree.

Populus tremuloides

Quaking Aspen

Zones: 2-6

Light Needs:

Mature Size:

Growth Rate: rapid

deciduous tree

Needs: Grow in full sun or part shade. Trees grow best in well-drained, fertile soil but they'll grow in any soil that isn't waterlogged.

Good for: accent use, groves, natural areas, hillsides, new construction areas

More Choices: pages 34, 42, 63, 71, and 73

Outstanding Features:

- Leaves shake and shimmer in the breeze
- Leaves turn a brilliant golden yellow in fall
- Transplants easily and grows quickly

When breezes blow, the leaves of Quaking Aspen shake, shimmer, and whisper to the wind. Yellow autumn leaves are showy against silvery trunks. Trees are very adaptable to a range of growing conditions and fast-growing. Unfortunately they are short-lived. The usual life span is under 35 years.

Prunus cerasifera 'Newport'

Newport Plum

Zones: 4-8

Light Needs:

Mature Size:

Growth Rate: rapid

deciduous flowering tree

Needs: Plant in any average soil that drains well. Trees aren't particular about soil pH. Grow in full sun. Prune after flowering to shape and maintain size.

Good for: specimen use, seasonal accents, patio trees, courtyards, entries, planting in clusters at corners of lots or in shrub beds, small areas

More Choices: pages 34, 40, 41, 63, 71, 72, and 73

'Thundercloud'

Outstanding Features:

- Reddish purple summer foliage
- Pale pink to white flowers in spring
- Compact size for small landscape situations

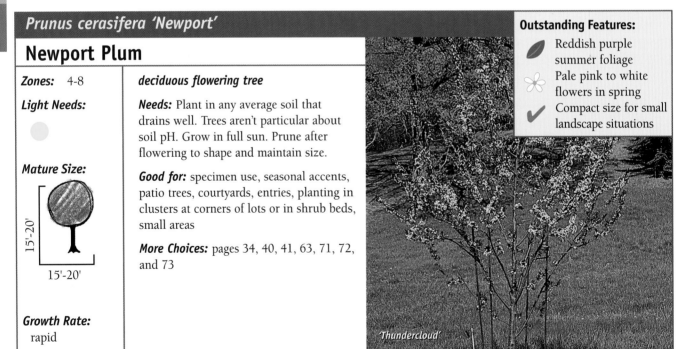

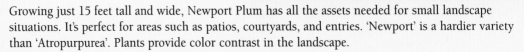

Growing just 15 feet tall and wide, Newport Plum has all the assets needed for small landscape situations. It's perfect for areas such as patios, courtyards, and entries. 'Newport' is a hardier variety than 'Atropurpurea'. Plants provide color contrast in the landscape.

Prunus maackii

Amur Chokecherry

Zones: 2-6

Light Needs:

Mature Size:

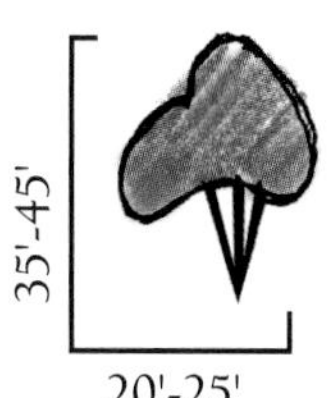

Growth Rate: medium to rapid

deciduous flowering tree

Needs: Plant in well-drained soil in full sun or partial shade. Naturally rounded canopy needs little or no pruning.

Good for: specimen use, seasonal accent, adding winter interest, attracting birds, fall color

More Choices: pages 34, 36, 63, 71, and 73

Outstanding Features:

- Shiny, cinnamon-colored, peeling bark
- Dense racemes of white spring flowers
- Thrives in cold regions of the country

It seems the colder the better for this spring flowering tree. White flowers are followed by small fruits ripening to black in August. Birds love them. Fruit can stain paving; avoid planting near walkways or patios. Yellow fall color completes the growing season display. The ornamental features of this tree don't end with leaf drop; shiny, cinnamon-colored bark brightens drab winter scenes. As trees mature, the bark exfoliates providing additional winter interest.

Prunus padus commutata

Mayday Tree

Zones: 3-6

Light Needs:

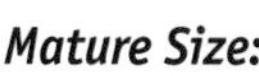

Mature Size:

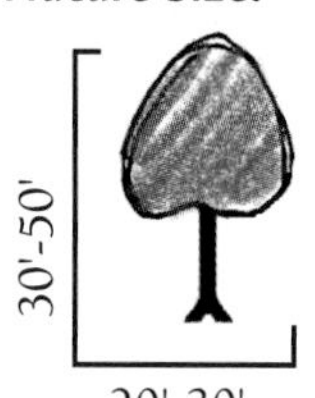

Growth Rate: medium

deciduous flowering tree

Needs: Plant in moist, well-drained soil that's somewhat fertile. Grow best in full sun. Little pruning is needed if mature size was taken into account prior to planting. Trees are low-branching. Thrives where summers are cool.

Good for: specimen use, seasonal accents, attracting birds, including in shrub beds

More Choices: pages 34, 71, and 73

Outstanding Features:

- Fragrant white flowers in midspring
- Leaves turn bronze or yellow in fall
- Small black fruits attract birds

If you're prone to early bouts of spring fever, plant a Mayday tree. Leaves are emerging while most trees are still bare; flowers open earlier than other kinds of Birdcherry trees. May also be sold as European Birdcherry—Mayday is a particular selection. One of the earliest trees to unfurl its leaves in the Midwest. Leaves turn shades of bronze and yellow in the fall.

Pseudotsuga menziesii

Douglas Fir

Outstanding Features:

- Classic, pyramidal shape; impressive size
- Evergreen needles stay fresh year-round
- Pendulous cones are light brown in color

Zones: 4-6

Light Needs:

Mature Size:

40'-80' × 12'-20'

Growth Rate: medium

evergreen tree

Needs: Plant in well-drained, moist soil with an acidic pH. Trees will not tolerate dry, poor soils or windy conditions. Grow in full sun.

Good for: specimen use, large groves, corners of yards, large estates, screening views, mass plantings

More Choices: pages 30, 34, and 40

Options: 'Fastigiata'—very upright, conical shape; 40' to 80' high, spread to 20'
var. *glauca*—needles are blue-green; 40' to 80' high, spread 12' to 20'
'Oudemansii'—15' to 30' high, spread 12' to 20'

Grow this stately tree where it will have room to grow up to its fullest potential. Slightly curving branches grow in pyramidal fashion. A traditional forest tree that makes the transition to the landscape beautifully. Trees are not suitable for use in windbreaks. May be sold as *P. douglasii*.

Pyrus calleryana 'Bradford'

Bradford Pear

Outstanding Features:

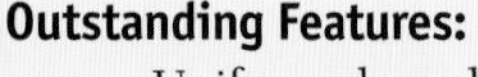

- Uniform shape like big lollipops
- White spring flowers before leaves

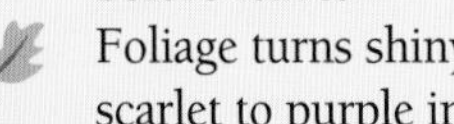

- Foliage turns shiny scarlet to purple in fall

Zones: 4-8

Light Needs:

Mature Size:

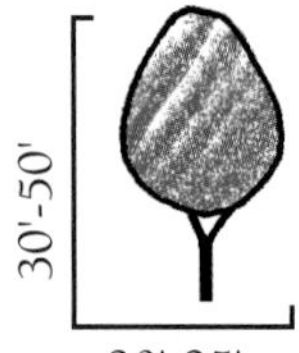

30'-50' × 20'-35'

Growth Rate: rapid

deciduous tree

Needs: Plant in any soil that's well-drained and receives full sun. Trees tolerate city conditions including polluted air and reflected heat from paving. Roots are well-behaved and won't buckle paving. Prune in late winter or early spring.

Good for: parking, lawns, and street trees, specimens, patios, courtyards, entries, lining driveways, growing in large planting beds, providing seasonal accent

More Choices: pages 31, 34, 43, 63, 71, 72, and 73

Bradford Pear combines all the features desired in an ornamental tree—rapid growth, spring bloom, summer shade, fruitless, and autumn color. Weak-wooded. Flowers have unpleasant odor. See the next page for pruning information that will help minimize winter damage. Try these cultivars in the landscape. 'Aristocrat'—less prone to splitting, 30' to 35' high, 20' to 25' wide; 'Capital'—fall leaves coppery, 40' high by 15' wide; 'Chanticleer'—less susceptible to freeze damage than 'Bradford', 30' high by 20' wide; 'Cleveland Select'—blooms very young, 30' to 35' high, 20' wide; 'Autumn Blaze'—35' tall by 20' wide, red fall color.

Pruning Bradford Pear

These ornamental pear trees are known for their uniformly shaped canopies. Pruning to remove narrow crotch angles is essential to keep trees from splitting apart during icy weather.

STUFF YOU'LL NEED

✔ Pruning saw
✔ Work gloves

What to Expect

You may be advised by tree care companies to flat-top your Bradford Pears. No tree should be flat-topped as a method of pruning. Tie canopies together when freezing rain is predicted to prevent splitting.

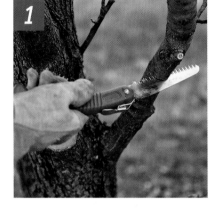

1 **To remove branches,** make the first cut with a pruning saw from the underside of the branch, about a foot from the trunk. Saw about a third of the way through. This cut stops the branch from ripping and splitting the bark.

2 **Make the second cut** about an inch farther out along the branch than the first one. Cut from the top of the branch until it comes off.

3 **Remove the remaining branch stub** by cutting upward from the bottom. Make your cut on the outside of the branch bark ridge (where the branch joins the trunk and bark is slightly raised). Trees heal best when pruned here.

4 **Watersprouts are vigorous shoots** that grow straight up from larger branches. They cross other branches and rub against them causing damage to both. Remove them with loppers or hand pruners in either spring or summer.

Quercus alba

White Oak

Outstanding Features:

- Purple fall color, leaves remain on tree
- Spreading canopies provide dense shade
- Long-lived, durable tree in the landscape

Zones: 3-9

Light Needs:

Mature Size:

Growth Rate: slow to medium

deciduous tree

Needs: Plant in acidic soil that's moist and well-drained. Grow in full sun. Avoid planting in areas where construction has compacted soils. Make pruning cuts in late winter or early spring.

Good for: shade tree use, large specimen trees, natural areas, woodlands

More Choices: pages 34, 38, 40, 71, and 73

Large landscapes deserve at least one White Oak to provide generations of leafy shade. Dark green summer foliage turns in the fall to a reddish wine color and finally to brown. Leaves are large, coarse, and may remain on the tree throughout the winter. Wood is sturdy.

Quercus coccinea

Scarlet Oak

Outstanding Features:

- Rounded, spreading canopies with age
- Leaves turn bright red in fall
- Impressive size is best suited for large areas

Zones: 4-9

Light Needs:

Mature Size:

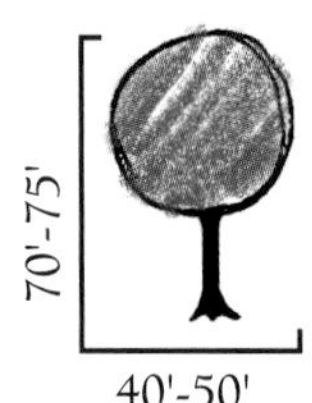

Growth Rate: medium to rapid

deciduous tree

Needs: Plant in acidic soil that's moist and well-drained. It will tolerate dry, sandy soils. Grow in full sun. Prune in late winter or early spring.

Good for: shade, lawn, large specimen use, natural areas, woodland landscapes

More Choices: pages 31, 34, 63, 71, and 73

For dense, summer shade and bright, fall color, add Scarlet Oak to your yard. Trees grow to an impressive size that works well with multistory homes and buildings. Young trees have a pyramidal form with a strong, central leader and pendulous, lower branches that drop off as the tree matures.

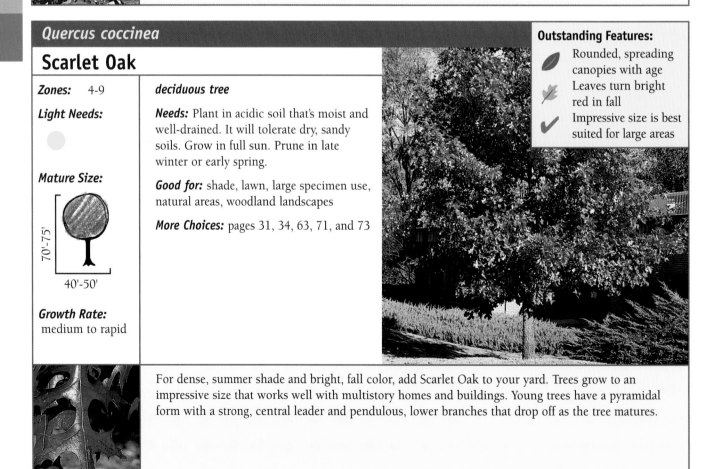

Quercus palustris

Pin Oak

Zones: 4-8

Light Needs:

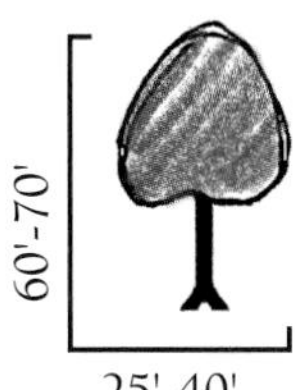

Mature Size:

Growth Rate: rapid

deciduous tree

Needs: Plant in moist, acidic soil—dry soil is OK, but not alkaline. Grow trees in full sun or partial shade. Endures confined roots, reflected heat from paving, and air pollution.

Good for: shade and street tree use, lining driveways, parking areas, urban conditions, parks, and golf courses

More Choices: pages 31, 34, 36, 38, 39, 40, 43, 63, 71, 72, and 73

Outstanding Features:

- One of the fastest growing oaks
- Tolerates a range of difficult conditions
- Pendulous branches, pyramidal form

In acidic soils there is nothing better than Pin Oak for a big, fast-growing shade tree. Roots won't buckle paving. Foliage turns scarlet in fall; brown leaves remain until spring. Surround with shade-tolerant groundcover, mulch, or paving; shade is too dense for a nice lawn. Remove lower branches for parking or walking beneath trees. Iron chlorosis is a common ailment of trees grown in alkaline soils. It is difficult to nearly impossible to remedy on a long-term basis. Select another tree species more suited to alkaline locations.

Quercus rubra

Northern Red Oak

Zones: 4-7

Light Needs:

Mature Size:

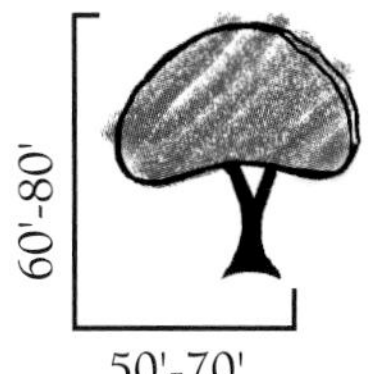

Growth Rate: rapid

deciduous tree

Needs: Plant in acidic soil that's moist but well-drained. Easy to transplant because it doesn't produce a taproot. Tolerates polluted city air. Plant in full sun.

Good for: shade and street tree use (in sites not confined by paving), specimen trees, large estates, open areas

More Choices: pages 34, 40, 43, 63, 71, 72, and 73

Outstanding Features:

- Glossy leaves turn dark red in fall
- Tolerates Midwest growing conditions
- Dense, rounded canopy provides shade

Though it's native to many parts of the United States, Northern Red Oak grows particularly well in the Midwest. Trees produce large, rounded canopies upon maturity. New foliage has a pinkish or reddish color when unfolding, turning dark green in summer. Foliage is coarse-textured and lobed. Fall color varies from dark to bright red depending on environmental conditions. Trees produce dense shade; it may be difficult to grow grass beneath the leafy canopies.

Salix alba 'Tristis'

Golden Weeping Willow

Outstanding Features:

- Pendulous branches sweep the ground
- Yellow-gold foliage during warm months
- Grows quickly; suitable for wet sites

Zones: 3-8

Light Needs:

Mature Size:

Growth Rate: rapid

deciduous tree

Needs: Grow in moist or wet soil in full sun. Tolerates a wide range of soil pH. Can withstand cold winter temperatures. Wood is weak and limbs break apart easily. Plan on gathering fallen limbs and small branches regularly.

Good for: specimen use, planting beside ponds or streams, wet areas, hillsides, large spaces,

More Choices: pages 34, 39, 42, 63, and 73

With it's large, rounded form and golden, weeping branches, this tree has a dramatic impact on the landscape. Plant near water to mirror the scene. Roots are invasive; avoid planting this tree near water lines, drain lines, or septic fields. Also sold as *Salix* x *sepulcralis chrysocoma*.

Salix babylonica

Weeping Willow

Outstanding Features:

- Pendulous branches sweep the ground
- Grows quickly to provide screening
- Large, dramatic form in the landscape

Zones: 4-8

Light Needs:

Mature Size:

Growth Rate: rapid

deciduous tree

Needs: Plant in soil that's wet or dry, fertile or poor. Lush, fast growth occurs when grown in moist locations. Grow in full sun. Leaves will shed prematurely during droughts.

Good for: specimen trees, beside ponds or streams, damp, boggy areas, hillsides, large spaces

More Choices: pages 23, 31, 34, 38, 39, 42, 63, and 73

Options: 'Niobe'—golden bark

If you have a large pond, you need a weeping willow to reflect on the water's surface. Streamerlike stems dangle to the water; roots love the soggy soil. Roots are invasive; don't plant this tree near waterlines, swimming pools, drain lines, or septic fields. Though they grow quickly, trees may be short-lived. Leaves, twigs, and branches drop frequently resulting in the need for constant cleanup.

Salix 'Golden Curls'

Corkscrew Willow

Outstanding Features:

- Young stems are twisted and yellow-orange
- Graceful, arching form; curled foliage
- Grows quickly and tolerates cold winters

Zones: 4-8

Light Needs:

Mature Size:

12'-15'

12'-15'

Growth Rate: rapid

deciduous tree

Needs: Tolerates most soils, though moist, well-drained soils are best. Trees won't thrive in shallow, alkaline soil. Grow in full sun to partial shade. Cut plants back early each spring to encourage the growth of stems with bright winter color.

Good for: specimen use, accent, winter interest, natural areas

More Choices: pages 34, 36, 63, and 73

Options: *S. matsudana* 'Tortuosa'—contorted branches, 50' tall by 25' wide 'Scarlet Curls'—contorted stems are reddish; leaves are curled contorted branches

Known for their twisty, contorted branches, Corkscrew Willows add interest to winter scenes when limbs are bare and exposed. 'Golden Curls' contributes brightly colored twigs, too. Great for growing in moist locations near water. May be sold as 'Erythroflexuosa'.

Sorbus aucuparia

European Mountain Ash

Outstanding Features:

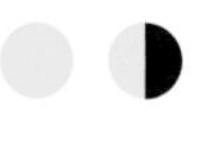

- Clusters of white flowers in spring
- Orange-red berries in summer
- Fine-textured leaves; attractive in fall

Zones: 4-7

Light Needs:

Mature Size:

30'-50'

15'-25'

Growth Rate: medium

deciduous flowering tree

Needs: Plant in fertile soil that's moist but well-drained. Neutral to acidic soil is best. Grow in full sun or partial shade. This tree thrives where summers are cool. Plants are not tolerant of summer heat or drought.

Good for: specimen use, seasonal accent, patio trees, courtyards, entries, attracting birds to the landscape

More Choices: pages 23, 34, 36, 39, 40, 71, 72, and 73

Options: *S. decora* (Showy Mountain Ash)—white flowers, red berries, orange-red fall foliage; Zones 3-8

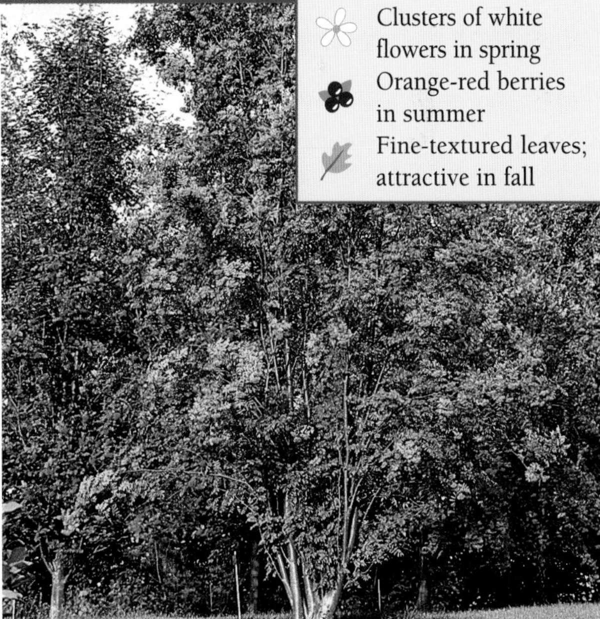

Three seasons of color make this tree a good choice for cooler climates. White spring flowers are followed by orange-red summer fruit and finally by yellow-red fall foliage. The scent of the flowers is unpleasant to some. Birds love the fruit and consume it as quickly as it ripens. Available as single or multitrunked trees.

Syringa reticulata

Japanese Tree Lilac

Zones: 3-7

Light Needs:

Mature Size:

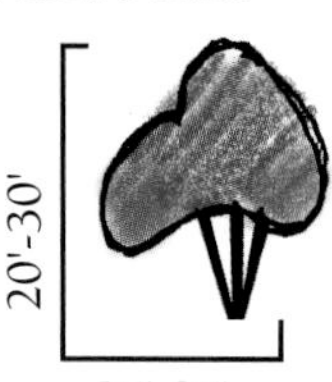

Growth Rate: medium

deciduous tree

Needs: Plant in well-drained, slightly acidic soil. Grow in full sun for best bloom. Remove spent flowers to keep plants looking neat. Prune unwanted branches in late winter or early spring. This tree thrives where summers are cool.

Good for: small specimen trees, seasonal accents, entries, patios, planting beside the corners of houses, planted in groups for screening and as backgrounds to deciduous shrubs and perennials

More Choices: pages 34, 40, 71, 72, and 73

Options: 'Summer Snow'—compact, rounded crown; profuse flowers

Outstanding Features:

- Creamy white flowers early to midsummer
- Dark green, heart-shaped leaves
- Resistant to borers, scale, and mildew

A Japanese Tree Lilac in bloom is a sight to see. Covered with snowy white flowers, the dark leaves provide the ideal backdrop. Trees thrive in areas with cold winters and cool summers. The flower show may be stronger on alternate years. Bark is a glossy, reddish-brown color. Additional varieties to consider include: 'Ivory Silk'—flowers appear on younger plants and 'Regent'—abundant flower production, uniform shape.

Taxus cuspidata 'Capitata'

Pyramidal Japanese Yew

Zones: 4-7

Light Needs:

Mature Size:

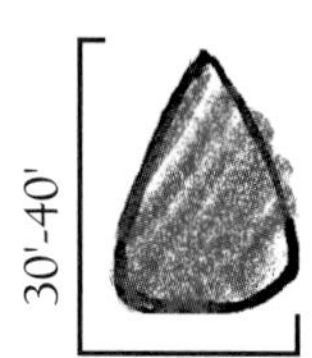

Growth Rate: slow

evergreen tree

Needs: Plant in any type of soil that's well-drained. This yew will grow in either sun or shade. Tolerates the dust and smoke of the city. Prune as much or as little as you like, whenever you like, to shape plants into dense, green canopies.

Good for: coastal areas, dry shade, city conditions, high hedges, screening to provide privacy or to block poor views, creating an evergreen background

More Choices: pages 23, 30, 34, 36, 38, 43, and 72

Outstanding Features:

- Dense evergreen foliage for screening
- Tolerates a range of harsh conditions
- Naturally pyramidal form tolerates pruning

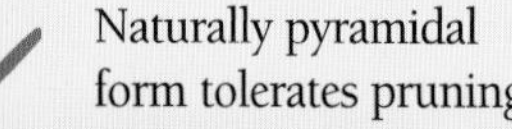

This evergreen tree can survive nearly any type of growing condition—except standing water. Dense, needlelike leaves remain dark green throughout the year. They make dense, year-round screens for privacy or to block unwanted views.

Thuja occidentalis

American Arborvitae

Zones: 2-7

Light Needs:

Mature Size:

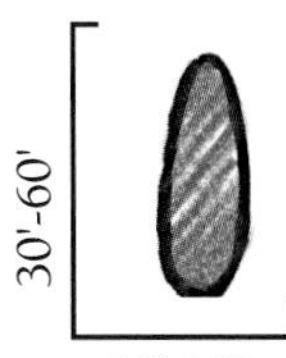

Growth Rate: slow-medium

evergreen tree

Needs: Plant in full sun in moist, well-drained soil; tolerates alkaline soils well. Protect from winter winds, snow, and ice. Prune to shape shrubs during the warm growing season.

Good for: specimen shrub, screen, foundation planting, anchoring the corner of planting beds

More Choices: pages 30, 34, 39, 41, and 45

Options: 'Emerald'—narrow, pyramidal shrub or small tree; leaves stay bright green through winter; 10' to 15' high, 3' to 4' wide; Zones 3-8

'Emerald'

Outstanding Features:

- Easy to maintain in desired shapes
- Easily established; low-maintenance
- Good foliage color throughout the winter

These low-care evergreens come in an assortment of shapes and sizes. There's easily one to fit every landscape setting. Many varieties have good foliage color throughout the winter months. Heavy snow or ice can break shrubs; knock snow away with a broom when it occurs. Also try: 'Pyramidalis'—narrow pyramidal shape; new leaves bright green; 12' to 15' high, 3' to 4' wide; Zones 3-8; 'Techny'—slow-growing, pyramidal form, 15' high, green all year.

Tilia americana

American Linden

Zones: 2-8

Light Needs:

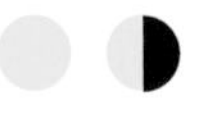

Mature Size:

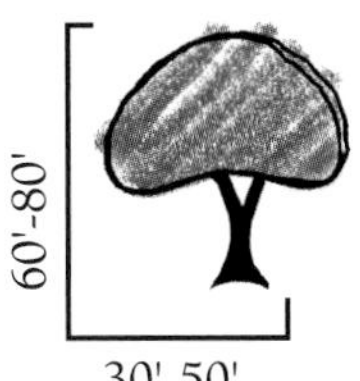

Growth Rate: medium

deciduous tree

Needs: Plant in moist soil that's well-drained. Trees grow best in alkaline soil but will tolerate some acidity. Will grow in shallow, rocky soil but mature size may be reduced. Grow in full sun or partial shade. Dislikes polluted air but withstands cold winters. Easy to transplant.

Good for: specimen use, shade trees, large estates, natural areas, wooded sites

More Choices: pages 34, 36, 39, 41, 71, and 72

Options: 'Redmond'—dense, pyramidal canopy; 45' tall by 25' wide
'Fastigiata'—conical form, upright form

Outstanding Features:

- Dark green foliage has lighter underside
- Fragrant, pale-yellow flowers in summer
- Pyramidal in youth rounded at maturity

Growing wild from Canada to Alabama, this tree is easy to transplant and grows very large. Coarse-textured leaves provide dense shade. Well suited for large areas. Selected varieties are more appropriate for home landscapes. May be sold as Basswood. Trees often reach 100' tall with age.

Chapter 5

shrubs

Graham Thomas Rose (Rosa Graham Thomas) Page 150

Shrubs add beauty to your landscape throughout the seasons. Plant groupings of the same shrubs together to show them at their best. For year-round interest, choose shrubs with various seasonal characteristics for grouping in different areas of your yard.

Burning Bush (Euonymus alatus) Page 133

Depend on Shrubs

Whether you're new to landscaping or have been working in your yard for years, this chapter helps you select, plant, and care for shrubs. The following pages offer tips and techniques. Landscaping decisions are a challenge because of the variety of available shrubs. But this chapter—complete with selection guides listing shrubs for specific purposes and growing conditions—makes it easier to buy the right shrub, plant it in the right place, and keep it thriving.

Provide the Framework

Rely on shrubs to supply the framework your landscape needs. Shrubs define spaces and hold the composition together. Use them to establish unity (see pages 12-13), provide background, screen unwanted views, complement your house, enhance privacy, and provide attractive accents. The selection guides help you select a palette of shrubs to beautify your landscape. They also provide ideas about solving problems identified when you made your site analysis. The guides match plants to the growing conditions of your yard and orchestrate a changing seasonal show of form and color.

Prepare to Purchase After you've chosen your shrubs for planting, you'll need to determine their arrangement in your planting beds. Start by finding out the growth rate and mature plant size. Shrub descriptions begin on page 124. Knowing these facts helps you space your shrubs correctly. As a general rule, set plants so that the distance between them—measuring from the center of one plant to the center of the next plant—is equal to or slightly less than the plant's mature spread. This gives shrubs room to grow and provide the desired massed effect without large gaps at maturity. Space slow-growing species a little closer together.

On paper, draw your planting beds to scale. Fill in with circles also drawn to scale and touching slightly that represent your plants at maturity. Remember they won't

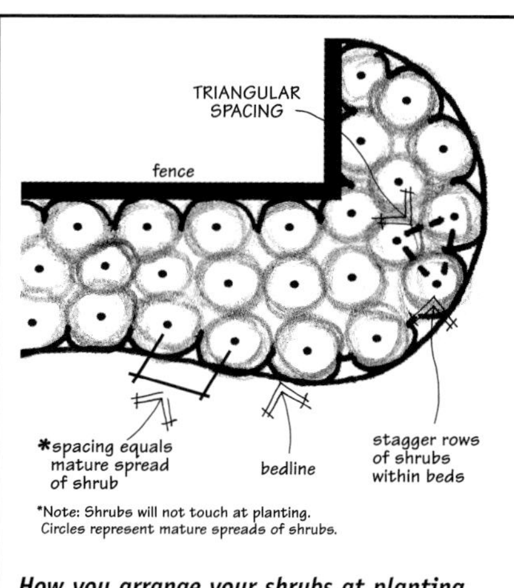
TRIANGULAR SPACING
fence
*spacing equals mature spread of shrub
bedline
stagger rows of shrubs within beds
*Note: Shrubs will not touch at planting. Circles represent mature spreads of shrubs.

How you arrange your shrubs at planting time has a big influence on how evident your bedlines become. The front row of the bed is the most important, so start there.

touch at planting time. Count the circles to determine how many shrubs of each type you will need before going to the store.

Prepare to Plant Arrange shrubs in the actual planting bed while still in their containers. You can finalize their spacing without worrying about shrubs drying out. (Always remove pots just before planting. Take only one plant out of its pot at a time.) First, position shrubs to follow the bedlines. This reinforces the shape of the bedline you spent so much time designing. Next, place shrubs in the back of the bed to follow elements that define this area, such as a fence or the wall of your home. Finally, fill the center by setting a second row behind the shrubs following the bedline. Stagger their placement in a triangular pattern (see diagram) so that no two shrubs line up. Work front to back, making adjustments and rearranging rows to avoid gaps. Before digging holes, move containers around until you're completely satisfied. Turn each shrub so that its best side faces the most important angle of view. Professionals take time with this phase. You should, too. You'll live with your decisions for a long time.

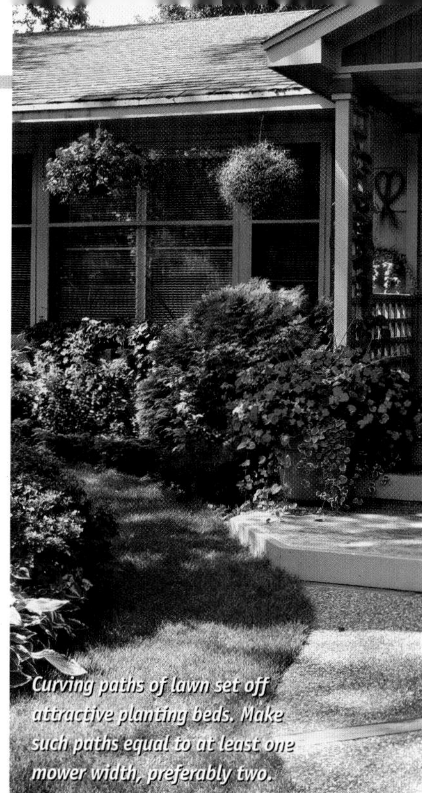

Curving paths of lawn set off attractive planting beds. Make such paths equal to at least one mower width, preferably two.

Wisdom of the Aisles

Plan before you plant. Placing plants correctly in the landscape is just as important as choosing the right ones. If this step has got you stumped, consider hiring a designer to help. Always ask to be taken to view completed landscapes before agreeing to design fees. Show the designer yards that you like, too. Landscape architects are professionals licensed to prepare plans to guide planting, grading, and construction. Garden designers aren't licensed but usually have a love of plants. (Expect to pay more for a plan produced by a landscape architect than for one drawn by a garden designer.) Design/build contractors will usually provide free designs as long as you hire them to do the work.

Hedges

Hedges are as functional as they are great-looking. Will yours be formal or informal, tall growing for screening and privacy or low growing for outlining a planting bed? Use this list to help guide your selections. On the pages referenced, look for photos and information about shrubs that include your growing zone.

Shrubs for hedging

Common Name	Zones	Page	Common Name	Zones	Page
Adelaide Hoodless Rose *Rosa 'Adelaide Hoodless'*	2-9	148	**Green Lustre Japanese Holly** *Ilex crenata 'Green Lustre'*	4-6	135
Amur Privet *Ligustrum amurense*	3-7	139	**Green Mound Alpine Currant** *Ribes alpinum 'Green Mound'*	2-7	147
Anglojap Yew *Taxus x media 'Densiformis'*	4-7	162	**Henry Kelsey Rose** *Rosa 'Henry Kelsey'*	3-9	150
Arrowwood Viburnum *Viburnum dentatum*	3-8	165	**Hick's Upright Yew** *Taxus x media 'Hicksii'*	4-7	163
Betty Prior Rose *Rosa 'Betty Prior'*	4-9	148	**Japanese Barberry** *Berberis thunbergii*	4-8	128
Bridalwreath Spirea *Spiraea prunifolia*	5-8	158	**Miss Kim Lilac** *Syringa patula 'Miss Kim'*	3-7	161
Carefree Beauty Rose *Rosa Carefree Beauty*	4-8	149	**Morden Centennial Rose** *Rosa 'Morden Centennial'*	2-9	152
Common Lilac *Syringa vulgaris*	3-7	162	**Northern Bayberry** *Myrica pensylvanica*	2-6	141
Compact Amer. Cranberrybush *Viburnum trilobum 'Alfredo'*	2-7	167	**Parson's Juniper** *Juniperus chinensis 'Parsonii'*	3-9	137
Coralberry *Symphoricarpos orbiculatus*	4-7	159	**Sir Thomas Lipton Rose** *Rosa 'Sir Thomas Lipton'*	2-7	153
Cornelian Cherry *Cornus mas*	4-8	131	**Tam Juniper** *Juniperus sabina 'Tamariscifolia'*	3-7	138
Cutleaf Lilac *Syringa x laciniata*	4-8	160	**Winterberry** *Ilex verticillata*	3-9	136
Dwarf Norway Spruce *Picea abies 'Pumila'*	3-8	142	**Wintergreen Boxwood** *Buxus microphylla 'Wintergreen'*	4-6	128
Emerald Arborvitae *Thuja occidentalis 'Emerald'*	2-7	163	**Yukon Belle Firethorn** *Pyracantha angustifolia Yukon Belle*	4-9	145

Availability varies by area and conditions (see page 21). Check with your garden center.

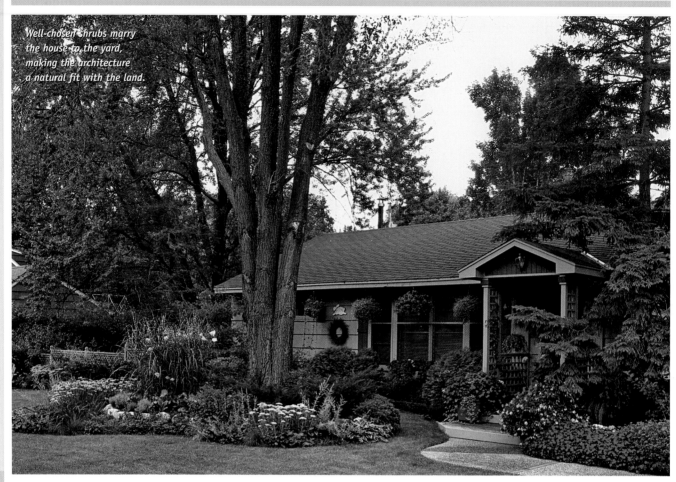

Well-chosen shrubs marry the house to the yard, making the architecture a natural fit with the land.

Foundation Planting

Plants growing close to your house are known as foundation plantings. Their primary functions are hiding the base of the house and connecting your home to the rest of the landscape. Shrubs provide numerous options for dressing up your home. Break out of the old mold— think about designs other than planting a straight hedge across the front of your home.

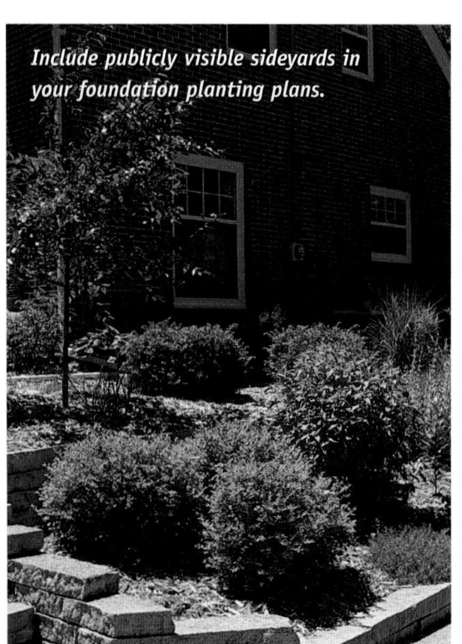

Include publicly visible sideyards in your foundation planting plans.

Bedlines First Your house should seem nestled into the landscape. For all but the most contemporary styles of architecture, which might call for angular lines, smoothly curving bedlines soften the straight lines of houses. This complements architecture, making houses become part of their settings.

Start planning your foundation planting by designing the bedline (see pages 46-47). A design plan results in a much more attractive project than if you limit yourself to following the shape of the house or keeping an old landscape. After drawing a rough sketch for the bedlines around your home, take a step back and look at your house. You'll want to enhance attractive features such as windows, stone chimneys, and the front-door area. Things you wish you didn't see—exposed foundations, meters, blank walls, and dingy siding—are candidates for screening.

Next, go inside your home and look out the windows. Do you keep the blinds shut to block glare or provide privacy? Use landscaping to solve such problems. Windows that you frequently look through should offer an attractive view. It's important that everyday living spaces, such as the kitchen, breakfast room, and den, have views. Make notes about what you see from them. If there's nothing to look at, it's time to add fresh landscaping for an attractive view. Remember this as you fine tune your sketches of bedlines, making the necessary adjustments.

Filling Beds Shrubs are the primary ingredient of most foundation plantings. If properly selected, they fit well beneath windows and grow together to form neat groups. Groups of shrubbery, known as masses, grow to form a single unit where individual plants are not noticed. Massing shrubs complements house size better than separate plants do. Resist the urge to prune each shrub into an individual plant; instead, let the shrubs grow together and trim only as needed to shape the mass.

Position shrubs in foundation plantings to follow bedlines, not the house. Fill curved beds with a curving arrangement of plants. If you already have a straight-line foundation planting, add more of the same shrubs in front of the hedge to stagger its shape. Then, add front layers of shorter plants arranged to follow the bedlines. Let the architecture of your house influence where you put accent plants. Fill in niches, frame attractive windows and doors, or add charming touches to porch posts and walls with trees, shrubs, groundcovers, and vines. (See page 207 to select appropriate vines that will grow on your home without damaging it.)

Foundation Shrubs

Select shrubs that include your range within their zones. Then, find more information on the pages specified. You'll need to know the mature size, rate of growth, and natural form of any plant you select to grow near your house. Don't choose naturally arching plants if what you want is a tightly clipped look.

Shrubs for foundation planting

Common Name	Zones	Page	Common Name	Zones	Page
Amur Privet *Ligustrum amurense*	3-7	139	Gray Dogwood *Cornus racemosa*	4-7	131
Anglojap Yew *Taxus x media 'Densiformis'*	4-7	162	Green Mound Alpine Currant *Ribes alpinum 'Green Mound'*	2-7	147
Carefree Beauty Rose *Rosa Carefree Beauty*	4-8	149	Inkberry *Ilex glabra 'Compacta'*	3-10	136
Carolina Azalea *Azalea carolinianum*	4-9	126	Japanese Barberry *Berberis thunbergii*	4-8	128
Catawba Rhododendron *Rhododendron catawbiense*	4-8	146	Limemound Spirea *Spiraea japonica Limemound*	4-9	158
Compact Amer. Cranberrybush *Viburnum trilobum 'Alfredo'*	2-7	167	Little Giant Arborvitae *Thuja occidentalis 'Little Giant'*	3-7	164
Cornelian Cherry *Cornus mas*	4-8	131	Mohican Viburnum *Viburnum lantana 'Mohican'*	4-8	165
Cornell Pink Azalea *Azalea mucronulatum 'Cornell Pink'*	4-7	127	Northern Bayberry *Myrica pensylvanica*	2-6	141
Dwarf Balsam Fir *Abies balsamea 'Nana'*	3-6	124	Northern Lights Azalea *Azalea 'Northern Lights'*	4-7	127
Dwarf Norway Spruce *Picea abies 'Pumila'*	3-8	142	Sea Green Juniper *Juniperus chinensis 'Sea Green'*	4-8	138
Emerald Arborvitae *Thuja occidentalis 'Emerald'*	2-7	163	Shrubby Cinquefoil *Potentilla fruticosa*	2-7	144
Exbury Azalea *Azalea 'Exbury Hybrids'*	4-7	126	Wintergreen Boxwood *Buxus microphylla 'Wintergreen'*	4-6	128

Availability varies by area and conditions (see page 21). Check with your garden center.

Some trees are not good near your home. Trees that grow large or have weak wood or invasive roots are poor choices for foundation planting. However, many small ornamental trees are just right for creating attractive focal points seen from main windows. They also offer a sense of shelter to people nearing your house along a walkway. The need to establish a transition between indoor and outdoor spaces is important, too; the sheltering effect of small trees helps do just that. Lastly, well-placed small trees help bring tall, multistory homes into human scale, making people feel more comfortable coming to your door.

Underplant such trees with shrubs and groundcovers to give your foundation planting a layered look that's sure to be an improvement over the single-row hedge style. Layers of shorter plants help to define your bedline plan and wrap your home with broad sweeps of plantings. Build a framework of evergreen plants for a solid background that enhances your home year-round and provides an anchor for landscape composition. Deciduous shrubs and small trees as well as annuals and perennials can be added in the foreground.

The foundation planting complements the casual, shingled style of this home.

Planting a Container Shrub

Planting shrubs correctly isn't difficult. Follow these steps to give your new plant the best possible start. Don't worry if you have an entire bed to fill. The more shrubs you plant, the more efficient and quicker you'll become at planting them.

STUFF YOU'LL NEED

- ✔ Sharpshooter or round-point shovel
- ✔ Topsoil or decomposed organic matter, such as compost
- ✔ Bagged gypsum for heavy clay soil

Optional:

- ✔ Tarp for collecting soil
- ✔ Wheelbarrow for mixing backfill soil
- ✔ Garden gloves

What to Expect

Workers hired to dig these holes might try to talk you out of making the holes as wide as they should be. Remain firm and your shrubs will thrive as a result.

1

1 Pick a spot to plant your new shrub. Make sure growing conditions match the needs of your plant. There should be enough space around the area for the shrub to grow undisturbed for many years to come.

Dig a hole twice as wide as the plant's container. This will give roots room to grow into the good, loosened soil before venturing through into native soil. Dig the hole only as deep as the container is tall to prevent planting too deep.

2

2 Carefully remove the shrub from its plastic pot and lay it on the ground. (Don't tug on the plant to pull it out.) If the roots are pot-bound, use the shovel blade to score the root ball. The root ball should retain the container's shape. Scoring encourages feeder roots to grow beyond the root ball, establishing the plant faster. If your plant seems loose, cut away the bottom and set the plant in the hole. Slice the sides and gently remove the pot. This will help prevent damage to young roots.

New plants need daily watering for the first few weeks, especially during hot weather. In cooler seasons, you can water every other day for the first week. After that, cut back to once a week for 2 to 3 months, then reduce to once a month, until shrubs have weathered a full growing season. Water faithfully unless nature supplies at least one-half inch of water during the week. Once established, properly sited plants will need supplemental water only during hot, dry spells.

3

3 Set the shrub in the hole to check the depth. The top of the root ball—where stems emerge from the soil— should be level with the surface of the undisturbed ground around the hole. If your shrub sits too low, the hole is too deep. Planting your shrub at this level causes stems to rot. Remove the plant and shovel additional soil into the bottom of the hole. Press loose soil firmly to prevent settling later. Put the plant into the hole to check the depth again. If the top of the root ball sits too high, remove the plant and dig the hole deeper. An exception to this step occurs when planting in heavy clay soils. In these locations, plant shrubs an inch or two higher than the level of the undisturbed soil to prevent water from collecting around roots.

Handling Your Shrub

▲ **Good** Always carry new plants by their nursery containers.

▲ **Not Good** Holding shrubs by their branches can stress and break roots and stems.

4 **Mix topsoil or composted organic matter** with the soil you dug from the hole, usually at a ratio of 1:1. In areas with high rainfall and heavy clay soil, reduce the amount of organic matter in the mix to 4:1.

Shovel the mixed soil around the plant, filling the hole completely. Don't tamp the soil in place because that can destroy porosity. Water to settle the soil. Add additional soil mixture as needed after settling.

Use excess soil to form a moat 3 to 4 inches high around the perimeter of the hole. Pat it firmly in place to keep water from running off the inside surface.

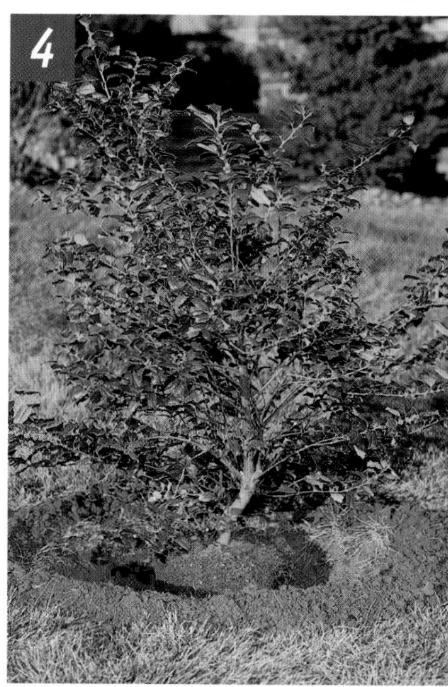

Good idea! **Put the best face on things.** Before backfilling, turn your shrub so that its best side is facing the direction from which it will be viewed. Once the dirt's in the hole, it's harder to adjust the shrub's direction.

5 **Mulch the area inside the moat with a 2- to 3-inch layer of organic matter.** Mulching retains moisture, cools the soil, and prevents weeds around the plant. Hay, pine straw, ground bark, compost, or shredded leaves are ideal. (Avoid bark nuggets, which float and wash away.) Use less mulch around stems. Mulch that fills the crotches of low stems can cause fungal problems.

Water your new shrub thoroughly. Lay a garden hose at the base of the plant and turn the water on to a gentle stream. Fill the moat slowly several times, letting water soak in.

Planting Shrubs on Slopes

Shrubs should always be planted upright, even if they're on sloping ground. Most upright stems will naturally reach for the vertical position as they grow, even if they have to bend to do so. Dig holes for shrubs on sloping sites much the way you would on a level site. Make sure plants are positioned straight up and down once they are placed in the hole. Build the soil moat only on the downhill side of the plant. The top of the moat should be level with the uphill soil. This prevents water from rushing down past the shrub before getting a chance to soak in. If your soil is heavy clay, omit the moat, but build up the soil to form a level planting area before setting your new shrub in place.

Pruning Evergreen Shrubs

Hold those clippers! There are things you need to know before pruning your evergreen shrubs.

First, determine what types of evergreens you have planted. Needled evergreens have needles surrounding plant stems. They are short or long, soft or stiff depending on the plant. Broad leaf evergreens have leaves ranging from the large leaves of rhododendrons to the small leaves of boxwood.

Pruning Style

Next, decide if the plant is going to, or should, have an informal or formal look. Plants informally pruned are not sheared into shapes the way shrubbery in formal gardens often are. Both needled and broad leaf evergreens can be pruned to maintain a naturalistic, informal style. Shrubs with small leaves and naturally compact forms are good choices for shearing into a formal style, as are many needled shrubs.

STUFF YOU'LL NEED

- ✔ Hand pruners for pencil-thick branches
- ✔ Loppers for bigger branches
- ✔ Hedge trimmers for shearing
- ✔ Sharpening stone
- ✔ Garden gloves

What to Expect

If you find it necessary to trim your shrubs late in the growing season, don't be surprised if fresh growth appears and then turns brown during a cold snap. While unsightly, the plant is unharmed.

Selective Pruning

When you're finished pruning selectively, all cuts will be concealed by foliage.

Selective pruning removes wayward branches while retaining a plant's natural form.

Why: To keep shrubs neat and control their size while maintaining natural, informal forms.

When: Prune needled evergreen shrubs in late winter or early spring. Prune flowering, broad leaf evergreens right after bloom.

How: Reach inside shrubs and look to find where each long shoot emerges from stiff, older wood. Make pruning cuts here, inside the shrub, removing only the flexible shoot. (Cuts on stiff, older wood will not sprout again.) Do not leave any stubs. Make cuts toward the tops of plants where sunlight prompts the most new growth. Avoid pruning evergreens severely at the bottom where there's less sunlight.

Shearing

Shearing cuts the surface of a plant instead of individual branches.

To give shrubs a tightly clipped, formal look, shear them on the surface, shaping them into the desired form. Plants suitable for shearing grow new twigs and leaves from each cut, making foliage thick and dense.

Why: To create a formal, sculpted look in the landscape.

When: Shear in warm weather, promoting fresh growth. Clip frequently to keep shrubs neatly trimmed and to control the size of evergreen shrubs.

How: Angle the blades of sharpened hedge trimmers as needed to cut the surface and to shape it. Stand back frequently to assess your work. Electric hedge trimmers make shearing large hedges easy. Use care to avoid overdoing it and whittling your shrubs away to bare branches.

Pinching

Pinching soft, new growth controls the size of evergreen shrubs.

Bright green sprouts on pines, spruce, and fir are called candles. Pinching by hand is the best way to control plant size and keep these evergreens neat without browning the tips.

Why: To control size and shape quickly and neatly during the early part of the growing season.

When: Pinch soft, new growth on nonflowering evergreens in late spring or early summer before the shoots "harden off," becoming stiff and woody.

How: Clasp the stem of the plant where the new growth is attached to the older wood. Pinch off the portion of new growth you want removed, even the entire shoot. Buds for next year's growth will form at this point.

Design Tip

Know the mature form of a young plant before you prune. Check the shrub encyclopedia or ask a garden staffer to describe its natural mature form. Many beautiful plants have been ruined by improper pruning.

The larger the leaf, the less pruning an evergreen shrub requires. Broad leaf evergreens with big leaves aren't well suited for shearing. Ragged, brown-edged foliage and blunted stems producing few leaves will result. If you want shrubs that can be clipped neatly into smooth forms, choose evergreens with naturally compact shapes. These shrubs have either needled foliage or small leaves.

Trim flowering evergreen shrubs when flowers fade. Use hand pruners to cut off the dead blooms and tips of small branches. This keeps plants from becoming shaggy and overgrown. Trimming prompts fresh growth and flower bud development for next year.

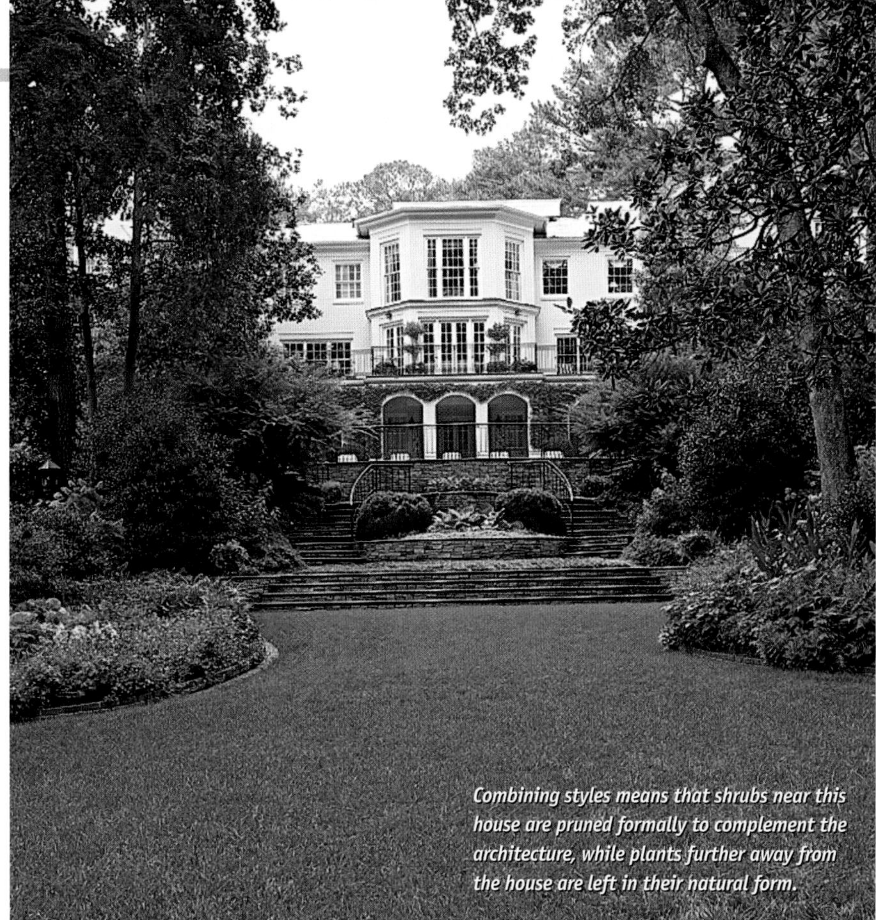

Combining styles means that shrubs near this house are pruned formally to complement the architecture, while plants further away from the house are left in their natural form.

Homer's Hindsight

I pruned my azaleas in autumn one year, long after they had finished blooming. The next spring, my shrubs had no flowers! Without realizing it, I had cut off all the new flower buds. Now I've learned that azaleas and lilacs bloom on "old wood." They form buds on this year's stems for next year. Pruning my azaleas and lilacs immediately after flowering ensures a beautiful display of flowers every spring.

Pruning Hedges

▲ ***Wrong*** Pruning hedges wider at the top than at the bottom results in lower branches with thin, spindly foliage over time. This is caused by the top of the plant shading the bottom of the plant too much.

▲ ***Right*** A hedge pruned narrower at the top than the bottom will stay lush and full from the ground up. Sunlight can reach plants from all angles.

Pruning Flowering Shrubs

Flowering shrubs need occasional shaping. Keep them under control without sacrificing flowers or form.

Selective Pruning

Prune spring-flowering shrubs when blossoms fade to avoid cutting off next year's flowers.

Prune spring flowering shrubs as soon as flowers fade. Many spring-flowering shrubs, such as lilacs, bloom on "old wood." They develop next year's flower buds on this year's growth. If you wait too late in the season to prune, you will remove next spring's show of blossoms. Summer blooming shrubs can be pruned in the spring before new growth begins.

Unless a shrub is severely overgrown and warrants hard pruning, make selective pruning your goal. Selective pruning reduces size and refines shape. No cuts are evident.

Reaching into shrubs to make cuts will hide unsightly stubs and preserve natural forms.

To prune selectively, locate an overgrown branch. Reach into the center of the plant so the cut is made deep within the shrub. Make your cut just above a leaf or where the stem emerges from a main branch. New growth will begin at this point. Pruning this way achieves three things. First, foliage hides ugly stubs from view. Second, removal of individual branches preserves the plant's natural form. Finally, selective pruning encourages prolific flowering. Sunlight reaches the center of the plant, promoting growth of new buds and leaves.

Give flowering shrubs a light pruning whenever you notice stray stems that have gone awry, giving your plant a hairy look. Use selective pruning methods to remove such branches so the natural form of the plant is preserved. (But don't get carried away and cut too much if flowering is long finished.)

Shearing a flowering shrub—cutting the outer edge of a branch to change a shrub's size and shape—eventually damages the plant. Dense, twiggy growth emerges from the multiple cuts, shading the center of the shrub. In time, leaves and flowers grow only along the outside edges of the plant, giving it a thin, scalped look. Some flowering shrubs send up long, stray shoots in protest, making trimming necessary all over again to eliminate the odd appearance of the plant.

STUFF YOU'LL NEED

- ✔ Bypass hand pruners
- ✔ Bypass loppers
- ✔ Rubbing alcohol

What to Expect

Avoid the temptation to switch from hand tools to electric trimmers. Unless you're trimming a big, formally clipped hedge, you'll be disappointed if you use them on most shrubs.

Wisdom of the Aisles

Rubbing alcohol is a bargain shopper's dream for plant disease prevention. Fill a spray bottle with the alcohol and make it a habit to spritz pruning tools to sterilize them between cuts, even when you're working on just a single plant. Non-sterilized tools can transfer diseases from one branch to another and spread infections throughout your entire landscape.

Pruning Hydrangeas

Hydrangeas can be trimmed in fall. Hydrangeas hold their big, beautiful blooms well into autumn. Flowers fade from white, pink, or blue to various shades of cream, pinkish brown, or tan. Leave them on shrubs to enjoy them in your yard. If you need to give your shrub a trim, wait until flowers have completely dried on their stems before pruning. Then you can use the cut, dried flowers in arrangements inside your home. However, you should plan to do major pruning on most hydrangeas in spring to avoid cutting off next year's flowers.

Annabelle Hydrangea (Hydrangea arborescens 'Annabelle') *Page 134*

Some plants are naturally arching, loose, and airy. Resist the urge to cut them into tight shapes.

Hard Pruning

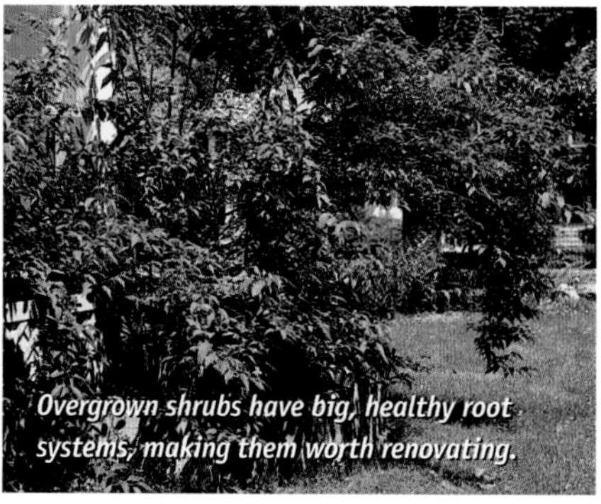
Overgrown shrubs have big, healthy root systems, making them worth renovating.

There are times when drastic measures are justified. Neglected shrubs become large and develop poor shape. You could just start over with a new plant, but don't let your eyes convince you that the old shrub is hopeless. What you can't see is the most valuable part of the plant.

Overgrown shrubs have had time to establish big, healthy root systems. It will take years for a replacement plant to do as well.

You can start over and still save the most valuable part of the shrub. But in doing so, you have to be ruthless. Prune individual branches nearly to the ground. Stagger cutting heights some so that all branches won't be at the same level. This will make the new growth appear to fill out faster.

Late winter or early spring, before new growth emerges, is the ideal time for hard pruning. (You can do it any time of year except just before a freeze.) Pruning this severely might result in no flowers for a season or two. In the meantime, you'll be amazed and pleased at how quickly your shrub can recover and how much better it looks despite your apparent abuse.

Homer's Hindsight

In the past, I used hand pruners for all my pruning jobs. I didn't want to stop what I was doing to go back into the garage and find the loppers for use on thicker stems. After a while, I noticed that many of the cuts I made with hand pruners were jagged and my hands were sore after pruning. Now I take both my loppers and my hand pruners with me when working in the yard so I'm prepared for branches of any size.

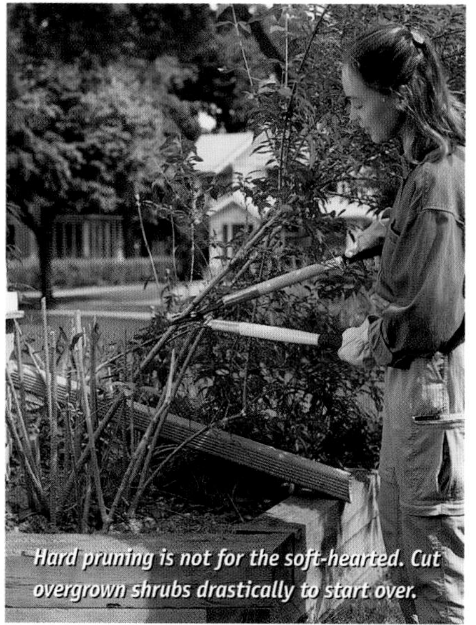
Hard pruning is not for the soft-hearted. Cut overgrown shrubs drastically to start over.

TOOL TIP

Good pruning tools make the job easier and are better for your shrubs.

Bypass hand pruners: This tool operates with a scissors action to make a clean cut. Hand pruners are operated with one hand, so they should be used only for cutting minor branches. You can buy them in various sizes to match your needs. For example, one-inch pruners are suitable for cutting one-inch-thick branches. Trying to force pruners to cut through too-big stems can cause wood and stems to rip, leaving a jagged edge that becomes an entry point for insects or disease.

Anvil hand pruners: Unlike bypass pruners, which operate with both blades moving, anvil pruners have one fixed side. This is the anvil against which the sharp, movable blade presses to make the cut. Although anvil hand pruners cost less than bypass pruners, they aren't desirable pruning tools. Pressing branches against the anvil to cut them results in mashed, torn stems and jagged cuts. This pruner also requires greater hand strength than bypass pruners.

Bypass loppers: Operated with both hands, the long handles on loppers give you greater leverage to cut larger branches. Sharp bypass blades work like scissors for smooth, clean cuts. Use loppers whenever stems are too thick for hand pruners. Use a pruning saw if you can't easily position the lopper blades around the branch.

Bundling Shrubs for Winter

Tender shrubs growing in your landscape need your help to survive winter temperatures and harsh winds. Here's how to bundle them snugly until spring. Late autumn, just before weather turns cold for the season, is the time to do this job.

1 **Give your shrub a good drink of water before you wrap it for winter.** Lay a slowly trickling hose at the base of the plant to thoroughly soak the soil around roots. Water in the soil will freeze in a block in winter and thaw in spring, providing roots with water. You'll unwrap shrubs in spring after the last frost, usually mid-April.

2 **Tuck burlap under the shrub you plan to bundle.** You'll be wrapping the plant from the bottom up so branches don't get pulled into unnatural positions. Practice folding the burlap around the shrub. If the fabric is too big, trim it now.

If you haven't bundled shrubs before, get a buddy to help. Hold the branches together while your helper pulls the burlap around them. Then, ask him to hold the seams tightly together while you pin the bundle together with nails.

STUFF YOU'LL NEED

- ✔ Burlap – large enough to cover shrubs completely
- ✔ Nails (about 10d size)
- ✔ Scissors
- ✔ Hose within reach of water source

What to Expect

Bundling shrubs isn't difficult once you get the hang of it. But your first attempts might be less than tidy. Keep trying—you'll get better with practice.

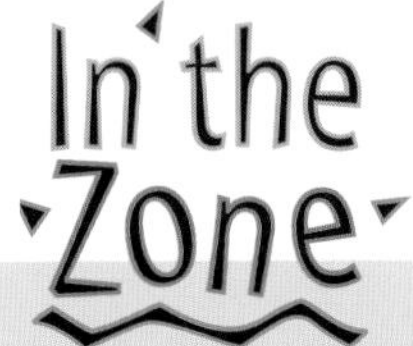

Why bundle?

Tender shrubs that are left exposed to winter weather will suffer. Cold temperatures and harsh winds dry foliage, damaging it and making it appear as though it were burned.

3 Pull the burlap together to form a tight bundle around shrub, concealing all greenery. Where the burlap overlaps and forms a seam, "pin" it together with nails. Start pinning at the bottom and work your way to the top. Keep a firm grip while pinning; if you don't make your bundles tight enough, they'll eventually droop and slide off.

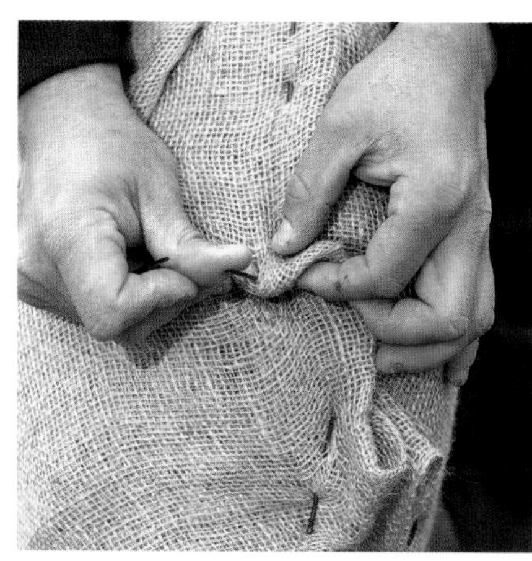

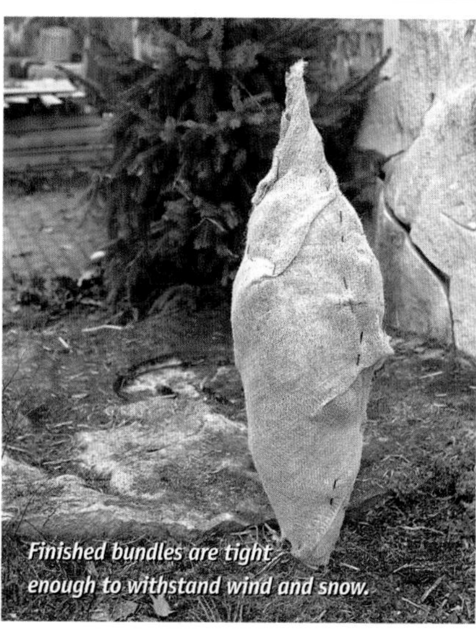

Finished bundles are tight enough to withstand wind and snow.

Bundle these shrubs

–see pages 60-61 for winterizing roses

Common Name	Zones Needing Bundling	Page
Amur Privet *Ligustrum amurense*	4 & colder	139
Anglojap Yew *Taxus x media 'Densiformis'*	4 & colder	162
Bird's Nest Spruce *Picea abies 'Nidiformis'*	2 & 3	142
Carol Mackie Daphne *Daphne x burkwoodii 'Carol Mackie'*	4 & colder	132
Carolina Azalea *Azalea carolinianum*	4 & colder	126
Catawba Rhododendron *Rhododendron catawbiense*	4 & colder	146
Cornell Pink Azalea *Azalea mucronulatum 'Cornell Pink'*	4 & colder	127
Dwarf Alberta Spruce *Picea glauca 'Conica'*	4 & colder	143
Dwarf Balsam Fir *Abies balsamea 'Nana'*	4 & colder	124
Dwarf Flowering Almond *Prunus glandulosa 'Rosea'*	4 & colder	144
Dwarf Hinoki False Cypress *Chamaecyparis obtusa 'Nana Gracilis'*	4 & colder	129
Dwarf Norway Spruce *Picea abies 'Pumila'*	4 & colder	142
Emerald Arborvitae *Thuja occidentalis 'Emerald'*	2 & 3	163
Exbury Azalea *Azalea 'Exbury Hybrids'*	4 & colder	126
Green Mound Alpine Currant *Ribes alpinum 'Green Mound'*	2 & 3	147
Hetz's Midget Arborvitae *Thuja occidentalis 'Hetz's Midget'*	2 & 3	164
Hick's Upright Yew *Taxus x media 'Hicksii'*	4 & colder	163
Little Giant Arborvitae *Thuja occidentalis 'Little Giant'*	3 & colder	164
Northern Lights Azalea *Azalea 'Northern Lights'*	4 & colder	127
Summersweet *Clethra alnifolia*	4 & colder	130
Vermont Sun Forsythia *Forsythia mandshurica 'Vermont Sun'*	4 & colder	133
White Forsythia *Abeliophyllum distichum*	4 & colder	124
Wintergreen Boxwood *Buxus microphylla 'Wintergreen'*	4 & colder	128

Deer Damage

Hungry deer will dine on just about anything in your yard.

There's no magical list of plants you can use to grow a deer-proof landscape. However, it helps to know that deer are particularly fond of arborvitae, birches, dogwoods, hostas, and yews. They seem less inclined to munch on plants with thorns, fuzzy foliage, or leathery leaves. Barberries, cinquefoils, forsythias, lilacs, junipers, spireas, and spruces are not favorite deer food. You can reduce deer damage by applying odor and taste repellents, but effectiveness will be limited by what the weather is like, how hungry deer are, how often you reapply, and how familiar deer become with the product. (When using repellents, purchase several and rotate their use.) Even though fencing won't stop a determined deer, using physical barriers to keep deer out of your landscape is your best bet for protecting it.

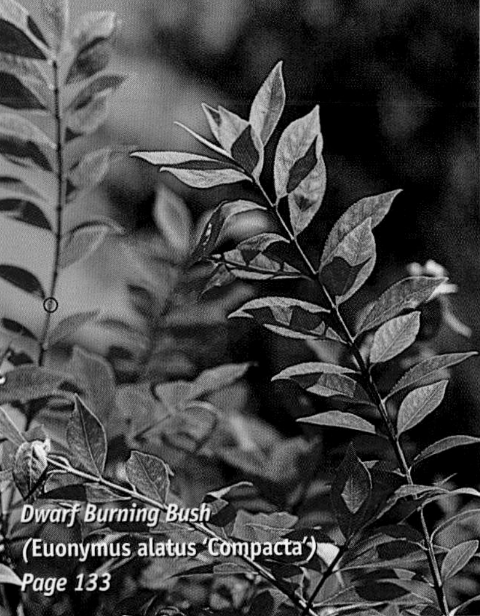
Dwarf Burning Bush
(Euonymus alatus 'Compacta')
Page 133

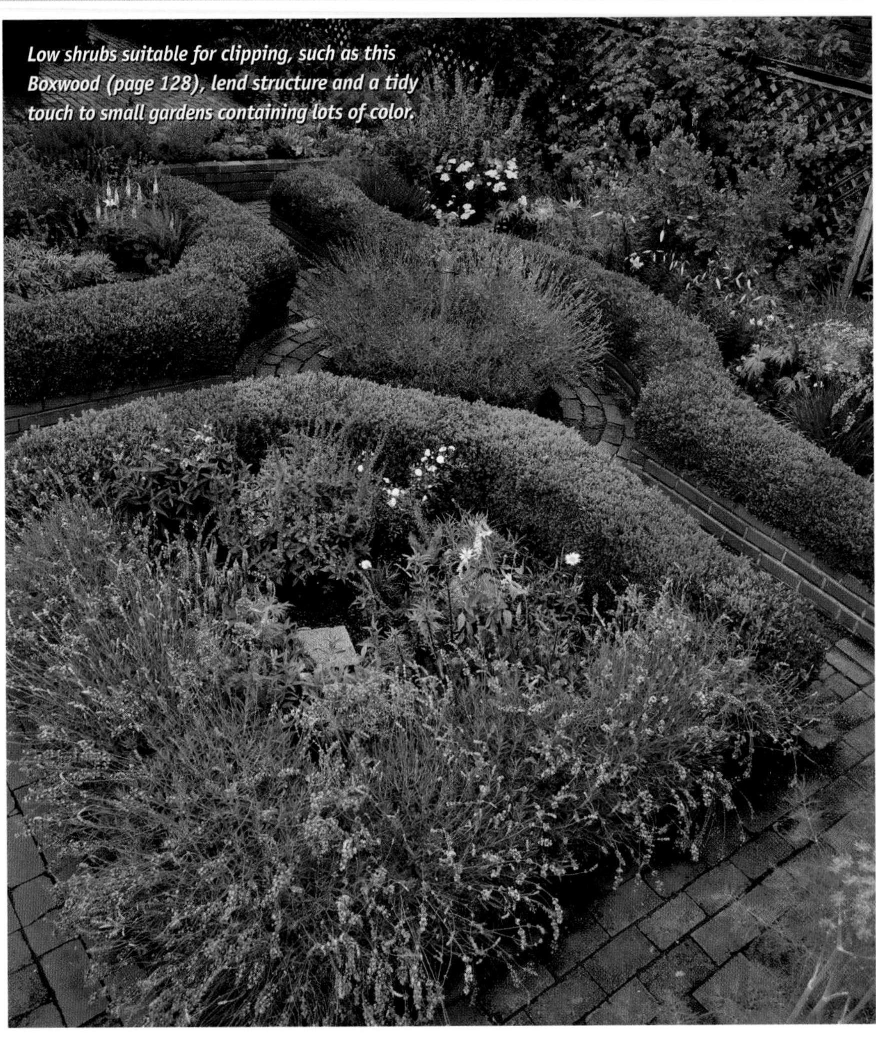
Low shrubs suitable for clipping, such as this Boxwood (page 128), lend structure and a tidy touch to small gardens containing lots of color.

Northern Lights Azalea
(Azalea 'Northern Lights')
Page 127

Choosing Shrubs by Characteristics

Identify particular plant characteristics that meet your needs.
A plant's growth rate, its mature form, and foliage texture are other traits to consider when selecting shrubs. Availability varies by area and site conditions (see page 21). Check with your garden center.

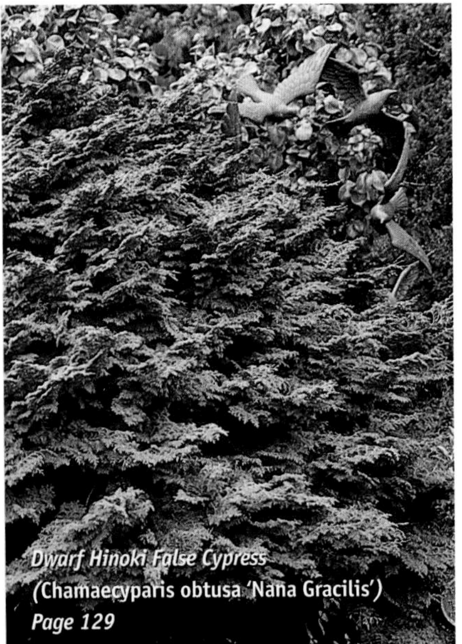
Dwarf Hinoki False Cypress
(Chamaecyparis obtusa 'Nana Gracilis')
Page 129

Fragrant flowering shrubs

Common Name	Zones	Page
Adelaide Hoodless Rose *Rosa 'Adelaide Hoodless'*	2-9	148
Arnold's Red Tatarian Honeysuckle *Lonicera tatarica 'Arnold's Red'*	3-9	140
Betty Prior Rose *Rosa 'Betty Prior'*	4-9	148
Carefree Beauty Rose *Rosa Carefree Beauty*	4-8	149
Carol Mackie Daphne *Daphne x burkwoodii 'Carol Mackie'*	4-8	132
Common Lilac *Syringa vulgaris*	3-7	162
Common Witch Hazel *Hamamelis virginiana*	3-8	134
Cutleaf Lilac *Syringa x laciniata*	4-8	160
Fru Dagmar Hastrup Rose *Rosa 'Fru Dagmar Hastrup'*	2-9	149
Graham Thomas Rose *Rosa Graham Thomas*	5-9	150
Henry Kelsey Rose *Rosa 'Henry Kelsey'*	3-9	150
Hunter Rose *Rosa 'Hunter'*	4-8	151
Margo Koster Rose *Rosa 'Margo Koster'*	5-8	151
Miss Kim Lilac *Syringa patula 'Miss Kim'*	3-7	161
Morden Centennial Rose *Rosa 'Morden Centennial'*	2-9	152
Northern Lights Azalea *Azalea 'Northern Lights'*	4-7	127
Purple-Leaf Sand Cherry *Prunus x cistena*	2-8	145
Rosa Rubrifolia *Rosa rubrifolia*	4-9	155
Sir Thomas Lipton Rose *Rosa 'Sir Thomas Lipton'*	2-7	153
Summersweet *Clethra alnifolia*	3-9	130
Sweetshrub *Calycanthus floridus*	4-9	129
Therese Bugnet Rose *Rosa 'Therese Bugnet'*	3-9	154
White Forsythia *Abeliophyllum distichum*	4-8	124
White Rugosa Rose *Rosa rugosa 'Alba'*	3-10	155
William Baffin Rose *Rosa 'William Baffin'*	2-9	154

Slow-growing shrubs

Common Name	Zones	Page
Anglojap Yew *Taxus x media 'Densiformis'*	4-7	162
Bird's Nest Spruce *Picea abies 'Nidiformis'*	2-7	142
Black Chokeberry *Aronia melanocarpa*	4-9	125
Blue Star Juniper *Juniperus squamata 'Blue Star'*	4-8	139
Carol Mackie Daphne *Daphne x burkwoodii 'Carol Mackie'*	4-8	132
Catawba Rhododendron *Rhododendron catawbiense*	4-8	146
Common Lilac *Syringa vulgaris*	3-7	162
Cornell Pink Azalea *Azalea mucronulatum 'Cornell Pink'*	4-7	127
Dwarf Alberta Spruce *Picea glauca 'Conica'*	2-8	143
Dwarf Balsam Fir *Abies balsamea 'Nana'*	3-6	124
Dwarf Burning Bush *Euonymus alatus 'Compacta'*	3-8	133
Dwarf Hinoki False Cypress *Chamaecyparis obtusa 'Nana Gracilis'*	4-8	129
Emerald Arborvitae *Thuja occidentalis 'Emerald'*	2-7	163
Exbury Azalea *Azalea 'Exbury Hybrids'*	4-7	126
Gray Dogwood *Cornus racemosa*	4-7	131
Green Lustre Japanese Holly *Ilex crenata 'Green Lustre'*	4-6	135
Hetz's Midget Arborvitae *Thuja occidentalis 'Hetz's Midget'*	2-8	164
Little Giant Arborvitae *Thuja occidentalis 'Little Giant'*	3-7	164
Miss Kim Lilac *Syringa patula 'Miss Kim'*	3-7	161
Mugo Pine *Pinus mugo*	2-7	143
Northern Lights Azalea *Azalea 'Northern Lights'*	4-7	127
Purple-Leaf Sand Cherry *Prunus x cistena*	2-8	145
Shrubby Cinquefoil *Potentilla fruticosa*	2-7	144
Summersweet *Clethra alnifolia*	3-9	130
Sweetshrub *Calycanthus floridus*	4-9	129
Vermont Sun Forsythia *Forsythia mandshurica 'Vermont Sun'*	4-8	133
Winterberry *Ilex verticillata*	3-9	136
Wintergreen Boxwood *Buxus microphylla 'Wintergreen'*	4-6	128

Annabelle Hydrangea (Hydrangea arborescens 'Annabelle') Page 134

Rapid-growing shrubs

Common Name	Zones	Page
Adelaide Hoodless Rose *Rosa 'Adelaide Hoodless'*	2-9	148
Amur Privet *Ligustrum amurense*	3-7	139
Arnold's Red Tatarian Honeysuckle *Lonicera tatarica 'Arnold's Red'*	3-9	140
Arrowwood Viburnum *Viburnum dentatum*	3-8	165
Blackhaw Virburnum *Viburnum prunifolium*	3-9	167
Bridalwreath Spirea *Spiraea prunifolia*	5-8	158
Compact Amer. Cranberrybush *Viburnum trilobum 'Alfredo'*	2-7	167
Coralberry *Symphoricarpos orbiculatus*	4-7	159
Coral Embers Willow *Salix alba 'Britzensis'*	2-8	156
Cornelian Cherry *Cornus mas*	4-8	131
Cut-Leaf Staghorn Sumac *Rhus typhina 'Laciniata'*	3-8	147
French Pussy Willow *Salix caprea 'Kilmarnock'*	4-8	156
Green Mound Alpine Currant *Ribes alpinum 'Green Mound'*	2-7	147
Henry Kelsey Rose *Rosa 'Henry Kelsey'*	3-9	150
Hick's Upright Yew *Taxus x media 'Hicksii'*	4-7	163
Morden Centennial Rose *Rosa 'Morden Centennial'*	2-9	152
Nearly Wild Rose *Rosa 'Nearly Wild'*	2-9	152
Northern Bayberry *Myrica pensylvanica*	2-6	141
PeeGee Hydrangea *Hydrangea paniculata 'Grandiflora'*	3-8	135
Redtwig Dogwood *Cornus alba*	2-8	130
Russian Cypress *Microbiota decussata*	3-7	140
Sir Thomas Lipton Rose *Rosa 'Sir Thomas Lipton'*	2-7	153
Snowberry *Symphoricarpos albus*	3-7	159
White Forsythia *Abeliophyllum distichum*	4-8	124
White Rugosa Rose *Rosa rugosa 'Alba'*	3-10	155
William Baffin Rose *Rosa 'William Baffin'*	2-9	154
Yellow-Twig Dogwood *Cornus stolonifera 'Flaviramea'*	3-8	132
Yukon Belle Firethorn *Pyracantha angustifolia Yukon Belle*	4-9	145

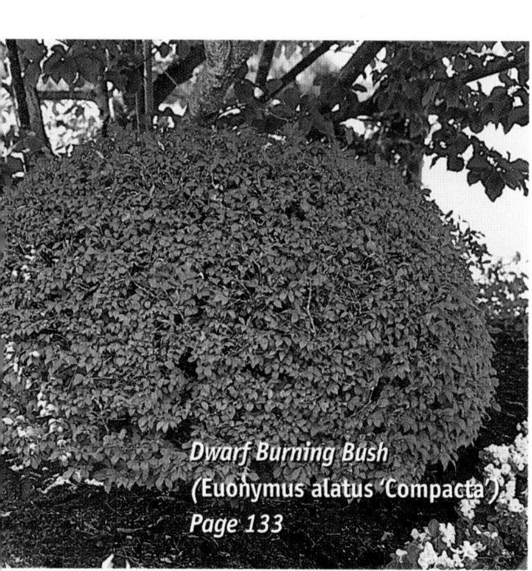

Dwarf Burning Bush (Euonymus alatus 'Compacta') Page 133

Fine-textured shrubs

Common Name	Zones	Page
Anglojap Yew *Taxus x media 'Densiformis'*	4-7	162
Blue Star Juniper *Juniperus squamata 'Blue Star'*	4-8	139
Compact Amer. Cranberrybush *Viburnum trilobum 'Alfredo'*	2-7	167
Cut-Leaf Staghorn Sumac *Rhus typhina 'Laciniata'*	3-8	147
Cutleaf Lilac *Syringa x laciniata*	4-8	160
Dwarf Alberta Spruce *Picea glauca 'Conica'*	2-8	143
Dwarf Hinoki False Cypress *Chamaecyparis obtusa 'Nana Gracilis'*	4-8	129
Emerald Arborvitae *Thuja occidentalis 'Emerald'*	2-7	163
Green Lustre Japanese Holly *Ilex crenata 'Green Lustre'*	4-6	135
Japanese Barberry *Berberis thunbergii*	4-8	128
Mugo Pine *Pinus mugo*	2-7	143
Parson's Juniper *Juniperus chinensis 'Parsonii'*	3-9	137
Russian Cypress *Microbiota decussata*	3-7	140
Sea Green Juniper *Juniperus chinensis 'Sea Green'*	4-8	138
Tam Juniper *Juniperus sabina 'Tamariscifolia'*	3-7	138
The Fairy Rose *Rosa 'The Fairy'*	4-9	153
Wintergreen Boxwood *Buxus microphylla 'Wintergreen'*	4-6	128
Yukon Belle Firethorn *Pyracantha angustifolia Yukon Belle*	4-9	145

Coarse-textured shrubs

Common Name	Zones	Page
Annabelle Hydrangea *Hydrangea arborescens 'Annabelle'*	3-9	134
Black Chokeberry *Aronia melanocarpa*	4-9	125
Blackhaw Virburnum *Viburnum prunifolium*	3-9	167
Catawba Rhododendron *Rhododendron catawbiense*	4-8	146
Common Lilac *Syringa vulgaris*	3-7	162
Doublefile Viburnum *Viburnum plicatum tomentosum*	4-8	166
European Cranberrybush *Viburnum opulus 'Roseum'*	3-8	166
White Forsythia *Abeliophyllum distichum*	4-8	124

Arborvitae (pages 163-164) adds a distinctive shape to the landscape year-round.

Choose shrubs to add color, texture, line, and form to your landscape.

Snowberry (Symphoricarpos albus) Page 159

Wintergreen Boxwood (Buxus microphylla 'Wintergreen') Page 128

Choosing Shrubs by Needs

Put shrubs to work in your landscape. The guides on these pages are organized by different landscaping needs. (See pages 30-31 to find lists of shrubs for privacy.) Go to the shrub encyclopedia for detailed information about individual shrubs. Availability varies by area and conditions (see page 21). Check with your garden center.

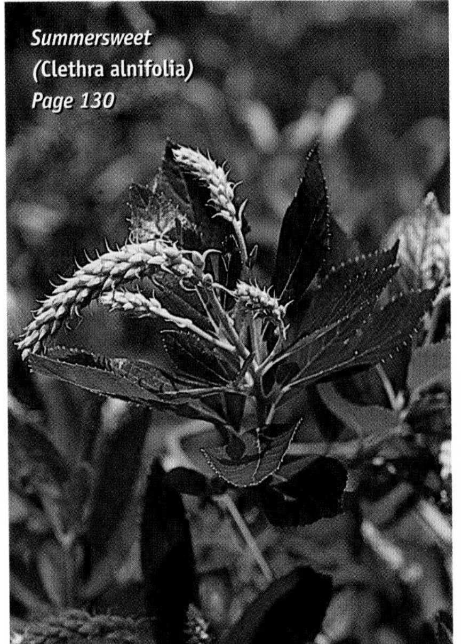
Summersweet (Clethra alnifolia) Page 130

Shrubs for mass planting

Common Name	Zones	Page
Anglojap Yew *Taxus x media 'Densiformis'*	4-7	162
Annabelle Hydrangea *Hydrangea arborescens 'Annabelle'*	3-9	134
Anthony Waterer Spirea *Spiraea japonica 'Anthony Waterer'*	3-9	157
Betty Prior Rose *Rosa 'Betty Prior'*	4-9	148
Black Chokeberry *Aronia melanocarpa*	4-9	125
Blackhaw Virburnum *Viburnum prunifolium*	3-9	167
Bridalwreath Spirea *Spiraea prunifolia*	5-8	158
Carolina Azalea *Azalea carolinianum*	4-9	126
Compact Amer. Cranberrybush *Viburnum trilobum 'Alfredo'*	2-7	167
Cornell Pink Azalea *Azalea mucronulatum 'Cornell Pink'*	4-7	127
Doublefile Viburnum *Viburnum plicatum tomentosum*	4-8	166
Dwarf Burning Bush *Euonymus alatus 'Compacta'*	3-8	133
Exbury Azalea *Azalea 'Exbury Hybrids'*	4-7	126
Graham Thomas Rose *Rosa Graham Thomas*	5-9	150
Hunter Rose *Rosa 'Hunter'*	4-8	151
Inkberry *Ilex glabra 'Compacta'*	3-10	136
Mohican Viburnum *Viburnum lantana 'Mohican'*	4-8	165
Nearly Wild Rose *Rosa 'Nearly Wild'*	2-9	152
Northern Lights Azalea *Azalea 'Northern Lights'*	4-7	127
Shibori Spirea *Spiraea japonica 'Shibori'*	4-8	157
Shrubby Cinquefoil *Potentilla fruticosa*	2-7	144
Sir Thomas Lipton Rose *Rosa 'Sir Thomas Lipton'*	2-7	153
Summersweet *Clethra alnifolia*	3-9	130
Vermont Sun Forsythia *Forsythia mandshurica 'Vermont Sun'*	4-8	133

Shrubs for entries, courtyards, and patios

Common Name	Zones	Page
Adelaide Hoodless Rose *Rosa 'Adelaide Hoodless'*	2-9	148
Anglojap Yew *Taxus x media 'Densiformis'*	4-7	162
Annabelle Hydrangea *Hydrangea arborescens 'Annabelle'*	3-9	134
Anthony Waterer Spirea *Spiraea japonica 'Anthony Waterer'*	3-9	157
Arnold's Red Tatarian Honeysuckle *Lonicera tatarica 'Arnold's Red'*	3-9	140
Blackhaw Virburnum *Viburnum prunifolium*	3-9	167
Bridalwreath Spirea *Spiraea prunifolia*	5-8	158
Carol Mackie Daphne *Daphne x burkwoodii 'Carol Mackie'*	4-8	132
Carolina Azalea *Azalea carolinianum*	4-9	126
Common Lilac *Syringa vulgaris*	3-7	162
Compact Amer. Cranberrybush *Viburnum trilobum 'Alfredo'*	2-7	167
Cutleaf Lilac *Syringa x laciniata*	4-8	160
Doublefile Viburnum *Viburnum plicatum tomentosum*	4-8	166
Dwarf Alberta Spruce *Picea glauca 'Conica'*	2-8	143
Dwarf Balsam Fir *Abies balsamea 'Nana'*	3-6	124
Dwarf Burning Bush *Euonymus alatus 'Compacta'*	3-8	133
Dwarf Norway Spruce *Picea abies 'Pumila'*	3-8	142
European Cranberrybush *Viburnum opulus 'Roseum'*	3-8	166
Graham Thomas Rose *Rosa Graham Thomas*	5-9	150
Green Lustre Japanese Holly *Ilex crenata 'Green Lustre'*	4-6	135
Henry Kelsey Rose *Rosa 'Henry Kelsey'*	3-9	150
Hetz's Midget Arborvitae *Thuja occidentalis 'Hetz's Midget'*	2-8	164
Hunter Rose *Rosa 'Hunter'*	4-8	151
Inkberry *Ilex glabra 'Compacta'*	3-10	136
Limemound Spirea *Spiraea japonica Limemound*	4-9	158
Miss Kim Lilac *Syringa patula 'Miss Kim'*	3-7	161
Morden Centennial Rose *Rosa 'Morden Centennial'*	2-9	152
Nearly Wild Rose *Rosa 'Nearly Wild'*	2-9	152
Parson's Juniper *Juniperus chinensis 'Parsonii'*	3-9	137
Sea Green Juniper *Juniperus chinensis 'Sea Green'*	4-8	138
Shibori Spirea *Spiraea japonica 'Shibori'*	4-8	157
Sweetshrub *Calycanthus floridus*	4-9	129
Tam Juniper *Juniperus sabina 'Tamariscifolia'*	3-7	138
The Fairy Rose *Rosa 'The Fairy'*	4-9	153
Wintergreen Boxwood *Buxus microphylla 'Wintergreen'*	4-6	128

Compact American Cranberrybush (Viburnum trilobum 'Alfredo') Page 167

Dwarf Norway Spruce (Picea abies 'Pumila') Page 142

Shrubs for woodland gardens

Common Name	Zones	Page
Arrowwood Viburnum *Viburnum dentatum*	3-8	165
Black Chokeberry *Aronia melanocarpa*	4-9	125
Blackhaw Virburnum *Viburnum prunifolium*	3-9	167
Compact Amer. Cranberrybush *Viburnum trilobum 'Alfredo'*	2-7	167
Coralberry *Symphoricarpos orbiculatus*	4-7	159
Cornell Pink Azalea *Azalea mucronulatum 'Cornell Pink'*	4-7	127
Cut-Leaf Staghorn Sumac *Rhus typhina 'Laciniata'*	3-8	147
Doublefile Viburnum *Viburnum plicatum tomentosum*	4-8	166
European Cranberrybush *Viburnum opulus 'Roseum'*	3-8	166
Mohican Viburnum *Viburnum lantana 'Mohican'*	4-8	165
Northern Lights Azalea *Azalea 'Northern Lights'*	4-7	127
Serviceberry *Amelanchier alnifolia*	4-5	125
Snowberry *Symphoricarpos albus*	3-7	159
Summersweet *Clethra alnifolia*	3-9	130
Sweetshrub *Calycanthus floridus*	4-9	129
Vermont Sun Forsythia *Forsythia mandshurica 'Vermont Sun'*	4-8	133
White Forsythia *Abeliophyllum distichum*	4-8	124

Shrubs for formal gardens

Common Name	Zones	Page
Adelaide Hoodless Rose *Rosa 'Adelaide Hoodless'*	2-9	148
Amur Privet *Ligustrum amurense*	3-7	139
Anglojap Yew *Taxus x media 'Densiformis'*	4-7	162
Annabelle Hydrangea *Hydrangea arborescens 'Annabelle'*	3-9	134
Blackhaw Virburnum *Viburnum prunifolium*	3-9	167
Dwarf Alberta Spruce *Picea glauca 'Conica'*	2-8	143
Dwarf Balsam Fir *Abies balsamea 'Nana'*	3-6	124
Dwarf Norway Spruce *Picea abies 'Pumila'*	3-8	142
Emerald Arborvitae *Thuja occidentalis 'Emerald'*	2-7	163
European Cranberrybush *Viburnum opulus 'Roseum'*	3-8	166
Green Lustre Japanese Holly *Ilex crenata 'Green Lustre'*	4-6	135
Green Mound Alpine Currant *Ribes alpinum 'Green Mound'*	2-7	147
Hetz's Midget Arborvitae *Thuja occidentalis 'Hetz's Midget'*	2-8	164
Hick's Upright Yew *Taxus x media 'Hicksii'*	4-7	163
Inkberry *Ilex glabra 'Compacta'*	3-10	136
Limemound Spirea *Spiraea japonica Limemound*	4-9	158
Little Giant Arborvitae *Thuja occidentalis 'Little Giant'*	3-7	164
Morden Centennial Rose *Rosa 'Morden Centennial'*	2-9	152
Mugo Pine *Pinus mugo*	2-7	143
Russian Cypress *Microbiota decussata*	3-7	140
Sweetshrub *Calycanthus floridus*	4-9	129
The Fairy Rose *Rosa 'The Fairy'*	4-9	153
Wintergreen Boxwood *Buxus microphylla 'Wintergreen'*	4-6	128

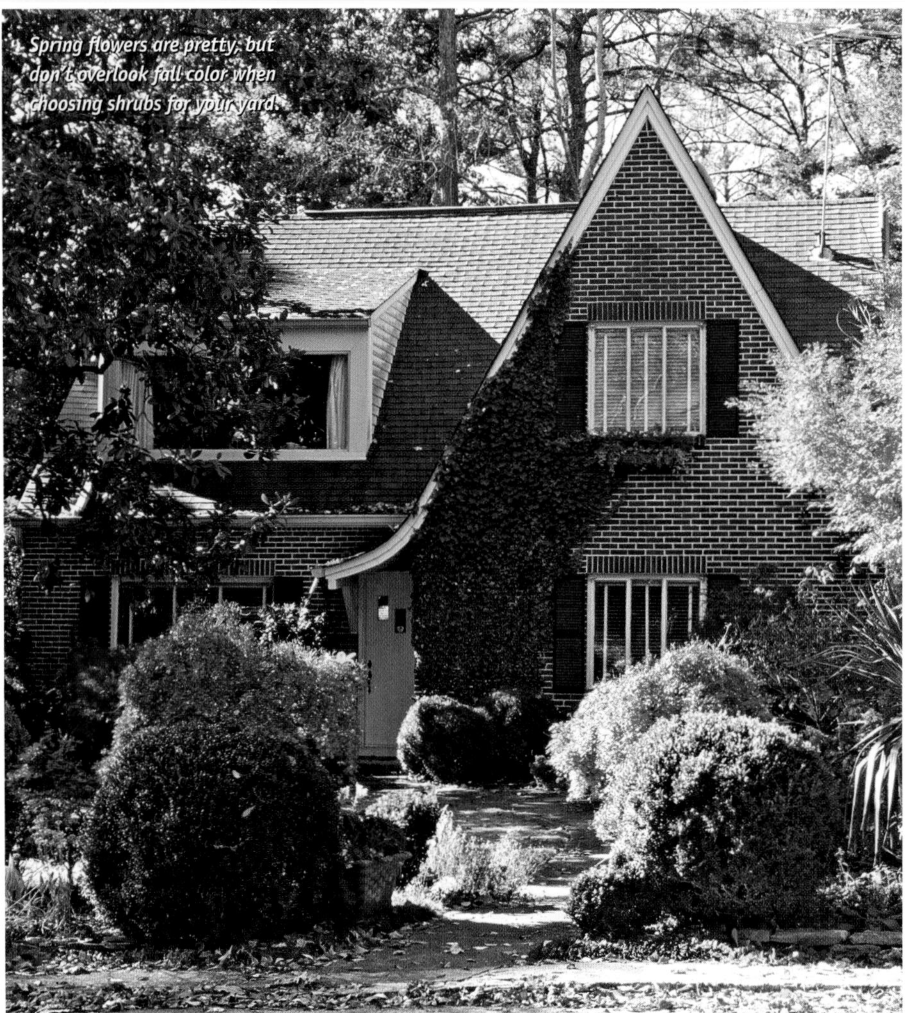
Spring flowers are pretty, but don't overlook fall color when choosing shrubs for your yard.

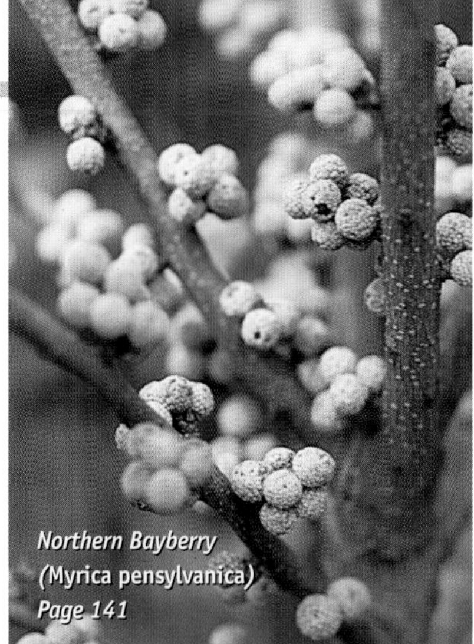
Northern Bayberry (Myrica pensylvanica) Page 141

Hunter Rose (Rosa 'Hunter') Page 151

Choosing Shrubs for Seasonal Interest

Decorate your yard throughout the seasons with shrubs. Fragrant flowers, colorful foliage, and desirable fruit add interest to the landscape throughout spring, summer, fall, and winter.

Spring-flowering shrubs

Common Name	Zones	Page
Annabelle Hydrangea *Hydrangea arborescens ‘Annabelle’*	3-9	134
Anthony Waterer Spirea *Spiraea japonica ‘Anthony Waterer’*	3-9	157
Arnold's Red Tatarian Honeysuckle *Lonicera tatarica ‘Arnold's Red’*	3-9	140
Arrowwood Viburnum *Viburnum dentatum*	3-8	165
Black Chokeberry *Aronia melanocarpa*	4-9	125
Blackhaw Virburnum *Viburnum prunifolium*	3-9	167
Bridalwreath Spirea *Spiraea prunifolia*	5-8	158
Carol Mackie Daphne *Daphne x burkwoodii ‘Carol Mackie’*	4-8	132
Carolina Azalea *Azalea carolinianum*	4-9	126
Catawba Rhododendron *Rhododendron catawbiense*	4-8	146
Common Lilac *Syringa vulgaris*	3-7	162
Compact Amer. Cranberrybush *Viburnum trilobum ‘Alfredo’*	2-7	167
Cornelian Cherry *Cornus mas*	4-8	131
Cornell Pink Azalea *Azalea mucronulatum ‘Cornell Pink’*	4-7	127
Cutleaf Lilac *Syringa x laciniata*	4-8	160
Doublefile Viburnum *Viburnum plicatum tomentosum*	4-8	166
Dwarf Flowering Almond *Prunus glandulosa ‘Rosea’*	4-8	144
European Cranberrybush *Viburnum opulus ‘Roseum’*	3-8	166
Exbury Azalea *Azalea ‘Exbury Hybrids’*	4-7	126
Gray Dogwood *Cornus racemosa*	4-7	131
Green Mound Alpine Currant *Ribes alpinum ‘Green Mound’*	2-7	147
Henry Kelsey Rose *Rosa ‘Henry Kelsey’*	3-9	150
Limemound Spirea *Spiraea japonica Limemound*	4-9	158
Miss Kim Lilac *Syringa patula ‘Miss Kim’*	3-7	161
Mohican Viburnum *Viburnum lantana ‘Mohican’*	3-8	165
Morden Centennial Rose *Rosa ‘Morden Centennial’*	2-9	152
Nearly Wild Rose *Rosa ‘Nearly Wild’*	2-9	152
Northern Lights Azalea *Azalea ‘Northern Lights’*	4-7	127
Oriental Photinia *Photinia villosa*	4-7	141
Persian Lilac *Syringa x persica*	3-7	161
Purple-Leaf Sand Cherry *Prunus x cistena*	2-8	145
Serviceberry *Amelanchier alnifolia*	4-5	125
Sweetshrub *Calycanthus floridus*	4-9	129
Vermont Sun Forsythia *Forsythia mandshurica ‘Vermont Sun’*	4-8	133
White Forsythia *Abeliophyllum distichum*	4-8	124
White Rugosa Rose *Rosa rugosa ‘Alba’*	3-10	155
William Baffin Rose *Rosa ‘William Baffin’*	2-9	154
Wintergreen Boxwood *Buxus microphylla ‘Wintergreen’*	4-6	128

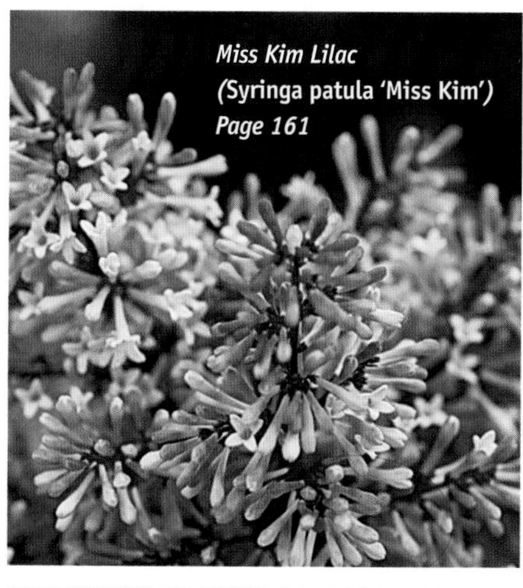
Miss Kim Lilac (Syringa patula 'Miss Kim') Page 161

Summer-flowering shrubs

Common Name	Zones	Page
Adelaide Hoodless Rose *Rosa 'Adelaide Hoodless'*	2-9	148
Annabelle Hydrangea *Hydrangea arborescens 'Annabelle'*	3-9	134
Anthony Waterer Spirea *Spiraea japonica 'Anthony Waterer'*	3-9	157
Arrowwood Viburnum *Viburnum dentatum*	3-8	165
Betty Prior Rose *Rosa 'Betty Prior'*	4-9	148
Black Chokeberry *Aronia melanocarpa*	4-9	125
Carefree Beauty Rose *Rosa Carefree Beauty*	4-8	149
Carolina Azalea *Azalea carolinianum*	4-9	126
Coralberry *Symphoricarpos orbiculatus*	4-7	159
Cut-Leaf Staghorn Sumac *Rhus typhina 'Laciniata'*	3-8	147
Fru Dagmar Hastrup Rose *Rosa 'Fru Dagmar Hastrup'*	2-9	149
Graham Thomas Rose *Rosa Graham Thomas*	5-9	150
Henry Kelsey Rose *Rosa 'Henry Kelsey'*	3-9	150
Hunter Rose *Rosa 'Hunter'*	4-8	151
Margo Koster Rose *Rosa 'Margo Koster'*	5-8	151
Miss Kim Lilac *Syringa patula 'Miss Kim'*	3-7	161
Mohican Viburnum *Viburnum lantana 'Mohican'*	3-8	165
Morden Centennial Rose *Rosa 'Morden Centennial'*	2-9	152
Nearly Wild Rose *Rosa 'Nearly Wild'*	2-9	152
Oriental Photinia *Photinia villosa*	4-7	141
PeeGee Hydrangea *Hydrangea paniculata 'Grandiflora'*	3-8	135
Rosa Rubrifolia *Rosa rubrifolia*	4-9	155
Shrubby Cinquefoil *Potentilla fruticosa*	2-7	144
Sir Thomas Lipton Rose *Rosa 'Sir Thomas Lipton'*	2-7	153
Summersweet *Clethra alnifolia*	3-9	130
Sweetshrub *Calycanthus floridus*	4-9	129
The Fairy Rose *Rosa 'The Fairy'*	4-9	153
Therese Bugnet Rose *Rosa 'Therese Bugnet'*	3-9	154
White Rugosa Rose *Rosa rugosa 'Alba'*	3-10	155
William Baffin Rose *Rosa 'William Baffin'*	2-9	154
Yukon Belle Firethorn *Pyracantha angustifolia Yukon Belle*	4-9	145

Shrubs with autumn color

Common Name	Zones	Page
Arrowwood Viburnum *Viburnum dentatum*	3-8	165
Black Chokeberry *Aronia melanocarpa*	4-9	125
Blackhaw Virburnum *Viburnum prunifolium*	3-9	167
Bridalwreath Spirea *Spiraea prunifolia*	5-8	158
Common Witch Hazel *Hamamelis virginiana*	3-8	134
Compact Amer. Cranberrybush *Viburnum trilobum 'Alfredo'*	2-7	167
Cornell Pink Azalea *Azalea mucronulatum 'Cornell Pink'*	4-7	127
Cut-Leaf Staghorn Sumac *Rhus typhina 'Laciniata'*	3-8	147
Doublefile Viburnum *Viburnum plicatum tomentosum*	4-8	166
Dwarf Burning Bush *Euonymus alatus 'Compacta'*	3-8	133
Exbury Azalea *Azalea 'Exbury Hybrids'*	4-7	126
Japanese Barberry *Berberis thunbergii*	4-8	128
Limemound Spirea *Spiraea japonica Limemound*	4-9	158
Mohican Viburnum *Viburnum lantana 'Mohican'*	3-8	165
Northern Lights Azalea *Azalea 'Northern Lights'*	4-7	127
Oriental Photinia *Photinia villosa*	4-7	141
Russian Cypress *Microbiota decussata*	3-7	140
Serviceberry *Amelanchier alnifolia*	4-5	125
Shrubby Cinquefoil *Potentilla fruticosa*	2-7	144
Summersweet *Clethra alnifolia*	3-9	130
Sweetshrub *Calycanthus floridus*	4-9	129
Therese Bugnet Rose *Rosa 'Therese Bugnet'*	3-9	154
Yellow-Twig Dogwood *Cornus stolonifera 'Flaviramea"*	3-8	132

Winterberry (Ilex verticillata) Page 136

Shrubs with winter fruit

Common Name	Zones	Page
Carefree Beauty Rose *Rosa Carefree Beauty*	4-8	149
Compact Amer. Cranberrybush *Viburnum trilobum 'Alfredo'*	2-7	167
Japanese Barberry *Berberis thunbergii*	4-8	128
Northern Bayberry *Myrica pensylvanica*	2-6	141
Oriental Photinia *Photinia villosa*	4-7	141
Rosa Rubrifolia *Rosa rubrifolia*	4-9	153
Winterberry *Ilex verticillata*	3-9	136

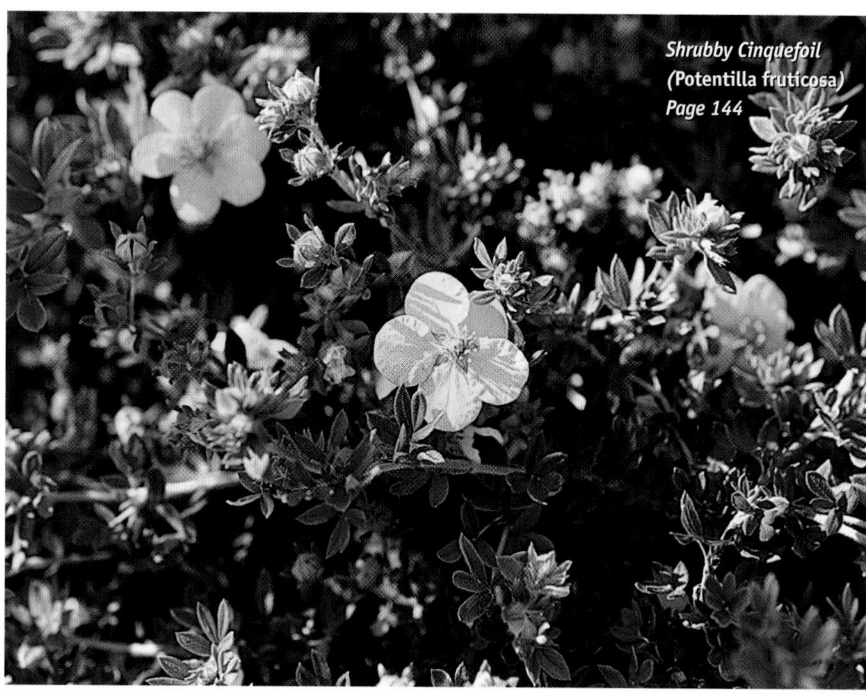
Shrubby Cinquefoil (Potentilla fruticosa) Page 144

Abeliophyllum distichum

White Forsythia

Zones: 4-8

Light Needs:

Mature Size: 3'-5' × 3'-4'

Growth Rate: medium to rapid

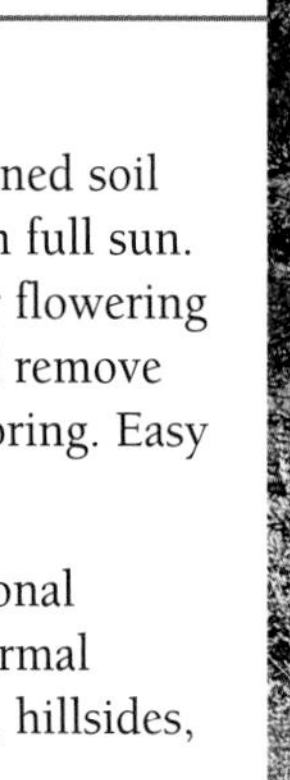

deciduous flowering shrub

Needs: Plant in fertile, well-drained soil that's acidic or alkaline. Grow in full sun. Prune heavily immediately after flowering to control size. Cutting late will remove flower buds for the following spring. Easy to transplant.

Good for: specimen shrub, seasonal accent, late winter interest, informal deciduous screen, natural areas, hillsides, sunny areas

More Choices: pages 31, 35, 41, 42, 117, 118, 119, 121, and 122

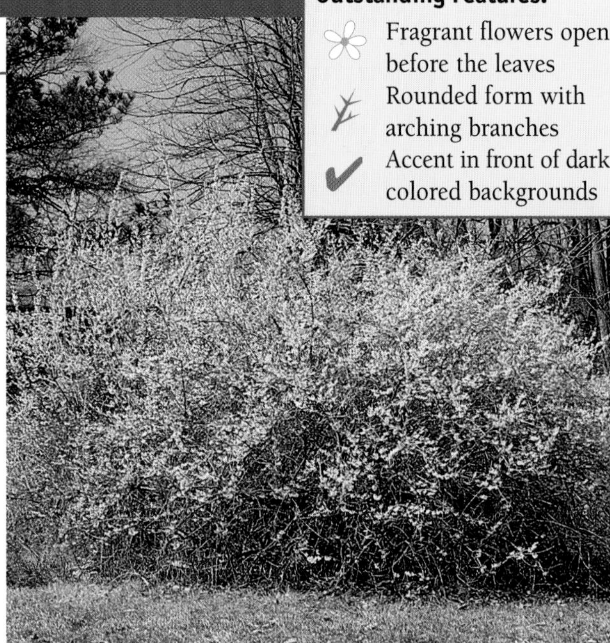

Outstanding Features:

- Fragrant flowers open before the leaves
- Rounded form with arching branches
- Accent in front of dark colored backgrounds

This ugly duckling becomes a swan when covered with fragrant, white flowers. Blooms have just a blush of pale pink. One of the first shrubs to bloom; flowers appear in March and early April. Plant in front of a dark background for contrast. Prune annually immediately after flowering to encourage new vigorous growth and abundant blooms next year.

Abies balsamea 'Nana'

Dwarf Balsam Fir

Zones: 3-6

Light Needs:

Mature Size:

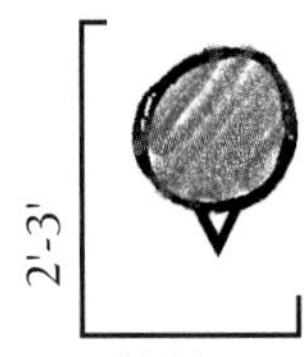

Growth Rate: slow

evergreen shrub

Needs: Plant in fertile soil that's moist but well-drained. Slightly acidic soil is best. Grow in partial shade. Plants are well adapted to cold locations. Provide supplemental water when conditions are dry or when growing in warmer areas.

Good for: foundation planting, low background for perennials, shrub beds, beside patios, along walkways, narrow areas, rock gardens, specimen planting

More Choices: pages 23, 30, 36, 41, 109, 117, 119, and 120

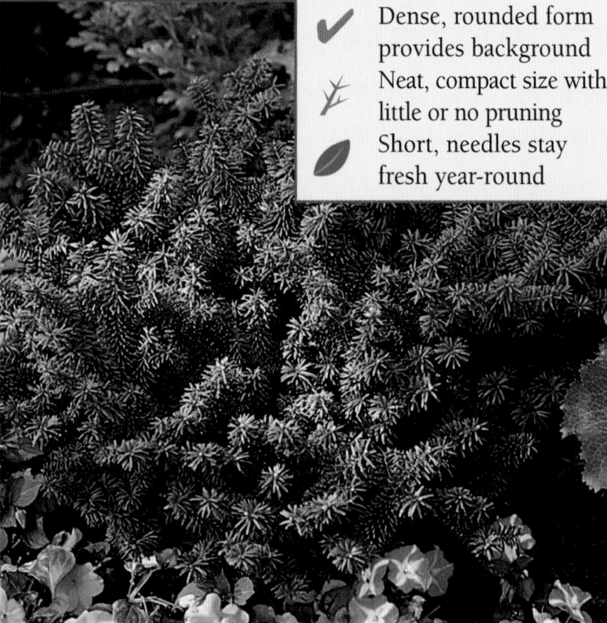

Outstanding Features:

- Dense, rounded form provides background
- Neat, compact size with little or no pruning
- Short, needles stay fresh year-round

Sometimes a green plant is just what's needed in the landscape. Dwarf Balsam Fir fills the bill and stays tidy at just 3 feet high. Use it around foundations and in planting beds, or position it in a dwarf conifer collection. This shrub thrives where summers are cool and moist. Water regularly in the warmer areas of its growing range, especially during dry periods.

Amelanchier alnifolia

Serviceberry

Zones: 4-5

Light Needs:

Mature Size:

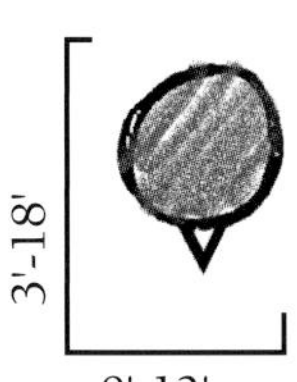

Growth Rate: medium

deciduous flowering shrub

Needs: Plant in full sun or partial shade in moist, well-drained, fertile soil. Will tolerate drier locations as well. Shrubs will grow in either acid or alkaline soil. This shrub rarely requires pruning.

Good for: specimen use, hedges, woodland areas, planting near ponds and streams, shrub borders, attracting birds

More Choices: pages 35, 36, 41, 121, 122, and 123

Options: 'Regent'—compact shrub with sweet fruit and attractive foliage. Grows 4' to 6' high, spreads 12' wide.

Outstanding Features:

- Star-shaped flowers in early spring
- Edible fruit ripens in July, attracting birds
- Red and yellow foliage color in the fall

Choose Serviceberry for beautiful spring flowers, which blanket the bush with white stars in early spring. Plants in flower are especially showy when planted against an evergreen hedge. Bluish-purple fruit ripens in July and is attractive to birds as well as humans. Rounded, green leaves turn brilliant red and yellow in autumn. Once Serviceberry is planted, it's basically carefree. Fallen fruit can stain paving surfaces, so it is best to keep this shrub away from patios, driveways, and walkways.

Aronia melanocarpa

Black Chokeberry

Zones: 4-9

Light Needs:

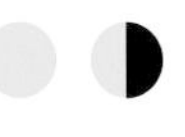

Mature Size:

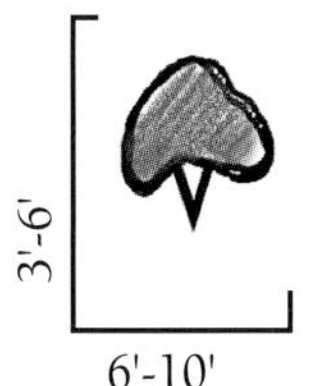

Growth Rate: slow

deciduous flowering shrub

Needs: Plant in any moist soil except shallow, alkaline sites. These swamp natives tolerate wet areas with heavy soil; they'll also endure dry, sandy conditions. Grow in full sun or partial shade. Fruiting is heavier in full sun.

Good for: natural areas, edges of woodlands, wet areas, planting beside sunny ponds, shrub beds, massing

More Choices: pages 34, 36, 38, 39, 40, 42, 119, 120, 121, 122, and 123

Options: Red Chokeberry, *A. arbutifolia*—red berries, red to purple fall color 'Brilliant'—berries, bright red, fall foliage

Outstanding Features:

- White flowers in late spring and summer
- Large, purplish-black fruit in fall and winter
- Leaves turn wine red in autumn

You'll enjoy this easy-to-grow shrub throughout the seasons. White, spring flowers are followed by black berries and wine-colored, fall foliage. Fruit persists through much of fall and early winter. This plant rarely requires pruning, but you'll need to give it room to grow. Forming thickets of leggy stems, plants are perfect for naturalizing, but are unsuitable for formal gardens. For a shrub with glossy foliage that turns red in fall, choose 'Elata'.

Azalea carolinianum

Carolina Azalea

Outstanding Features:
- Wide range of flower colors available
- Foliage stays green year-round
- Provides seasonal accent in spring

Zones: 4-9

Light Needs:

Mature Size:

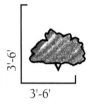

Growth Rate: slow

evergreen flowering shrub

Needs: Grow in full sun. Plant in fertile, acidic, moist, and well-drained soil. Set new shrubs slightly higher to prevent water from collecting around roots. Mulch to keep roots moist. Provide extra water during dry periods and in autumn. Prune as soon as flowering finishes by removing selected woody stems; do not shear.

Good for: seasonal accents, background use, foundation plantings, growing along fences, entries, walkways, beside patios, massing in planting beds

More Choices: pages 34, 40, 109, 117, 120, 121, 122, and 123

Welcome spring to your yard with plantings of Carolina Azaleas. These shrubs feature flowers in springtime shades. Leaves stay shiny green throughout the year. Can grow in Zone 4 with winter protection. Avoid planting azaleas where they'll be exposed to harsh winds or strong winter sun. Also try: var. *album*—white flowers; var. *luteum*—yellow flowers.

Azalea 'Exbury Hybrids'

Exbury Azalea

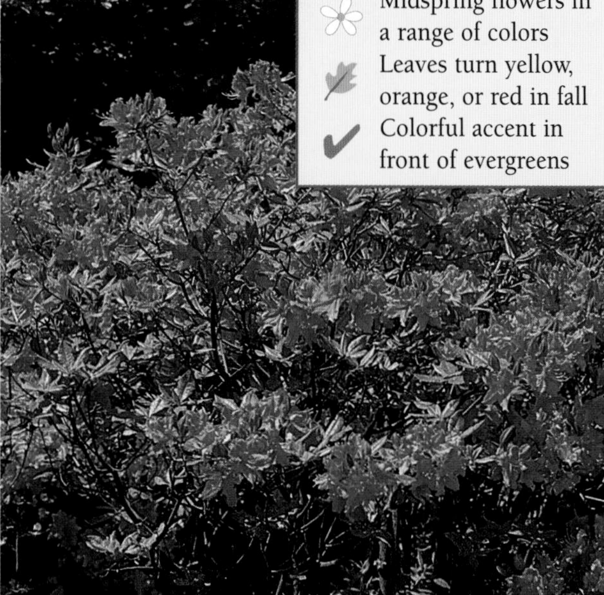

Outstanding Features:
- Midspring flowers in a range of colors
- Leaves turn yellow, orange, or red in fall
- Colorful accent in front of evergreens

Zones: 4-7

Light Needs:

Mature Size:

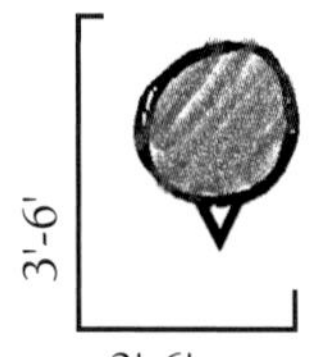

Growth Rate: slow

deciduous flowering shrub

Needs: Plant in fertile, acidic soil that's moist but well-drained. Set new shrubs slightly higher than existing ground to prevent water from collecting around roots. Mulch to keep roots moist. Supply extra water during dry periods and in autumn. Grow in full sun. Remove selected woody stems after flowering; do not shear.

Good for: seasonal accents, foundation planting, hedges, massing, planting along fences, long driveways, and beneath trees

More Choices: pages 35, 41, 109, 117, 119, 120, 122, and 123

These azaleas will add color to your yard in the spring when blossoms open and again in autumn when the leaves put on their fall show. Choose rose-pink, red, orange, white, or yellow flower colors. Plants are also known as Knap Hill or Rothschild Hybrids. Look for these cultivars: 'Berry Rose'—rose-pink blossoms, 'Firefly'—red flowers; 'Gibraltar'—bright orange flowers, and 'White Swan'—white blooms.

Azalea mucronulatum 'Cornell Pink'

Cornell Pink Azalea

Outstanding Features:

- Lush pink flowers in early spring
- Leaves turn yellow to crimson in fall
- An azalea tolerant of cold climates

Zones: 4-7

Light Needs:

Mature Size:

Growth Rate: slow

deciduous flowering shrub

Needs: Plant in fertile, acidic soil that's moist but well-drained. Set new shrubs slightly higher than existing ground to prevent water from collecting around roots. Mulch well to keep roots moist. Supply extra water during dry periods and in autumn. Grow in full sun. Remove woody stems after flowering; do not shear.

Good for: specimen use, seasonal accents, foundation plantings (with evergreen shrubs), massing, filling in planting beds, natural areas

More Choices: pages 34, 40, 109, 117, 119, 120, 121, 122, and 123

Include these shrubs for early spring color. Flowers open before leaves unfurl, blanketing the plant in bright pink. One of the earliest azaleas to bloom. Plant these shrubs in a protected location away from winter sun. This is especially important in colder climates where warming rays may coax buds into opening too early. Freezing temperatures will damage or kill the blooms before you can enjoy them.

Azalea 'Northern Lights'

Northern Lights Azalea

Outstanding Features:

- Spring flowers available in a range of colors
- Bronze, burgundy, or purple foliage in fall
- Cold-tolerant accent for the spring garden

Zones: 4-7

Light Needs:

Mature Size:

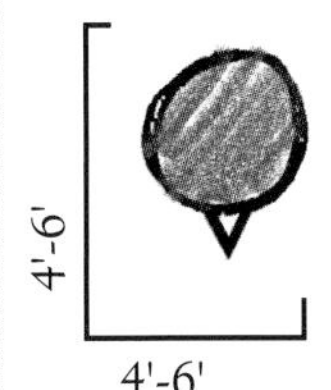

Growth Rate: slow

deciduous flowering shrub

Needs: Grow in full sun. Plant in fertile, moist, well-drained, acidic soil. Set new shrubs slightly higher than existing ground to prevent water from collecting around roots. Mulch. Supply extra water during dry weather and again in autumn. Prune when flowers have finished to remove woody stems; do not shear.

Good for: seasonal accents, informal deciduous hedges, foundation plantings (with evergreen shrubs), massing, natural areas, filling in planting beds

More Choices: pages 35, 41, 109, 117, 118, 119, 120, 121, 122, and 123

Developed at the University of Minnesota, these azaleas can take the cold. Buds will withstand temperatures down to 45 below zero and still produce abundant blooms when spring arrives. Flowers possess a clovelike fragrance. Additional selections include: 'Golden Lights'—golden flowers in late spring, bronzy-red fall foliage; 'Northern Hi-Lights'—creamy white and yellow flowers in late spring, burgundy to purple fall foliage; 'Orchid Lights'—lilac flowers in early spring, insignificant fall color; 'Rosy Lights'—rosy flowers in late spring, insignificant fall color; and 'White Lights'—pink buds open to white blossoms in late spring, bronzy-purple fall foliage.

Berberis thunbergii

Japanese Barberry

Zones: 4-8

Light Needs:

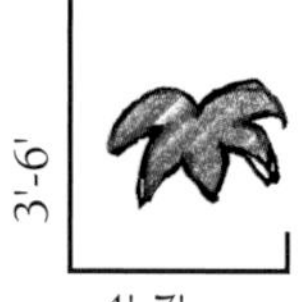

Mature Size:

Growth Rate: medium

deciduous shrub

Needs: Plant anywhere except in standing water. Japanese Barberry performs best in full sun in well-drained, fertile soil. Prune to shape after flowering. Plants tolerate urban conditions very well.

Good for: hedges, barriers, foundation planting, or border shrub

More Choices: pages 35, 36, 39, 107, 109, 119, and 123

Options: var. *atropurpurea*—reddish or purple leaves, turning red in fall
'Crimson Pygmy'—deep red leaves turn orange-scarlet in fall, 2' to 3' tall and wide
'Rose Glow'—rose-red leaves in fall

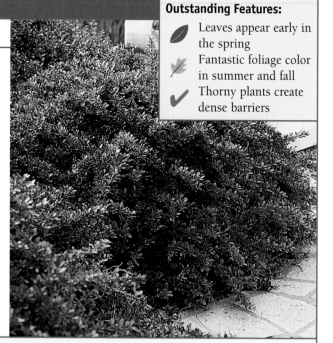

Outstanding Features:
- Leaves appear early in the spring
- Fantastic foliage color in summer and fall
- Thorny plants create dense barriers

This spiny shrub will grow anywhere. It can tolerate tight root quarters, urban pollution, and neglect. Green summer foliage turns shades of orange, scarlet, or reddish-purple in the fall. Spines are sharp and make effective barrier plantings, but avoid planting them where children play. The variety 'Thornless' is a better selection for these areas. Turning orange-red in the fall, it grows 3' to 5' high by 4' to 6' wide; stems are thornless. Plants tend to collect blowing debris and require cleaning out in the spring. Growth in Zone 8 is limited.

Buxus microphylla 'Wintergreen'

Wintergreen Boxwood

Zones: 4-6

Light Needs:

Mature Size:

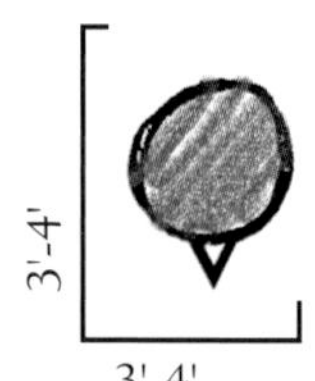

Growth Rate: slow

evergreen shrub

Needs: Plant in fertile soil that's moist but well-drained. Avoid soggy soil and mulch to keep roots cool. Plants are shallow-rooted and deep cultivation should be avoided. Grow in full sun or partial shade.

Good for: edging flowerbeds, formal gardens, foundation plantings, low hedges, planting beside patios, along walkways, in courtyards or entries, winter interest

More Choices: pages 35, 36, 107, 109, 117, 119, 121, and 122

Options: 'Green Pillow'—forms a small, rounded, green cushion

Outstanding Features:
- Shears well, stays neat, compact, and low
- Foliage remains dark green in winter
- Tolerates cold temperatures and sun

This shrub earns its place in the landscape for year-round beauty. Its tidy form stays neat summer through winter and looks great under snow. Plants make beautiful low hedges or edges. Also known as Korean Boxwood or Littleleaf Boxwood. 'Wintergreen' is a particularly hardy selection that doesn't discolor during the winter.

Calycanthus floridus

Sweetshrub

Zones: 4-9

Light Needs:

Mature Size:

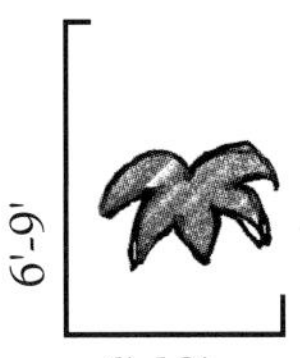

Growth Rate: slow

deciduous flowering shrub

Needs: Plant in any soil type; shrubs grow best in deep, moist, loamy soil. Grow in sun or shade. Flowering is best and plants grow largest in full sun. Prune after flowering in the spring to remove older wood. Pest resistant.

Good for: massing, specimen use, fragrance, planting beside entries, windows, porches, patios, benches, gates, parking areas, courtyards; edges of woodlands, shrub beds

More Choices: pages 35, 36, 39, 118, 119, 121, 122, and 123

Options: 'Athens'—yellow-green flowers

Outstanding Features:

- Flowers bear a spicy or fruity scent
- Bright green leaves turn yellow in fall
- Adaptable to moist soils and shade

Let this old-fashioned shrub welcome you home with its spicy perfume. Small, reddish-brown flowers unleash their fruity fragrance during warm, summer months. Purchase plants while in bloom to ensure a pleasing fragrance. Shrubs grown from seed may have an unreliable smell; some are unpleasant. Plants are easy to grow and form a rounded outline. Also sold as Carolina Allspice.

Chamaecyparis obtusa 'Nana Gracilis'

Dwarf Hinoki False Cypress

Zones: 4-8

Light Needs:

Mature Size:

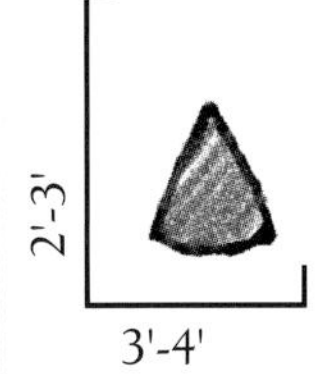

Growth Rate: slow

evergreen shrub

Needs: Plant in full sun in moist, well-drained, acidic soil. Plants will tolerate alkaline soils. Protect from wind.

Good for: specimen use, rock gardens, planters, adding upright, evergreen shape

More Choices: pages 35, 41, 117, and 119

Options: 'Nana Lutea'—golden-yellow leaves; 12" high, 10" wide

Outstanding Features:

- Dark green needles and diminutive size
- Pyramidal form makes a beautiful specimen
- Tolerates moist, acidic soil locations

This slow-growing evergreen adds unchanging beauty to any yard. Foliage and form remains the same through the seasons and through the years. It looks like a tiny Christmas tree. This shrub is easy to grow; aside from occasional watering during times of drought, no care is needed.

Clethra alnifolia

Summersweet

Zones: 3-9

Light Needs:

Mature Size:

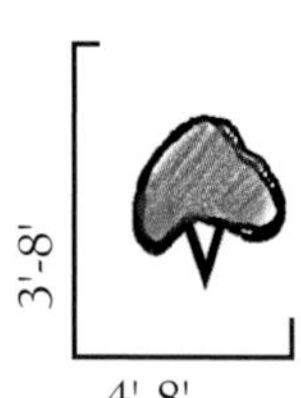

Growth Rate: slow

deciduous flowering shrub

Needs: Plant in moist, acidic soil. Mix organic matter in at planting time; mulch with a 3-inch-thick layer of compost each spring. Water regularly during the growing season. Grow in partial shade. Prune in late summer after flowering to keep plants dense and oval-shaped.

Good for: massing in shady beds, woodlands, swampy spots, natural areas, beside ponds, streams, shrub borders

More Choices: pages 23, 36, 39, 41, 117, 118, 119, 120, 121, and 123

Options: 'Ruby Spice'—dark pink flowers

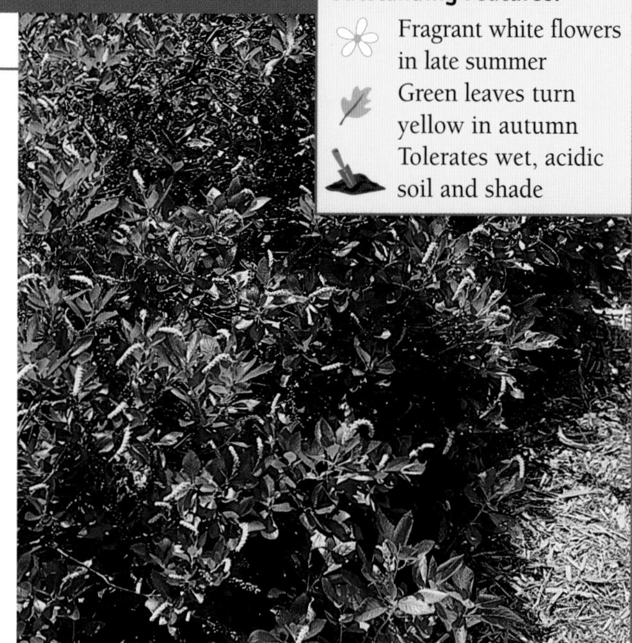

Outstanding Features:

- Fragrant white flowers in late summer
- Green leaves turn yellow in autumn
- Tolerates wet, acidic soil and shade

Don't let soggy soils or shady sites deter you. Summersweet will thrive in these locations. Fragrant flowers occur at a time when few other shrubs are blooming, usually from July to August. Shrubs get quite large and form an oval outline. They sucker to form colonies of clean, healthy plants. Plants may be sold as Sweet Pepperbush. Summersweet is fragrant.

Cornus alba

Redtwig Dogwood

Zones: 2-8

Light Needs:

Mature Size:

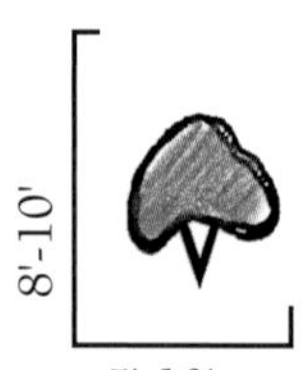

Growth Rate: rapid

deciduous shrub

Needs: Plant in full sun in moist, well-drained soil. Will tolerate partial shade. The red stem color is brightest on young wood. Prune all stems to within 4" to 6" of the ground in early spring, before new growth begins.

Good for: shrub borders, along fences or driveways, around ponds, large displays

More Choices: pages 35, 39, and 119

Options: *Cornus stolonifera* 'Cardinal'—showy red twigs, 6' tall, 12' wide
'Elegantissima'—gray-green leaves with irregular, twisted white margins
'Aurea'—leaves are soft yellow

'Argenteo-marginata'

Outstanding Features:

- Winter interest against evergreen background
- Fast growth and soil adaptability
- Usefulness in large planting areas

Brighten your yard's winter appeal with Redtwig Dogwood. The new stems have a greenish color with just a hint of red. With the onset of cool weather, stems turn bright red, the perfect color to linger and glow against winter snows after the leaves blow away in the fall. The more sun plants receive, the brighter the twig color will be.

Cornus mas

Cornelian Cherry

Outstanding Features:

- Bright yellow flowers open early in spring
- Edible berries attract birds to the landscape
- Adaptable to various soil and pH types

Zones: 4-8

Light Needs:

Mature Size:

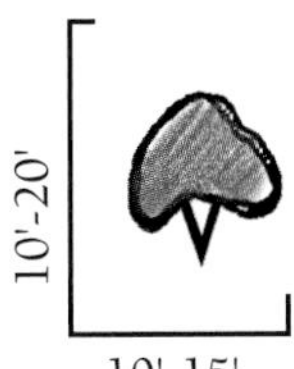

Growth Rate: medium to rapid

deciduous flowering shrub

Needs: Plant in full sun in moist, well-drained soil. Prune any dead or damaged stems in late winter or early spring; prune to shape after flowering. Pest-free.

Good for: specimen use, shrub borders, hedges, screens, foundation plantings, small, ornamental trees

More Choices: pages 34, 107, 109, 119, and 122

Options: 'Aureo-elegantissima'—leaves are yellow or brushed with pink
'Variegata'—leaf margins are creamy white

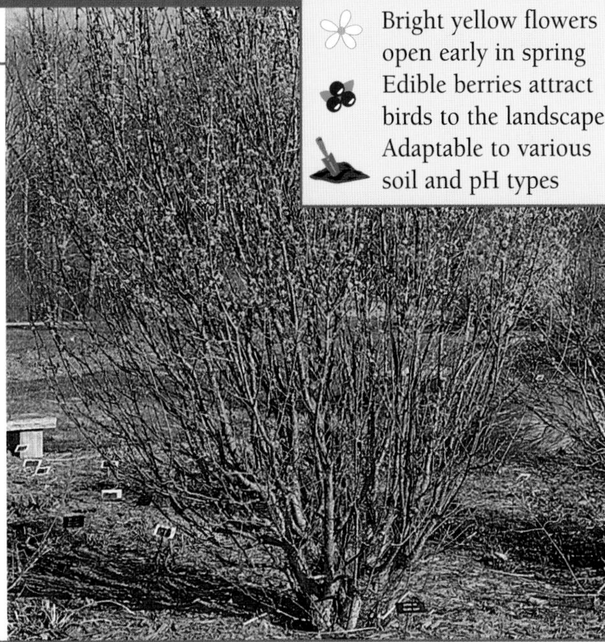

Cornelian Cherry steals the show in early spring with golden blooms that burst open even before forsythia. Edible, cherry red fruit ripens in midsummer and can be made into flavorful preserves. Or, let the birds enjoy the fruit. These shrubs require little or no care after plants become established. Plants are attractive planted against a dark green or red background.

Cornus racemosa

Gray Dogwood

Outstanding Features:

- Winter interest from bark and flower stems
- White flowers open in late May
- White berries ripen in fall and attract birds

Zones: 4-7

Light Needs:

Mature Size:

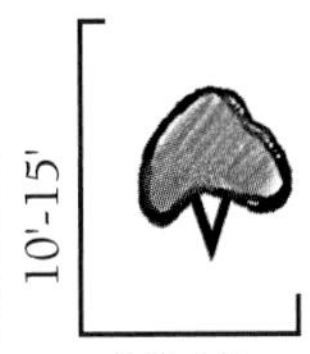

Growth Rate: slow to rapid

deciduous flowering shrub

Needs: Plant in full sun in moist, well-drained soil. Prune any dead or damaged stems in late winter or early spring; prune to shape after flowering. It suckers and can be difficult to maintain in small settings.

Good for: shrub borders, hedges, poor soils, naturalized areas, winter interest, massed plantings

More Choices: pages 35, 109, 119, and 122

Options: 'Slavinii'—dwarf with twisted leaves; 2' to 3' high, suckering spread

Spring flowers turn into white, berrylike fruits that are savored by numerous species of birds. After the fruits are gone and leaves have fallen, the stems that held the fruits become visible. The pinkish stems contrast with the gray stems of the shrub, and the result is picture perfect—all winter long. Three-year-old and older stems develop the gray bark color; younger wood is reddish brown. In colder climates, shield from northwest winds by planting in a protected area, not out in the open.

Cornus stolonifera 'Flaviramea'

Yellow-Twig Dogwood

Zones: 3-8

Light Needs:

Mature Size:

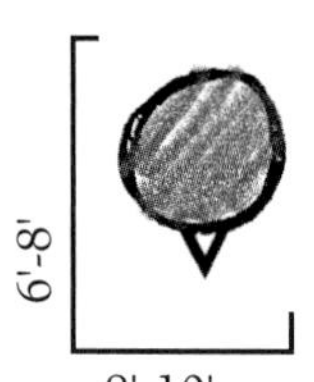

Growth Rate: rapid

deciduous shrub

Needs: Plant in full sun or part shade in moist or wet soil. The yellow stem color is brightest on young wood. Prune all stems to within 4" to 6" of the ground in early spring, before new growth begins.

Good for: shrub borders, mass plantings, use along drives or fences

More Choices: pages 35, 36, 39, 119, and 123

Options: 'Isanti'—bright red stems; 5' to 6' high, 8' to 10' wide; Zones 3-8

Outstanding Features:

- Yellow-green twigs provide color contrast
- Fall leaves are reddish-purple in color
- Fast growth; adaptable to wet soils

Plant Yellow-Twig Dogwood to brighten winter scenes around your home. This plant requires nothing more than well-drained soil and well-timed pruning in early spring to encourage growth of new, yellow stems. Use with caution in the landscape. The color effect can be overwhelming.

Daphne x burkwoodii 'Carol Mackie'

Carol Mackie Daphne

Zones: 4-8

Light Needs:

Mature Size:

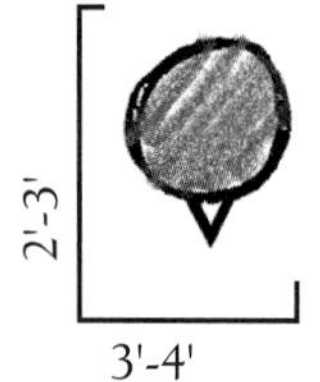

Growth Rate: slow

semievergreen shrub

Needs: Plant in full sun or part shade in cool, moist soil. Neutral to slightly alkaline soil yields best growth. Mulch to keep roots cool. Prune to remove dead wood or to shape immediately after flowering.

Good for: specimen shrubs, small yards, rock gardens, raised planting beds, entries, outdoor living areas

More Choices: pages 34, 36, 39, 41, 117, 118, 119, 121, and 122

Outstanding Features:

- Clusters of light pink flowers in spring
- Leaves are delicately edged in cream
- Maintain foliage well into winter

Waxy, perfumed pink blooms cover this shrub in spring, scenting an entire yard with their sweet fragrance. The leaves are deep green edged in cream. Roots require cool soil that is well-drained. Once that need is met, get set for years of springtime scents and summertime beauty.

Euonymus alatus 'Compacta'

Dwarf Burning Bush

Zones: 3-8

Light Needs:

Mature Size:

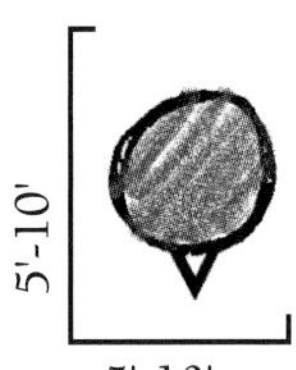

Growth Rate: slow

deciduous shrub

Needs: Plant in any well-drained soil, acidic or alkaline. Grow in full sun or partial shade. Pruning is seldom needed or desired. Maintain plants in their natural rounded form.

Good for: specimen shrubs, seasonal accents, deciduous screens, massing, parking areas, beside patios, along walkways or paths, hedges

More Choices: pages 31, 34, 36, 41, 43, 119, 120, 121, and 123

Options: Burning Bush (not dwarf; no 'Compacta' in botanical name)—12' to 15' high, 10' to 12' wide

Outstanding Features:

- Flame red foliage color in fall
- Leaves grow in horizontal layers
- Naturally dense, rounded outline

If you enjoy fall color, you ought to plant some Burning Bush. Leaves on these shrubs turn brilliant red in autumn. Also sold as Dwarf Winged Euonymus, so named for corky ridges present on stems.

Forsythia mandshurica 'Vermont Sun'

Vermont Sun Forsythia

Zones: 4-8

Light Needs:

Mature Size:

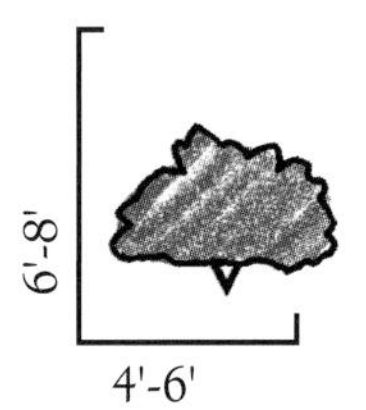

Growth Rate: slow

deciduous flowering shrub

Needs: Plant in moist, well-drained soil, though shrubs will adapt to most soil types. Grow in full sun. After flowering, prune established shrubs by removing one-third of the stems back to the ground each year. This will rejuvenate growth and encourage flowers the next spring.

Good for: seasonal accent, informal screens or hedges, hillsides, natural areas, massing, shrub beds

More Choices: pages 31, 35, 36, 42, 117, 119, 120, 121, and 122

Options: *F. ovata* 'Northern Gold'—hardy to –25 degrees F

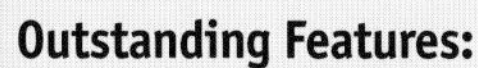

Outstanding Features:

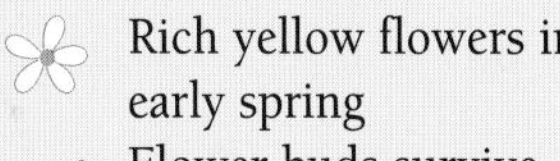

- Rich yellow flowers in early spring
- Flower buds survive harsh winters
- Foliage turns yellow, pink, and red in fall

Vermont Sun Forsythia is the ideal forsythia for colder regions. Its yellow flowers in early spring make an attractive shrub border or screen. Flower buds will withstand temperatures as low as 30 below zero and open about one week before other types of forsythia. Foliage turns beautiful shades of yellow, pink, and red in the fall.

Hamamelis virginiana

Common Witch Hazel

Zones: 3-8

Light Needs:

Mature Size:

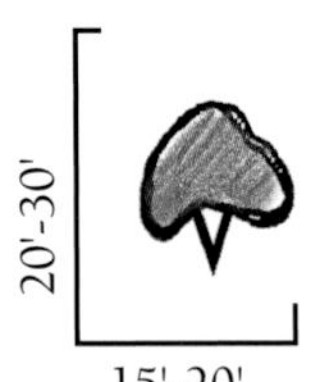

Growth Rate: medium

deciduous flowering shrub

Needs: Plant in full sun or partial shade in well-drained, fertile soil. It will not thrive in dry soils. Tolerant of city conditions. This shrub will get big; give it room to grow. Prune in late winter or early spring to remove dead or damaged wood.

Good for: shrub borders, large foundation plantings or massing, naturalized areas, fragrance, shaded areas

More Choices: pages 34, 36, 118, and 123

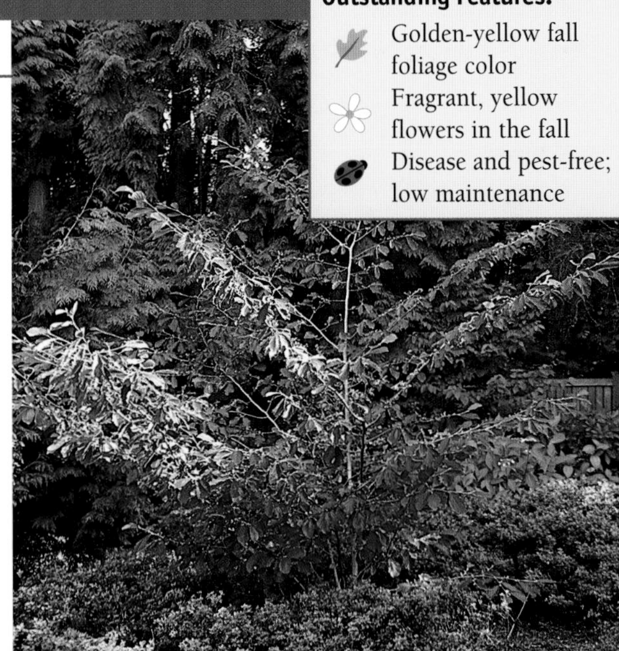

Outstanding Features:

- Golden-yellow fall foliage color
- Fragrant, yellow flowers in the fall
- Disease and pest-free; low maintenance

Add flower fragrance to the scents experienced in autumn by planting Common Witch Hazel. The flowers open in fall from October to November. Green summer foliage turns a spectacular yellow in fall. Plants grown in full sun have a rounded shape while those grown in shade are more open and irregular. Can be used as a small tree or large shrub in the landscape.

Hydrangea arborescens 'Annabelle'

Annabelle Hydrangea

Zones: 3-9

Light Needs:

Mature Size:

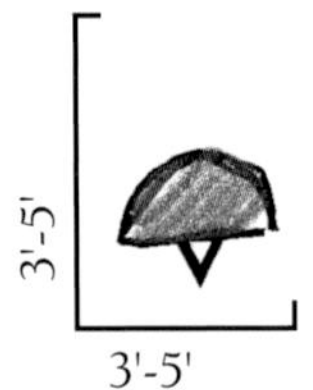

Growth Rate: rapid

deciduous shrub

Needs: Plant in fertile, slightly acidic soil that's well-drained but moist. Water regularly. Grow in full sun or partial shade—blooms best in sun but may require afternoon shade in hotter regions. Prune in late winter or early spring, cutting stems just above a bud to remove one-quarter of stem length.

Good for: specimen shrubs, seasonal accent, massing, entries, courtyards, beside patios, include in flower or shrub beds, fill in narrow spaces between walkways and walls

More Choices: pages 34, 36, 39, 40, 43, 119, 120, 121, 122, and 123

Outstanding Features:

- Big, showy flowers last from spring into fall
- Grows quickly to fill in planting beds
- Tolerates both cold and hot temperatures

Get the soil right and this shrub is easy to grow. Big blossoms are showy from spring into fall and change colors with the seasons. They start off apple green in late spring, then become white, then back to green, and finally fade to pink-blushed beige in cool weather. Position these shrubs where you can enjoy them throughout the growing season. Flowers may reach nearly a foot in diameter. Cut blossoms dry well.

Hydrangea paniculata 'Grandiflora'

PeeGee Hydrangea

Zones: 3-8

Light Needs:

Mature Size:

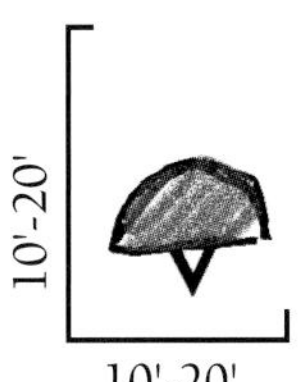

Growth Rate: rapid

deciduous flowering shrub

Needs: Plant in rich soil that's moist but well-drained. Slightly acidic soils are best. Shrubs will adapt to any soil condition except soggy. Grow in full sun or partial shade. Avoid pruning by giving plants plenty of room; shrubs grow vigorously and get large enough to be trained into small trees.

Good for: specimen shrub, seasonal accent, informal deciduous screen, coarse-textured background, planting in front of blank walls or fences

More Choices: pages 31, 35, 36, 41, 119, and 123

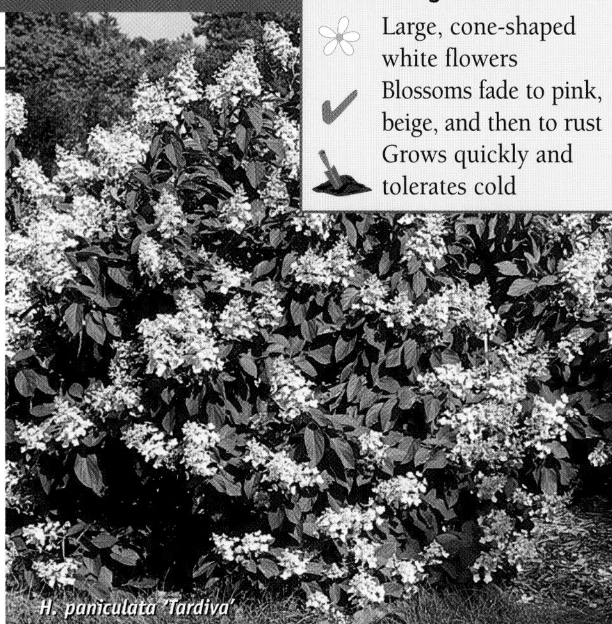

H. paniculata 'Tardiva'

Outstanding Features:

- Large, cone-shaped white flowers
- Blossoms fade to pink, beige, and then to rust
- Grows quickly and tolerates cold

Plant this tough, fast-growing shrub where it has room to get big. Plants fade into the background until midsummer flowers put them in the spotlight. Flowers are produced on new wood. Flower heads can reach 12 to 18 inches in length. Plants should be pruned to 5 or 10 main shoots to produce the largest heads. Ultimate plant size is quite variable. Also try: 'Tardiva'—flowers in fall.

Ilex crenata 'Green Lustre'

Green Lustre Japanese Holly

Zones: 4-6

Light Needs:

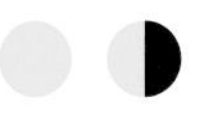

Mature Size:

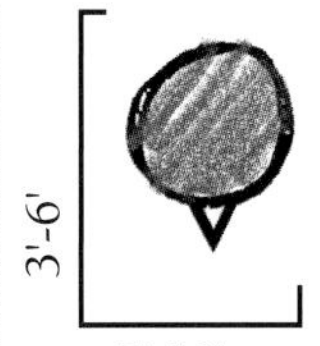

Growth Rate: slow

evergreen shrub

Needs: Plant in either full sun or partial shade in fertile, moist soil that's high in organic matter. Prefers acidic soils. Alkaline soil (high pH) will cause leaves to turn yellow; add peat at planting if it's necessary to lower pH. Prune to shape shrubs in summer, after the new growth is mature. Tolerates city conditions and confined growing spaces.

Good for: specimen use, hedging, screening, massing in planting beds

More Choices: pages 30, 35, 36, 43, 107, 119, and 121

'Convexa'

Outstanding Features:

- Shiny green leaves throughout the year
- Dense, solid growth makes a solid screen
- Adaptability to urban growing conditions

This holly is hardy and sturdy. Its dense branching habit and thick leaf cover make it an excellent choice for creating a privacy screen or barrier hedge. Japanese Holly adapts well to urban growing conditions and to small yards. Though it prefers acidic soil, it will tolerate neutral soil pH. This holly isn't difficult to grow or to maintain. Grow this shrub in the warmer areas of Zone 4 by planting in a location shielded from harsh winter winds.

Ilex glabra 'Compacta'

Inkberry

Zones: 3-10

Light Needs:

Mature Size:

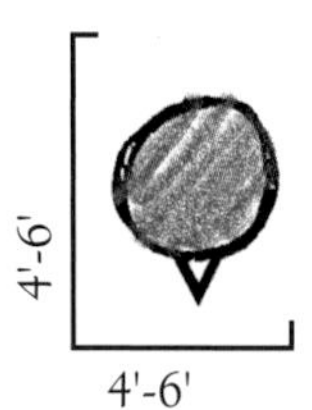

Growth Rate: slow to medium

evergreen shrub

Needs: Plant in acidic soil that's moist but well-drained. Grow in full sun or partial shade. Pest and disease-resistant. Shear or prune heavily as needed to maintain compact size.

Good for: foundation planting, screening, massing, winter interest, providing background, seaside landscapes, formal or informal gardens, parking areas, poolside, planting beside patios, and walkways

More Choices: pages 23, 30, 35, 36, 39, 41, 43, 45, 109, 120, and 121

Outstanding Features:

- Glossy leaves stay dark green year-round
- Tolerates heat, snow, salt, and pruning
- Dense, compact form; tight branching

Few shrubs are as adaptable as glossy-leaved Inkberry. You can grow it at the beach, in snow, in alkaline or acidic soils, in sunny or shady spots. Also sold as Gallberry. Compact varieties are more desirable for home landscape use. Select these unless you want a 10' tall shrub: 'Nigra'—3' to 4' tall; 'Shamrock'—5' to 6' tall. Thrives in the Eastern United States.

Ilex verticillata

Winterberry

Zones: 3-9

Light Needs:

Mature Size:

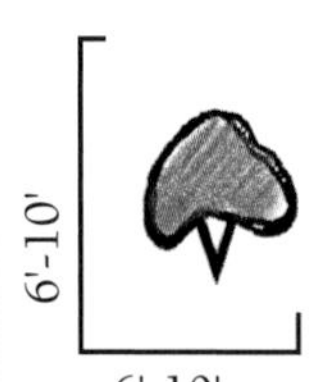

Growth Rate: slow

deciduous flowering shrub

Needs: Plant in full sun or partial shade in fertile, moist soil that's high in organic matter. Plants prefer an acidic soil pH. They will adapt to wet soils.

Good for: wet, boggy areas, winter interest, screens or hedges, attracting birds, training as a small tree, massing

More Choices: pages 31, 35, 36, 39, 41, 107, 119, and 123

Options: 'Sparkleberry'—quarter-inch berries; 15' high by 12' wide; Zones 5-9 'Winter Red'—dark green leaves turn bronze in fall; berries last until spring; 8' high by 10' wide; Zones 3-9

Outstanding Features:

- Big, bright red berries persist through winter
- Fruit attracts birds to the landscape
- Grows in wet, swampy soil conditions

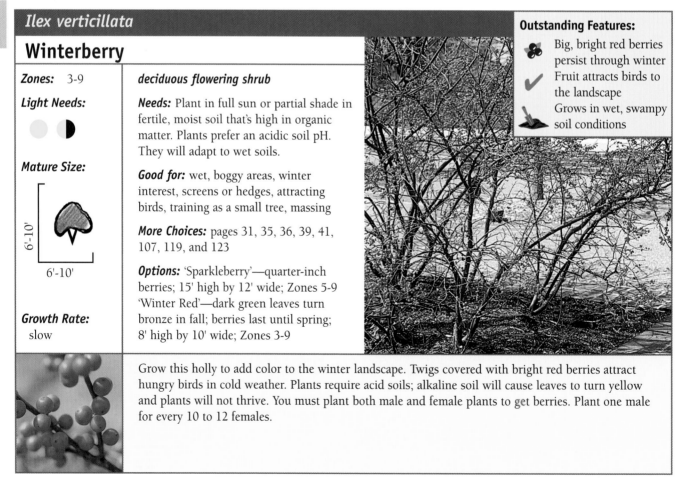

Grow this holly to add color to the winter landscape. Twigs covered with bright red berries attract hungry birds in cold weather. Plants require acid soils; alkaline soil will cause leaves to turn yellow and plants will not thrive. You must plant both male and female plants to get berries. Plant one male for every 10 to 12 females.

Juniperus chinensis 'Old Gold'

Old Gold Juniper

Outstanding Features:

- Bronze-gold foliage year-round
- Compact, spreading shape; little pruning
- Tolerates heat and cold

Zones: 4-10

Light Needs:

Mature Size: 2'-3' × 3'-4'

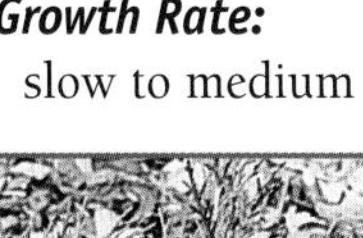

Growth Rate: slow to medium

evergreen shrub

Needs: Plant in any soil that's well-drained, including acidic or alkaline. Hot, dry and poor soil is fine; avoid wet soil. Not for extreme heat or desert conditions. Grow in full sun.

Good for: specimen plants, dry areas, hillsides, winter interest, Xeriscaping, arid landscapes

More Choices: pages 35, 39, 41, 42, and 43

Options: 'Spartan'—20' tall pyramidal shrub, green foliage, fast-growing

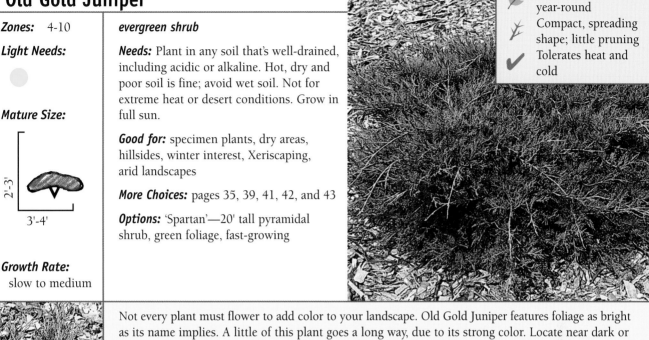

Not every plant must flower to add color to your landscape. Old Gold Juniper features foliage as bright as its name implies. A little of this plant goes a long way, due to its strong color. Locate near dark or neutral backgrounds. Foliage may clash with house color or the foliage of other variegated plants.

Juniperus chinensis 'Parsonii'

Parson's Juniper

Outstanding Features:

- Forms a low-growing mound of grey-green
- Maintains leaf color through the seasons
- Low maintenance and adaptability

Zones: 3-9

Light Needs:

Mature Size: 2'-3' × 3'-4'

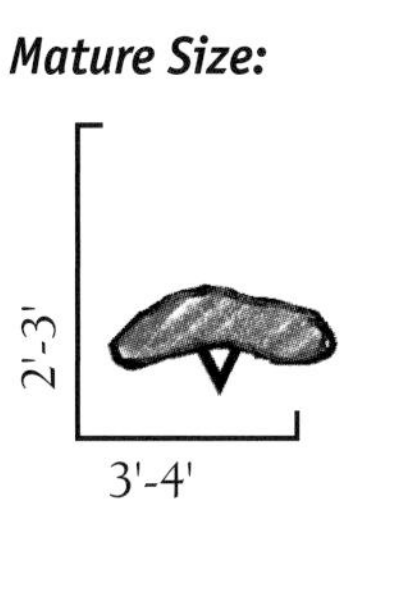

Growth Rate: slow to medium

evergreen shrub

Needs: Plant in full sun in moist, well-drained soil. Junipers will also grow in chalky, sandy soils that are dry. Little pruning is needed.

Good for: low growing hedge, low plantings along a walkway, or surrounding a patio or deck

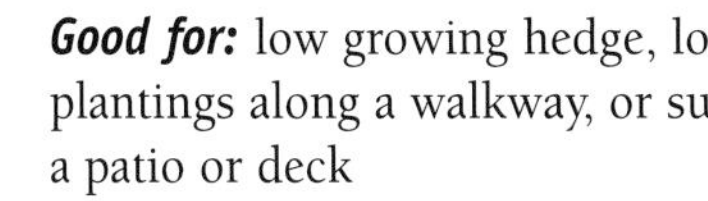

More Choices: pages 23, 35, 39, 42, 43, 107, 119, and 121

Junipers earn their keep in the landscape. Once established, they are carefree. Occasional pruning to remove any dead or damaged growth is all that is needed. Don't overwater.

Juniperus chinensis 'Sea Green'

Sea Green Juniper

Zones: 4-8

Light Needs:

Mature Size:

Growth Rate: slow to medium

evergreen shrub

Needs: Plant in full sun in moist to dry, well-drained soil. Junipers will also grow in chalky, sandy soils that are dry. Little pruning is needed.

Good for: foundation plantings around homes or decks or porches

More Choices: pages 23, 35, 39, 42, 45, 119, and 121

Outstanding Features:

- Easily transplanted and grown
- Graceful and elegant, fountainlike form
- Foliage darkens with cooler temperatures

Easy and evergreen—that pretty much sums up Sea Green Juniper. Grow it for year-round frothy foliage in moist or poor soils in full sun.

Juniperus sabina 'Tamariscifolia'

Tam Juniper

Zones: 3-7

Light Needs:

Mature Size:

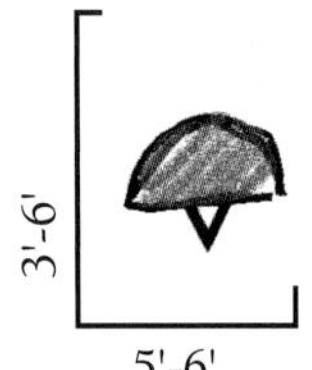

Growth Rate: slow to medium

evergreen shrub

Needs: Plant in full sun in well-drained soil. Grows well in chalky, sandy soils that are dry. It also can take urban growing conditions. Little pruning is needed. Remove dead or damaged branches or shape anytime from early summer to fall.

Good for: low growing hedges, planting along walkways, surrounding patios or decks, mass plantings

More Choices: pages 35, 39, 45, 107, 119, and 121

Options: 'Arcadia'—leaves are grass green; 1' high by 4' wide; Zones 3-7

Outstanding Features:

- Rounded mound of blue-green branches
- Maintains leaf color through the seasons
- Tolerates poor, dry soil conditions with ease

Skandia

This easy-to-grow evergreen requires no effort to grow or to maintain. Simply plant it, water it in, and let it grow. Tam Juniper grows in a mounded shape, making it the perfect choice for including as part of a foundation planting or for rounding the corner of a house or deck.

Juniperus squamata 'Blue Star'

Blue Star Juniper

Outstanding Features:

- Tight mound of silvery blue-green foliage
- Maintains leaf color through the seasons.
- Slow growth rate; doesn't get out of hand

Zones: 4-8

Light Needs:

Mature Size:

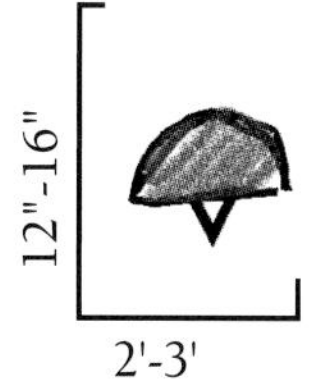

Growth Rate: slow

evergreen shrub

Needs: Plant in full sun in well-drained chalky, sandy, or dry soils. It grows well in urban growing conditions. Very little pruning or additional care is required.

Good for: specimen use, rock garden plantings, planting along walkways

More Choices: pages 34, 39, and 119

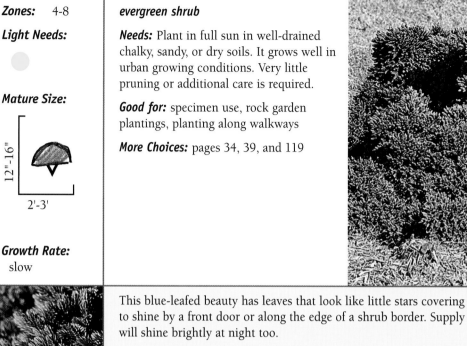

This blue-leafed beauty has leaves that look like little stars covering the branches of the shrub. Use it to shine by a front door or along the edge of a shrub border. Supply some night-lighting and leaves will shine brightly at night too.

Ligustrum amurense

Amur Privet

Outstanding Features:

- Neat, dense foliage takes shearing well
- Adaptable to various soil conditions
- Easy to transplant and grow in the landscape

Zones: 3-7

Light Needs:

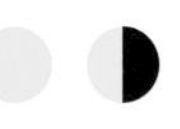

Mature Size:

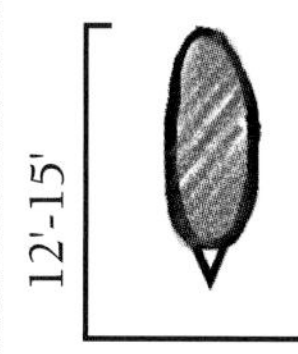

Growth Rate: rapid

deciduous shrub

Needs: Plant in any soil except those that are very wet. Grow in full sun or partial shade. Shrubs tolerate poor, dry, or compacted soils, polluted air, salt, and reflected heat from paving. They take shearing well. Prune in summer.

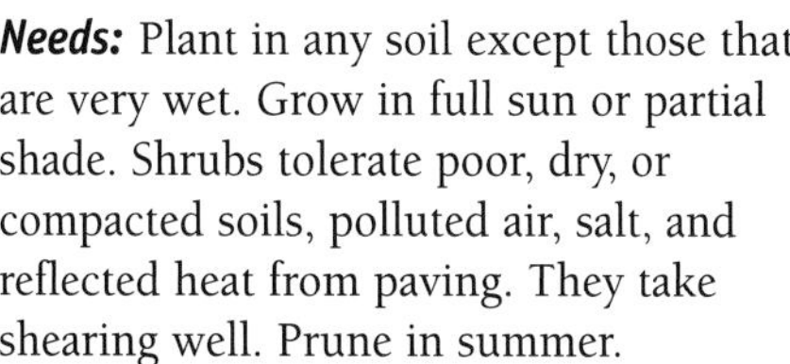

Good for: hedging, screening, foundation planting, formal or informal landscapes, background plantings

More Choices: pages 23, 31, 34, 36, 38, 107, 109, 117, 119, and 121

Some plants are common with good reason. Amur Privet is easy to grow, tolerates a range of conditions, and can be sheared into neat hedges. Thrives even under tough Midwest growing conditions. Odor from small flowers in summer can be objectionable. Pruning in formal shapes often removes flowers.

Lonicera tatarica 'Arnold's Red'

Arnold's Red Tatarian Honeysuckle

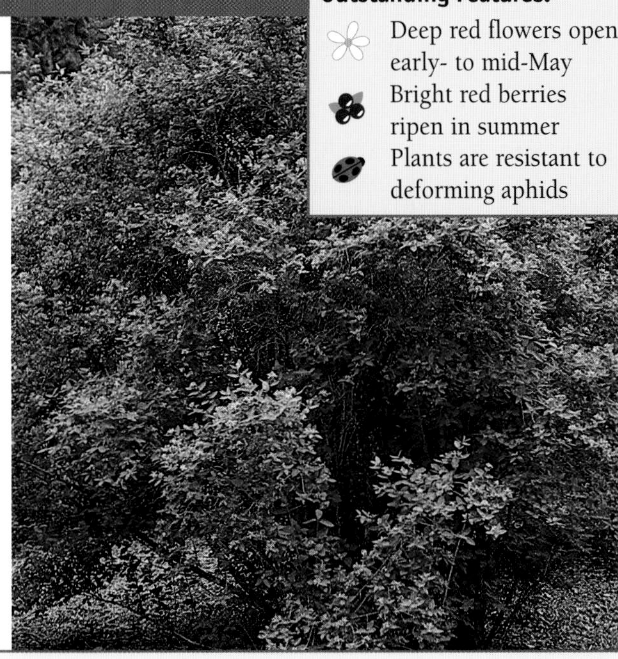

Outstanding Features:

- Deep red flowers open early- to mid-May
- Bright red berries ripen in summer
- Plants are resistant to deforming aphids

Zones: 3-9

Light Needs:

Mature Size:

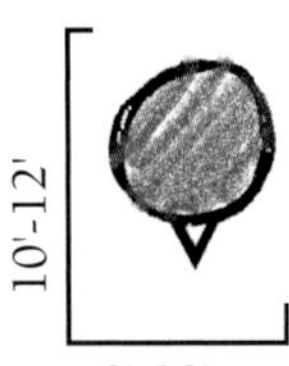

Growth Rate: medium to rapid

deciduous flowering shrub

Needs: Plant in full sun or partial shade in well-drained, fertile soil. Prune annually after flowering to shape and maintain size. Prune anytime to tame wayward stems.

Good for: hedges, dense screens, or fence row planting; use near outdoor living areas for fragrance

More Choices: pages 31, 34, 45, 118, 119, 121, and 122

Options: 'Alba' or 'Parvifolia'—fragrant white flowers
'Hack's Red'—deep purplish-red flowers
'Virginalis'—rose-pink buds and the largest flowers of any *L. tatarica* form

When 'Arnold's Red' bursts into bloom, the effect is that of a red waterfall. Blossoms give way to bright red berries that are a favorite among birds. This shrub is easy to establish and easy to care for. Fallen fruit can stain paving. Use near outside living areas but not right beside them. Dense masses of branches can catch all kinds of wind-borne trash; spring cleanup will be needed especially if planted in open areas or near roadsides.

Microbiota decussata

Russian Cypress

Outstanding Features:

- Low, spreading form covers the ground
- Green foliage changes color for winter
- Tolerates harsh winters without injury

Zones: 3-7

Light Needs:

Mature Size:

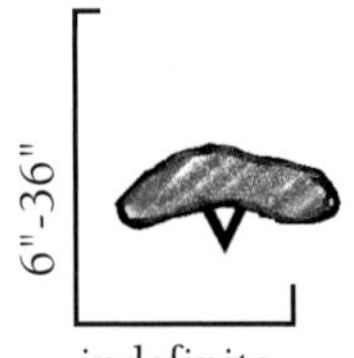

Growth Rate: rapid

evergreen shrub

Needs: Plant in moist well-drained soil. Grow in full sun or partial shade. Pruning is rarely needed; cut to remove stray growth as it occurs. Plants are disease- and pest-free.

Good for: including in the front layer of shrub beds; filling blank spots on hillsides; planting beneath low windows, parking areas; cold, dry, or windswept areas; winter interest

More Choices: pages 35, 36, 42, 119, 121, and 123

This Siberian native isn't fazed by cold weather, diseases, or insects. Scaly green foliage merely blushes with a reddish or purplish brown tinge in winter. They return to their midgreen color when warm weather returns. Plants grow low and wide and are useful in a wide variety of landscaping situations.

Myrica pensylvanica

Northern Bayberry

Zones: 2-6

Light Needs:

Mature Size:

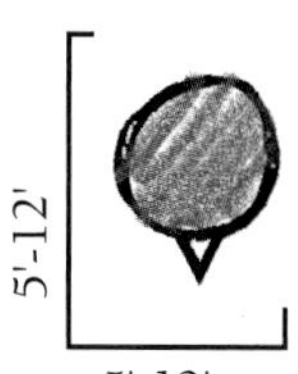

Growth Rate: medium to rapid

evergreen to deciduous shrub

Needs: Plant in full sun or partial shade. This shrub is easy to grow and adapts to a variety of soils, thriving in heavy clay, sandy, fertile, or poor soil. Prune in late winter to remove dead wood and to shape shrubs. To produce fruit, both female and male plants need to be included (check plant tags).

Good for: hedges, screens, fence rows, foundation plantings, use along streets, seaside areas, dried flower arrangements

More Choices: pages 23, 30, 31, 35, 36, 39, 45, 107, 109, 119, and 123

Outstanding Features:

- Aromatic, silvery berries persist through winter
- Tolerance of poor, salty soil conditions
- Attractive used with broad leaf evergreens

Northern Bayberry is one tough shrub, surviving in any kind of soil and withstanding harsh salt spray and soil salts. Its bright green leaves release a bayberry scent when rustled or crushed. Aromatic berries ripen in late summer and fall and linger on branches through winter into spring. They make a lovely addition to fall or holiday flower arrangements. Plants are evergreen in warmer areas and deciduous in colder climates.

Photinia villosa

Oriental Photinia

Zones: 4-7

Light Needs:

Mature Size:

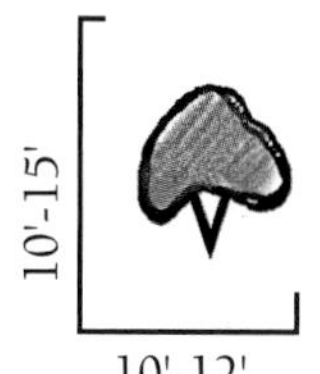

Growth Rate: medium

deciduous flowering shrub

Needs: Plant in well-drained, acidic soil. Grow in full sun to partial shade. Rarely needs pruning.

Good for: specimen use, background plantings, deciduous screens, attracting birds, winter interest, seasonal accent, pruning into a small trees, shrub borders

More Choices: pages 31, 35, 36, 41, 122, and 123

Outstanding Features:

- Dark green leaves, turn red in fall
- White flowers bloom May into June
- Red fruit ripens in fall and lingers into winter

This shrub gets large, so give it plenty of room to grow. You'll enjoy spring flowers, reddish fall foliage, and bright red berries. Plants can be pruned to form an attractive small tree for use around patios and in foundation plantings. They can be susceptible to fire blight. Prune and destroy dying branches; sterilize tools between cuts. Apply a spray containing streptomycin or basic copper sulfate in spring before buds open if this disease is a problem in your area. Reapply throughout bloom.

Picea abies 'Nidiformis'

Bird's Nest Spruce

Outstanding Features:

- Slow growth, spreading more out than up
- Interesting plant form creates a living "nest"
- Tolerates cool climates and moist soils

Zones: 2-7

Light Needs:

Mature Size:

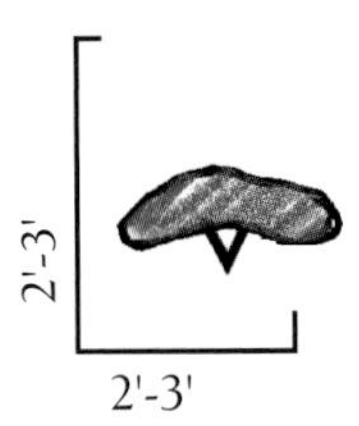

Growth Rate: slow

evergreen shrub

Needs: Plant in full sun in moist, well-drained soil. Spruces do not grow well in polluted, dry conditions. Prune to remove damaged wood or to shape the shrub.

Good for: specimen use, mass plantings, growing along walkways and drives, rock gardens, and perennial borders

More Choices: pages 34, 39, 117, and 119

Bird's Nest Spruce is an excellent plant for small gardens. Its slow growth rate and short stature make it a natural choice for planting in areas where you do not want to block views. Plant this low growing shrub and then forget about it. It's really that easy.

Picea abies 'Pumila'

Dwarf Norway Spruce

Outstanding Features:

- Broad, compact form rarely needs pruning
- Dense, evergreen foliage for year-round appeal
- Tolerates severe winters, cold, and snow

Zones: 3-8

Light Needs:

Mature Size:

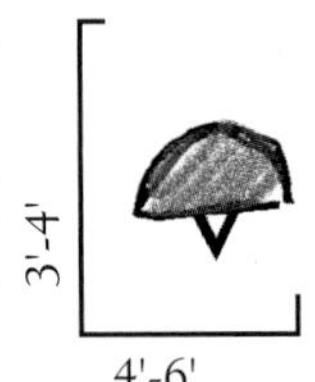

Growth Rate: medium to rapid

evergreen shrub

Needs: Plant in sandy, acidic soil that's moist but well-drained. Grow in full sun. This plant is cold-tolerant and thrives where summers are cool.

Good for: foundation planting, hedges, background use, planting in shrub beds, winter interest, entries, corners of porches, patios, or low decks

More Choices: pages 35, 39, 41, 107, 109, 117, and 121

Here's a cold-hardy shrub with a broad, rounded form that looks great even under snow. Grow this evergreen where you need a plant with year-round presence.

Picea glauca 'Conica'

Dwarf Alberta Spruce

Zones: 2-8

Light Needs:

Mature Size:

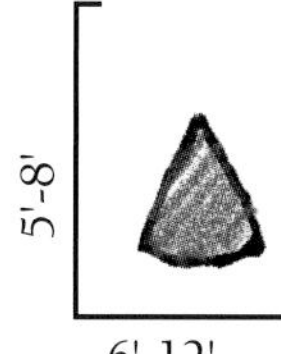

Growth Rate: slow

evergreen shrub

Needs: Plant in neutral to acidic soil that's moist but well-drained. Grow in full sun or partial shade. Provide regular watering in hot areas. If growing in containers, make sure pots drain well. Rarely needs pruning; cut stray branches on occasion to maintain shape.

Good for: single specimen, matched pairs, anchoring corners of flowerbeds, formal gardens, entries, courtyards, beside walkways, gates and patios, growing in containers or confined spaces

More Choices: pages 34, 36, 39, 40, 43, 117, 119, and 121

Outstanding Features:

- Tidy, conical shape adds contrast
- Small and slow-growing
- Bluish green foliage stays fresh year-round

If you want a topiary but don't have time to train one, this is the plant for you. Slow-growing dwarf shrubs resemble tidy, miniature trees. These little shrubs often stay as small as 2 or 3 feet tall for many years. Easily grown.

Pinus mugo

Mugo Pine

Zones: 2-7

Light Needs:

Mature Size:

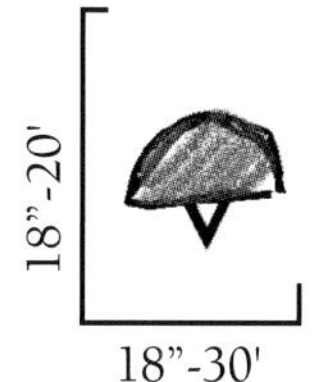

Growth Rate: slow

evergreen shrub

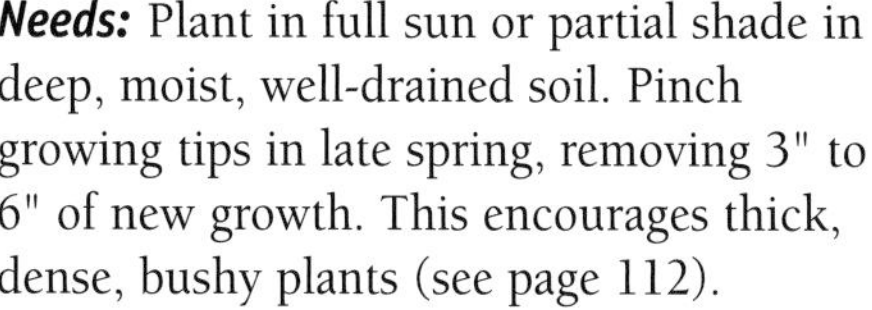

Needs: Plant in full sun or partial shade in deep, moist, well-drained soil. Pinch growing tips in late spring, removing 3" to 6" of new growth. This encourages thick, dense, bushy plants (see page 112).

Good for: specimen use, mass planting, combining with perennials and alpines in rock gardens, year-round texture

More Choices: pages 35, 36, 39, 45, 119, and 121

Options: 'Compacta'—4' tall by 5' wide; Zones 2-7
'Gnome'—15" tall by 3' wide; Zones 2-7
'Mops'—7' to 10' high, 8' wide; Zones 2-7

Outstanding Features:

- Rich, deep green needles year-round
- Slow growth makes maintenance easy
- Wide variety of heights are available

Mugo Pine grows slowly and makes a good filler for planting beds. There are many different varieties and forms of Mugo Pine available that range in heights from just over a foot to tree size. Be sure to read plant labels so that you can select the growth habit you desire. If you want one that stays small, select a variety that grows less than a few feet tall. If you are looking for a larger plant or even a small tree there are selections to fill your needs as well.

Potentilla fruticosa

Shrubby Cinquefoil

Zones: 2-7

Light Needs:

Mature Size:

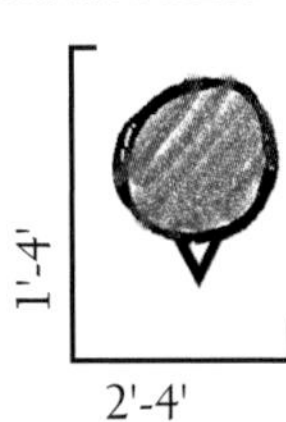

Growth Rate: slow

deciduous flowering shrub

Needs: Plant in any kind of soil that is well-drained. Though full sun yields best flowering, this shrub will also grow in partial shade. Remove one-third of the stems in late winter or early spring for best flowering.

Good for: low hedges, shrub borders, foundation use, or mass planting

More Choices: pages 35, 36, 109, 119, 120, and 123

Options: 'Abbottswood'—white flowers; bluish-green leaves; 30" tall, 4' wide 'Goldfinger'—bright yellow flowers; dark green leaves

Outstanding Features:

- Extended flowering from summer to frost
- Bright green foliage, yellow-brown in fall
- Tolerates the extremes from cold to hot

This bloomer keeps going and going, from early summer until frost. The flowers of Shrubby Cinquefoil come in all shades, from white to yellow to pink and orange. The shrub stays a neat size—under 4'—and grows in all types of soil from poor to rich. Amazing cold tolerance allows this plant to grow where winter temperatures dip to a frigid 50 below zero. Additional varieties to look for include: 'Jackman's Variety'—bright yellow flowers, 3' or 4' high; 'Primrose Beauty'—primrose flowers; 3' high; 'Tangerine'—yellow-flushed-red flowers, 2' high and 4' wide.

Prunus glandulosa 'Rosea'

Dwarf Flowering Almond

Zones: 4-8

Light Needs:

Mature Size:

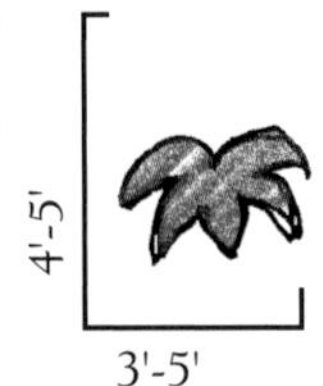

Growth Rate: medium

deciduous flowering shrub

Needs: Plant in full sun in fertile, moist, well-drained soil. Full sun yields best flowering, but this shrub will grow in partial shade. Prune annually after flowering to shape the shrub. Remove any dead wood in early spring.

Good for: specimen use, shrub or perennial border, seasonal interest

More Choices: pages 34, 36, 117, and 122

Outstanding Features:

- Pink blossoms appear before leaves unfurl
- Great in combination with spring perennials
- Easily transplanted and grown

In midspring, dull twigs transform into wands of bloom, turning Dwarf Flowering Almond into a cloud of double, pink blossoms. Plants look scraggly when not in bloom; skirt them with low-growing bloomers such as Catmint, Alpine Strawberries, or Flower Carpet Roses.

Prunus x cistena

Purple-Leaf Sand Cherry

Zones: 2-8

Light Needs:

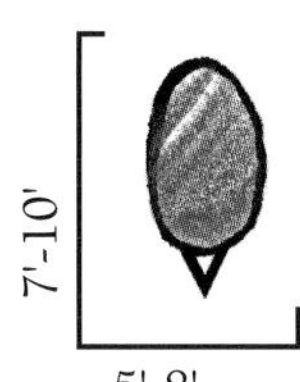

Mature Size:

7'-10'
5'-8'

Growth Rate: slow

deciduous flowering shrub

Needs: Plant in any soil that's moist but well-drained. Grow in full sun. Trim in spring after flowering to shape plants and maintain desired size.

Good for: hedges, screens, specimen use, background planting in perennial beds

More Choices: pages 31, 35, 118, 119, and 122

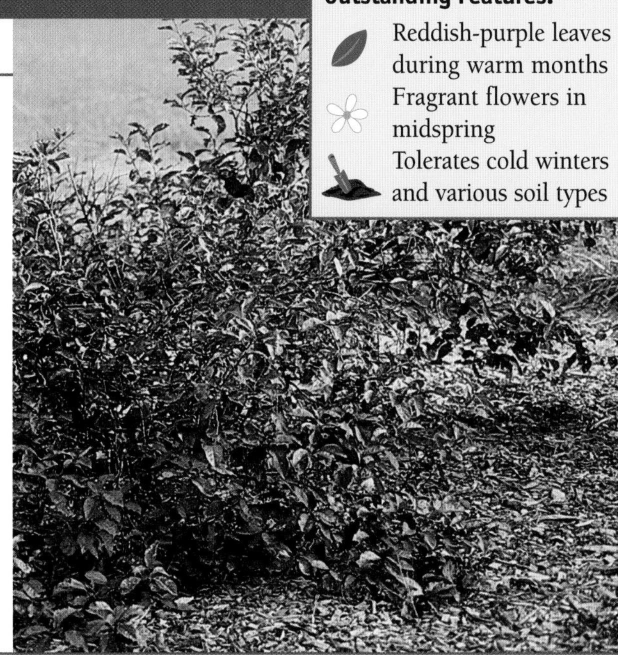

Outstanding Features:

- Reddish-purple leaves during warm months
- Fragrant flowers in midspring
- Tolerates cold winters and various soil types

Plant a few of these shrubs and you'll have a hedge—and a purple one, at that. Broad plants take shaping well and bloom with pinkish-white flowers in midspring. Shrubs sometimes produce purple, cherrylike fruit in summer. Place shrubs where purple foliage creates a desired color contrast and won't clash with the color of the your house.

Pyracantha angustifolia Yukon Belle

Yukon Belle Firethorn

Zones: 4-9

Light Needs:

Mature Size:

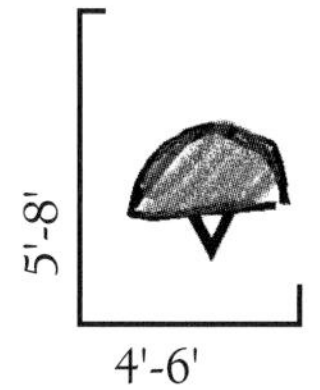

5'-8'
4'-6'

Growth Rate: medium to rapid

semievergreen to evergreen shrub

Needs: Plant in fertile, moist, well-drained soil. Full sun yields best flowering and fruiting, but this shrub will grow in partial shade. Prune as needed in any season. Plant this shrub where you want it, because once this shrub is established, it doesn't take well to transplanting.

Good for: hedges, barriers, espalier on a wall or chimney as shown here.

More Choices: pages 35, 36, 107, 119, and 123

Options: 'Gnome'—orange berries; to 6' high and wide; Zones 4-9

Outstanding Features:

- White flowers cover the shrub in early summer
- Bright orange berries ripen in autumn
- Attractive trained on walls and chimneys

This thorny shrub spills out fountains of white flowers in early summer. Bright, orange berries follow in autumn and linger through winter, long after the leaves are gone. Birds love this shrub because of its berries and protection for nests. This shrub is very thorny. Avoid placing it in areas where children play or near walkways.

Pruning Rhododendrons

When the flowers of these evergreen shrubs fade, bend and snap them off at their bases. (Be careful to remove only the soft flower part, not the stiff wood from which it grew.) Getting rid of old flowers is called deadheading. When you deadhead a rhododendron, you encourage the plant to produce new leaves and form fresh flower buds for next year's show.

Prune dead, leafless branches from rhododendrons during any season. Make the cuts on dead wood just above its connection to the main, live stem. Sterilize tools with rubbing alcohol between cuts in order to avoid spreading possible disease.

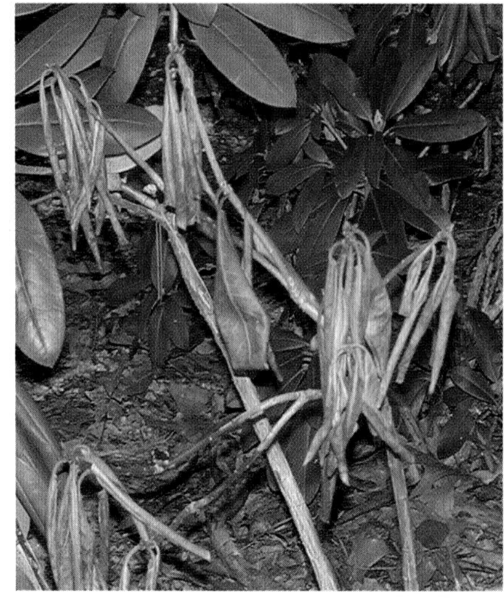

Dead leaves on the branches indicate dieback, a fungal problem. Cut away dead branches, making each cut a few inches below the problem to avoid cutting into and leaving infected wood. Sterilize tools between pruning cuts. Destroy cuttings. The following spring, after blooming, spray a fungicide containing basic copper sulfate. Repeat applications twice at two-week intervals.

Rhododendron catawbiense

Catawba Rhododendron

Zones: 4-8

Light Needs:

Mature Size:

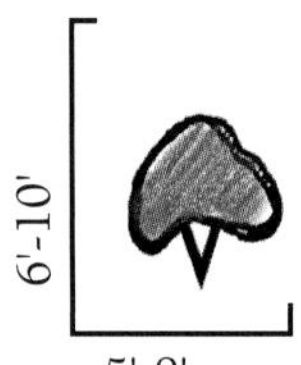

Growth Rate: slow

evergreen flowering shrub

Needs: Plant in moist, well-drained, acidic, fertile soil. Rhododendrons can take full sun in colder areas; in warmer climates, partial shade is best. Water plants in fall. Mulch beneath shrubs to help soil stay moist. Prune to remove dead branches after new growth has emerged. Snap off flowers after they fade.

Good for: specimen shrub, screen, massed, or foundation planting

More Choices: pages 30, 34, 36, 40, 109, 117, 119, and 122

Outstanding Features:

- Spring flowers in shades of lilac-purple
- Leaves stay green all year-round
- Broad, rounded outline, dense plant

The bright, lilac-purple blossoms of Catawba Rhododendron are breathtaking against the dark green leaves. Catawba Rhododendron can take cold weather without sacrificing flower buds, but protect it from drying winter winds. Cultivar options: 'P.J.M.'—lavender-pink flowers, shade- and drought-tolerant, 6' high to 4' wide, Zones 4-8; 'P.J.M. White'—white flowers, leaves turn burgundy in winter, 3' to 4' high and wide, Zones 4-8; 'Mollis' Hybrids—large, waxy blooms; many flower colors, deciduous, 4' to 5' high and wide Zones 4-8.

Rhus typhina 'Laciniata'

Cut-Leaf Staghorn Sumac

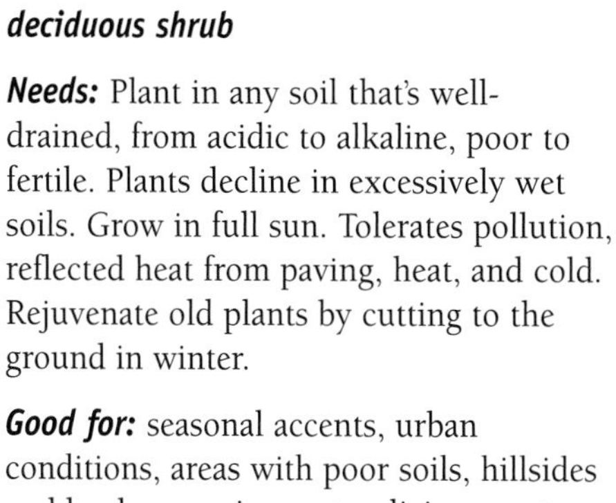

Zones: 3-8

Light Needs:

Mature Size:

15'-25' (height) × 15'-25' (width)

Growth Rate: rapid

deciduous shrub

Needs: Plant in any soil that's well-drained, from acidic to alkaline, poor to fertile. Plants decline in excessively wet soils. Grow in full sun. Tolerates pollution, reflected heat from paving, heat, and cold. Rejuvenate old plants by cutting to the ground in winter.

Good for: seasonal accents, urban conditions, areas with poor soils, hillsides and banks, massing, naturalizing, waste areas, specimen use

More Choices: pages 34, 39, 40, 41, 42, 43, 119, 121, and 123

Outstanding Features:

- Fine-textured, deeply cut, ferny leaves
- Dark green foliage turn orange-red in fall
- Rusty-red fruit adds winter interest

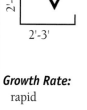

For a surprisingly tropical look in cold climates, grow Cut-Leaf Staghorn Sumac. The lacy leaves resemble fronds. This shrub will grow in any soil that isn't soggy. An excellent selection for problem areas. Use with care in landscape settings; its interesting texture can easily be overused. May be sold as 'Red Autumn Lace'.

Ribes alpinum 'Green Mound'

Green Mound Alpine Currant

Zones: 2-7

Light Needs:

Mature Size:

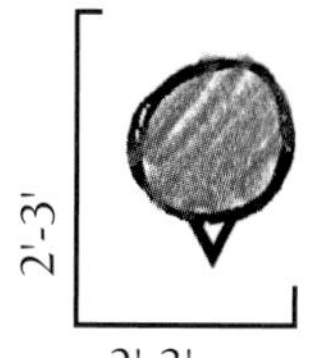

2'-3' (height) × 2'-3' (width)

Growth Rate: rapid

deciduous flowering shrub

Needs: Plant in any kind of soil, including acidic to alkaline, fertile to poor, wet to dry. Grow in sun or shade. Trim hedges anytime; removal of flowers isn't a concern. Easy to transplant and grow.

Good for: deciduous hedges, lower layers in front of evergreens, foundation plantings, shrub beds, filling in bare areas, seasonal accents

More Choices: pages 23, 35, 36, 39, 41, 45, 107, 109, 117, 119, 121, and 122

Options: Clove currant, *R. odoratum*—6' to 8' high, scented flowers, Zones 4 to 6

Outstanding Features:

- Compact size and mounded form
- Plants require very little maintenance
- Tolerates harsh winters and growing conditions

Grow this plant for its neat, compact form and maintenance-free care. Shrubs thrive in cold weather, all types of soil, sun or shade and everything in between. 'Green Mound' is a male form and has better disease resistance than most female varieties. Fruiting is rare. Plants thrive in the Upper Midwest.

Rosa 'Adelaide Hoodless'

Adelaide Hoodless Rose

Zones: 2-9

Light Needs:

Mature Size:

2'-3' × 2'-3'

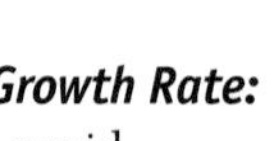

Growth Rate: rapid

deciduous flowering shrub

Needs: Plant in well-drained, slightly acidic soil. Grow in full sun. Water generously during the growing season, taking care not to water the foliage. Fertilize with rose food when blooming begins and monthly thereafter. Stop feeding six weeks before first anticipated frost. Remove spent flowers to encourage additional blooms. Stop deadheading four to six weeks before the first frost.

Good for: specimen shrub use, seasonal accents, entries, courtyards, planting beside patios, informal hedges

More Choices: pages 34, 40, 107, 118, 119, 121, and 123

Outstanding Features:

- Large clusters of red flowers in summer
- Plants are covered with glossy leaves
- With protection, tolerates harsh winters

You can grow this prolific bloomer in areas that are too cold for many roses. Clusters of bright red flowers cover mounding shrubs each summer. Three-inch flowers are semi-double and may repeat again in autumn. Plants are susceptible to blackspot especially in wet years. This disease can defoliate plants. Remove infected leaves from the plant and around the growing area. Spray regularly with an all-purpose or rose disease fungicide until wet weather ceases.

Rosa 'Betty Prior'

Betty Prior Rose

Zones: 4-9

Light Needs:

Mature Size:

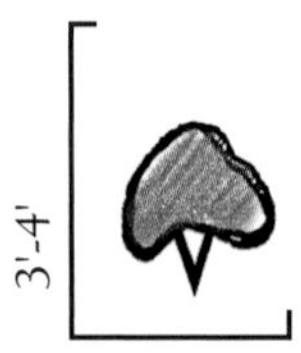

Growth Rate: medium

deciduous flowering shrub

Needs: Plant roses in full sun in moist, well-drained, fertile soil. Prune to remove dead branches and to shape shrubs after buds swell in spring. Clip faded blooms for nonstop flowers until late summer. Fertilize with rose food when blooming starts.

Good for: specimen shrub, hedge, or massed planting. Space plants 18 inches apart for a hedge of bloom. It will also grow well in a large container.

More Choices: pages 34, 107, 118, 120, and 123

Outstanding Features:

- Large flowers are deep pink and fragrant
- Cold-hardy and easy care
- Compact size and form

Want a hedge that is as beautiful as it is functional? Plant a row of Betty Prior roses. Pink blossoms are 2 to 3 inches wide and appear from summer until frost. When planting roses, it's helpful to add super phosphate or bonemeal to the soil in the planting hole to promote root growth.

Rosa Carefree Beauty

Carefree Beauty Rose

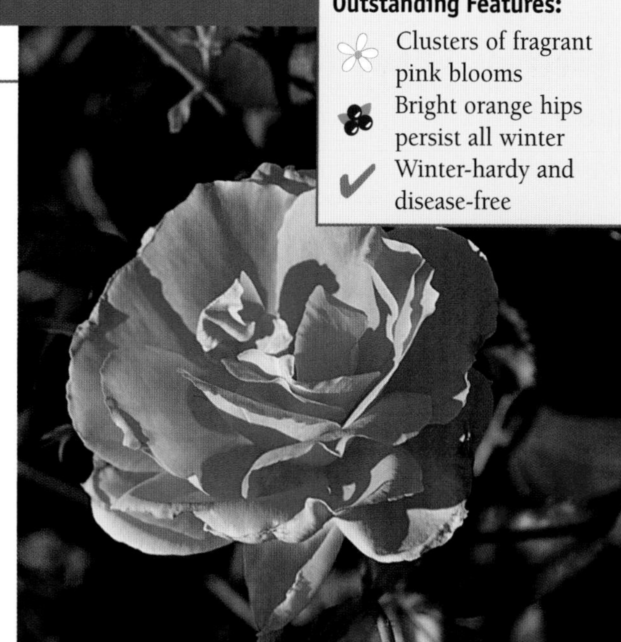

Outstanding Features:

- Clusters of fragrant pink blooms
- Bright orange hips persist all winter
- Winter-hardy and disease-free

Zones: 4-8

Light Needs:

Mature Size:

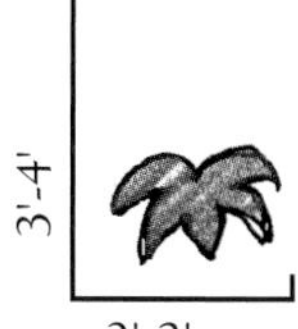

Growth Rate: medium

deciduous shrub

Needs: Plant in full sun in moist, well-drained, fertile soil. Prune to remove dead branches after buds swell in spring. Clip spent blooms to encourage ongoing flowering. Fertilize with rose food when blooming starts.

Good for: specimen shrub, hedge, or foundation planting. To grow as a hedge, space plants 18 inches apart.

More Choices: pages 34, 107, 109, 118, and 123

The name says it all: Carefree Beauty. Flowers open continually from summer until frost—large, double, rose-pink blooms packed with perfume. No spraying needed; they are completely disease-free. When planting roses, it's helpful to add super phosphate or bonemeal to the soil in the planting hole to promote root growth. This is probably the most famous of Griffith Buck's roses.

Rosa 'Fru Dagmar Hastrup'

Fru Dagmar Hastrup Rose

Outstanding Features:

- One of the most disease-resistant roses
- Single flowers in shades of silvery pink
- Flowers have a rich clove scent

Zones: 2-9

Light Needs:

Mature Size:

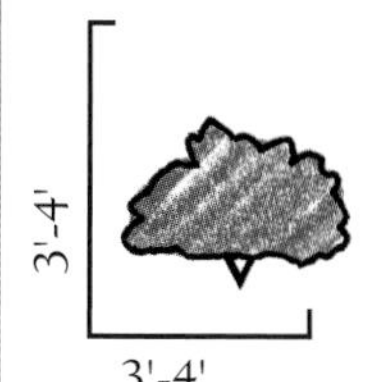

Growth Rate: medium

deciduous flowering shrub

Needs: This rose prefers sandy, light soil. It will survive in warm, coastal climates as well as cold. Prune in early spring each year to remove old, worn-out stems that have stopped bearing blooms. Fertilize with rose food when blooming starts and repeat monthly. Remove spent flowers to encourage additional blooms. Discontinue fertilization and deadheading four to six weeks before the first anticipated frost.

Good for: specimen shrub or hedge. It's also a good plant to include in the back of a perennial bed.

More Choices: pages 23, 35, 39, 42, 118, and 123

Large, single, pale pink blooms first appear in June and continue opening all summer long. At the end of the season, large scarlet hips cover the bush. Leaves are a deep green in summer, then develop shades of maroon and gold in the fall. This is a highly disease-resistant rose.

Rosa Graham Thomas

Graham Thomas Rose

Zones: 5-9

Light Needs:

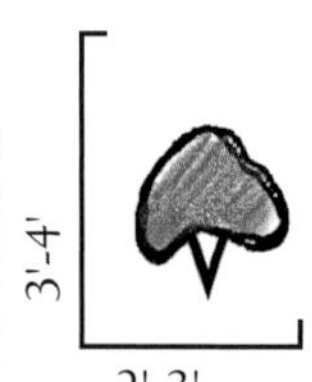

Mature Size:

3'-4'

2'-3'

Growth Rate: medium

deciduous flowering shrub

Needs: Plant roses in full sun in moist, well-drained, fertile soil. The only required pruning is removing nonflowering stems in spring. Remove faded blooms to get more flowers.

Good for: specimen shrub, hedge, massed planting, near sitting areas to enjoy fragrance

More Choices: pages 35, 118, 120, 121, and 123

Outstanding Features:

- 3-inch-wide, golden-yellow, double blooms
- Old-fashioned rose fragrance
- Compact size and form

This David Austin rose boasts the fragrance of an old-fashioned rose in a shrub form that blooms repeatedly during the growing season. Flowers are golden yellow and double-petalled; they appear all through the growing season, including during the heat of summer. Grow where the fragrance can be enjoyed to the fullest. When grown in ideal conditions, plants may become large with age.

Rosa 'Henry Kelsey'

Henry Kelsey Rose

Zones: 3-9

Light Needs:

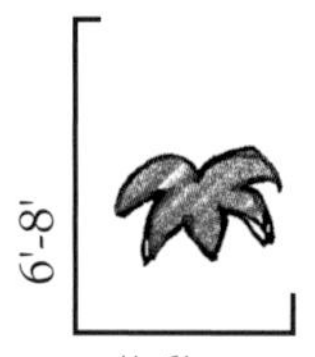

Mature Size:

6'-8'

4'-6'

Growth Rate: rapid

deciduous flowering shrub

Needs: Plant in well-drained, slightly acidic soil. Grow in full sun. Water during the growing season, taking care not to water the foliage. Fertilize with rose food when blooming starts and repeat monthly. Remove spent flowers to encourage additional bloom. Stop feeding and deadheading six weeks before first anticipated frost.

Good for: hedges, specimen use, accents, entries, covering blank walls, posts or fences, vertical growth

More Choices: pages 35, 41, 107, 118, 119, 121, 122, and 123

Outstanding Features:

- Fragrant, warm-red flowers in clusters
- Glossy, dark green leaves resist mildew
- Arching, spreading form; can also climb

Bred to take the cold, this red rose blooms heavily and scents the air with sweet perfume. Canes arch and spread and can be trained to climb or allowed to sprawl. Flowers on and off, summer through fall. Foliage may develop black spot during warm, damp weather. Remove infected leaves from the plant and growing area. Spray regularly with an all-purpose or rose disease fungicide until wet weather ceases. Modern hardy shrub rose; *R. kordesii.*

Rosa 'Hunter'

Hunter Rose

Zones: 4-8

Light Needs:

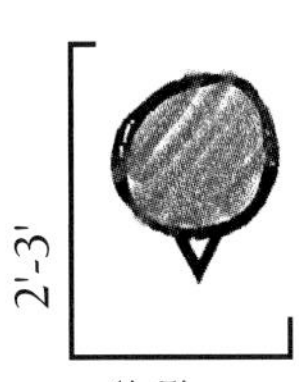

Mature Size:

Growth Rate: medium to rapid

deciduous flowering shrub

Needs: Plant in well-drained, slightly acidic soil. Grow in full sun. Water during the growing season, taking care not to wet the foliage. Fertilize with rose food when blooming starts and repeat monthly. Stop feeding six weeks before first anticipated frost. Remove spent flowers regularly to encourage additional bloom. Stop removing spent blooms four to six weeks before the first anticipated frost.

Good for: specimen use, seasonal accents, informal hedges, massing, planting beside patios and decks

More Choices: pages 35, 41, 118, 120, 121, and 123

Outstanding Features:

- Brilliant red flowers are over 3 inches wide
- Compact, tidy form for use in small areas
- Disease-resistant and cold-tolerant

Big, double, red flowers occur in clusters of 5 to 10 in June. This heaviest bloom is followed up with light encores in late summer and early fall. A hybrid *R. rugosa*, Hunter has disease resistance and cold tolerance.

Rosa 'Margo Koster'

Margo Koster Rose

Zones: 5-8

Light Needs:

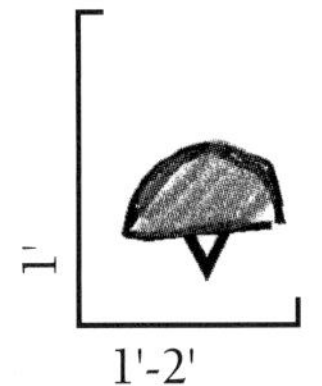

Mature Size:

1'

1'-2'

Growth Rate: medium

deciduous flowering shrub

Needs: Plant roses in full sun in moist, well-drained, fertile soil. Fertilize with rose food when blooming starts.

Good for: an edging plant, a low hedge, or a specimen. Use it to edge a perennial border, skirt evergreen shrubs, or in well-drained soil near a water garden.

More Choices: pages 35, 118, and 123

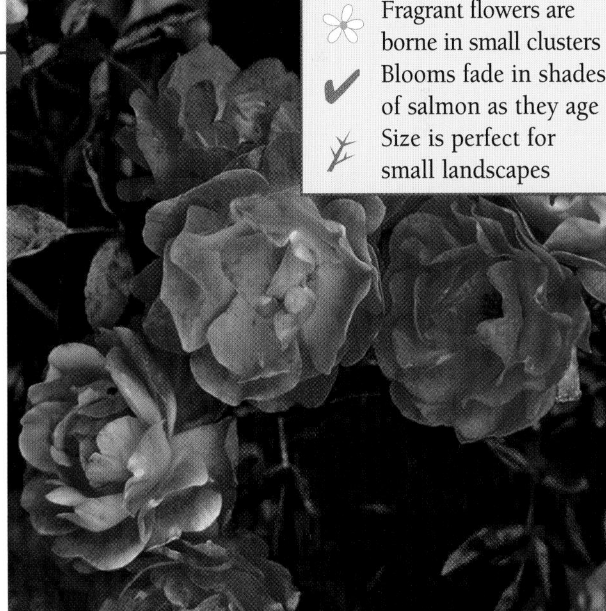

Outstanding Features:

- Fragrant flowers are borne in small clusters
- Blooms fade in shades of salmon as they age
- Size is perfect for small landscapes

Growing a mere 12 inches high, Margo Koster is a perfect choice to edge a walkway, patio, or shrub border. The stems are nearly thornless and flowers open in shades of salmon all summer long. This rose is a low-maintenance plant. Also try: 'Nearly Wild'—nearly nonstop, pink blossoms.

Rosa 'Morden Centennial'

Morden Centennial Rose

Outstanding Features:

- Leaves are dark green and semiglossy
- Clusters of pink rosettelike flowers
- Produces abundant amounts of rose hips

Zones: 2-9

Light Needs:

Mature Size: 2'-3' × 2'-3'

Growth Rate: rapid

deciduous flowering shrub

Needs: Plant in well-drained, slightly acidic soil. Grow in full sun. Water during the growing season, taking care not to get the foliage wet. Prune very little during the first year to encourage root growth instead of stems. Prune older plants by cutting long shoots just above a node during the growing season.

Good for: specimen use, warm season accents, low hedges, edging, foundation plantings, shrub beds, courtyards, entries, planting beside patios

More Choices: pages 35, 41, 107, 118, 119, 121, 122, and 123

Here's a hardy shrub rose that blooms from late spring into the fall. Pink flowers are followed by numerous hips that provide added seasonal interest. Rosette shaped, double blooms are lightly scented and measure 2 to 3 inches across. Blooms occur in clusters over the entire bush. This modern shrub rose was bred in Canada so you know it's hardy.

Rosa 'Nearly Wild'

Nearly Wild Rose

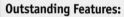

Outstanding Features:

- Fragrant, medium pink flowers cover plants
- Bushy growth spreads for fast coverage
- Tolerates severely cold winter temperatures

Zones: 2-9

Light Needs:

Mature Size: 3'-5' × 3'-5'

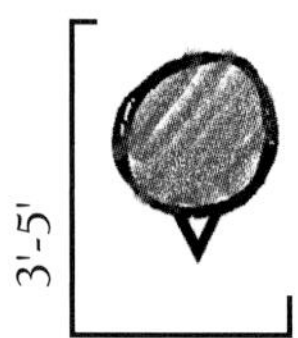

Growth Rate: rapid

deciduous flowering shrub

Needs: Plant in well-drained, slightly acidic soil. Grow in full sun. Water generously, taking care not to wet the foliage. Fertilize when blooming starts and repeat monthly. Remove spent blossoms to encourage repeated bloom. Stop fertilizing and deadheading four to six weeks before the first frost. Prune to rejuvenate.

Good for: slopes, front layers of shrub beds, growing over stone walls or low fences, seasonal accents, specimen use, entries, parking areas, massing

More Choices: pages 35, 41, 42, 119, 120, 121, 122, and 123

This sturdy little spreading rose puts on a show throughout spring, summer, and fall. Numerous, single blossoms cover shrubs nearly nonstop with pink. A floribunda type, plants die back in winter but reappear to grow vigorously and bloom heavily during the summer.

Rosa 'Sir Thomas Lipton'

Sir Thomas Lipton Rose

Outstanding Features:

- White, 3-inch-wide, double flowers
- Large, arching form; long canes
- Vigorous grower; tolerates some shade

Zones: 2-7

Light Needs:

Mature Size:

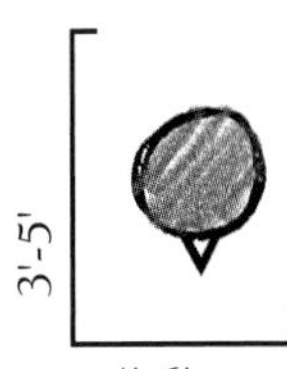

Growth Rate: rapid

deciduous flowering shrub

Needs: Plant in well-drained, slightly acidic soil. Grow in full sun or partial shade. Water generously during the growing season, taking care not to get the foliage wet. Fertilize with rose food when blooming starts and repeat monthly. Remove spent flowers to encourage additional bloom. Stop fertilizing and deadheading four to six weeks before the first anticipated frost.

Good for: screening, informal hedges, background for flowerbeds, massing, seasonal accents

More Choices: pages 31, 35, 36, 41, 42, 107, 118, 119, 120, and 123

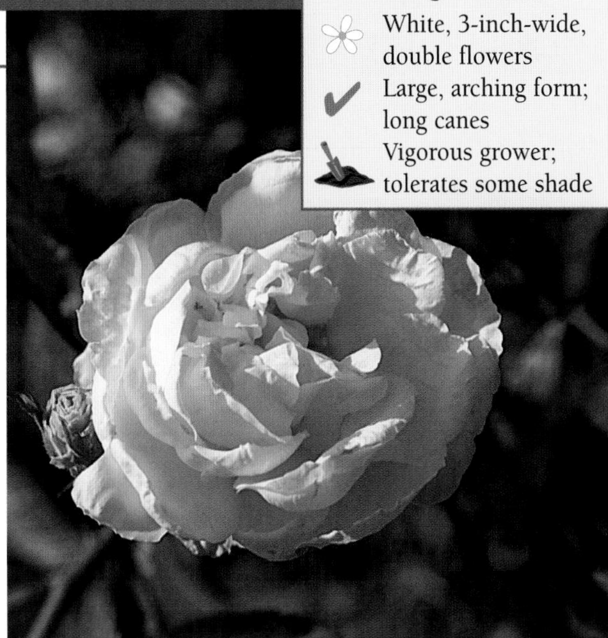

Hedges don't have to be boring. Grow one that blooms and provides summer appeal. Sir Thomas Lipton grows quite large and forms an effective barrier with spiny stems. The biggest show of double blooms occurs in June; flowers repeat sporadically into fall. A hybrid rugosa type.

Rosa 'The Fairy'

The Fairy Rose

Outstanding Features:

- Clusters of pink blooms all summer
- Extremely cold-hardy; tolerates below zero
- Flowering ability even in partial shade

Zones: 4-9

Light Needs:

Mature Size:

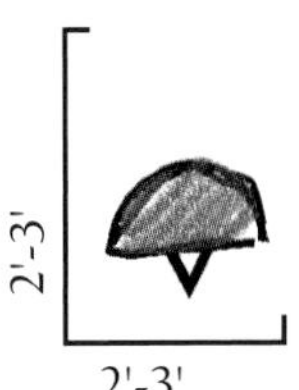

Growth Rate: medium

deciduous flowering shrub

Needs: Plant in moist, well-drained, fertile soil in full sun or partial shade. Fertilize with rose food when blooming starts and repeat monthly. Remove spent flowers to encourage additional flowering. Discontinue fertilizing and deadheading four to six weeks before the first anticipated frost.

Good for: specimen shrub or low hedge. The Fairy is a perfect rose to grow in large container such as a whiskey barrel planter.

More Choices: pages 35, 36, 43, 119, 121, and 123

Though the dainty flowers appear delicate, this rose is hardy to 40 degrees below zero. Small, double pink blossoms open summer through fall. This rose will even bloom in partial shade.

Rosa 'Therese Bugnet'

Therese Bugnet Rose

Zones: 3-9

Light Needs:

Mature Size:

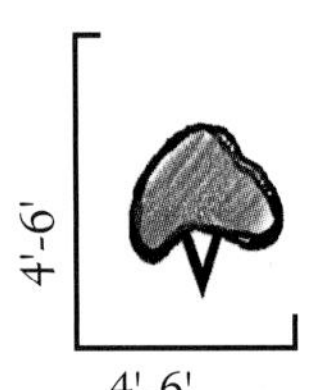

Growth Rate: medium

deciduous flowering shrub

Needs: 'Therese Bugnet' tolerates sandy, light, poor soils. Prune sparingly in early spring each year only to remove old, worn-out stems that have stopped bearing blooms. Fertilize with rose food when blooming starts and repeat monthly. Remove spent flowers to encourage additional blooms. Discontinue fertilization and deadheading four to six weeks before the first anticipated frost.

Good for: hedging or specimen shrub

More Choices: pages 23, 35, 39, 42, 118, and 123

Outstanding Features:

- Pink, ruffled flowers are 4 inches wide
- Wonderfully fragrant flowers
- Dark green foliage turning red in fall

Large, fully double, pink blooms are rich with fragrance. Leaves are a lustrous green in summer and then deep red in the fall. Therese Bugnet can grow and bloom in poor soil and even in shade. If your yard is hard on roses, Therese Bugnet is the choice for you.

Rosa 'William Baffin'

William Baffin Rose

Zones: 2-9

Light Needs:

Mature Size:

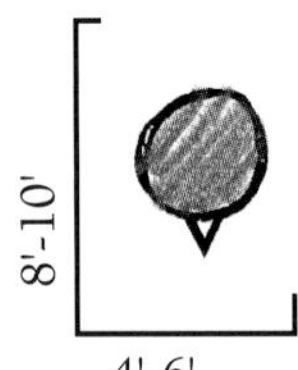

Growth Rate: rapid

deciduous flowering shrub

Needs: Plant in well-drained, slightly acidic soil. Grow in full sun. Water generously during the growing season; avoid getting the foliage wet. Give this rose plenty of room to grow. Disease-resistant and cold-hardy.

Good for: informal hedges, massing, hillsides, barriers, open areas, informal landscapes, seasonal accents, tying trailers to posts or fences for vertical growth

More Choices: pages 35, 41, 118, 119, 120, 122, and 123

Outstanding Features:

- Deep pink flowers in spring to early summer
- Giant clusters contain thirty flowers or more
- Disease-resistant foliage; arching canes

Grow this rose where you've got room for an enthusiastic plant; canes grow vigorously and can be trained to climb. Strawberry-pink flowers cover shrubs in clusters. Blooms appear in spring and summer. Plants have glossy-midgreen, disease resistant foliage. This is a low-maintenance rose for large areas. *R. kordesii* shrub rose.

Rosa rubrifolia

Rosa Rubrifolia

Zones: 4-9

Light Needs:

Mature Size:

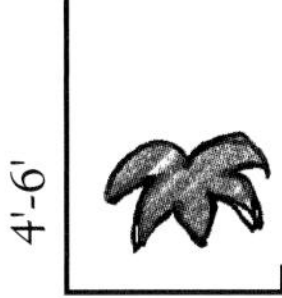

Growth Rate: medium

deciduous flowering shrub

Needs: Plant roses in full sun in moist, well-drained, fertile soil. Prune stray stems as needed. Fertilize with rose food when blooming starts and repeat monthly. Remove spent flowers to encourage additional bloom. Discontinue fertilizing and deadheading four to six weeks before the first anticipated frost.

Good for: specimen shrub or hedge. Plant it where you can see it from inside your home for year-round view.

More Choices: pages 35, 118, and 123

Outstanding Features:

- Bright pink flowers are fragrant
- Nearly thornless, purple-red stems
- Scarlet hips linger throughout winter

Single flowers open to a bright, flamingo pink in early summer. Petal tips are pink with white bases. After they fade, the purple-tinged leaves take center stage, highlighted against bright, purple-red arching stems. In fall, hips ripen to a scarlet red color and last all winter. May be sold as *Rosa glauca.*

Rosa rugosa 'Alba'

White Rugosa Rose

Zones: 3-10

Light Needs:

Mature Size:

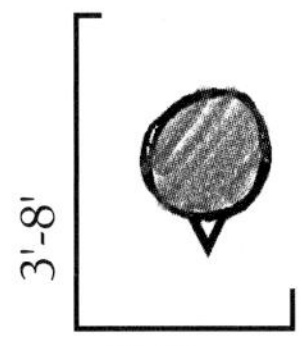

Growth Rate: rapid

deciduous flowering shrub

Needs: Plant in well-drained, slightly acidic soil. Grow in full sun. Give it plenty of room to grow. Disease-resistant for low maintenance rose care.

Good for: hedges, seaside landscapes, massing, hillsides, barriers, open areas, informal landscapes

More Choices: pages 23, 35, 41, 42, 118, 119, 120, 122, and 123

Options: *R. rugosa* var. *alboplena*—double, white flowers opening from pink buds

Outstanding Features:

- Pale pink buds open to single white flowers
- Large red hips may be up to an inch across
- Withstands heat, cold, wind, and salt spray

Roses at the beach? You betcha—this one will grow just about anywhere the sun shines. You'll enjoy clusters of cupped, white flowers from spring into fall. Sweetly scented blooms add fragrance to the landscape. Stems are prickly; avoid using near traffic areas. Leathery, dark-green leaves appear wrinkled. Also known as Sea Tomato, Ramanas Rose, or Hedgehog Rose. This species shrub rose is not grafted.

Salix alba 'Britzensis'

Coral Embers Willow

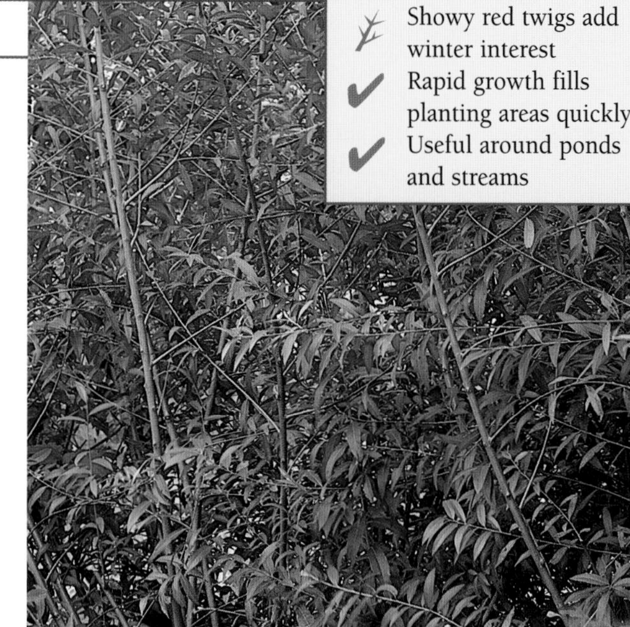

Outstanding Features:

- Showy red twigs add winter interest
- ✔ Rapid growth fills planting areas quickly
- ✔ Useful around ponds and streams

Zones: 2-8

Light Needs:

Mature Size:

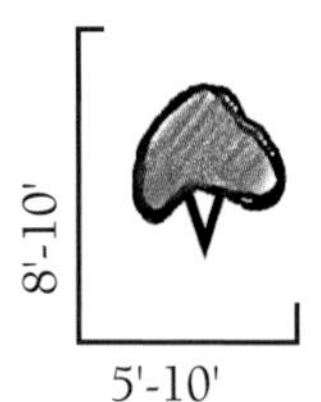

8'-10' × 5'-10'

Growth Rate: rapid

deciduous shrub

Needs: Plant in full sun in moist, well-drained soil. Tolerates wet soil. The red stem color is most prominent on young wood; prune all stems to within a few inches of the ground in early spring before new growth begins.

Good for: shrub beds, mass planting against evergreen backgrounds, wet locations, around ponds and streams

More Choices: pages 23, 34, 39, and 119

The new stems on this shrub are bright red and are most effective during winter months after the leaves fall. Stems covered in snow add winter interest. Coral Embers Willow grows in any well-drained soil as well as moist locations. The most intense color shows up on young stems. Trim plants back severely in late winter to encourage vigorous, new growth.

Salix caprea 'Kilmarnock'

French Pussy Willow

'Pendula'

Outstanding Features:

- Plump fuzzy buds on bare stems in spring
- Thrives in soggy, wet soil conditions
- ✔ Grows fast to form an interesting ornamental

Zones: 4-8

Light Needs:

Mature Size:

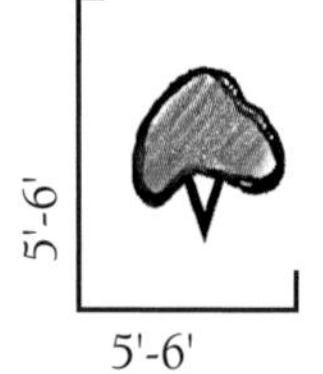

5'-6' × 5'-6'

Growth Rate: rapid

deciduous flowering shrub

Needs: Plant in any kind of soil—damp or wet soils are best. Grow in full sun. Prune immediately after bloom to control size if necessary. Pruning at this time will not destroy next year's show.

Good for: wet, boggy areas, planting beside streams, ponds, or downspouts, seasonal specimens, forcing cut branches indoors in spring arrangements

More Choices: pages 35, 39, and 119

If there's a place in your yard that stays wet, you've got the perfect location for French Pussy Willow. Decorative, furry buds cover stems in early spring before the leaves emerge. 'Kilmarnock' is a male form that produces abundant buds. The fuzzy buds are actually the male catkins or flowers. Plants may also be sold as *S. caprea* 'Pendula' or as Goat Willow.

Spiraea japonica 'Anthony Waterer'

Anthony Waterer Spirea

Zones: 3-9

Light Needs:

Mature Size:

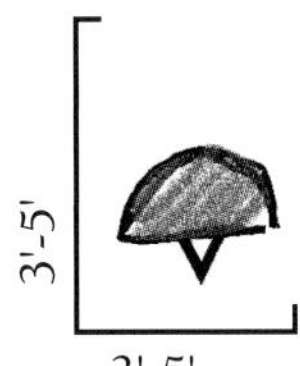

Growth Rate: medium to rapid

deciduous flowering shrub

Needs: Plant in full sun to partial shade in any well-drained soil. Prune back in spring before new growth begins.

Good for: parking areas, entries, specimen plants, beside patios, background to summer flowerbeds, facing for taller shrubs, massed plantings, low hedges

More Choices: pages 34, 36, 39, 43, 120, 121, 122, and 123

Options: 'Little Princess'—rounded shape, about 30" high, pink flowers
'Alpina'—12" to 30" high

'Little Princess'

Outstanding Features:

- Dark pink blooms in late spring and summer
- New foliage is reddish purple in color
- Durable and adaptable in any setting

Not all spireas have white flowers in early spring. This one boasts dark pink blooms when spring is fading into summer. For durability nothing can take the place of spirea in home landscapes. May be sold as *S.* x *bumalda* 'Anthony Waterer'.

Spiraea japonica Limemound

Limemound Spirea

Zones: 4-9

Light Needs:

Mature Size:

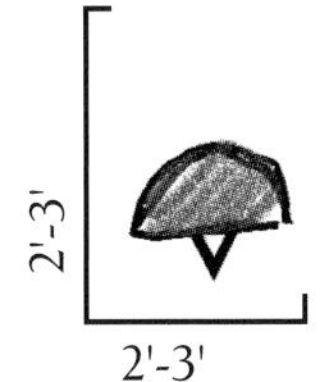

Growth Rate: rapid

deciduous flowering shrub

Needs: Plant in full sun and well-drained soil. No pruning is required but plants can be pruned off near the ground in late winter or spring to encourage dense, compact plants.

Good for: entries, parking areas, accents, or the front layer of shrub beds

More Choices: pages 35, 43, 109, 121, 122, and 123

Options: 'Golden Princess'—golden yellow colored leaves
'Gold Mound'—heat-tolerant, 30" to 40" high, pink flowers

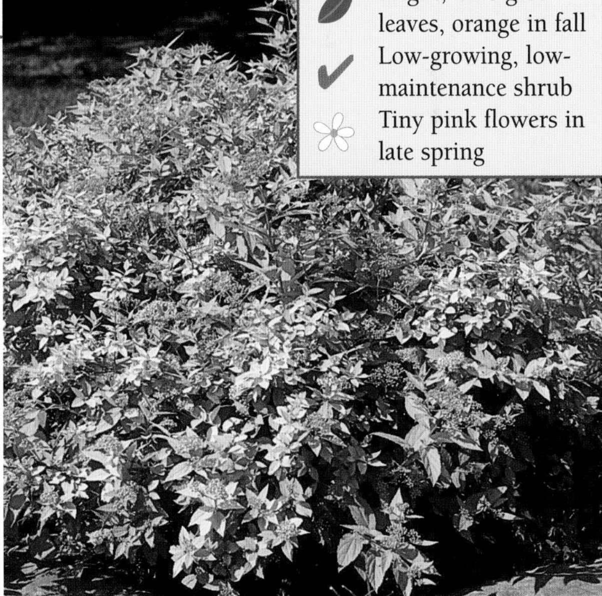

Outstanding Features:

- Bright, lime-green leaves, orange in fall
- Low-growing, low-maintenance shrub
- Tiny pink flowers in late spring

True to its name, Limemound Spirea is a little lump of bright, lime-green foliage. Tiny blooms cover plants in late spring and leaves turn bright orange in fall. Plants provide interest no matter what the season. If desired, prune plants back in the spring before new growth begins.

Spiraea japonica 'Shibori'

Shibori Spirea

Zones: 4-8

Light Needs:

Mature Size:

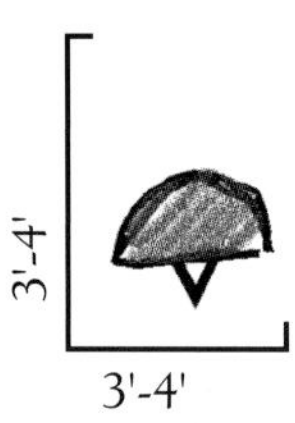

Growth Rate: medium

deciduous flowering shrub

Needs: Plant in full sun to partial shade in well-drained soil. Spirea will not tolerate wet sites. Prune in spring before new growth begins. Blooms best in full sun.

Good for: entries, groups behind flowerbeds, specimen plants, beside patios and low decks, low hedges

More Choices: pages 35, 36, 120, and 121

Outstanding Features:

- Pink and white flowers blooming together
- Easy to grow, very adaptable
- Wide range of landscape uses

Can't decide between pink or white flowers? This spirea blooms in both colors at the same time. Like all spirea, Shibori is adaptable for a variety of uses in the home landscape.

Spiraea prunifolia

Bridalwreath Spirea

Zones: 5-8

Light Needs:

Mature Size:

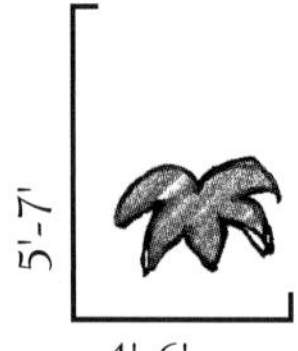

Growth Rate: rapid

deciduous flowering shrub

Needs: Plant in full sun to partial shade in soil that's moderately fertile and doesn't stay wet. Prune with a light hand, over-pruning spoils the naturally arching form. Give plants room to grow.

Good for: entries, informal hedges, specimen plants, or as a background to spring flowerbeds

More Choices: pages 31, 34, 36, 43, 107, 119, 120, 121, 122, and 123

Outstanding Features:

- Many tiny buttonlike blooms in spring
- Arching branches form informal hedges
- Leaves turn orange-red in autumn

Little white flowers cover the arching branches early each spring. A perfect backdrop for spring flowering bulbs. Shiny dark green foliage turns orange-red in fall. Best used in informal areas.

Symphoricarpos albus

Snowberry

Outstanding Features:

- White berries dangle from stems in fall
- Adaptable to heavily shaded areas
- Good for stabilizing banks and slopes

Zones: 3-7

Light Needs:

Mature Size:

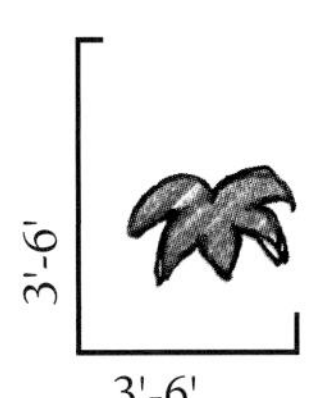

Growth Rate: rapid

deciduous flowering shrub

Needs: Snowberry grows in sun or shade, in any type of soil, and in areas where air pollution is high. Prune in early spring to stimulate flowering on new growth. Plants will sucker and spread.

Good for: informal landscapes, woodland areas, hillsides to stabilize soil, wildlife habitat plantings

More Choices: pages 23, 35, 36, 39, 42, 43, 119, and 121

Snowberry earns its name from the abundance of white berries that cover its stems in fall. This shrub is tolerant of difficult growing conditions; use it in shady locations, on steep banks, and in areas where air pollution is high.

Symphoricarpos orbiculatus

Coralberry

Outstanding Features:

- Summer flowers look like tiny roses
- Purplish-red berries linger through winter
- Tolerates heavy shade as well as pollution

Zones: 4-7

Light Needs:

Mature Size:

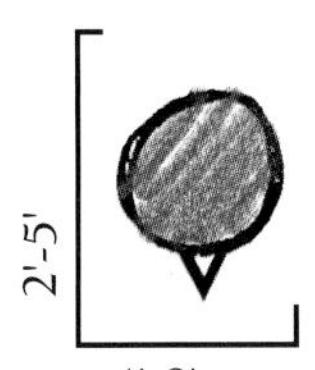

Growth Rate: rapid

deciduous flowering shrub

Needs: Plant in sun or shade in soil that is fertile or poor, moist or dry. Prune in early spring to stimulate prolific flowering.

Good for: shrub borders, informal hedges, screens, woodland plantings, stabilizing hillsides and banks, attracting birds, winter interest

More Choices: pages 31, 34, 36, 39, 42, 107, 119, 121, and 123

Coralberry thrives in any growing condition. Moist or dry soil, full sun to dense shade, alkaline or acidic—it can easily fit into any yard. Winter berries attract birds. Place plants where you can view the feeding from inside. Best flowering occurs on new shoots; prune annually to encourage vigorous new growth.

Rejuvenating Overgrown Lilacs

An overgrown lilac is worth rescuing. Mature roots and hardy trunks make the plant valuable, even if the crown is misshapen. Combine severe pruning with patience to turn an overgrown shrub into a specimen plant.

1 Wait until the shrub is totally bare and temperatures have dipped below freezing. Cut away water sprouts – those stems that grow straight up and don't bloom. Remove them at ground level or flush with the branch or trunk where they emerge. Use hand pruners on small stems, loppers if it's a struggle.

2 It's time to be ruthless. Using loppers, cut the shrub down to about one-third or one-half its current size.

3 Now that the shrub is at a manageable size, it's time to make final cuts. Use a pruning saw to cut thick trunks about 2 feet above ground level, leaving these stubs.

Stuff You'll Need

- ✔ Bypass hand pruners
- ✔ Bypass loppers
- ✔ Pruning saw

What to Expect

Don't expect flowers the spring after you hard-prune a lilac. New growth will produce flower buds next year, though severe pruning may result in two bloomless years.

Get the 'Full Scoop'

Selective pruning

If your lilac requires just a little trim, make cuts in spring immediately after flowers finish blooming. This will avoid removing next year's flower buds. Don't cut your lilacs back to stubs each year. If you do, you'll never enjoy any flowers. Instead, make selective cuts on an annual basis.

–see pages 112-113

Syringa x laciniata

Cutleaf Lilac

Zones: 4-8

Light Needs:

Mature Size:

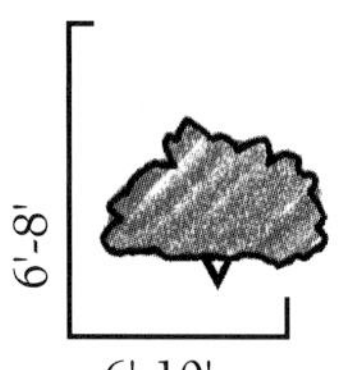

Growth Rate: medium

deciduous flowering shrub

Needs: Plant in full sun or partial shade in well-drained, fertile soil. Best flowering occurs in full sun. Add composted leaves or peat moss to soil at planting time to boost fertility. Remove faded blooms to keep plants looking neat. Prune after flowering to shape the shrub and encourage new vigorous growth.

Good for: shrub borders, informal hedges, screens, specimen use, near entries or sitting areas

More Choices: pages 31, 34, 36, 107, 118, 119, 121, and 122

Outstanding Features:

- Purplish, fragrant flowers in late spring
- Leaves look like they have been cut
- Adaptable to cold and warm climates

Cutleaf Lilac is the best lilac to grow in the warmer parts of the country, even Zone 8. This shrub flowers in late spring with sweet, fragrant blooms. Use this blooming shrub to frame a porch or other outdoor seating area and enjoy the flowers' perfume to the fullest. Lacy foliage looks like it has been cut with scissors. The foliage is an added asset for this plant.

Syringa patula 'Miss Kim'

Miss Kim Lilac

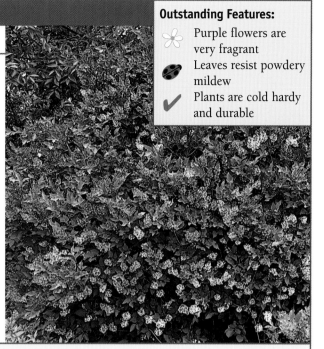

Outstanding Features:
- Purple flowers are very fragrant
- Leaves resist powdery mildew
- Plants are cold hardy and durable

Zones: 3-7

Light Needs:

Mature Size:

6'-8'

4'-5'

Growth Rate: slow

deciduous flowering shrub

Needs: Plant in full sun to partial shade in well-drained, fertile soil. Clip off blooms after they fade. Prune only if needed, after flowering, to shape the shrub.

Good for: shrub borders, informal hedges, screens, specimen use, planting near outdoor seating areas for fragrance

More Choices: pages 31, 35, 36, 107, 118, 119, 121, 122, and 123

This late-blooming lilac features single, pale lavender flowers that are rich with perfume. Leaves are glossy green in summer, then turn a burgundy-red in fall. Miss Kim can survive winter temperatures of 40 degrees below zero. A nice lilac for smaller locations.

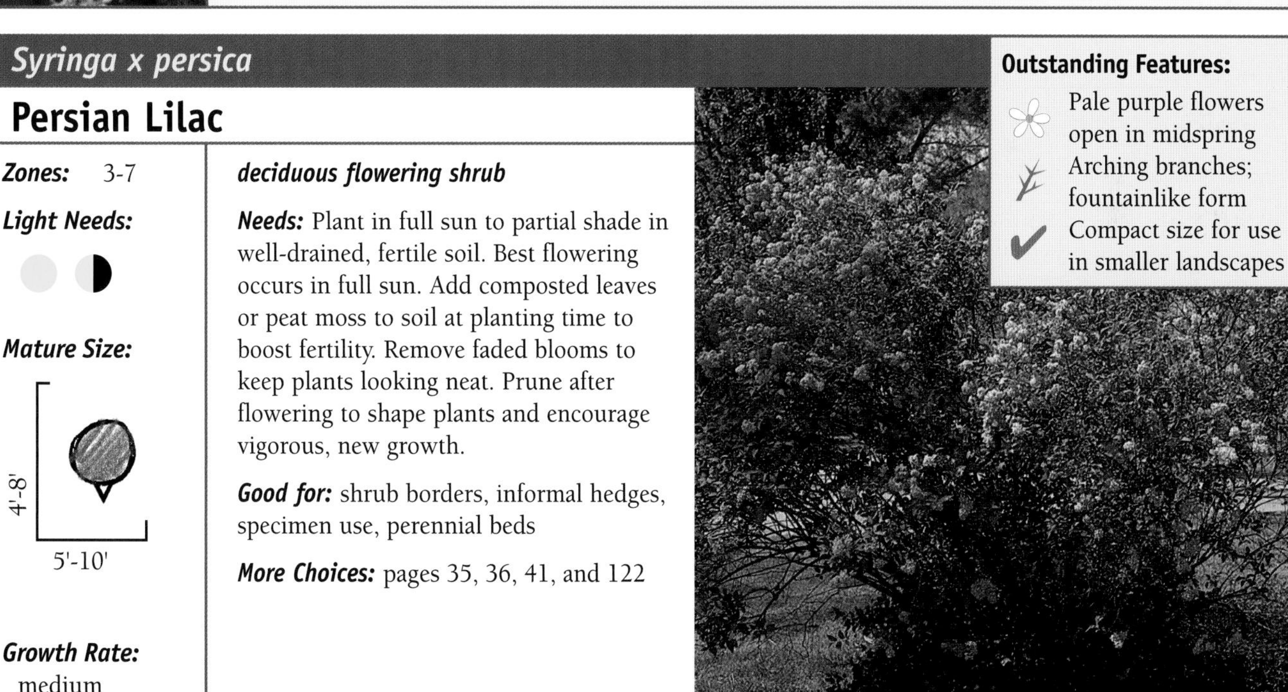

Syringa x persica

Persian Lilac

Outstanding Features:
- Pale purple flowers open in midspring
- Arching branches; fountainlike form
- Compact size for use in smaller landscapes

Zones: 3-7

Light Needs:

Mature Size:

4'-8'

5'-10'

Growth Rate: medium

deciduous flowering shrub

Needs: Plant in full sun to partial shade in well-drained, fertile soil. Best flowering occurs in full sun. Add composted leaves or peat moss to soil at planting time to boost fertility. Remove faded blooms to keep plants looking neat. Prune after flowering to shape plants and encourage vigorous, new growth.

Good for: shrub borders, informal hedges, specimen use, perennial beds

More Choices: pages 35, 36, 41, and 122

This shrub has the same sweet, fragrant blooms as its larger lilac cousins but with a little more grace. Pale-purple flowers grow in clusters at the tips of branches. Good for shrub borders and hedges. Plant Virginia Bluebells beneath the bushes for an even sweeter spring scene.

Syringa vulgaris

Common Lilac

Zones: 3-7

Light Needs:

Mature Size:

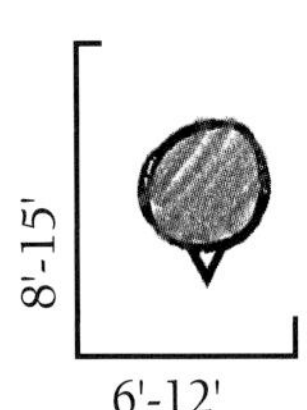

Growth Rate: medium

deciduous flowering shrub

Needs: Plant in full sun to partial shade in well-drained, fertile soil. Best flowering occurs in full sun. Add composted leaves or peat moss to soil at planting time to boost fertility. Remove faded blooms to keep plants looking neat. Prune after flowering to shape the shrub and encourage vigorous new growth.

Good for: shrub borders, informal hedges, screening, specimen use, planting beside entries or patios

More Choices: pages 34, 36, 39, 43, 45, 107, 118, 119, 121, and 122

Outstanding Features:

- Spring flowers are extremely fragrant
- Numerous colors from which to choose
- Dense hedges for privacy and screening

French hybrids offer big double flowers in a variety of colors including wine, pink, white, and deep purple. Powdery mildew is common on lilacs, but won't kill plants. Look for these varieties: *S. vulgaris* var. *alba*—white flowers; 'Arch McKean'—reddish-purple flowers, produces nearly no suckers; 'Charm Lilac'—pink flowers; 'Ellen Willmott'—double white flowers; 'Little Boy Blue'—single sky-blue flowers, 4' to 5' high, 5' to 6' wide; 'Primrose'—yellow flowers; 'Wedgwood Blue'—lilac pink buds open to true, blue flowers, 6' high, 6' to 8' wide.

Taxus x media 'Densiformis'

Anglojap Yew

Zones: 4-7

Light Needs:

Mature Size:

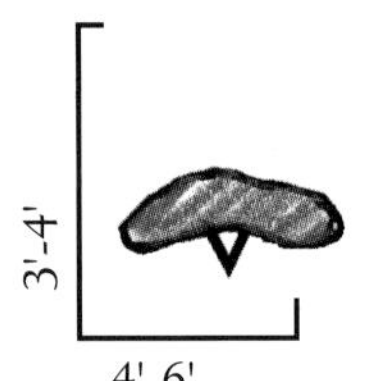

Growth Rate: slow

evergreen shrub

Needs: Plant in soil that's acidic to neutral and moist but well-drained. Shrubs won't thrive in soggy soil. Grows well in full sun, partial or dense shade. Easily transplanted and grown.

Good for: foundation plantings, low hedges, informal or formal gardens, massing, providing background in perennial and shrub beds, parking areas, planting beside patios and driveways, adding winter interest

More Choices: pages 34, 36, 40, 107, 109, 117, 119, 120, and 121

Outstanding Features:

- Dense, bushy form provides background
- Bright green needles are evergreen
- Cold-hardy and easy to grow

Here's a dense, shrubby plant that fills a variety of landscaping needs. Fluffy, needlelike foliage stays bright green, year-round. Plants grow twice as wide as they will tall and thrive in the growing conditions found in the Midwest and Northeast. Many cultivars and forms are available. May also be sold as English-Japanese Yew or as Spreading Yew.

Taxus x media 'Hicksii'

Hick's Upright Yew

Zones: 4-7

Light Needs:

Mature Size:

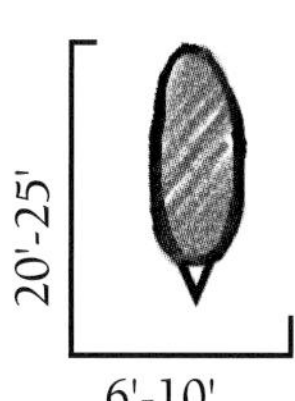

Growth Rate: slow

columnar evergreen shrub

Needs: Plant in sun or shade in moist, sandy, acidic soil. Soil must be well-drained. Add composted leaves or peat moss to soil at planting time to boost soil acidity. Prune to shape the shrub during summer or early fall.

Good for: hedges, screens, or specimen use; adding formal accent to entrances; forming a living fence

More Choices: pages 30, 35, 36, 41, 45, 107, 117, 119, and 121

Options: *T.* x *media* 'Densiformis'—dense and spreading, 4 to 6 feet wide

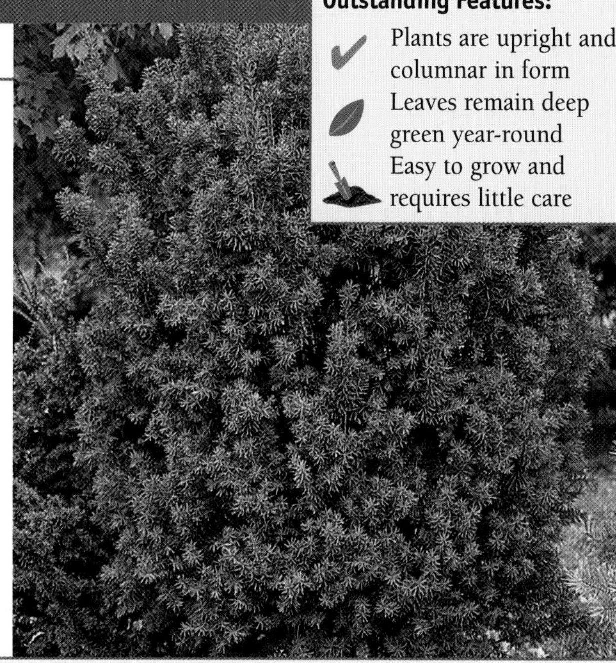

Outstanding Features:

- Plants are upright and columnar in form
- Leaves remain deep green year-round
- Easy to grow and requires little care

This is a perfect shrub to screen a fence or patio in a small yard. Its upright, narrow growth forms a dense screen without using up a lot of horizontal area. Plants add a formal touch wherever they are planted. Very low maintenance.

Thuja occidentalis 'Emerald'

Emerald Arborvitae

Zones: 2-7

Light Needs:

Mature Size:

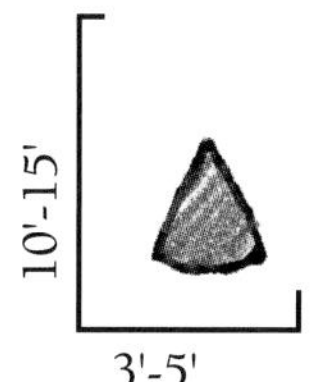

Growth Rate: slow to medium

evergreen shrub

Needs: Plant in any soil that isn't extremely wet. Rocky, poor, dry, or highly alkaline soils are fine. Grow in full sun. Prune to shape during summer months.

Good for: specimen use, accents, anchoring the corners of planting beds, formal gardens, foundation plantings, winter interest, hedges, screening

More Choices: pages 30, 35, 39, 41, 45, 107, 109, 117, 119, and 121

Options: 'Globosa'—rounded shape, 4'-6' high and wide
'Golden Globe'—bright golden foliage, 3' high and wide

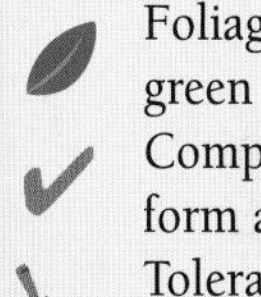

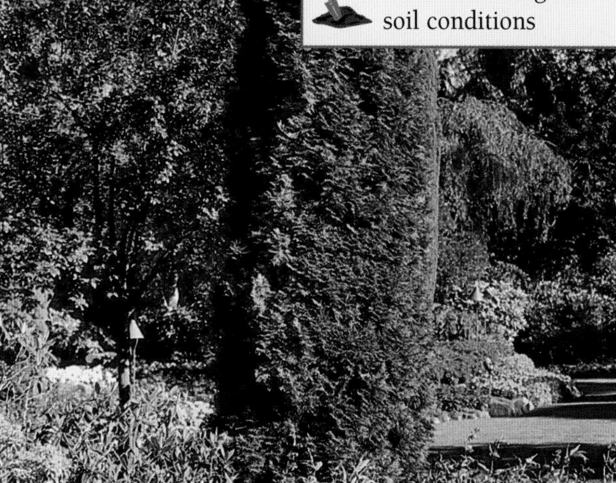

Outstanding Features:

- Foliage stays bright green through winter
- Compact, pyramidal form adds formality
- Tolerates a range of soil conditions

Choose this evergreen shrub for its narrow, upright form, which punctuates the landscape. You'll love the bright green foliage that remains even in winter. Protect for harsh winds, snow, and ice to prevent permanent damage. Plants can be susceptible to spider mites. At first sign of fading foliage or silky webbing, spray with an insecticide that lists spider mites on the label. Thrives in Eastern North America. May also be sold as 'Smaragd'.

Thuja occidentalis 'Hetz's Midget'

Hetz's Midget Arborvitae

Zones: 2-8

Light Needs:

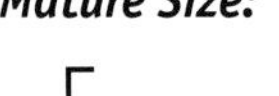

Mature Size:

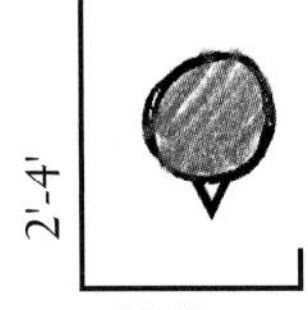

Growth Rate: slow to medium

evergreen shrub

Needs: For best growth, plant in full sun and provide moist, fertile, well-drained soil. Limestone soil is fine. Prune to shape the shrub in spring or late summer. Protect plants from strong winter winds.

Good for: specimen use, lining a walkway, small entry plantings

More Choices: pages 35, 39, 117, 119, and 121

Outstanding Features:

- Slow growth doesn't outgrow its location
- Rounded shape adds interest and form
- Foliage maintains rich color, year-round

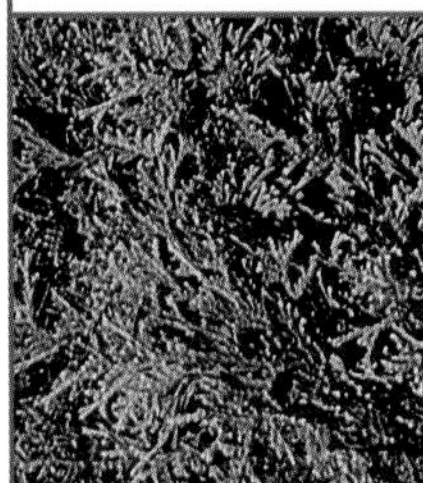

This tiny shrub stays short and tidy making it an ideal choice for a small entry plantings, lining a walkway, or siting in rock gardens. Its leaves remain rich green throughout the seasons. Heavy, wet snow or ice can break shrubs apart; knock snow away with a broom when it occurs. Plants are cold tolerant but less vigorous in the warmer areas of its growing range.

Thuja occidentalis 'Little Giant'

Little Giant Arborvitae

Zones: 3-7

Light Needs:

Mature Size:

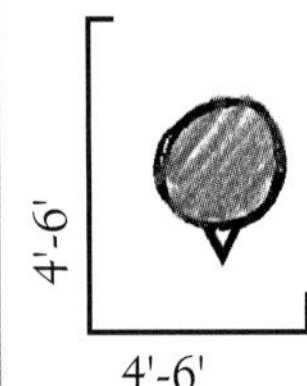

Growth Rate: slow to medium

evergreen shrub

Needs: Plant in any soil type that isn't extremely wet. Rocky, poor, dry, or alkaline conditions are fine. Grow in full sun. Prune to shape during warm months. Protect from harsh winds, ice, and snow.

Good for: specimen use, anchoring shrub and perennial planting beds, foundations

More Choices: pages 30, 35, 39, 41, 45, 109, 117, 119, and 121

Options: 'Emerald'—narrow pyramidal, green foliage; 10' to 15' high, 3' to 4' wide
'Globosa'—gray green foliage, rounded shape; 4' to 6' high and wide
'Golden Globe'—bright golden foliage

Outstanding Features:

- Compact, spherical growth adds form
- Tolerates a range of soils and conditions
- Evergreen foliage adds year-round appeal

Here's a plant that looks like a big, green ball in the landscape. Its evergreen foliage and rounded form make it eye-catching throughout the year. Plants are susceptible to spider mites. At first sign of fading foliage or silky webbing, spray with an insecticide labeled for spider mites. Thrives in Eastern North America.

Viburnum dentatum

Arrowwood Viburnum

Zones: 3-8

Light Needs:

Mature Size:

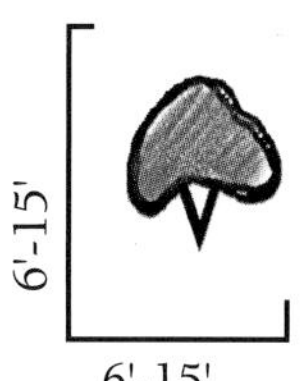

Growth Rate: medium to rapid

deciduous flowering shrub

Needs: Plant in soil that's moist but well-drained. Shrubs will adapt to a variety of other soils. Grow in full sun or partial shade. Give this plant plenty of room to grow as it suckers readily. Salt tolerant.

Good for: deciduous hedges, screening, coastal areas, attracting birds, providing a background for garden rooms, shrub and flowerbeds

More Choices: pages 23, 31, 34, 36, 39, 40, 107, 119, 121, 122, and 123

Outstanding Features:

- Clusters of tiny, white flowers in late spring
- Dark green leaves turn yellow or red in fall
- Adaptable to many growing conditions

Here's a flowering shrub that's tough and durable. It is cold-hardy, adaptable, and gets big quickly. Plant it to create a living wall in your landscape or for other utilitarian uses. Birds enjoy the bluish-black fruits that ripen in late summer and fall. Plants sucker freely and may need restriction from growing out of their given area.

Viburnum lantana 'Mohican'

Mohican Viburnum

Zones: 3-8

Light Needs:

Mature Size:

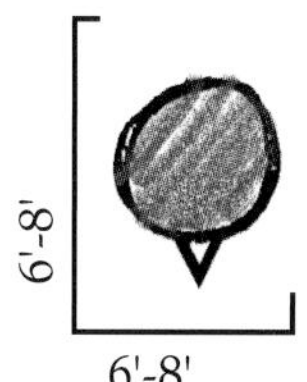

Growth Rate: medium

deciduous flowering shrub

Needs: Plant in slightly acidic soil that's moist but well-drained; however, shrubs will adapt to other soils, including clay. Grow in full sun or partial shade. Resists bacterial leaf spot.

Good for: shrub beds, background plantings, seasonal accents, massing, attracting birds, foundation plantings with evergreens, natural areas

More Choices: pages 35, 36, 39, 41, 109, 120, 121, 122, and 123

Outstanding Features:

- Clusters of white flowers in late spring
- Orange-red fruit and red foliage in fall
- Compact, dense form for home landscapes

With its white flowers, coarse textured, dark green foliage, and orange-red fruit, this hardy and adaptable shrub is at home just about anywhere in the landscape. Flower display lasts about a week in the spring. Fruit display is effective for a month in late summer. Fall color is quite attractive. Compact plants thrive in Midwestern and Northeastern gardens.

Viburnum opulus 'Roseum'

European Cranberrybush

Zones: 3-8

Light Needs:

Mature Size:

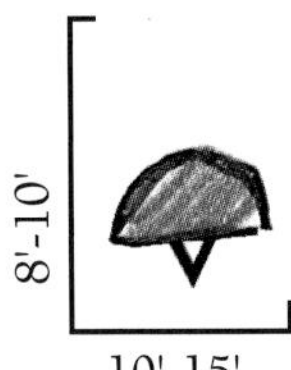

Growth Rate: medium

deciduous flowering shrub

Needs: Plant in wet or well-drained soil. This cold-hardy plant doesn't tolerate heat well; grow in afternoon shade in hotter climates, full sun elsewhere.

Good for: specimen plants, seasonal accents, focal points, large courtyards or entries, anchoring planting beds, contrasting with evergreen backgrounds, corners of houses, or yards

More Choices: pages 35, 39, 119, 121, and 122

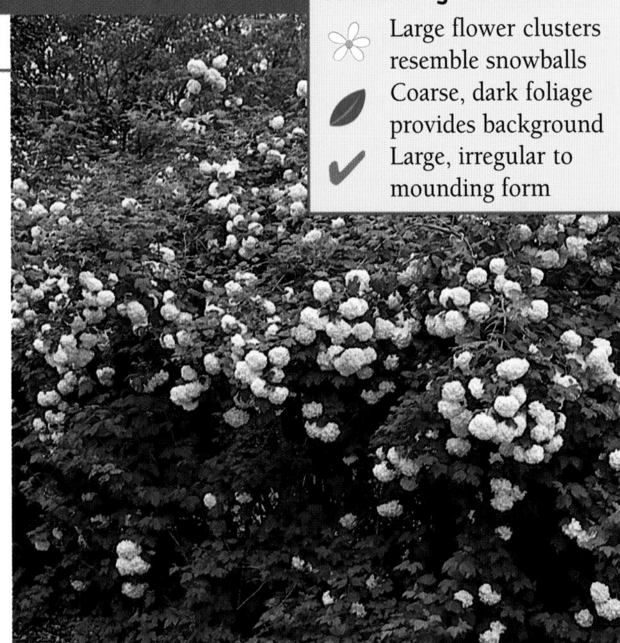

Outstanding Features:

- Large flower clusters resemble snowballs
- Coarse, dark foliage provides background
- Large, irregular to mounding form

Grow, don't throw, snowballs in the spring. A blizzard of blossoms—puffy, white, and round—covers this large shrub, commanding attention in the spring. Shrubs tolerate wet soil. Very easy to grow in almost any soil. Susceptible to aphids. Spray with insecticide or insecticidal soap to control. Sometimes sold as Snowball Viburnum or 'Sterile'.

Viburnum plicatum tomentosum

Doublefile Viburnum

Zones: 4-8

Light Needs:

Mature Size:

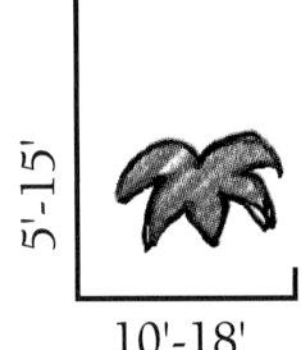

Growth Rate: rapid

deciduous flowering shrub

Needs: Plant in fertile soil that's moist but well-drained. Grow in full sun to partial shade. Water regularly.

Good for: specimen plants, seasonal accents, massing, corners of houses or yards, in front of fences, balancing vertical plants, beside patios, natural areas

More Choices: pages 34, 36, 119, 120, 121, 122, and 123

Outstanding Features:

- Lacy white flowers in late spring
- Clusters of red berries late summer to fall
- Branches grow in horizontal layers

For white flowers, red berries, tiered branches, all layered together in a spring display—plant Doublefile Viburnum. You'll get all that plus scarlet fall foliage. Leaves are coarse-textured. Blooms as well in partial shade as it does in full sun. Shrubs can be pruned to form a small tree. May be planted in warmer parts of Zone 4.

Viburnum prunifolium

Blackhaw Viburnum

Zones: 3-9

Light Needs:

Mature Size:

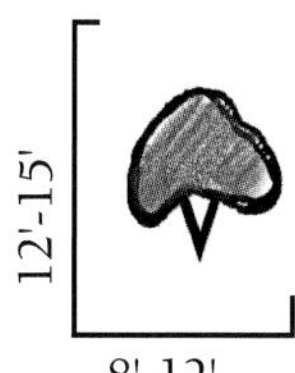

Growth Rate: slow to medium

deciduous flowering shrub

Needs: Plant in slightly acidic soil that's moist but well-drained; however, shrubs will adapt to other soil types. Will tolerate dry soils. Grow in full sun or partial shade. Resists mildew.

Good for: specimen use, seasonal accents, including in shrub beds, courtyards, entries, areas beside patios, gates, fences, or walls, natural areas, massing, attracting birds to the landscape

More Choices: pages 34, 36, 41, 119, 120, 121, 122, and 123

Outstanding Features:

- Creamy white flowers in spring
- Dark green leaves turn reddish purple in fall
- Pink fruit ripening to blue-black in autumn

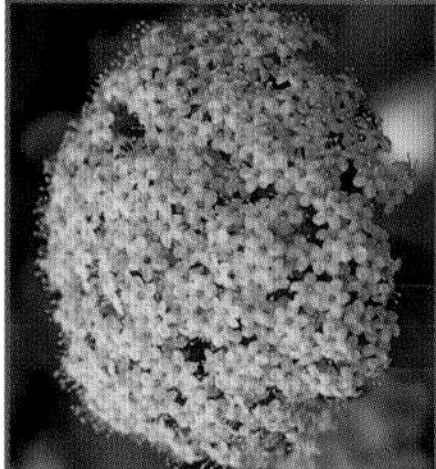

Whether you live where winters are cold or summers are hot, this shrub will adapt to your climate. You'll enjoy creamy colored flowers in the spring, edible berries in the fall, and colorful autumn foliage. Fall foliage varies from purplish to shining red to deep red or bronze. This large growing shrub can be pruned in the form of a small tree.

Viburnum trilobum 'Alfredo'

Compact American Cranberrybush

Zones: 2-7

Light Needs:

Mature Size:

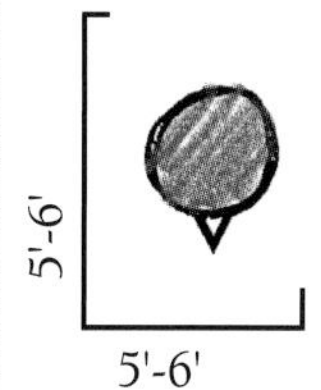

Growth Rate: rapid

deciduous flowering shrub

Needs: Plant in slightly acidic soil that's moist but well-drained; however, shrubs will adapt to other soils. Grow in full sun or partial shade. Resists aphids better than European Cranberrybush.

Good for: hedges, shrub beds, foundation planting, massing, planting beside patios, attracting birds, naturalizing, filling in empty corners of yards

More Choices: pages 34, 36, 39, 40, 43, 107, 109, 119, 120, 121, 122, and 123

'Wentworth'

Outstanding Features:

- White flower clusters in spring
- Brilliant red foliage in fall
- Decorative, red fruit in fall and winter

Here's a hardworking shrub that's easy to grow. Flowers, berries, and bright, fall foliage decorate the seasons. Dense, rounded form keeps the plant looking neat with minimal care. Branches are fine-textured.

Chapter 6

groundcovers and vines

Ever wonder why some landscapes have a gardenlike feeling while others seem to be basic and dull? Groundcovers and vines add lush layers and finishing touches to your yard. These plants also have a problem-solving practical side, too. Vines screen views and add privacy. Groundcovers anchor slopes, fill planting beds, and cover bare spots where grass won't grow.

Adding the Final Layers

This section explains how to add the final layers to your planting beds. Groundcovers and vines refine landscape compositions and make them appear filled out and complete. This chapter helps you choose groundcovers to control erosion, add texture and seasonal interest, and cover bare areas where grass won't grow. Selection guides indicate which groundcovers are best for growing in large beds and which are suitable for growing in confined areas, such as courtyards and entryways. For groundcovers suitable for growing in sun or shade, see pages 35 and 37.

Add pockets of groundcover for finishing touches at steps.

You'll find information about vines, too. Adding vines and climbers puts color and texture at eye level and above. They can also be used to shelter a location, enhance privacy, screen poor views, and add shade. The inclusion of vines in a landscape is an extra step professional designers take to make new landscape installations look natural and more mature.

Groundcover

Any plant that grows close to the ground—spreading vines, prostrate plants, dwarf shrubs, and low perennials—is considered a groundcover. The selection guides and detailed information within individual plant descriptions enable you to find the plants best suited to your purpose. Local garden center staff can help, too.

Plant groundcovers after all your trees and shrubs are in place. Low-growing plants fill in empty spaces beneath taller plants, giving planting beds a finished look and preventing weeds from taking over. However, groundcovers are more than just fillers. Planting an entire bed with nothing but groundcover gives the landscape a simple, sophisticated look. To achieve this effect, make sure that bedlines are smooth and well-defined. Beds of groundcover are excellent for framing lawns with foliage that differs from grass in color, texture, or height.

Plant groundcover through slits in landscape fabric on steep slopes.

Groundcovers are also handy for edging walkways, patios, and planting beds containing taller plants. Grow them in neat rows or let them spill over the edges of paving for a softer look. Some groundcovers are suitable for tucking into the crevices of rock gardens or between stepping stones. Others look best in beds all alone, set in front of a background of trees and shrubs. When you're laying out bedlines and adding trees and shrubs to your landscape, remember to save room for the last layer of the planting bed.

Slopes When planting groundcovers on slopes, cover the soil surface with landscape fabric to keep topsoil from washing away while plants are young. (Avoid plastic, which heats the soil and must be removed later.) Use any landscape fabric that will decompose over time. Lay it on the slope and cut slits through the fabric where you want the new plants to grow. For steep angles or windy areas, nail the fabric in place with spikes. Water new groundcovers thoroughly at planting and apply supplemental irrigation if necessary until plants are established.

TOOL TIP

For hands-and-knees digging jobs, anything that increases comfort is valuable.

Make things easy on your hands with a hand trowel that's designed with ergonomic features to make gripping and holding easier.

Kneepads to strap on over your gardening clothes can offer relief. If you can't find these items in the garden department, check the hardware department or where floor tiles and mortar are sold.

Planting Groundcovers

Though you don't have to dig deep holes, planting groundcover is labor intensive.

Planting small plants means getting down on your hands and knees. If possible, till the bed area to make planting easier and establishment quicker. Spread soil amendments such as organic matter on the surface and work it into the soil. A loose planting bed is best for small plants sold in 4-inch pots or cell packs. Planting groundcover is labor-intensive. If you hire someone to do the planting, you might find yourself paying more for the work than for the plants.

Dig individual holes as you would for a shrub if you're planting larger groundcovers, such as those grown in 1- or 3-gallon containers. Regardless of container size, arrange the plants to fill an area before you remove them from their pots. This keeps them from drying out. Set plants in a staggered formation—like laying bricks. Avoid lining plants in perfect rows. The goal is to fill the bed with greenery, not to create a geometrical pattern that will remain recognizable for months or even years. Always set the first row of groundcover plants to follow the shape of the bedline. Set plants back from the edge of the bed a distance equal to half their mature spread. Plants then have room to grow without crossing the bedline.

Replace worn paths with stepping stones and groundcovers.

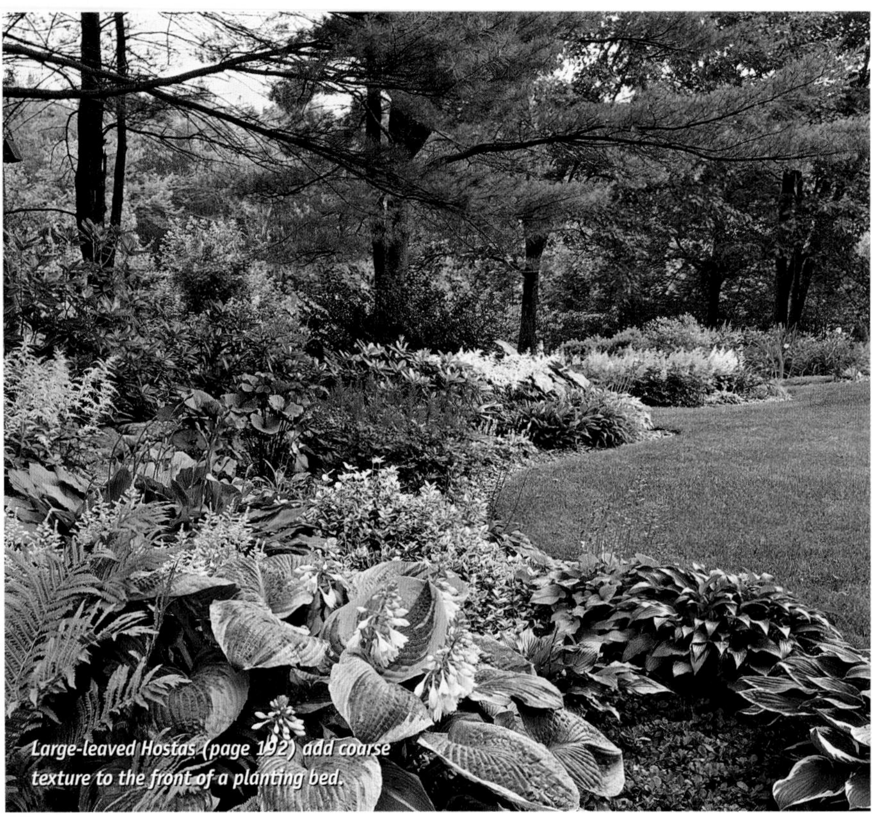
Large-leaved Hostas (page 192) add coarse texture to the front of a planting bed.

Blue Star Bellflower (Campanula poscharskyana) Page 184

Andorra Compact Juniper (Juniperus horizontalis 'Plumosa Compacta') Page 194

Choosing Groundcovers by Characteristics

The more you know about groundcovers that grow in your area, the more likely you are to pick ones with characteristics desirable for your yard. Groundcovers listed as evergreen keep their foliage year-round. Perennial groundcover disappears in late fall or early winter and comes back in spring. Coarse-textured groundcovers frame lawns, add depth to the foreground of small, confined spaces, and contrast with finer textured plants, including fine-textured groundcovers. If you want seasonal color in your yard, look at the grouped list of flowering groundcover in this chapter.

Fine-textured groundcover

Common Name	Zones	Page
Allegheny Foam Flower *Tiarella cordifolia*	4-9	204
Andorra Compact Juniper *Juniperus horizontalis 'Plumosa Compacta'*	3-9	194
Bar Harbor Juniper *Juniperus horizontalis 'Bar Harbor'*	3-9	193
Bath's Pink *Dianthus gratianopolitanus 'Bath's Pink'*	4-9	187
Bloody Cranesbill *Geranium sanguineum*	3-8	191
Blue Chip Juniper *Juniperus horizontalis 'Blue Chip'*	3-9	193
Blue Rug Juniper *Juniperus horizontalis 'Wiltonii'*	3-9	194
Catmint *Nepeta x faassenii*	4-8	197
Cliff Green *Paxistima canbyi*	3-7	199
Cypress Spurge *Euphorbia cyparissias*	4-8	188
Dwarf Blue Fescue *Festuca glauca*	4-9	188
Dwarf Japanese Garden Juniper *Juniperus procumbens 'Nana'*	4-9	195
Germander *Teucrium prostratum*	4-9	204
Goldmoss *Sedum acre*	4-9	202
Hay-Scented Fern *Dennstaedtia punctilobula*	3-8	186
Kinnikinick *Arctostaphylos uva-ursi*	2-7	181
Littleleaf Periwinkle *Vinca minor*	4-8	205
Maidenhair Fern *Adiantum pedatum*	3-8	177
Moss Phlox *Phlox subulata*	2-9	200
Mountain Sandwort *Arenaria montana*	3-6	181
Rockcress *Arabis caucasica*	3-7	180
Sea Thrift *Armeria maritima*	3-8	182
Siberian Forget-Me-Not *Anchusa myosotidiflora*	3-7	179
Silver Brocade Artemisia *Artemisia stelleriana 'Silver Brocade'*	3-9	182
Snow-in-Summer *Cerastium tomentosum*	3-7	185

Coarse-textured groundcover

Common Name	Zones	Page
Bunchberry *Cornus canadensis*	2-7	186
Coral Bells *Heuchera sanguinea*	3-8	191
Hosta *Hosta species*	3-8	192
Lady's Mantle *Alchemilla mollis*	4-7	178
Lamb's Ear *Stachys byzantina*	4-8	203
Lily-of-the-Valley *Convallaria majalis*	2-9	185
Pachysandra *Pachysandra terminalis*	4-9	198
Saxifrage *Bergenia cordifolia*	3-8	184
Stonecrop *Sedum spectabile*	3-10	202
Sweet Woodruff *Asperula odorata*	4-8	183

Availability varies by area and conditions (see page 21). Check with your garden center.

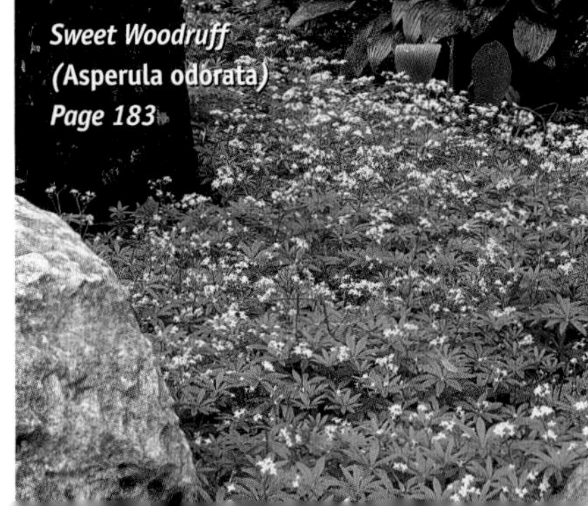
Sweet Woodruff (Asperula odorata) Page 183

Perennial groundcover

Common Name	Zones	Page
Ajuga *Ajuga reptans*	3-9	178
Allegheny Foam Flower *Tiarella cordifolia*	4-9	204
Alpine Strawberry *Fragaria vesca*	3-9	189
Basket-of-Gold *Aurinia saxatilis*	4-8	183
Bath's Pink *Dianthus gratianopolitanus 'Bath's Pink'*	4-9	187
Blanket Flower *Gaillardia x grandiflora*	2-9	190
Bloody Cranesbill *Geranium sanguineum*	3-8	191
Blue Star *Amsonia tabernaemontana*	3-9	179
Blue Star Bellflower *Campanula poscharskyana*	4-9	184
Bunchberry *Cornus canadensis*	2-7	186
Catmint *Nepeta x faassenii*	4-8	197
Coral Bells *Heuchera sanguinea*	3-8	191
Creeping Phlox *Phlox stolonifera*	2-8	199
Cypress Spurge *Euphorbia cyparissias*	4-8	188
Dwarf Blue Fescue *Festuca glauca*	4-9	188
Forget-Me-Not *Myosotis scorpioides*	3-8	197
Goldmoss *Sedum acre*	4-9	202
Hay-Scented Fern *Dennstaedtia punctilobula*	3-8	186
Hosta *Hosta species*	3-8	192
Lamb's Ear *Stachys byzantina*	4-8	203
Lily-of-the-Valley *Convallaria majalis*	2-9	185
Maidenhair Fern *Adiantum pedatum*	3-8	177
Moss Phlox *Phlox subulata*	2-9	200
Mountain Sandwort *Arenaria montana*	3-6	181
Partridge Berry *Mitchella repens*	4-9	196
Pink Panda Strawberry *Fragaria 'Pink Panda'*	3-9	189
Rockcress *Arabis caucasica*	3-7	180
Saixfrage *Bergenia cordifolia*	3-8	184
Sea Thrift *Armeria maritima*	3-8	182
Siberian Forget-Me-Not *Anchusa myosotidiflora*	3-7	179
Silver Brocade Artemisia *Artemisia stelleriana 'Silver Brocade'*	3-9	182
Snow-in-Summer *Cerastium tomentosum*	3-7	185
Snow-on-the-Mountain *Aegopodium podagraria 'Variegatum'*	3-9	177
Spotted Dead Nettle *Lamium maculatum*	3-9	196
Spring Cinquefoil *Potentilla tabernaemontani*	4-8	200
Stonecrop *Sedum spectabile*	3-10	202
Sundrop Primrose *Oenothera missouriensis*	4-8	198
Sweet Woodruff *Asperula odorata*	4-8	183
Waldesteinia *Waldsteinia ternata*	3-8	205
Wintergreen *Gaultheria procumbens*	3-8	190
Yellow Archangel *Lamiastrum galeobdolon 'Variegatum'*	3-9	195

Evergreen groundcover

Common Name	Zones	Page
Allegheny Foam Flower *Tiarella cordifolia*	4-9	204
Andorra Compact Juniper *Juniperus horizontalis 'Plumosa Compacta'*	3-9	194
Bar Harbor Juniper *Juniperus horizontalis 'Bar Harbor'*	3-9	193
Basket-of-Gold *Aurinia saxatilis*	4-8	183
Blue Chip Juniper *Juniperus horizontalis 'Blue Chip'*	3-9	193
Blue Rug Juniper *Juniperus horizontalis 'Wiltonii'*	3-9	194
Bog Rosemary *Andromeda polifolia*	2-6	180
Cliff Green *Paxistima canbyi*	3-7	199
Creeping Phlox *Phlox stolonifera*	2-8	199
Dwarf Japanese Garden Juniper *Juniperus procumbens 'Nana'*	4-9	195
Germander *Teucrium prostratum*	4-9	204
Goldmoss *Sedum acre*	4-9	202
Kinnikinick *Arctostaphylos uva-ursi*	2-7	181
Littleleaf Periwinkle *Vinca minor*	4-8	205
Moss Phlox *Phlox subulata*	2-9	200
Mountain Sandwort *Arenaria montana*	3-6	181
Pachysandra *Pachysandra terminalis*	4-9	198
Partridge Berry *Mitchella repens*	4-9	196
Purple-Leaf Wintercreeper *Euonymus fortunei 'Coloratus'*	3-9	187
Rockcress *Arabis caucasica*	3-7	180
Sea Thrift *Armeria maritima*	3-8	182
Waldesteinia *Waldsteinia ternata*	3-8	205

Rockcress (Arabis caucasica) Page 180

Flowering groundcover

Common Name	Zones	Page
Ajuga *Ajuga reptans*	3-9	178
Alba Meidiland Rose *Rosa Alba Meidiland*	4-8	201
Allegheny Foam Flower *Tiarella cordifolia*	4-9	204
Alpine Strawberry *Fragaria vesca*	3-9	189
Basket-of-Gold *Aurinia saxatilis*	4-8	183
Bath's Pink *Dianthus gratianopolitanus 'Bath's Pink'*	4-9	187
Blanket Flower *Gaillardia x grandiflora*	2-9	190
Bloody Cranesbill *Geranium sanguineum*	3-8	191
Blue Star *Amsonia tabernaemontana*	3-9	179
Blue Star Bellflower *Campanula poscharskyana*	4-9	184
Bog Rosemary *Andromeda polifolia*	2-6	180
Bunchberry *Cornus canadensis*	2-7	186
Catmint *Nepeta x faassenii*	4-8	197
Cliff Green *Paxistima canbyi*	3-7	199
Coral Bells *Heuchera sanguinea*	3-8	191
Creeping Phlox *Phlox stolonifera*	2-8	199
Cypress Spurge *Euphorbia cyparissias*	4-8	188
Flower Carpet Rose *Rosa 'Flower Carpet'*	4-10	201
Forget-Me-Not *Myosotis scorpioides*	3-8	197
Germander *Teucrium prostratum*	4-9	204
Goldmoss *Sedum acre*	4-9	202
Kinnikinick *Arctostaphylos uva-ursi*	2-7	181
Lady's Mantle *Alchemilla mollis*	4-7	178
Lamb's Ear *Stachys byzantina*	4-8	203
Lily-of-the-Valley *Convallaria majalis*	2-9	185
Littleleaf Periwinkle *Vinca minor*	4-8	205
Moss Phlox *Phlox subulata*	2-9	200
Mountain Sandwort *Arenaria montana*	3-6	181
Pachysandra *Pachysandra terminalis*	4-9	198
Partridge Berry *Mitchella repens*	4-9	196
Pink Panda Strawberry *Fragaria 'Pink Panda'*	3-9	189
Prostrate Chenault Coralberry *Symphoricarpos x chenaultii 'Hancock'*	4-7	203
Rockcress *Arabis caucasica*	3-7	180
Saxifrage *Bergenia cordifolia*	3-8	184
Sea Thrift *Armeria maritima*	3-8	182
Siberian Forget-Me-Not *Anchusa myosotidiflora*	3-7	179
Snow-in-Summer *Cerastium tomentosum*	3-7	185
Snow-on-the-Mountain *Aegopodium podagraria 'Variegatum'*	3-9	177
Spotted Dead Nettle *Lamium maculatum*	3-9	196
Spring Cinquefoil *Potentilla tabernaemontani*	4-8	200
Stonecrop *Sedum spectabile*	3-10	202
Sundrop Primrose *Oenothera missouriensis*	4-8	198
Sweet Woodruff *Asperula odorata*	4-8	183
Waldesteinia *Waldsteinia ternata*	3-8	205
Wintergreen *Gaultheria procumbens*	3-8	190
Yellow Archangel *Lamiastrum galeobdolon 'Variegatum'*	3-9	195

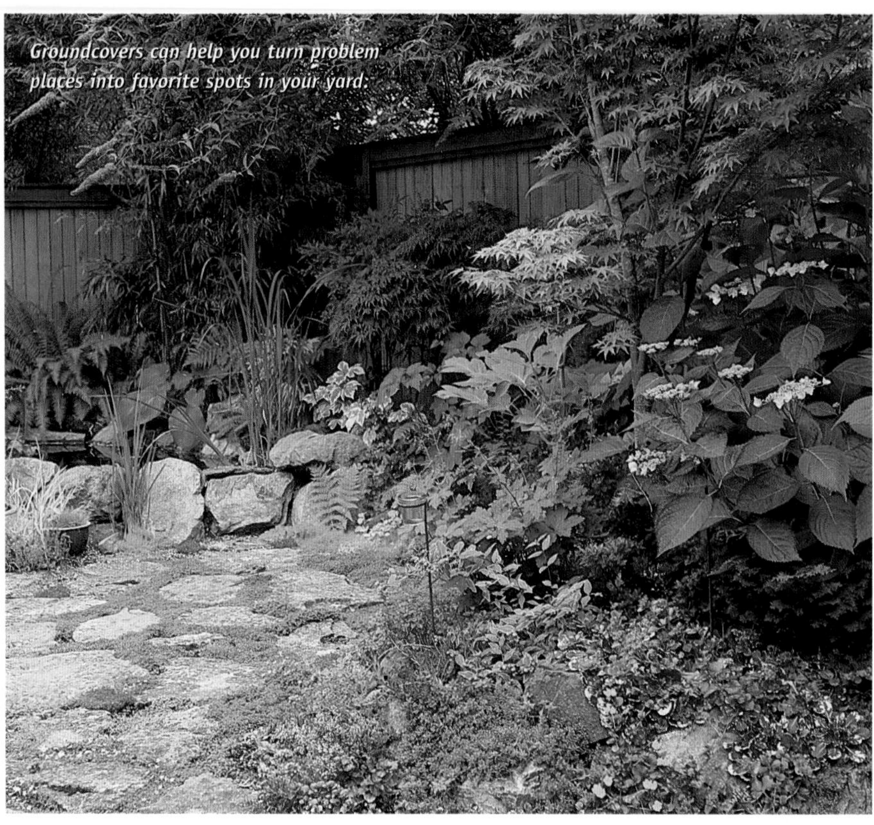
Groundcovers can help you turn problem places into favorite spots in your yard.

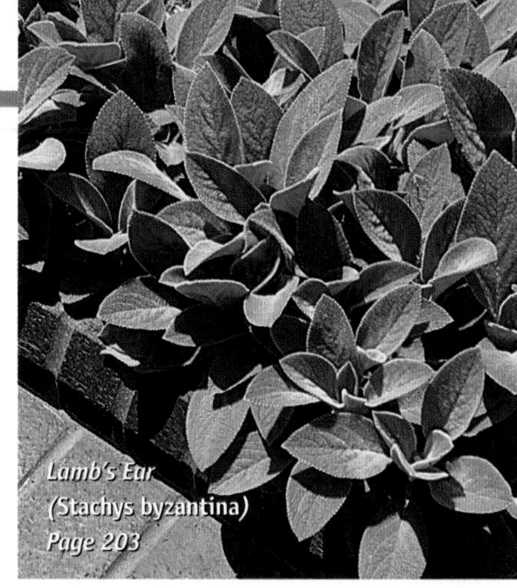
Lamb's Ear (Stachys byzantina) Page 203

Littleleaf Periwinkle (Vinca minor) Page 205

Choosing Groundcovers for Special Areas

Use these lists to find groundcovers that will fulfill your needs. Photographs of plants and detailed information can be found on the page numbers listed. Look for plants that include your growing zone within their range. To find your climate zone, turn to page 5.

Availability varies by area and conditions (see page 21). Check with your garden center.

Lady's Mantle (Alchemilla mollis) Page 178

Groundcover for edging patios, entries, and garden beds

Common Name	Zones	Page
Alba Meidiland Rose *Rosa Alba Meidiland*	4-8	201
Alpine Strawberry *Fragaria vesca*	3-9	189
Andorra Compact Juniper *Juniperus horizontalis 'Plumosa Compacta'*	3-9	194
Bar Harbor Juniper *Juniperus horizontalis 'Bar Harbor'*	3-9	193
Basket-of-Gold *Aurinia saxatilis*	4-8	183
Bath's Pink *Dianthus gratianopolitanus 'Bath's Pink'*	4-9	187
Blanket Flower *Gaillardia x grandiflora*	2-9	190
Bloody Cranesbill *Geranium sanguineum*	3-8	191
Blue Chip Juniper *Juniperus horizontalis 'Blue Chip'*	3-9	193
Blue Rug Juniper *Juniperus horizontalis 'Wiltonii'*	3-9	194
Blue Star Bellflower *Campanula poscharskyana*	4-9	184
Catmint *Nepeta x faassenii*	4-8	197
Coral Bells *Heuchera sanguinea*	3-8	191
Dwarf Blue Fescue *Festuca glauca*	4-9	188
Dwarf Japanese Garden Juniper *Juniperus procumbens 'Nana'*	4-9	195
Germander *Teucrium prostratum*	4-9	204
Goldmoss *Sedum acre*	4-9	202
Hosta *Hosta species*	3-8	192
Kinnikinick *Arctostaphylos uva-ursi*	2-7	181
Lady's Mantle *Alchemilla mollis*	4-7	178
Lamb's Ear *Stachys byzantina*	4-8	203
Lily-of-the-Valley *Convallaria majalis*	2-9	185
Moss Phlox *Phlox subulata*	2-9	200
Pink Panda Strawberry *Fragaria 'Pink Panda'*	3-9	189
Purple-Leaf Wintercreeper *Euonymus fortunei 'Coloratus'*	3-9	187
Rockcress *Arabis caucasica*	3-7	180
Saxifrage *Bergenia cordifolia*	3-8	184
Sea Thrift *Armeria maritima*	3-8	182
Silver Brocade Artemisia *Artemisia stelleriana 'Silver Brocade'*	3-9	182
Snow-in-Summer *Cerastium tomentosum*	3-7	185
Spring Cinquefoil *Potentilla tabernaemontani*	4-8	200
Sundrop Primrose *Oenothera missouriensis*	4-8	198

Groundcover for woodland areas

Common Name	Zones	Page
Allegheny Foam Flower *Tiarella cordifolia*	4-9	204
Alpine Strawberry *Fragaria vesca*	3-9	189
Bog Rosemary *Andromeda polifolia*	2-6	180
Bunchberry *Cornus canadensis*	2-7	186
Cliff Green *Paxistima canbyi*	3-7	199
Creeping Phlox *Phlox stolonifera*	2-8	199
Forget-Me-Not *Myosotis scorpioides*	3-8	197
Hay-Scented Fern *Dennstaedtia punctilobula*	3-8	186
Hosta *Hosta species*	3-8	192
Lily-of-the-Valley *Convallaria majalis*	2-9	185
Littleleaf Periwinkle *Vinca minor*	4-8	205
Maidenhair Fern *Adiantum pedatum*	3-8	177
Partridge Berry *Mitchella repens*	4-9	196
Prostrate Chenault Coralberry *Symphoricarpos x chenaultii 'Hancock'*	4-7	203
Snow-on-the-Mountain *Aegopodium podagraria 'Variegatum'*	3-9	177
Sweet Woodruff *Asperula odorata*	4-8	183
Waldesteinia *Waldsteinia ternata*	3-8	205
Wintergreen *Gaultheria procumbens*	3-8	190
Yellow Archangel *Lamiastrum galeobdolon 'Variegatum'*	3-9	195

Groundcover for small, confined spaces

Common Name	Zones	Page
Alpine Strawberry *Fragaria vesca*	3-9	189
Andorra Compact Juniper *Juniperus horizontalis 'Plumosa Compacta'*	3-9	194
Bar Harbor Juniper *Juniperus horizontalis 'Bar Harbor'*	3-9	193
Bath's Pink *Dianthus gratianopolitanus 'Bath's Pink'*	4-9	187
Blanket Flower *Gaillardia x grandiflora*	2-9	190
Bloody Cranesbill *Geranium sanguineum*	3-8	191
Blue Chip Juniper *Juniperus horizontalis 'Blue Chip'*	3-9	193
Blue Rug Juniper *Juniperus horizontalis 'Wiltonii'*	3-9	194
Catmint *Nepeta x faassenii*	4-8	197
Coral Bells *Heuchera sanguinea*	3-8	191
Dwarf Japanese Garden Juniper *Juniperus procumbens 'Nana'*	4-9	195
Germander *Teucrium prostratum*	4-9	204
Goldmoss *Sedum acre*	4-9	202
Hosta *Hosta species*	3-8	192
Lamb's Ear *Stachys byzantina*	4-8	203
Maidenhair Fern *Adiantum pedatum*	3-8	177
Moss Phlox *Phlox subulata*	2-9	200
Silver Brocade Artemisia *Artemisia stelleriana 'Silver Brocade'*	3-9	182
Stonecrop *Sedum spectabile*	3-10	202

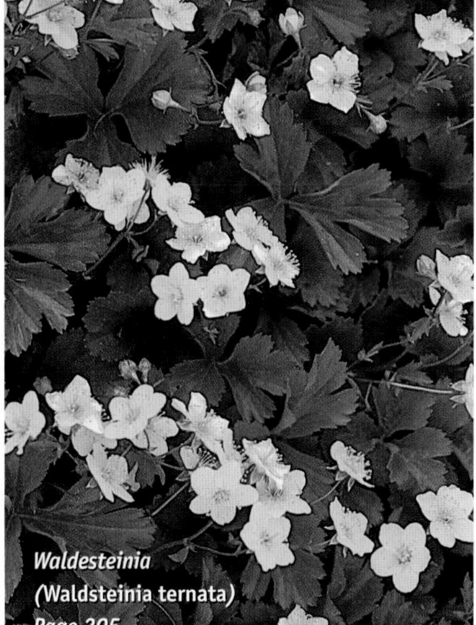

Waldesteinia (Waldsteinia ternata) Page 205

Groundcover for slopes

Common Name	Zones	Page
Alba Meidiland Rose *Rosa Alba Meidiland*	4-8	201
Alpine Strawberry *Fragaria vesca*	3-9	189
Andorra Compact Juniper *Juniperus horizontalis 'Plumosa Compacta'*	3-9	194
Bar Harbor Juniper *Juniperus horizontalis 'Bar Harbor'*	3-9	193
Basket-of-Gold *Aurinia saxatilis*	4-8	183
Bath's Pink *Dianthus gratianopolitanus 'Bath's Pink'*	4-9	187
Blanket Flower *Gaillardia x grandiflora*	2-9	190
Blue Chip Juniper *Juniperus horizontalis 'Blue Chip'*	3-9	193
Blue Rug Juniper *Juniperus horizontalis 'Wiltonii'*	3-9	194
Blue Star Bellflower *Campanula poscharskyana*	4-9	184
Cliff Green *Paxistima canbyi*	3-7	199
Cypress Spurge *Euphorbia cyparissias*	4-8	188
Goldmoss *Sedum acre*	4-9	202
Littleleaf Periwinkle *Vinca minor*	4-8	205
Moss Phlox *Phlox subulata*	2-9	200
Partridge Berry *Mitchella repens*	4-9	196
Prostrate Chenault Coralberry *Symphoricarpos x chenaultii 'Hancock'*	4-7	203
Purple-Leaf Wintercreeper *Euonymus fortunei 'Coloratus'*	3-9	187
Snow-in-Summer *Cerastium tomentosum*	3-7	185
Snow-on-the-Mountain *Aegopodium podagraria 'Variegatum'*	3-9	177
Spring Cinquefoil *Potentilla tabernaemontani*	4-8	200
Stonecrop *Sedum spectabile*	3-10	202

Groundcover for rock gardens

Common Name	Zones	Page
Basket-of-Gold *Aurinia saxatilis*	4-8	183
Bath's Pink *Dianthus gratianopolitanus 'Bath's Pink'*	4-9	187
Bog Rosemary *Andromeda polifolia*	2-6	180
Catmint *Nepeta x faassenii*	4-8	197
Cliff Green *Paxistima canbyi*	3-7	199
Dwarf Blue Fescue *Festuca glauca*	4-9	188
Germander *Teucrium prostratum*	4-9	204
Goldmoss *Sedum acre*	4-9	202
Moss Phlox *Phlox subulata*	2-9	200
Mountain Sandwort *Arenaria montana*	3-6	181
Partridge Berry *Mitchella repens*	4-9	196
Rockcress *Arabis caucasica*	3-7	180
Sea Thrift *Armeria maritima*	3-8	182
Silver Brocade Artemisia *Artemisia stelleriana 'Silver Brocade'*	3-9	182
Spring Cinquefoil *Potentilla tabernaemontani*	4-8	200
Stonecrop *Sedum spectabile*	3-10	202

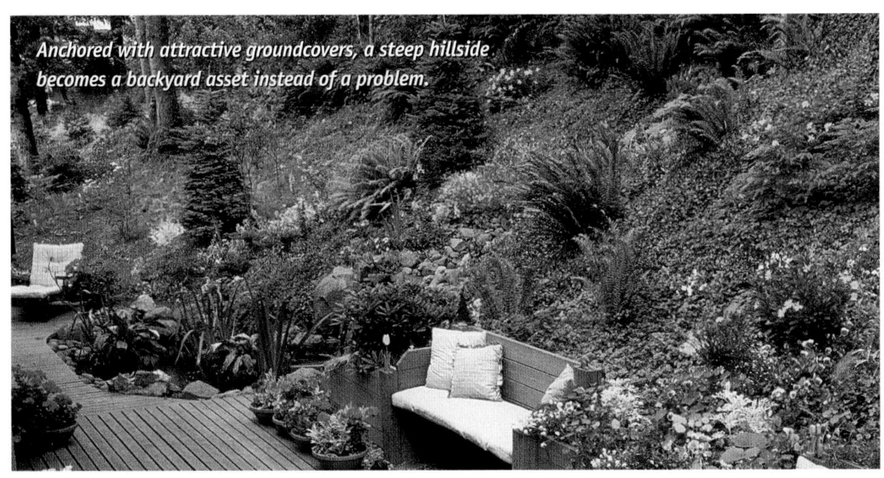

Anchored with attractive groundcovers, a steep hillside becomes a backyard asset instead of a problem.

Artemisia (Artemisia spp.) Page 182

Winterizing Groundcovers

Give your groundcover beds a layer of protection against winter's chill. A little extra effort in the fall will pay off in spring when you're ready to enjoy greenery again.

STUFF YOU'LL NEED

Late fall:
- ✔ Bales of straw
- ✔ Hose or sprinkler

Early spring:
- ✔ Granular pre-emergent herbicide
- ✔ Gloves
- ✔ Leaf rake

What to Expect

You'll find straw for sale at many stores for use in outdoor autumn decorations. Make sure the straw you buy for mulching is clean and dry, not dark and damp.

1 Water groundcover thoroughly before mulching for winter. This offsets autumn dry spells and gets the ground moist before it freezes. Groundwater that is frozen will be available to roots when it thaws early next spring. If you turn your hose on too hard, much of the water will flow across the surface instead of soaking down to roots. Use a watering wand attached to the end of your hose, a sprinkler, or a hose that's turned on just enough to emit a gentle stream of water.

2 Spread a 6- to 10-inch-thick layer of clean straw over the watered groundcover bed. Cover plants entirely and fluff the straw to trap air beneath it.

Wisdom of the Aisles

Pre-emergent Herbicide

This type of product is ideal for use in groundcover beds. It kills plants that have not yet germinated but it won't harm existing plants. Your groundcovers are unaffected but newly emerging weeds will die. This keeps your plants from having to compete with weeds for water and nutrients, resulting in a bed that's lush and tidy. You can apply pre-emergent herbicide at any time of year, but including it in your landscape's spring cleaning will nip weeds before they get a chance to grow.

Unless the straw shows signs of fungus (white or powdery discoloration), recycle it. Add this organic matter to your compost pile next spring.

In the Zone

Don't take the easy way out and rake fallen leaves on top of your groundcover plants.

▲ ***Wrong*** Layers of leaves compressed by winter precipitation smothers plants. Moisture held in place by leaves on top of the soil creates an ideal setting for fungal problems to flourish. And lastly, you're not really saving yourself any work. Leaves that aren't shredded aren't going to decay over the winter so you'll have to rake them off of groundcover beds in spring and dispose of leaves then.

Fresh, clean straw is the best material to use when bedding down groundcovers for winter.

BUYER'$ GUIDE

One bale of straw can cover about 100 square feet with a 10-inch-thick layer. Take rough measurements of your groundcover beds before you go to the store so you'll know how many bales to purchase.

3 In early spring when the final freeze is over and the ground thaws, use a leaf rake to gently uncover the bed of groundcover. Apply a granular pre-emergent herbicide to the bed, scratching it into the soil around plants and watering thoroughly after application. Follow package directions for application rates and safety measures.

4 After giving your groundcover bed a good drink of water, replenish mulch around plants. Tuck organic matter between plants, nestling it against base of stems. Mulch will help preserve moisture, suppress weed growth, and keep soil temperatures even. You'll need to get down on your hands and knees to do this job correctly. If you drop mulch from above, it can clog the crowns of plants, causing disease and inviting soft-bodied pests such as slugs and snails.

Design Tip — *Adding New Plants*

Spring is the best time to add new plants to your groundcover beds. This will give them the benefit of a full growing season before winter sets in again. If you plant in the fall, the root systems of young plants might not be developed enough to anchor them well. Such plants can be heaved out of the soil during freeze-thaw cycles. This results in dry, exposed roots and damaged plants.

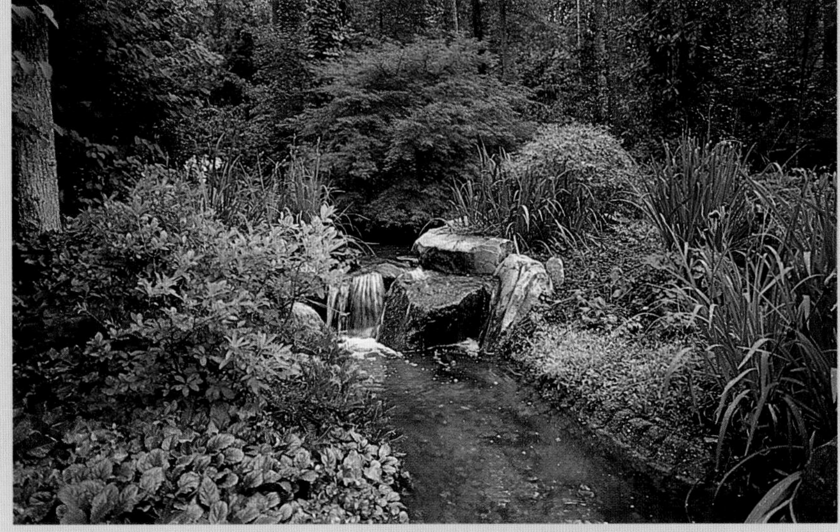

Dividing Groundcover Clumps

Dividing clump-forming groundcovers keeps plants vigorous and increases the quantity of plants you have to cover the ground. If your beds are already filled, share with a neighbor.

STUFF YOU'LL NEED

- ✔ Sharp shovel
- ✔ Utility knife (optional)
- ✔ Work boots
- ✔ Garden hose with sprayer attachment

What to Expect

You won't need to divide every year. Plants that decline, fail to bloom, or appear crowded should be divided. Every three years is usually enough.

1

1 In late spring or early summer, dig up overgrown clumps of groundcover from crowded beds. Dig and divide one clump at a time to keep roots from drying out. Spray roots with a stiff stream of water to wash soil away from roots. This makes it easier to see what you're doing.

2

2 Lay the plant on its side. Position the sharp shovel blade against the clump of roots and press down to cut it in half. (Large clumps can be divided several times.) You may need to supplement your efforts with a utility knife if roots are thick and tangled.

3

3 Gently pull the severed root mass apart with your hands to form two plants. Each plant should have its own roots and leaves.

4 Replant your newly divided groundcovers right away to keep plants from drying out. (Water immediately after planting.) If you want to save them to set in beds later or to give away, plant divided groundcovers temporarily in containers of potting soil or top soil and water thoroughly. Store potted plants in an area with light conditions that match those of the bed from which you removed plants. You'll need to water potted plants a little more frequently than those growing in the ground.

Design Tip

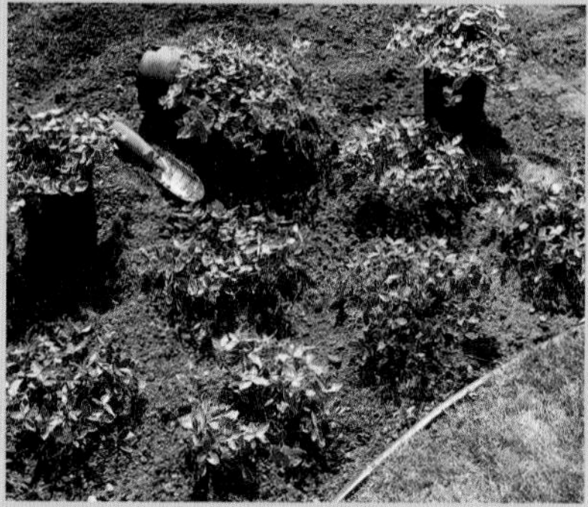

Arrange new groundcover plants in beds before removing pots. This will help you get the spacing right before planting. (Remove pots and install plants one at a time.) Set the first row of plants to follow the shape of your bedline; set them back from the edge a distance that's equal to one-half the species' mature spread so plants have room to grow. Working from front to back, set groundcover in alternating rows to create a staggered formation. Doing so helps plants fill in to cover ground quickly. It's OK to fudge as needed to fill odd-shaped areas; the staggered formation is a goal, not a firm rule.

Adiantum pedatum

Maidenhair Fern

Outstanding Features:

- Bright green, fine-textured foliage
- Thrives in damp, shady locations
- Returns every year in the spring

Zones: 3-8

Light Needs:

Mature Size:

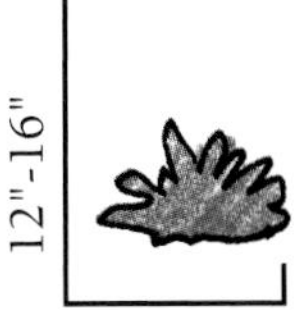

Growth Rate: medium

perennial

Needs: Plant in moist soil that's rich in organic matter. Soil should be neutral or slightly acidic. Grow in partial to dense shade; protect from afternoon sun in hotter climates. Mulch for winter.

Good for: natural areas, damp sites, woodland paths, shady courtyards and entries, textural contrast among plants or stones, narrow confined spaces, shady ponds, creeks, or using near downspouts

More Choices: pages 37, 41, 43, 170, 171, and 173

Add this plant to shady, damp spots and you'll be rewarded with bright green, delicate fronds. Leaflets seem to hover above dark, purplish stems. The fine-texture combines nicely with Hostas. May be sold as Northern Maidenhair Fern.

Aegopodium podagraria 'Variegatum'

Snow-on-the-Mountain

Outstanding Features:

- Lustrous, green leaves are edged with white
- Grows rapidly to cover ground completely
- Small, white flowers in early summer

Zones: 3-9

Light Needs:

Mature Size:

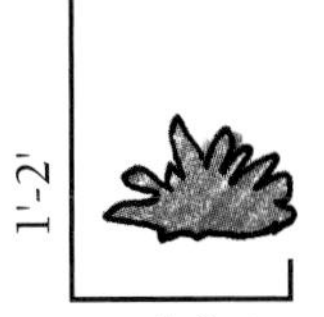

Growth Rate: rapid

perennial

Needs: Plant in any kind of soil. It will grow in full sun, partial or dense shade; protect from afternoon sun in hotter climates. Tolerates full sun where summers are cool.

Good for: filling in where grass won't grow, massing, erosion control, hillsides, dry shade around tree roots, naturalized areas, large planting beds, brightening dim, shaded areas

More Choices: pages 37, 39, 41, 42, 171, and 173

Here's a groundcover that performs well in sun or shade. Green-and-white foliage spreads quickly; vigorous growth is a hallmark of this plant. Keep this isolated from other types of groundcover and perennials. Its vigorous growth will choke other plants out. Also sold as Variegated Bishop's Weed or Goutweed. Remove any solid green foliage that appears.

Ajuga reptans

Ajuga

Zones: 3-9

Light Needs:

Mature Size:

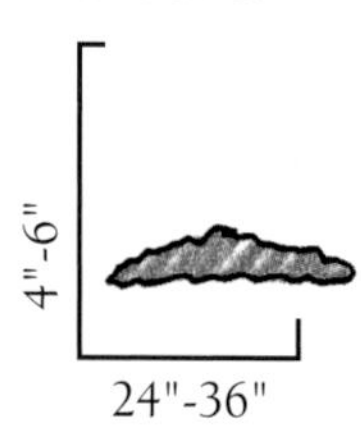

Growth Rate: medium to rapid

semievergreen perennial (evergreen in hot areas)

Needs: Plant in any soil that's moist but well-drained. Plants won't thrive in soggy soil or in drought conditions. Grow in partial shade.

Good for: rock gardens, edging patios, stepping-stone paths, formal or informal gardens, front layer of planting beds

More Choices: pages 35, 37, and 171

Options: 'Alba'—white flowers
'Burgundy Lace'—dark pink flowers
'Atropurpurea'—blue flowers, bronze
'Tricolor'—pink, cream, green leaves

Outstanding Features:

- Fast growing cover for shaded locations
- Flowers combine well with spring blooms
- Wide availability of foliage variations

Spring brings spikes of sky blue flowers. Ajuga will grow where grass won't. Dry or dense shade is not a problem for this adaptable, low-growing groundcover. Ajuga will spread easily into lawns. Avoid locating it where it will take advantage of this situation.

Alchemilla mollis

Lady's Mantle

Zones: 4-7

Light Needs:

Mature Size:

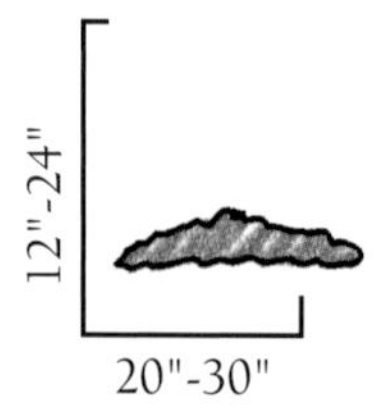

Growth Rate: medium

perennial

Needs: Plant in well-drained fertile, moist soil. Partial shade is best in hotter areas; plants can take full sun in cooler regions.

Good for: edging flower and shrub beds, planting at the base of shrubs or trees, lining walkways

More Choices: pages 37, 170, 171, and 172

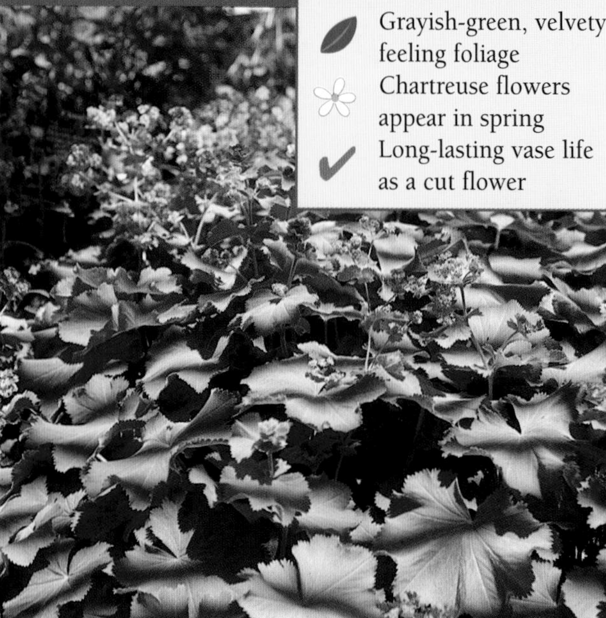

Outstanding Features:

- Grayish-green, velvety feeling foliage
- Chartreuse flowers appear in spring
- Long-lasting vase life as a cut flower

Lady's Mantle is a good, low plant for in-between areas that are both shady and sunny. Chartreuse blooms are set off by silky gray-green leaves. Morning dew or rain caught by the leaves is a beautiful site. Plants are drought tolerant.

Amsonia tabernaemontana

Blue Star

Zones: 3-9

Light Needs:

Mature Size:

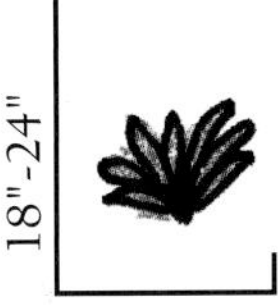

18"-24"

12"-18"

Growth Rate: medium

perennial

Needs: Plant in well-drained soil. Avoid excessively fertile soil or extra fertilization. Growth will be floppy and open if over fertilized. Trim plants back after flowering to increase density. Pick a spot that's partially shaded if your summer temperatures are warm.

Good for: wildflower gardens, perennial beds, entries, along fences, around decks, or at the foot of rock walls

More Choices: pages 37 and 171

Outstanding Features:

- Blue starlike blossoms begin in late spring
- Narrow green leaves turn golden in autumn
- Adapts well to poor soil conditions

Starry blue flowers cover this perennial from late spring and continue through the middle of summer. Its upright form makes a nice addition to areas where shorter groundcovers may be hidden from view. Cool blue flowers are a nice contrast with other, brighter colored blooms.

Anchusa myosotidiflora (also listed as *Brunnera macrophylla*)

Siberian Forget-Me-Not

Zones: 3-7

Light Needs:

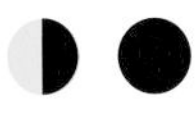

Mature Size:

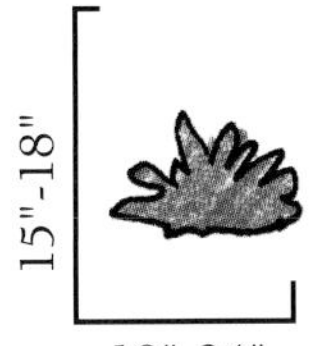

15"-18"

18"-24"

Growth Rate: medium to rapid

perennial

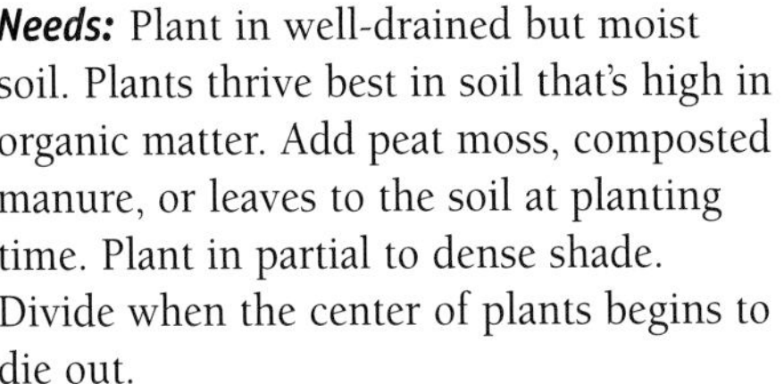

Needs: Plant in well-drained but moist soil. Plants thrive best in soil that's high in organic matter. Add peat moss, composted manure, or leaves to the soil at planting time. Plant in partial to dense shade. Divide when the center of plants begins to die out.

Good for: planting beneath trees, filling in shady flowerbeds

More Choices: pages 37, 170, and 171

Outstanding Features:

- Bright blue blooms appear in spring
- Form a problem-free carpet of green
- Self-seeds freely to fill in an area over time

Siberian Forget-Me-Not is at home in shady, organic soils beneath trees. Springtime blue flowers appear year after year. Plants self-sow and increase in number for an attractive cover.

Andromeda polifolia (also listed as *Andromeda rosmarinifolia*)

Bog Rosemary

Zones: 2-6

Light Needs:

Mature Size:

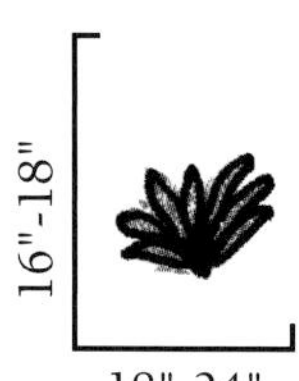

Growth Rate: slow

evergreen shrub

Needs: Plant in well-drained, fertile, moist, acidic soil. Increase soil acidity by adding peat moss or composted oak leaves to the soil at planting time. Mulch well to conserve moisture. Plant in full sun or partial shade for best growth.

Good for: shady beds, rock gardens, woodland areas, moist locations

More Choices: pages 35, 37, 41, 171, and 173

Options: 'Alba'—abundant white blooms; 6" high, 8" wide
'Compacta'—pink blooms, glaucous leaves; 12" high, 8" wide

Outstanding Features:

- Tiny, balloon-shaped flowers cover plants
- Leaves remain dark green year-round
- Tolerates moist, acidic growing conditions

As long as soil is acidic, dampness doesn't bother Bog Rosemary. White to pink flowers open in spring and continue through early summer. Leaves stay green in all seasons.

Arabis caucasica

Rockcress

Zones: 3-7

Light Needs:

Mature Size:

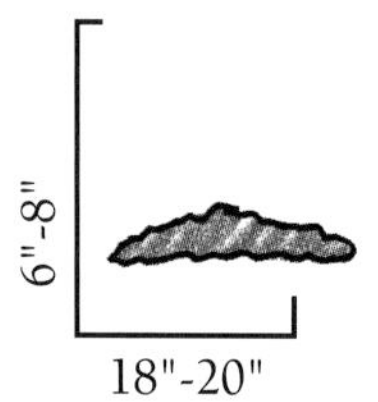

Growth Rate: medium to rapid

evergreen perennial

Needs: Plant in any soil that's well-drained in full sun or partial shade. Trim plants after flowering to promote vigorous growth. Cut stems back by two-thirds.

Good for: trailing over walls, planting beside paths, edging the front of planting beds, rock gardens

More Choices: pages 35, 37, 170, 171, 172, and 173

Options: 'Variegata'—white-edged foliage; slow grower; plant in light shade
'Flore Pleno'—double, white flowers
'Rosabella'—rose-pink flowers, compact growth habit

Outstanding Features:

- Flowers are white and sweetly fragrant
- Leaves on trailing stems are evergreen
- Foliage is covered with fine hairs

The trailing stems of Rockcress are covered with white flowers each spring. Leaves remain on the plants all year, even in Zone 3. Prune plants after flowering for dense growth.

Arctostaphylos uva-ursi

Kinnikinick or Bearberry

Zones: 2-7

Light Needs:

Mature Size:

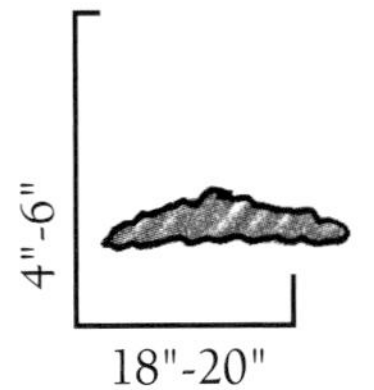

Growth Rate: slow

evergreen shrub

Needs: Plant in poor, sandy, infertile soil in full sun or partial shade. Plants rarely require pruning and never need fertilizer.

Good for: planting near paving, seaside gardens, foundation plantings, perennial beds, poor soils, attracting birds

More Choices: pages 23, 35, 37, 39, 170, 171, and 172

Options: ' 'Massachusetts'—pale pink flowers
'Vancouver Jade'—dark green leaves turn dark red in fall; pink flowers

Outstanding Features:

- White flowers are tinged with pink
- Bright red berries attract birds to the area
- Well known for being a low maintenance plant

This low evergreen can take sun, cold, poor soil, and heat without any help from you. Kinnikinick blooms mid- to late-spring and produces red berries in the fall. Low maintenance plants are ideal for sites you don't have time for, yet want to look good.

Arenaria montana

Mountain Sandwort

Zones: 3-6

Light Needs:

Mature Size:

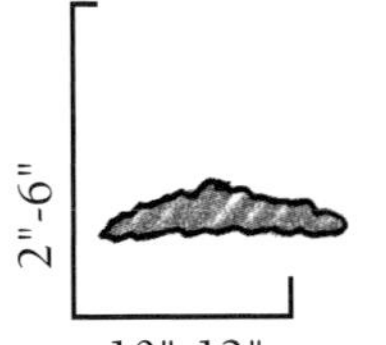

Growth Rate: slow to medium

evergreen perennial

Needs: Plant in full sun in well-drained, yet moist soil. Soils with low fertility are preferred. Plants are not drought tolerant and will need supplemental water during dry periods.

Good for: rock gardens, sunny niches, tucking into crevices of stone walls

More Choices: pages 35, 39, 170, 171, and 173

Options: *A. purpurascens* (Pink Sandwort)—pink flowers; 2" tall by 8" wide; Zones 4-7

Outstanding Features:

- White flowers open in late spring to summer
- Mounds of gray-green leaves last year-round
- Plants adapt to poor soils

Sandwort will grow in sunny spots and poor soil too. Mounds of tiny, gray-green leaves last throughout the year. White flowers appear in mid- to late-spring. Provide extra water during dry spells or plants will not survive.

Armeria maritima

Sea Thrift

Zones: 3-8

Light Needs:

Mature Size:

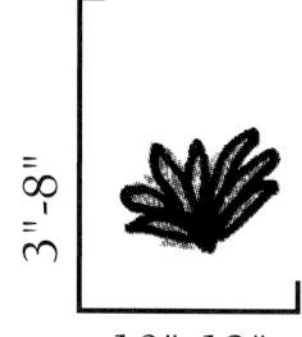

Growth Rate: slow to medium

evergreen perennial

Needs: Plant in full sun in well-drained soil, including sand. Grow plants in afternoon shade in hot regions. Divide when the centers of plants begin to die out and flowering is reduced.

Good for: coastal areas, rock gardens, edging planting beds

More Choices: pages 23, 37, 39, 170, 171, 172, and 173

Options: 'Alba'—white flowers; 6" high
'Dusseldorf Pride'—rose-pink blooms; about 10" high
'Laucheana'— intermittent blooms of deep rose-pink; 4" to 6" high

Outstanding Features:

- Leaves grow in grasslike tufts
- Flowerheads shaped like lollipops in spring
- Tolerates poor, dry, sandy soil conditions

Sea Thrift thrives by the sea as well as in any garden that has plenty of sunshine and sandy soil. This grasslike evergreen features bright pink flowers during hot months. Foliage grows just a few inches tall. Flowering stems rise above the foliage.

Artemisia stelleriana

Silver Brocade Artemisia

Zones: 3-9

Light Needs:

Mature Size:

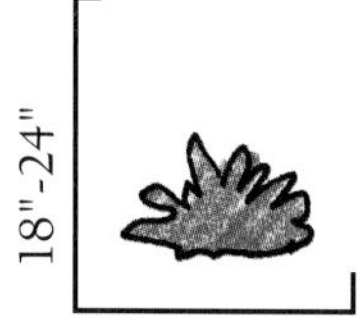

Growth Rate: medium

evergreen perennial

Needs: Plant in well-drained soil in full sun. Poor, sandy soils and coastal conditions are fine. Remove flower stalks to keep plants bushy. Artemisia is grown more for foliage. Divide in spring or fall when centers of crowded clumps die out.

Good for: entry areas, fronts of beds, planting near colorful or dark green plants, complementing white gardens

More Choices: pages 23, 35, 43, 170, 171, 172, and 173

Options: *A. ludoviciana*—Zones 4-7;
A schmidtiana—(Silver Mound), Zones 4-10

Outstanding Features:

- Silvery foliage combines with white
- Tolerates dry, sandy soil conditions
- Soft texture is great for touching

Choose this low-growing plant for a sandy, sunny yard. There are several species and varieties each boasting silvery leaves year-round. The soft texture of the foliage is very touchable. Kids love it.

Asperula odorata (also listed as Galium odoratum)

Sweet Woodruff

Outstanding Features:

- Bright green leaves shaped like hands
- Starry flowers blanket plants in spring
- Plants spread quickly to cover bare areas

Zones: 4-8

Light Needs:

Mature Size:

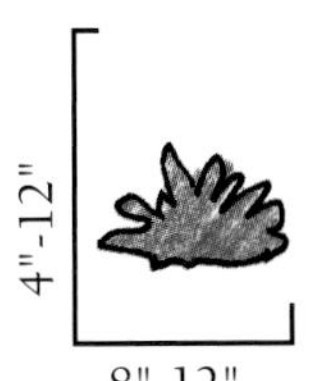

Growth Rate: medium to rapid

perennial

Needs: Plant in well-drained, humus-rich, acidic soil—increase soil acidity by adding peat moss or composted oak leaves to the soil at planting time. Or, mulch with pine straw. Grows well in full sun or partial shade. The hotter the climate, the more shade that's required

Good for: massing beneath shade trees, use along walkways, fronts of flowerbeds

More Choices: pages 35, 37, 41, 170, 171, and 173

This groundcover grows quickly in rich soil, making it a good choice to fill in bare areas. Little, white blossoms spread like snowflakes across a blanket of green in spring.

Aurinia saxatilis

Basket-of-Gold

Outstanding Features:

- Bright yellow flowers in late spring
- Tolerates drought and rocky soil
- Low clumps of gray-green foliage

Zones: 4-8

Light Needs:

Mature Size:

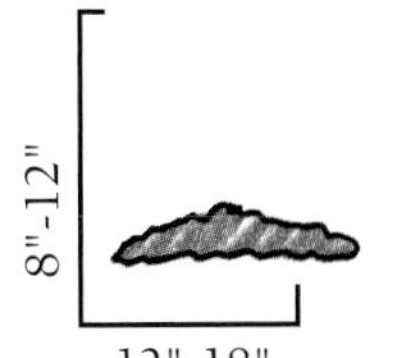

Growth Rate: rapid

evergreen perennial

Needs: Plant in any soil that's dry, including rocky soil. Grow in full sun. Trim after flowering to keep plants neat and compact. Do not fertilize. Water only during extreme periods of drought.

Good for: rock gardens, slopes, raised planters, planting beds, edging walkways or patios, entries, parking areas, arid landscapes, Xeriscaping, cascading over retaining walls

More Choices: pages 35, 39, 42, 171, 172, and 173

Options: 'Variegata'—leaves are edged with pale green; 10" high

Plant this evergreen cover in dry, rocky spots. You'll enjoy attractive clusters of bright yellow flowers from spring into summer. Not for areas that are hot and humid. May also be sold as Cloth-of-Gold or Gold Dust. Sometimes listed as *Alyssum saxatile*. Also try: 'Tom Thumb'—3" to 6" high.

Bergenia cordifolia

Saxifrage

Zones: 3-8

Light Needs:

Mature Size:

Growth Rate: medium to rapid

perennial

Needs: Plant in moist but well-drained soil, in full sun or partial shade. The cooler the climate, the more sun plants can tolerate. Before new growth emerges, remove leaves burned by winter cold.

Good for: mass planting, edging perennial beds and borders, along walkways

More Choices: pages 35, 37, 170, 171, and 172

Options: 'Bressingham Ruby'—ruby red flowers; purplish leaves in winter, compact 'Bressingham White'—apple-blossom pink flowers fade to white

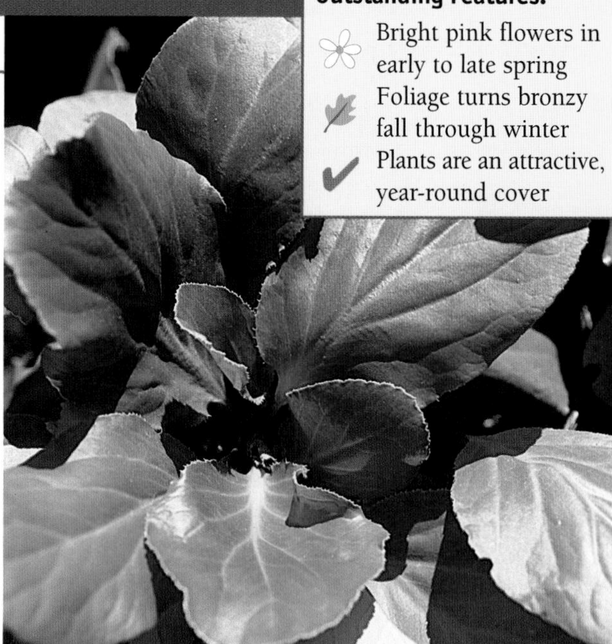

Outstanding Features:

- Bright pink flowers in early to late spring
- Foliage turns bronzy fall through winter
- Plants are an attractive, year-round cover

Saxifrage offers something for every season—bell-shaped flowers in spring, bright green foliage in summer, and bronzy-red leaves in fall and winter. Add organic matter to the soil at planting time to help retain moisture.

Campanula poscharskyana

Blue Star Bellflower

Zones: 4-9

Light Needs:

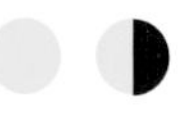

Mature Size:

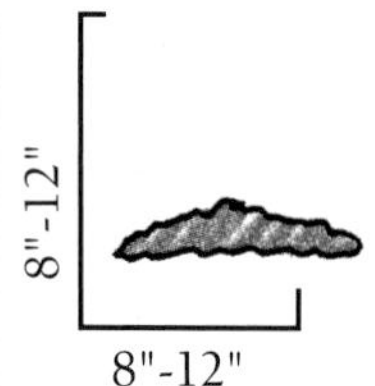

Growth Rate: medium to rapid

evergreen perennial

Needs: Plant in any normal garden soil. Grow in full sun or partial shade; flowering is best in full sun. Plants are drought-resistant and durable.

Good for: filling planting beds, covering bare spots, slopes, raised planters, sprawling over retaining walls, parking areas, entries, patio plantings

More Choices: pages 35, 37, 41, 42, 171, 172, and 173

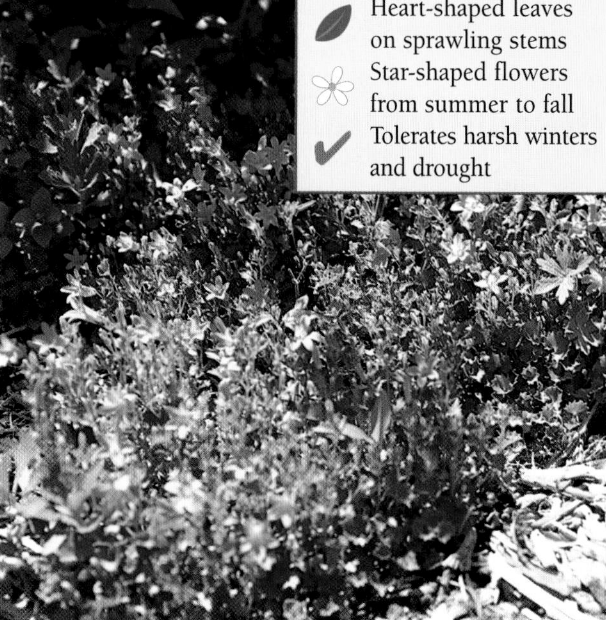

Outstanding Features:

- Heart-shaped leaves on sprawling stems
- Star-shaped flowers from summer to fall
- Tolerates harsh winters and drought

Grow this groundcover for a carpet of year-round foliage. Spreading plants are decorated with 1-inch-wide blue flowers during warm weather. Plant only in areas where you want them to spread. They can become too invasive for flowerbeds. May be sold as Serbian Bellflower. If slugs become a problem, control them with slug bait or diatomaceous earth.

Cerastium tomentosum

Snow-in-Summer

Outstanding Features:
- Snowy white blossoms from spring to summer
- Silvery white leaves form mats of foliage
- Tolerates dry, sandy, poor soil

Zones: 3-7

Light Needs:

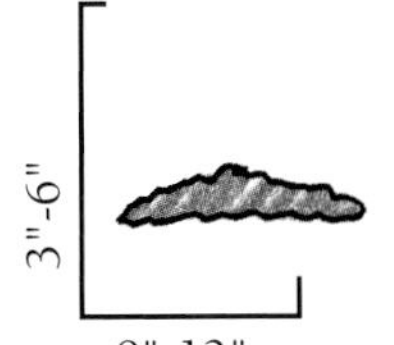

Mature Size:

Growth Rate: rapid

evergreen perennial

Needs: Plant in any well-drained soil with low fertility. Sandy soils suit it fine. Plants won't survive in soggy soil. Grow in full sun. Prune after flowers have faded to keep plants neat and full.

Good for: dry soils, hillsides, banks, berms, raised planters, planting beds, Xeriscaping, arid areas, entries, growing beside walkways or patios, sprawling over and out of walls

More Choices: pages 35, 39, 42, 170, 171, 172, and 173

Just as the name suggests, snowy white blossoms cover these plants from late spring through early summer. This groundcover thrives in dry soil. Plants may be short-lived in hot, humid areas. Divide plants to fill in thin patches and bare areas.

Convallaria majalis

Lily-of-the-Valley

Outstanding Features:
- Bell-shaped, fragrant spring flowers
- Coarse-textured, dark green foliage
- Fast growing; tolerates moist conditions

Zones: 2-9

Light Needs:

Mature Size:

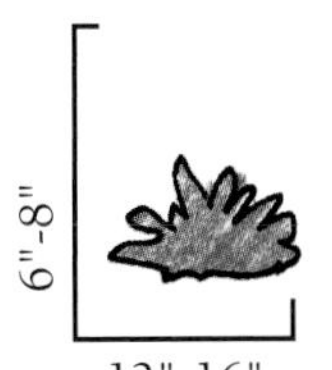

Growth Rate: slow to rapid

perennial

Needs: Plant in any soil that's moist or receives regular watering. Grow in partial to dense shade; protect from afternoon sun in hotter climates. Tolerates full sun where summers are cool and moisture is adequate. Mulch to conserve moisture and control weeds.

Good for: shady beds, growing beneath trees or shrubs, filling in bare spots, use beside shady patios, entries, or courtyards, woodland gardens, natural areas

More Choices: pages 37, 39, 170, 171, 172, and 173

This easy-to-grow perennial spreads to cover plenty of bare ground. Delicate spring flowers show off against coarse-textured leaves. Dig and divide crowded beds in fall. Share extra plants with friends.

Cornus canadensis

Bunchberry

Zones: 2-7

Light Needs:

Mature Size:

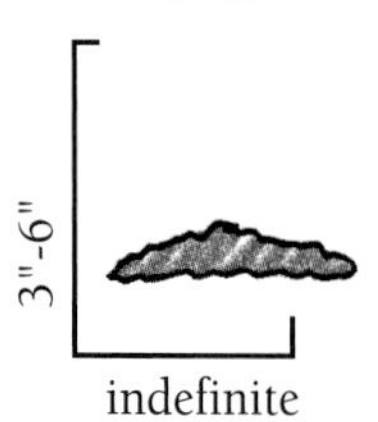

3"-6"

indefinite

Growth Rate: slow to medium

deciduous flowering shrub

Needs: Plant in well-drained, fertile, acidic soil. Choose a spot in partial to full shade and where moisture is available. Plants can be hard to get started; improve soil acidity with peat, composted oak leaves, or pine straw mulch at planting time. Regions with cool summers are best.

Good for: shady beds, woodland gardens, planting under acid-loving shrubs and trees, cool locations

More Choices: pages 37, 41, 170, 171, and 173

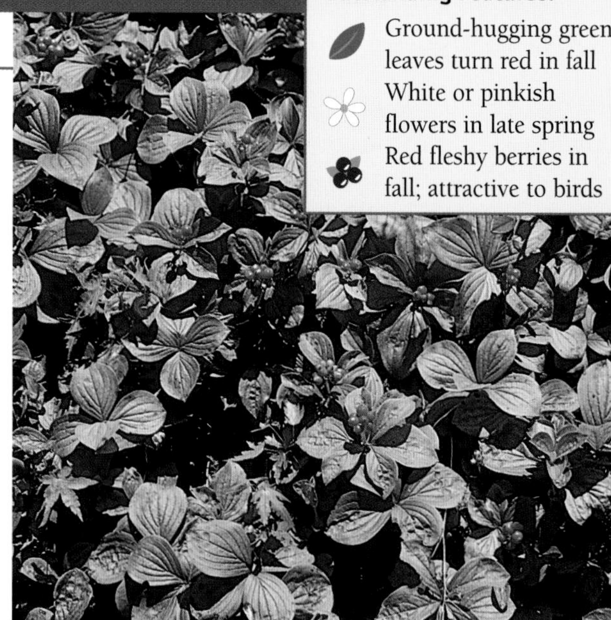

Outstanding Features:

- Ground-hugging green leaves turn red in fall
- White or pinkish flowers in late spring
- Red fleshy berries in fall; attractive to birds

This low-growing relative of the dogwood blooms in spring. White summer flowers are followed by red berries. A little more challenging to get started than other groundcovers but worth the extra effort.

Dennstaedtia punctilobula

Hay-Scented Fern

Zones: 3-8

Light Needs:

Mature Size:

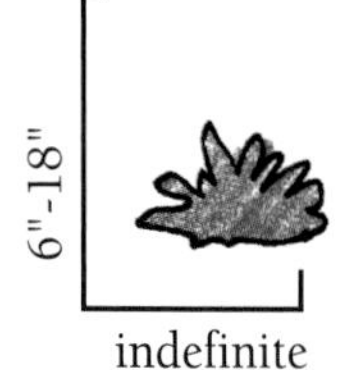

6"-18"

indefinite

Growth Rate: rapid

perennial

Needs: Plant in acidic soil; adapts to poor, dry soil. Grow in partial to dense shade. Established plants require little watering.

Good for: shade gardens, massing, contrasting with coarse-textured plants, large planting beds, natural areas, shaded woodlands

More Choices: pages 37, 39, 41, 170, 171, and 173

Outstanding Features:

- Feathery, light green fronds are fine-textured
- Foliage turns shades of yellow in fall
- Adaptable plants spread quickly

Fill in bare, shady spots with this fast-growing fern that isn't picky about the soil in which it grows. You'll enjoy arching, feathery fronds that are green in summer and yellow in autumn. Make sure you've allowed plenty of room for this fern to spread.

Diagnthus gratianopolitanus 'Bath's Pink'

Bath's Pink

Zones: 4-9

Light Needs:

Mature Size:

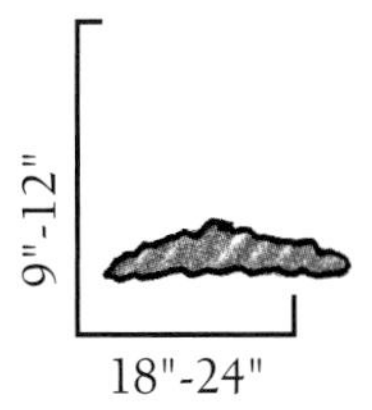

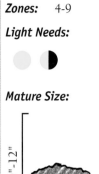

Growth Rate: medium to rapid

perennial

Needs: Plant in well-drained soil; plants won't thrive in soggy soil. Grow in full sun or partial shade. Too much shade discourages flowering. Pluck or shear wilted blooms to extend flowering and tidy up sprawling plants.

Good for: hillsides, growing over retaining walls, raised beds, berms, rock gardens, bordering planting beds, patios, or walkways, courtyards, Xeriscaping

More Choices: pages 35, 37, 39, 41, 42, 43, 170, 171, 172, and 173

Outstanding Features:

- Fine-textured leaves are blue-green
- Pink, fringed flowers cover foliage in spring
- Tolerates heat, humidity, and drought

Plant this fragrant groundcover in sloping soil where water can drain quickly away. Pink flowers adorn blue-green mats of foliage each spring. If deadheaded, flowering will continue for more than six weeks. Almost indestructible.

Euonymus fortunei 'Coloratus'

Purple-Leaf Wintercreeper

Zones: 3-9

Light Needs:

Mature Size:

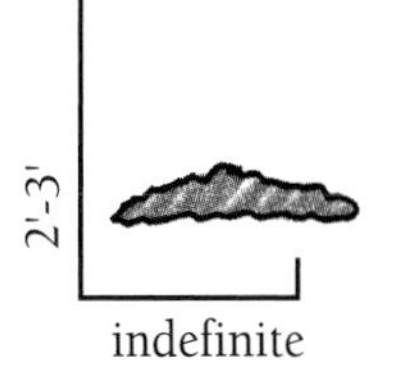

Growth Rate: rapid

evergreen perennial

Needs: Plant in full sun in any soil that is well-drained. Tolerant of high and low soil pH. Trim midspring to keep it in bounds and to remove dead or damaged stems. Underplant with spring bulbs. Mulch for winter in colder growing zones.

Good for: filling in bare spots beneath trees, hillsides, dry areas surrounded with paving, hot areas

More Choices: pages 35, 41, 42, 43, 171, 172, and 173

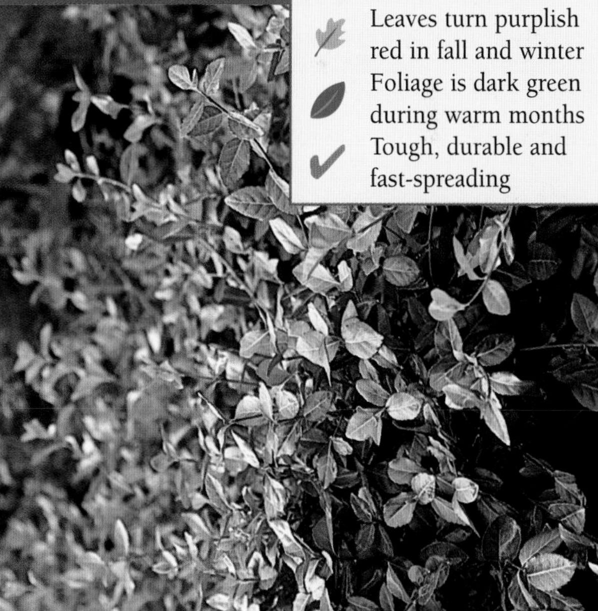

Outstanding Features:

- Leaves turn purplish red in fall and winter
- Foliage is dark green during warm months
- Tough, durable and fast-spreading

This sprawling groundcover isn't picky about soil. Plant it in full sun so green foliage will turn wine red in fall and winter. Make sure you want this one, it spreads vigorously. Control possible scale infestations with an insecticide spray labeled for euonymus.

Euphorbia cyparissias

Cypress Spurge

Zones: 4-8

Light Needs:

Mature Size:

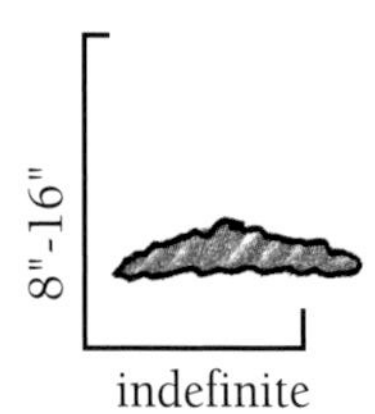

Growth Rate: rapid

perennial

Needs: Plant in full sun or partial shade in well-drained soil. Tolerates dry, infertile growing conditions.

Good for: hillsides, dry areas, raised planters, banks, large planting beds

More Choices: pages 35, 37, 42, 170, 171, and 173

Options: 'Orange Man'—flowers and fall leaves both tinted orange

Outstanding Features:

- Neat mounds of sea green foliage
- Yellow spring flowers blanket plants
- Adapts well to poor growing conditions

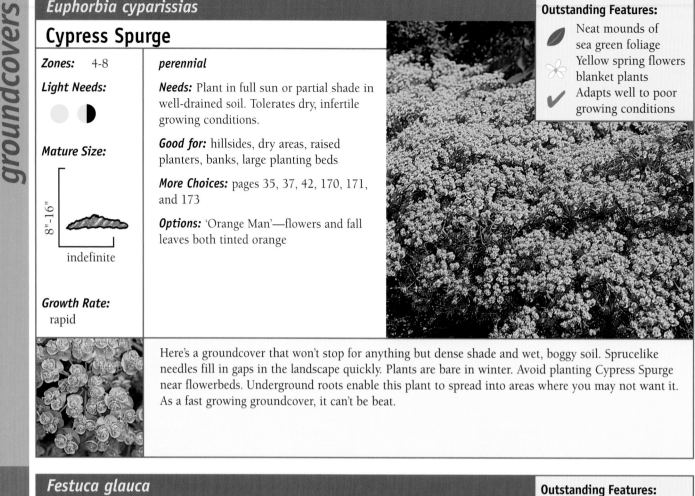

Here's a groundcover that won't stop for anything but dense shade and wet, boggy soil. Sprucelike needles fill in gaps in the landscape quickly. Plants are bare in winter. Avoid planting Cypress Spurge near flowerbeds. Underground roots enable this plant to spread into areas where you may not want it. As a fast growing groundcover, it can't be beat.

Festuca glauca

Dwarf Blue Fescue

Zones: 4-9

Light Needs:

Mature Size:

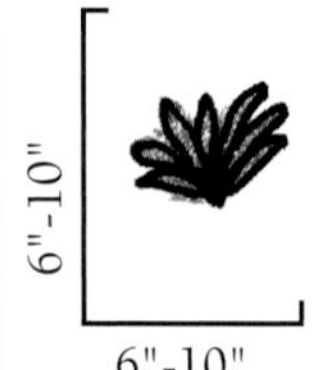

Growth Rate: medium to rapid

perennial

Needs: Plant in full sun in any well-drained soil. Dig and divide plants every two or three years. Trim plants to the ground in early spring to allow emergence of new growth and clean plants up.

Good for: rock gardens, parking areas, entries, edging walkways, perennial beds, planting in front of evergreen shrubs and leggy roses

More Choices: pages 35, 39, 170, 171, and 172

Options: 'Elijah Blue'—6" to 10" high and wide; powdery blue foliage

Outstanding Features:

- Blue, grassy foliage in fine-textured tufts
- Tough, durable, and drought-tolerant
- Foliage color contrasts with other plants

Add a little blue to your yard with Dwarf Blue Fescue. This ornamental grass is drought-tolerant and easy to grow. It forms tufts of fine-textured bluish leaves. Position plants close together to form a dense groundcover. Space them further apart for individual plant appearance.

Fragaria 'Pink Panda'

Pink Panda Strawberry

Outstanding Features:
- Pink flowers through warm months
- Small, edible berries are sweet and tasty
- Glossy green foliage forms quick cover

Zones: 3-9

Light Needs:

Mature Size:

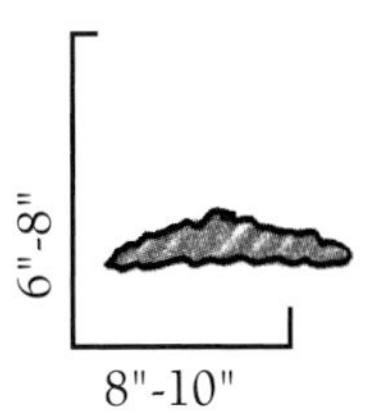

Growth Rate: rapid

perennial

Needs: Plant in full sun or partial shade in fertile, well-drained soil. Divide by digging up tiny, rooted plants and clipping connecting stems. In spring, remove any dead or winter-damaged leaves before new growth emerges. Mulch plants in cold winters to help keep them evergreen.

Good for: entries, planting beside patios and along walkways, containers

More Choices: pages 35, 37, 171, and 172

If you have fertile, well-drained soil in partial shade, consider Pink Panda Strawberry. Enjoy pink flowers, miniature berries, and spreading foliage. Plants spread by runners that root wherever they touch soil. Needs room to spread.

Fragaria vesca

Alpine Strawberry

Outstanding Features:

White flowers appear in late spring

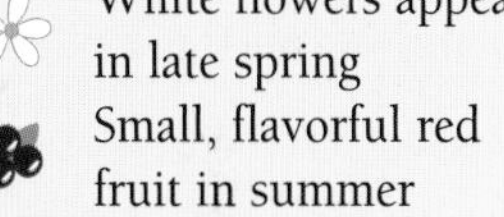
Small, flavorful red fruit in summer

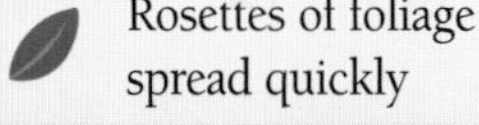
Rosettes of foliage spread quickly

Zones: 3-9

Light Needs:

Mature Size:

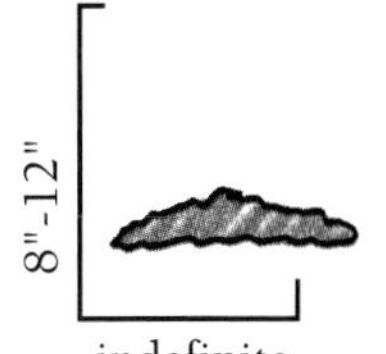

Growth Rate: medium to rapid

perennial

Needs: Plant in well-drained, fertile soil. Strawberries tolerate acidic soil but thrive in alkaline soil. Grow in full sun where summers are cool. Cover with mulch in late fall to prevent winter injury.

Good for: filling in empty areas, shrub beds, planting beneath roses, confined spaces, natural areas, slopes, raised planters, berms, planting beside patios

More Choices: pages 35, 37, 41, 42, 43, 171, 172, and 173

Alpine Strawberry, usually grown for its flavorful fruit, also makes a fine groundcover. Add it to herb gardens or window boxes for flowers and fruit in late spring and summer. Plant where it has plenty of room to spread.When purchasing strawberry plants for their fruit, keep in mind that June-bearing plants produce a single crop of larger berries in the spring while ever-bearing plants produce two crops of smaller berries, one in the spring and another in late summer and fall.

Gaillardia x grandiflora

Blanket Flower

Zones: 2-9

Light Needs:

Mature Size:

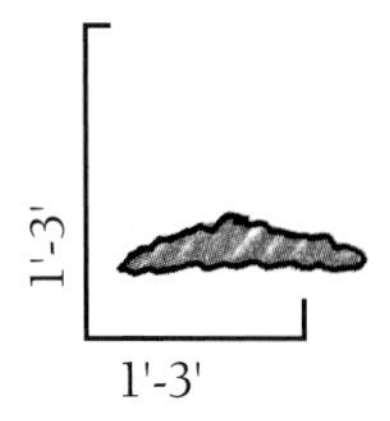

Growth Rate: rapid

perennial

Needs: Plant in any soil that's well-drained. Poor, dry, and sandy soil is fine. Grow in full sun.Tolerates heat and drought. Divide every few years in the spring. Salt-tolerant.

Good for: seaside gardens, hillsides, ditches, raised beds, berms, parking areas, seasonal accent, use along sunny walkways or patios, containers, covering bare, dry hot spots

More Choices: pages 23, 35, 39, 42, 43, 171, 172, and 173

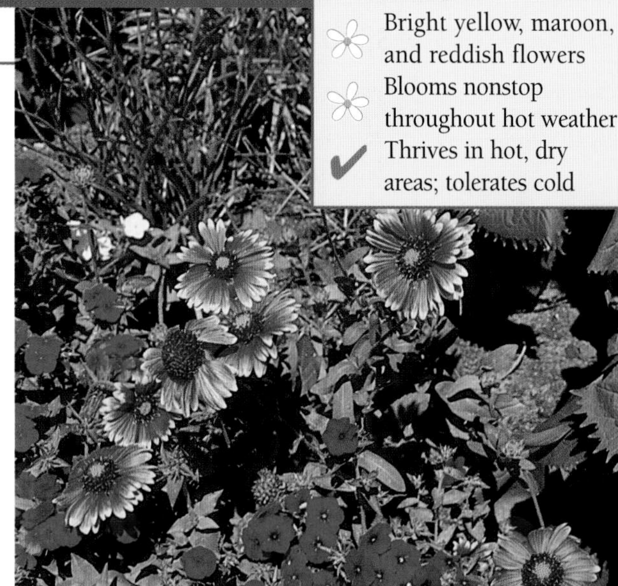

Outstanding Features:

- Bright yellow, maroon, and reddish flowers
- Blooms nonstop throughout hot weather
- Thrives in hot, dry areas; tolerates cold

You can grow this bright bloomer anywhere soil stays dry. Hot, warm, or cold climates, it doesn't matter. Fiery flowers appear summer through frost. Flowers well even without regular deadheading.

Gaultheria procumbens

Wintergreen

Zones: 3-8

Light Needs:

Mature Size:

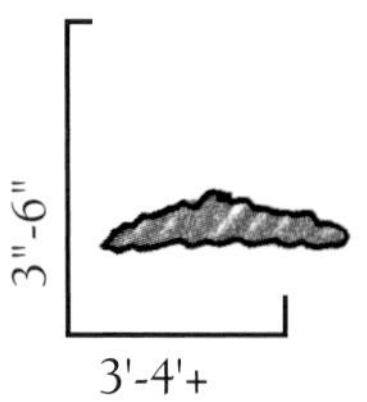

Growth Rate: slow to medium

perennial

Needs: Plant in fertile, well-drained soil that's moist and acidic. Increase soil acidity by adding peat moss or composted oak leaves to the soil at planting time. Mulch with pine products to help conserve moisture. Wintergreen grows best in partial shade—plants in full sun need extra water.

Good for: woodland areas, planting beneath acid-loving shrubs and trees, wintergreen fragrance, locating between stepping stones

More Choices: pages 37, 41, 171, and 173

Outstanding Features:

- White or pale-pink flowers in summer
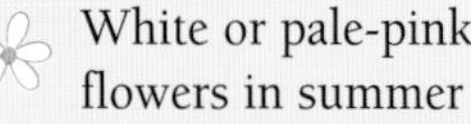
- Red, aromatic, edible berries in winter
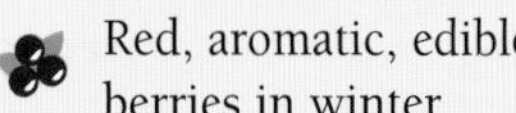
- Wintergreen fragrance from leaves and fruit

Though it's a little picky about where it grows, Wintergreen requires very little maintenance if the situation is right. This groundcover is famous for fragrance, delicate flowers, and red winter berries.

Geranium sanguineum

Bloody Cranesbill

Zones: 3-8

Light Needs:

Mature Size:

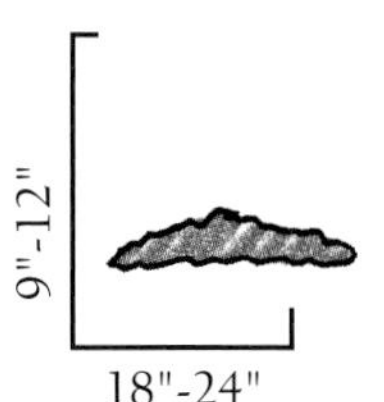

9"-12"

18"-24"

Growth Rate: medium

perennial

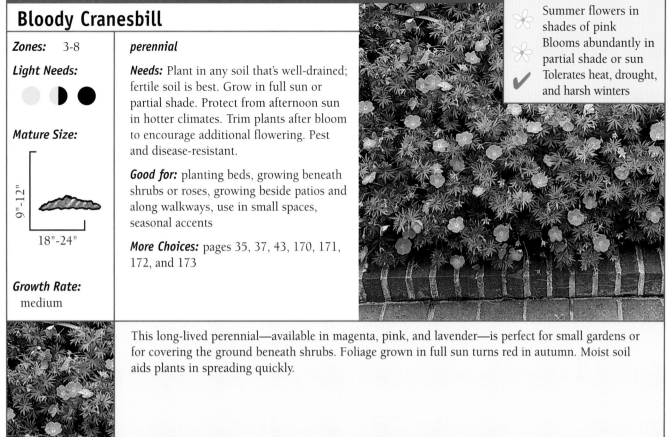

Needs: Plant in any soil that's well-drained; fertile soil is best. Grow in full sun or partial shade. Protect from afternoon sun in hotter climates. Trim plants after bloom to encourage additional flowering. Pest and disease-resistant.

Good for: planting beds, growing beneath shrubs or roses, growing beside patios and along walkways, use in small spaces, seasonal accents

More Choices: pages 35, 37, 43, 170, 171, 172, and 173

Outstanding Features:

- Summer flowers in shades of pink
- Blooms abundantly in partial shade or sun
- Tolerates heat, drought, and harsh winters

This long-lived perennial—available in magenta, pink, and lavender—is perfect for small gardens or for covering the ground beneath shrubs. Foliage grown in full sun turns red in autumn. Moist soil aids plants in spreading quickly.

Heuchera sanguinea

Coral Bells

Zones: 3-8

Light Needs:

Mature Size:

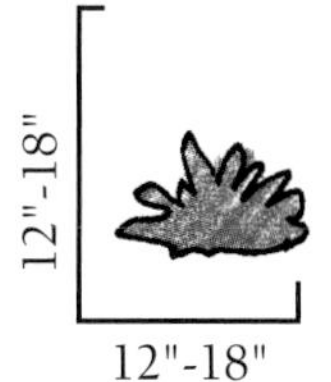

12"-18"

12"-18"

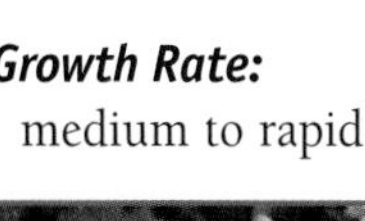

Growth Rate: medium to rapid

evergreen perennial

Needs: Plant in well-drained, fertile soil. Coral bells will not thrive in acidic soil; add lime to raise soil pH. In hotter climates, provide partial shade. Grow in full sun elsewhere, but keep plants moist.

Good for: perennial beds, edging planting beds and walks, filling in narrow areas, combining with spring-blooming bulbs, foliage effect

More Choices: pages 35, 37, 41, 43, 170, 171, 172, and 173

Outstanding Features:

- Bell-shaped blooms open in warm weather
- Evergreen foliage; attractively colored
- Attracts hummingbirds and bees

Forming tidy mounds of heart-shaped leaves, this is grown more for the foliage than the flowers. Numerous cultivars are available with variations of foliage color. Delicate blooms in red, pink, or white open on stalks in spring or summer.

Hosta spp.

Hosta

Outstanding Features:

Coarse-textured, puckery leaves

Thrives in all levels of shade and sun

Colorful foliage; both solid and variegated

Zones: 3-8

Light Needs:

Mature Size:

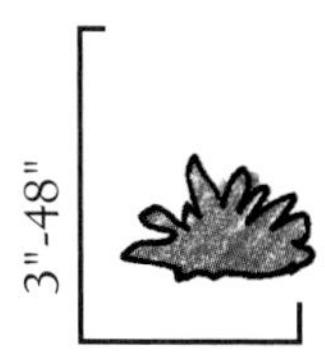

Growth Rate: rapid

perennial

Needs: Plant in rich, moist soil. Mix compost into the soil at planting time and mulch with humus each spring. Grow in partial or dense shade. Sun tolerance varies with the cultivar grown. Supply extra water during dry periods.

Good for: shade gardens, front layer of planting beds, natural areas, massing, specimen use, coarse-textured accent, shady courtyards, entries, or patio areas

More Choices: pages 37, 43, 170, 171, 172, and 173

Options: 'Blue Angel'—oval, bluish green leaves; 36" tall by 48" wide; white flowers; 36" tall by 48" wide
'Blue Moon'—blue-green leaves; 4" tall by 12" wide; pale mauve flowers
'Diamond Tiara'—thin, wavy, olive-green leaves splashed with gray-green and edged with creamy white; 14" tall by 26" wide; violet flowers
'Frances Williams'—heart-shaped, puckered, blue-green foliage with yellowish margins; 24" tall by 36" wide; white flowers
'Golden Prayers'—deep yellow, slightly puckered leaves; 14" tall by 24" wide; pale lavender flowers
'Kabitan'—lance-shaped, bright yellow leaves edged with green; 8" tall by 10" wide; violet flowers
'Love Pat'—heart-shaped, thick, puckered foliage; 18" tall by 36" wide; off-white flowers
'Ryan's Big One'—heart-shaped, grayish blue leaves are thick and deeply puckered; 34" tall by 60" wide; white flowers
'Sugar and Cream'—wavy, heart-shaped, green leaves are edged with cream; 30" tall and wide; white flowers
'Zounds'—puckered, thick, yellow, heart-shaped foliage, 22" tall by 36" wide; pale lavender-blue flowers

If you find composing with textures to be an elusive concept, plant beds filled with hostas. These large-leaved plants add coarse texture, a variety of hues, and erect stems of often fragrant flowers. Use variegation with care to avoid clashing foliage colors.

Juniperus horizontalis 'Bar Harbor'

Bar Harbor Juniper

Zones: 3-9

Light Needs:

Mature Size:

10"-12"

4'-6'

Growth Rate: slow

evergreen shrub

Needs: Plant in full sun in well-drained soil. Slightly alkaline soil is preferred. Little pruning required—remove dead or damaged branches as needed. Extra watering is not required.

Good for: parking areas, coastal gardens, raised planters, hillsides, beside patios, and filling in hot, dry beds, bare spots, and foundations

More Choices: pages 23, 35, 41, 42, 43, 170, 171, 172, and 173

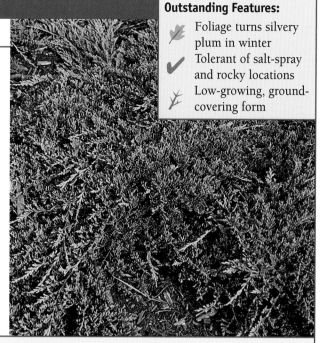

Outstanding Features:

- Foliage turns silvery plum in winter
- Tolerant of salt-spray and rocky locations
- Low-growing, ground-covering form

This spreading shrub tolerates heat, salt, and drought plus turns shades of plum in winter. Makes a handsome groundcover. Twig blight can be a problem. Remove affected branches and destroy. Rinse pruners in alcohol between cuts.

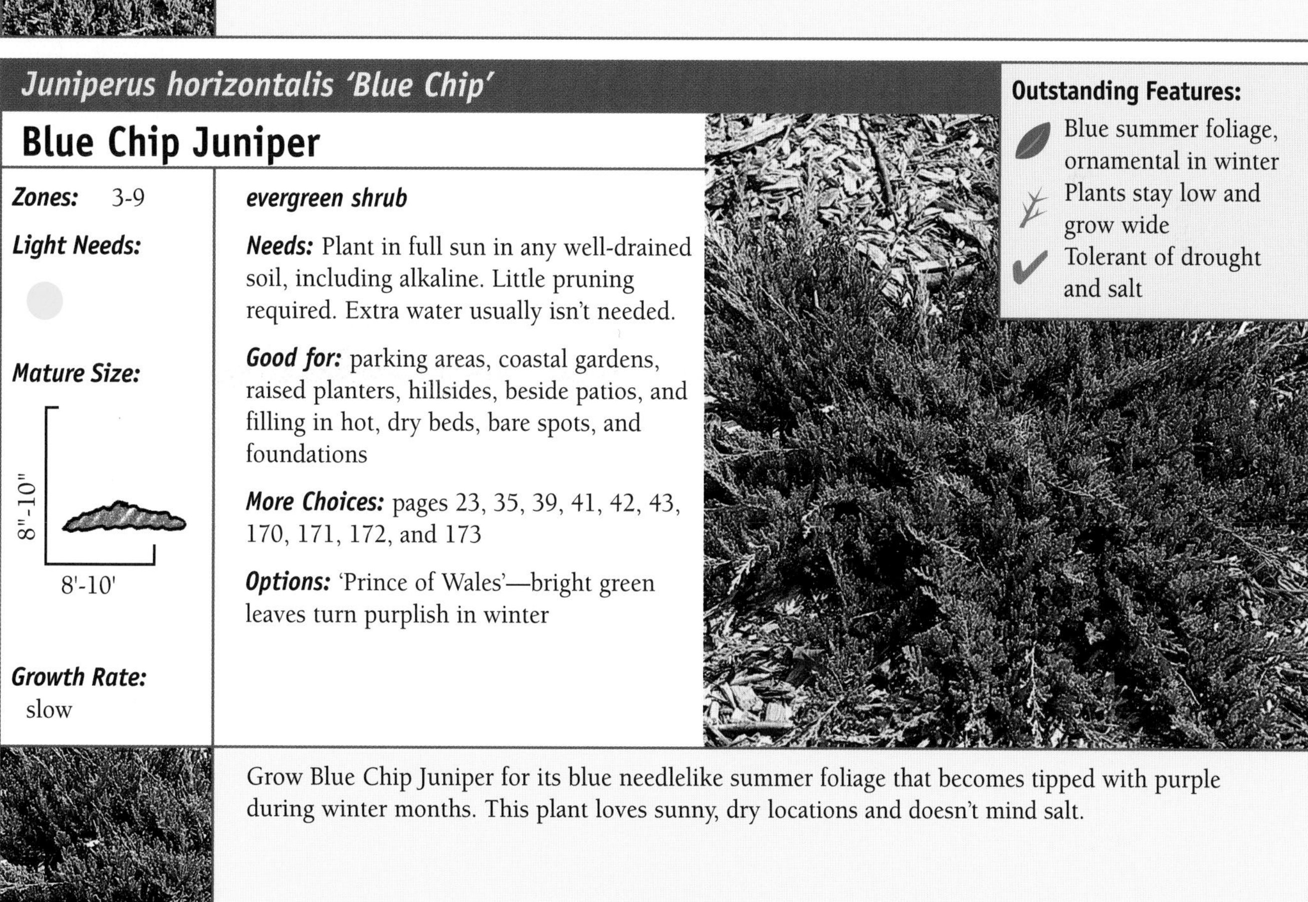

Juniperus horizontalis 'Blue Chip'

Blue Chip Juniper

Zones: 3-9

Light Needs:

Mature Size:

8"-10"

8'-10'

Growth Rate: slow

evergreen shrub

Needs: Plant in full sun in any well-drained soil, including alkaline. Little pruning required. Extra water usually isn't needed.

Good for: parking areas, coastal gardens, raised planters, hillsides, beside patios, and filling in hot, dry beds, bare spots, and foundations

More Choices: pages 23, 35, 39, 41, 42, 43, 170, 171, 172, and 173

Options: 'Prince of Wales'—bright green leaves turn purplish in winter

Outstanding Features:

- Blue summer foliage, ornamental in winter
- Plants stay low and grow wide
- Tolerant of drought and salt

Grow Blue Chip Juniper for its blue needlelike summer foliage that becomes tipped with purple during winter months. This plant loves sunny, dry locations and doesn't mind salt.

Juniperus horizontalis 'Plumosa Compacta'

Andorra Compact Juniper

Zones: 3-9

Light Needs:

Mature Size: 12"-18" × 6'-10'

Growth Rate: slow

evergreen shrub

Needs: Plant in full sun in any well-drained soil, including alkaline. Little pruning is required—remove dead or damaged branches as needed. Extra water isn't
usually needed.

Good for: parking areas, coastal gardens, raised planters, hillsides, locating beside patios, filling in hot, dry beds and bare spots, foundations

More Choices: pages 23, 35, 41, 42, 43, 170, 171, 172, and 173

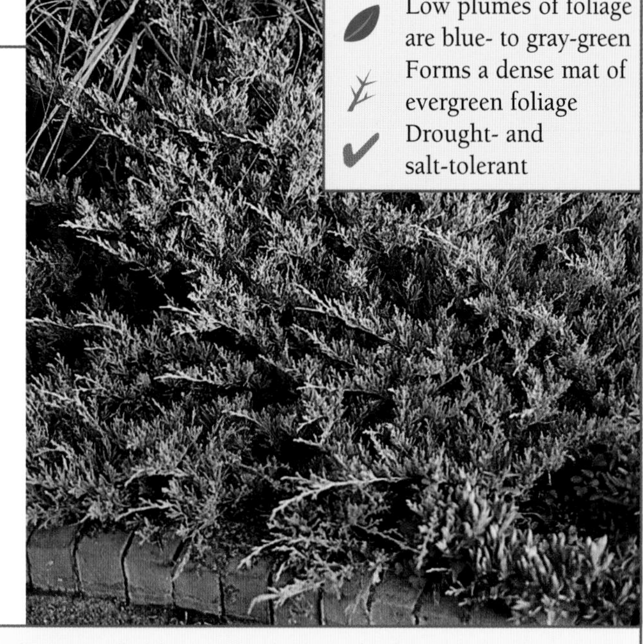

Outstanding Features:

- Low plumes of foliage are blue- to gray-green
- Forms a dense mat of evergreen foliage
- Drought- and salt-tolerant

If you're looking for a groundcover for a bed surrounded by paving, look no further. This juniper won't mind the reflected heat as long as the soil drains well. Plants stay full in the center without dying out. Susceptible to twig blight when environmental conditions are right.

Juniperus horizontalis 'Wiltonii'

Blue Rug Juniper

Zones: 3-9

Light Needs:

Mature Size:

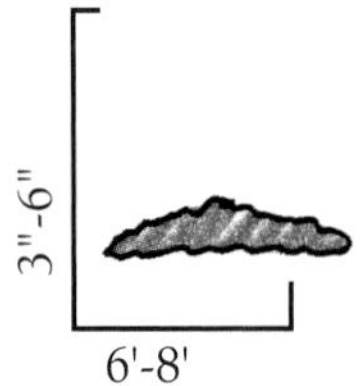

3"-6" × 6'-8'

Growth Rate: slow

evergreen shrub

Needs: Plant in full sun in any well-drained soil, including alkaline. Little pruning required—remove dead or damaged branches as needed. Extra water usually isn't needed.

Good for: parking areas, coastal gardens, dry planting beds, edging beside walkways and patios, planting behind retaining walls

More Choices: pages 23, 35, 41, 42, 43, 170, 171, 172, and 173

Outstanding Features:

- Flat, spreading growth creeps along ground
- Blue foliage turns purplish in winter
- Drought- and salt-tolerant

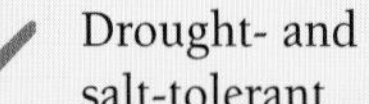

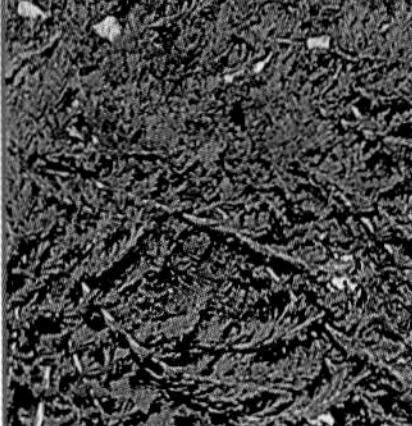

Here's a plant that's aptly named. Its intense blue foliage is flat just like a rug. Grow this juniper in hot, dry soil to carpet difficult spots or drape over retaining walls. This plant is susceptible to twig blight when environmental conditions are right.

Juniperus procumbens 'Nana'

Dwarf Japanese Garden Juniper

Outstanding Features:

- Fine-textured bluish green foliage
- Tolerates heat and car exhaust
- Stays low with dense compact growth

Zones: 4-9

Light Needs:

Mature Size:

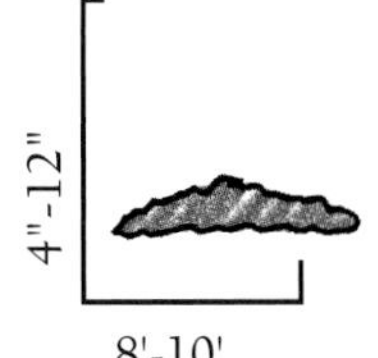

Growth Rate: slow to medium

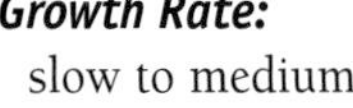

evergreen shrub

Needs: Plant in full sun in any well-drained soil, including acidic or alkaline. Little pruning required—remove dead or damaged branches as needed. Extra water is usually not required.

Good for: parking areas, planting beds, growing beside walkways and patios

More Choices: pages 35, 41, 43, 170, 171, 172, and 173

Options: 'Nana Greenmound'—resembles bright green cushions, 4" to 6" tall, 6' to 8' wide

This ground-hugging juniper has branches that are densely packed with blue-green foliage. Plants thrive in heat and dry soil; they'll even tolerate pollution. The brighter the sunlight, the better for this sun-loving plant.

Lamiastrum galeobdolon 'Variegatum'

Yellow Archangel

Outstanding Features:

- Silver and green leaves grows in dense shade
- Trailing stems cover bare ground quickly
- Adapts well to dry shade beneath trees

Zones: 3-9

Light Needs:

Mature Size:

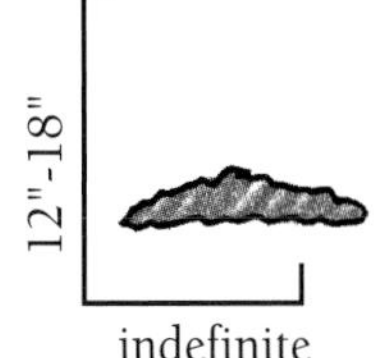

Growth Rate: rapid

perennial

Needs: Plant in moist, well-drained soil in dense or partial shade. Plants adapt to dry shade as well. Cut plants back after summer flowers fade to promote thick foliage growth.

Good for: planting beneath trees, covering bare, shady slopes; banks, containers

More Choices: pages 37, 171, and 173

Options: 'Herman's Pride'—green foliage with silver mottling, less invasive

Deep shade doesn't have to mean bare ground. Yellow Archangel will cover shady locations with silvery foliage quickly. Hooded, yellow flowers appear in late spring and early summer. Avoid planting in flowerbeds; this plant can be quite invasive. Dig out stems when they creep into areas you don't want them. Control slugs with diatomaceous earth, traps, or poisonous bait.

Lamium maculatum

Spotted Dead Nettle

Zones: 3-9

Light Needs:

Mature Size:

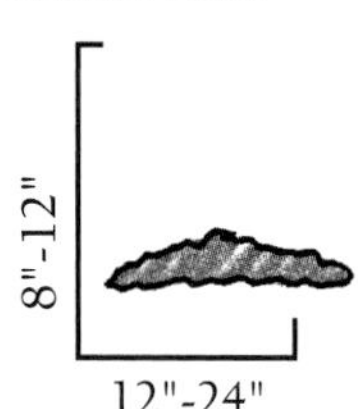

Growth Rate: rapid

perennial

Needs: Plant in deep or partial shade in any soil that's well-drained. Plants will grow in full sun in colder climates as long as the soil stays consistently moist.

Good for: planting beneath trees and covering bare, shady spots—even places with dry soil.

More Choices: pages 37, 39, 43, and 171

Options: 'White Nancy'—white flowers
'Beacon Silver'—pale pink blooms
'Pink Pewter'—pink flowers

Outstanding Features:

- Leaves have white or silvery centers
- Pink or purple blooms spring to summer
- Trailing stems cover shady ground quickly

Even shady spots kept dry by thirsty tree roots are no problem for this plant. Choose Spotted Dead Nettle for its silvery leaves and durability. Plants can be very vigorous and may outgrow some garden situations. As a groundcover, vigourous growth is highly desireable.

Mitchella repens

Partridge Berry

Zones: 4-9

Light Needs:

Mature Size:

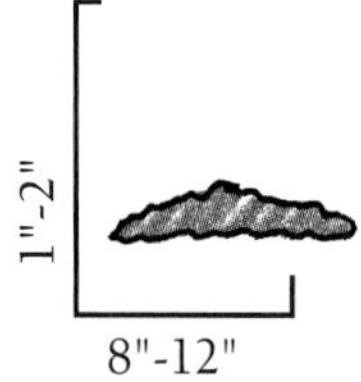

Growth Rate: medium to rapid

evergreen

Needs: Plant in rich, acidic soil that's moist but well-drained. Increase soil acidity by adding peat moss or composted oak leaves to the soil at planting time. Mulch to help conserve moisture. Grow in partial or dense shade. Water regularly.

Good for: shaded slopes, woodlands, shrub beds, natural areas, mass plantings, rock gardens

More Choices: pages 37, 41, 42, 171, and 173

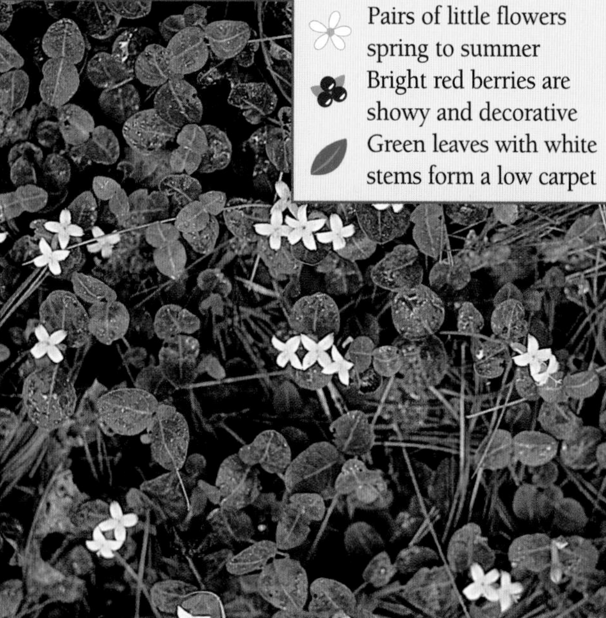

Outstanding Features:

- Pairs of little flowers spring to summer
- Bright red berries are showy and decorative
- Green leaves with white stems form a low carpet

Here's a shade-loving groundcover that's native to eastern North America. In the right soil conditions, it grows easily to form a dark green carpet highlighted with red berries. This plant is low-growing, with dainty flowers and fire-red berries nestled in foliage at your feet. Try growing Partridge Berry on a shaded upward slope, in a raised bed, or behind a retaining wall to bring its ornamental characteristics closer to eye-level. Sometimes called Running Box or Twinberry.

Myosotis scorpioides

Forget-Me-Not

Zones: 3-8

Light Needs:

Mature Size:

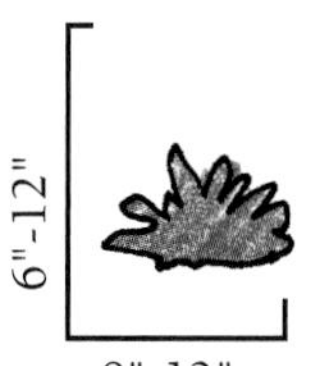

6"-12"

8"-12"

Growth Rate: rapid

perennial

Needs: Plant in fertile, moist soil. Partial shade is best, but full sun will do in cooler areas when moisture is consistent. Cut plants back after flowering to promote compact growth.

Good for: moist areas, planting beside water features, edges of woodlands, near downspouts, banks of streams

More Choices: pages 35, 37, 39, 171, and 173

Options: *M. sylvatica* (Annual Forget-Me-Not)—bedding plant, short-lived but reseeds readily, Zones 5-9

Outstanding Features:

- Dainty blue flowers with yellow eyes
- Grows in moist, partially-shaded areas
- Comes back reliably year after year

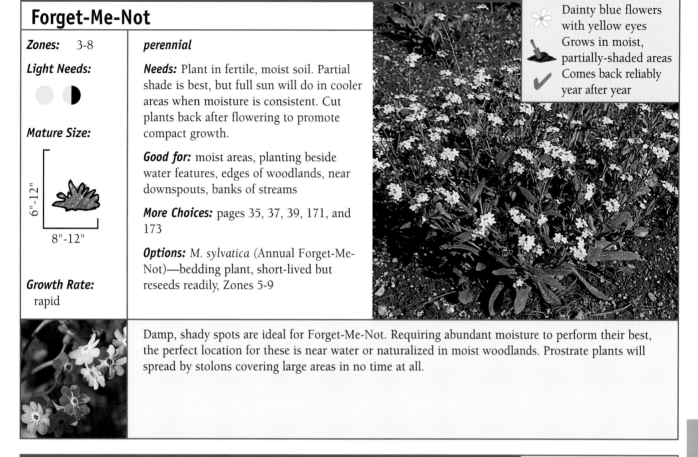

Damp, shady spots are ideal for Forget-Me-Not. Requiring abundant moisture to perform their best, the perfect location for these is near water or naturalized in moist woodlands. Prostrate plants will spread by stolons covering large areas in no time at all.

Nepeta x faassenii

Catmint

Zones: 4-8

Light Needs:

Mature Size:

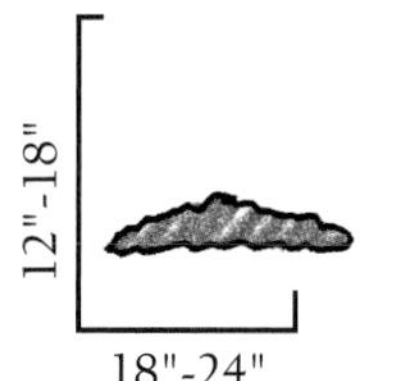

12"-18"

18"-24"

Growth Rate: rapid

perennial

Needs: Plant in well-drained, sandy soil in full sun or partial shade. Cut plants back after bloom to encourage a second flowering later. Dig and divide in early spring to make new plantings.

Good for: Xeriscaping, rock gardens, filling in hot spots, edging planting beds, walkways, entries, or patios.

More Choices: pages 35, 37, 42, 43, 170, 171, 172, and 173

Options: 'Six Hills Giant'—violet blue blooms; 24" to 36" tall, 24" wide

Outstanding Features:

- Grows in hot sun and dry, sandy soil

- Great in combination with yellow and pink
- Cascading gray-green foliage is aromatic

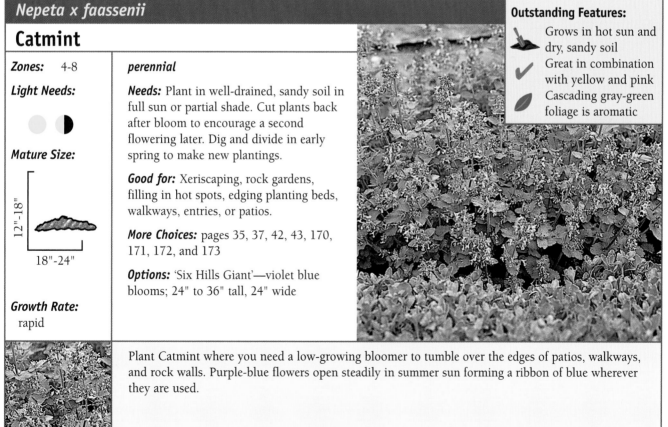

Plant Catmint where you need a low-growing bloomer to tumble over the edges of patios, walkways, and rock walls. Purple-blue flowers open steadily in summer sun forming a ribbon of blue wherever they are used.

Oenothera missouriensis

Sundrop Primrose

Outstanding Features:

- Large, bright yellow flowers in summer
- Tolerates heat, sun, and poor soil
- Spreads quickly to cover large areas

Zones: 4-8

Light Needs:

Mature Size:

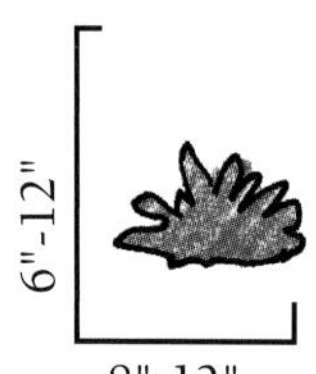

Growth Rate: rapid

perennial

Needs: Plant in any soil that drains well, including poor, rocky sites. Full sun is necessary for flowering. Mulch in late fall in areas with cold winters. Remove faded flowers to encourage additional blooms. For more plants, dig and divide in early spring or fall.

Good for: entry areas, parking areas, edging planting beds, walkways, rock walls, and patios

More Choices: pages 35, 39, 171, and 172

Options: *O. speciosa* (Evening Primrose)—spreading perennial, pink flowers

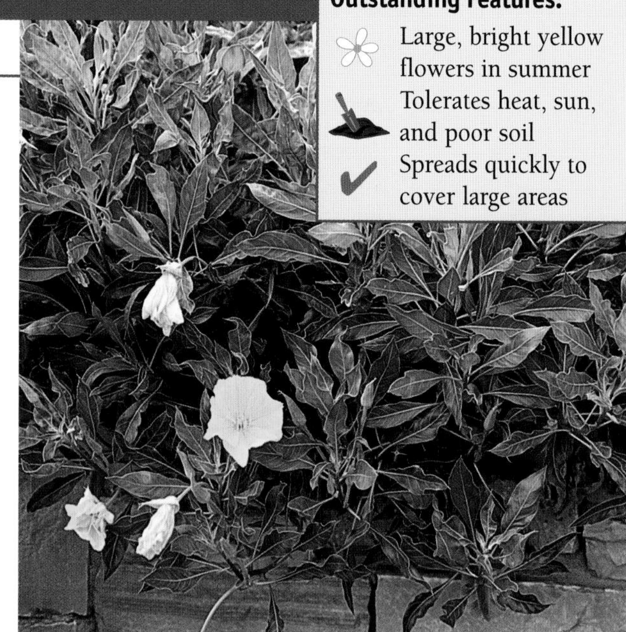

Big, bright-yellow flowers earn this plant its name. How appropriate to have drops of sunshine covering red tinted foliage. It grows in hot, dry spots and comes back year after year. Blossoms attract butterflies and hummingbirds. Sometimes listed as *O. macrocarpa*.

Pachysandra terminalis

Pachysandra

Outstanding Features:

- Covers acidic, shady, bare areas
- Rich green leaves stay low and neat
- Small white flowers in late spring

Zones: 4-9

Light Needs:

Mature Size:

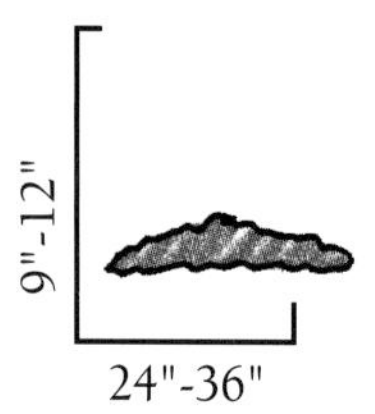

Growth Rate: rapid

perennial

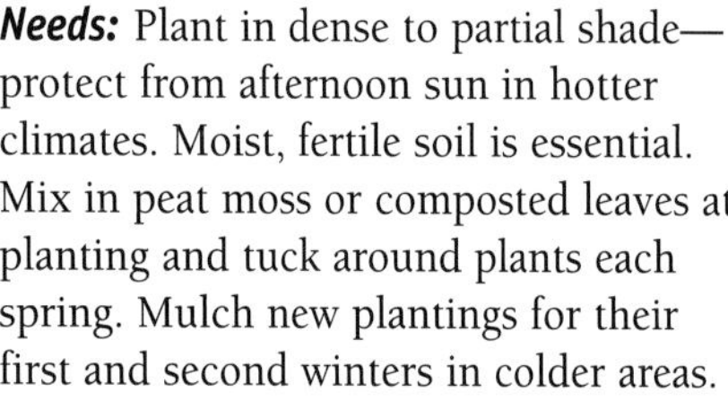

Needs: Plant in dense to partial shade—protect from afternoon sun in hotter climates. Moist, fertile soil is essential. Mix in peat moss or composted leaves at planting and tuck around plants each spring. Mulch new plantings for their first and second winters in colder areas.

Good for: filling in shady spots where grass won't grow, planting beneath trees, raised beds, growing in shade gardens

More Choices: pages 37, 170, and 171

This groundcover fills in bare, shady spots where grass won't grow—but only if the soil is moist. Plants make a good companion to hostas. Both are coarse-textured, grow in shade, and like the same type of growing conditions.

Paxistima canbyi

Cliff Green

Zones: 3-7

Light Needs:

Mature Size:

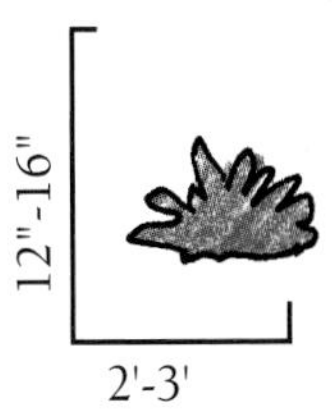

Growth Rate: slow to medium

evergreen shrub

Needs: Plant in rich soil that's moist but well-drained for best growth. Plants will adapt to dry, alkaline soil conditions. Grow in full sun or partial shade.

Good for: rock gardens, mountain areas, slopes, woodlands, natural areas, adding fine texture, filling beds with foliage

More Choices: pages 35, 37, 39, 41, 170, 171, and 173

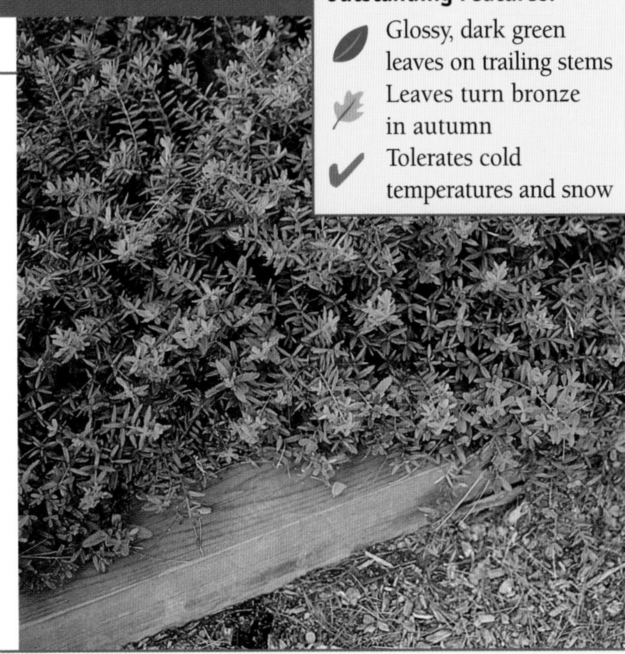

Outstanding Features:

- Glossy, dark green leaves on trailing stems
- Leaves turn bronze in autumn
- Tolerates cold temperatures and snow

This plant doesn't need blooms to provide an eye-catching show. Fine-textured foliage provides color and accent when planted beneath trees and shrubs. Small clusters of spring flowers are greenish white. May be sold as Rat-Stripper.

Phlox stolonifera

Creeping Phlox or Woodland Phlox

Zones: 2-8

Light Needs:

Mature Size:

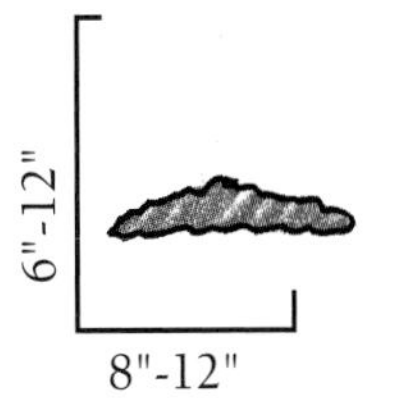

Growth Rate: rapid

evergreen perennial

Needs: Plant in fertile, moist soil in partial to deep shade. Plants in cooler climates can tolerate more sun.

Good for: combining with spring flowering bulbs, shady areas, woodland plantings, growing at the base of shrubs and trees, moist locations

More Choices: pages 37, 41, 171, and 173

Options: 'Blue Ridge'—sky blue flowers; 12" tall stems
'Bruce's White'—white flowers with attractive yellow eye; 6" tall
'Sherwood Purple'—fragrant purple-blue flowers; 6" tall

Outstanding Features:

- Becomes a carpet of flowers in spring
- Foliage forms a dense matted groundcover
- Grows in deep to partially shaded areas

True Creeping Phlox is the most shade tolerant of all phlox—either partial or deep shade. It thrives with abundant moisture forming a dense groundcover that combines beautifully with spring flowering bulbs and shrubs. Together the three plant types will put on quite a color show. Moisture is a requirement for this species; plants will not thrive in dry shade.

Phlox subulata

Moss Phlox

Outstanding Features:

- Becomes a carpet of flowers in spring
- Evergreen foliage forms a dense mat
- Grows in sunny, dry places

Zones: 2-9

Light Needs:

Mature Size:

Growth Rate: rapid

evergreen perennial

Needs: Plant in full sun. Soil that is average, poor, rocky, or dry is fine. Dig and divide plants in fall to increase plant numbers. Or, let them spread naturally.

Good for: Xeriscaping, slopes, ditches, erosion control, edging planting beds, rock gardens, entries, creeping over walls

More Choices: pages 35, 39, 42, 43, 170, 171, 172, and 173

Options: 'Emerald Blue'—blue flowers
'Emerald Pink'—soft pink flowers
'Crimson Beauty'—crimson flowers
'White Delight'—large white flowers

This thick, low groundcover is the answer to dry hillsides and ditches. Grow Creeping Phlox in full sun in poor, dry, even rocky soil. Plants are carpeted with white, pink, or lavender blooms in spring. Often sold as Creeping Phlox. It pays to learn a word or two of Latin when different plants have the same common name. Though they're both called Creeping Phlox, make sure you buy *Phlox subulata* for sunny, dry areas and *Phlox stolonifera* for shady, moist spots.

Potentilla tabernaemontani

Spring Cinquefoil

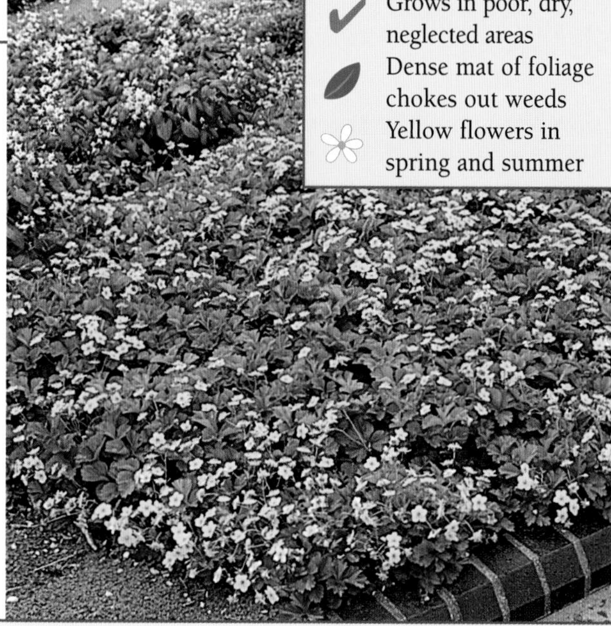

Outstanding Features:

- Grows in poor, dry, neglected areas
- Dense mat of foliage chokes out weeds
- Yellow flowers in spring and summer

Zones: 4-8

Light Needs:

Mature Size:

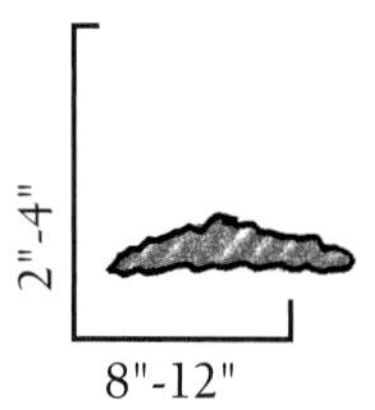

Growth Rate: medium to rapid

perennial

Needs: Spring Cinquefoil will grow in soil that's rich or poor, even rocky, as long as it's dry. Full sun yields best flowering. Prune after blooms fade to reduce invasive tendencies. Divide in spring or fall.

Good for: Xeriscaping, rock gardens, slopes, edging planting beds, dry banks, rock walls

More Choices: pages 35, 39, 42, 171, 172, and 173

Spring Cinquefoil thrives in dry, neglected areas. Vigorous growth forms a dense cover that reduces weed growth. Yellow flowers bloom nearly nonstop during warm summer months. Division is easy—just dig up a clump and plant it where you want additional sunny, yellow blooms.

Rosa Alba Meidiland

Alba Meidiland Rose

Zones: 4-8

Light Needs:

Mature Size:

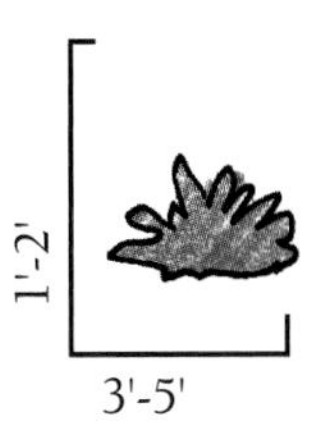

Growth Rate: medium

deciduous shrub

Needs: Plant in moist, fertile, well-drained soil. Sun or partial shade. Add super phosphate or bonemeal to the planting hole to promote rapid root growth. Reapply every fall. No pruning needed, but plants will need plenty of room.

Good for: slopes, planting behind retaining walls, use along walkways, patios, the front layer of foundation plantings, around low decks, and in raised planters

More Choices: pages 35, 37, 42, 171, 172, and 173

Outstanding Features:

- Clusters of creamy colored, double blooms
- Mounded form spreads quickly
- Blooms in sun or partial shade

This sounds too good to be true, but it isn't. This rose cascades thickly to cover the ground with fragrant flowers and shiny green foliage. Flowers appear from summer through fall.

Rosa 'Flower Carpet'

Flower Carpet Rose

Zones: 4-10

Light Needs:

Mature Size:

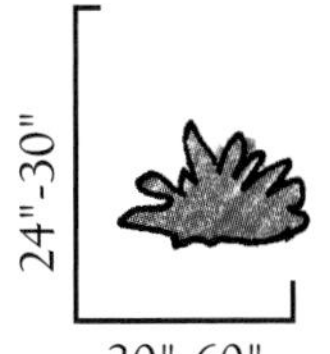

Growth Rate: medium

deciduous shrub

Needs: Plant in full sun in fertile, well-drained soil. No spraying for diseases is required. Let plants grow together to form a large mass. Remove branches that want to grow straight up.

Good for: filling in bare sunny areas, growing in the front layer of planting beds, growing on berms, low barriers

More Choices: pages 35, 43, and 171

Options: 'Flower Carpet Pink'
'Flower Carpet White'
'Flower Carpet Appleblossom'

Outstanding Features:

- Available in a wide range of flower colors
- Disease-resistant, shiny green leaves
- Easy to grow; ideal for the novice rose grower

You don't need to know a lot about roses to succeed with these. Spreading plants need sun and soil that drains well. Often sold in pink plastic pots. Plants are thorny. Use two or three plants per square yard for a thick groundcover.

Sedum acre

Goldmoss

Zones: 4-9

Light Needs:

Mature Size:

2"-4"

indefinite

Growth Rate: rapid

evergreen perennial

Needs: Plant in any soil that's well-drained; slightly alkaline soil is best. Adapts to poor, dry soil conditions. Grow in full sun. Tolerates cold temperatures, drought, and reflected heat from paving.

Good for: slopes, ditches, rock gardens, tucking into crevices in paving or walls, parking areas, cascading over retaining walls, filling hot, dry areas, confined spaces, containers

More Choices: pages 35, 39, 41, 42, 43, 170, 171, 172, and 173

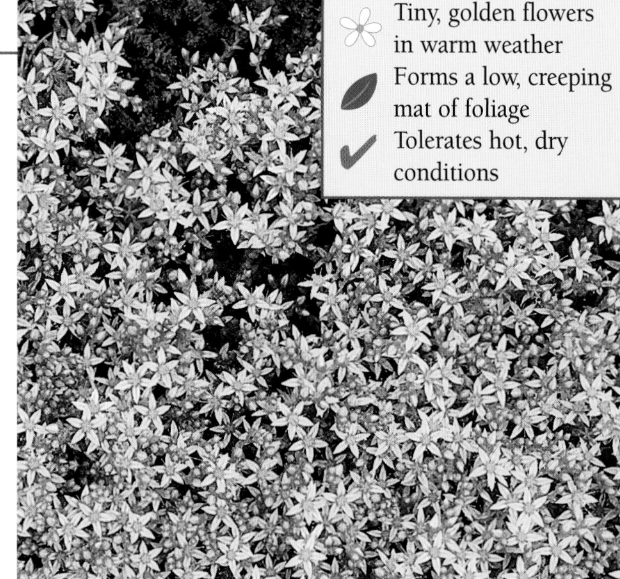

Outstanding Features:

- Tiny, golden flowers in warm weather
- Forms a low, creeping mat of foliage
- Tolerates hot, dry conditions

Here's a fast-growing groundcover that grows where many plants cannot: in hot, dry pockets or barren slopes. Creeping plants produce golden-colored, star-shaped flowers all summer long. May be sold as Stonecrop because of its ability to grow in poor sites.

Sedum spectabile

Stonecrop

Zones: 3-10

Light Needs:

Mature Size:

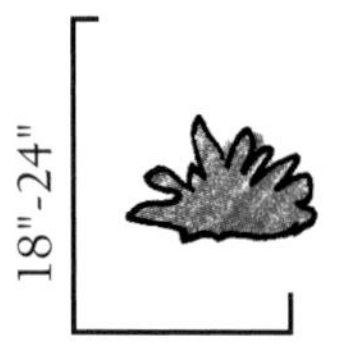

18"-24"

18"-24"

Growth Rate: medium to rapid

perennial

Needs: Plant in poor, dry soils that drain well—plants won't tolerate damp conditions. Grow in full sun. Divide when clumps grow from outer edges instead of the center. Cut plants back in June for smaller, compact plants with additional flowers—and stems that don't flop over.

Good for: rock gardens, arid landscapes, Xeriscaping, slopes, entries, planting beds

More Choices: pages 35, 39, 42, 43, 170, 171, and 173

Options: 'Autumn Joy'—rusty fall flowers; 12" to 24" tall, 18" wide

Outstanding Features:

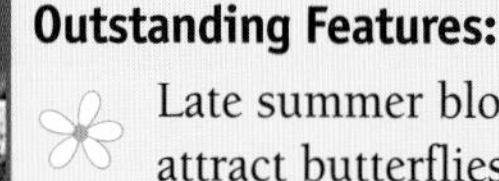

- Late summer blooms attract butterflies
- Grows with little water; very drought-tolerant
- Thick, fleshy leaves add coarse texture

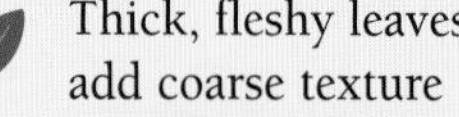

Here's a plant that loves poor, dry soil—even rocky or sandy soils suit this plant. Grow Stonecrop in hot spots to enjoy thick foliage and clusters of late summer flowers. Blooms attract large numbers of butterflies. Support for stems may be needed for plants growing in partial shade and unpinched plants. Additional selections include: 'Brilliant'—bright pink flowers, 18" tall and wide; 'Ruby Glow'—red flowers, purple-gray leaves, 8" tall, 18" wide.

Stachys byzantina

Lamb's Ear

Zones: 4-8

Light Needs:

Mature Size:

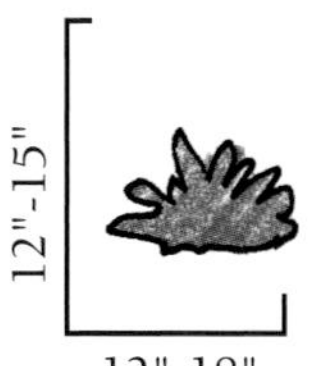

Growth Rate: medium to rapid

perennial

Needs: Plant in moist well-drained soil. Best growth occurs in soils of low fertility. Grow in full sun (with afternoon shade in hotter climates). Trim heat-damaged plants to encourage new growth. Mulch plants in late fall where winters are cold. Divide plants every three to four years.

Good for: entries, children's gardens, moonlight gardens, edging planting beds, patios, walkways

More Choices: pages 35, 43, 170, 171, 172, and 173

Options: 'Big Ears'—big leaves resist rot
'Silver Carpet'—4" high; no flower spikes

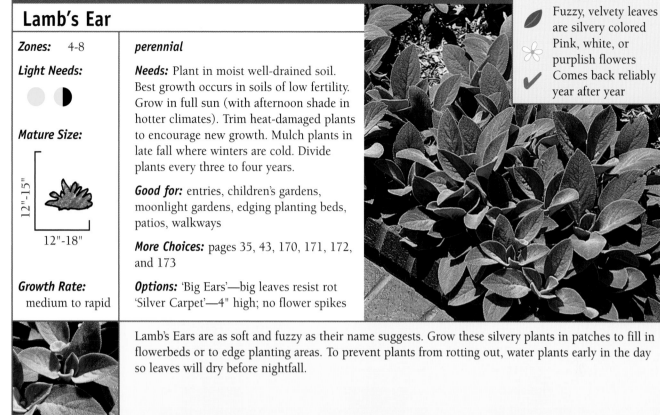

Outstanding Features:

- Fuzzy, velvety leaves are silvery colored
- Pink, white, or purplish flowers
- Comes back reliably year after year

Lamb's Ears are as soft and fuzzy as their name suggests. Grow these silvery plants in patches to fill in flowerbeds or to edge planting areas. To prevent plants from rotting out, water plants early in the day so leaves will dry before nightfall.

Symphoricarpos x chenaultii 'Hancock'

Prostrate Chenault Coralberry

Zones: 4-7

Light Needs:

Mature Size:

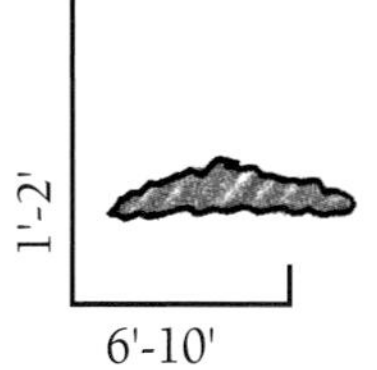

Growth Rate: rapid

deciduous shrub

Needs: Plant in soil that's moist or dry, fertile or poor. Tolerates alkaline soil pH and will thrive in sun or shade. Prune in early spring to stimulate abundant bloom.

Good for: slopes, erosion control, woodland gardens, planting beds, bird habitats

More Choices: pages 35, 37, 39, 42, 43, 171, and 173

Outstanding Features:

- Tolerates a wide range of soil conditions
- Multitudes of blooms in summer
- Pink and white berries attract birds

Grow this plant to cover ground that's moist or dry, in full sun or shade. Its self-layering habit forms a broad mound of foliage. White or pink flowers and berries add seasonal appeal. Tolerates air pollution.

Teucrium prostratum or chamaedrys

Germander

Zones: 4-9

Light Needs:

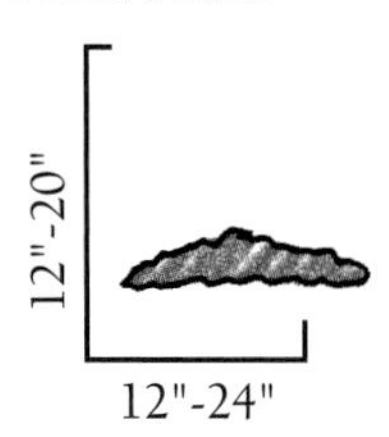

Mature Size:

12"-20" × 12"-24"

Growth Rate: medium to rapid

evergreen shrub

Needs: Grow in full sun. Plant in well-drained, alkaline to neutral soil. Work lime into soil to increase alkalinity. For formal hedges, cut plants in early spring to within a few inches of the ground.

Good for: formal knot gardens, edging rose, herb, or flowerbeds, rock gardens, entries, edging patios or walkways

More Choices: pages 35, 41, 43, 170, 171, 172, and 173

T. chamaedrys

Outstanding Features:

- Tolerates pruning to form a low hedge
- Grows well in alkaline soil conditions
- Carmine-rose blooms in mid to late summer

Grow Germander where you want a little row of green. Plants adapt to both a formal or informal way of life. Trim into desired forms or allow them to remain in their natural mounded form.

Tiarella cordifolia

Allegheny Foam Flower

Zones: 4-9

Light Needs:

Mature Size:

6"-12" × 12"-24"

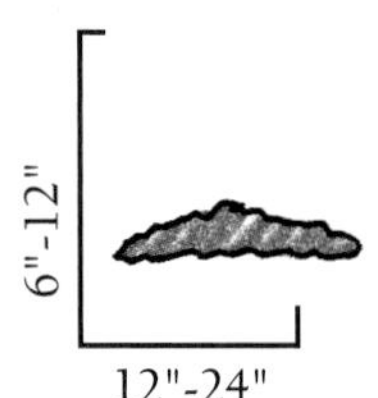

Growth Rate: rapid

evergreen perennial

Needs: Grow in deep or partial shade. Plant in well-drained, moist, fertile, slightly acidic soil. Mix in peat moss or composted leaves at planting and apply a 3-inch-thick layer to the soil surface each spring. Avoid sunny, dry, alkaline conditions. Plants prefer cool locations.

Good for: moist shaded areas, planting beneath acid loving shrubs and trees, woodland gardens, rock gardens, perennial flower borders

More Choices: pages 37, 41, 170, 171, and 173

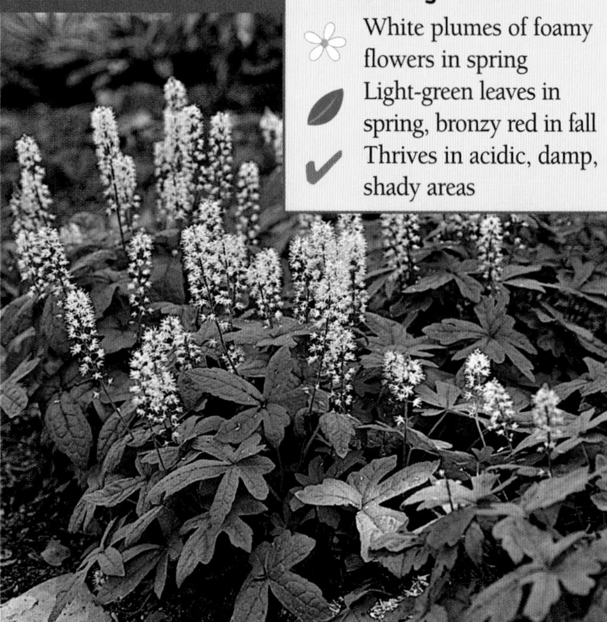

Outstanding Features:

- White plumes of foamy flowers in spring
- Light-green leaves in spring, bronzy red in fall
- Thrives in acidic, damp, shady areas

Brighten those damp, shady spots with Allegheny Foam Flower. Feathery white flowers appear in spring above light green foliage. When grown with the proper conditions, plants spread quickly to make large, lush patches. Plants spread by underground stems and can quickly take over in moist, shady areas.

Vinca minor

Littleleaf Periwinkle

Zones: 4-8

Light Needs:

Mature Size:

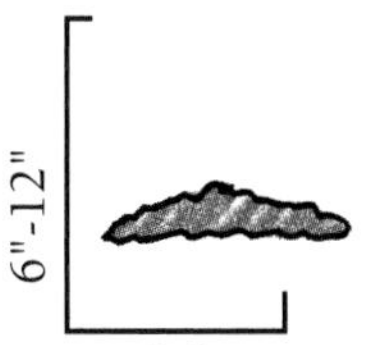

Growth Rate: rapid

evergreen

Needs: Grow in sun or partial shade north of Zone 7; southward, grow in full or partial shade. Plant in well-drained, moist, fertile soil high in organic matter. Mix in peat moss or composted leaves at planting time. Mulch to help conserve moisture.

Good for: bare, shady spots, hillsides, erosion control on banks, beneath trees, woodland gardens, underplanting with spring bulbs

More Choices: pages 35, 37, 42, 43, 170, 171, and 173

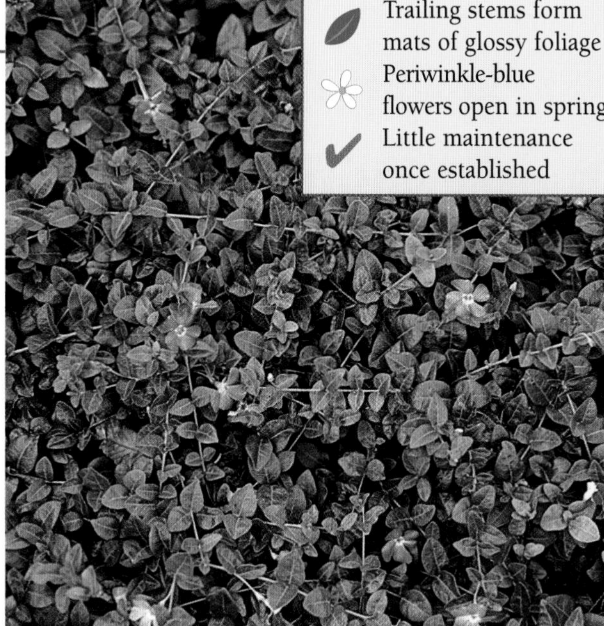

Outstanding Features:

- Trailing stems form mats of glossy foliage
- Periwinkle-blue flowers open in spring
- Little maintenance once established

Fill in bare, shady areas with a dense blanket of glossy green leaves. Plants are tough and adapted to a wide range of growing conditions. Grows slowly in poor soil. Lavender-blue flowers appear each spring. Not recommended for coastal areas. May also be sold as Creeping Myrtle.

Waldsteinia ternata

Waldsteinia

Zones: 3-8

Light Needs:

Mature Size:

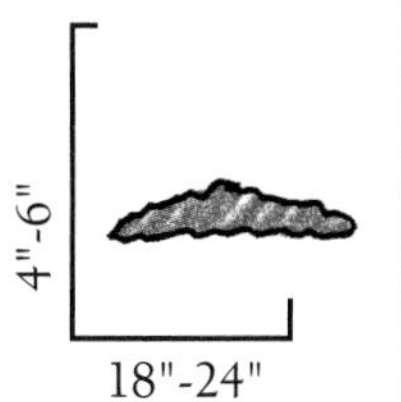

Growth Rate: medium

semievergreen perennial

Needs: Plant in moist, rich soil, in partial to dense shade. Plants spread quickly under ideal conditions and tolerate even dry, sunny areas.

Good for: woodland gardens, massing, shade gardens, shaded slopes, edging perennial beds and borders

More Choices: pages 35, 37, 171, and 173

Outstanding Features:

- Clusters of bright yellow flowers
- Glossy leaves form an evergreen carpet
- Thrives in shade and moist conditions

Grow this groundcover to brighten shaded areas with a carpet of green and sunny, yellow flowers. Waldesteinia resembles its relative the strawberry with fringed, triplet leaves. They spread by rhizomes and stolons. Plants are semievergreen in colder climates, renewing foliage in the spring. Sometimes sold as Barren Strawberry. May be labeled *W. siberica* or *W. trifolia*.

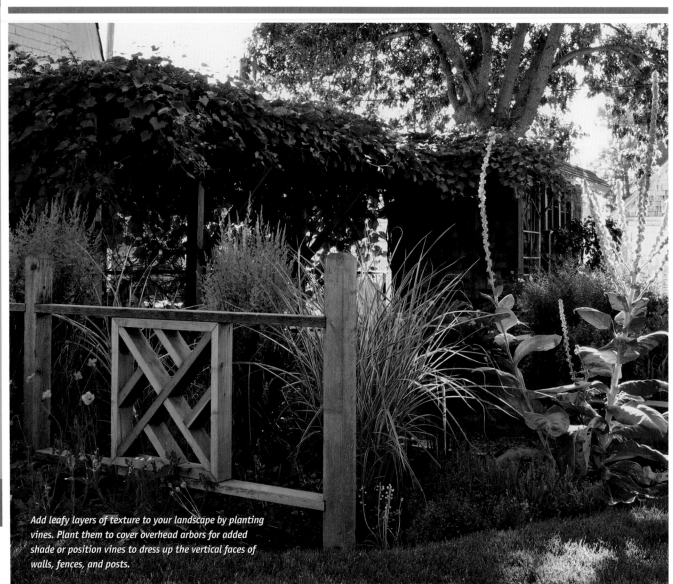

Add leafy layers of texture to your landscape by planting vines. Plant them to cover overhead arbors for added shade or position vines to dress up the vertical faces of walls, fences, and posts.

Vines

Add charming finishing touches to your landscape with the addition of vines. Observe landscapes in books and magazines, as well as eye-catching yards in your neighborhood. They usually have vines, sprawling up a post or over a wall, polishing off the composition with the lush look that makes you think an experienced gardener must live there.

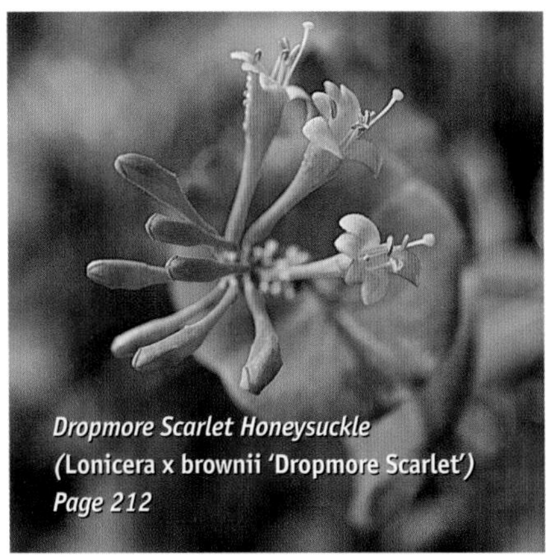

Dropmore Scarlet Honeysuckle (Lonicera x brownii 'Dropmore Scarlet') Page 212

Give your landscape that green-thumb look by learning about vines. Some climb by adhesive disks that will damage wood or stucco. Others climb by tendrils or twining stems, making them better choices for such supports. The selection guides make it easy to pick the right vine for your yard. See pages 38-41 for vines for various soil types, page 35 for vines to grow in sun, page 37 for vines to grow in shade, and pages 30-31 for vines for privacy.

American Bittersweet (Celastrus scandens) Page 211

Vines for low-water landscapes

Common Name	Zones	Page
American Bittersweet *Celastrus scandens*	3-8	211
Boston Ivy *Parthenocissus tricuspidata*	4-8	213
Trumpet Vine *Campsis radicans*	4-9	210
Virginia Creeper *Parthenocissus quinquefolia*	4-9	213

Evergreen vines

Common Name	Zones	Page
Dropmore Scarlet Honeysuckle *Lonicera x brownii 'Dropmore Scarlet'*	3-7	212

Deciduous vines

Common Name	Zones	Page
American Bittersweet *Celastrus scandens*	3-8	211
Boston Ivy *Parthenocissus tricuspidata*	4-8	213
Climbing Hydrangea *Hydrangea petiolaris*	4-7	211
Hardy Kiwi *Actinidia arguta*	4-8	210
Trumpet Honeysuckle *Lonicera sempervirens*	4-9	212
Trumpet Vine *Campsis radicans*	4-9	210
Virginia Creeper *Parthenocissus quinquefolia*	4-9	213

Vines for wooden structures

Common Name	Zones	Page	Type
American Bittersweet *Celastrus scandens*	3-8	211	Twiner
Hardy Kiwi *Actinidia arguta*	4-8	210	Twiner
Trumpet Honeysuckle *Lonicera sempervirens*	4-9	212	Twiner
Virginia Creeper *Parthenocissus quinquefolia*	4-9	213	Sticker

Vines to avoid on wooden structures

Common Name	Zones	Page	Type
Boston Ivy *Parthenocissus tricuspidata*	4-8	213	Sticker
Climbing Hydrangea *Hydrangea petiolaris*	4-7	211	Sticker
Trumpet Vine *Campsis radicans*	4-9	210	Twiner

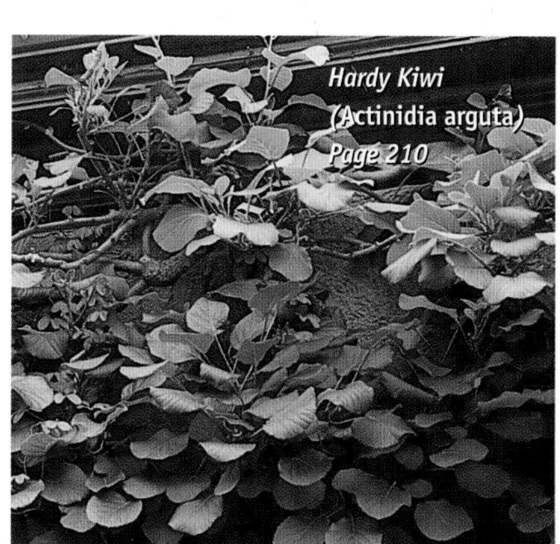

Hardy Kiwi (Actinidia arguta) Page 210

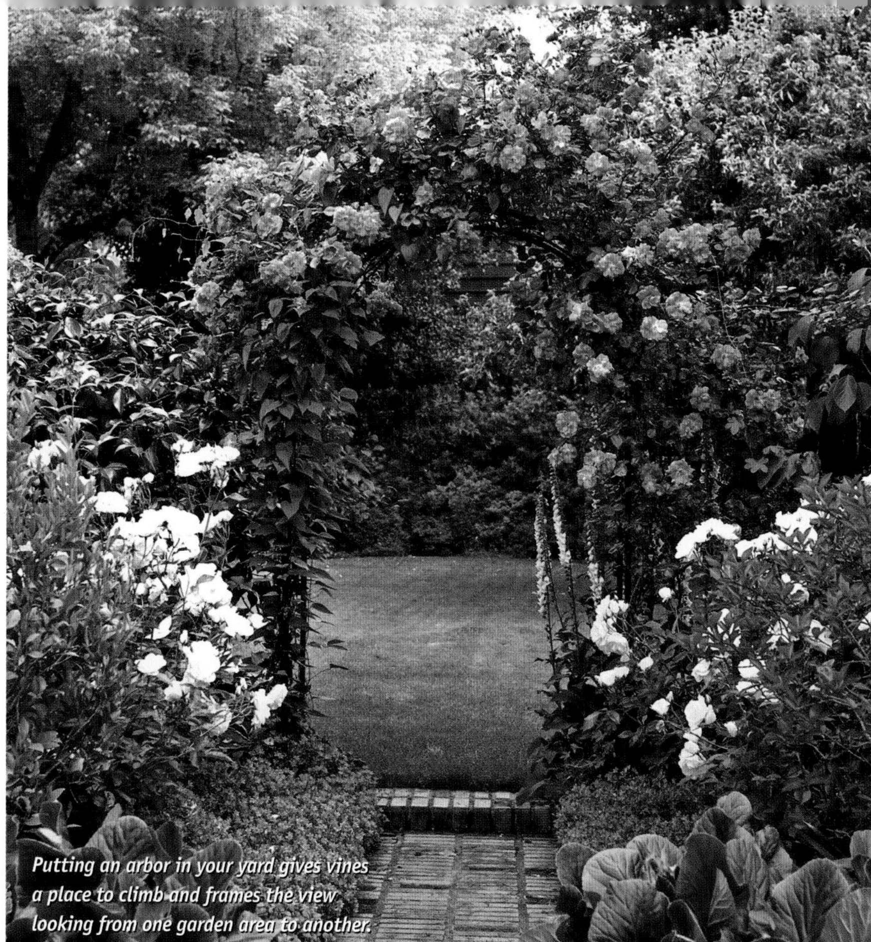

Putting an arbor in your yard gives vines a place to climb and frames the view looking from one garden area to another.

Twiners vs. Stickers

Twining vines grab onto whatever is handy to pull themselves up. Some twining vines have stems that wrap themselves around supports. Other vines have straight stems but grow coiling tendrils that reach out to anchor the vine as it grows. Most twining vines won't hurt wooden structures, but beware of any vine that's described as rapid-growing and vigorous. Such a vine might develop strong, heavy stems that can eventually crush wooden structures.

Twining vines don't grow well on flat walls because there's nothing for them to coil around. They do better on arbors, posts, and trellises. If you want to grow a twining vine on a flat, vertical surface such as the back of your garage, attach a lattice panel to the wall. Insert 1-inch-thick blocks of wood, called spacers, between the lattice and the wall so that there is airspace between them. This provides a route for vines to follow as they weave their way through the lattice.

Sticking vines grow their own adhesive. Some grow aerial rootlets that plaster the vine against hard surfaces while others grow suction discs on the ends of special stems. Both methods allow vines to grow up flat supports, such as walls made of masonry or stone. However, you should think twice before planting sticking vines to grow up walls made of masonry, stucco, or stone because this kind of vine can damage hard surfaces. If you're willing to go to the trouble of repointing mortar after a number of years, then sticking vines are worth the beauty they add to flat walls. If you've already got a sticking vine growing on a flat wall, don't pull it off; you could do more damage during removal than the vine is causing. You'll also find it difficult to remove completely stubborn rootlets or discs that are left behind.

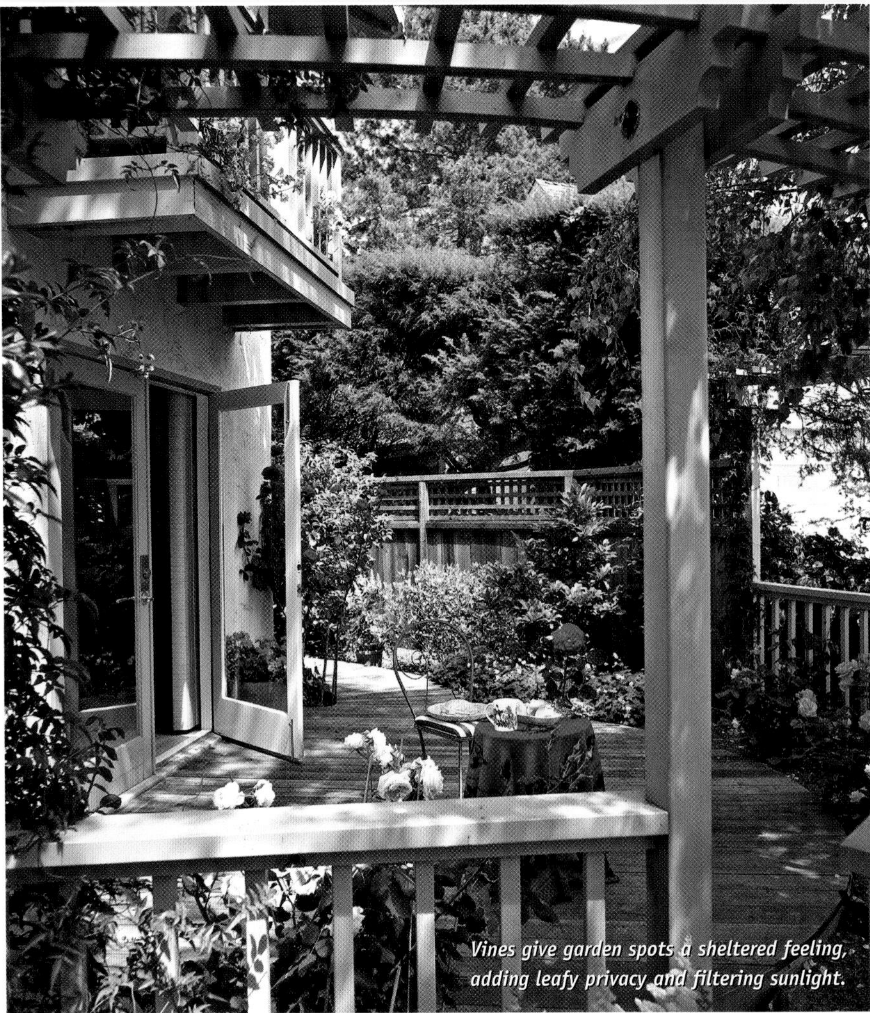
Vines give garden spots a sheltered feeling, adding leafy privacy and filtering sunlight.

Boston Ivy (Parthenocissus tricuspidata) Page 213

Trumpet Honeysuckle (Lonicera sempervirens) Page 212

Choosing Vines for Seasonal Interest

Planting vines and climbers adds color and texture to your landscape season after season. The selection guides that follow will help you choose vines for their flowers, colorful foliage, fragrance, and showy fruit in spring, summer, and fall.

Climbing Hydrangea (Hydrangea petiolaris) Page 211

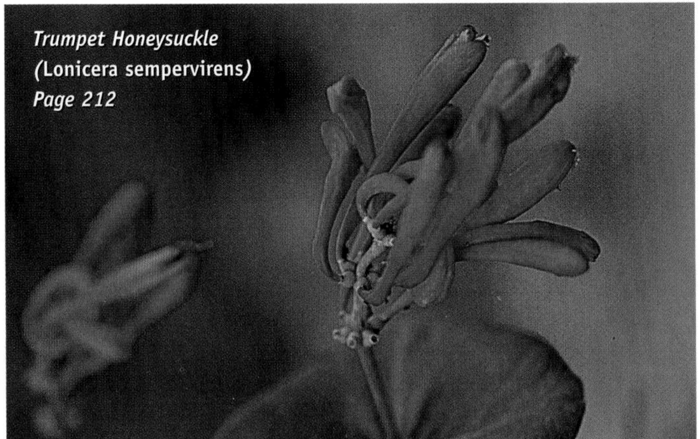
Trumpet Honeysuckle (Lonicera sempervirens) Page 212

Spring-flowering vines

Common Name	Zones	Page
Dropmore Scarlet Honeysuckle *Lonicera x brownii 'Dropmore Scarlet'*	3-7	212
Trumpet Vine *Campsis radicans*	4-9	210

Summer-flowering vines

Common Name	Zones	Page
Climbing Hydrangea *Hydrangea petiolaris*	4-7	211
Dropmore Scarlet Honeysuckle *Lonicera x brownii 'Dropmore Scarlet'*	3-7	212
Trumpet Honeysuckle *Lonicera sempervirens*	4-9	212

Vines for autumn interest

◆ Showy fall fruit

Common Name	Zones	Page
American Bittersweet *Celastrus scandens*	3-8	211
Boston Ivy *Parthenocissus tricuspidata*	4-8	213
Trumpet Honeysuckle *Lonicera sempervirens*	4-9	212

◆Colorful fall foliage

Common Name	Zones	Page
Boston Ivy *Parthenocissus tricuspidata*	4-8	213
Virginia Creeper *Parthenocissus quinquefolia*	4-9	213

Rapid-growing vines

Common Name	Zones	Page
American Bittersweet *Celastrus scandens*	3-8	211
Boston Ivy *Parthenocissus tricuspidata*	4-8	213
Hardy Kiwi *Actinidia arguta*	4-8	210
Trumpet Honeysuckle *Lonicera sempervirens*	4-9	212
Trumpet Vine *Campsis radicans*	4-9	210
Virginia Creeper *Parthenocissus quinquefolia*	4-9	213

Availability varies by area and conditions (see page 21). Check with your garden center.

Pruning Vines

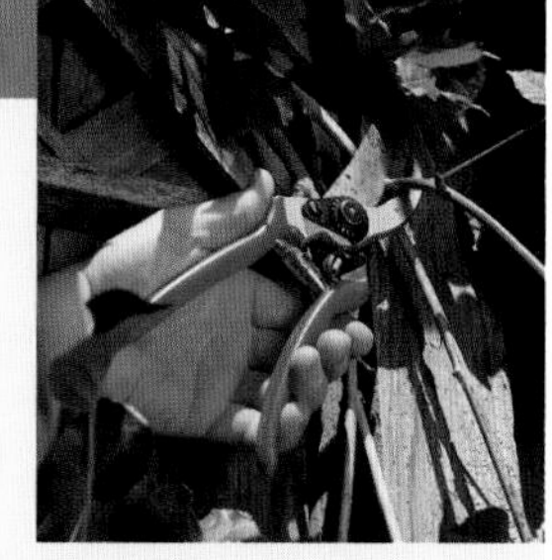

The first time you'll need to prune a vine is immediately after planting it. Though you might feel as though you're reducing your investment, you'll spur the vine onto new and faster growth if you cut it back to about half the size it was when you bought it. Most vines won't need much pruning for a season or two after that as they grow into their new homes. But if stems appear leggy with few leaves or flowers, trim them back to encourage new growth to develop more branches. However, most vines will eventually require trimming to shape them and keep their size under control. Here's how to prune the vines you'll find within the plant encyclopedia pages of this book.

- **American Bittersweet** (*Celastrus scandens*)

Late winter or early spring is the time to cut back this vine to keep it in bounds, but trimming in fall produces pretty cuttings for arrangements. Trim stems as needed to keep vines the size and shape you desire. Overgrown vines require yearly pruning to keep them under control.

- **Climbing Hydrangea** (*Hydrangea petiolaris*)

Trim these vines only as needed to keep them growing in the area you want and to keep their aerial rootlets off wooden structures. Make cuts after flowering.

- **Hardy Kiwi** (*Actinidia arguta*)

No regular pruning is required except to maintain size. Trim stems back immediately after flowering to avoid cutting off next year's blossoms.

- **Trumpet Honeysuckle** (*Lonicera sempervirens*) and
- **Dropmore Scarlet Honeysuckle** (*Lonicera x brownii* 'Dropmore Scarlet')

Prune these vines only if they've outgrown their allotted space. You can cut them any time except just before a freeze, but the best time to prune honeysuckle is right after flowering finishes.

- **Trumpet Vine** (*Campsis radicans*)

Prune as needed in late winter or early spring to control this vigorous vine's size and reduce its weight. Cut back side shoots to develop a strong main framework of woody stems. Leave stubs with three or four buds when cutting off shoots.

- **Virginia Creeper** (*Parthenocissus quinquefolia*) and
- **Boston Ivy** (*Parthenocissus tricuspidata*)

Let these vines grow, but cut them back as needed to keep them off wooden structures. If you must control their size, cut the growing ends of stems back in early winter. Repeat if necessary at the beginning of summer. Never cut these vines at the base; if you do, you'll end up with the hard-to-remove dead stems clinging to the wall.

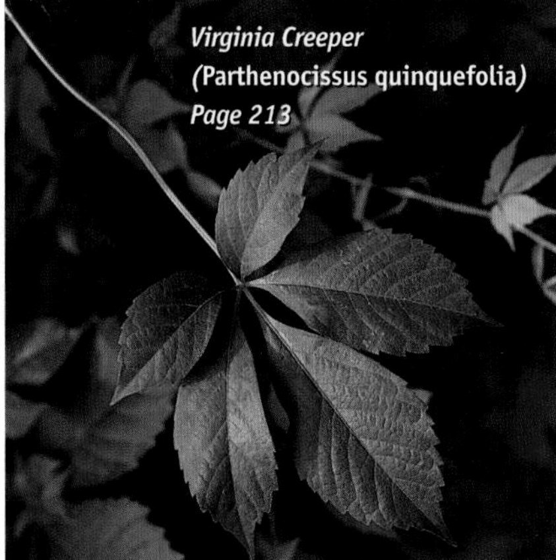

Virginia Creeper (Parthenocissus quinquefolia) Page 213

Climbing Hydrangea (Hydrangea petiolaris) Page 211

Actinidia arguta

Hardy Kiwi

Zones: 4-8

Light Needs:

Mature Size:

Growth Rate: rapid

deciduous vine

Needs: Plant in full sun or partial shade in any kind of soil. Growth rate is fastest in rich soil. To slow it down, plant in a poor location. Prune any time during the growing season to keep it in bounds.

Good for: screening, privacy, covering a fence, trellis, or arbor

More Choices: pages 31, 35, 37, 207, and 209

Options: 'Issai'— bears purple seed pods; *A. chinensis* (also sold as *A. deliciosa*; Chinese Gooseberry or Kiwi Fruit)—bears edible fruit. Grow both male and female plants for fruit production.

Outstanding Features:

- Fast-growing screen for unsightly views
- Thick, beautiful, disease-free foliage
- Won't harm wood or supporting structures

For quick cover-ups, Hardy Kiwi is made to order. This deciduous, twining vine is not picky about its growing conditions. Poor or fertile, wet or dry, this vine will take off wherever it is planted. Attractive foliage adds coarse, textural background in the landscape. White flowers open in early summer. They are fragrant but not showy. Small fruit ripens from September to October. For added protection in colder climates, plant on southern walls only. *A. kolomikta* (Variegated Kiwi Vine)—green leaves with pink and white blotches; grows to 15' high; Zones 5-8.

Campsis radicans

Trumpet Vine

Zones: 4-9

Light Needs:

Mature Size:

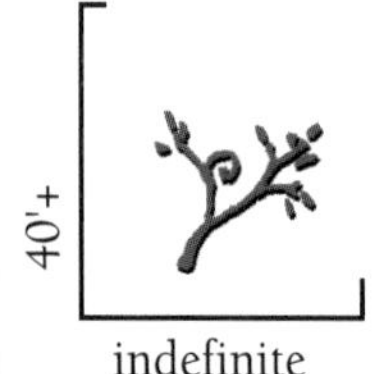

Growth Rate: rapid

deciduous flowering vine

Needs: Plant in any growing condition; Trumpet Vine grows in sun, shade, rich soil, or poor. It will even thrive in sidewalk cracks. Prune as needed to control size and spread. Mow over shoots that appear in the lawn.

Good for: camouflaging eyesores, attracting hummingbirds, growing on tall, blank masonry walls

More Choices: page 31, 35, 37, 39, 42, 207, and 209

Options: 'Flava'—yellow flowers
'Praecox'—red flowers

Outstanding Features:

- Grow in any soil type and amount of light
- Blossoms attract hummingbirds
- Fast-growing for covering blank walls

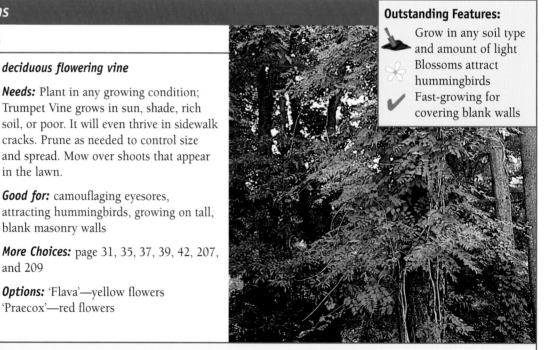

This blooming beauty of a vine is as easy as a weed to grow. Shiny green leaves and orange flowers are attractive from spring until frost. Plant on sturdy forms of support. Rampant growth can destroy arbors and fences or choke trees. Keep away from rooftops.

Celastrus scandens

American Bittersweet

Outstanding Features:

- Ornamental red-and-yellow fruit in fall
- Vines cover arbors and fences quickly
- Good for cutting and use in arrangements

Zones: 3-8

Light Needs:

Mature Size:

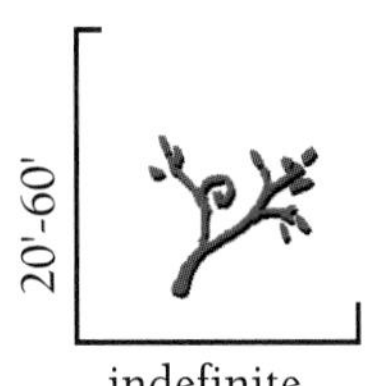

20'-60'

indefinite

Growth Rate: rapid

deciduous vine

Needs: Plant in any kind of soil, damp or dry. Grows in sun or shade, but full sun yields the most fruit. Sturdy support is needed. Prune to control size and shape. Plant both male and female plants for fruit production.

Good for: autumn accent, growing on fences, trellises, arbors, natural areas, hiding scars in the landscape

More Choices: page 31, 35, 37, 39, 42, 207, and 209

Maturing in autumn, bright red berries are nestled inside yellow capsules. Fruiting vines are widely used in dried arrangements during fall and winter. Plants are easy to grow and very vigorous. Locate them carefully in the landscape, vines can girdle the trunks of young trees, killing them.

Hydrangea petiolaris

Climbing Hydrangea

Outstanding Features:

- Lacy caps of white flowers in summer
- Coarse leaves, unusual growth habit
- Grows on hard surfaces without support

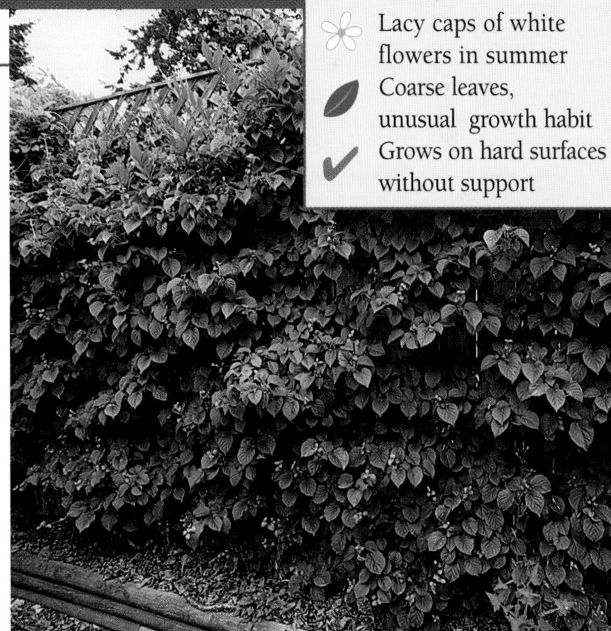

Zones: 4-7

Light Needs:

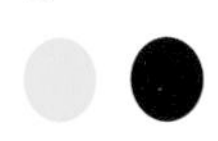

Mature Size:

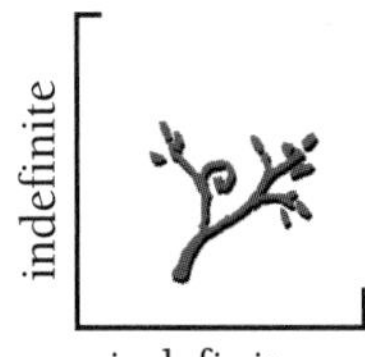

indefinite

indefinite

Growth Rate: slow to medium

deciduous flowering vine

Needs: Plant in fertile, well-drained, moist soil in either full sun or shade. Prune as needed in late winter or early spring to control growth. Tolerates alkaline soil.

Good for: adding texture to brick or stone walls, chimneys, courtyard walls, and tree trunks, seasonal accent, providing a coarse-textured background

More Choices: page 35, 37, 43, 207, and 209

This hydrangea is an easy growing, beautiful vine. It will cover buildings or tree trunks with yards of foliage and flowers. Older stems develop exfoliating bark. The combination of flowers, foliage, and bark make this plant ideal for all seasons.

Lonicera sempervirens

Trumpet Honeysuckle

Zones: 4-9

Light Needs:

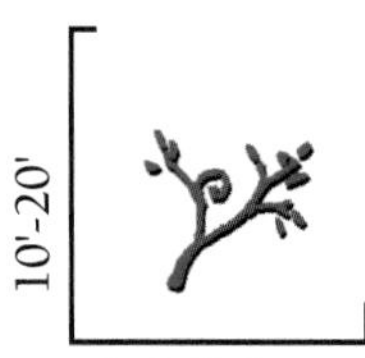

Mature Size:

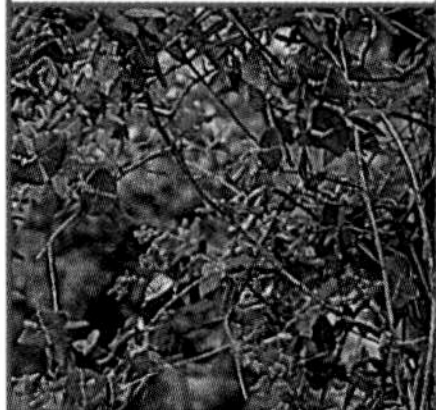

Growth Rate: rapid

deciduous flowering vine (evergreen in frost-free zones)

Needs: Plant in well-drained, moist soil that's rich in organic matter. Water regularly especially during dry spells. Grow in full sun. Prune in late winter or early spring to control growth as needed.

Good for: entries, courtyards, sitting areas; covering fences, trellises, arbors, rails, and posts; attracting hummingbirds to the garden

More Choices: pages 31, 35, 207, and 209

Outstanding Features:

- Red to yellow-orange summer flowers
- Bright red berries ripen in fall
- Twining stems won't damage wood

Grow this gently twisting climber to cover fences, posts, arbors, or rails with blue-green foliage and scarlet summer flowers. Easy to grow and nondamaging to garden structures.

Lonicera x brownii 'Dropmore Scarlet'

Dropmore Scarlet Honeysuckle

Zones: 3-7

Light Needs:

Mature Size:

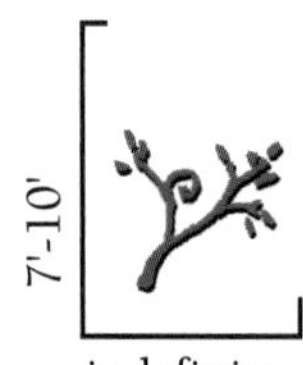

Growth Rate: medium

semievergreen flowering vine

Needs: Plant in any type of soil that's well-drained. Grow in full sun. Water during dry periods. Fertilize using a balanced liquid fertilizer at half-strength every two months. New plants may require strings to help them start scaling posts.

Good for: climbing chain-link fences, trellises, scaling picket or privacy fences, arbors, posts, seasonal accents

More Choices: pages 30, 35, 207, and 209

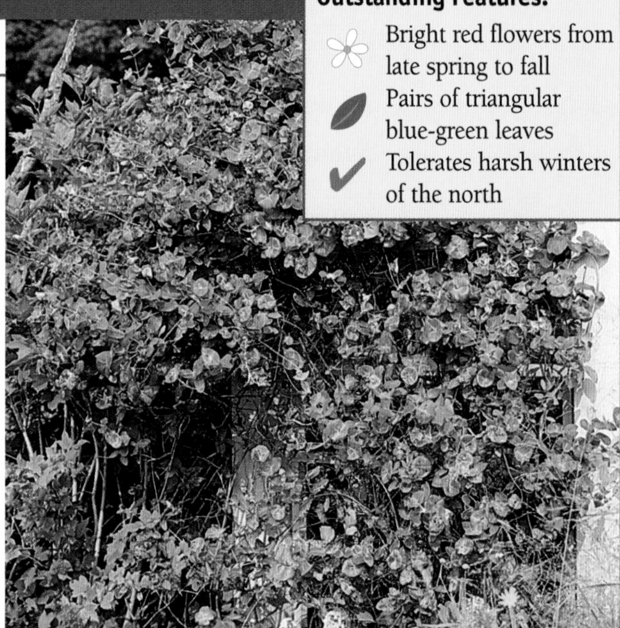

Outstanding Features:

- Bright red flowers from late spring to fall
- Pairs of triangular blue-green leaves
- Tolerates harsh winters of the north

Enjoy the trumpet-shaped flowers as well as the hummingbirds they attract from June all the way through September. Twining stems climb and clamber on vertical structures. This vine won't damage wood. Control major aphid infestations if they occur with insecticide or insecticidal soap. May also be sold as Scarlet Trumpet Honeysuckle.

Parthenocissus quinquefolia

Virginia Creeper

Zones: 4-9

Light Needs:

Mature Size:

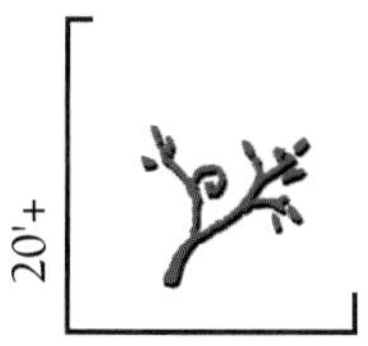

20'+

indefinite

Growth Rate: rapid

deciduous vine

Needs: Grow in any soil, from alkaline to acidic, dry to moist. Rocky soil is fine. Plant in full sun or partial shade. More sun yields brighter fall color. Tolerates heat, drought, and salt spray.

Good for: natural areas, seaside gardens, masonry or stone walls, fences, buildings, hiding blank walls, adding coarse texture, backgrounds, seasonal accents, groundcover for erosion control

More Choices: pages 31, 35, 37, 39, 41, 42, 207, and 209

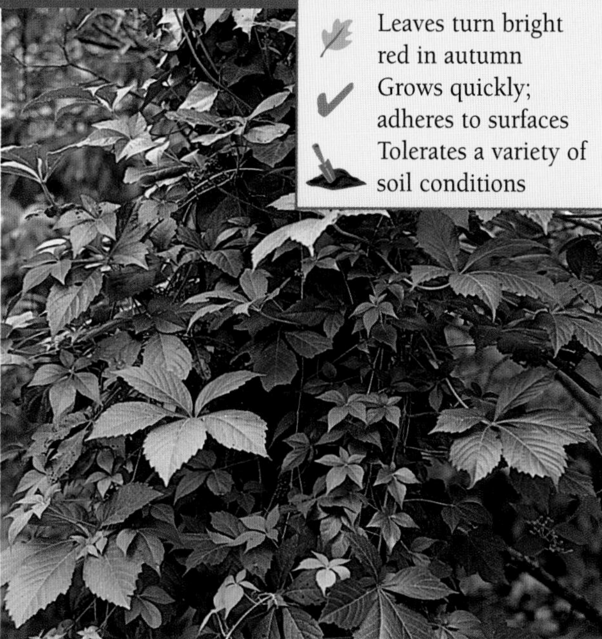

Outstanding Features:

- Leaves turn bright red in autumn
- Grows quickly; adheres to surfaces
- Tolerates a variety of soil conditions

This five-leafed native vine is easy to grow. Plant where it can climb on solid surfaces. This plant is often mistaken for poison ivy. The old saying leaves of three let it be; leaves of five let it thrive applies to this plant. *Parthenocissus* var. Englemannii boasts burgundy fall color and is hardy to Zone 3.

Parthenocissus tricuspidata

Boston Ivy

Zones: 4-8

Light Needs:

Mature Size:

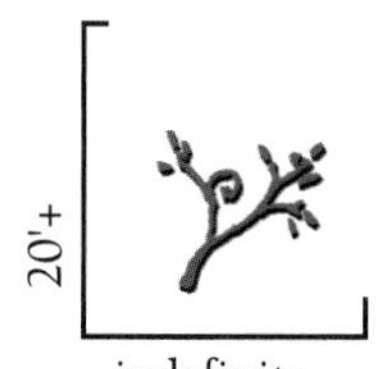

20'+

indefinite

Growth Rate: rapid

deciduous vine

Needs: Grow in any soil, from alkaline to acidic, dry to moist. Plant in full sun or partial shade. Full sun brings out intense fall color. Plants may require additional water in hotter climates.

Good for: growing on masonry walls, fences, buildings, adding coarse texture, seasonal accents, giving new homes an aged look

More Choices: pages 31, 35, 37, 39, 41, 42, 207, and 209

Outstanding Features:

- Rich, dark wine red fall color
- Glossy, rich green summer leaves
- Vines adhere to solid surfaces

Grow this vine to enjoy foliage that changes with the seasons. Large leaves are green in summer turning rich, red in fall. Bare winter stems lend pattern to hard surfaces for vertical interest. Adhesive disks can damage wood.

index

General Index

A

Accent plants, 13, 73
Acidic soil
- balancing, 51
- plants for, 40–41

Alkaline soil
- balancing, 51
- plants for, 41

Architect, landscape, 7
Austin, David, 150
Autumn interest
- shrubs for, 123
- vines for, 209

B

Base map, 16, *16*
Beds
- around trees, 69
- construction, 48–49
- design, 44–45
- drainage, 53
- edging, 49, *49*, 172
- groundcovers and, 49, *49*, 172, 176
- preparation, 50–51
- raised, 51
- for shrubs, 106–109
- weed prevention, 51

Buck, Griffith, 149
Budget, 17

C

Cameras, 16
Catch basins, 53
Clay soil
- amending, 51
- plants for, 39

Climate zones, 4
Color
- as accent, 13
- as design element, *10*, 10-12
- house color, choosing plants for, 11
- repetition of, 12

Composting leaves, 73
Contrast as a design element, 13
Courtyards, shrubs for, 121

D

De-icers, chemical, 23
Deadheading, 146
Deciduous plants for screening, 29, 31
Deer damage, 117
Design
- accents, 13
- beds, 46–47
- color, *10*, 10-12
- form, *10*, 11-12, *12*
- line, 11
- planning, 6–7
- prioritizing plans, 18–19
- professional help, 7
- site assessment, 16–17
- style, 14–15
- symmetry, 14
- texture, *10*, 10-12
- unity, 12, *12*

Digging bar, 68
Dividing groundcover clumps, 176
Downspouts, 53
Drainage, 23, 53
Dry sites, plants for, 38–39, 42, 207

E

Edging, 49, *49*
Entries
- edging, groundcovers for, 172
- shrubs for, 121

Evergreens
- groundcover, 171
- pruning, 112–113
- for screening, 28, *28*, 30-31
- shrubs, 30, 112–113
- trees, 30
- vines, 30, 207

Exposure, 17

F

Fall foliage
- shrubs for, 123
- trees for, 71
- vines for, 209

Fertilizing, 54–55
- with natural fertilizers, 55
- roses, 59
- with synthetic fertilizers, 54–55
- troubleshooting, 55

Flowering plants. *See also specific plants*
- groundcover, 171
- shrubs, fragrant, 118
- shrubs, pruning, 114–115
- shrubs, spring-flowering, 122
- shrubs, summer-flowering, 123
- trees, spring-flowering, 71
- trees, summer-flowering, 71
- vines, spring-flowering, 209
- vines, summer-flowering, 209

Form as design element, 10-12, *12*
Formal gardens
- shrubs for, 121
- style, 14-15, *14, 15*

Foundation plantings, 108–109, *108, 109*
French drains, 53

G

Grass, removing from beds, 48–49, *48, 49*
Groundcovers, 168–205
- for acidic soil, 41
- for alkaline soil, 41
- for clay soil, 39
- coarse-textured, 170
- design use of, 7
- dividing, 176
- for dry sites, 39, 42
- for edging, 172
- encyclopedia of choices, 177–205
- evergreen, 171
- fine-textured, 170
- flowering, 171
- for full sun, 35
- perennial, 171
- planting, 169, 175, 176
- for rock gardens, 173
- for shade, 37
- for slopes, 42, 169, 173
- for small spaces, 43, 173
- for urban areas, 43
- watering, 174–175
- for wet soil, 39
- winterizing, 174–175
- for woodlands, 173
- for zone 2, 22
- for zone 3, 25
- for zone 4, 27

H

Hedges
- pruning, 113
- selection guide, 107

Herbicide, 51, 174
Hoes, 50

I

Informal style, 15, *15*, 44–45
Irrigation, 52

L

Landscape architect, 7
Leaves, composting, 73
Limestone, 51
Line as design element, 11

M

Map, base, 16, *16*
Mass plantings, shrubs for, 120
Minnesota Tip method of protecting roses, 60-61
Mulch, 51, 57, 111, 174–175

N

Nitrogen, 54, 55

P

Patios
- edging, groundcovers for, 172
- shrubs for, 121
- trees for, 72

Peat moss, 51
Percolation test, 38
Perennial groundcovers, 171
PH, soil, 40–41, 51
Phosphorus, 54, 55
Pinching, 112
Planning, 6–7. *See also* Design
- budget, 17
- needs inventory, 17
- prioritizing, 18–19, 30
- site analysis, 16–17

Planting
- bed construction, 48–49
- bed design, 46–47
- bed preparation, 50–51
- fall, 65
- groundcovers, 169
- preparation, 107
- roses, bare-root, 56
- roses, climbing, 57
- roses, containerized, 57
- shrubs, 107, 110–111
- trees, 65–69

Potassium, 54, 55
Privacy. *See also* Screening
- filtering views, 28–29
- needs, defining, 28
- plant selection guides, 30–31

Private spaces, landscaping, 18–19, *18, 19, 29*
Pruning
- azaleas, 113
- Bradford pear, 99
- deadheading, 146
- evergreen shrubs, 112–113
- flowering shrubs, 114–115
- hard, 115
- hedges, 113
- hydrangeas, 114
- pinching, 112
- rhododendrons, 146
- roses, 58–59
- selective, 112, 114
- shearing, 112
- tools, 115
- trees, 68
- vines, 209

Public spaces, landscaping, 18-19, *18*

R

Repetition, value of, 12–13
Rock gardens, groundcover for, 173
Root stimulator, 54

S

Salt-tolerant plants, 23
Screening
- deciduous shrubs for, 31

deciduous trees for, 31
deciduous vines for, 31
evergreen shrubs for, 30
evergreen trees for, 30
evergreen vines for, 30
filtering views, 28–29
needs, defining, 28
plant selection guides, 30–31
Selection guides - groundcovers
for acidic soil, 41
for alkaline soil, 41
for clay soil, 39
coarse-textured, 170
for dry soil, 39, 42
for edging entries, patios, garden beds, 172
evergreen, 171
fine-textured, 170
flowering, 171
for full sun, 35
perennial, 171
for rock gardens, 173
salt-tolerant, 23
for shade, 37
for slopes, 42
for small spaces, 43, 173
for urban areas, 43
for wet soil, 39
for woodland areas, 173
zone 2, 22
zone 3, 25
zone 4, 27
Selection guides - shrubs
for acidic soil, 40–41
for alkaline soil, 41
for autumn color, 123
bundling for winter protection, 117
for clay soil, 39
coarse-textured, 119
for dry sites, 38–39, 42
for entries, courtyards, and patios, 121
fine-textured, 119
for formal gardens, 121
foundation, 109
fragrant-flowering, 118
for full sun, 34–35
hedges, 107
for mass plantings, 120
rapid-growing, 119
salt-tolerant, 23
for screening, deciduous, 31
for screening, evergreen, 30
for shade, 36–37
for slopes, 42
slow-growing, 119
for small spaces, 43
spring-flowering, 122
summer-flowering, 123
for urban areas, 43
for wet soil, 39
for windbreaks, 45
for winter fruit, 123
for woodland gardens, 121
zone 2, 22
zone 3, 24–25
zone 4, 26–27
Selection guides - trees
accent, 73
for acidic soil, 40
for alkaline soil, 41
for clay soil, 39
for dry soil, 38, 42
for fall foliage, 71
for filtering views, 31
for full sun, 34
for open areas, 73
patio, 72
rapid-growing, 63
salt-tolerant, 23
for screening, evergreen, 30
shade, 36, 73
for slopes, 42
for small spaces, 43
spring-flowering, 71
street, 72
summer-flowering, 71
for urban areas, 43
for wet soil, 39
for windbreaks, 45
for winter interest, 71
zone 2, 22
zone 3, 24
zone 4, 26
Selection guides - vines
for acidic soil, 41
for alkaline soil, 41
for autumn interest, 209
deciduous, 207
for dry sites, 39, 42, 207
evergreen, 207
for full sun, 35
rapid-growing, 209
salt-tolerant, 23
for screening, deciduous, 31
for screening, evergreen, 30
for shade, 37
for small spaces, 43
spring-flowering, 209
summer-flowering, 209
for wood, 207
zone 3, 25
zone 4, 27
Selection of plants, 20–45
climate factors, 21
dry sites, 42
maintenance requirements and, 21
needs, determining, 20
salt-tolerant, 23
screening and privacy, 28–31
slopes and, 42
for small spaces, 43
soil conditions and, 38–41
sunlight conditions and, 32–37
for urban areas, 43
for windbreaks, 44–45
Shade
groundcovers for, 37
requirements, 32–33
shrubs for, 36–37
trees for, 36, 73
vines for, 37
Shape. *See* Form
Shearing, 112
Shrubs, 106–167
for acidic soil, 40–41
for alkaline soil, 41
for autumn color, 123
beds, planning, 106–107
for clay soil, 39
coarse-textured, 119
deer damage, 117
design use of, 6
for dry sites, 38–39, 42
encyclopedia of choices, 124–167
for entries, courtyards, and patios, 121
fine-textured, 119
formal gardens, 121
foundation plantings, 108–109
fragrant-flowering, 118
for full sun, 34–35
hedges, 107
for mass plantings, 120
planting, 110–11
pruning, 112–115
rapid-growing, 119
for screening, deciduous, 31
for screening, evergreen, 30
for shade, 36
slopes, plant selection for, 42
slopes, planting on, 111
slow-growing, 119
for small spaces, 43
spacing, 106–107
spring-flowering, 122
summer-flowering, 123
for urban areas, 43
for wet soil, 39
for windbreaks, 45
for winter fruit, 123
winter protection, 116–117
for woodland gardens, 121
for zone 2, 22
for zone 3, 24–25
for zone 4, 26–27
Site analysis, 16–17
Slopes
groundcovers for, 169, 173
plant selection for, 42
planting groundcovers on, 169
planting shrubs on, 111
planting trees on, 67
Small spaces
groundcover for, 173
plant selection for, 43
Sod cutter, 49, *49*
Soil
acidic soil, plants for, 40–41
alkaline soil, plants for, 41
amending, 23, 50–51, 66, 68
assessment, 17
bed preparation, 50–51
clay soil, plants for, 39
drainage, 23
dry soil, plants for, 38–39
percolation test, 38
pH, 40–41, 51
wet soil, plants for, 39
Spring-flowering shrubs, 114, 122
Spring-flowering trees, 71
Spring-flowering vines, 209
Staking trees, 67
Straw, 174–175
Street trees, 72
Style
combined, 15
formal, 14-15, *14, 15*
informal, 15, *15,* 44–45
regional, 14
Summer-flowering shrubs, 123
Summer-flowering trees, 71
Summer-flowering vines, 209
Sunlight requirements, 32–37. *See also* Shade
groundcover for full sun, 35
shrubs for full sun, 34–35
trees for full sun, 34
vines for full sun, 35
Symmetry, 14, *14*

T

Terminology, 4
Texture
as design element, 10–12, *11, 12*
repetition of, 12
Tilling, 48, *48,* 50, *50*
Tools
camera, 16, *16*
digging bar, 68, *68*
hoes, 50, *50*
pruning, 115, *115*
shovels, 49, *49,* 67, *67*
sod cutter, 49, *49*
sterilizing with alcohol, 115

tiller, 48, *48*
Transplant shock, 68
Trees
accent, 73
for acidic soil, 40
for alkaline soil, 41
buying, 64–65
for clay soil, 39
composting leaves, 73
design use of, 6
for dry sites, 38, 42
for fall foliage, 71
for filtered views, 31
for full sun, 34
legacy, 63
mortality, 65
for open areas, 73
patio, 72
planting, season for, 65
planting balled-and-burlapped, 68–69
planting container-grown, 66–67
planting on a slope, 67
rapid-growing, 31, 63
for screening, evergreen, 30
for seasonality, 70–71
shade, 36, 73
for slopes, 42
for small spaces, 43
spring-flowering, 71
staking, 67
street, 72
summer-flowering, 71
transplant shock, 68
trimming, 68
for urban areas, 43
for wet soil, 39
for windbreaks, 45
for winter interest, 71
wrapping, 76
for zone 2, 22
for zone 3, 24
for zone 4, 26

U

Unity, design, *12*, 12–13
Urban areas, plants for, 43

V

Vines, 206–213
for acidic soil, 41
for alkaline soil, 41
for autumn interest, 209
deciduous, 207
design use of, 7
for dry sites, 39, 42, 207
encyclopedia of choices, 210–213
evergreen, 207
for full sun, 35
pruning, 209
rapid-growing, 31, 209
for screening, deciduous, 31
for screening, evergreen, 30
for shade, 37
for small spaces, 43
spring-flowering, 209
summer-flowering, 209
twining *versus* sticking, 207
for wood, 207
for zone 3, 25
for zone 4, 27

W

Watering
deep, 52
drainage, 53
groundcovers, 174–175
irrigation, 52
shrubs, 110-111, 116
timing, 52
trees, 65, 69
troubleshooting, 52
Weed prevention, 51
Wet soil, plants for, 39
Windbreaks, 44–45
positioning, 44
shrubs for, 45
snow accumulation and, 45
trees for, 45
Winter fruit, shrubs for, 123
Winter interest, trees for, 71
Winter protection
bundling shrubs for, 116-117
groundcover, 174–175
wrapping maple trees, 76
Woodland gardens
groundcover for, 173
shrubs for, 121

Plants by Common and Botanical Names

Numbers in **boldface** indicate Plant Encyclopedia entries. Numbers in *italics* indicate photographs.

A

Abies balsamea (Balsam fir), 30, 36, 40, 73, *74*, **74**
Abies balsamea 'Nana' (Dwarf balsam fir), 23, 30, 36, 41, 45, *45*, 109, 117, 119, 120, *124*, **124**
Abies concolor (White fir), 30, 34, 38, 45, *74*, **74**
Abies fraseri (Frasier fir), *20*, 30, 34, 36, *75*, **75**
Abies veitchii (Veitch fir), 30, 36, 40, 63, *75*, **75**
Abeliophyllum distichum (White forsythia), 31, 35, 41, 42, *42*, 117, 118, 119, 121, 122, *124*, **124**
Acer tataricum ginnala (Amur maple), 22, 34, 36, 71, 72, *77*, **77**
Acer platanoides (Norway maple), 34, 36, 39, 41, 43, 45, *77*, **77**
Acer rubrum (Red maple), 31, 36, 38, 40, 43, 63, 71, 72, 73, *78*, **78**
Acer saccharinum (Silver maple), 31, 34, 36, 39, 40, 41, 63, 71, 73, *78*, **78**
Acer saccharum (Sugar maple), 34, 36, 40, 71, 73, *79*, **79**
Actinidia arguta (Hardy kiwi), 31, 35, 37, 207, *207*, 209, *210*, **210**
Actinidia chinensis (Chinese Gooseberry), 210
Actinidia kolomikta (Variegated kiwi vine), 210
Adelaide Hoodless rose (*Rosa* 'Adelaide Hoodless'), 34, 40, 107, 118, 119, 121, 123, *148*, **148**
Adiantum pedatum (Maidenhair fern), 37, 41, 43, 170, 171, 173, *177*, **177**
Aegopodium podagraria 'Variegatum' (Snow-on-the-Mountain), 37, 39, 41, 42, 171, 173, *177*, **177**
Aesculus glabra (Ohio buckeye), 34, 36, 71, 73, *79*, **79**
Aesculus hippocastanum (Common horsechestnut), 34, 36, 39, 41, *41*, 71, 73, *80*, **80**
Aesculus x grandiflora (Apple serviceberry), 80
Ajuga (*Ajuga reptans*), 35, 37, 171, *178*, **178**
'Burgundy Glow," 178
'Pink Beauty,' 178
'Silver Beauty,' 178
Ajuga reptans (Ajuga), 35, 37, 171, *178*, **178**
Alba Meidiland rose (*Rosa* Alba Meidiland), 35, 37, 42, 171, 172, 173, *201*, **201**
Alchemilla mollis (Lady's mantle), 37, 170, 171, 172, *172*, *178*, **178**
Allegheny foam flower (*Tiarella cordifolia*), 37, 41, 170, 171, 173, *204*, **204**
Allegheny serviceberry (*Amelanchier laevis*), 34, 36, 39, 40, 43, 71, *81*, **81**
Almond. *See* Dwarf flowering almond
Alpine strawberry (*Fragaria vesca*), 35, 37, 41, 42, 43, 171, 172, 173, *189*, **189**
Alyssum saxatile. See Basket-of-gold
Amelanchier alnifolia (Serviceberry), 35, 36, 41, 121, 122, 123, *125*, **125**
Amelanchier canadensis (Shadblow serviceberry), 34, 36, 39, 40, 71, 73, *80*, **80**
Amelanchier laevis (Allegheny serviceberry), 34, 36, 39, 40, 43, 71, *81*, **81**
American arborvitae (*Thuja occidentalis*), 30, 34, 39, 41, *105*, **105**
'Emerald,' 105
'Pyramidalis,' 105
'Techny,' 105
American beech (*Fagus grandifolia*), 34, 36, 40, *44*, 45, 71, *87*, **87**
American bittersweet (*Celastrus scandens*), *25*, 31, 35, 37, 39, 42, *206*, 207, 209, *211*, **211**
pruning, 209
American hornbeam (*Carpinus caroliniana*), 34, 36, 39, 40, 43, 71, 72, 83, *84*, **84**
American linden (*Tilia americana*), 34, 36, 41, 71, 72, *105*, **105**
'Fastigiata,' 105
'Redmond,' 105
American Smoketree (*Cotinus obovatus*), 34, 38, 41, 43, 71, 72, 73, *85*, **85**
Ampelopsis brevipedunculata (Porcelain vine), 42
Amsonia tabernaemontana (Blue star), 37, 171, *179*, **179**
Amur chokecherry (*Prunus maackii*), 34, 36, 63, 71, 73, *73*, *97*, **97**
Amur maple (*Acer tataricum ginnala*), *22*, 34, 36, 71, 72, *77*, **77**
'Flame,' 77
'Red Fruit,' 77
Amur privet (*Ligustrum amurense*), 23, 31, 34, 36, 38, 39, 43, 107, 109, 117, 119, 121, *139*, **139**
Anchusa myosotidiflora (Siberian forget-me-not), 37, 170, 171, *179*, **179**
Andorra compact juniper (*Juniperus horizontalis* 'Plumosa Compacta'), 23, 35, 41, 42, 43, 170, 171, 172, 173, *194*, **194**
Andromeda polifolia (Bog rosemary), 35, 37, 41, 171, 173, *180*, **180**
Andromeda rosmarinifolia. See Andromeda polifolia (Bog rosemary)
Anglojap yew (*Taxus x media* 'Densiformis'), 34, 36, 40, 107, 109, 117, 119, 120, 121, *162*, **162**
Annabelle hydrangea (*Hydrangea arborescens* 'Annabelle'), 34, 36, 39, 40, 43, *114*, 119, *119*, 120, 121, 122, 123, *134*, **134**
Anthony Waterer spirea (*Spiraea japonica* 'Anthony Waterer'), *12*, 34, 36, 39, 43, 121, 122, 123, *157*, **157**
Apple serviceberry (*Aesculus x grandiflora*), 80
Arabis caucasica (Rockcress), 35, 37, 170, 171, *171*, 172, 173, *180*, **180**
Arborvitae, *120*. *See also* American arborvitae; Emerald arborvitae; Hetz's Midget arborvitae; Little Giant arborvitae
Arctostaphylos uva-ursi (Kinnikinick or Bearberry), 23, 35, 37, 39, 170, 171, 172, *181*, **181**
Arenaria montana (Mountain sandwort), 35, 39, 170, 171, 173, *181*, **181**
Arenaria purpurascens (Pink sandwort), 181
Armeria maritima (Sea thrift), 23, *25*, 37, 39, 170, 171, 172, 173, *182*, **182**

Arnold's Red Tatarian honeysuckle (*Lonicera tatarica* 'Arnold's Red'), 31, 34, 118, 119, 121, 122, *140*, **140**

Aronia arbutifolia (Red chokeberry), 125

Aronia melanocarpa (Black chokeberry), 34, 36, 38, 39, 40, 42, 119, 120, 121, 122, 123, *125*, **125**

Arrowwood viburnum (*Viburnum dentatum*), 23, 31, 34, 36, 40, 107, 119, 121, 122, 123, *165*, **165**

Artemisia ludoviciana, 182

Artemisia schmidtiana, 182

Artemisia spp., *173*

Artemisia stelleriana (Silver brocade artemisia), 23, 35, 43, 170, 171, 172, 173, *182*, **182**

Ash. *See* Green ash

Aspen. *See* Quaking aspen

Asperula odorata (Sweet Woodruff), 35, 37, *37*, 41, 170, *170*, 171, 173, *183*, **183**

Aurinia saxatilis (Basket-of-gold), 35, 39, 42, 171, 172, 173, *183*, **183**

Azaleas (*Azalea* spp.)

- *Azalea carolinianum* (Carolina azalea), 34, 40, 109, 117, 120, 121, 122, 123, *126*, **126**
- *Azalea* 'Exbury Hybrids' (Exbury azalea), 35, *40*, 41, 109, 117, 119, 120, 122, 123, *126*, **126**
- *Azalea mucronulatum* 'Cornell Pink' (Cornell Pink azalea), 34, 40, 109, 117, 119, 120, 121, 122, 123, *127*, **127**
- *Azalea*
  - 'Northern Lights' (Northern Lights azalea), 35, 41, 109, 117, 118, *118*, 119, 120, 121, 122, 123, *127*, **127**
  - 'Golden Lights,' 127
  - 'Northern Hi-Lights,' 127
  - 'Orchid Lights,' 127
  - pruning, 113
  - 'Rosy Lights,' 127
  - 'White Lights,' 127

B

Balsam fir (*Abies balsamea*), 30, 36, 40, 73, *74*, **74**

Bar Harbor juniper (*Juniperus horizontalis* 'Bar Harbor'), 23, 35, 41, 42, 43, 170, 171, 172, 173, *193*, **193**

Barberry. *See* Japanese barberry

Barren strawberry. *See* Waldesteinia (*Waldesteinia ternata*)

Basket-of-gold (*Aurinia saxatilis*), 35, 39, 42, 171, 172, 173, *183*, **183**

- 'Tom Thumb,' 183
- 'Variegata,' 183

Bath's Pink (*Dianthus gratianopoliatanus* 'Bath's Pink'), 35, 37, 39, 41, 42, 43, 170, 171, 172, 173, *187*, **187**

Bayberry. *See* Northern bayberry

Bearberry. *See* Kinnikinick (*Arctostaphylos uva-ursi*)

Beech. *See* American beech

Berberis thunbergii (Japanese barberry), 35, 36, 39, 107, 109, 119, 123, *128*, **128**

Bergenia cordifolia (Saxifrage), *20*, 35, 37, 170, 171, 172, *184*, **184**

Betty Prior rose (*Rosa* 'Betty Prior'), 34, 107, 118, 120, 123, *148*, **148**

Betula nigra (River birch), 31, 34, 36, 38, *38*, 39, 40, 63, 71, *71*, 72, 73, *81*, **81**

Betula papyrifera (Canoe birch), 34, 40, 63, 71, *82*, **82**

Betula pendula (European white birch), 34, 36, 40, 41, 63, 71, *82*, **82**

Betula mandschurica japonica 'Whitespire' (Whitespire birch), *21*, 34, 38, 40, 63, 71, 72, *83*, **83**

Birch

- Canoe birch (*Betula papyrifera*), 34, 40, 63, 71, *82*, **82**
- European white birch (*Betula pendula*), *21*, 34, 36, 40, 41, 63, 71, *82*, **82**
- River birch (*Betula nigra*), 31, 34, 36, 38, *38*, 39, 40, 63, 71, *71*, 72, 73, *81*, **81**
- Whitespire birch (*Betula mandschurica japonica* 'Whitespire'), 34, 38, 40, 63, 71, 72, *83*, **83**

Bird's Nest spruce (*Picea abies* 'Nidiformis'), 34, 39, 117, 119, *142*, **142**

Bittersweet. *See* American bittersweet

Black chokeberry (*Aronia melanocarpa*), 34, 36, 38, 39, 40, 42, 119, 120, 121, 122, 123, *125*, **125**

- 'Brilliant,' 125

Blackhaw viburnum (*Viburnum prunifolium*), 34, 36, 41, 119, 120, 121, 122, 123, *167*, **167**

Blanket flower (*Gaillardia x grandiflora*), 23, 35, 39, 42, 43, 171, 172, 173, *190*, **190**

Bloody cranesbill (*Geranium sanguineum*), 35, 37, 43, 170, 171, 172, 173, *191*, **191**

Blue Chip juniper (*Juniperus horizontalis* 'Blue Chip'), 23, 35, 39, 41, 42, 43, 170, 171, 172, 173, *193*, **193**

Blue Rug juniper (*Juniperus horizontalis* 'Wiltonii'), 23, 35, 41, 42, 43, 170, 171, 172, 173, *194*, **194**

Blue star (*Amsonia tabernaemontana*), 37, 171, *179*, **179**

Blue star bellflower (*Campanula poscharskyana*), 35, 37, 41, 42, *170*, 171, 172, 173, *184*, **184**

Blue Star juniper (*Juniperus squamata* 'Blue Star'), 34, 39, 119, *139*, **139**

Bog rosemary (*Andromeda polifolia*), 35, 37, 41, 171, 173, *180*, **180**

- 'Alba,' 180
- 'Compacta,' 180

Boston ivy (*Parthenocissus tricuspidata*), 31, 35, 37, 39, 41, 42, 207, *208*, 209, *213*, **213**

- pruning, 209

Boxwood, *128*. *See also* Wintergreen boxwood

Bradford pear (*Pyrus calleryana* 'Bradford'), 31, 34, 43, 63, 71, 72, 73, *98*, **98**

- pruning, 99

Bridalwreath spirea (*Spiraea prunifolia*), 31, 34, 36, 107, 119, 121, *158*, **158**

Brunnera macrophylla. *See* Siberian forget-me-not

Buckeye. *See* Ohio buckeye

Bunchberry (*Cornus canadensis*), 37, 41, 170, 171, 173, *186*, **186**

Burning bush (*Euonymus alatus*), *106*

- Dwarf burning bush (*Euonymus alatus* 'Compacta'), 31, 34, 36, 41, 43, *118*, 119, *119*, 120, 121, 123, *133*, **133**

Buxus microphylla 'Wintergreen' (Wintergreen boxwood), 35, 36, 107, 109, 117, 119, *120*, 121, 122, *128*, **128**

C

Calycanthus floridus (Sweetshrub), *20*, 35, 36, 39, 118, 119, 121, 122, 123, *129*, **129**

Campanula poscharskyana (Blue star bellflower), 35, 37, 41, 42, *170*, 171, 172, 173, *184*, **184**

Campsis radicans (Trumpet vine), *27*, 31, 35, 37, 39, 42, 207, 209, **210**, *210*, *210*, **210**

Canoe birch (*Betula papyrifera*), 34, 40, 63, 71, *82*, **82**

Carefree Beauty rose (*Rosa* Carefree Beauty), 34, 107, 109, 118, 123, *149*, **149**

Carol Mackie daphne (*Daphne x burkwoodii* 'Carol Mackie'), 34, 36, 39, 41, 117, 118, 119, 121, 122, *132*, **132**

Carolina allspice. *See* Sweetshrub (*Calycanthus floridus*)

Carolina azalea (*Azalea carolinianum*), 34, 40, 109, 117, 120, 121, 122, 123, *126*, **126**

Carpinus betulus (European hornbeam), 34, 36, 39, 40, 41, 43, 71, 72, *83*, **83**

Carpinus caroliniana (American hornbeam), 34, 36, 39, 40, 43, 71, 72, 83, *84*, **84**

Catawba rhododendron (*Rhododendron catawba*), 30, 34, 36, 40, *40*, 109, 117, 119, 122, *146*, **146**

- Mollis hybrids, 146
- 'P.J.M.', 146
- 'P.J.M. White,' 146

Catmint (*Nepeta x faassenii*), 35, 37, 42, 43, 170, 171, 172, 173, *197*, **197**

- 'Six Hills Giant,' 197

Cedar. *See* Eastern red cedar

Celastrus scandens (American bittersweet), *25*, 31, 35, 37, 39, 42, *206*, 207, 209, *211*, **211**

Cerastium tomentosum (Snow-in-Summer), 35, 39, 42, 170, 171, 172, 173, *185*, **185**

Cercidiphyllum japonicum (Katsura tree), 34, 40, 41, 63, 71, 72, *84*, **84**

Cercis canadensis (Redbud), 31, 34, 36, 39, 40, 41, 43, 63, *70*, 71, 72, 73, *85*, **85**

Cercis canadensis 'Alba' (White flowering redbud), *85*

Chamaecyparis obtusa 'Nana Gracilis' (Dwarf Hinoki false cypress), 35, 39, 41, 117, *118*, 119, *129*, **129**

Chenault coralberry. *See* Prostrate Chenault coralberry (*Symphoricarpos x chenaultii* 'Hancock')

Cherry. *See* Cornelian cherry

Chinese Gooseberry (*Actinidia chinensis*), 210

Chokeberry

- Black chokeberry (*Aronia melanocarpa*), 34,36, 38, 39, 40, 42, 119, 120, 121, 122, 123, *125*, **125**
- Red chokeberry (*Aronia arbutifolia*), 125

Chokecherry

- Amur chokecherry (*Prunus maackii*), 34, 36, 63, 71, 73, *73*, *97*, **97**

Cinquefoil

- Shrubby cinquefoil (*Potentilla fruticosa*), 35, 36, 109, 119, 120, 123, *144*, **144**
- Spring cinquefoil (*Potentilla tabernaemontani*), 35, 39, 42, 171, 172, 173, *200*, **200**

Clethra alnifolia (Summersweet), 23, 36, 39, 41, 117, 118, 119, 120, *120*, 121, 123, *130*, **130**

Cliff green (*Paxistima canbyi*), 35, 37, 39, 41, 170, 171, 173, *199*, **199**

Climbing hydrangea (*Hydrangea petiolaris*), *29*, 35, *35*, 37, 43, 207, *208*, 209, *209*, *211*, **211**

- pruning, 209

Cloth-of-gold. *See* Basket-of-gold (*Aurinia saxatilis*)

Clove currant (*Ribes odoratum*), 147

Cockspur hawthorn (*Crataegus crus-galli* 'Inermis'), 23, 34, 36, 39, 40, 41, 43, 71, 72, 73, *86*, **86**

Colorado blue spruce (*Picea pungens glauca*), 30, 34, 45, *93*, **93**

- 'Hoopsii,' 93
- 'Koster,' 93

Common lilac (*Syringa vulgaris*), 34, 36, 39, 107, 118, 119, 121, 122, *161*, **161**

- 'Arch McKean,' 161

'Charm Lilac,' 161
'Ellen Willmott,' 161
'Little Boy Blue,' 161
'Primrose,' 161
var. *alba,* 161
'Wedgewood Blue,' 161
Common witch hazel. *See* Witch hazel, common *(Hamamelis virginiana)*
Compact American cranberry bush (*Viburnum trilobum* 'Alfredo'), *121*
Concolor fir. *See* White fir *(Abies concolor)*
Convallaria majalis (Lily-of-the-valley), 37, 39, 170, 171, 172, 173, *185,* **185**
Coral bells *(Heuchera sanguinea),* 35, 37, 41, 43, 170, 171, 172, 173, *191,* **191**
Coral Embers willow (*Salix alba* 'Britzensis'), 23, 34, 39, 119, *156,* **156**
Coralberry. *See* Prostrate Chenault coralberry (*Symphoricarpos x chenaultii* 'Hancock')
Coralberry *(Symphoricarpos orbiculatus),* 31, 34, 36, 39, 42, 107, 119, 121, 123, 159, **159**
Corkscrew willow (*Salix* 'Golden Curls'), 34, 36, 63, 73, *103,* **103**
Cornelian cherry *(Cornus mas)*
'Aureo-elegantissima,' 131
'Variegata,' 131
Cornell Pink azalea (*Azalea mucronulatum* 'Cornell Pink'), 34, 40, 109, 117, 119, 120, 121, 122, 123, *127,* **127**
Cornus alba (Redtwig dogwood), 35, 39, 119, *130,* **130**
Cornus canadensis (Bunchberry), 37, 41, 170, 171, 173, *186,* **186**
Cornus mas (Cornelian cherry), 34, 107, 109, 119, 122, *131,* **131**
Cornus racemosa (Gray dogwood), 35, 109, 119, 122, *131,* **131**
Cornus stolonifera 'Flaviramea' (Yellow-Twig dogwood), 35, 36, 39, 119, 123, *132,* **132**
Cornus stolonifera 'Cardinal,' 130
Cotinus americanus. See Cotinus obovatus (American Smoketree)
Cotinus coggygria, 85
Cotinus obovatus (American Smoketree), 34, 38, 41, 43, 71, 72, 73, *85,* **85**
Crabapple
Japanese flowering crabapple *(Malus floribunda),* 34, 41, 43, 71, *71,* 72, 73, *91,* **91**
Plumleaf crabapple *(Malus prunifolia),* 34, 40, 43, 71, 73, *91,* **91**
Crataegus crus-galli 'Inermis' (Cockspur hawthorn), 23, 34, 36, 39, 40, 41, 43, 71, 72, 73, *86,* **86**
Crataegus phaenopyrum (Washington hawthorn), 34, 36, 38, 40, 41, 43, 71, 72, 73, 86, **86**
Creeping myrtle. *See* Littleleaf periwinkle *(Vinca minor)*
Creeping phlox *(Phlox stolonifera),* 37, 41, 171, 173, *199,* **199**
'Blue Ridge,' 199
'Bruce's White,' 199
'Sherwood Purple,' 199
Cutleaf lilac *(Syringa x laciniata),* 31, 34, 36, 107, 118, 119, 121, 122, *161,* **161**
Cut-Leaf staghorn sumac (*Rhus typhina* 'Laciniata'), 34, 39, 40, 41, 42, 43, 119, 121, 123, *147,* **147**
Cypress spurge *(Euphorbia cyparissias),* 35, 37, 42, 170, 171, 173, *188,* **188**
'Orange Man,' 188

D

Daphne x burkwoodii 'Carol Mackie' (Carol Mackie daphne), 34, 36, 39, 41, 117, 118, 119, 121, 122, *132,* **132**
Dead nettle. *See* Spotted dead nettle
Dennstaedtia punctilobula (Hay-Scented fern), 37, 39, 41, 170, 171, 173, *186,* **186**
Dianthus gratianopoliatanus 'Bath's Pink' (Bath's Pink), 35, 37, 39, 41, 42, 43, 170, 171, 172, 173, *187,* **187**
Dogwood
Gray dogwood *(Cornus racemosa),* 35, 109, 119, 122, *131,* **131**
Redtwig dogwood *(Cornus alba),* 35, 39, 119, *130,* **130**
Yellow-Twig dogwood (*Cornus stolonifera* 'Flaviramea'), 35, 36, 39, 119, 123, *132,* **132**
Doublefile viburnum (*Viburnum plicatum tomentosum*), 34, *34,* 36, 119, 120, 121, 122, 123, *166,* **166**
Douglas fir *(Pseudotsuga menziesii),* 30, 34, 40, *98,* **98**
'Fastigiata,' 98
'Oudemansii,' 98
Dropmore scarlet honeysuckle (*Lonicera x brownii* 'Dropmore Scarlet'), 30, 35, *206,* 207, 209, *212,* **212**
pruning, 209
Dwarf Alberta spruce (*Picea glauca* 'Conica'), 34, 36, 39, 40, 43, 117, 119, 121, *143,* **143**
Dwarf balsam fir (*Abies balsamea* 'Nana'), 23, 30, 36, 41, 45, *45,* 109, 117, 119, 120, *124,* **124**
Dwarf blue fescue *(Festuca glauca),* 35, 39, 170, 171, 172, *188,* **188**
'Elijah Blue,' 188
Dwarf burning bush (*Euonymus alatus* 'Compacta'), 31, 34, 36, 41, 43, *118,* 119, *119,* 120, 121, 123, *133,* **133**
Dwarf flowering almond (*Prunus glandulosa* 'Rosea'), 34, 36, 117, 122, *144,* **144**
Dwarf Hinoki false cypress (*Chamaecyparis obtusa* 'Nana Gracilis'), 35, 39, 41, 117, *118,* 119, *129,* **129**
'Nana Lutea,' 129
Dwarf Japanese garden juniper (*Juniperus procumbens* 'Nana'), 35, 41, 43, *43,* 170, 171, 172, 173, *195,* **195**
Dwarf Norway spruce (*Picea abies* 'Pumila'), 35, 39, 41, 107, 109, 117, 121, *121,* *142,* **142**
Dwarf winged Euonymus. *See* Dwarf burning bush (*Euonymus alatus* 'Compacta')

E

Eastern red cedar *(Juniperus virginiana),* 23, 30, 34, 38, 39, 40, 41, 42, 45, 71, 73, *90,* **90**
Elaeagnus angustifolia (Russian olive), 23, 34, 40, 42, 63, 71, 72, *87,* **87**
Emerald arborvitae (*Thuja occidentalis* 'Emerald'), 30, 35, 39, 41, 45, 107, 109, 117, 119, 121, *163,* **163**
Euonymus alatus (Burning bush), *106*
Euonymus alatus 'Compacta' (Dwarf burning bush), 31, 34, 36, 41, 43, *118,* 119, *119,* 120, 121, 123, *133,* **133**
Euonymus fortunei 'Coloratus' (Purple-Leaf winter creeper), 35, 41, 42, 43, 171, 172, 173, *187,* **187**
Euphorbia cyparissias (Cypress spurge), 35, 37, 42, 170, 171, 173, *188,* **188**
European birdcherry. *See* Mayday tree
European cranberrybush (*Viburnum opulus* 'Roseum'), 35, 39, 119, 121, 122, *166,* **166**
European hornbeam *(Carpinus betulus),* 34, 36, 39, 40, 41, 43, 71, 72, *83,* **83**
'Asplenifolia,' 83
'Columnaris,' 83
'Fastigiata,' 83
European mountain ash *(Sorbus aucuparia),* 23, 34, 36, *36,* 39, 40, 71, 72, 73, *103,* **103**
European white birch *(Betula pendula), 21,* 34, 36, 40, 41, 63, 71, *82,* **82**
Evening primrose *(Oenothera speciosa),* 198
Exbury azalea (*Azalea* 'Exbury Hybrids'), 35, *40,* 41, 109, 117, 119, 120, 122, 123, *126,* **126**
'Berry Rose,' 126
'Firefly,' 126
'Gibraltar,' 126
'White Swan,' 126

F

Fagus grandifolia (American beech), 34, 36, 40, *44,* 45, 71, *87,* **87**
Fagus sylvatica pendula, 87
Fagus sylvatica 'Purpurea Tricolor,' 87
Fairy rose (*Rosa* 'The Fairy'), 35, 36, 43, 119, 121, 123, *153,* **153**
Fern
Hay-Scented fern *(Dennstaedtia punctilobula),* 37, 39, 41, 170, 171, 173, *186,* **186**
Maidenhair fern *(Adiantum pedatum),* 37, 41, 43, 170, 171, 173, *177,* **177**
Fescue. *See* Dwarf blue fescue *(Festuca glauca)*
Festuca glauca (Dwarf blue fescue), 35, 39, 170, 171, 172, *188,* **188**
Fir
Balsam fir *(Abies balsamea),* 30, 36, 40, 73, *74,* **74**
Douglas fir *(Pseudotsuga menziesii),* 30, 34, 40, *98,* **98**
Dwarf balsam fir (*Abies balsamea* 'Nana'), 23, 30, 36, 41, 45, *45,* 109, 117, 119, 120, *124,* **124**
Frasier fir *(Abies fraseri), 20,* 30, 34, 36, *75,* **75**
Veitch fir *(Abies veitchii),* 30, 36, 40, 63, *75,* **75**
White fir *(Abies concolor),* 30, 34, 38, 45, *74,* **74**
Firethorn. *See* Yukon Belle firethorn (*Pyracantha angustifolia* Yukon Belle)
Flower carpet rose (*Rosa* 'Flower Carpet'), 35, 43, *43,* 171, *201,* **201**
Forget-me-not *(Myosotis scorpioides),* 35, 37, 39, 171, 173, *197,* **197**
Forsythia mandschurica 'Vermont Sun' (Vermont sun forsythia), 31, 35, 36, 42, 117, 119, 120, 121, 122, *133,* **133**
Forsythia ovata 'Northern Gold' (Northern Gold forsythia), 133
Fragaria 'Pink Panda' (Pink Panda strawberry), 35, 37, 171, 172, *189,* **189**
Fragaria vesca (Alpine strawberry), 35, 37, 41, 42, 43, 171, 172, 173, *189,* **189**
Frasier fir *(Abies fraseri), 20,* 30, 34, 36, *75,* **75**
Fraxinus americana Autumn Purple, 88
Fraxinus pennsylvanica (Green ash), 31, 34, 38, 39, 40, 41, 43, 63, 71, 72, 73, *88,* **88**
French pussy willow (*Salix caprea* 'Kilmarnock'), 35, 39, 119, *156,* **156**
Fru Dagmar Hastrup rose (*Rosa* 'Fru Dagmar Hastrup'), 23, 35, 39, 42, 118, 123, *149,* **149**

G

Galium odoratum. See Asperula odorata (Sweet Woodruff)
Gallberry. *See* Inkberry (*Ilex glabra* 'Compacta')

Gaultheria procumbens (Wintergreen), 37, 41, 171, 173, *190*, **190**
Geranium sanguineum (Bloody cranesbill), 35, 37, 43, 170, 171, 172, 173, *191*, **191**
Germander (*Teucrium prostratum*), 35, 41, 43, 170, 171, 172, 173, *204*, **204**
Ginkgo (*Ginkgo biloba*), 34, 38, 39, 40, 41, 43, *70*, 71, 72, 73, *88*, **88**
  'Autumn Gold,' 88
  'Fastigiata,' 88
Gleditsia triacanthos inermis (Honeylocust), 23, 34, 41, 43, 63, 71, 72, *72*, 73, *89*, **89**
Goat willow. *See* French pussy willow (*Salix caprea* 'Kilmarnock')
Gold dust. *See* Basket-of-gold (*Aurinia saxatilis*)
Golden weeping willow (*Salix alba* 'Tristis'), 23, 34, 39, 42, 63, 73, *102*, **102**
Goldmoss (*Sedum acre*), 35, 39, 41, 42, 43, 170, 171, 172, 173, *202*, **202**
Gooseberry. *See* Chinese gooseberry
Goutweed. *See* Snow-on-the-Mountain (*Aegopodium podagraria* 'Variegatum')
Graham Thomas rose (*Rosa* Graham Thomas), 35, *106*, 118, 120, 121, 123, *150*, **150**
Gray dogwood (*Cornus racemosa*), 35, 109, 119, 122, *131*, **131**
  'Slavinii,' 131
Green ash (*Fraxinus pennsylvanica*), 31, 34, 38, 39, 40, 41, 43, 63, 71, 72, 73, *88*, **88**
  'Marshall's Seedless,' 88
Green Lustre Japanese holly (*Ilex crenata* 'Green Lustre'), 30, 35, 36, 43, 45, 107, 119, 121, *135*, **135**
Green Mound alpine currant (*Ribes alpinum* 'Green Mound'), 23, 35, 36, 39, 41, *41*, 107, 109, 117, 119, 121, 122, *147*, **147**

H

Hamamelis virginiana (Common witch hazel), 34, 36, 109, 118, 123, *134*, **134**
Hardy kiwi (*Actinidia arguta*), 31, 35, 37, 207, *207*, 209, *210*, **210**
  'Issai,' 210
  pruning, 209
Hawthorn
  Cockspur hawthorn (*Crataegus crus-galli 'Inermis'*), 23, 34, 36, 39, 40, 41, 43, 71, 72, 73, *86*, **86**
  Washington hawthorn (*Crataegus phaenopyrum*), 34, 36, 38, 40, 41, 43, 71, 72, 73, *86*, **86**
Hay-Scented fern (*Dennstaedtia punctilobula*), 37, 39, 41, 170, 171, 173, *186*, **186**
Hedgehog rose. *See* Rugosa rose (*Rosa rugosa*)
Henry Kelsey rose (*Rosa* 'Henry Kelsey'), 35, 41, 107, 118, 119, 121, 122, 123, *150*, **150**
Hetz's Midget arborvitae (*Thuja occidentalis* 'Hetz's Midget'), 35, 39, 117, 119, 121, *164*, **164**
Heuchera sanguinea (Coral bells), 35, 37, 41, 43, 170, 171, 172, 173, *191*, **191**
Hick's upright yew (*Taxus x media* 'Hicksii'), 30, 35, 36, 41, 45, 107, 117, 119, 121, *163*, **163**
Holly. *See* Green Lustre Japanese holly
Honeylocust (*Gleditsia triacanthos inermis*), 23, 34, 41, 43, 63, 71, 72, *72*, 73, *89*, **89**
  'Shademaster,' 89
  'Skyline,' 89
  'Sunburst,' 89
Honeysuckle
  Arnold's Red Tatarian honeysuckle (*Lonicera tatarica* 'Arnold's Red'), 31, 34, 118, 119, 121, 122, *140*, **140**
  Dropmore scarlet honeysuckle (*Lonicera x brownii* 'Dropmore Scarlet'), 30, 35, *206*, 207, 209, *212*, **212**
  Scarlet trumpet honeysuckle (*See* Dropmore scarlet honeysuckle (*Lonicera x brownii* 'Dropmore Scarlet'))
  Trumpet honeysuckle (*Lonicera sempervirens*), 31, 35, 207, *208*, 209, *212*, **212**
Hornbeam. *See* American hornbeam; European hornbeam
Horsechestnut, common (*Aesculus hippocastanum*), 34, 36, 39, 41, *41*, 71, 73, *80*, **80**
Hosta (*Hosta* spp.), 13, 37, 43, 170, *170*, 171, 172, 173, *192*, **192**
Hunter rose (*Rosa* 'Hunter'), 35, 41, 118, 120, 121, *122*, 123, *151*, **151**
Hydrangea petiolaris (Climbing hydrangea), *29*, 35, 37, 43, 207, *208*, 209, *209*, *211*, **211**
Hydrangea arborescens 'Annabelle' (Annabelle hydrangea), 34, 36, 39, 40, 43, *114*, 119, *119*, 120, 121, 122, 123, *134*, **134**
Hydrangea paniculata 'Grandiflora' (PeeGee hydrangea), 31, 35, 36, 41, 119, 123, *135*, **135**
Hydrangea paniculata 'Tardiva,' 135
Hydrangeas, pruning, 114

I

Ilex crenata 'Green Lustre' (Green Lustre Japanese holly), 30, 35, 36, 43, 45, 107, 119, 121, *135*, **135**
Ilex glabra 'Compacta' (Inkberry), 23, 30, 35, 36, 41, 43, 45, 109, 120, 121, *136*, **136**
Ilex verticullata (Winterberry), *25*, 31, 35, 36, 39, 41, 107, 119, 123, *136*, **136**
Inkberry (*Ilex glabra* 'Compacta'), 23, 30, 35, 36, 41, 43, 45, 109, 120, 121, *136*, **136**
  'Nigra,' 136
  'Shamrock,' 136
Ivy. *See* Boston ivy

J

Jack pine (*Pinus banksiana*), 30, 34, 38, 39, 40, 45, *94*, **94**
Japanese barberry (*Berberis thunbergii*), 35, 36, 39, 107, 109, 119, 123, *128*, **128**
  'Crimson Pygmy,' 128
  'Rose Glow,' 128
  'Thornless,' 128
  var. *atropurpurea*, 128
Japanese flowering crabapple (*Malus floribunda*), 34, 41, 43, 71, *71*, 72, 73, *91*, **91**
Japanese tree lilac (*Syringa reticulata*), *34*, *40*, *71*, *72*, *73*, *104*, **104**
  'Ivory Silk,' 104
  'Regent,' 104
  'Summer Snow,' 104
Juniperus chinensis 'Old Gold' (Old Gold juniper), 35, 39, 41, 42, 43, *137*, **137**
Juniperus chinensis 'Parsonii' (Parson's juniper), 23, 35, 39, 42, 43, 107, 119, 121, *137*, **137**
Juniperus chinensis 'Sea Green' (Sea Green juniper), 23, 35, 39, 42, 45, 119, 121, *138*, **138**
Juniperus chinensis 'Spartan,' 137
Juniperus chinensis 'Torulosa' (Hollywood juniper), *29*
Juniperus horizontalis 'Bar Harbor' (Bar Harbor juniper), 23, 35, 41, 42, 43, 170, 171, 172, 173, *193*, **193**
Juniperus horizontalis 'Blue Chip' (Blue Chip juniper), 23, 35, 39, 41, 42, 43, 170, 171, 172, 173, *193*, **193**
Juniperus horizontalis 'Plumosa Compacta' (Andorra compact juniper), 23, 35, 41, 42, 43, 170, 171, 172, 173, *194*, **194**
Juniperus horizontalis 'Prince of Wales' (Prince of Wales juniper), 193
Juniperus horizontalis 'Wiltonii' (Blue Rug juniper), 23, 35, 41, 42, 43, 170, 171, 172, 173, *194*, **194**
Juniperus procumbens 'Nana' (Dwarf Japanese garden juniper), 35, 41, 43, *43*, 170, 171, 172, 173, *195*, **195**
Juniperus procumbens 'Nana Greenmound,' 195
Juniperus sabina 'Tamariscifolia' (Tam juniper), 35, 39, 45, 107, 119, 121, *138*, **138**
Juniperus scopulorum 'Skyrocket' (Skyrocket juniper), 30, 34, 38, 42, 43, 45, 73, *89*, **89**
Juniperus squamata 'Blue Star' (Blue Star juniper), 34, 39, 119, *139*, **139**
Juniperus virginiana (Eastern red cedar), 23, 30, 34, 38, 39, 40, 41, 42, 45, 71, 73, *90*, **90**

K

Katsura tree (*Cercidiphyllum japonicum*), 34, 40, 41, 63, 71, 72, *84*, **84**
Kinnikinick (*Arctostaphylos uva-ursi*), 23, 35, 37, 39, 170, 171, 172, *181*, **181**
  'Snow Camp,' 181
  'Vancouver Jade,' 181
Kiwi. *See* Hardy kiwi
Korean boxwood. *See* Wintergreen boxwood (*Buxus microphylla* 'Wintergreen')

L

Lacebark pine (*Pinus bungeana*), 30, 34, 40, 41, 45, 71, *94*, **94**
Lady's mantle (*Alchemilla mollis*), 37, 170, 171, 172, *172*, *178*, **178**
Lamb's ear (*Stachys byzantina*), 35, 43, 170, 171, 172, *172*, 173, *203*, **203**
Lamiastrum galeobdolon 'Variegatum' (Yellow archangel), 37, 171, 173, *195*, **195**
Lamium maculatum (Spotted dead nettle), 37, 39, 43, 171, *196*, **196**
Ligustrum amurense (Amur privet), 23, 31, 34, 36, 38, 39, 43, 107, 109, 117, 119, 121, *139*, **139**
Lilacs
  Common lilac (*Syringa vulgaris*), 34, 36, 39, 107, 118, 119, 121, 122, *161*, **161**
  Cutleaf lilac (*Syringa x laciniata*), 31, 34, 36, 107, 118, 119, 121, 122, *161*, **161**
  Miss Kim lilac (*Syringa patula* 'Miss Kim'), 31, 35, 36, 107, 118, 119, 121, 122, 123, *123*, *160*, **160**
  Persian lilac (*Syringa x persica*), 35, 36, 41, 122, *162*, **162**
  rejuvenating overgrown, 160
Lily-of-the-valley (*Convallaria majalis*), 37, 39, 170, 171, 172, 173, *185*, **185**
Limemound spirea (*Spiraea* japonica Limemound), 35, 43, 121, 122, 123, *158*, **158**
Linden. *See* American linden
Little Giant arborvitae (*Thuja occidentalis* 'Little Giant'), 30, 35, 39, 41, 45, 109, 117, 119, 121, *164*, **164**
Littleleaf boxwood. *See* Wintergreen boxwood (*Buxus microphylla* 'Wintergreen')
Littleleaf periwinkle (*Vinca minor*), 35, 37, 42, 43, 170, 171, *172*, 173, *205*, **205**
Lonicera sempervirens (Trumpet honeysuckle), 31, 35, 207, *208*, 209, *212*, **212**
Lonicera tatarica
  'Alba,' 141
  'Arnold's Red' (Arnold's Red Tatarian honeysuckle), 31, 34, 118, 119, 121, 122, *140*, **140**
  'Hack's Red,' 141
  'Virginalis,' 141

scarlet honeysuckle), 30, 35, *206*, 207, 209, *212*, **212**

M

Magnolia stellata (Star magnolia), 36, 40, 43, 71, 73, *90*, **90**
Maidenhair fern *(Adiantum pedatum)*, 37, 41, 43, 170, 171, 173, *177*, **177**
Malus floribunda (Japanese flowering crabapple), *13*, 34, 41, 43, 71, *71*, 72, 73, *91*, **91**
Malus 'Pink Spires,' 91
Malus prunifolia (Plumleaf crabapple), 34, 40, 43, 71, 73, *91*, **91**
Malus x robusta 'Red Siberian,' 91
Maples
  Amur maple *(Acer tataricum ginnala)*, *22*, 34, 36, 71, 72, *77*, **77**
  Norway maple *(Acer platanoides)*, 34, 36, 39, 41, 43, 45, *77*, **77**
  Red maple *(Acer rubrum)*, 31, 36, 38, 40, 43, 63, 71, 72, 73, *78*, **78**
  Silver maple *(Acer saccharinum)*, 31, 34, 36, 39, 40, 41, 63, 71, 73, *78*, **78**
  Sugar maple *(Acer saccharum)*, 34, 36, 40, 71, 73, *79*, **79**
  wrapping for winter protection, 76
Margo Koster rose (*Rosa* 'Margo Koster'), 35, 118, 123, *151*, **151**
Mayday tree *(Prunus padus commutata)*, 34, 71, 73, *97*, **97**
Microbiota decussata (Russian cypress), 35, 36, 42, 119, 121, 123, *140*, **140**
Miss Kim lilac (*Syringa patula* 'Miss Kim'), 31, 35, 36, 107, 118, 119, 121, 122, 123, *123*, *160*, **160**
Mitchella repens (Partridge berry), 37, 41, 42, 171, 173, *196*, **196**
Mohican viburnum (*Viburnum lantana* 'Mohican'), 35, 36, 39, 41, 109, 120, 121, 122, 123, *165*, **165**
Morden Centennial rose (*Rosa* 'Morden Centennial'), 35, 41, 107, 118, 119, 121, 122, 123, *152*, **152**
Moss phlox *(Phlox subulata)*, *22*, 35, 39, 42, 43, 170, 171, 172, 173, *200*, **200**
  'Crimson Beauty,' 200
  'Emerald Blue,' 200
  'Emerald Pink,' 200
  'White Delight,' 200
Mountain ash. *See* European mountain ash
Mountain sandwort *(Arenaria montana)*, 35, 39, 170, 171, 173, *181*, **181**
Mugo pine *(Pinus mugo)*, 35, 36, 39, 45, 119, 121, *143*, **143**
  'Compacta,' 143
  'Gnome,' 143
  'Mops,' 143
Musclewood. *See* American hornbeam
Myosotis scorpioides (Forget-me-not), 35, 37, 39, 171, 173, *197*, **197**
Myosotis sylvatica (Annual forget-me-not), 197
Myrica pensylvanica (Northern bayberry), 23, 30, 31, 35, 36, 39, 45, 107, 109, 119, *122*, 123, *141*, **141**

N

Nearly Wild rose (*Rosa* 'Nearly Wild'), 35, 41, 42, *59*, 119, 120, 121, 122, 123, *152*, **152**
Nepeta x faassenii (Catmint), 35, 37, 42, 43, 170, 171, 172, 173, *197*, **197**
Newport plum (*Prunus cerasifera* 'Newport'), 6, *34*, *40*, *41*, *63*, *71*, *72*, *96*, **96**
Northern bayberry *(Myrica pensylvanica)*, 23, 30, 31, 35, 36, 39, 45, 107, 109, 119, *122*, 123, *141*, **141**
Northern Gold forsythia (*Forsythia ovata* 'Northern Gold'), 133
Northern Lights azalea (*Azalea* 'Northern Lights'), 35, 41, 109, 117, 118, *118*, 119, 120, 121, 122, 123, *127*, **127**
Northern maidenhair fern. *See* Maidenhair fern
Northern red oak *(Quercus rubra)*, 34, 40, 43, 63, 71, 72, 73, *101*, **101**
Norway maple *(Acer platanoides)*, 34, 36, 39, 41, 43, 45, *77*, **77**
  'Crimson King,' 77
  'Deborah,' 77
  'Royal Red,' 77
  'Schwedleri,' 77
Norway spruce *(Picea abies)*, 30, 34, 39, 40, 45, 63, *92*, **92**
  'Aurea,' 92

O

Oak
  Northern red oak *(Quercus rubra)*, 34, 40, 43, 63, 71, 72, 73, *101*, **101**
  Pin oak *(Quercus palustris)*, 31, 34, 36, 38, 39, 40, 43, 63, 71, 72, 73, *101*, **101**
  Scarlet oak *(Quercus coccinea)*, 31, 34, 63, 71, 73, *100*, **100**
  White oak *(Quercus alba)*, 34, 38, 40, *63*, 71, 73, *100*, **100**
Oenothera macrocarpa. See Oenothera missouriensis (Sundrop primrose)
Oenothera missouriensis (Sundrop primrose), 35, 39, 171, 172, *198*, **198**
Oenothera speciosa (Evening primrose), 198
Ohio buckeye *(Aesculus glabra)*, 34, 36, 71, 73, *79*, **79**
Old Gold juniper (*Juniperus chinensis* 'Old Gold'), 35, 39, 41, 42, 43, *137*, **137**
Olive. *See* Russian olive
Oriental photinia *(Photinia villosa)*, 31, 35, 36, 41, 122, 123, *141*, **141**

P

Pachysandra *(Pachysandra terminalis)*, 37, 170, 171, *198*, **198**
Paper birch. *See* Canoe birch
Parson's juniper (*Juniperus chinensis* 'Parsonii'), 23, 35, 39, 42, 43, 107, 119, 121, *137*, **137**
Parthenocissus quinquefolia (Virginia creeper), 31, 35, 37, 39, 41, 42, 207, 209, *209*, *213*, **213**
Parthenocissus tricuspidata (Boston ivy), 31, 35, 37, 39, 41, 42, 207, *208*, 209, *213*, **213**
Partridge berry *(Mitchella repens)*, 37, 41, 42, 171, 173, *196*, **196**
Paxistima canbyi (Cliff green), 35, 37, 39, 41, 170, 171, 173, *199*, **199**
Pear *(Pyrus)*
  'Aristocrat,' 98
  'Bradford,' 31, 34, 43, 63, 71, 72, 73, *98*, **98**
  'Capital,' 98
  'Chanticleer,' 98
  'Cleveland Select,' 98
PeeGee hydrangea (*Hydrangea paniculata* 'Grandiflora'), *24*, 31, 35, 36, 41, 119, 123, *135*, **135**
Periwinkle. *See* Littleleaf periwinkle *(Vinca minor)*
Persian lilac *(Syringa x persica)*, 35, 36, 41, 122, *162*, **162**
Phlox stolonifera (Creeping phlox), 37, 41, 171, 173, *199*, **199**
Phlox subulata (Moss phlox), *22*, 35, 39, 42, 43, 170, 171, 172, 173, *200*, **200**
Photinia villosa (Oriental photinia), 31, 35, 36, 41, 122, 123, *141*, **141**
Picea abies (Norway spruce), 30, 34, 39, 40, 45, 63, *92*, **92**
Picea abies 'Nidiformis' (Bird's Nest spruce), 34, 39, 117, 119, *142*, **142**
Picea abies 'Pumila' (Dwarf Norway spruce), 35, 39, 41, 107, 109, 117, 121, *121*, *142*, **142**
Picea glauca (White spruce), 30, 34, 36, 39, 40, 45, *92*, **92**
Picea glauca 'Conica' (Dwarf Alberta spruce), 34, 36, 39, 40, 43, 117, 119, 121, *143*, **143**
Picea pungens glauca (Colorado blue spruce), 30, 34, 45, *93*, **93**
Picea rubens (Red spruce), 30, 34, 36, 40, 71, 73, *93*, **93**
Pin oak *(Quercus palustris)*, 31, 34, 36, 38, 39, 40, 43, 63, 71, 72, 73, *101*, **101**
Pink Panda strawberry (*Fragaria* 'Pink Panda'), 35, 37, 171, 172, *189*, **189**
Pink sandwort *(Arenaria purpurascens)*, 181
Pinus banksiana (Jack pine), 30, 34, 38, 39, 40, 45, *94*, **94**
Pinus bungeana (Lacebark pine), 30, 34, 40, 41, 45, 71, *94*, **94**
Pinus mugo (Mugo pine), 35, 36, 39, 45, 119, 121, *143*, **143**
Pinus strobus (White pine), 30, 34, 38, 39, *39*, 45, *45*, 63, *95*, **95**
Pinus sylvestris (Scots pine), 30, 34, 38, 45, 71, *95*, **95**
Plum. *See* Newport plum
Plumleaf crabapple *(Malus prunifolia)*, 34, 40, 43, 71, 73, *91*, **91**
Populus tremuloides (Quaking aspen), 34, 42, 63, 71, 73, *96*, **96**
Porcelain vine *(Ampelopsis brevipedunculata)*, 42
Potentilla fruticosa (Shrubby cinquefoil), 35, 36, 109, 119, 120, 123, *123*, *144*, **144**
Potentilla tabernaemontani (Spring Cinquefoil), 35, 39, 42, 171, 172, 173, *200*, **200**
Primrose
  Evening primrose *(Oenothera speciosa)*, 198
  Sundrop primrose *(Oenothera missouriensis)*, 35, 39, 171, 172, *198*, **198**
Prince of Wales juniper (*Juniperus horizontalis* 'Prince of Wales'), 193
Privet. *See* Amur privet
Prostrate Chenault coralberry (*Symphoricarpos x chenaultii* 'Hancock'), 35, 37, 39, 42, 43, 171, 173, *203*, **203**
Prunus cerasifera 'Newport' (Newport plum), 6, *34*, *40*, *41*, *63*, *71*, *72*, *96*, **96**
Prunus glandulosa 'Rosea' (Dwarf flowering almond), 34, 36, 117, 122, *144*, **144**
Prunus maackii (Amur chokecherry), 34, 36, 63, 71, 73, *73*, *97*, **97**
Prunus padus commutata (Mayday tree), 34, 71, 73, *97*, **97**
Prunus x cistena (Purple-Leaf sand cherry), *22*, 31, 35, 118, 119, 122, *145*, **145**
Pseudotsuga menziesii (Douglas fir), 30, 34, 40, *98*, **98**
  var. *glauca*, 98
Purple-Leaf sand cherry *(Prunus x cistena)*, *22*, 31, 35, 118, 119, 122, *145*, **145**
Purple-Leaf wintercreeper (*Euonymus fortunei* 'Coloratus'), 35, 41, 42, 43, 171, 172, 173, *187*, **187**
Pussy willow. *See* French pussy willow
Pyracantha angustifolia Yukon Belle (Yukon Belle firethorn), 35, 36, 107, 119,

Pyracantha angustifolia Yukon Belle (Yukon Belle firethorn), 35, 36, 107, 119, 123, *145,* **145**
Pyramidal Japanese yew (*Taxus cuspidata* 'Capitata'), 23, 30, 34, 36, 38, 43, 72, *104,* **104**
Pyrus calleryana 'Bradford' (Bradford pear), 31, 34, 43, 63, 71, 72, 73, *98,* **98**

Q
Quaking aspen (*Populus tremuloides*), 34, 42, 63, 71, 73, *96,* **96**
Quercus alba (White oak), 34, 38, 40, *63,* 71, 73, *100,* **100**
Quercus coccinea (Scarlet oak), 31, 34, 63, 71, 73, *100,* **100**
Quercus palustris (Pin oak), 31, 34, 36, 38, 39, 40, 43, 63, 71, 72, 73, *101,* **101**
Quercus rubra (Northern red oak), 34, 40, 43, 63, 71, 72, 73, *101,* **101**

R
Ramanas rose. *See* Rugosa rose (*Rosa rugosa*)
Red Autumn Lace. *See* Cut-Leaf staghorn sumac (*Rhus typhina* 'Laciniata')
Red chokeberry (*Aronia arbutifolia*), 125
Red maple (*Acer rubrum*), 31, 36, 38, 40, 43, 63, 71, 72, 73, *78,* **78**
'Autumn Flame,' 78
'Bowhall,' 78
'Columnare,' 78
'October Glory,' 78
'Red Sunset,' 78
Red oak. *See* Northern red oak
Red spruce (*Picea rubens*), 30, 34, 36, 40, 71, 73, *93,* **93**
Redbud (*Cercis canadensis*), 31, 34, 36, 39, 40, 41, 43, 63, 71, 72, 73, *85,* **85**
'Alba,' *70,* 85, *85*
'Forest Pansy,' 85
Redtwig dogwood (*Cornus alba*), 35, 39, 119, *130,* **130**
'Aurea,' 130
'Elegantissima,' 130
Rhododendron catawba (Catawba rhododendron), 30, 34, 36, 40, *40,* 109, 117, 119, 122, *146,* **146**
pruning, 146
Rhus typhina 'Laciniata' (Cut-Leaf staghorn sumac), 34, 39, 40, 41, 42, 43, 119, 121, 123, *147,* **147**
Ribes alpinum 'Green Mound' (Green Mound alpine currant), 23, 35, 36, 39, 41, *41,* 107, 109, 117, 119, 121, 122, *147,* **147**
Ribes odoratum (Clove currant), 147
River birch (*Betula nigra*), 31, 34, 36, 38, *38,* 39, 40, 63, 71, *71,* 72, 73, *81,* **81**
'Heritage,' 81
Rockcress (*Arabis caucasica*), 35, 37, 170, 171, *171,* 172, 173, *180,* **180**
'Flore Pleno,' 180
'Rosabella,' 180
'Variegata,' 180
Rocky Mountain juniper. *See* Skyrocket juniper
Rosa 'Adelaide Hoodless' (Adelaide Hoodless rose), 34, 40, 107, 118, 119, 121, 123, *148,* **148**
Rosa Alba Meidiland (Alba Meidiland rose), 35, 37, 42, 171, 172, 173, *201,* **201**
Rosa Carefree Beauty (Carefree Beauty rose), 34, 107, 109, 118, 123, *149,* **149**
Rosa 'Betty Prior' (Betty Prior rose), 34, 107, 118, 120, 123, *148,* **148**
Rosa 'Flower Carpet' (Flower carpet rose), 35, 43, *43,* 171, *201,* **201**
Rosa Graham Thomas (Graham Thomas rose), 35, *106,* 118, 120, 121, 123, *150,* **150**
Rosa 'Henry Kelsey' (Henry Kelsey rose), 35, 41, 107, 118, 119, 121, 122, 123, *150,* **150**
Rosa 'Hunter' (Hunter rose), 35, 41, 118, 120, 121, *122,* 123, *151,* **151**
Rosa kordesii, 150, 154
Rosa 'Margo Koster' (Margo Koster rose), 35, 118, 123, *151,* **151**
Rosa 'Morden Centennial' (Morden Centennial rose), 35, 41, 107, 118, 119, 121, 122, 123, *152,* **152**
Rosa 'Nearly Wild' (Nearly Wild rose), 35, 41, 42, *59,* 119, 120, 121, 122, 123, *152,* **152**
Rosa 'The Fairy' (The Fairy rose), 35, 36, 43, 119, 121, 123, *153,* **153**
Rosa rubrifolia, 35, 118, 123, *155,* **155**
Rosa rugosa 'Alba' (White rugosa rose), 23, 35, 41, 42, 118, 119, 120, 122, 123, *155,* **155**
Rosa 'Fru Dagmar Hastrup' (Fru Dagmar Hastrup rose), 23, 35, 39, 42, 118, 123, *149,* **149**
Rosa 'Therese Bugnet' (Therese Bugnet rose), 23, 35, 39, 42, 118, 123, *154,* **154**
Rosa rugosa var. *alboplena,* 155
Rosa 'Sir Thomas Lipton' (Sir Thomas Lipton rose), 31, 35, 36, 41, 42, 107, 118, 119, 120, 123, *153,* **153**
Rosa 'William Baffin' (William Baffin rose), 35, 41, 42, 118, 119, 120, 122, 123, *154,* **154**
Rosemary. *See* Bog rosemary
Roses (*Rosa*)
Adelaide Hoodless, 34, 40, 107, 118, 119, 121, 123, *148,* **148**
Alba Meidiland, 35, 37, 42, 171, 172, 173, *201,* **201**
Betty Prior, 34, 107, 118, 120, 123, *148,* **148**
Carefree Beauty, 34, 107, 109, 118, 123, *149,* **149**
climbing, 57, *207*
The Fairy, 35, 36, 43, 119, 121, 123, *153,* **153**
feeding, 59
Flower Carpet, 35, 43, *43,* 171, *201,* **201**
Fru Dagmar Hastrup, 23, 35, 39, 42, 118, 123, *149,* **149**
Graham Thomas, 35, 118, 120, 121, 123, *150,* **150**
Henry Kelsey, 35, 41, 107, 118, 119, 121, 122, 123, *150,* **150**
Hunter, 35, 41, 118, 120, 121, 123, *151,* **151**
light requirements, 33
Margo Koster, 35, 118, 123, *151,* **151**
Morden Centennial, 35, 41, 107, 118, 119, 121, 122, 123, *152,* **152**
Nearly Wild, 35, 41, 42, *59,* 119, 120, 121, 122, 123, *152,* **152**
planting bare-root, 56
planting containerized, 57
problem solving, 59
pruning, 58
rugosa, 23, 35, 41, 42, 118, 119, 120, 122, 123, *153,* **153**
Sir Thomas Lipton, 31, 35, 36, 41, 42, 107, 118, 119, 120, 123, *153,* **153**
Therese Bugnet, 23, 35, 39, 42, 118, 123, *154,* **154**
winter protection, 57, 60–61
Rugosa rose (*Rosa rugosa*), 23, 35, 41, 42, 118, 119, 120, 122, 123, *153,* **153**
Running box. *See* Partridge berry (*Mitchella repens*)
Russian cypress (*Microbiota decussata*), 35, 36, 42, 119, 121, 123, *140,* **140**
Russian olive (*Elaeagnus angustifolia*), 23, 34, 40, 42, 63, 71, 72, *87,* **87**

S
Salix alba 'Tristis' (Golden weeping willow), 23, 34, 39, 42, 63, 73, *102,* **102**
Salix alba 'Britzensis' (Coral Embers willow), 23, 34, 39, 119, *156,* **156**
Salix babylonica (Weeping willow), 31, *31,* 34, 38, 39, 42, 63, *72,* 73, *102,* **102**
Salix caprea 'Kilmarnock' (French pussy willow), 35, 39, 119, *156,* **156**
Salix caprea 'Pendula.' *See Salix caprea* 'Kilmarnock' (French pussy willow)
Salix 'Golden Curls' (Corkscrew willow), 34, 36, 63, 73, *103,* **103**
Salix matsudana 'Tortuosa,' 103
Salix 'Scarlet Curls' (Corkscrew willow), 103
Sand cherry. *See* Purple-Leaf sand cherry
Sandwort. *See* Pink sandwort
Saxifrage (*Bergenia cordifolia*), *20,* 35, 37, 170, 171, 172, *184,* **184**
'Bressingham Ruby,' 184
'Bressingham White,' 184
Scarlet oak (*Quercus coccinea*), 31, 34, 63, 71, 73, *100,* **100**
Scarlet trumpet honeysuckle. *See* Dropmore scarlet honeysuckle (*Lonicera x brownii* 'Dropmore Scarlet')
Scots pine (*Pinus sylvestris*), 30, 34, 38, 45, 71, *95,* **95**
'Aurea,' 95
'Edwin Hiller,' 95
'Fastigiata,' 95
Sea Green juniper (*Juniperus chinensis* 'Sea Green'), 23, 35, 39, 42, 45, 119, 121, *138,* **138**
Sea thrift (*Armeria maritima*), 23, *25,* 37, 39, 170, 171, 172, 173, *182,* **182**
'Alba,' 182
'Dusseldorf Pride,' 182
'Laucheana,' 182
Sea tomato. *See* Rugosa rose (*Rosa rugosa*)
Sedum acre (Goldmoss), 35, 39, 41, 42, 43, 170, 171, 172, 173, *202,* **202**
Sedum spectabile (Stonecrop), 35, 39, 42, 43, 170, 171, 173, *202,* **202**
Serbian bellflower. *See* Blue star bellflower (*Campanula poscharskyana*)
Serviceberry (*Amelanchier alnifolia*), 35, 36, 41, 121, 122, 123, *125,* **125**. *See also* Allegheny serviceberry; Apple serviceberry; Shadblow serviceberry
'Regent,' 125
Shadblow serviceberry (*Amelanchier canadensis*), 34, 36, 39, 40, 71, 73, *80,* **80**
Shibori spirea (*Spiraea japonica* 'Shibori'), 35, 36, 121, *157,* **157**
Showy crabapple. *See* Japanese flowering crabapple
Showy mountain ash (*Sorbus decora*), 103
Shrubby cinquefoil (*Potentilla fruticosa*), 35, 36, 109, 119, 120, 123, *123, 144,* **144**
'Abbotswood,' 144
'Goldfinger,' 144
'Jackmannii,' 144
'Primrose Beauty,' 144
'Tangerine,' 144
Siberian forget-me-not (*Anchusa myosotidiflora*), 37, 170, 171, *179,* **179**
Silver brocade artemisia (*Artemisia stelleriana*), 23, 35, 43, 170, 171, 172, 173, *182,* **182**
Silver maple (*Acer saccharinum*), 31, 34, 36, 39, 40, 41, 63, 71, 73, *78,* **78**
'Silver Queen,' 78
'Skinneri,' 78
Sir Thomas Lipton rose (*Rosa* 'Sir Thomas Lipton'), 31, 35, 36, 41, 42, 107, 118, 119, 120, 123, *155,* **155**

Skyrocket juniper (*Juniperus scopulorum* 'Skyrocket'), 30, 34, 38, 42, 43, 45, 73, *89*, **89**
Smoketree. *See* American smoketree
Snowberry (*Symphoricarpos albus*), 23, 35, 36, 42, 43, 119, *120*, 121, 159, **159**
Snow-in-Summer (*Cerastium tomentosum*), 35, 39, 42, 170, 171, 172, 173, *185*, **185**
Snow-on-the-Mountain (*Aegopodium podagraria* 'Variegatum'), 37, 39, 41, 42, 171, 173, *177*, **177**
Sorbus aucuparia (European mountain ash), 23, 34, 36, *36*, 39, 40, 71, 72, 73, *103*, **103**
Sorbus decora (Showy mountain ash), 103
Southern balsam fir. *See* Frasier fir
Spiraea japonica 'Alba,' 157
Spiraea japonica 'Anthony Waterer' (Anthony Waterer spirea), *12*, 34, 36, 39, 43, 121, 122, 123, *157*, **157**
Spiraea japonica 'Golden Princess,' 158
Spiraea japonica 'Goldmound,' 158
Spiraea japonica Limemound (Limemound spirea), 35, 43, 121, 122, 123, *158*, **158**
Spiraea japonica 'Little Princess' (Little Princess spirea), 157, *157*
Spiraea japonica 'Shibori' (Shibori spirea), 35, 36, 121, *157*, **157**
Spiraea prunifolia (Bridalwreath spirea), 31, 34, 36, 107, 119, 121, *158*, **158**
Spotted dead nettle (*Lamium maculatum*), 37, 39, 43, 171, *196*, **196**
  'Beacon Silver,' 196
  'Pink Pewter,' 196
  'White Nancy,' 196
Spring Cinquefoil (*Potentilla tabernaemontani*), 35, 39, 42, 171, 172, 173, *200*, **200**
Spruce
  Bird's Nest spruce (*Picea abies* 'Nidiformis'), 34, 39, 117, 119, *142*, **142**
  Colorado blue spruce (*Picea pungens glauca*), 30, 34, 45, *93*, **93**
  Dwarf Alberta spruce (*Picea glauca* 'Conica'), 34, 36, 39, 40, 43, 117, 119, 121, *143*, **143**
  Dwarf Norway spruce (*Picea abies* 'Pumila'), 35, 39, 41, 107, 109, 117, 121, *142*, **142**
  Norway spruce (*Picea abies*), 30, 34, 39, 40, 45, 63, *92*, **92**
  Red spruce (*Picea rubens*), 30, 34, 36, 40, 71, 73, *93*, **93**
  White spruce (*Picea glauca*), 30, 34, 36, 39, 40, 45, *92*, **92**
Spurge. *See* Cypress spurge
Stachys byzantina (Lamb's ear), 35, 43, 170, 171, 172, *172*, 173, *203*, **203**
Star magnolia (*Magnolia stellata*), 36, 40, 43, 71, 73, *90*, **90**
Stonecrop (*Sedum spectabile*), 35, 39, 42, 43, 170, 171, 173, *202*, **202**
  'Autumn Joy,' 202
  'Brilliant,' 202
Strawberry
  Alpine strawberry (*Fragaria vesca*), 35, 37, 41, 42, 43, 171, 172, 173, *189*, **189**
  Pink Panda strawberry (*Fragaria* 'Pink Panda'), 35, 37, 171, 172, *189*, **189**
Sugar maple (*Acer saccharum*), 34, 36, 40, 71, 73, *79*, **79**
  'Bonfire,' 79
  'Flax Mill Majesty,' 79
  'Green Column,' 79
  'Green Mountain,' 79
  'Legacy,' 79
Sumac. *See* Cut-Leaf staghorn sumac (*Rhus typhina* 'Laciniata')
Summersweet (*Clethra alnifolia*), 23, 36, 39, 41, 117, 118, 119, 120, *120*, 121, 123, *130*, **130**
  'Ruby Spice,' 130
Sundrop primrose (*Oenothera missouriensis*), 35, 39, 171, 172, *198*, **198**
Sweet pepperbush. *See* Summersweet (*Clethra alnifolia*)
Sweet Woodruff (*Asperula odorata*), 35, 37, *37*, 41, 170, *170*, 171, 173, *183*, **183**
Sweetshrub (*Calycanthus floridus*), *20*, 35, 36, 39, 118, 119, 121, 122, 123, *129*, **129**
  'Athens,' 129
Symphoricarpos albus (Snowberry), 23, 35, 36, 42, 43, 119, *120*, 121, 159, **159**
Symphoricarpos orbiculatus (Coralberry), 31, 34, 36, 39, 42, 107, 119, 121, 123, 159, **159**
Symphoricarpos x chenaultii 'Hancock' (Prostrate Chenault coralberry), 35, 37, 39, 42, 43, 171, 173, *203*, **203**
Syringa patula 'Miss Kim' (Miss Kim lilac), 31, 35, 36, 107, 118, 119, 121, 122, 123, *123*, *160*, **160**
Syringa reticulata (Japanese tree lilac), *34*, *40*, *71*, *72*, *73*, *104*, **104**
Syringa vulgaris (Lilac, common), 34, 36, 39, 107, 118, 119, 121, 122, *161*, **161**
Syringa x laciniata (Cutleaf lilac), 31, 34, 36, 107, 118, 119, 121, 122, *161*, **161**
Syringa x persica (Persian lilac), 35, 36, 41, 122, *162*, **162**

T

Tam juniper (*Juniperus sabina 'Tamariscifolia'*), 35, 39, 45, 107, 119, 121, *138*, **138**
  'Arcadia,' 138
Taxus cuspidata 'Capitata' (Pyramidal Japanese yew), 23, 30, 34, 36, 38, 43, 72, *104*, **104**
Taxus x media 'Densiformis' (Anglojap yew), 34, 36, 40, 107, 109, 117, 119, 120, 121, *162*, **162**
Taxus x media 'Hicksii' (Hick's upright yew), 30, 35, 36, 41, 45, 107, 117, 119, 121, *163*, **163**
Teucrium chamaedrys. See Teucrium prostratum (Germander)
Teucrium prostratum (Germander), 35, 41, 43, 170, 171, 172, 173, *204*, **204**
Therese Bugnet rose (*Rosa* 'Therese Bugnet'), 23, 35, 39, 42, 118, 123, *154*, **154**
Thuja occidentalis (American arborvitae), 30, 34, 39, 41, *105*, **105**
Thuja occidentalis 'Emerald' (Emerald arborvitae), 30, 35, 39, 41, 45, 107, 109, 117, 119, 121, *163*, 164, **163**
Thuja occidentalis 'Globosa,' 163, 164
Thuja occidentalis 'Golden Globe,' 163, 164
Thuja occidentalis 'Hetz's Midget' (Hetz's Midget arborvitae), 35, 39, 117, 119, 121, *164*, **164**
Thuja occidentalis 'Little Giant' (Little Giant arborvitae), 30, 35, 39, 41, 45, 109, 117, 119, 121, *164*, **164**
Tiarella cordifolia (Allegheny foam flower), 37, 41, 170, 171, 173, *204*, **204**
Tilia americana (American linden), 34, 36, 41, 71, 72, *105*, **105**
Trumpet honeysuckle (*Lonicera sempervirens*), 31, 35, 207, *208*, 209, *212*, **212**
  pruning, 209
Trumpet vine (*Campsis radicans*), *27*, 31, 35, 37, 39, 42, 207, 209, *210*, **210**
  'Flava,' 210
  'Praecox,' 210
  pruning, 209
Twinberry. *See* Partridge berry (*Mitchella repens*)

V

Variegated Bishop's weed. *See* Snow-on-the-Mountain (*Aegopodium podagraria* 'Variegatum')
Variegated kiwi vine (*Actinidia kolomikta*), 210
Veitch fir (*Abies veitchii*), 30, 36, 40, 63, *75*, **75**
Vermont Sun forsythia (*Forsythia mandschurica* 'Vermont Sun'), 31, 35, 36, 42, 117, 119, 120, 121, 122, *133*, **133**
Viburnum dentatum (Arrowwood viburnum), 23, 31, 34, 36, 40, 107, 119, 121, 122, 123, *165*, **165**
Viburnum lantana 'Mohican' (Mohican viburnum), 35, 36, 39, 41, 109, 120, 121, 122, 123, *165*, **165**
Viburnum opulus 'Roseum' (European cranberry-bush), 35, 39, 119, 121, 122, *166*, **166**
Viburnum plicatum tomentosum (Doublefile viburnum), 34, *34*, 36, 119, 120, 121, 122, 123, *166*, **166**
Viburnum prunifolium (Blackhaw viburnum), 34, 36, 41, 119, 120, 121, 122, 123, *167*, **167**
Viburnum trilobum 'Alfredo' (Compact American cranberrybush), 34, 36, 40, 107, 109, 119, 120, 121, *121*, 122, 123, *167*, **167**
Vinca minor (Littleleaf periwinkle), 35, 37, 42, 43, 170, 171, *172*, 173, *205*, **205**
Virginia creeper (*Parthenocissus quinquefolia*), 31, 35, 37, 39, 41, 42, 207, 209, *209*, *213*, **213**
  pruning, 209

W

Waldesteinia (*Waldesteinia ternata*), 35, 37, 171, 173, *173*, *205*, **205**
Waldsteinia siberica. See Waldesteinia (*Waldesteinia ternata*)
Waldsteinia trifolia. See Waldesteinia (*Waldesteinia ternata*)
Washington hawthorn (*Crataegus phaenopyrum*), 34, 36, 38, 40, 41, 43, 71, 72, 73, *86*, **86**
Weeping willow (*Salix babylonica*), 31, *31*, 34, 38, 39, 42, 63, *72*, 73, *102*, **102**. *See also* Golden weeping willow
White fir (*Abies concolor*), 30, 34, 38, 45, *74*, **74**
White flowering redbud (*Cercis canadensis* 'Alba'), *85*
White forsythia (*Abeliophyllum distichum*), 31, 35, 41, 42, *42*, 117, 118, 119, 121, 122, *124*, **124**
White oak (*Quercus alba*), 34, 38, 40, *63*, 71, 73, *100*, **100**
White pine (*Pinus strobus*), 30, 34, 38, 39, *39*, 45, *45*, 63, *95*, **95**
White rugosa rose (*Rosa rugosa* 'Alba'), 23, 35, 41, 42, 118, 119, 120, 122, 123, *155*, **155**
White spruce (*Picea glauca*), 30, 34, 36, 39, 40, 45, *92*, **92**
Whitespire birch (*Betula mandschurica japonica* 'Whitespire'), 34, 38, 40, 63, 71, 72, *83*, **83**
William Baffin rose (*Rosa* 'William Baffin'), 35, 41, 42, 118, 119, 120, 122, 123, *154*, **154**
Winterberry (*Ilex verticullata*), 31, 35, 36, 39, 41, 107, 119, 123, *136*, **136**
  'Sparkleberry,' 136
  'Winter Red,' *25*, 136
Wintercreeper, Purple–Leaf wintercreeper (*Euonymus fortunei* 'Coloratus')
Wintergreen (*Gaultheria procumbens*), 37, 41, 171, 173, *190*, **190**
Wintergreen boxwood (*Buxus microphylla* 'Wintergreen'), 35, 36, 107, 109, 117, 119, *120*, 121, 122, *128*, **128**
  'Green Pillow,' 128